Lecture Notes in Computer Science 16056

Founding Editors

Gerhard Goos
Juris Hartmanis

Editorial Board Members

Elisa Bertino, *Purdue University, West Lafayette, IN, USA*
Wen Gao, *Peking University, Beijing, China*
Bernhard Steffen , *TU Dortmund University, Dortmund, Germany*
Moti Yung , *Columbia University, New York, NY, USA*

The series Lecture Notes in Computer Science (LNCS), including its subseries Lecture Notes in Artificial Intelligence (LNAI) and Lecture Notes in Bioinformatics (LNBI), has established itself as a medium for the publication of new developments in computer science and information technology research, teaching, and education.

LNCS enjoys close cooperation with the computer science R & D community, the series counts many renowned academics among its volume editors and paper authors, and collaborates with prestigious societies. Its mission is to serve this international community by providing an invaluable service, mainly focused on the publication of conference and workshop proceedings and postproceedings. LNCS commenced publication in 1973.

Vincent Nicomette · Abdelmalek Benzekri ·
Nora Boulahia-Cuppens · Jaideep Vaidya
Editors

Computer Security – ESORICS 2025

30th European Symposium
on Research in Computer Security
Toulouse, France, September 22–24, 2025
Proceedings, Part IV

Editors
Vincent Nicomette
INSA Toulouse
Toulouse, France

Abdelmalek Benzekri
Université Toulouse- Paul Sabatier
Toulouse, France

Nora Boulahia-Cuppens
Polytechnique Montreal
Montreal, QC, Canada

Jaideep Vaidya
Rutgers University
Newark, NJ, USA

ISSN 0302-9743　　　　　　　ISSN 1611-3349　(electronic)
Lecture Notes in Computer Science
ISBN 978-3-032-07900-8　　　ISBN 978-3-032-07901-5　(eBook)
https://doi.org/10.1007/978-3-032-07901-5

© The Editor(s) (if applicable) and The Author(s), under exclusive license to Springer Nature Switzerland AG 2026

This work is subject to copyright. All rights are solely and exclusively licensed by the Publisher, whether the whole or part of the material is concerned, specifically the rights of translation, reprinting, reuse of illustrations, recitation, broadcasting, reproduction on microfilms or in any other physical way, and transmission or information storage and retrieval, electronic adaptation, computer software, or by similar or dissimilar methodology now known or hereafter developed.
The use of general descriptive names, registered names, trademarks, service marks, etc. in this publication does not imply, even in the absence of a specific statement, that such names are exempt from the relevant protective laws and regulations and therefore free for general use.
The publisher, the authors and the editors are safe to assume that the advice and information in this book are believed to be true and accurate at the date of publication. Neither the publisher nor the authors or the editors give a warranty, expressed or implied, with respect to the material contained herein or for any errors or omissions that may have been made. The publisher remains neutral with regard to jurisdictional claims in published maps and institutional affiliations.

This Springer imprint is published by the registered company Springer Nature Switzerland AG
The registered company address is: Gewerbestrasse 11, 6330 Cham, Switzerland

If disposing of this product, please recycle the paper.

Preface

It is our great pleasure to welcome you to the thirtieth edition of the European Symposium on Research in Computer Security (ESORICS 2025). This symposium was founded to further the progress of research in computer, information and cyber security and in privacy, by establishing a European forum for bringing together researchers in this area, by promoting the exchange of ideas with system developers and by encouraging links with researchers in related areas.

Since its inception in 1990, ESORICS has been hosted in a series of European countries and has established itself as the premiere European research event in computer security. Starting biannually in 1990 in Toulouse, the symposium has been held annually since 2002. We are delighted to welcome you to the 30th edition of the symposium in Toulouse, where it was first held.

As one of the longest-running reputable conferences focused on security research, ESORICS 2025 attracted numerous high-quality submissions from all over the world, with authors affiliated with diverse academic, non-profit, governmental, and industrial entities. After two rounds of submissions, each followed by an extensive reviewing period, we wound up with an excellent program, covering a broad range of timely and interesting topics. A total of 605 unique submissions were received: 150 in the first round and 475 in the second (of which 20 were invited resubmissions). Three to four reviewers per submission in a single-blind review driven by selfless and dedicated PC members (and external reviewers) collectively did an amazing job providing thorough and insightful reviews. Some PC members even "went the extra mile" by reviewing more than their share. The end result was 100 accepted submissions: 10 and 90, in the first and second rounds, respectively – giving an overall acceptance rate of 16.52%.

The ESORICS 2025 technical program was organized into 27 tracks held in 3 parallel sessions as well as 3 impressive keynote talks by internationally prominent and active researchers across academia and industry: Carlos Aguilar, Pierangela Samarati, and V. S. Subrahmanian. The program testifies to the level of excellence and stature of ESORICS.

Putting together ESORICS 2025 was a team effort. We would like to express our sincere gratitude to:

- Authors and contributors: without high-quality submissions from the authors, the success of the conference would not have been possible.
- PC members and additional reviewers: for the effort they put into the evaluation and high-quality in-depth reviews.
- Organization Chairs: Denise Gross from ICO, Justine Praneuf from LAAS-CNRS, Charlotte Sébastien from Université de Toulouse, and Tifanny Vest from Université de Toulouse for all of their efforts in organizing the conference and managing all of the logistics.
- Publicity Chairs: Paria Shirani from the University of Ottawa, Canada, Wenjuan Li from Hong Kong Polytechnic University, China, and Sebastien Bardin from Software

Safety and Security Lab, CEA, France, for their efforts in spreading the word about ESORICS 2025.
- Web Chairs: Charlotte Sébastien from Université de Toulouse and Tifanny Vest from Université de Toulouse for their efforts and continuous and quick updates of the website.
- Workshops Chair Romain Laborde from IRIT, Université de Toulouse for handling the workshops organization and being involved in other organizational aspects.
- Sponsor Chair Giorgia Macilotti from Airbus Protect for helping to arrange sponsorship for the symposium.
- The ESORICS Steering Committee and in particular, the Steering Committee Chair Joaquin Garcia-Alfaro for providing advice with numerous organizational issues.
- Easychair for providing an excellent conference management system.

In closing, we believe that ESORICS 2025 was an overall success and we hope that all attendees enjoyed the symposium and their stay in Toulouse, France.

July 2025

Vincent Nicomette
Abdelmalek Benzekri
Nora Boulahia-Cuppens
Jaideep Vaidya

Organization

General Chairs

Vincent Nicomette — LAAS-CNRS, INSA de Toulouse, France
Abdelmalek Benzekri — IRIT, Université de Toulouse, France

Program Chairs

Nora Boulahia-Cuppens — Polytechnique Montréal, Canada
Jaideep Vaidya — Rutgers University, USA

Publicity Chairs

Paria Shirani — University of Ottawa, Canada
Wenjuan Li — Education University of Hong Kong, China
Sebastien Bardin — CEA, France

Organization Chairs

Denise Gross — ICO, France
Justine Praneuf — LAAS-CNRS, France
Charlotte Sébastien — Université de Toulouse, France
Tifanny Vest — Université de Toulouse, France

Workshops Chair

Romain Laborde — IRIT, Université de Toulouse, France

Sponsor Chair

Giorgia Macilotti — Airbus Protect, France

Web Chairs

Charlotte Sébastien   Université de Toulouse, France
Tifanny Vest   Université de Toulouse, France

Steering Committee

Joachim Biskup	University of Dortmund, Germany
Frédéric Cuppens	Polytechnique Montréal, Canada
Sabrina De Capitani di Vimercati	Università degli Studi di Milano, Italy
Joaquin Garcia-Alfaro (Chair)	Institut Polytechnique de Paris, France
Dieter Gollmann	Hamburg University of Technology, Germany
Sushil Jajodia	George Mason University, USA
Sokratis Katsikas	Norwegian University of Science and Technology, Norway
Mirek Kutylowski	Wrocław University of Technology, Poland
Javier Lopez	Universidad de Málaga, Spain
Jean-Jacques Quisquater	Université catholique de Louvain, Belgium
Peter Y. A. Ryan	University of Luxembourg, Luxembourg
Pierangela Samarati	Università degli Studi di Milano, Italy
Einar Snekkenes	Norwegian University of Science and Technology, Norway
Michael Waidner	Technische Universität Darmstadt, Germany
Edgar Weippl	University of Vienna & SBA Research, Austria

Program Committee

Andrea Agiollo (Round 2)	TU Delft, The Netherlands
Massimiliano Albanese	George Mason University, USA
Cristina Alcaraz	University of Málaga, Spain
Abdelrahaman Aly	Technology Innovation Institute, United Arab Emirates
Shengwei An (Round 2)	Virginia Tech, USA
Hafiz Asif (Round 2)	Hofstra University, Rutgers University, USA
Mikael Asplund	Linköping University, Sweden
Vijay Atluri	Rutgers University, USA
Daniel Augot (Round 1)	Inria Saclay, France
Samiha Ayed (Round 2)	Université de technologie de Troyes, France
Sebastien Bardin	CEA LIST, France
Alessandro Barenghi	Politecnico di Milano, Italy

Ken Barker (Round 1)	University of Calgary, Canada
Giampaolo Bella (Round 2)	University of Catania, Italy
Abdelmalek Benzekri	Université de Toulouse, France
Elisa Bertino	Purdue University, USA
Clara Bertolissi (Round 2)	Aix-Marseille University, France
Bruhadeshwar Bezawada (Round 2)	Southern Arkansas University, USA
Smriti Bhatt (Round 2)	Purdue University, USA
Giuseppe Bianchi (Round 2)	University of Rome "Tor Vergata", Italy
Alex Biryukov	University of Luxembourg, Luxembourg
Jorge Blasco (Round 1)	Universidad Politécnica de Madrid, Spain
Carlo Blundo	Università degli Studi di Salerno, Italy
Tamara Bonaci (Round 2)	Northeastern University, USA
Rainer Böhme (Round 2)	University of Innsbruck, Austria
Pino Caballero-Gil	University of La Laguna, Spain
Maurantonio Caprolu (Round 2)	King Abdullah University of Science and Technology, Saudi Arabia
Xavier Carpent	University of Nottingham, UK
Aldar C.-F. Chan (Round 2)	University of Hong Kong, China
Bo Chen (Round 2)	Michigan Technological University, USA
Rongmao Chen (Round 2)	National University of Defense Technology, China
Xiaofeng Chen (Round 2)	Xidian University, China
Yuan Cheng (Round 2)	University of Nottingham Ningbo China, China
Sherman S. M. Chow (Round 2)	Chinese University of Hong Kong, China
Pietro Colombo (Round 2)	Università dell'Insubria, Italy
Michal Choras (Round 1)	Bydgoszcz University of Science and Technology, Poland
Mauro Conti	University of Padua, Italy
Bruno Crispo (Round 2)	University of Trento, Italy
Michel Cukier (Round 2)	University of Maryland, USA
Frédéric Cuppens	Polytechnique Montréal, Canada
Tooska Dargahi	Manchester Metropolitan University, UK
Saptarshi Das (Round 2)	Pennsylvania State University, USA
Sabrina De Capitani di Vimercati	Universita' degli Studi di Milano, Italy
Hervé Debar	Télécom SudParis, France
Jose Maria De Fuentes (Round 1)	Universidad Carlos III de Madrid, Spain
Soumyadeep Dey (Round 2)	IIT Kharagpur, India
Roberto Di Pietro (Round 2)	King Abdullah University of Science and Technology, Saudi Arabia
Tassos Dimitriou (Round 2)	Kuwait University, Kuwait
Xuhua Ding (Round 1)	Singapore Management University, Singapore

Josep Domingo-Ferrer — Universitat Rovira i Virgili, Spain
Andreas Ekelhart (Round 1) — Secure Business Austria, Austria
Santiago Escobar (Round 2) — Universitat Politècnica de València, Spain
David Espes (Round 2) — Université de Bretagne Ouest, France
Shuya Feng (Round 2) — University of Connecticut, USA
Anna Lisa Ferrara — Università degli studi del Molise, Italy
Josep Lluís Ferrer Gomila (Round 2) — Universitat de les Illes Balears, Spain
Philip W. L. Fong (Round 2) — University of Calgary, Canada
Olga Gadyatskaya — University of Leiden, The Netherlands
Debin Gao — Singapore Management University, Singapore
Joaquin Garcia-Alfaro — Institut Polytechnique de Paris, France
Essam Ghadafi — Newcastle University, UK
Giorgio Giacinto — University of Cagliari, Italy
Alberto Giaretta (Round 1) — Örebro Universitet, Sweden
Dieter Gollmann — Hamburg University of Technology, Germany
Lorena González Manzano — Universidad Carlos III de Madrid, Spain
Dimitris Gritzalis (Round 1) — Athens University of Economics & Business, Greece
Stefanos Gritzalis (Round 2) — University of Piraeus, Greece
Maanak Gupta (Round 2) — Tennessee Tech University, USA
M. Emre Gursoy (Round 2) — Koç University, Turkey
Gregory Gutin (Round 2) — Royal Holloway, University of London, UK
Hannes Hartenstein (Round 2) — Karlsruhe Institute of Technology, Germany
Hongxin Hu (Round 2) — University at Buffalo, SUNY, USA
Xinyi Huang (Round 2) — Fujian Normal University, China
Hugo Jonker — Open University of the Netherlands, The Netherlands
Sokratis Katsikas — Norwegian University of Science and Technology, Norway
Stefan Katzenbeisser — University of Passau, Germany
Jörg Keller — FernUniversität in Hagen, Germany
Latifur Khan (Round 2) — University of Texas at Dallas, USA
Hiroaki Kikuchi — Meiji University, Japan
Hyoungshick Kim (Round 2) — Sungkyunkwan University, South Korea
Ram Krishnan (Round 2) — University of Texas at San Antonio, USA
Marina Krotofil — Maersk, Switzerland
Christopher Kruegel (Round 2) — University of California Santa Barbara, USA
Alptekin Küpçü — Koç University, Turkey
Romain Laborde — Université de Toulouse, France
Peeter Laud — Cybernetica AS, Estonia
Maryline Laurent — Télécom SudParis, France

Zeyu Lei (Round 2)	Purdue University, USA
Shujun Li (Round 2)	University of Kent, UK
Wenting Li (Round 2)	Peking University, China
Jun Li (Round 2)	Università of Oregon, USA
Kaitai Liang	Delft University of Technology, The Netherlands
Hoon Wei Lim (Round 2)	NCS Group, Singapore
Dan Lin (Round 2)	Vanderbilt University, USA
Peng Liu (Round 2)	Pennsylvania State University, USA
Giovanni Livraga	University of Milan, Italy
Valeria Loscri	Inria, France
Wenjing Lou (Round 2)	Virginia Tech, USA
Rongxing Lu (Round 2)	Queen's University, Canada
Haibing Lu (Round 2)	Santa Clara University, USA
Xiapu Luo (Round 2)	Hong Kong Polytechnic University, China
Eduard Marin	Telefónica Research, Spain
Jean-Yves Marion	Université de Lorraine, France
Fabio Martinelli (Round 2)	IIT-CNR, Italy
Amir Masoumzadeh (Round 2)	University at Albany - SUNY, USA
Barbara Masucci	University of Salerno, Italy
Wojciech Mazurczyk	Warsaw University of Technology, Poland
David Megías	Universitat Oberta de Catalunya, Spain
Weizhi Meng	Lancaster University, UK
Donika Mirdita (Round 2)	Fraunhofer Secure Information Technology, Germany
Chris Mitchell (Round 2)	Royal Holloway, University of London, UK
Barsha Mitra (Round 2)	BITS Pilani Hyderabad Campus, India
Sudip Mittal (Round 2)	Mississippi State University, USA
Meisam Mohammady (Round 2)	Iowa State University, USA
Haralambos Mouratidis (Round 2)	University of Essex, UK
Guillermo Navarro-Arribas	Autonomous University of Barcelona, Spain
Jianting Ning (Round 2)	Singapore Management University, Singapore
Antonino Nocera	University of Pavia, Italy
Gabriele Oligeri	Hamad Bin Khalifa University, Qatar
Melek Önen (Round 2)	EURECOM, France
Philippe Owezarski	LAAS-CNRS, France
Balaji Palanisamy (Round 2)	University of Pittsburgh, USA
Stefano Paraboschi (Round 2)	Università di Bergamo, Italy
Sikhar Patranabis (Round 2)	IBM Research India, India
Günther Pernul (Round 2)	Universität Regensburg, Germany
Josef Pieprzyk	CSIRO/Data61, Australia
Joachim Posegga	University of Passau, Germany
Mir Mehedi Pritom (Round 2)	Tennessee Tech University, USA

Megha Quamara (Round 2) — King's College London, UK
Silvio Ranise (Round 2) — University of Trento, Italy
Kai Rannenberg (Round 2) — Goethe University Frankfurt, Germany
Siddharth Prakash Rao (Round 2) — Nokia Bell Labs, Finland
Danda B. Rawat (Round 2) — Howard University, USA
Indrakshi Ray (Round 1) — Colorado State University, USA
Indrajit Ray (Round 2) — Colorado State University, USA
Peter Rønne — University of Luxembourg, Luxembourg
Carlos Rubio Medrano (Round 2) — Texas A&M University, USA
Peter Y. A. Ryan — University of Luxembourg, Luxembourg
Reihaneh Safavi-Naini — University of Calgary, Canada
Pierangela Samarati — Università degli Studi di Milano, Italy
Neetesh Saxena — Cardiff University, UK
Neta Rozen-Schiff (Round 2) — Hebrew University of Jerusalem, Israel
Dominique Schröder — Universität Erlangen-Nürnberg, Germany
Jörg Schwenk — Ruhr-Universität Bochum, Germany
Savio Sciancalepore — Eindhoven University of Technology, The Netherlands
R. Sekar (Round 2) — Stony Brook University, USA
Basit Shafiq (Round 2) — Lahore University of Management Sciences, Pakistan
Ankit Shah (Round 2) — Indiana University, USA
Siamak Shahandashti — University of York, UK
Alessandro Sorniotti (Round 1) — IBM Research Europe, Switzerland
Shantanu Sharma (Round 2) — New Jersey Institute of Technology, USA
Wenbo Shen (Round 2) — Zhejiang University, China
Weidong Shi (Round 2) — University of Houston, USA
Arunesh Sinha (Round 2) — Rutgers University, USA
Jayesh Soni (Round 2) — Florida International University, USA
Angelo Spognardi — Sapienza Università di Roma, Italy
Riccardo Spolaor — Shandong University, China
Natalia Stakhanova (Round 2) — University of Saskatchewan, Canada
Thorsten Strufe (Round 2) — Karlsruhe Institute of Technology, Germany
Wenhai Sun (Round 2) — Purdue University, USA
Shamik Sural (Round 2) — Indian Institute of Technology Kharagpur, India
Luis Suárez (Round 2) — Ericsson, Canada
Qiang Tang (Round 2) — University of Sydney, Australia
Nadia Tawbi — Laval University, Canada
Vicenc Torra — Umeå University, Sweden
Jacob Torrey (Round 2) — Thinkst Applied Research, USA
Ari Trachtenberg (Round 2) — Boston University, USA
Stacey Truex (Round 2) — Denison University, USA

Jalaj Upadhyay (Round 2)	Johns Hopkins University, USA
Tobias Urban (Round 2)	Westphalian University of Applied Sciences, Germany
Daniele Venturi	Sapienza University of Rome, Italy
Rakesh Verma (Round 2)	University of Houston, USA
Tran Viet Xuan Phuong (Round 2)	University of Arkansas at Little Rock, USA
Joao P. Vilela (Round 2)	University of Porto, Portugal
Di Wang (Round 2)	State University of New York at Buffalo, USA
Haining Wang (Round 2)	Virginia Tech, USA
Cong Wang (Round 2)	City University of Hong Kong, China
Xinyue Wang (Round 2)	Renmin University of China, China
Lingyu Wang (Round 2)	Concordia University, Canada
Han Wang (Round 2)	University of Kansas, USA
Wenqi Wei (Round 2)	Fordham University, USA
Edgar Weippl	University of Vienna, Austria
Avishai Wool (Round 1)	Tel Aviv University, Israel
Christos Xenakis (Round 2)	University of Piraeus, Greece
Yang Xiang (Round 2)	Swinburne University of Technology, Australia
Yue Xiao (Round 2)	IBM Research, USA
Shouhuai Xu (Round 2)	University of Colorado Colorado Springs, USA
Runhua Xu (Round 2)	Beihang University, China
Peng Xu (Round 2)	Huazhong University of Science and Technology, China
Guomin Yang (Round 2)	Singapore Management University, Singapore
Zhihao Yao (Round 2)	New Jersey Institute of Technology, USA
Roland Yap (Round 2)	National University of Singapore, Singapore
Miuyin Yong Wong (Round 2)	Georgia Institute of Technology, USA
Chuan Yue (Round 2)	Colorado School of Mines, USA
Stefano Zanero (Round 1)	Politecnico di Milano, Italy
Yuan Zhang (Round 2)	Fudan University, China
Zhikun Zhang (Round 2)	Zhejiang University, China
Kehuan Zhang (Round 2)	Chinese University of Hong Kong, China
Liang Zhao (Round 2)	Emory University, USA
Ziming Zhao (Round 2)	Northeastern University, USA
Yunlei Zhao (Round 2)	Fudan University, China
Jianying Zhou (Round 2)	Singapore University of Technology and Design, Singapore
Sencun Zhu (Round 2)	Pennsylvania State University, USA
Rui Zhu (Round 2)	Indiana University, USA

Additional Reviewers

Abbadini, Marco
Abdelgawad, Mahmoud
Abdullahi, Ahmed
Abu Jabal, Amani
Afzal, Zeeshan
Aghayarzadeh, Hamed
Agrawal, Anand
Ahmed, Basharat
Ahmed, Faisal
Akbar, Khandakar Ashrafi
Akbarzadeh, Aida
Al Kadri, Mhd Omar
Al Mahmud, Tamim
Alborch Escobar, Ferran
Alhaidari, Abdulrahman
Allami, Ali
Almani, Dimah
Almasan, Paul
Almutaitri, Abeer
Amaral Simões, Sancho
Arazzi, Marco
Armanuzzaman, Md
Arriaga, Afonso
Arrus, Aurora
Aryal, Kshitiz
Aung, Yan Lin
Avizheh, Sepideh
Azizli, Elmaddin
Bacho, Renas
Baecker, Ruben
Bashir, Shadaab Kawnain
Belguith, Sana
Benaloh, Josh
Beneš, Martin
Beretta, Michele
Berlato, Stefano
Bertrand, Léo
Bertrand, Simon
Bezawada, Bruhadeshwar
Bianchi, Federica
Binosi, Lorenzo
Binte Haq, Hina
Birashk, Amin

Biswas, Chinmoy
Bisways, Chinmoy
Boyapally, Harishma
Carlson, Trevor E.
Carminati, Michele
Carvalho, Tânia
Casagrande, Marco
Castiglione, Arcangelo
Castiglione, Gianpietro
Catuogno, Luigi
Cecconello, Stefano
Charlès, Alex
Chaturvedi, Bhuvnesh
Chawla, Abhimanyu
Chekole, Eyasu Getahun
Chen, Depeng
Chen, Juntao
Chen, Yumin
Chen, Zeyu
Chong, Chun Jie
Chouchoulis, Ioannis
Chu, Hien Thi Thu
Cihangiroglu, Mert
Cimato, Stelvio
Collu, Matteo Gioele
Cui, Hui
Cunha, Mariana
Dai, Jiongyu
Dai, Xushu
Daneshmand, Arash
Dang, Hai-Van
Das, Debayan
Das, Prajit Kumar
Das Chowdhury, Partha
Daudén-Esmel, Cristòfol
Deidda, Nicola
Demetrio, Luca
Demir, Nurullah
Demirkiran, Ferhat
Dey, Kunal
Di Gennaro, Marco
Di Paolo, Edoardo
Ding, Weikang

Dipta, Debopriya Roy
Dolati, Mahdi
Donadel, Denis
Droll, Jan
Du, Linkang
Du, Minxin
Duck, Gregory
Dunbar, Arthur
Eichhammer, Philipp
Erinola, Nurullah
Esposito, Sergio
Facchinetti, Dario
Fadavi, Mojtaba
Falanji, Reyhane
Falebita, Oluwatosin
Faraj, Omair
Farasat, Talaya
Feng, Hanwen
Ferrari, Stefano
Ferré-Queralt, Joan
Flamini, Andrea
Fotiadis, Georgios
Fouotsa, Tako Boris
Galeazzi, Alessandro
Gao, Yang
Garbelini, Matheus
García Díaz, Jorge Francisco
García Fernández, Pablo
George, Aleena Elsa
Ghorbel, Bassem
Ghosh, Soumyadyuti
Giannakopoulos, Thrasyvoulos
Giapantzis, Konstantinos
Gimenez, Pierre-François
Glas, Magdalena
Golinelli, Matteo
Gomes, Catarina
Gowdanakatte, Shwetha
Grill, Johannes
Grisafi, Michele
Groszschaedl, Johann
Grundmann, Matthias
Guiot, Miquel
Guo, Jinduo
Gupta, Deepti

Haefner, Kyle
Haffar, Rami
Haffey, Preston
Hamm, Peter
Hamm And Lieberknecht, Two Subreviewers Peter And Ann-Kristin
Han, Qiang
Han, Yanni
Haque, Md Shahedul
Hassanpour, Seyedeh Bahereh
Herranz, Javier
Hopkins, Jacob
Hore, Soumyadeep
Hosseini, Henry
Hou, Chenxi
Howard, Samuel
Hu, Chengcong
Huang, Mengdie
Huang, Qiqing
Huang, Zhicheng
Huso, Ingrid
Ibarrondo, Alberto
In, Junbeom
Ioannidis, Thodoris
Irfan, Muhammad
Jacob, Florian
Jacqmin, Quentin
Jiang, Shan
Jiang, Yuning
Jin, Heng
Jorba, Josep
Kaaniche, Nesrine
Kammueller, Florian
Kanpak, Halil Ibrahim
Karim Imtiaz
Katsis Charalampos
Kei, Andes Y. L.
Kembu, Vignesh Kumar
Kermabon-Bobinnec, Hugo
Kern, Sascha
Khan, Younas
Kimm, Hanke
Koffas, Stefanos
Koohpayeh Araghi, Tanya
Korichi, Youcef

Kouko, Gildas
Kumar, Gulshan
Kumari, Komal
Kunwar, Pradip
Lalande, Jean-Francois
Lara, Carlos
Laura Madison, Axel Durbet
Le Mouel, Florian
Leinweber, Marc
Lerch-Hostalot, Daniel
Li, Adrian Shuai
Li, Fagen
Li, Xiang
Li, Xiaoguo
Li, Yamin
Li Calsi, Davide
Liang, Yu
Ligier, Damien
Lin, Chao
Litzinger, Sebastian
Liu, Gaoxiang
Liu, Jiahao
Liu, Jianghua
Loh, Jia-Chng
Lombard-Platet, Marius
Longo, Riccardo
Lopez Morales, Efren
Lotto, Alessandro
Luchini, Chiara
Luo, Nanqing
Lybarger, Kevin
Löbner, Sascha
Ma, Jack P. K.
Ma, Jinhua
Ma, Wanlun
Ma, Zheyuan
Maehren, Marcel
Maffei, Ivo
Maitra, Sudip
Makropodis, Ioannis
Maldonado, Mark
Manzanares-Salor, Benet
Martins, Óscar
Marty, Pierre
Massidda, Emmanuele

McCarthy, Andrew
Meadows, Catherine
Meng, Qiaoran
Mercer, Rebekah
Merzdovnik, Georg
Michaud, Quentin
Mishra, Nimish
Mishra, Sagar
Mitra, Shaswata
Mohammadi, Sareh
Mondragon, Jennifer
Mostafiz, Mir Imtiaz
Mura, Raffaele
Müller, Mathis
Nagasubramaniam, Piyush
Nath, Souradip
Nelson, Jonathan
Neudert, Raphael
Nguyen, Hieu
Nicolazzo, Serena
Niknia, Ahad
Niow, Choon Hock
Noble, Daniel
P., Vinod
Palihawadana, Chamath
Pan, Ying-Yu
Panebianco, Francesco
Panja, Somnath
Patel, Raj
Paudel, Diwas
Persiano, Giuseppe
Pimpinella, Giovanni
Podder, Rakesh
Praharaj, Lopamudra
Preatoni, Riccardo
Psychogyiou, Aikaterini
Pucher, Michael
Puchta, Alexander
Pérez-Ramos, Edgar
Qiu, Tian Qu, Jiashu
Quadrio, Giacomo
Quinci, Arianna
Qureshi, Amna
Raciti, Mario
Rasul, Md Fazle

Regano, Leonardo
Reijsbergen, Daniel
Rizzi, Matteo
Rosenblattl, Jakob
Rossi, Matthew
Roy, Shovan
Russo, Luigi
Saadi Dadmarzi, Hamidreza
Sacchetta, Juri
Saha, Rahul
Samdaliri, Mahya
Sanna, Alessandro
Saqlain, Sabbir Ahmed
Sato, Shingo
Sauger, Gabriel
Senn, Judith
Serra-Ruiz, Jordi
Sha, Kailun
Shafir, Lior
Shahriar, Md Hasan
Sharif, Amir
Shen, Zilin
Shepherd, Carlton
Shi, Shanghao
Siemer, Jan Niklas
Singh, Animesh
Singh, Gurjot
Sinha, Sayani
Skandylas, Charilaos
Skrobot, Marjan
Song, Yongcheng
Song, Zirui
Soria-Comas, Jordi
Spadafora, Chiara
Spiesberger, Patrick
Srivastava, Gautam
Stifter, Nicholas
Streicher, Klaus
Stylianou, Ioannis
Sun, Shihua
Sözen Esen, Derya
Thomas, Julian
Thomas, Tony
Tian, Guohua
Tian, Jianwen

Tippe, Pascal
Todd, James
Torabi, Sadegh
Tripathi, Himanshu
Trombetta, Alberto
Tsado, Yakubu
Tuck, Bryan
Tureček, Philip
Udovenko, Aleksei
Valeriani, Lorenzo
Vasilopoulos, Dimitrios
Wan, Guoan
Wang, Cheng-Long
Wang, Hongxiao
Wang, Jingzhe
Wang, Lulu
Wang, Shuo
Wang, Wenli
Wang, Xinhai
Wang, Yuyu
Wazan, Ahmad Samer
Wen, Tian
Wong, Harry W. H.
Wu, Jiaojiao
Wu, Pengfei
Xie, Xinhong
Xu, Chenming
Xu, Difei
Xu, Peng
Xu, Shengmin
Xue, Haiyang
Yan, Yingfei
Yang, Fan
Yang, Yang
Yang, Zeyu
Yin, Zihao
Younas, Affan
Yu, Chia-Mu
Yu, Hexuan
Yu, Tianchi
Yuan, Quan
Yuan, Wei
Yuan, Yijun
Zari, Oualid
Zhang, Bokang

Zhang, Chaoyu
Zhang, Ke
Zhang, Zicheng
Zhao, Rui

Zhou, Ming
Zhu, Rui
Zhu, Xiaogang
Özfatura, Kerem

Contents – Part IV

Transparency and Consent Challenges in mHealth Apps:
An Interdisciplinary Study of Privacy Policies, Data Sharing,
and Dark Patterns 1
   *Mehrdad Bahrini, Alexander Herbst, Merle Freye, Matthias Kohn,
Karsten Sohr, and Rainer Malaka*

Don't Hash Me Like That: Exposing and Mitigating Hash-Induced
Unfairness in Local Differential Privacy 22
   Berkay Kemal Balioglu, Alireza Khodaie, and M. Emre Gursoy

Functional Credentials: A Practical Construction for the European Digital
Identity 43
   Giovanni Bartolomeo

Privacy-Preserving k-Nearest Neighbor Query: Faster and More Secure 63
   *Jialin Chi, Cheng Hong, Axin Wu, Tianqi Sun, ZheChen Li, Min Zhang,
and Dengguo Feng*

Breaking Verifiability and Vote Privacy in CHVote 86
   Véronique Cortier, Alexandre Debant, and Pierrick Gaudry

Zero-Click SnailLoad: From Minimal to No User Interaction 106
   *Stefan Gast, Nora Puntigam, Simone Franza,
Sudheendra Raghav Neela, Daniel Gruss, and Johanna Ullrich*

Analysis of Input-Output Mappings in Coinjoin Transactions
with Arbitrary Values 126
   Jiri Gavenda, Petr Svenda, Stanislav Bobon, and Vladimir Sedlacek

Email Cloaking: Deceiving Users and Spam Email Detectors with Invisible
HTML Settings 147
   *Bingyang Guo, Mingxuan Liu, Yihui Ma, Ruixuan Li, Fan Shi,
Min Zhang, Baojun Liu, Chengxi Xu, Haixin Duan, Geng Hong,
Min Yang, and Qingfeng Pan*

BlowPrint: Blow-Based Multi-factor Biometrics for Smartphone User
Authentication 169
   *Howard Halim, Eyasu Getahun Chekole, Daniël Reijsbergen,
and Jianying Zhou*

GET-AID: Graph-Enhanced Transformer for Provenance-Based Advanced
Persistent Threats Investigation and Detection 190
  *Zhicheng Huang, Fengyuan Xu, Jiahong Yang, Wenting Li,
  Zonghua Zhang, Chenbin Zhang, Meng Ma, and Ping Wang*

The Economics of Deception: Structural Patterns of Rug Pull Across DeFi
Blockchains 211
  *Bhavani Kalal, Abdulrahman Alhaidari, Balaji Palanisamy,
  and Shamik Sural*

Privacy-Preserving Trajectory Data Publication Via Differentially-Private
Representation Learning 233
  Youcef Korichi, Josée Desharnais, Sébastien Gambs, and Nadia Tawbi

Fine-Grained, Privacy-Augmenting LI-Compliance in the LAKE Standard 253
  *Pascal Lafourcade, Elsa López Pérez, Charles Olivier-Anclin,
  Cristina Onete, Clément Papon, and Mališa Vučinić*

RIPOST: Two-Phase Private Decomposition for Multidimensional Data 274
  Ala Eddine Laouir and Abdessamad Imine

Correcting the Record on Leakage Abuse Attacks: Revisiting the Subgraph
Attacks with Sound Evaluation 294
  Takumi Namiki, Takumi Amada, Mitsugu Iwamoto, and Yohei Watanabe

Efficient and Secure Sleepy Model for BFT Consensus 314
  Pengkun Ren, Hai Dong, Zahir Tari, and Pengcheng Zhang

An Algebraic Approach to Asymmetric Delegation and Polymorphic
Label Inference 334
  Silei Ren, Coşku Acay, and Andrew C. Myers

An Efficient Security-Enhanced Accountable Access Control for Named
Data Networking 354
  Jianfei Sun, Yuxian Li, Xuehuan Yang, Guomin Yang, and Robert Deng

Dobby: A Privacy-Preserving Time Series Data Analytics System
with Enforcement of Flexible Policies 374
  Yansen Xin, Rui Zhang, Zhenglin Fan, and Ze Jia

A User-Centric, Privacy-Preserving, and Verifiable Ecosystem for Personal
Data Management and Utilization 395
  Osama Zafar, Mina Namazi, Yuqiao Xu, Youngjin Yoo, and Erman Ayday

Imitater: An Efficient Shared Mempool Protocol with Application
to Byzantine Fault Tolerance 415
    Qingming Zeng, Mo Li, Ximing Fu, Hui Jiang, and Chuanyi Liu

Premining in the Shadows: How Hidden Blocks Weaken the Security
of Proof-of-Work Chains 433
    Wanying Zeng, Lijia Xie, and Xiao Zhang

Author Index 453

Transparency and Consent Challenges in mHealth Apps: An Interdisciplinary Study of Privacy Policies, Data Sharing, and Dark Patterns

Mehrdad Bahrini[1]($\boxtimes$), Alexander Herbst[1], Merle Freye[2], Matthias Kohn[2], Karsten Sohr[1], and Rainer Malaka[1]

[1] Digital Media Lab, TZI, University of Bremen, Bremen, Germany
{mbahrini,herbst1,sohr,malaka}@uni-bremen.de
[2] Institute for Information, Health and Medical Law, University of Bremen, Bremen, Germany
{mfreye,kohn}@uni-bremen.de

Abstract. Health, fitness, and medical apps have become increasingly popular to help users manage their well-being. However, their widespread use raises significant concerns about data privacy, given the sensitive nature of the information they process. In this study, we evaluate the transparency and regulatory compliance of such apps by focusing on three key aspects: actual data transmission behavior, claims made in privacy policies—particularly concerning third-country recipients—and the presence of dark patterns in their user interfaces. We combine network traffic analysis with a systematic review of privacy policies to examine whether data is transmitted before consent and whether recipients align with disclosures. In addition, we analyze interface designs for manipulative elements that can hinder informed consent. Our results reveal discrepancies between stated and observed data flows, instances of pre-consent data transmission, and recurring dark patterns. These findings highlight critical transparency gaps and underscore the need for stronger enforcement and user-centered privacy design.

Keywords: mHealth Apps · GDPR Compliance · Dynamic Analysis · Static Analysis · Privacy Policies · Dark Patterns · Data Sharing

1 Introduction

Mobile Health applications (mHealth apps) have become increasingly prevalent as people seek convenient ways to achieve health goals and receive tailored health guidance. However, the growing integration of these apps into daily life raises significant concerns about personal data protection and transparency, especially given the sensitive nature of the information handled [3,20,49]. Existing studies highlight discrepancies between the stated privacy policies and observed data handling practices. For example, researchers analyzed 36 mental health apps and observed that although 23 apps disclosed third-party data sharing, 33 apps transmitted data externally, with only a fraction clearly stating such practices in their privacy policies [30]. Similarly, studies discovered that some popular Android apps continued to send sensitive data, such as advertising IDs and GPS locations, to promotion companies even when advertising tracking was disabled [13]. These findings demonstrate a widespread misalignment between declared and actual data practices, underscoring critical transparency and compliance gaps. Although previous studies examined general third-party data sharing [8,14,27], our study takes a more targeted approach by examining not just *if* data is shared, but also *where* it is sent and *when*. We specifically examine data transmissions to third countries and whether such transfers precede explicit user consent, resulting in our initial research questions: *1) To what extent do data recipients listed in mHealth app privacy policies align with observed data transmission patterns, including transfers to third countries?* and *2) Does any data transmission occur before users consent to privacy policies?*.

Beyond data transmission patterns, we explore dark patterns in privacy policy interfaces of mHealth apps. Dark patterns are manipulative design tactics that undermine user autonomy by obscuring, misleading, or coercing decisions [37]. Examples include Missing Consent Notices, Disguised Data Collection, Obfuscation, Forced Action, Privacy Zuckering, Misdirection, and Forced Registration, each methodically reducing transparency and user control over personal data [12,26,28]. Considering the security and ethical implications of these tactics, we ask: *3) What is the prevalence of dark patterns in privacy policy forms of mHealth apps?* Finally, we assess the comprehensiveness and clarity of information presented in privacy policies, which builds on insights from previous questions to determine the degree of user-informed awareness. Our fourth research question thus examines: *4) How comprehensive are the privacy policies of mHealth apps in delineating information regarding data recipients, international data transfers, and personal data utilization?* We structure our study methodology into three key components to address these questions. First, we curate a set of 20 widely used mHealth apps according to clearly defined selection criteria. Second, we analyze the apps' privacy policies in-depth, comparing their stated practices against actual data transmissions obtained from hybrid analyses (static and dynamic). Third, we closely scrutinize consent forms and privacy interfaces for the presence of dark patterns and other manipulative design elements. This holistic approach enables us to provide comprehensive insights into transparency and regulatory compliance, enhancing both user autonomy and data security.

This work makes four key contributions. First, we present empirical evidence from a comparative analysis of 20 widely used mHealth apps, revealing discrepancies between the data handling practices described in their privacy policies and the actual behaviors observed through technical analysis. Second, we systematically identify dark patterns in consent and privacy interfaces using a manual heuristic approach grounded in established taxonomies, uncovering how interface design may mislead users or obscure privacy-relevant decisions. Third, we evaluate the transparency of privacy policies from a user-centered perspective through content analysis, assessing how information about data recipients, international transfers, and data usage is communicated. Fourth, we adopt an interdisciplinary perspective that integrates insights from information security, human-computer interaction, and legal regulatory frameworks, offering a holistic understanding of privacy and usability challenges.

2 Related Work

The interdisciplinary nature of this study spans technical analysis, legal frameworks, and user interface design, which together provide a comprehensive understanding of data privacy issues in mHealth apps. Previous research has examined various aspects of privacy and security in this domain, including app behaviors [16], consent mechanisms [44], and interface manipulation [28]. Furthermore, studies have highlighted security shortcomings, such as weak encryption [50], hard-coded secrets [46], insecure communication channels [40], and excessive permissions [29]. Based on this foundation, Forsberg and Iwaya conducted an in-depth security assessment of ten top-ranked health apps, identifying widespread technical vulnerabilities, including insecure encryption methods, hard-coded API keys, and extensive data sharing with third-party domains [22]. Their study focused primarily on the technical security posture of widely used apps. In contrast, the present study adopts a broader interdisciplinary approach by combining static and dynamic technical analysis with investigating privacy policy compliance and dark patterns in consent interfaces. Analyzing 20 available mHealth apps in Germany, this study emphasizes how personal data is transmitted, how user consent is shaped through interface design, and how well privacy disclosures align with observed behaviors.

Beyond technical vulnerabilities, existing research has emphasized the importance of privacy policies in shaping the user's understanding of data practices, while also revealing significant shortcomings and inconsistencies in the privacy practices of mHealth apps [2,9,48,49]. Several studies have further examined the compliance of the General Data Protection Regulation (GDPR) in mobile applications, particularly focusing on the transparency and completeness of privacy policies [11,20,39,43]. Although initial work has addressed these issues, more systematic investigations are needed to compare disclosed privacy practices with actual data collection and sharing behaviors using static and dynamic analysis [54]. In addition, the usability of security settings and privacy policies has emerged as a critical concern in mHealth apps [29,36].

Even though many apps formally comply with the GDPR disclosure requirements, studies have shown that their privacy features are often difficult for users to understand due to complex legal language, excessive length, and complicated settings [41,55]. Users are typically required to agree on privacy policies to access digital tools and services; however, readability analyses indicate that these agreements are often not comprehensible to most adults and even less so to younger users [15]. This lack of transparency creates opportunities for the use of dark patterns and manipulative interface designs that nudge users toward decisions that may not align with their privacy preferences or best interests. Dark patterns have been increasingly documented in digital interfaces, particularly within consent dialogs, privacy settings, and account registrations [17]. These manipulative designs exploit cognitive biases to encourage greater data sharing or hinder the exercise of privacy rights [35]. Common types include Missing Consent Notices, Disguised Data Collection, Obfuscation, Forced Action, Misdirection, and Forced Registration [37]. Practices such as hiding privacy information behind additional clicks or visually emphasizing "Accept All" options are widespread [42]. Although previous research has addressed technical flaws, privacy policies, or dark patterns—sometimes in combination [31]—this study provides an integrated analysis that combines hybrid code analysis, privacy policy evaluation, and dark pattern detection in widely used mHealth apps.

3 Methodology

This study used a multifaceted methodology to analyze a set of mHealth apps available in Germany, focusing on their underlying codes, detecting dark patterns, and evaluating compliance with privacy policies. The technical analysis was conducted using a hybrid approach, combining static and dynamic methods. The static analysis delves into the APK files of the apps without execution, employing tools such as MobSF [1] to dissect their code and structural components. On the other hand, dynamic analysis involves the active execution of apps to observe real-time behaviors and user interactions, especially concerning the transmission of personal data. This process was facilitated by network monitoring software, which allowed for detailed observation and data collection. To prepare for dynamic analysis, an Android smartphone was rooted and configured, with specific permissions activated and monitoring tools installed, creating a controlled environment conducive to a thorough examination. In addition to technical analysis, the privacy policy user interfaces of the apps were scrutinized for the presence of dark patterns or manipulative design elements intended to deceive or drive users into certain actions. Finally, the privacy policies of the selected apps underwent a thorough review to identify involved third parties, types of collected personal data, and potential data transfer destinations. Note that under the GDPR (Art. 6(1)), user consent is only one of several legal bases for personal data processing [53]. Our subsequent analyses focus on apps that explicitly state consent as the legal basis, in accordance with Art. 6(1)(a).

App Selection: For this study, we selected 20 mobile apps from the Google Play Store, focusing on the categories "Health and Fitness" and "Medical" categories due to their handling of sensitive data, emphasizing the need for transparent and secure communication with users [52]. To ensure a comprehensive study, we chose apps that appeal to a diverse audience and represent various user demographics. In addition, accessibility played a pivotal role in our selection process. Therefore, all chosen apps had to be provided for free, ensuring that users could download and use them without any cost. Our experimental design prioritized independent analysis, avoiding the necessity of input from medical professionals. Hence, apps requiring interaction with medical personnel, such as appointment scheduling or video consultations, were excluded. Similarly, apps focused on medical personnel training were also omitted. We excluded specific categories of apps to maintain a focus on general health and fitness. These included COVID-19 apps, especially those affiliated with the Robert Koch Institute, as well as apps associated with DiGA (Digitale Gesundheitsanwendungen, translated as "Digital Health Applications"), which target managing specific health conditions and are typically used by people covered by statutory health insurances. Furthermore, service apps of statutory health insurance companies in Germany were excluded to provide relevance to a broader public audience. With reference to our selection criteria, the apps were determined based on their download count using AndroidRank [7] data. The apps chosen from the "Health and Fitness" and "Medical" categories are presented in Table 1.

Table 1. Health, Fitness, and Medical Apps

Rank	Name	Developer	Downloads
Health & Fitness			
1.	Samsung Health	Samsung Electronics Co., Ltd.	1B
2.	Period Calendar Period Tracker	Simple Design Ltd.	100M
3.	Home Workout No Equipment	Leap Fitness Group	100M
4.	Zepp Life (MiFit)	Anhui Huami Information Technology Co., Ltd.	100M
5.	MyFitnessPal: Calorie Counter	MyFitnessPal, Inc.	100M
6.	Six Pack in 30 Days	Leap Fitness Group	100M
7.	Google Fit: Activity Tracking	Google LLC	100M
8.	Flo Ovulation & Period Tracker	Flo Health Inc.	100M
9.	Sweatcoin	Sweatco Ltd.	100M
10.	Lose Weight App for Men	Leap Fitness Group	100M
Medical			
1.	Period Tracker and Calendar	SimpleInnovation	10M
2.	amma: Pregnancy & Baby Tracker	PERIOD TRACKER & PREGNANCY AND BABY CALENDAR	10M
3.	Blood Pressure	Klimaszewski Szymon	10M
4.	Ada check your health	Ada Health	10M
5.	Period and Ovulation Tracker	SMSROBOT LTD	10M
6.	Pregnancy App	Amila	5M
7.	MyTherapy Pill Reminder	MyTherapy	5M
8.	Ladytimer Ovulation Calendar	Vipos Apps	5M
9.	Medscape	WebMD, LLC	5M
10.	Ovia Pregnancy & Baby Tracker	Ovia Health	1M

Static Analysis: We employed the Mobile Security Framework (MobSF) in the static analysis stage to investigate the selected apps. MobSF is a versatile tool designed for penetration testing, malware analysis, and static security assessments. Although MobSF provides a wide array of functionalities, we focus here on elucidating the pertinent features we utilized. One key aspect of MobSF is its capability to inspect the permissions requested by an app extracted from the "AndroidManifest.xml" file. These permissions delineate the actions for which an app seeks the consent of the user, such as accessing location information or camera functionality. Our goal is to determine whether these permissions imply the collection of personal data, which can then be cross-referenced with disclosures in privacy policies. Moving forward, we explore network security within the "Security Analysis" section of MobSF's results for each individual app. The findings may flag potential vulnerabilities necessitating further investigation. Furthermore, MobSF facilitates the identification of communication channels between the analyzed apps and distributed servers. It includes details such as server location, IP address, and domain name, helping to identify server operators and their industry affiliations, whether it involves advertising or providing services. This information is crucial for assessing whether data transmission crosses borders.

Dynamic Analysis: The technique used in dynamic analysis draws inspiration from the approach outlined by Claesson and Bjørstad [13]. We set up our testing environment using a Google Pixel 2 XL running Android 10, connected to a home network. During the dynamic analysis stage, we analyzed app network communications in real-time using Burp Suite [45], a comprehensive tool developed by PortSwigger for web or application security testing and analysis of HTTP traffic. To set up our analysis, we configured Burp Suite's proxy server with port 8082. This configuration enables us to intercept and inspect outgoing messages from the mobile device within the Burp Suite interface. The network settings on the smartphone were then adjusted so that all outgoing traffic was routed through the same port. Since most of the outgoing network traffic is actually encrypted using the HTTPS protocol, decrypting these messages was crucial for our analysis. One common method involves installing a self-signed certificate via the Burp Suite to facilitate a Man-in-the-Middle attack. This process installs a certificate that allows the examined app to trust Burp Suite as an intermediary, enabling the decryption of the network traffic. Despite Android 10 permitting the installation of self-signed certificates, it segregates them into two distinct storage areas. These certificates are stored in the user certificate storage, yet apps installed on the device solely trust certificates from the Trusted Credential Storage [5]. Therefore, the decryption of network messages becomes impossible. To bypass this security measure, we rooted the Android smartphone. A rooted device grants us the ability to execute privileged actions that are typically inaccessible. This is achieved by running processes with UID zero, causing all privileged processes to disregard permission checks from the system's kernel. In addition, we gain the ability to manipulate system files, including adding, editing, or deleting them.

The preparation of the device for rooting is a necessary step. Android complicates direct alterations to the kernel system, prompting users to modify the bootloader [6] instead. The bootloader initializes and launches the kernel on a device while monitoring its status. In order to acquire separate permissions, a program must be installed on the bootloader, necessitating the initial unlocking of the bootloader to allow the initiation of third-party programs directly. This step can be accomplished through the developer options provided by Android.

Upon unlocking the bootloader, Magisk [33] was installed. Magisk serves as a tool for modifying Android devices without altering the core system, which is known as systemless rooting. This approach requires users to completely control their devices without directly impacting the system itself. Unlike traditional rooting methods, Magisk is initialized directly by the bootloader upon device startup, avoiding direct system modifications. In particular, this technique circumvents detection by various apps designed to identify rooted devices, including Google's SafetyNet [4]. Installing Magisk on the bootloader enabled a rooted environment for testing while maintaining original app functionality.

Following its installation on the bootloader, a fully privileged Magisk daemon with UID:0 is executed during the booting process. This daemon can grant root privileges to any process requiring them. Moreover, Magisk supports the installation of extensions. For analytical purposes, the Magisk Trust User Certs extension [32] was installed. This module enables the installation of all user-installed certificates into the Trusted Credential Storage during system startup, ensuring that all apps on the device trust these certificates. Consequently, in conjunction with Burp Suite, all encrypted outgoing and incoming HTTPS messages can be decrypted directly from the device.

After the device has been prepared, network activities are monitored using Burp Suite. Serving as an intercepting HTTPS proxy, Burp Suite renders encrypted TLS data in a comprehensible format. Among the transmitted data, certain personally identifiable information, such as the local IP address, country, and language, can be observed coming from the host *branch.io*, a service commonly used for mobile deep linking and attribution. It should be noted that many of these transmitted messages are further encoded in an unreadable format. Although encoding differs from encryption, it is commonly utilized to minimize the file size of transmitted data. Common encoding schemes found in HTTPS messages include URL, Base64, ASCII Hex, Octal, Binary, or GZIP. Decoding messages usually involves identifying the encoding method, often omitted during transmission, complicating the decoding process. Burp Suite offers tools to identify the encoding format and decode accordingly. Although frequently used in the analysis, it is worth mentioning that some messages, primarily those from Google, could not be decoded, rendering them unreadable.

We created a test persona named *Petra Muster* to facilitate dynamic analysis. Then we have generated various health data points for this person, including weight, age, gender, temperature, and date of birth. Furthermore, technical data such as the Google Advertising ID and the Device ID were collected to facilitate locating them in the data stream of network transmissions.

At the outset of the dynamic analysis, the app is freshly installed and left to run for five minutes without any interaction. Throughout this period, network transmissions are closely monitored. As the next step, the app is executed until consent to the privacy policy is required. If personal data are found to be transmitted at this stage, it is considered a breach of the privacy policy, as consent has not yet been obtained. In addition, an examination is conducted to ensure that the language of the privacy policy displayed matches the language of execution. Then consent is granted, and the app is executed through all its functionality to determine whether the transmitted data and the destinations of these transmissions align with the terms outlined in the privacy policy. Lastly, it is verified whether the app offers a mechanism for users to revoke consent to the privacy policy within its interface.

Dark Patterns Analysis: One focus of this study was on uncovering dark patterns embedded within consent agreements. We captured screenshots of all privacy policy agreement interfaces through dynamic analysis, subjecting them to detailed scrutiny afterward. Initially, we conducted an exhaustive examination to identify potential dark patterns and documented their occurrences. Subsequently, we synthesized a comprehensive list of recurring dark patterns, streamlining the classification process for app privacy policies. This compiled inventory encompassed a variety of possible dark patterns, including Misdirection, Forced Action, Obfuscation, Disguised Data Collection, Missing Notices and Options, and Forced Registration [35].

Privacy Policies Analysis: We examined the privacy policies of selected applications through a systematic process. Firstly, we thoroughly reviewed each privacy policy, carefully examining the disclosed information regarding third-party recipients, third countries involved in data processing, and the types of personal data collected. Next, we meticulously cataloged all third-party recipients mentioned in the privacy policies. These entities ranged from specific corporations like Google or Facebook to more general designations such as "business partners" or "companies for purposes of analytics." Subsequently, we analyzed the section on data processing outside the originating country.

We identified all mentioned foreign countries and determined the legal basis associated with data processing in these jurisdictions. Whether explicitly named or described using terms like "Outside the European Economic Area" we documented these instances. Lastly, we cataloged all types of personal data and health-related information mentioned in the privacy policies. We then compared our findings with data obtained from both static and dynamic analyses. This comparative analysis allowed us to highlight any inconsistencies or discrepancies between the disclosed privacy policies and the actual operational practices of the respective applications. Figure 1 visually summarizes the investigation process.

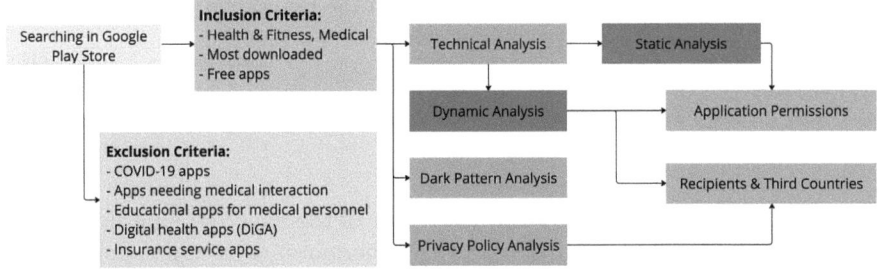

Fig. 1. Overview of analysis steps and objectives.

4 Empirical Findings

Recipients of Transmitted Data: One of the essential parts of our analysis was examining the data recipients with whom communication was established. We categorized these recipients by analyzing the results of static and dynamic analyses, evaluating the privacy policies, and conducting subsequent Whois searches online. In particular, a recipient can belong to multiple categories, reflecting the multifaceted nature of their involvement. The identified recipients fell into distinct groups:

- *Advertising Companies:* Specialized entities leveraging data for targeted advertising.
- *Analytical Services:* Providers that collect, measure, and analyze user behavior within the app for insights and personalized marketing.
- *Information Providers:* Offering users valuable information, such as dietary habits, sleep patterns, and crisis assistance.
- *Governmental Bodies:* Dispensing information and standards at the governmental level.
- *Service Providers:* Offering a range of technical services for apps, including cloud computing, development tools, and artificial intelligence.
- *Social Media Platforms:* Facilitating social interactions on networks such as Facebook, X (formerly Twitter), and Instagram.
- *Potentially Malicious Entities:* Hosts posing security risks, such as fraudulent activity or malware distribution.
- *Partners:* Likely contractual collaborators contributing to app development or functionality.

Table 2 summarizes the categorization of recipients in the analysis. Interestingly, recipients categorized as "advertising companies" were frequently encountered, totaling 49 instances. This finding highlights a widespread dependency on numerous advertising entities, averaging 2.45 per app. Moreover, our analysis of the "Sweatcoin" app revealed communication with potentially harmful hosts, "dewrain" and "akisinn," flagged as possible malware by MobSF. However, no conclusive result was given for these hosts in the subsequent Whois search.

Table 2. Number of Recipients Found in the Respective Categories

Category	Count	Category	Count	Category	Count	Category	Count
Service Providers	178	Partners	72	Advertising Companies	49	Analytical Services	38
Social Media	29	Information Providers	16	Governmental Bodies	4	Potentially Malicious	2

Data Transfers to Third Countries: Most of the analyzed apps were developed or designed for users in the USA. Furthermore, each app communicates with Google in different capacities, be it as an advertising company or an analytical service. Although Google's locations are distributed, they all have at least one base in the USA. As a result, all 20 apps sent their data to the USA. In addition, Table 3 presents that 40% of the communications are sent to Ireland. Ireland is favored as the headquarters of many major industries in Europe due to its favorable climate for server cooling and low corporate tax rates [18,23].

Table 3. Server Locations of Third-Party Recipients

Country	Count	Country	Count	Country	Count	Country	Count	Country	Count
USA	20	Ireland	8	Australia	6	Sweden	5	China	4
France	3	Netherlands	3	Singapore	3	Japan	2	Russia	2
Spain	2	Switzerland	2	UK	2	Finland	1	North Macedonia	1
Turkey	1	Brazil	1	India	1	Canada	1		

Transmitted Data Without Consent: Our static analysis revealed that most of the examined apps communicate with servers outside the EU. The destination of the transmitted data is significant, as the GDPR permits transfers to third countries only under specific conditions, such as an adequacy decision (Art. 45), appropriate safeguards (Art. 46), or, in some cases, the data subject's explicit consent (Art. 49(1)(a)). Another critical aspect involves observing the transmission of personal data, mainly focusing on data sent *before* obtaining consent for its processing. This result was obtained through dynamic analysis. However, it is essential to note that the identified data may present a partial result, as only the data found or decrypted during the investigation are represented. Table 4 summarizes all the data that were transmitted before users consented to the privacy policies in our analyzed apps. According to the GDPR, "personal data" is defined as information that can lead to the identification of an individual [51]. The findings indicate that the Google Advertising ID was identified in 13 of the analyzed apps. This ID serves as a unique identifier for advertising purposes, assigned to each Android device via Google Play. Although it can be reset, deactivation is not an option [25]. The European Commission classifies this information as personal data, referring to it as "the advertising identifier of your phone" [19]. In addition, hardware details were detected in 13 apps, while data about the country, languages, or time zones were found in 9 apps. For example, hardware information was transmitted to a Facebook server in the "Period Tracker and Calendar" app (developed by SimpleInnovation). The transferred message included an indication labeled "ROOTED:1," suggesting that the app may detect a rooted smartphone, along with details about the device model. Although a Magisk module was intended to conceal the rooted status, our analysis revealed that certain apps could still detect it. Furthermore, the investigation showed the transmission of local IP addresses. A local IP address, also known as an internal or private IP address, is a numerical label assigned to devices within a local network, such as a home or office network. However, when users leave a home network, they typically switch to mobile data, where a dynamic IP address is assigned to facilitate communication between servers and mobile devices. Nonetheless, evidence indicates dynamic IP addresses can be categorized as personally identifiable information [10].

Consent Dialogs and Dark Patterns: We examined the privacy policies of the apps to identify potential dark patterns. In the case of "Blood Pressure" (Developed by K. Szymon) and "Ladytimer Ovulation Calendar" (Developed by Vipos Apps), users were not provided with an option to consent to the privacy policy. No window was displayed to inform users about the processing of personal data or to obtain consent. Access to the privacy policy was only possible through the settings of the respective apps. Consequently, these apps were excluded from this aspect of the analysis. Although the app "Period Calendar Period Tracker" (Developed by Simple Design Ltd.) did present a consent window for the privacy policy, it appeared only upon the second launch of the app, indicating a potential software issue. Nevertheless, data processing was observed during the first launch. Despite this discrepancy, the app was still examined for dark patterns, and the results were documented during the second launch. In total, 18 out of 20 apps underwent an analysis to identify the presence of dark patterns. Table 4 shows the result of the study, revealing that every app analyzed exhibited at least one instance of a dark pattern.

Table 4. Data Transmitted without Consent and Dark Patterns

Personal Data	Count	Dark Patterns	Count
Google Advertisement ID	13	Misdirection	12
Hardware Information	13	Obfuscation	11
Country/Language/Timezone	9	Forced Action	9
Local IP Address	2	Missing Notices and Options	8
		Forced Registration	7
		Disguised Data Collection	3

The most prevalent dark pattern identified was Misdirection, which uses design elements to distract users' attention from crucial information. For instance, in Fig. 2, example (a) shows a screenshot of the Sweatcoin app (developed by Sweatco Ltd.), where different colors are used for various buttons. The "Registrieren mit Google" (translated as "Register with Google") button is prominently highlighted with a white background, making it more visually appealing and likely to be selected by users, even though they also have the option to register with other accounts. Below these two options is the privacy policy explanation, rendered in a gray font without additional design elements, making it less noticeable. A similar manipulation is seen in example (c), where users are prompted to click the "Einwilligen" (translated as "Consent") button. Another variation of Misdirection appears in example (b), where sensitive data collection details are listed, whereas an "Accept All" checkbox is provided to encourage users to skip reading the details. This design nudges users to consent to all options directly, thus bypassing the detailed information about the collected data.

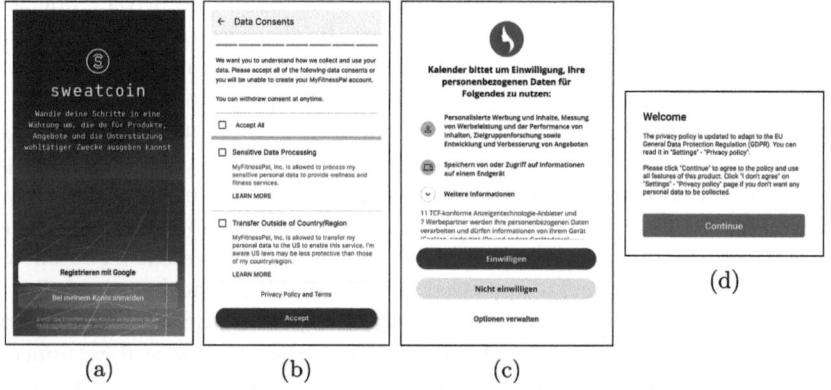

Fig. 2. Privacy policy screenshots.

In the case of Obfuscation, important information is deliberately withheld. In example (a), the privacy policy screen design provides no information directly to users, requiring them to open a link to read the privacy policy and learn about handling their personal data. Similarly, example (d) fails to present any information within the dialog. It does not provide access to the privacy policy, leaving users without any means to obtain the necessary information. In addition, important information is only partially displayed. In examples (b) and (c), while some details are listed, users must click the "LEARN MORE" button in example (b) and the "Optionen verwalten" (translated as "Manage options") button in example (c) to access comprehensive information. However, neither example (b) nor example (c) provides a complete picture of all sensitive data collected.

In the case of Forced Action, users are not given the option to decline, tempting them to perform a specific action to continue using the app. Examples (a), (b), and (d) do not allow users to refuse the collection of personal data while still using the app. In examples (a) and (d), there are no design elements that permit rejection. Although example (b) includes checkboxes that users can leave unchecked, the app becomes unusable if they do so. However, example (c) offers an option to decline the collection of sensitive data while continuing to use the app. Furthermore, some apps, including "MyFitnessPal" (developed by MyFitnessPal, Inc.), explicitly inform users during account creation about the privacy policy and their right to revoke consent at any time. However, they fail to mention that this requires deleting the account. By this point, users may have become habituated to the app, making it more challenging to delete their accounts. Among the 18 apps analyzed, eight neglected to offer privacy choices, provide check boxes for distinct personal data categories or empower users to govern their data rights. With the exception of example (b), none of the showcased apps allows users to specifically consent to categories of information such as health, fitness, or location data. Instead, users are prompted for broad consent, lacking the capacity to tailor their consent for different data types.

In the case of Forced Registration, users are required to register and create an account. This dark pattern often appears alongside Forced Action, yet they are distinct. While examples (a), (b), and (d) illustrate instances of Forced Action, example (d) does not require an account to use the app. The app works without an account as long as consent to the privacy policy is given. However, seven apps required account creation, allowing the developer to store data about the users.

Finally, we examined the scenario of Disguised Data Collection, where the user's personal data is collected without explicit consent to the privacy policy. Figure 3 example (a) indicates that the user agrees to the privacy policy by creating an account. However, when combined with other dark patterns like Misdirection, users may not fully grasp that they are consenting to the privacy policy during this stage of app usage. In addition, it was noted that the design of consent dialogs varies even among apps from the same company. Three different apps from the Leap Fitness Group were thoroughly analyzed. Although the consent dialogs of the apps "30 days sixpack" and "Lose Weight for App for Men" (both developed by Leap Fitness Group) remained consistent and provided users with some information regarding the use of their data, the confirmation dialog for the app "Home Workout - No Equipment" (also developed by Leap Fitness Group) appeared outdated and offered no information to the user. In the analysis of "Home Workout - No Equipment" (see Fig. 3 - (b)) and "Period Calendar Period Tracker" (see Fig. 2 - (d)), it was observed that although users are presented with an interface element to provide consent, they are not offered an option to access the privacy policy (e.g., via a link). In these apps, users are required to consent to the privacy policy before having the chance to review it.

Revocation and Language: Another dimension of our analysis delved into the presentation of privacy policies across different languages and the extent to which users could retract their consent. Among the 20 analyzed applications, two did not allow users to access the privacy policy, narrowing down our evaluation to 18 apps. Interestingly, seven apps lacked mechanisms for users to modify or

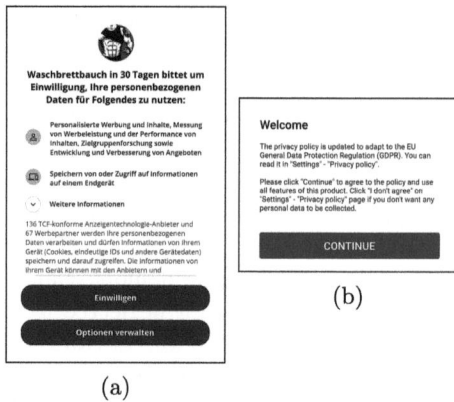

Fig. 3. Privacy policy interfaces within apps developed by Leap Fitness Group.

retract their consent once granted. Subsequently, we thoroughly examined the language used in presenting these privacy policies. Of the remaining 18 apps, only two were exclusively available in English, necessitating their exclusion from this linguistic analysis. Interestingly, all 16 apps in this analysis offered German language support, with their interface elements exclusively presented in German. However, it should be mentioned that the privacy policies of 10 of these apps were only written in English. This discrepancy underscores a potential language barrier for German-speaking users, particularly those with limited English skills, who may need help comprehending the handling of their personal data in the majority (63%) of the apps studied, except during the initial consent dialog.

Privacy Policy Analysis: This part compares static and dynamic analyses with privacy policy disclosures to evaluate their accuracy and transparency.

– *Data Transfers to Third Countries:* Data transfers to third countries were compared through static analysis with the corresponding privacy policy disclosures. In two instances, privacy policies did not mention data transfers despite evidence of such transfers in the static analysis. Overall, 55% of the examined apps did not specify particular countries, opting instead for general categories like "European Union" or "operating offices." Moreover, combinations of third countries and categories were common, such as repeated mentions of the USA alongside the European Union, making it challenging for users to track data transfers accurately. Despite efforts to catalog identified countries and compare them with defined categories and explicitly named countries, only a 75% match was achieved. This discrepancy indicates that in five apps, users could not learn about data transfers to third countries. The lack of precise or missing information about data transfers significantly hampers transparency, as vague or evasive language leaves users uninformed about the actual destinations of their personal data.

- *Recipients of Transmitted Data:* The recipients of transmitted data were also categorized. Although each privacy policy listed names or categories of potential recipients, an 85% overall match was found between static analysis results and privacy policy disclosures. Privacy policies tended to list recipients primarily in categories, with 60% of the apps using categories instead of explicitly naming recipients. These categories often employed broad terms like "Service Partners," "Analytics Partners," or "Advertisement Partners." Interestingly, 55% of these categories included more than ten potential recipients, raising questions about whether these categories might be overly broad. Conversely, 40% of the privacy policies listed only two or fewer recipients in a category, suggesting that individual recipients could be named for clarity. Moreover, 55% of the apps listed more categories than exactly identified recipients, mentioning categories for recipients that may not exist, potentially undermining transparency. We also examined whether prominent and frequently used companies related to data sharing, especially in advertising networks or tracking services like "Google Analytics," were explicitly named. Such companies were explicitly named in only 75% of the examined cases, raising the question of whether capturing widespread advertising companies and tracking services in more general categories instead of explicitly naming them enhances user transparency.
- *Requested Personal Data:* The requested personal data was analyzed, revealing challenges in comparing it with the corresponding apps. Permissions obtained through static analysis and MobSF provided minimal information about personal data, often limited to the user's location information. However, this finding could not be confirmed in the dynamic analysis. Permissions defined in the AndroidManifest.xml do not specify the actual data accessed, which limits the effectiveness of static analysis in detecting personal data transmission. Additionally, no flow of personal data was identified during app operation. This could be because the data is encoded or encrypted, making it difficult to use the applied analysis methods. Therefore, no definitive conclusion could be drawn regarding the conformity of the personal data requested in the privacy policies compared to the actual app execution.
- *Consent Dialogs and Dark Patterns:* The study showed that personal data, particularly the Advertising ID, was identified even before consent in 13 of the examined apps. This finding raises questions about the definition and protection of personal data. Furthermore, privacy policy consent dialogs were examined for dark patterns, revealing their presence in each examined app. These dark patterns, primarily forms of Forced Action and Obfuscation, suggest that users are often coerced into agreeing without sufficient information.

5 Discussion

This study examined privacy practices in mHealth apps by analyzing the alignment between stated privacy policies and observed behaviors, the timing of data transmissions relative to user consent, the prevalence of manipulative interface design, and the comprehensiveness of privacy disclosures. Through a combination of static and dynamic analysis, interface evaluation, and legal assessment, we contribute an interdisciplinary perspective that bridges technical, legal, and human-centered considerations in line with previous research efforts [13, 22, 27, 30, 37]. An important finding concerns the gap between disclosed data recipients in privacy policies and actual data transmission behaviors. Although most apps broadly categorized third parties as "service providers" or "partners," only 85% of observed communications could be traced back to disclosed recipients. Furthermore, many privacy policies relied on vague categorizations without explicitly naming companies, complicating a user's understanding of who processes their data and potentially causing reduced trust in mHealth apps [3]. This practice mirrors concerns already raised by Forsberg and Iwaya [22], and by Minssen et al. [38] w.r.t. the opacity of data-sharing in mHealth apps.

Previous analyses in healthcare apps have similarly reported that privacy disclosures often fall short of capturing real data practices [48]. The lack of transparency regarding data flows to third countries, particularly the United States and Ireland, persists despite the GDPR requirements for clear international data transfer disclosures [34]. Our findings highlight that legal compliance in letters does not guarantee transparency in practice. In parallel, the investigation into data transmission timing revealed troubling behaviors. Personal data—most notably, the Google Advertising ID—was transmitted in 65% of apps before users consented, echoing findings by Claesson and Bjørstad [13] and Grundy et al. [27]. Although it is disputed whether device identifiers alone constitute personal data [10], the aggregation potential of that information raises significant privacy risks. Moreover, while our technical analysis primarily detected identifiers and device metadata rather than sensitive health information, limitations in capturing encrypted and encoded transmissions suggest that actual risks could be underestimated. In addition, definitional challenges surrounding the classification of personal data under the GDPR, as discussed by researchers [21], further complicate the regulatory framing of such transmission behaviors.

Examining user interfaces, we observed that every app analyzed employed at least one dark pattern, often involving Misdirection, Forced Action, or Obfuscation. Such tactics, including emphasizing "Accept All" options or concealing critical privacy choices, compromise a user's ability to make informed decisions. These results extend previous dark pattern investigations [17, 35, 37], confirming that manipulative consent design remains pervasive even in contexts involving sensitive health data. In particular, apps often presented consent dialogs that superficially satisfied regulatory requirements while functionally undermining user autonomy. The intersection of the legal compliance theater and deceptive design patterns warrants closer scrutiny from regulators and researchers. The analysis of privacy policies further revealed significant deficits in language accessibility and information granularity. Although most apps localized user interfaces into German, a majority offered privacy policies only in English. Given the importance of clear, understandable communication under the GDPR [15, 55], this practice likely impedes informed consent for many users. Moreover, privacy disclosures often failed to detail the categories of personal data collected or allowed only broad, bundled consents, contravening the principle of specific consent.

Our study revealed several challenges and limitations. While the analysis includes 20 highly downloaded mHealth apps, this selection may not fully represent the entire mHealth app market. We primarily relied on MobSF for static analysis, as alternative tools were scarce. Although the JADX [47] decompiler was available, its cryptic output made it impractical, forcing us to abandon this option. In dynamic analysis, rooting the mobile device was necessary, albeit risky. Although initial considerations included device emulation through platforms such as the Android Studio Simulator and Genymotion [24], their unreliability led us to favor physical devices despite MobSF offering dynamic analysis options for both. Moreover, some apps could detect rooted or emulated devices, potentially altering their behavior. Despite installing a Magisk module to conceal root access, detection remained possible, compromising data transmission reliability. Identifying personal data beyond the Google Advertising ID posed challenges due to encoded transmissions, particularly to Google servers, impeding our assessment of personal data handling during technical analysis. During the experiment setup, isolating app activities from background system transmissions proved daunting despite monitoring outgoing network activities with Burp Suite. Although efforts were made to minimize the influence of background activity, we could not guarantee distortion-free results.

The key findings of this study include systemic transparency and usability failures within mHealth apps. From a regulatory perspective, clearer enforcement mechanisms are needed to ensure that data recipients and third-country transfers are disclosed with specificity and that consent is obtained before personal data processing. Technical standards should enforce that consent events occur before network transmissions of data. Furthermore, dark patterns in consent interfaces should be explicitly prohibited in health-related applications, where the stakes for user autonomy and data protection are especially high.

6 Conclusion

Our study reveals a troubling gap between the declared and actual privacy practices in mHealth apps. Vague disclosures, premature data transmission, and manipulative consent designs challenge the core principles of informed consent and user autonomy. These findings point to systemic issues in privacy governance and app design. Future work should investigate how redesigning consent flows and policy structures, potentially supported by automated or AI-assisted analysis methods, can meaningfully improve transparency and support regulatory compliance at scale.

Acknowledgment. This work was funded by the Klaus Tschira Stiftung.

References

1. Abraham, A., et al.: Mobile security framework (mobsf) (2024). https://github.com/MobSF/Mobile-Security-Framework-MobSF
2. Alfawzan, N., Christen, M., Spitale, G., Biller-Andorno, N.: Privacy, data sharing, and data security policies of women's mhealth apps: scoping review and content analysis. JMIR Mhealth Uhealth **10**(5), e33735 (2022). https://doi.org/10.2196/33735
3. Alhammad, N., Alajlani, M., Abd-alrazaq, A., Epiphaniou, G., Arvanitis, T.: Patients' perspectives on the data confidentiality, privacy, and security of mhealth apps: systematic review. J. Med. Internet Res. **26**, e50715 (2024). https://doi.org/10.2196/50715
4. Android Developers: Protect against security threats with safetynet (2024). https://developer.android.com/privacy-and-security/safetynet
5. Android Developers: Security with network protocols (2024). https://developer.android.com/privacy-and-security/security-ssl
6. Android Open Source Project: Bootloader overview (2024). https://source.android.com/docs/core/architecture/bootloader
7. AndroidRank: Android apps market data, history, and rankings (2024). https://www.androidrank.org
8. Bauer, M., et al.: Smartphones in mental health: a critical review of background issues, current status and future concerns. Int. J. Bipolar Disorders **8**(1), 2 (2020). https://doi.org/10.1186/s40345-019-0164-x
9. Benjumea, J., Ropero, J., Rivera-Romero, O., Dorronzoro-Zubiete, E., Carrasco, A.: Privacy assessment in mobile health apps: scoping review. JMIR Mhealth Uhealth **8**(7), e18868 (2020). https://doi.org/10.2196/18868
10. Borgesius, F.Z.: The Breyer case of the court of justice of the European union: IP addresses and the personal data definition. Eur. Data Prot. L. Rev. **3**, 130 (2017)
11. Braghin, C., Cimato, S., Della Libera, A.: Are mhealth apps secure? A case study. In: 2018 IEEE 42nd Annual Computer Software and Applications Conference (COMPSAC), vol. 02, pp. 335–340 (2018). https://doi.org/10.1109/COMPSAC.2018.10253
12. Bösch, C., Erb, B., Kargl, F., Kopp, H., Pfattheicher, S.: Tales from the dark side: privacy dark strategies and privacy dark patterns. Proc. Privacy Enhancing Technol. **2016**, 237–254 (2016). https://doi.org/10.1515/popets-2016-0038
13. Claesson, A., Bjørstad, T.E.: "Out of control" – a review of data sharing by popular mobile apps. Technical report, Norwegian Consumer Council, Oslo (2020)
14. Cory, T., Rieder, W., Huynh, T.M.: A qualitative analysis framework for mhealth privacy practices. In: 2024 IEEE European Symposium on Security and Privacy Workshops (EuroS&PW), pp. 24–31 (2024). https://doi.org/10.1109/EuroSPW61312.2024.00010
15. Das, G., Cheung, C., Nebeker, C., Bietz, M., Bloss, C.: Privacy policies for apps targeted toward youth: descriptive analysis of readability. JMIR Mhealth Uhealth **6**(1), e3 (2018). https://doi.org/10.2196/mhealth.7626
16. Dehling, T., Gao, F., Schneider, S., Sunyaev, A.: Exploring the far side of mobile health: information security and privacy of mobile health apps on IOS and android. JMIR Mhealth Uhealth **3**(1), e8 (2015). https://doi.org/10.2196/mhealth.3672
17. Di Geronimo, L., Braz, L., Fregnan, E., Palomba, F., Bacchelli, A.: UI Dark Patterns and Where to Find Them: A Study on Mobile Applications and User Perception, pp. 1–14. Association for Computing Machinery, New York (2020). https://doi.org/10.1145/3313831.3376600

18. Dodd, E.: A natural progression? Why there are so many data centres in Ireland—buzz.ie (2023). https://www.buzz.ie/news/irish-news/data-centres-ireland-economy-energy-25529167. Accessed 30 May 2024
19. European Commission: What is personal data?—commission.europa.eu (2024). https://commission.europa.eu/law/law-topic/data-protection/reform/what-personal-data_en. Accessed 31 May 2024
20. Fan, M., et al.: An empirical evaluation of GDPR compliance violations in Android mhealth apps. In: 2020 IEEE 31st International Symposium on Software Reliability Engineering (ISSRE), pp. 253–264 (2020). https://doi.org/10.1109/ISSRE5003.2020.00032
21. Finck, M., Pallas, F.: They who must not be identified–distinguishing personal from non-personal data under the GDPR. Int. Data Privacy Law **10**(1), 11–36 (2020)
22. Forsberg, A., Iwaya, L.H.: Security analysis of top-ranked mhealth fitness apps: an empirical study. In: Horn Iwaya, L., Kamm, L., Martucci, L., Pulls, T. (eds.) Secure IT Systems, pp. 364–381. Springer, Cham (2025)
23. Fox, K.: Ireland's data centers are an economic lifeline. But environmentalists say they're wrecking the planet | CNN Business—edition.cnn.com (2022). https://edition.cnn.com/2022/01/23/tech/ireland-data-centers-climate-intl-cmd/index.html. Accessed 30 May 2024
24. Genymobile SAS: Genymotion: Android emulator for desktop and cloud (2024). https://www.genymotion.com
25. Google: Advertising ID - Play Console Help—support.google.com (2024). https://support.google.com/googleplay/android-developer/answer/6048248?hl=en. Accessed 31 May 2024
26. Gray, C.M., Kou, Y., Battles, B., Hoggatt, J., Toombs, A.L.: The dark (patterns) side of UX design. In: Proceedings of the 2018 CHI Conference on Human Factors in Computing Systems, CHI 2018, pp. 1–14. Association for Computing Machinery, New York (2018). https://doi.org/10.1145/3173574.3174108
27. Grundy, Q., Chiu, K., Held, F., Continella, A., Bero, L., Holz, R.: Data sharing practices of medicines related apps and the mobile ecosystem: traffic, content, and network analysis. BMJ **364** (2019). https://doi.org/10.1136/bmj.l920
28. Gunawan, J., Pradeep, A., Choffnes, D., Hartzog, W., Wilson, C.: A comparative study of dark patterns across web and mobile modalities. Proc. ACM Hum.-Comput. Interact. **5**(CSCW2) (2021). https://doi.org/10.1145/3479521
29. Haggag, O., Grundy, J., Abdelrazek, M., Haggag, S.: A large scale analysis of mhealth app user reviews. Empir. Softw. Eng. **27**(7), 196 (2022). https://doi.org/10.1007/s10664-022-10222-6
30. Huckvale, K., Torous, J., Larsen, M.E.: Assessment of the data sharing and privacy practices of smartphone apps for depression and smoking cessation. JAMA Netw. Open **2**(4), e192542–e192542 (2019). https://doi.org/10.1001/jamanetworkopen.2019.2542
31. Iwaya, L.H., Babar, M.A., Rashid, A., Wijayarathna, C.: On the privacy of mental health apps: an empirical investigation and its implications for app development. Empir. Softw. Eng. **28**(1), 2 (2022). https://doi.org/10.1007/s10664-022-10236-0
32. Jeroen Beckers (NVISO.eu): Magisktrustusercerts: Always trust user certificates (2024). https://github.com/NVISOsecurity/MagiskTrustUserCerts
33. Wu, J., et al.: Magisk documentation (2024). https://topjohnwu.github.io/Magisk
34. Juliussen, B.A., Kozyri, E., Johansen, D., Rui, J.P.: The third country problem under the GDPR: enhancing protection of data transfers with technology. Int. Data Privacy Law **13**(3), 225–243 (2023). https://doi.org/10.1093/idpl/ipad013

35. Luguri, J., Strahilevitz, L.J.: Shining a light on dark patterns. J. Legal Anal. **13**(1), 43–109 (2021). https://doi.org/10.1093/jla/laaa006
36. Malki, L.M., Kaleva, I., Patel, D., Warner, M., Abu-Salma, R.: Exploring privacy practices of female mhealth apps in a post-roe world. In: Proceedings of the 2024 CHI Conference on Human Factors in Computing Systems, CHI 2024. Association for Computing Machinery, New York (2024). https://doi.org/10.1145/3613904.3642521
37. Mathur, A., Kshirsagar, M., Mayer, J.: What makes a dark pattern... dark? Design attributes, normative considerations, and measurement methods. In: Proceedings of the 2021 CHI Conference on Human Factors in Computing Systems, CHI 2021. Association for Computing Machinery, New York (2021). https://doi.org/10.1145/3411764.3445610
38. Minssen, T., Rajam, N., Bogers, M.: Clinical trial data transparency and GDPR compliance: implications for data sharing and open innovation. Sci. Public Policy **47**(5), 616–626 (2020)
39. Muchagata, J., Ferreira, A.: Translating GDPR into the mhealth practice. In: 2018 International Carnahan Conference on Security Technology (ICCST), pp. 1–5 (2018). https://doi.org/10.1109/CCST.2018.8585546
40. Müthing, J., Brüngel, R., Friedrich, C.M.: Server-focused security assessment of mobile health apps for popular mobile platforms. J. Med. Internet Res. **21**(1), e9818 (2019). https://doi.org/10.2196/jmir.9818
41. Neal, D., Gaber, S., Joddrell, P., Brorsson, A., Dijkstra, K., Dröes, R.M.: Read and accepted? Scoping the cognitive accessibility of privacy policies of health apps and websites in three European countries. Digit. Health **9**, 12 (2023). https://doi.org/10.1177/20552076231152162
42. Nouwens, M., Liccardi, I., Veale, M., Karger, D., Kagal, L.: Dark patterns after the GDPR: scraping consent pop-ups and demonstrating their influence. In: Proceedings of the 2020 CHI Conference on Human Factors in Computing Systems, CHI 2020, pp. 1–13. Association for Computing Machinery, New York (2020). https://doi.org/10.1145/3313831.3376321
43. Papageorgiou, A., Strigkos, M., Politou, E., Alepis, E., Solanas, A., Patsakis, C.: Security and privacy analysis of mobile health applications: the alarming state of practice. IEEE Access **6**, 9390–9403 (2018). https://doi.org/10.1109/ACCESS.2018.2799522
44. Parker, L., Halter, V., Karliychuk, T., Grundy, Q.: How private is your mental health app data? An empirical study of mental health app privacy policies and practices. Int. J. Law Psychiatry **64**, 198–204 (2019). https://doi.org/10.1016/j.ijlp.2019.04.002
45. PortSwigger Ltd.: Burp suite: Web application security testing software (2024). https://portswigger.net/burp
46. Priambodo, D.F., Ajie, G.S., Rahman, H.A., Nugraha, A.C.F., Rachmawati, A., Avianti, M.R.: Mobile health application security assessment based on owasp top 10 mobile vulnerabilities. In: 2022 International Conference on Information Technology Systems and Innovation (ICITSI), pp. 25–29 (2022). https://doi.org/10.1109/ICITSI56531.2022.9970949
47. Skylot: Jadx: Dex to java decompiler (2024). https://github.com/skylot/jadx
48. Sunyaev, A., Dehling, T., Taylor, P.L., Mandl, K.D.: Availability and quality of mobile health app privacy policies. J. Am. Med. Inform. Assoc. **22**(e1), e28–e33 (2014). https://doi.org/10.1136/amiajnl-2013-002605

49. Tangari, G., Ikram, M., Ijaz, K., Kaafar, M.A., Berkovsky, S.: Mobile health and privacy: cross sectional study. BMJ **373** (2021). https://doi.org/10.1136/bmj.n1248
50. Tangari, G., Ikram, M., Sentana, I.W.B., Ijaz, K., Kaafar, M.A., Berkovsky, S.: Analyzing security issues of Android mobile health and medical applications. J. Am. Med. Inform. Assoc. **28**(10), 2074–2084 (2021). https://doi.org/10.1093/jamia/ocab131
51. Voigt, P., Von dem Bussche, A.: The EU General Data Protection Regulation (GDPR). A Practical Guide, vol. 10, 1st edn. Springer, Cham (2017)
52. Wykes, T., Schueller, S.: Why reviewing apps is not enough: transparency for trust (T4T) principles of responsible health app marketplaces. J. Med. Internet Res. **21**(5), e12390 (2019). https://doi.org/10.2196/12390
53. Xiang, A., Pei, W., Yue, C.: Policychecker: analyzing the GDPR completeness of mobile apps' privacy policies. In: Proceedings of the 2023 ACM SIGSAC Conference on Computer and Communications Security, CCS 2023, pp. 3373–3387. Association for Computing Machinery, New York (2023). https://doi.org/10.1145/3576915.3623067
54. Zhao, W., Shahriar, H., Clincy, V., Bhuiyan, Z.A.: Security and privacy analysis of mhealth application: a case study. In: 2020 IEEE 19th International Conference on Trust, Security and Privacy in Computing and Communications (TrustCom), pp. 1882–1887 (2020). https://doi.org/10.1109/TrustCom50675.2020.00257
55. Zhou, L., Bao, J., Watzlaf, V., Parmanto, B.: Barriers to and facilitators of the use of mobile health apps from a security perspective: mixed-methods study. JMIR Mhealth Uhealth **7**(4), e11223 (2019). https://doi.org/10.2196/11223

Don't Hash Me Like That: Exposing and Mitigating Hash-Induced Unfairness in Local Differential Privacy

Berkay Kemal Balioglu, Alireza Khodaie, and M. Emre Gursoy(✉)

Department of Computer Engineering, Koç University, Istanbul, Turkey
{bbalioglu23,akhodaie22,emregursoy}@ku.edu.tr

Abstract. Local differential privacy (LDP) has become a widely accepted framework for privacy-preserving data collection. In LDP, many protocols rely on hash functions to implement user-side encoding and perturbation. However, the security and privacy implications of hash function selection have not been previously investigated. In this paper, we expose that the hash functions may act as a source of unfairness in LDP protocols. We show that although users operate under the same protocol and privacy budget, differences in hash functions can lead to significant disparities in vulnerability to inference and poisoning attacks. To mitigate hash-induced unfairness, we propose Fair-OLH (F-OLH), a variant of OLH that enforces an entropy-based fairness constraint on hash function selection. Experiments show that F-OLH is effective in mitigating hash-induced unfairness under acceptable time overheads.

Keywords: Privacy · local differential privacy · protocol fairness · inference attacks · poisoning attacks · privacy technologies and mechanisms

1 Introduction

Local Differential Privacy (LDP) has become a widely adopted framework for collecting user data while providing strong privacy guarantees [9,25,26]. By perturbing each user's data locally before transmission, LDP protocols eliminate the need for a trusted data collector. Many LDP mechanisms were proposed in the literature, and several prominent deployments of LDP exist in the real world, e.g., in Chrome, Apple iOS, and Microsoft Windows [11,12].

While LDP protocols offer formal privacy guarantees, recent research has highlighted that several privacy and security risks remain. Adversaries can utilize protocol outputs to make predictions regarding users' true values via inference attacks [4,13,14], or inject manipulated reports to skew aggregate statistics estimated by the data collector via poisoning attacks [6,8,17,24]. To implement encoding and perturbation, many LDP protocols such as OLH rely on hash functions. However, the security and privacy implications of hash function selection, e.g., its impacts on inference and poisoning attacks, have not been investigated.

B. K. Balioglu and A. Khodaie—These authors contributed equally to this work.

© The Author(s), under exclusive license to Springer Nature Switzerland AG 2026
V. Nicomette et al. (Eds.): ESORICS 2025, LNCS 16056, pp. 22–42, 2026.
https://doi.org/10.1007/978-3-032-07901-5_2

In this paper, for the first time (to the best of our knowledge), we expose that hash functions can act as a source of unfairness in LDP. We show that even when users operate under the same protocol and privacy budget ε, differences in hash functions can lead to significant disparities in vulnerability to inference and poisoning attacks. In particular, users whose hash functions exhibit low uniformity (i.e., yielding skewed distributions of hash outputs) are more negatively affected by inference attacks and cause more severe damage via poisoning attacks. We experimentally demonstrate these traits using three subpopulations (High-ENT, Low-PIS, and High-PIS), which represent balanced, unfairly advantaged, and unfairly disadvantaged groups according to their hash functions. Results with five datasets, a state-of-the-art inference attack (BIA [14]), and poisoning attack (MGA [6]) show that: (i) Low-PIS users are 1.5–2 times more vulnerable to BIAs, and (ii) High-PIS users' impact via MGAs can be 3–4 times higher than others.

To mitigate hash-induced unfairness, we propose a fair variant of the well-known OLH protocol, called Fair-OLH (F-OLH). The main idea of F-OLH is to enforce each user's hash function to have sufficiently high fairness, measured in terms of entropy. In F-OLH, the user keeps drawing hash functions from the underlying hash family until a suitable hash function that satisfies the fairness threshold ρ is found. The remainder of user-side perturbation and server-side estimation in F-OLH is similar to OLH.

We show that F-OLH is effective in mitigating hash-induced unfairness. As ρ gets stricter, different subpopulations' vulnerabilities to BIAs converge to one another. Furthermore, the utility loss caused by MGAs is substantially reduced in F-OLH compared to OLH. On the other hand, since F-OLH enforces the user to draw hash functions until a suitable hash function is found, it brings an increased time cost. We experimentally establish that this time cost is related to the domain size, privacy budget ε, as well as the threshold ρ, since finding hash functions which satisfy stricter ρ is more time-consuming. Experiment results show that although the execution time of F-OLH is larger than OLH, it still remains acceptable, and replacing OLH by F-OLH in a practical deployment is unlikely to cause a noticeable problem.

Contributions. In summary, our main contributions include:

- We expose the problem of hash-induced unfairness in LDP for the first time, using a state-of-the-art inference attack (BIA) and poisoning attack (MGA).
- To mitigate hash-induced unfairness, we propose a fair variant of OLH, a popular and well-known LDP protocol, called Fair-OLH (F-OLH).
- We provide extensive results demonstrating that F-OLH reduces disparate impacts of BIAs and MGAs, thereby achieving better fairness, without introducing prohibitive time costs.

2 Background and Preliminaries

2.1 Local Differential Privacy

Local Differential Privacy (LDP) is a widely used notion for safeguarding users' privacy in data collection. Unlike central differential privacy (DP) which assumes the existence of a trusted data collector, LDP ensures that each user locally perturbs their data on their own device before sharing the perturbed version with the data collector. In a typical LDP setting, a population of users, denoted by $\mathcal{U}$, interacts with a server that aggregates the received data. Each user $u \in \mathcal{U}$ holds a true value $v_u \in \mathcal{D}$, where $\mathcal{D}$ represents the domain of possible values. To satisfy LDP, each user applies a randomized mechanism Ψ to perturb their v_u before sending the result to the server. The server can estimate population-level aggregate statistics from the received responses, but cannot reconstruct any individual's true value.

Definition 1 (ε-LDP]). *A randomized mechanism Ψ satisfies ε-LDP if and only if, for any two possible inputs $v_1, v_2 \in \mathcal{D}$, the following condition holds:*

$$\forall y \in Range(\Psi): \quad \frac{Pr[\Psi(v_1) = y]}{Pr[\Psi(v_2) = y]} \leq e^\varepsilon \tag{1}$$

where $Range(\Psi)$ represents the set of all possible outputs of Ψ.

LDP is typically implemented using well-known LDP protocols such as GRR, BLH, OLH, RAPPOR, OUE, and SS [1,10,14,22]. In many of the protocols, v_u is encoded into a lower-dimensional artifact such as a bitvector, integer, or a single bit. For example, RAPPOR and OUE encode v_u into a bitvector [12,22]; BLH and OLH encode v_u into a bit and integer, respectively [14,22]. To facilitate this encoding, hash functions are commonly used. This paper focuses on the privacy and security impacts associated with the choice of these hash functions. In particular, we will utilize the Optimized Local Hashing (OLH) protocol to demonstrate the impacts, since OLH is a popular and state-of-the-art protocol that is commonly used in recent works [23,26].

Optimized Local Hashing (OLH) was introduced by Wang et al. [22]. It utilizes a set of hash functions $\mathcal{H}$, where each hash function $H \in \mathcal{H}$ maps values from $\mathcal{D}$ to an integer in the range $[0, g-1]$. The default value of g is derived as $g = e^\varepsilon + 1$ in [22], which we also use in the rest of this paper.

In OLH, each user u randomly selects a hash function H_u from $\mathcal{H}$ and computes the integer $x_u = H_u(v_u)$. Then, the perturbation mechanism Ψ_{OLH} perturbs x_u into $x'_u \in [0, g-1]$ using the following probabilities:

$$Pr[x'_u = i] = \begin{cases} \frac{e^\varepsilon}{e^\varepsilon + g - 1}, & \text{if } x_u = i, \\ \frac{1}{e^\varepsilon + g - 1}, & \text{otherwise.} \end{cases} \tag{2}$$

The user sends the tuple $\langle H_u, x'_u \rangle$ to the server. After collecting tuples $\langle H_u, x'_u \rangle$ from users $u \in \mathcal{U}$, the server begins the aggregation and estimation phase. To perform estimation for some $v \in \mathcal{D}$, the server first finds $Sup(v)$, which is equal to the number of user tuples satisfying $x'_u = H_u(v)$. The server then finds the estimated frequency of v, denoted by $\tilde{f}(v)$, using the formula:

$$\tilde{f}(v) = \frac{(e^\varepsilon + g - 1) \cdot (g \cdot Sup(v) - |\mathcal{U}|)}{(e^\varepsilon - 1) \cdot (g - 1) \cdot |\mathcal{U}|} \tag{3}$$

Algorithm 1. Bayesian Inference Attack on OLH
Input: $\mathcal{D}, \mathcal{O}_u = \{\langle H_u^1, x_u^1\rangle, ..., \langle H_u^n, x_u^n\rangle\}$
Output: Predicted value v_u^p
1: **for** $v \in \mathcal{D}$ **do**
2:     Initialize $score(v) = 0$
3: **for** $i \in [1, n]$ **do**
4:     **for** $v \in \mathcal{D}$ **do**
5:         **if** $H_u^i(v) = x_u^i$ **then**
6:             $score(v) = score(v) + 1$
7: Find $v_u^p = \mathrm{argmax}_v \ score(v)$
8: **return** v_u^p

2.2 Bayesian Inference Attack

There are several recent security and privacy attacks on LDP protocols, such as reidentification attacks [21], pool inference attacks [13], and poisoning attacks [8,17,24]. Among them, we utilize two applicable attacks to demonstrate hash-induced unfairness in LDP: one privacy attack (Bayesian Inference Attack) and one poisoning attack (Maximal Gain Attack).

Bayesian Inference Attack (BIA) was first proposed in [14], and later extended and used in [3,4,15]. Having observed one or more protocol outputs originating from the user's true value v_u, the attacker aims to infer the most likely value that resulted in the observed outputs via Bayesian inference. More formally, let $\mathcal{O}_u$ denote the protocol outputs that the adversary observed from u. In the case of OLH, if data is collected once, then $\mathcal{O}_u = \langle H_u, x_u'\rangle$. If data is collected multiple times longitudinally, then we write $\mathcal{O}_u = \{\langle H_u^1, x_u^1\rangle, \langle H_u^2, x_u^2\rangle, ..., \langle H_u^n, x_u^n\rangle\}$. Armed with $\mathcal{O}_u$, the goal of the adversary is to predict v_u. Denoting the adversary's prediction by v_u^p, according to the Bayes theorem:

$$v_u^p = \mathrm{argmax}_{\hat{v}\in\mathcal{D}} \ \Pr[\hat{v}|\mathcal{O}_u] = \mathrm{argmax}_{\hat{v}\in\mathcal{D}} \ \frac{\Pr[\mathcal{O}_u|\hat{v}] \cdot \Pr[\hat{v}]}{\Pr[\mathcal{O}_u]} \quad (4)$$

$$= \mathrm{argmax}_{\hat{v}\in\mathcal{D}} \ \Pr[\mathcal{O}_u|\hat{v}] \cdot \Pr[\hat{v}] \quad (5)$$

$$\propto \mathrm{argmax}_{\hat{v}\in\mathcal{D}} \ \Pr[\mathcal{O}_u|\hat{v}] \quad (6)$$

From the definition of the OLH protocol, we know that for all pairs of values $v_j, v_k \in \mathcal{D}$ such that $H_u(v_j) = H_u(v_k)$, it holds that: $\Pr[x_u^i|v_j] = \Pr[x_u^i|v_k]$. In other words, the two values v_j, v_k that are both within the preimage set of the hash function H_u are equally likely. Second, consider that a certain x_u^i was reported to the server, and we divide $\mathcal{D}$ into two disjoint subsets $\mathcal{D}_1, \mathcal{D}_2$ such that $\mathcal{D}_1 = \{v|v \in \mathcal{D}, H_u^i(v) = x_u^i\}$ and $\mathcal{D}_2 = \mathcal{D}\setminus \mathcal{D}_1$. Then, due to Eq. 2, it holds that: $\Pr[v_u \in \mathcal{D}_1] > \Pr[v_u \in \mathcal{D}_2]$.

Combining these observations, the BIA for OLH can be implemented as shown in Algorithm 1. The algorithm initializes the score of each $v \in \mathcal{D}$ as 0. Then, for each observed $\langle H_u^i, x_u^i\rangle$, the algorithm computes the preimage of x_u^i

Algorithm 2. Maximal Gain Attack on OLH

Input: $\mathcal{D}, T, \kappa, \mathcal{H}$
Output: $\langle H_u, x'_u \rangle$ for a poisoning user u
1: Initialize max_mp_size as 0
2: Initialize current $\langle H_u, x'_u \rangle$ as null
3: **for** κ number of iterations **do**
4:     Randomly select a hash function H from family $\mathcal{H}$
5:     Initialize $counts$ as a list of integers, containing all zeros, with length g
6:     **for** $\bar{v} \in T$ **do**
7:         $x \leftarrow H(\bar{v})$
8:         $counts[x] \leftarrow counts[x] + 1$
9:     $mp\_size \leftarrow \max(counts)$
10:    $mp\_size\_index \leftarrow \arg\max(counts)$
11:    **if** $mp\_size > max\_mp\_size$ **then**
12:        Assign $\langle H_u, x'_u \rangle \leftarrow \langle H, mp\_size\_index \rangle$
13:        Assign $max\_mp\_size \leftarrow mp\_size$
14: **return** $\langle H_u, x'_u \rangle$
---

according to H_u^i, i.e., the subset of values in the domain which would result in x_u^i when hashed using H_u^i. The scores of each of those values are incremented by 1. Finally, the attacker selects the highest scoring value and returns it as the predicted v_u^p. This strategy conforms to the aforementioned observations because (i) those values that are in the preimage set are more likely than those that are not, and (ii) all values in the preimage set are equally likely; therefore, their scores are incremented by $+1$.

2.3 Maximal Gain Attack

LDP protocols are vulnerable to poisoning attacks in which attackers inject manipulated data to distort the estimated statistics on the server side (e.g., $\tilde{f}(v)$). Poisoning attacks can be untargeted, aiming to degrade the overall accuracy of frequency estimation, or targeted, focusing on inflating or reducing the estimated frequencies of attacker-chosen items.

Maximal Gain Attack (MGA) is a seminal poisoning attack introduced in [6]. In MGA, there exist a set of target items $T = \{\bar{v}_1, \bar{v}_2, ..., \bar{v}_t\}$ where $T \subset \mathcal{D}$. The attacker's goal is to promote the items in T, i.e., increase their estimated frequencies. Denoting by $\tilde{f}_b$ and $\tilde{f}_a$ the frequencies estimated by the LDP protocol before and after attack, MGA defines the frequency gain $\Delta \tilde{f}(\bar{v})$ as $\Delta \tilde{f}(\bar{v}) = \tilde{f}_a(\bar{v}) - \tilde{f}_b(\bar{v})$. Then, the overall Gain of the attack is: Gain $= \sum_{\bar{v} \in T} \Delta \tilde{f}(\bar{v})$. The attacker's goal is to maximize Gain.

Recall from the BIA that when a certain $\langle H_u, x'_u \rangle$ is reported to the server and we divide $\mathcal{D}$ into two $\mathcal{D}_1, \mathcal{D}_2$ such that $\mathcal{D}_1 = \{v | v \in \mathcal{D}, H_u(v) = x'_u\}$ and $\mathcal{D}_2 = \mathcal{D} \setminus \mathcal{D}_1$, it holds that: $\Pr[v_u \in \mathcal{D}_1] > \Pr[v_u \in \mathcal{D}_2]$. Because of this, the strategy that maximizes Gain in OLH is to find the $\langle H_u, x'_u \rangle$ which maps as many of the items in T to the same x'_u as possible (from an attacker's perspective, the best scenario is when $\forall \bar{v}_i \in T$, $H_u(\bar{v}_i) = x'_u$). This enables $Sup(\bar{v}_i)$ to increase $\forall \bar{v}_i \in T$ when performing server-side estimation in OLH. Consequently, $\tilde{f}(\bar{v})$ is also increased, and the attack becomes more successful.

Following [6], MGA for OLH can be implemented as shown in Algorithm 2, i.e., malicious user u determines their $\langle H_u, x'_u \rangle$ using Algorithm 2. The inputs are the domain $\mathcal{D}$, target items T, iteration count parameter κ, and the hash function family $\mathcal{H}$. Following [6], the value of κ can be 1000. In each of the κ total number of iterations, a hash function H is drawn from $\mathcal{H}$. Then, the algorithm studies how many items from $\bar{v} \in T$ this H hashes to each integer in $[0, g-1]$. These item counts are stored in a list called *counts*. The maximum count (denoted by *mp_size* in Algorithm 2) and the index of the maximum count (denoted by *mp_size_index*) are found from *counts*. If the current *mp_size* exceeds the previously found maximum *max_mp_size*, then $\langle H_u, x'_u \rangle$ is updated using the current hash function H and the current *mp_size_index*. At the end of κ iterations performing the above, $\langle H_u, x'_u \rangle$ stores the hash function that hashes the maximum number of items from T to x'_u. This $\langle H_u, x'_u \rangle$ is the tuple which maximizes Gain; therefore, it is produced as the output of Algorithm 2.

3 Exposing Hash-Induced Unfairness in LDP

In this section, we empirically show that the impacts of BIA and MGA can differ significantly under the same ε budget, due to variations in hash functions. First, we describe our experiment setup (datasets and metrics) in Sect. 3.1. Second, we describe the construction of subpopulations from $\mathcal{U}$ in Sect. 3.2. Third, we experimentally demonstrate the impacts of BIAs and MGAs on different subpopulations in Sect. 3.3.

3.1 Experiment Setup

<u>Datasets.</u> We used three real-world datasets (Adult, BMS-POS, and Kosarak) and two synthetically generated datasets (Gaussian and Uniform) in our experiments. All implementations were done in Python. In all figures, we report average results from 10 experiments to account for LDP randomness.

Adult: We used the Adult dataset from the UCI Machine Learning Repository[1], which contains demographic and employment-related information about individuals. We dropped records with missing data, yielding $|\mathcal{U}| = 45222$, and then used the cross product of age and gender attributes as $\mathcal{D}$.

BMS-POS: The BMS-POS dataset contains sales data from a large electronics retailer, comprising 515596 transactions and 1657 distinct items sold[2]. For our experiments, we retained only the top 100 most frequently purchased items, hence $|\mathcal{D}| = 100$. After this filtering, we had $|\mathcal{U}| = 400577$ users remaining.

---
[1] https://archive.ics.uci.edu/dataset/2/adult.
[2] https://github.com/cpearce/HARM/blob/master/datasets/BMS-POS.csv.

Kosarak: The Kosarak dataset consists of click-stream data from a Hungarian online news portal[3]. Since many URLs appeared infrequently (e.g., only once or twice), we pre-processed the dataset by selecting the 128 most frequently visited URLs and discarded the rest, hence $|\mathcal{D}| = 128$. For users with multiple URLs remaining in their click stream sequence, we assigned the most frequently visited URL as their v_u.

Gaussian: We generated multiple synthetic Gaussian datasets by sampling data points from Gaussian distributions with mean $\mu = 50$ and varying standard deviation $\sigma = 1, 5, 7$, and 10. By default, we used $|\mathcal{D}| = 100$ and $|\mathcal{U}| = 100000$. The default σ is $\sigma = 7$, but we report results with varying σ as well.

Uniform: Lastly, we generated synthetic Uniform datasets where users' values are drawn from a Uniform distribution. We used $|\mathcal{U}| = 100000$ and varied the domain size $|\mathcal{D}|$ between 100 and 2000.

Metrics. We used the Attack Success Rate (ASR) metric to measure the success of a BIA, and the ULoss metric to measure the success of a MGA.

ASR captures the ratio of the population for which the attacker's predicted v_u^p is correct. Higher ASR indicates lower privacy for users.

$$\text{ASR} = \frac{\text{\# of users } u \in \mathcal{U} \text{ such that } v_u = v_u^p}{|\mathcal{U}|} \quad (7)$$

Since the goal of a MGA is to distort items' frequencies, the ULoss metric is defined to measure the differences between items' original and aggregated frequencies. The ℓ_1 distance is used as the distance measure:

$$\text{ULoss} = \sum_{v \in \mathcal{D}} |\tilde{f}(v) - f(v)| \quad (8)$$

3.2 Division of Users into Subpopulations

Since our goal is to expose unfairness in LDP caused by hash function behaviors, we divide the total user population $\mathcal{U}$ into subpopulations based on how the users' hash functions behave. More specifically, we construct three subpopulations: High-ENT, Low-PIS, and High-PIS, as explained below.

High-ENT (High Entropy) consists of users whose hash functions H_u distribute the values in $\mathcal{D}$ in a more uniform manner. To quantify uniformity, we use the notion of entropy. Higher entropy indicates a more uniform distribution of $\mathcal{D}$ into possible hash outputs $[0, g-1]$. We use the process outlined in Algorithm 3 to calculate the entropy of a hash function H. Initially, we set the counts of all $i \in [0, g-1]$ to zero. For each value v in $\mathcal{D}$, we apply the hash function on v to obtain $x \leftarrow H(v)$, where $x \in [0, g-1]$. We then increment $count(x)$ by 1. After going through all $v \in \mathcal{D}$, we obtain the $counts$ storing how many elements in $\mathcal{D}$ hash to each integer i. We convert $count(i)$ to $prob(i)$ (lines 6–7), and compute the entropy of the hash function, denoted by $\mathcal{E}_{\text{comp}}$, on line 8.

---

[3] https://www.philippe-fournier-viger.com/spmf/index.php?link=datasets.php

Algorithm 3. Calculating the Entropy of a Hash Function

Input: Hash function H, domain $\mathcal{D}$
Output: Computed entropy of this hash function $\mathcal{E}_{\text{comp}}$
1: **for** $i = 0$ to $g - 1$ **do**
2:     Initialize $count(i) = 0$
3: **for** $v \in \mathcal{D}$ **do**
4:     $x \leftarrow H(v)$
5:     $count(x) \leftarrow count(x) + 1$
6: **for** $i = 0$ to $g - 1$ **do**
7:     $prob(i) \leftarrow \frac{count(i)}{|\mathcal{D}|}$
8: $\mathcal{E}_{\text{comp}} \leftarrow -\sum_{i=0}^{g-1} prob(i) \times \log(prob(i))$
9: **return** $\mathcal{E}_{\text{comp}}$

Given the total user population $\mathcal{U}$, the High-ENT subpopulation is constructed as follows. For each user $u \in \mathcal{U}$, we feed the user's hash function H_u into Algorithm 3 to obtain the entropy for this user, $\mathcal{E}_{\text{comp}}^u$. After obtaining the entropies for all users $\mathcal{E}_{\text{comp}}^{u_1}, \mathcal{E}_{\text{comp}}^{u_2}, ..., \mathcal{E}_{\text{comp}}^{u_{|\mathcal{U}|}}$ we sort them in descending order. We select the top 10% of the users with the highest entropies to constitute the set of users in High-ENT.

Low-PIS (Low Preimage Size). Recall from the OLH protocol that we have $x_u = H_u(v_u)$ for user u. The preimage set of H_u, which we denote by P_u, can be defined as: $P_u = \{v | v \in \mathcal{D}, H_u(v) = x_u\}$. In other words, P_u is the set of values in the domain that hash to the same outcome as v_u. Low-PIS consists of users whose hash functions yield low P_u. Given the total user population $\mathcal{U}$, the Low-PIS subpopulation is constructed as follows. For each user $u \in \mathcal{U}$, we calculate the P_u for this user. After obtaining all preimage set sizes $P_{u_1}, P_{u_2}, ..., P_{u_{|\mathcal{U}|}}$, we sort them in descending order. We select the bottom 10% of the users with the lowest preimage set sizes to constitute the set of users in Low-PIS.

High-PIS (High Preimage Size). We use the same preimage set sizes P_u as in Low-PIS, but this time, we focus on the opposite end, i.e., users whose hash functions yield high P_u. After obtaining $P_{u_1}, P_{u_2}, ..., P_{u_{|\mathcal{U}|}}$ and sorting them in descending order, we select the top 10% of the users with the highest preimage set sizes to constitute the set of users in High-PIS.

Summary. We summarize the intuition behind High-ENT, Low-PIS, and High-PIS as follows. Users in High-ENT are those users in $\mathcal{U}$ whose hash functions yield the most uniform-like output distributions, i.e., values in $\mathcal{D}$ are as evenly distributed as possible over the output space $[0, g - 1]$. On the other hand, Low-PIS and High-PIS both correspond to cases where hash function non-uniformity is high, i.e., certain outputs are more likely than others. Yet, they represent two opposite ends: In High-PIS, non-uniformity is high *and* there are many hash collisions with $x_u = H_u(v_u)$. In Low-PIS, non-uniformity is high *but* as opposed to High-PIS, there are very few hash collisions with x_u.

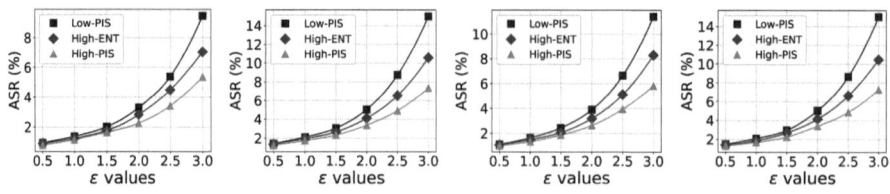

Fig. 1. BIA results on Adult, BMS-POS, Kosarak, and Gaussian datasets.

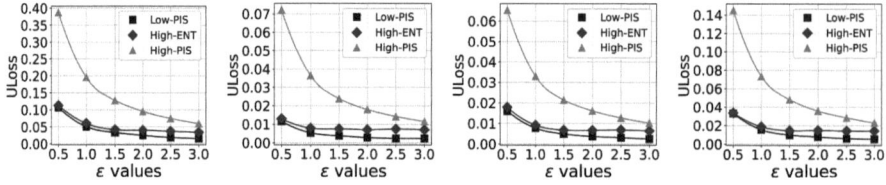

Fig. 2. MGA results on Adult, BMS-POS, Kosarak, and Gaussian datasets.

3.3 Impacts of BIA and MGA on Different Subpopulations

We execute BIAs on the three subpopulations (High-ENT, Low-PIS, and High-PIS) and measure their ASRs separately. Results with varying ε are shown in Fig. 1. The results show that significant differences in ASR can be observed for different subpopulations, especially when ε is increased. When ε is low, all subpopulations' ASRs remain low, therefore the differences between them are not too visible in the graphs (though they exist). As $\varepsilon \geq 2$, the differences become more visible. When $\varepsilon = 3$, ASRs for Low-PIS are typically 2x higher than High-PIS and 1.5x higher than High-ENT. These validate that the behaviors of hash functions indeed have a substantial impact on ASRs, and users in the Low-PIS population can be twice as vulnerable to a BIA compared to High-PIS users, despite using the same LDP protocol and ε budget.

It is intuitive that Low-PIS users have higher vulnerability than others. By definition of Low-PIS, users in this subpopulation use hash functions with small preimage sets P_u. From Algorithm 1, we observe that if P_u is small, then lines 5–6 of the algorithm will increment the scores of fewer different values, since the condition on line 5 will be satisfied by only those $v \in P_u$. Hence, the argmax on line 7 will recover the correct prediction. However, for High-PIS users, since P_u is large, lines 5–6 of Algorithm 1 will increment the scores of many different values, and consequently, the argmax on line 7 will necessitate random tie-breaking or pick an incorrect prediction. High-ENT's ASR falls between these two subpopulations, because P_u in High-ENT is neither as small as Low-PIS, nor as large as High-PIS. For example, P_u in High-ENT can be close to $\frac{|\mathcal{D}|}{g}$, whereas it is larger in High-PIS and smaller in Low-PIS. Making a correct prediction from a larger set is more difficult, hence lower ASR in High-PIS.

Next, we execute MGAs on the three subpopulations and measure their ULoss separately. To make MGA untargeted, we use $T = \mathcal{D}$. Results of this

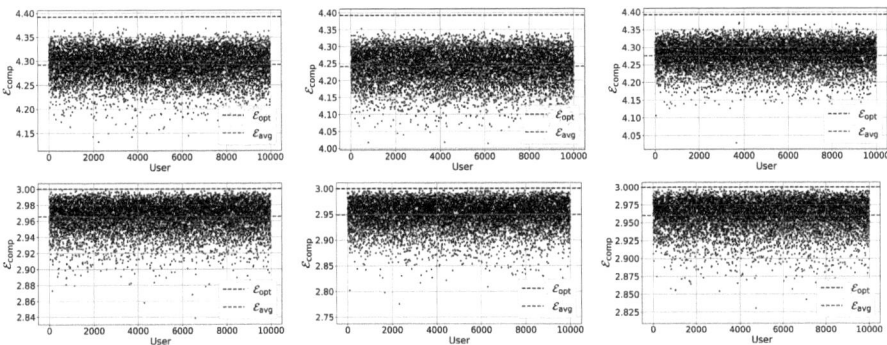

Fig. 3. Entropy of users' hash functions compared to $\mathcal{E}_{\text{avg}}$ and $\mathcal{E}_{\text{opt}}$. First row is with $\varepsilon = 3$, second row is with $\varepsilon = 2$. Datasets from left to right: Adult, BMS-POS, Kosarak.

experiment with varying ε are shown in Fig. 2. According to the results, again there are significant differences in ULoss for different subpopulations. ULoss of High-PIS is especially much higher than Low-PIS and High-ENT. Conversely, Low-PIS exhibits the lowest ULoss, while the ULoss of High-ENT falls between Low-PIS and High-PIS. Consequently, we find that if the malicious user in a MGA is a High-PIS user, they can achieve a much more successful attack than a Low-PIS or High-ENT user, e.g., the attack can increase ULoss by 3-4 times more when $\varepsilon \leq 1$. Since the Adult dataset has the smallest domain size, it is easier under the MGA attack for the High-PIS population to find a hash seed that maps most (if not all) domain values into a single output. This allows the attacker to manipulate frequencies more effectively, leading to greater ULoss.

The reason behind these results is that the hash function and the resulting P_u are important in MGA as well. Consider lines 6-10 of Algorithm 2. When P_u is large, it becomes more likely that many $\bar{v} \in T$ are also members of P_u. Consequently, the final $\langle H_u, x'_u \rangle$ returned by Algorithm 2 affects the resulting frequencies $\tilde{f}(v)$ more. This causes a larger discrepancy between $\tilde{f}(v)$ and $f(v)$, resulting in higher ULoss. This trend is quite amplified in High-PIS; therefore, High-PIS has much higher ULoss than High-ENT and Low-PIS.

4 F-OLH: Mitigating Hash-Induced Unfairness

Having shown that users' membership in Low-PIS or High-PIS yields substantial differences in terms of BIA and MGA, we now shift our direction towards how these disparate impacts (unfairness) can be mitigated. To address this problem, we propose a fair variant of OLH, called Fair-OLH (F-OLH).

4.1 Intuition Behind F-OLH

Considering that the unfairness is caused by the hash functions of different users behaving differently, we ask: How differently do different users' hash functions

Algorithm 4. Fair-OLH (F-OLH)

Input: Domain $\mathcal{D}$, true value v_u, budget ε, hash function family $\mathcal{H}$, fairness ratio ρ
Output: Result of user-side perturbation $\langle H_u, x'_u \rangle$
1: $g \leftarrow e^{\varepsilon} + 1$
2: $\mathcal{E}_{\text{opt}} \leftarrow -\sum_{i=0}^{g-1} \frac{1}{g} \times \log(\frac{1}{g})$
3: $H_u \leftarrow$ Draw a hash function from $\mathcal{H}$
4: $\mathcal{E}_{\text{comp}} \leftarrow$ Call Algorithm 3 with H_u and $\mathcal{D}$
5: **while** $\frac{\mathcal{E}_{\text{opt}}}{\mathcal{E}_{\text{comp}}} > \rho$ **do**
6: $\quad H_u \leftarrow$ Draw a hash function from $\mathcal{H}$
7: $\quad \mathcal{E}_{\text{comp}} \leftarrow$ Call Algorithm 3 with H_u and $\mathcal{D}$
8: $x_u \leftarrow H_u(v_u)$
9: Perturb x_u to $x'_u \in [0, g-1]$ such that: $\Pr[x'_u = i] = \begin{cases} \frac{e^{\varepsilon}}{e^{\varepsilon}+g-1}, & \text{if } x_u = i, \\ \frac{1}{e^{\varepsilon}+g-1}, & \text{otherwise} \end{cases}$
10: Send $\langle H_u, x'_u \rangle$ to the server

behave in practice? Is it possible to enforce that all users' hash functions behave similarly in terms of entropy? To illustrate the answers to these questions, we provide the results in Fig. 3. We sampled 10000 users from the corresponding populations and computed the entropies of their hash functions $\mathcal{E}_{\text{comp}}$ using Algorithm 3. Each user's $\mathcal{E}_{\text{comp}}$ is denoted by a black dot in Fig. 3. Then, we computed the average entropy of all users, denoted by $\mathcal{E}_{\text{avg}}$ and drawn using a dashed red line. Finally, we computed the entropy of a hypothetical ideal hash function with maximum entropy, i.e., $\mathcal{D}$ is distributed evenly into outputs $[0, g-1]$. This is denoted by $\mathcal{E}_{\text{opt}}$ and drawn using a dashed blue line in Fig. 3.

We observe from Fig. 3 that when $\varepsilon = 2$, some users' $\mathcal{E}_{\text{comp}}$ can be close to $\mathcal{E}_{\text{opt}}$. When $\varepsilon = 3$, $\mathcal{E}_{\text{comp}}$ and $\mathcal{E}_{\text{opt}}$ are farther from one another because when ε is increased, the g parameter of the OLH protocol, which is tied to ε, also increases. Thus, the output space $[0, g-1]$ enlarges, and it becomes more difficult for a hash function to achieve perfect uniformity in a larger output space. We also observe from Fig. 3 that many users' hash functions behave similarly to $\mathcal{E}_{\text{avg}}$. Some have higher entropy and some have lower entropy than $\mathcal{E}_{\text{avg}}$, but they are usually not far from $\mathcal{E}_{\text{avg}}$. However, there also exist a few users whose $\mathcal{E}_{\text{comp}}$ is significantly low. These are the users who are typically members of the Low-PIS and High-PIS subpopulations, and therefore, they are the users with the highest amount of hash-induced unfairness. Therefore, our intuition is to design a solution which ensures $\mathcal{E}_{\text{comp}}$ is not too low. Indeed, our proposed F-OLH protocol stems from this principle.

4.2 Formalization of F-OLH

To mitigate hash-induced unfairness in LDP, we propose the Fair-OLH (F-OLH) protocol. The main idea of F-OLH is to enforce each user to select a hash function that ensures $\mathcal{E}_{\text{comp}}$ is not too low. For user u with a certain hash function H_u, we define the fairness ratio ρ_u as:

$$\rho_u = \frac{\mathcal{E}_{\text{opt}}}{\mathcal{E}_{\text{comp}}} \quad (9)$$

If ρ_u is greater than a system-wide threshold ρ, F-OLH enforces the user to select another hash function. If ρ_u with the newly selected hash function is again greater than ρ, another hash function is selected. This selection process keeps iterating until a suitable hash function that satisfies the ρ threshold is found. Afterwards, the user executes the OLH protocol with the suitable hash function that was found.

The pseudocode of F-OLH is given in Algorithm 4. The calculation of g is identical to OLH. Then, $\mathcal{E}_{\text{opt}}$ is computed assuming an optimal hash function which uniformly distributes $\mathcal{D}$ to $[0, g-1]$. Note that in such a hash function, the probability of each hash outcome is $\frac{1}{g}$. Then, between lines 3–7, the user searches for a suitable H_u which satisfies the $\frac{\mathcal{E}_{\text{opt}}}{\mathcal{E}_{\text{comp}}} \leq \rho$ condition by drawing hash functions from $\mathcal{H}$ and discarding those which do not satisfy the condition. Once a suitable hash function H_u is found, the user hashes their true value v_u using H_u to obtain x_u. The perturbation of x_u to x'_u is identical to OLH. Finally, the user sends $\langle H_u, x'_u \rangle$ to the server. We note that this algorithm describes the user-side execution of F-OLH. On the server side, the server collects $\langle H_u, x'_u \rangle$ from all users $u \in \mathcal{P}$. The server's aggregation and estimation process remains identical to OLH, which was explained at the end of Sect. 2.1.

From an implementation standpoint, current implementations of the OLH protocol typically use a Python library like XXHASH for hashing. In these implementations, drawing H_u from $\mathcal{H}$ means changing the hash seed used in XXHASH, since each different seed yields a different H_u. In F-OLH, we use a similar strategy to implement iterative drawing of different H_u from $\mathcal{H}$, i.e., we iterate over different seeds in XXHASH until Algorithm 4 finds a suitable H_u.

Finally, we note that when the user runs Algorithm 4, the while loop (lines 5–7) takes a longer time as the target ρ becomes smaller, since it becomes more difficult to find a hash function that meets the entropy constraint. To address this, F-OLH can be modified to guarantee loop termination in a bounded time. One approach is to always try a fixed number of $\mathcal{N}$ hash functions and select the one that appears fairest. Another approach is to impose a time limit, after which the user exits the loop and selects the best hash encountered.

4.3 Results of F-OLH on BIA and MGA

We again execute BIAs on the three subpopulations (High-ENT, Low-PIS, and High-PIS) and measure their ASRs. This time, as opposed to Sect. 3.3, we assume that the whole population uses F-OLH instead of OLH. Hence, High-ENT, Low-PIS, and High-PIS subpopulations also consist of users who use F-OLH. Results with varying ρ are shown in Fig. 4.

A key take-away message from Fig. 4 is that F-OLH is indeed effective in reducing the ASR differences between different subpopulations using the ρ

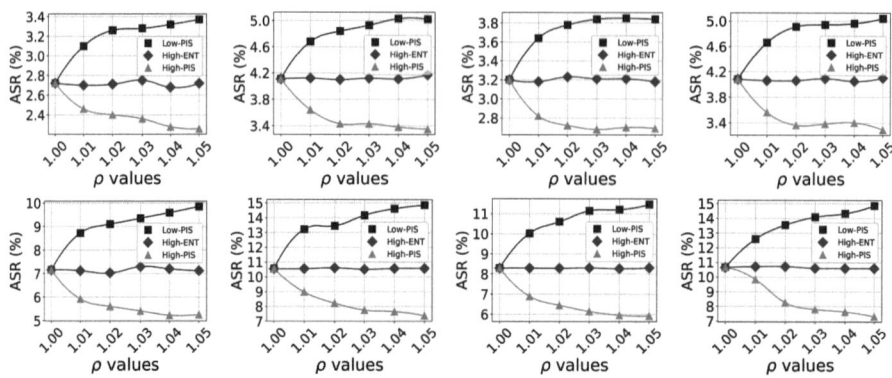

Fig. 4. BIA results on Adult, BMS-POS, Kosarak, and Gaussian datasets using F-OLH instead of OLH. Top row is with $\varepsilon = 2$, bottom row is with $\varepsilon = 3$.

threshold. For example, ASRs of Low-PIS, High-ENT, and High-PIS users are all equal when $\rho = 1$, indicating a fair outcome for all subpopulations. This is an intuitive result because $\rho = 1$ enforces all users' hash functions to behave like $\mathcal{E}_{\mathrm{opt}}$; therefore, there are no disparate impacts. On the other hand, as ρ is increased, the threshold becomes more relaxed. Consequently, we observe from Fig. 4 that the ASR differences between the three subpopulations increase as ρ is increased. This is also an intuitive result, since higher ρ allows the use of more non-uniform hash functions, i.e., hash functions which diverge from $\mathcal{E}_{\mathrm{opt}}$. As a result, unfairness in the user population increases, and the subpopulations start diverging from one another. While the differences between subpopulations are relatively small when $\rho = 1.01$, they enlarge as ρ is increased to 1.05. In fact, results with $\rho = 1.05$ approach the results in Fig. 1, implying that F-OLH converges to OLH, and it no longer provides much fairness benefit. Thus, we confirm that ρ values closer to 1 better address unfairness with respect to BIA.

In the next set of experiments, we compare the effectiveness of MGA on OLH and F-OLH under varying ρ using the ULoss metric. Since previous results (reported in Fig. 2) established that MGA is most effective on High-PIS by far, we focus our experiments here on the High-PIS subpopulation. The results, demonstrated in Fig. 5, demonstrate that the effectiveness of MGA decreases significantly when F-OLH is used. Notably, when $\rho = 1.01$, the effectiveness of MGA is nearly halved in F-OLH compared to OLH. As ρ increases, F-OLH again gradually converges to OLH (similar to BIA). The primary reason for this behavior is that under a strict ρ constraint, the maximum preimage set size P_u of a user ends up being much smaller in F-OLH compared to what it can be in OLH. As a result, MGA can manipulate fewer $\bar{v} \in T$, yielding smaller attack impact. It can also be observed from Fig. 5 that under small ε such as $\varepsilon = 0.5$, ULoss is generally larger and it can remain large despite the use of F-OLH with strict ρ. The reason behind this trend is that the ULoss caused by LDP itself is larger when ε is small. In other words, even if there was no attack like MGA,

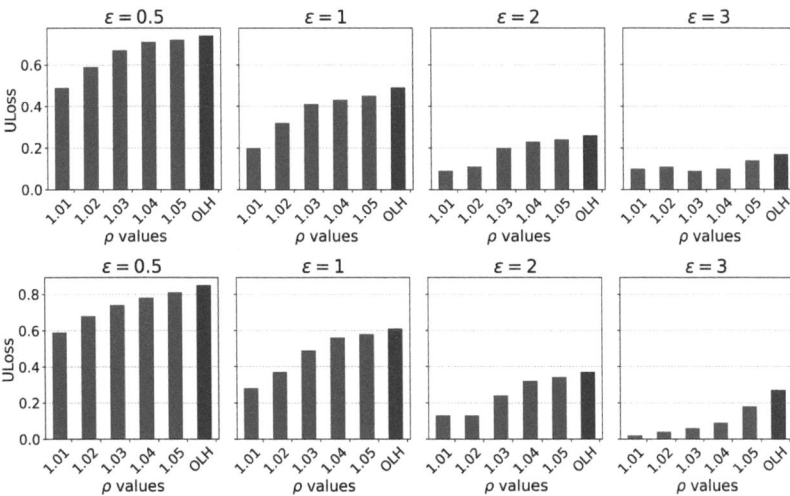

Fig. 5. MGA results using the proposed F-OLH protocol. Top row is with the Kosarak dataset, bottom row is with the Gaussian dataset.

there would have been substantial ULoss when ε is small, caused by LDP. Such fundamental (and natural) ULoss cannot be addressed by OLH or F-OLH.

Finally, we perform additional experiments on two real-world datasets (Kosarak and BMS-POS) to analyze how the real frequency distribution $f(v)$ compares with frequencies after MGA attacks on OLH and F-OLH. We also perform additional experiments using Gaussian datasets with different σ. (The results of the latter experiment are similar to Fig. 5). Due to the page limit, we provide the results and analysis of these experiments in the appendix.

4.4 Time Cost of F-OLH

In OLH, each user draws their hash function H_u from $\mathcal{H}$ once. However, in F-OLH, the user continues drawing hash functions from $\mathcal{H}$ until a hash function satisfying the ρ threshold is found. Thus, F-OLH has an additional time cost compared to OLH. In this section, we experimentally analyze this time cost.

In Fig. 6, we report the execution time comparison between OLH and F-OLH under varying ρ. In all plots, the value of ε is 2. We observe that when ρ is small, execution times are higher. This is because F-OLH needs more time to find a hash function that satisfies the strict ρ threshold, leading to increased computational overhead. As ρ increases, it is easier to find a hash function that satisfies the threshold; therefore, execution times of F-OLH begin to converge to OLH. However, execution times of F-OLH always remain higher than OLH due to the additional computation in F-OLH: even when the ρ constraint is relaxed, F-OLH still needs to call Algorithm 3 to compute $\mathcal{E}_{\text{comp}}$ and verify compliance with ρ. This computation, which exists in F-OLH but not in OLH, causes F-OLH's execution times to always be higher.

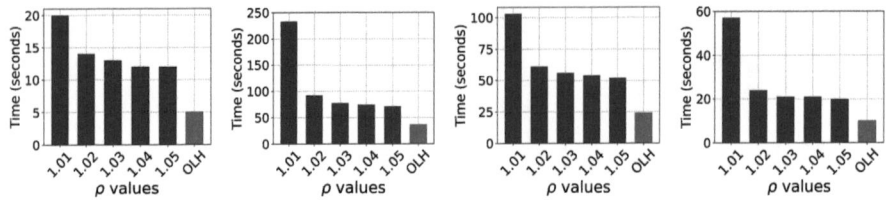

Fig. 6. Execution time comparison between F-OLH (blue bars) and OLH (orange bar) on Adult, BMS-POS, Kosarak, and Gaussian datasets. (Color figure online)

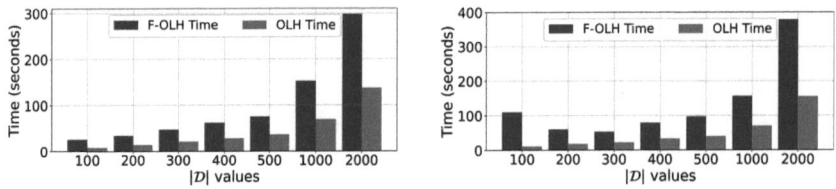

Fig. 7. Execution time comparison between F-OLH and OLH on Uniform datasets with varying domain sizes $|\mathcal{D}|$. $g = 5$ on the left, $g = 10$ on the right.

Next, we use the Uniform datasets to measure how the domain size $|\mathcal{D}|$ affects the execution times of OLH and F-OLH. The results of this experiment are shown in Fig. 7. We fixed $g = 5$ for the plot on the left (corresponding to approximately $\varepsilon = 1.5$) and $g = 10$ for the plot on the right (corresponding to approximately $\varepsilon = 2.2$). In both figures, $\rho = 1.01$. Again, we observe that in general, the execution times of F-OLH are higher than OLH. As the domain size increases, the execution time for both protocols increases. A notable outlier, however, is the case when $g = 10$ and $|\mathcal{D}| = 100$. In this case, the execution time is higher than many other $|\mathcal{D}|$. We found the reason behind this outlier is that it is challenging for F-OLH to find a suitable hash function which ensures a near-uniform distribution (so that $\rho = 1.01$ is satisfied) for a relatively small $|\mathcal{D}|$ and large $g = 10$. Many iterations of the while loop in Algorithm 4 are necessary to find a suitable hash function, thereby increasing execution time.

Based on these results, we arrive at the following conclusions: While larger $|\mathcal{D}|$ usually yields higher execution times, the values of ρ and g (which is tied to ε) are also important, especially in F-OLH. This is because ρ, g, and $|\mathcal{D}|$ all affect how difficult it is to find a hash function that satisfies the ρ constraint. We also note that the execution times reported in Figs. 6 and 7 are the results of simulating all users on one CPU sequentially. In the real world, users will be executing OLH or F-OLH in parallel on their own devices. Thus, the real-world execution time costs of the protocols will be close to the execution times reported in Figs. 6 and 7 divided by $|\mathcal{U}|$. Hence, the execution time for each user will remain in the order of milliseconds. This shows that in practice, replacing OLH by F-OLH will not lead to a noticeable execution time problem. In the appendix, we provide guidance regarding how to select ρ in a practical setting.

5 Related Work

Since our paper aims to expose and mitigate hash-induced unfairness in LDP protocols in terms of privacy and poisoning attacks, we survey related literature in three categories: (i) privacy attacks in LDP, (ii) poisoning attacks in LDP, (iii) intersection of fairness and LDP.

Privacy attacks in LDP typically aim to infer sensitive user information or assess practical privacy guarantees of LDP protocols against specific adversaries. Murakami et al. [21] examined re-identification risks in LDP. Gadotti et al. [13] introduced pool inference attacks to determine if a user's true value belongs to a certain pool based on the LDP protocol output. Gursoy et al. [14] analyzed LDP protocols using a Bayesian adversary model, and later extended this model to longitudinal data collection [15]. Arcolezi et al. [4] studied inference risks stemming from multidimensional data collection. Finally, Arcolezi and Gambs [2] proposed LDP-Auditor for empirically estimating the privacy loss of LDP mechanisms. Following the literature, this paper uses the Bayesian adversary model, which was proposed in [14] and later extended and used in [3,4,15].

Poisoning Attacks in LDP. In poisoning attacks, malicious users poison the LDP protocol to manipulate the statistics recovered by the data collector. The vulnerability of LDP protocols to poisoning was shown by Cheu et al. [8] and Cao et al. [6]. Poisoning attacks targeting mean and variance estimation were proposed in [17]. Li et al. [18] studied the robustness of LDP protocols designed for numerical attributes. Wu et al. [24] proposed poisoning attacks for key-value data, Imola et al. [16] studied poisoning attacks on graph analysis, and Zheng et al. [27] studied poisoning attacks against LDP-based privacy-preserving crowdsensing. Since we are working directly with LDP protocols (i.e., not an application such as key-value data or crowdsensing), in this paper, we use MGA from the literature [6] as the fundamental poisoning attack.

Fairness and LDP. There also exist some recent works at the intersection of LDP and fairness. Chen et al. [7] propose FairSP to achieve fair machine learning predictions while some sensitive attributes are protected with LDP. Mozannar et al. [20] study fair learning under privatized demographic data. Arcolezi et al. [5] and Makhlouf et al. [19] study the impacts of perturbing multidimensional records with LDP on fairness. However, all of these works consider fairness in terms of classification models (i.e., supervised machine learning) built from privatized data. None of the previous works consider fairness from the perspective of increased (or decreased) vulnerability to privacy and poisoning attacks. To the best of our knowledge, we are the first to study the unfairness of LDP protocols in terms of privacy protection and vulnerability to poisoning.

6 Conclusion

In this paper, we identified and analyzed hash-induced unfairness in LDP. We demonstrated that users employing non-uniform hash functions experience significantly different vulnerabilities to BIA and MGA attacks, despite using the same protocol and privacy parameters. To mitigate this disparity, we proposed Fair-OLH (F-OLH), a variant of OLH that enforces an entropy-based fairness constraint on hash function selection. Our experiments showed that F-OLH substantially reduces disparities among users, improving fairness in both BIA and MGA attacks, while maintaining acceptable time cost. These findings highlight the critical need to account for hash function behavior in LDP protocols. In future work, we plan to explore broader notions of fairness, explore more efficient methods for fair hash function selection, and propose fair variants of protocols other than OLH. In particular, we aim to extend our fairness-aware approach to other protocols, including those using different encoding types such as bitvector encoding, e.g., RAPPOR, OUE, BLH.

Acknowledgment. This study was supported by The Scientific and Technological Research Council of Turkiye (TUBITAK) under grant number 123E179. The authors thank TUBITAK for their support.

A   Additional Experiments with MGA

In Fig. 8, we present the results of MGA on BMS-POS and Kosarak, using 2000 malicious users for BMS-POS and 1000 malicious users for Kosarak (malicious user count is higher for BMS-POS since it consists of 400.000 users, almost twice of Kosarak). We observe from the plots that OLH exhibits an interesting behavior: frequencies of frequent values (high $f(v)$) are underestimated, while frequencies of infrequent values (low $f(v)$) are overestimated. However, F-OLH performs better than OLH, i.e., its overestimation and underestimation amounts are lower than those of OLH. This is because of the uniformity of hash functions used in F-OLH. Especially when ρ is small, F-OLH effectively "scales up" the

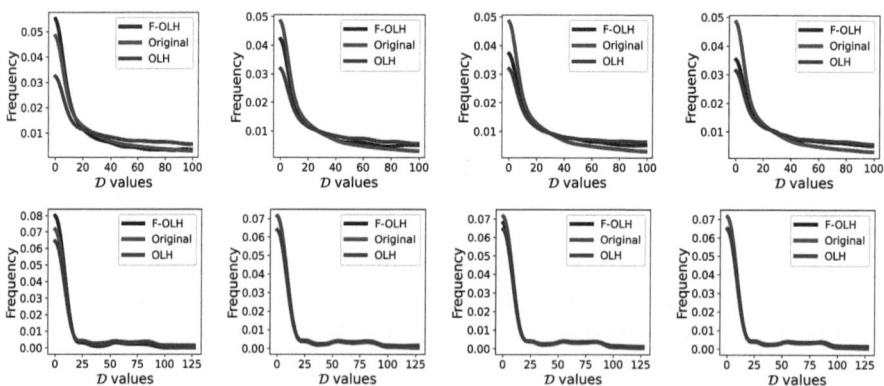

Fig. 8. Real frequencies $f(v)$ of items $v \in \mathcal{D}$ (red curve) versus estimated frequencies $\tilde{f}(v)$ under MGA attack with OLH (green curve) and F-OLH (blue curve). $\varepsilon = 0.5$, ρ values are $\rho = 1.01, 1.02, 1.03, 1.04$ from left to right. Top row: BMS-POS, bottom row: Kosarak dataset. (Color figure online)

frequencies, causing frequent values to be estimated higher whereas infrequent values are estimated lower. This characteristic fixes the underestimations and overestimations of OLH, thereby acting as a natural defense mechanism against MGA. It also allows F-OLH to maintain a frequency distribution that more closely resembles the original distribution, thereby yielding lower ULoss (Fig. 9).

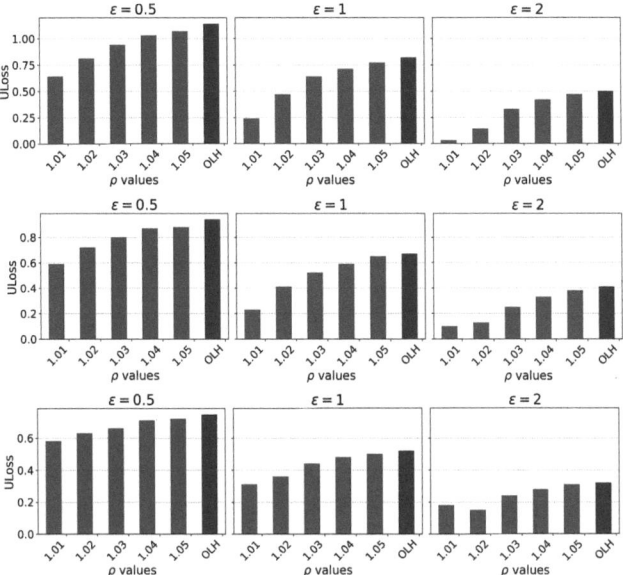

Fig. 9. MGA results of the proposed F-OLH protocol using different Gaussian datasets. First row is with $\sigma = 1$, second row is with $\sigma = 5$, third row is with $\sigma = 10$.

B Selection of the ρ Threshold

In the paper, we established that selecting ρ close to 1 improves fairness and resilience to both BIA and MGA attacks. However, it also has the adverse effect of increasing execution time. In this section, we provide guidance regarding how to select ρ. In particular, when selecting the value of ρ, we recommend performing the following analysis, which can be conducted in simulation using $\mathcal{D}$, ε, and $\mathcal{H}$ prior to actual data collection.

For user u with true value v_u and hash function H_u, recall that P_u denotes the preimage set. We define:

$$P_{max} = \max_{u \in \mathcal{U}} |P_u| \qquad P_{min} = \min_{u \in \mathcal{U}} |P_u| \qquad P_{avg} = \frac{1}{|\mathcal{U}|} \sum_{u \in \mathcal{U}} |P_u| \qquad (10)$$

In Table 1, we analyze how different choices of ρ affect P_{min}, P_{max}, and P_{avg} in F-OLH. We compare these values with theoretical bounds of $P_{min} = 1$, $P_{max} = |\mathcal{D}|$, and $P_{avg} = \frac{|\mathcal{D}|}{g}$, as well as those achieved by OLH. In general, it is desirable for OLH and F-OLH to have P_{avg} similar to the theoretical P_{avg}, since it implies higher uniformity of the hash function. On the other hand, it is desirable to have P_{min} and P_{max} that are distant from the theoretical P_{min} and P_{max}, since the theoretical P_{min} and P_{max} represent edge cases (maximum non-uniformity).

Table 1. P_{avg}, P_{min}, and P_{max} on BMS-POS and Kosarak datasets, $\varepsilon = 2$.

	P_{avg}	P_{min}	P_{max}		P_{avg}	P_{min}	P_{max}
Theoretical	12.50	1	100	Theoretical	16.00	1	128
$\rho = 1.01$	12.86	7	19	$\rho = 1.01$	16.30	9	24
$\rho = 1.02$	13.10	5	22	$\rho = 1.02$	16.58	6	26
$\rho = 1.03$	13.26	4	25	$\rho = 1.03$	16.64	5	31
$\rho = 1.04$	13.34	3	26	$\rho = 1.04$	16.71	4	33
$\rho = 1.05$	13.35	2	27	$\rho = 1.05$	16.74	3	35
OLH	13.37	2	31	OLH	16.74	3	36

It can be observed from Table 1 that as we decrease ρ in F-OLH, the values of P_{min}, P_{max}, and P_{avg} become more desirable. As we increase ρ, the values of P_{min}, P_{max}, and P_{avg} approach OLH, which is undesirable. It should be noted that even when $\rho = 1.01$, P_{avg} of F-OLH is different from the theoretical P_{avg}, but nevertheless, it is substantially lower than other ρ and OLH.

In general, the analysis in Table 1 can be used in ρ selection as follows. First, one should select ρ such that P_{avg} of F-OLH is not too different from the theoretical P_{avg}. Second, considering that P_{min} and P_{max} represent the unfair edge cases, the difference between them should be low. Using $\mathcal{H}$ and $\mathcal{D}$, the data collector can simulate P_{min}, P_{max}, and P_{avg} under varying ρ. Similar to Table 1, these values can be compared with their theoretical values and the outputs of OLH. The ρ value that yields sufficient divergence from OLH and similarity to the theoretical P_{avg} can be selected as the ρ to be used. It should be noted that as ρ gets smaller (i.e., stricter), it will be more difficult to find a hash function that satisfies this ρ, and the execution time will increase.

Next, we show how this analysis relates to the expected ASR of BIA. For BIA attack to succeed, the user's encoded value must remain unperturbed. Under OLH, the probability that a hashed value remains unperturbed is $\frac{e^\varepsilon}{e^\varepsilon+g-1}$. If an adversary knows the preimage set of the reported value, the success rate of random guess is $\frac{1}{|P_u|}$. Therefore, the expected attack success rate (ASR) is:

$$\mathbb{E}[\text{ASR}] = \frac{e^\varepsilon}{e^\varepsilon + g - 1} \cdot \frac{1}{P_{avg}} \qquad (11)$$

For example, in the BMS-POS dataset with $\varepsilon = 2$ and $\rho = 1.01$, Table 1 shows $P_{\text{avg}} = 12.86$. Substituting into the equation yields $\mathbb{E}[\text{ASR}] = 3.99$, which aligns with the result shown in Fig. 4. Similarly, for the Kosarak dataset with $P_{\text{avg}} = 16.30$, $\varepsilon = 2$, and $\rho = 1.01$, we obtain $\mathbb{E}[\text{ASR}] = 3.15$, again confirming the results in Fig. 4.

References

1. Arcolezi, H.H., Couchot, J.F., Al Bouna, B., Xiao, X.: Improving the utility of locally differentially private protocols for longitudinal and multidimensional frequency estimates. Digit. Commun. Netw. (2022)
2. Arcolezi, H.H., Gambs, S.: Revealing the true cost of locally differentially private protocols: an auditing perspective. Proc. Privacy Enhancing Technol. **2024**(4)
3. Arcolezi, H.H., Gambs, S.: Revisiting locally differentially private protocols: towards better trade-offs in privacy, utility, and attack resistance. arXiv preprint arXiv:2503.01482 (2025)
4. Arcolezi, H.H., Gambs, S., Couchot, J.F., Palamidessi, C.: On the risks of collecting multidimensional data under local differential privacy. Proc. VLDB Endow. (PVLDB) **16**(5), 1126–1139 (2023)
5. Arcolezi, H.H., Makhlouf, K., Palamidessi, C.: (local) differential privacy has no disparate impact on fairness. In: IFIP Annual Conference on Data and Applications Security and Privacy, pp. 3–21. Springer, Cham (2023)
6. Cao, X., Jia, J., Gong, N.Z.: Data poisoning attacks to local differential privacy protocols. In: 30th USENIX Security Symposium (USENIX Security 2021), pp. 947–964. USENIX Association (2021)
7. Chen, C., Liang, Y., Xu, X., Xie, S., Hong, Y., Shu, K.: When fairness meets privacy: fair classification with semi-private sensitive attributes. In: Workshop on Trustworthy and Socially Responsible Machine Learning, NeurIPS 2022
8. Cheu, A., Smith, A., Ullman, J.: Manipulation attacks in local differential privacy. In: 2021 IEEE Symposium on Security and Privacy (SP), pp. 883–900. IEEE (2021)
9. Cormode, G., Jha, S., Kulkarni, T., Li, N., Srivastava, D., Wang, T.: Privacy at scale: local differential privacy in practice. In: Proceedings of the 2018 International Conference on Management of Data, pp. 1655–1658. ACM (2018)
10. Cormode, G., Maddock, S., Maple, C.: Frequency estimation under local differential privacy. Proc. VLDB Endow. **14**(11), 2046–2058 (2021)
11. Ding, B., Kulkarni, J., Yekhanin, S.: Collecting telemetry data privately. In: Advances in Neural Information Processing Systems, pp. 3571–3580 (2017)
12. Erlingsson, Ú., Pihur, V., Korolova, A.: Rappor: randomized aggregatable privacy-preserving ordinal response. In: Proceedings of the 2014 ACM SIGSAC Conference on Computer and Communications Security, pp. 1054–1067 (2014)
13. Gadotti, A., Houssiau, F., Annamalai, M.S.M.S., de Montjoye, Y.A.: Pool inference attacks on local differential privacy: quantifying the privacy guarantees of apple's count mean sketch in practice. In: 31st USENIX Security Symposium (2022)
14. Gursoy, M.E., Liu, L., Chow, K.H., Truex, S., Wei, W.: An adversarial approach to protocol analysis and selection in local differential privacy. IEEE Trans. Inf. Forensics Secur. **17**, 1785–1799 (2022)
15. Gursoy, M.E.: Longitudinal attacks against iterative data collection with local differential privacy. Turk. J. Electr. Eng. Comput. Sci. **32**(1), 198–218 (2024)
16. Imola, J., Chowdhury, A.R., Chaudhuri, K.: Robustness of locally differentially private graph analysis against poisoning. arXiv preprint arXiv:2210.14376 (2022)

17. Li, X., Li, N., Sun, W., Gong, N.Z., Li, H.: Fine-grained poisoning attack to local differential privacy protocols for mean and variance estimation. In: 32nd USENIX Security Symposium (USENIX Security 2023), pp. 1739–1756 (2023)
18. Li, X., Li, Z., Li, N., Sun, W.: On the robustness of LDP protocols for numerical attributes under data poisoning attacks. arXiv preprint arXiv:2403.19510 (2024)
19. Makhlouf, K., Arcolezi, H.H., Zhioua, S., Brahim, G.B., Palamidessi, C.: On the impact of multi-dimensional local differential privacy on fairness. Data Min. Knowl. Disc. **38**(4), 2252–2275 (2024)
20. Mozannar, H., Ohannessian, M., Srebro, N.: Fair learning with private demographic data. In: International Conference on Machine Learning. PMLR (2020)
21. Murakami, T., Takahashi, K.: Toward evaluating re-identification risks in the local privacy model. Trans. Data Privacy **14**(3), 79–116 (2021)
22. Wang, T., Blocki, J., Li, N., Jha, S.: Locally differentially private protocols for frequency estimation. In: 26th USENIX Security Symposium (USENIX Security 2017), pp. 729–745. USENIX Association, Vancouver, BC (2017)
23. Wang, T., Lopuhaa-Zwakenberg, M., Li, Z., Skoric, B., Li, N.: Locally differentially private frequency estimation with consistency. In: Proceedings of the Network and Distributed System Security (NDSS) Symposium (2020)
24. Wu, Y., Cao, X., Jia, J., Gong, N.Z.: Poisoning attacks to local differential privacy protocols for key-value data. In: 31st USENIX Security Symposium (2022)
25. Xiong, X., Liu, S., Li, D., Cai, Z., Niu, X.: A comprehensive survey on local differential privacy. Secur. Commun. Netw. **2020**, 1–29 (2020)
26. Yang, M., Guo, T., Zhu, T., Tjuawinata, I., Zhao, J., Lam, K.Y.: Local differential privacy and its applications: a comprehensive survey. Comput. Standards Interfaces 103827 (2023)
27. Zheng, Z., Li, Z., Huang, C., Long, S., Li, M., Shen, X.: Data poisoning attacks and defenses to LDP-based privacy-preserving crowdsensing. IEEE Trans. Dependable Secure Comput. (2024)

Functional Credentials: A Practical Construction for the European Digital Identity

Giovanni Bartolomeo[1,2]

[1] CNIT NAM Lab., University of Rome Tor Vergata, Rome, Italy
giovanni.bartolomeo@uniroma2.it
[2] Department for Digital Transformation, Presidency of the Council of Ministers, Rome, Italy

Abstract. Extending Functional credentials introduced in 2018 by Deuber et al., we present a credential verification protocol supporting anonymous proof of predicates over attributes and efficient revocation by dynamic accumulators. Furthermore, we provide a light and fast adaptation of the protocol suitable for the European Digital Identity model.

Keywords: Anonymous Credentials · Attribute-Based Encryption · Cryptography

1 Introduction

Some wallet credential models, including mobile Driver's License (mDL) and Selective Disclosure Json Web Token (SD-JWT) used in the European Digital IDentity Wallet (EUDIW), provide basic privacy protection by implementing credentials as a signed list of randomized commitments to attributes. While the user (said credential "Holder" or "Prover") can selectively open the commitment to the credential Verifiers, any credential Issuer colluding with Verifiers can use the signature as a handle to correlate various presentations [8]. In 2024 a feedback on the EUDIW provided by the cryptographic community pointed out that Anonymous Credentials (ACs), in particular the ones based on BBS signature (e.g., [17] currently under standardization at IETF), have been specifically designed to achieve secure privacy-preserving authentication. ACs do not only remove any source of correlation between the credential (privately stored) and its presentation (*unlinkability*, as explicitly required by EU Regulation 2024/1183 art. 5a, 16), but also prevent trivial credential copy by the Verifier (being the credential in form of a private element and the presentation derived from it using a trapdoor function). Historically, several ACs were built on special multi-message signature schemes that support *selective disclosure*. However, selective disclosure is not the only desired feature. For example, a service may require that their users are over 18 years old and that they are based in one of the European Countries. In such a case, an *anonymous proof of predicates* proving user's attribute age and country satisfying the following policy: age > 18 AND country ONEOF {Austria, Belgium,..., Sweden} would be needed. Microsoft Research [14] and Google [9] have recently demonstrated such kind of proofs by implementing Zero Knowledge Succint Non-Interactive Argument of Knowledge (ZK-SNARKs) for EUDIW and mDL credentials. However, while these systems are indeed more versatile and offer the notable advantage of retaining the legacy Issuer infrastructure without changing the credential format, in practice ACs based on multi-message signature schemes (like BBS) provide several advantages for implementers: there is no need to design from scratch complex arithmetic circuits for proving statements; size of public parameters is smaller; schemes relying on signature and encryption are several magnitude orders faster in terms of performances, etc. In a 2018 paper, Functional credentials [7] were proposed as an extension of ACs providing efficient anonymous proof of predicates via functional encryption. We want to prove a practical realization of such a scheme for the EUDIW. Starting from Water's Ciphertext Policy Attribute-Based Encryption (CP-ABE) [18], we progressively: simplify the original Functional credential presentation protocol; add efficient anonymous revocation by dynamic accumulators [3]; provide a pairing-free construction; introduce Holder binding; these latter goals are being achieved projecting our scheme in the experimental setting proposed by Orange for the BBS signature [6].

2 Preliminaries

2.1 Revocable Functional Credentials

We first define (Revocable) Functional Credentials and illustrate their properties. A revocable functional credentials scheme for an attribute universe Ω and a family of policies Φ consists of the following probabilistic algorithms:

1. $\text{MSK}, \text{MPK} \leftarrow \text{KeyGen}(1^\lambda)$: The key generation algorithm takes input the security parameter $\lambda \in \mathbb{N}$ and outputs a key pair (MSK, MPK) of an Issuer (master key pair).
2. $\text{cred}_i, \text{MPK}' \leftarrow \text{GrantCred}(\text{MSK}, \text{S}_i)$: The grant credential algorithm takes input the master secret key MSK and a (non-empty) set of attributes $\text{S}_i \subset \Omega$ and outputs a credential cred_i with $i \in \mathbb{N}$ for the corresponding set of attributes, which is added to the set GrantedCred. It also outputs an updated master public key MPK'.
3. $b \leftarrow\, <\text{ShowCred}(\text{MPK}, \text{cred}_i, f), \text{VerifyCred}(\text{MPK}, f)>$: A two party protocol played between the Prover and the Verifier. ShowCred takes input the master public key MPK, a credential cred_i, and a policy $f \in \Phi$; VerifyCred inputs the master public key MPK and a policy f. The protocol outputs a bit (0 or 1).
4. $\text{MPK}' \leftarrow \text{Revoke}(\text{MPK}, \text{MSK}, \text{cred}_i)$: this (optional) step takes input MPK, MSK, and a credential $\text{cred}_i \in \text{GrantedCred}$ and produces an update of the master public key MPK'. cred_i is said a "revoked credential" and is added to the set Revoked. A non-revoked credentials is said a "valid credential".

By definition, for all $\lambda \in \mathbb{N}$, for all $(\mathtt{MSK}, \mathtt{MPK}) \in \mathtt{KeyGen}(1^\lambda)$ for all $\mathtt{S} \subset \Omega$, for all $\mathtt{cred} \in \mathtt{GrantedCred}$, for all $\mathtt{f} \in \Phi$ such that $\mathtt{f}(\mathtt{S}) = 1$, a Functional credentials scheme:

- is said *correct* if, assumed $\mathtt{cred} \notin \mathtt{Revoked}$ it holds that

$$\Pr[1 \leftarrow\, <\mathtt{ShowCred}(\mathtt{MPK}, \mathtt{cred}, \mathtt{f}), \mathtt{VerifyCred}(\mathtt{MPK}, \mathtt{f})>] = 1$$

- is said *unforgeable* if, chosen an arbitrary policy $\mathtt{f}$, any adversary having access to all system issued credentials $\mathtt{cred}_i \in \mathtt{GrantedCred}$ but the ones satisfying the policy (i.e., $\mathtt{f}(\mathtt{cred}_i) \neq 1$) and to all revoked credentials $\mathtt{cred}_j \in \mathtt{Revoked}$, has a negligible probability to succeed in the credential verification process.
- is said *anonymous* if, arbitrarily chosen a policy $\mathtt{f}$ and two Provers $\mathtt{P}_0$ and $\mathtt{P}_1$ respectively owing $\mathtt{cred}_i, \mathtt{cred}_j \in \mathtt{GrantedCred}$ s.t. $\mathtt{cred}_i, \mathtt{cred}_j \notin \mathtt{Revoked}$, both satisfying or not the policy (i.e., $\mathtt{f}(\mathtt{cred}_i) = \mathtt{f}(\mathtt{cred}_j)$), any adversary cannot distinguish between them.

Note that the scheme is adapted from [7] where we left off one optional feature described in the original paper (policy hiding).

2.2 CP-WATERS-KEM

We recall some notions from the original CP-ABE construction proposed by Waters in Section 5 of [18][1]. The construction makes use of a bilinear group, defined as follows:

Let G and G_T be two multiplicative cyclic groups of prime order p. Let g be a generator of G and e be a bilinear map: $e\colon G \times G \to G_T$. The bilinear map e has the following properties:

1. Bilinearity: for all $u, v \in G$ and $a, b \in Z_p$, we have $e(u^a, v^b) = e(u^b, v^a) = e(u, v)^{ab}$.
2. Non-degeneracy: $e(g, g) \neq 1$.

If the group operation in G and the bilinear map e are both efficiently computable, G is said a bilinear group.

The construction consists of four algorithms:

1. $(\mathtt{MPK}, \mathtt{MSK}) \leftarrow \mathtt{Setup}(1^\lambda)$: Using the security parameter λ, the algorithm outputs the master secret key MSK and the master public key MPK, and publishes the MPK.
   - The algorithm chooses a group G of prime order p and a generator g, random group elements $h_1, h_2, \ldots, h_u$ (where u is the maximum number of system attributes) and a bilinear pairing e such that $e\colon G \times G \to G_T$. In addition, it chooses random exponents $\alpha, a \in Z_p$.

---

[1] Here, we consider CP-WATERS-KEM in its small universe construct, however, an extension to the large universe (reported in Appendix A of [18]) is straightforward.

- The public key is $g, g^a, e(g,g)^\alpha, h_1, h_2, \ldots, h_u$ and the master secret key is a, α.
2. $\mathtt{SK} = (\mathtt{K}, \mathtt{L}, \forall_{x \in S}\ \mathtt{K}_x) \leftarrow \mathtt{KeyGen}(\mathtt{MPK}, \mathtt{MSK}, \mathtt{S})$: Key generation occurs by taking as input the public key MPK (which contains the public parameters and the attributes), the master secret key MSK and a set of attributes S that describe the key. The output is a randomized secret decryption key.
   - Chosen a random $t \in Z_p$ the algorithm simply generates and releases: $K = g^\alpha g^{at}$, $L = g^t$ and, for each $x \in S$, $K_x = h_x^t$ as the secret decryption key.
3. $(\mathtt{CT} = (\mathtt{C}, \forall_{k \in [1,\ldots l]}\ \mathtt{C}_k), \mu) \leftarrow \mathtt{Encrypt}(\mathtt{MPK}, \mathtt{M}^{l \times m}, \rho)$: The algorithm takes as input an access structure (M, ρ) and the public key MPK. M is an $l \times m$ matrix, while ρ is an injective function that associates each row of M with an attribute ρ_k (i.e., $\rho_k = \rho(k) \in S$); note that in this construction one attribute is associated with at most one row[2]. The output is a secret and the ciphertext.
   - Chosen a random[3] vector $\boldsymbol{v} = (s, y_2, \ldots, y_m)$ in Z_p^m and being M_k the k-th row of M, the algorithm computes $\lambda_k = M_k \cdot \boldsymbol{v}$.
   - Together with the access structure $(M; \rho)$, the algorithm makes public the ciphertext: $C = g^s$ and $C_k = g^{a\lambda_k} h_{\rho_k}^{-s}$
   - The algorithm computes the secret $\mu = e(g,g)^{\alpha s}$ and keeps it private.
4. $\mu \leftarrow \mathtt{Decrypt}(\mathtt{SK}, \mathtt{CT})$: Dually, the decryption takes as input the ciphertext CT generated at step 3 and the secret key SK generated at step 2. The output is the common secret $e(g,g)^{\alpha s}$ if and only if the set of attributes S satisfies the access structure or *null* otherwise.
   - For each k such that $\rho_k \in S$ (i.e., consider only attributes in S), compute ω_k such that $\sum_k \omega_k \lambda_k = s$ (there could different sets of $\{\omega_k\}$ satisfying this equation)
   - Compute the secret: $\mu = \dfrac{e(C,K)}{\prod_k [e(C_k,L)e(C,K_{\rho_k})]^{\omega_k}} = e(g,g)^{\alpha s}$

2.3 Verification Protocol

We use the above construction to implement the revocable Functional credentials scheme in Sect. 2.1. Note that in the following we use a challenge that encapsulates a random value generated anew for each use as a proof of freshness; thus the protocol is natively immune to replay attacks.

1. CP-ABE $\mathtt{Setup}(1^\lambda)$ algorithm takes place in order to generate the key pair (MPK, MSK).
2. $\mathtt{MPK'}, \mathtt{SK}_i \leftarrow \mathtt{KeyGen}(\mathtt{MPK}, \mathtt{MSK}, \mathtt{S})$ algorithm implements the granting of credentials by releasing $\mathtt{cred}_i = \mathtt{SK}_i$ corresponding to a (non-empty) set of attributes S. It also outputs an updated master public key MPK'.

---

[2] [18] proposes off-the-shelf techniques to cope with this limitation.
[3] In order to use pseudo-randomness, the algorithm can take as input an optional input seed $u \in \{0,1\}^k$ to a pseudo-random generator PRG. Later in the paper, we will use this feature to transform the ABKEM schema into a hybrid CCA-IND encryption schema.

3. To check credentials, chosen an access policy (i.e., a matrix $M^{l \times m}$, and a function ρ), a Verifier generates and encrypts a secret μ through the CP-ABE Encrypt(MPK, $M^{l \times m}, \rho$); and sends the resulting ciphertext CT to the Prover. Using a credential SK′, the Prover executes $\mu' \leftarrow$ Decrypt(SK′, CT) and sends the result to the Verifier. The Verifier outputs 1 if $\mu = \mu'$ and 0 otherwise.

Unfortunately, the (optional) revocation step KeyRemove(MPK, MSK, i) cannot be efficiently achieved by CP-WATERS-KEM alone, even if there exist some workarounds (we briefly review them in Sect. 4). In Sect. 3 we will provide a new CP-ABE construction that supports efficient revocation. But first we provide proof of the correctness, unforgeability, and anonymity of the above construction.

2.4 Correctness, Unforgeability and Anonymity

In this Section we observe that hybrid encryption via the Fujisaki-Okamoto transformation [10], which is used in the OpenABE framework [19] to make CP-WATERS-KEM secure under Chosen Ciphertext Attacks (IND-CCA), may also serve to ensure anonymity without incurring in few extra commitment steps introduced by the author of [7][4]. By proving that this transformation also ensures anonimity, we give developers the opportunity to easily build ACs by simply relying on ABE frameworks like [19], leveraging on their wide expressiveness of policies. The transformation uses two random numbers r_c and K_c both chosen by the encrypting party to generate randomness for encryption. The most relevant fact that we will use to prove anonymity is that there is a negligible probability that an attacker will produce a ciphertext that may decrypt and that this probability is the same as guessing a ciphertext without any knowledge of the randomness used to produce it (see [19], Lemma 3.1.5). The IND-CCA secure encryption algorithm is specified by the following steps:

- The encrypting party chooses an access structure AP and samples a secret K_c and a randomness r_c, and concatenates them to form the string $r_c||K_c||AP$
- Then, it runs the encryption algorithm of the original CP-WATERS-KEM to produce a secret $e(g,g)^{\alpha s}$ and a ciphertext CT. The seed $r_c||K_c||AP$ is used as a source of randomness $u \leftarrow$ PRG(H′($r_c||K_c||AP$), λ) for the encryption, where PRG is a pseudo-random generator, λ is the length of the returned random bit string ($u \in \{0,1\}^l$) and H′ is a collision-resistant hash function.
- The encrypting party uses the secret for XORing the concatenation $r_c||K_c$
  - Transform $r_c||K_c$ into bytes (octects).
  - Using the pseudo-random generator PRG and a collision-resistant hash function H, get $r \leftarrow$ PRG(H($e(g,g)^{\alpha s}$), λ).
  - Finally, compute $C = r \oplus (K_c||r_c)$

The IND-CCA secure decryption algorithm works as follows:

---

[4] We consider this result important in practice because many existing authentication protocols (such as HTTP and OAuth) relies on a three steps procedure (request-challenge-response), so avoiding any extra step would perfectly fit them.

- Run decryption of the original CP-WATERS-KEM or of the modified schema to decrypt the ciphertext CT and obtain the secret: $e(g,g)^{\alpha s}$.
- Use that secret to generate randomness $r \leftarrow$ PRG(H($e(g,g)^{\alpha s}$), λ).
- Use generated randomness r for XORing the ciphertext and retrieve K_c and r_c: $C \oplus r = (K_c || r_c)$.
- Re-run the CCA-secure encryption using $r_c || K_c || AP$ as a source of randomness and verify the result is equal to the received ciphertext CT. If this is true, the algorithm outputs a valid decryption; outputs $\perp$ otherwise.

Now we prove the following:

Theorem 1. *A polynomial-time adversary, acting as a Verifier, cannot distinguish between any two Provers with different CP-WATERS-KEM keys, if their (non-revoked) keys both satisfy (or not satisfy) the same access structure they are tested against.*

Proof. We start considering the following security game (adapted from [7]):

1. The Setup(1^λ) algorithm of CP-WATERS-KEM or the modified schema takes place. The public key PK is given to the adversary.
2. Any Prover P_i receives distinct secret keys K_i embedding some attributes.
3. The adversary is allowed to submit queries in the form $(r_c || K_c || AP)$ to an oracle O^1 which produces a random output u if this is the first time the input has been queried on. Otherwise, it returns the previous response. In addition, the oracle computes the ciphertext C using the CCA-secure encryption algorithm and records the couple $((r_c || K_c || AP), (C, u))$ in a table. This oracle operation runs throughout the whole game.
4. The adversary, acting as a Verifier V, arbitrarily chooses an access structure A^* and two Provers P_0 and P_1, such that their corresponding keys either both satisfy, or both not satisfy the chosen access structure.
5. Depending on an internal coin toss b, a second oracle O^2 impersonates Prover P_b in the verification algorithm.
6. Verifier V computes a CCA-secure ciphertext and sends it to O^2.
7. O^2 responds with the decrypted message m or with $\perp$.
8. The aforementioned steps (except the Setup) are repeated adaptively for any polynomial number of times on arbitrarily chosen access structure and arbitrarily chosen pairs of Provers.
9. The adversary tries a guess b' and wins the game if $b == b'$ (i.e., she is able to guess which Prover has responded).

Modify the game as follows: at step 7, when given a ciphertext C, oracle O^1 checks if C appears in the random oracle table. If so, it outputs the corresponding m = $(K_c || r_c)$ value in the table; otherwise, it outputs $\perp$ and rejects.

The difference between the original game and the modified one is negligible, as in the original game the oracle may decrypt even in case of a forged ciphertext (i.e., a ciphertext not computed using the CCA-secure encryption algorithm). However, since O^1 was not queried on $(r_c || K_c || AP)$, the probability that this event happens is bounded by the probability of apriori guessing a ciphertext output by an encryption for a given message without knowing the randomness used to encrypt.

Now, the following observations apply to this modified game:

- If the Verifier produces a genuine ciphertext C following the CCA-secure Encryption algorithm, she gets a correct decryption m if the attributes embedded in the secret key K_b satisfy the chosen access structure A^*, i.e. $A^*(K_b) = 1$. Thus, the presented schema satisfies by definition the correctness property.
- Viceversa, if the attributes embedded in the secret key K_b do not satisfy the chosen access structure A^*, i.e. $A^*(K_b) = 0$, the ciphertext wouldn't decrypt at all except for a negligible probability ϵ. Thus, the presented schema satisfies by definition the unforgeability property.

Furthermore, we observe that:

- The access structure A^* associated to the ciphertext C is always known to the challenger (given as input after being chosen by the adversary)
- Because a pseudo-random generator is used, the ciphertext C is deterministically computed from the public key PK and the access structure A^*
- The ciphertext C is uniformly distributed on the ciphertext space, because computed using the uniformly distributed randomness u in step 3.

Under the conditions above, suppose to modify the previous game replacing Prover P_b's behaviour as follows:

- if key K_b embeds attributes satisfying the access structure A^*, then message m is returned;
- otherwise $\bot$ is returned.

That is, P_b no longer evaluates the decryption using the key K_b rather it (deterministically) returns m or $\bot$ depending on the internal bit $A^*(K_b)$. Since $A^*(K_0) = A^*(K_1)$ (both keys satisfy or not satisfy the access structure), in the latter schema the random coin b of the oracle remains hidden in the information-theoretic sense. This implies that the advantage of any adversary is $1/2$ in distinguishing between P_0 and P_1. As the introduced modifications do not alter the advantage except for at most a negligible probability, the advantage of any adversary in the original game is negligibly close to $1/2$. $\square$

3 Revocation

Consider the CP-WATERS-KEM scheme reported in the previous Section. In the following we describe a revocation scheme preventing decryption of ciphertext created after the key has been revoked. To implement this scheme, CP-WATERS-KEM is slightly altered and combined with the cryptographic accumulator based on bilinear mappings described by Camenisch in [3].

The accumulator makes use of a set of indexes $\{i\}$ kept by the Authority and assigned to each secret key released. In the setup phase, the Authority initially creates an accumulator $acc_0 = 1$ and two initially empty public sets: $V = \{\}$ and $U = \{\}$, where U is the set of all indexes i that will be ever added to the accumulator (but may have been subsequently removed). The sequence $g^\gamma, \ldots, g^{\gamma^n}, g^{\gamma^{n+2}}, \ldots, g^{\gamma^{2n}}$ (but not $g^{\gamma^{n+1}}$) is made public by the Authority (e.g., as part of MPK). Appendix D of [3] suggests a practical technique to reduce the size of this sequence. The mathematical definition of the accumulator is the following:

$$acc_V = \prod_{j \in V} g^{\gamma^{n+1-j}} = g^{\frac{\sum_{j \in V} \gamma^{n+1+i-j}}{\gamma^i}}$$

$$W_i = \prod_{j \neq i} g^{\gamma^{n+1+i-j}} = g^{\sum_{j \neq i} \gamma^{n+1+i-j}}$$

$$\sum_{j \in V} \gamma^{n+1+i-j} = \gamma^{n+1} + \sum_{j \neq i} \gamma^{n+1+i-j} \Leftrightarrow i \in V$$

where $g \in G$ is a generator of the group G of prime order p, and γ is sampled from Z_p.

3.1 CP-WATERS-KEM Plus Accumulator

To include Camenisch's accumulator in the original CP-WATERS-KEM algorithms, the key generation algorithm associates an index i with each secret decryption key generated. The new index i is added to the accumulator. When the Authority needs to revoke a key, it simply removes the corresponding index i and updates the accumulator value. The authority needs also to update the term that is used as a basis to calculate the secret (distributed as part of the MPK), as it depends on the accumulator.

With the addition or removal of any accumulator element, the previously released keys become stale, and any party who has previously received a key shall update it. Therefore, a new UpdateSecretKey step is introduced in the schema. The update algorithm can be run locally and does not require any secret or computation from the Authority, so to reduce the Authority's workload.

More in details, the following modifications are needed:

1. $(\text{MPK}, \text{MSK}) \leftarrow \text{Setup}(1^\lambda)$:
   - The algorithm chooses a group G of prime order p and generator g, random group elements $h_1, h_2, \ldots, h_u$ (where u is the maximum number of system attributes) and a bilinear pairing e such that $e \colon G \times G \to G_T$. In addition, it chooses random exponents $a, b, \gamma \in Z_p$.
   - The algorithm initially creates an accumulator $acc_0 = 1$, and two initially empty public sets: $V = \{\}$ and $U = \{\}$, where U is the set of all indexes i that will be ever added to the accumulator (but may have been subsequently removed).
   - The public key is $g, g^b, h_1, h_2, \ldots, h_u, acc_V, acc_V^a$ and

   $$e(g,g)^{b\gamma^{n+1}}$$

   The master secret key is a, b, γ.

- Chosen $n < q \in N$ (see Sect. 3.3 for the parameter q), the sequence $g^\gamma, \ldots, g^{\gamma^n}, g^{\gamma^{n+2}}, \ldots, g^{\gamma^{2n}}$ (but not $g^{\gamma^{n+1}}$) is made public.

2. $(\text{MPK}', \text{SK}_\mathtt{i} = (K_\mathtt{i}, L_\mathtt{i}, \forall_{x \in S}\, K_{\mathtt{i},x}, W_\mathtt{i})) \leftarrow \text{KeyGen}(\text{MPK}, \text{MSK}, \text{S})$:
   - The algorithm includes i in the set V and U: $V = V_{old} \cup \{i\}$, $U = U_{old} \cup \{i\}$ and updates the accumulator $acc_V = \prod_{j \in V} g^{\gamma^{n+1-j}}$.
   - Chosen a random $t_i \in Z_p$, the algorithm computes the secret decryption key component $K_i = g^{abt_i + b\gamma^i}$, $L_i = g^{bt_i}$ and, for each $x \in S$, $K_{i,x} = h_x^{t_i}$.
   - Also, the algorithm releases a new key component (the witness): $W_i = \prod_{j \neq i} g^{\gamma^{n+1+i-j}}$.

3. $\text{MPK}' \leftarrow \text{KeyRemove}(\text{MPK}, \text{MSK}, \mathtt{i})$: A similar step is also executed when the Authority needs to revoke a key K_i. In this case, the algorithm simply removes i from the set V and updates the accumulator value acc_V.

   With the addition or removal of elements to the accumulator, previously released witnesses become stale and any Client who has previously received a witness W_i shall update it. Therefore, the following step is introduced into the schema:

4. $W'_\mathtt{i} \leftarrow \text{UpdateWitness}(\text{MPK}, V_{old}, V, W_\mathtt{i})$: The algorithm takes as input the old witness and updates it to match the new master public key MPK and the current set of authorized indices V. The new witness is locally computed using the following equation:

$$W'_i \leftarrow W_i \frac{\prod_{j \in V/V_{old}} g^{\gamma^{n+1+i-j}}}{\prod_{j \in V_{old}/V} g^{\gamma^{n+1+i-j}}}$$

note that the Client can compute this formula if and only if $i \in V \cap V_{old}$, as $g^{\gamma^{n+1}}$ is private (and part of the MSK); when $i \notin V \cap V_{old}$ this algorithm simply returns $W'_i = \perp$. Hence, a Client cannot update its W_i if i was originally not in the accumulator or is no more in the accumulator as a result of a revocation.

5. $(\text{CT} = (C', C'', \forall_{\mathtt{k} \in [1,\ldots 1]}\, C_\mathtt{k}), \mu) \leftarrow \text{Encrypt}(\text{MPK}, \mathtt{M}^{1 \times \mathtt{m}}, \rho)$: The algorithm takes as input an access structure (M, ρ) and the public key MPK, then:
   - Chosen a random vector $\mathbf{v} = (s, y_2, \ldots, y_m)$ in Z_p^n and being M_k the k-th row of M, the algorithm computes $\lambda_k = M_k \cdot \mathbf{v}$.
   - Together with a with description of (M, ρ), the algorithm makes public the ciphertext:

$$C' = g^{bs},\, C_k = acc_V^{a\lambda_k} h_{\rho_k}^{-s},\, C'' = acc_V^s = \left(\prod_{j \in V} g^{\gamma^{n+1-j}} \right)^s$$

   - Finally, the algorithm computes the secret

$$\mu = [e(g,g)^{b\gamma^{n+1}}]^s$$

and keeps it private.

6. $\mu \leftarrow$ Decrypt(SK_i, CT): Dually, the decryption takes as input the ciphertext CT and the secret key SK. The output is the secret if and only if the set of attributes S satisfies the access structure, or $\perp$ otherwise.
   - For each k such that $\rho_k \in S$ (i.e., consider only attributes in S), compute ω_k such that $\sum_k \omega_k \lambda_k = s$ (there could different sets of $\{\omega_k\}$ satisfying this equation)
   - Compute the secret:

$$\mu = \frac{e(C'', K_i)}{\prod_k [e(C_k, L_i)e(C', K_{i,\rho_k})]^{\omega_k} e(C', W_i)} =$$

$$[e(g,g)^{b\gamma^{n+1}}]^s$$

3.2 Correctness

To understand why decryption works, consider the solution equation, and note that the numerator is

$$e(C'', K) = e(g,g)^{\frac{\sum_{j \in V} \gamma^{n+1+i-j}}{\gamma^i} s(abt_i + b\gamma^i)} =$$

$$e(g,g)^{\frac{\sum_{j \in V} \gamma^{n+1+i-j}}{\gamma^i} sabt_i} e(g,g)^{bs \sum_{j \in V} \gamma^{n+1+i-j}} =$$

$$e(acc_V, g)^{sabt_i} e(g^{bs}, g)^{\sum_{j \in V} \gamma^{n+1+i-j}}$$

As in the original CP-ABKEM decryption algorithm, the factor $e(acc_V, g)^{sabt_i}$ cancels out with the first part of the denominator:

$$\prod_k [e(C_k, L)e(C', K_{\rho_k})]^{\omega_k} = \prod_k [e(acc_V^{a\lambda_k} h_{\rho_k}^{-s}, g^{bt_i}) e(g^{bs}, h_{\rho_k}^{t_i})]^{\omega_k} =$$

$$\prod_k e(acc_V, g)^{ab\lambda_k \omega_k t_i} = e(acc_V, g)^{sabt_i}$$

Regarding the factor $e(g^{bs}, g)^{\sum_{j \in V} \gamma^{n+1+i-j}}$ we note that, if and only if $i \in V$, we have:

$$e(g^{bs}, g)^{\sum_{j \in V} \gamma^{n+1+i-j}} = e(g^{bs}, g^{\gamma^{n+1} + \sum_{j \neq i} \gamma^{n+1+i-j}}) =$$

$$e(g^{bs}, g^{\gamma^{n+1}}) e(g^{bs}, W_i)$$

Partially canceling out with the factor $e(g^{bs}, W_i)$ in the denominator. Therefore, the result of the computation is $[e(g,g)^{b\gamma^{n+1}}]^s$.

3.3 Security

To prove security, we use a security game based on the one presented in Section 5 of [18]. The adversary chooses to be challenged on an encryption to an access structure A*, and can ask arbitrarily q times for any private key S that does not satisfy A*. However, the original model is extended by letting the adversary query for private keys that satisfy the access structure, with the restriction that each of those keys shall be revoked before the challenge:

- *Setup.* The challenger runs Setup algorithm and gives the public parameters, PK to the adversary.
- *Phase 1.* The adversary makes repeated private keys corresponding to sets of attributes $S_1, \ldots, S_{q'}$ (with $1 < q' < q$).
- *Revocation* Using the keyremove algorithm in the schema, any key may (or not) be revoked. *Phase 1* and *Revocation* may be arbitrarily interleaved.
- *Challenge.* The adversary submits two equal-length messages M_0 and M_1. In addition, the adversary gives a challenge access structure A* such that none of the sets $S_1, \ldots, S_{q'}$ from *Phase 1* satisfies the access structure, or such that any of those keys corresponding to sets satisfying the access structure has been revoked. The challenger flips a random coin β, and encrypts M_β under A*. The ciphertext CT* is given to the adversary.
- *Phase 2. Phase 1* is repeated with the restriction that none of sets of attributes $S_{q'+1}, \ldots, S_q$ satisfies the access structure corresponding to the challenge. Revocation may also occur in this phase.
- *Guess.* The adversary outputs a guess β' of β.

The advantage of the adversary in the above game is $\epsilon = \Pr[\beta' = \beta] - \frac{1}{2}$ and, by definition, the scheme is secure if all polynomial-time adversaries have at most a negligible advantage. We use a selective proof, therefore the above game is augmented by an initial step *Init* in which the adversary commits to the challenge access structure A* and to the final set of credentials that will eventually appear in the accumulator V^*.

Our security proof works under the General Diffie-Hellman Exponent Problem introduced by Boneh, Boyen and Goh in [2]. Let ν and σ be natural numbers, $P, Q \in Z_p^+[X_1, \ldots, X_n]^\sigma$ be two s-tuples (i.e., ordered sets) of n-variate polynomials over Z_p^+ and let $f \in Z_p^+[X_1, \ldots, X_\nu]$. The notation $P = (p_1, p_2, \ldots, p_\sigma), Q = (q_1, q_2, \ldots, q_\sigma)$ is used to refer to each set of polynomials and it is required that $p_1 = q_1 = 1$; f is said dependent on P and Q if there exist $\sigma^2 + \sigma$ constants $\{a\}_{i,j=1}^{\sigma}, \{b_k\}_{k=1}^{\sigma}$ such that

$$f^* = \sum_{i,j=1}^{\sigma} a_{i,j} p_i p_j + \sum_{k=1}^{\sigma} b_k q_k$$

f^* is independent of P and Q iff is not dependent on P and Q. Furthermore, consider a bilinear map $e : G_0 \times G_0 \to G_1$ and two injective maps ξ_0, ξ_1 of the additive group Z_p^+, i.e. $\xi_0, \xi_1 : Z_p^+ \to \{0,1\}^m$ such that $G_i = \{\xi_i(x) : x \in Z_p^+\}$, for $i = 0, 1$. Use $deg(f)$ to denote the degree of any function f and define $deg(P) =$

$max\{deg(f) : f \in P\}$. The Complexity Lower Bound theorem in Generic Bilinear Groups theorem states that, if f^* is independent of P and Q then, the advantage of any adversary A that makes a total of at most $q \in N$ queries to an oracle computing group operations in G_0, G_1 and the bilinear pairing $e : G_0 \times G_0 \to G_1$ in distinguishing $f^*(x_1, \ldots, x_n)$ from a random group element in Z_p cannot exceed $\frac{(q+2\sigma+2)^2 \cdot d}{2p}$, where $d = max(2 \cdot deg(P), deg(Q), deg(f))$. Consequently, the General (Decisional) Diffie-Hellman Exponent Problem, which is formulated as follows: given $g_0 \in G_0, g_1 \in G_1$,

$$(g_0^{P(x_1,\ldots,x_n)}, g_1^{Q(x_1,\ldots,x_n)}) \in G_0^s \times G_1^s$$

distinguish $g_1^{f^*(x_1,\ldots,x_n)} \in G_1$ from a random element in G_1, is a hard problem in the generic group model.

Using the aforementioned hardness assumption, in Appendix A we prove that chosen an access structure $\mathtt{A}^*$, no polynomial-time adversary can (selectively) break our system, provided that all keys satisfying $\mathtt{A}^*$ have been revoked before the challenge.

Note that the presented security model supports only chosen-plaintext attacks. The model is extended to handle chosen-ciphertext attacks by allowing for decryption queries in Phase 1 and Phase 2. To achieve chosen-ciphertext security we use the Fujisaki-Okamoto transformation (Sect. 2.4), which exactly applies as in the original paper [19] and provides correctness, unforgeability, and anonymity when our schema is used in conjunction with the protocol in Sect. 2.3 to implement revocable Functional credentials.

4 Related Works

A survey on revocation strategies for anonymous credentials is presented in [12]. Early attempts included time-based attributes contained in the credentials or re-issuing of credentials after a change in the key material. Similar approaches work as well for Functional credentials using predicate encryption. However, they may be unpractical in real-world contexts. Whitelist and blacklist approaches may also be used. To invalidate revoked credentials, the Issuer shall periodically update the white or black list. For predicate encryption, a trivial naive approach would be to directly implement whitelists or blacklists in the access policy (*Verifier-local revocation*). However, this would typically increase the length of the policy linearly with the number of credentials involved. More dangerously, this approach leaves the control on revocation to the Verifier, not to the Issuer. This is formally incorrect and can potentially expose the Prover to the risk of *backward linkability* (a similar problem was highlighted in group signature schemas [16]). For Functional credentials in particular, the Verifier can re-identify the Prover by specially crafted policies able to create correlation when the same credential is shown more than once.

Building on Dual-Policy Attribute-Based Encryption (DP-ABE), [1] presents a predicate encryption scheme that supports revocation by combining Boolean formula predicate encoding with broadcast encryption. The latter encoding takes care of revocation, while the former encodes the desired access structure. A drawback is that the setup, key generation, and encryption time grows polynomial with the number of users.

[5] reports several works considering the application of dynamic universal accumulators to anonymous credentials to implement blacklists. While these approaches require to prove in zero-knowledge that a Prover's non-membership witness satisfies the accumulator verification equation, the authors describe a different construction where both the accumulator and the anonymous credentials, previously described in [11], rely on the same construction (Structure-Preserving Signatures on Equivalence Classes). To the same extent, our approach is similar to their one, but we highlight the different scope, because [5] limits to consider *selective disclosure*, not proof of predicates. In terms of performance, scheme 2 in [11], using primitives `VerifyR` and `VerifySubset`, requires a total of $2 * (i + 2)$ pairing operations per number of credential entries i, plus two additional revocation-induced pairings (scheme 2 in [5]). Our scheme presented in Sect. 3.1, using the optimization described in [19], reduces the number of pairings to $k + 2$, with k being the number of attributes satisfying the policy, plus one more for checking the witness.

5 Our Pairing-Free, Holder-Bound Construction

Functional credentials are the natural evolution of ACs and share the view of credentials as no more signed objects publicly revealed to a Verifier (i.e., analogs of physical identity cards), rather as Issuer-derived keys, privately kept by the Holder, and difficult to clone. Some obstacles to their adoption may be due to the use of pairing-based cryptography and consequent (still) lack of regulatory Body approval (e.g., NIST, SOG-IS). Unfortunately, [15] rules out the existence of any non-trivial Identity-Based Encryption (hence, ABE which implies it) construction in generic groups. However, Orange has recently proposed a pairing-free *adaptation* of the BBS signature to traditional elliptic curve cryptography [6]. Similarly to the paradigm introduced by Chase in [4], in their construction Issuer and Verifier are allowed to collaborate (another possibility being "oblivious" [13] batch issuance of credentials by the Issuer; however, revocation would anyway imply Issuer and Verifier collaboration). In addition, they propose an implementation of proof of possession via a secure element that privately stores the credential's secret key $t \in Z_p$. Sampling a random $e \in Z_p$, the Prover is able to randomize an ECDSA signature with public key $\tilde{g}^{et}$ by splitting the computation between itself and the secure element. In the following, we argue that a similar adaptation exists for our scheme. We assume that in any Prover there is a secure element trusted by the Issuer, assigning the Prover a public key $\tilde{g}^{t_i} \in G$ and keeping secure the corresponding private key $t_i \in Z_p$ (the secure element can prove that $\tilde{g}^{t_i}$ is genuine to the Issuer, e.g., by including it in a certificate).

- $(\text{MPK}, \text{MSK}) \leftarrow \text{Setup}(1^\lambda)$: The algorithm samples random $a, \beta, \gamma, a_1, a_2, \ldots, a_u \in Z_p$ (where $\beta = \frac{1}{b} (mod\ p)$) as MSK. Chosen $n \in N$, a group G

of prime order p and generator $\tilde{g}$, it publishes $\tilde{g}$ and $\tilde{g}^{\gamma^{n+1}}$, creates two empty public sets: $V = \{\}$ and $U = \{\}$ and makes public the sequence $\tilde{g}^{\beta\gamma}, \ldots, \tilde{g}^{\beta\gamma^n}, \tilde{g}^{\beta\gamma^{n+2}}, \ldots, \tilde{g}^{\beta\gamma^{2n}}$.

- $(\text{MPK}', \text{SK}_\text{i} = (\text{K}_\text{i}, \text{L}_\text{i}, \forall_{\text{x} \in \text{S}}\, \text{K}_{\text{i},\text{x}}, \text{W}_\text{i})) \leftarrow \text{KeyGen}(\text{MPK}, \text{MSK}, \text{S})$: The algorithm associates an index i to each new generated secret key SK_i, by including i in the set V and U, then computes and releases the secret decryption key components: $K_i = (\tilde{g}^{t_i})^a \tilde{g}^{\gamma^i}$, $L_i = \tilde{g}^{t_i}$ and, for each $x \in S$, $K_{i,x} = (\tilde{g}^{t_i})^{\beta a_x}$, $W_i = \prod_{j \neq i} \tilde{g}^{\beta\gamma^{n+1+i-j}}$.
- $\text{MPK}' \leftarrow \text{KeyRemove}(\text{MPK}, \text{MSK}, \text{i})$: The algorithm removes i from the set V.
- $\text{W}'_\text{i} \leftarrow \text{UpdateWitness}(\text{MPK}, \text{V}_\text{old}, \text{V}, \text{W}_\text{i})$: Assumed $i \in V$, the new witness is computed locally using the equation:

$$W'_i \leftarrow W_i \frac{\prod_{j \in V/V_{old}} \tilde{g}^{\beta\gamma^{n+1+i-j}}}{\prod_{j \in V_{old}/V} \tilde{g}^{\beta\gamma^{n+1+i-j}}}$$

Otherwise the update operation returns $W'_i = \bot$.

- $\tilde{\text{SK}}_\text{i} = (\bar{\text{K}}_\text{i}, \bar{\text{L}}_\text{i}, \forall_{\text{k} \in [1,\ldots 1]}\, \bar{\text{K}}_{\text{i},\text{k}}, \bar{\text{W}}_\text{i}) \leftarrow \text{Randomize}(\text{SK}_\text{i} = (\text{K}_\text{i}, \text{L}_\text{i}, \forall_{\text{x} \in \text{S}}\, \text{K}_{\text{i},\text{x}}, \text{W}_\text{i}))$: additionally introduced algorithm run by the Prover after knowing the access structure; it samples a random element $e \in Z_p$ and raises all secret key components to it: $\bar{K}_i = K_i^e$, $\bar{L}_i = L_i^e$, for each k such that $\rho_k \in S$, $\bar{K}_{i,k} = (K_{i,k})^e$, otherwise samples random $\bar{K}_{i,k}$ from G, $\bar{W}_i = (W_i)^e$.
- $(\text{C} = (\text{C}', \forall_{\text{k} \in [1,\ldots 1]}\, \text{C}_\text{k}), (\bar{\text{K}}_{\text{i},\text{k}})^{\frac{s}{\beta}}, (\bar{\text{W}}_\text{i})^{\frac{s}{\beta}}, \mu) \leftarrow\, <\text{Encrypt}(\text{MPK}, \text{M}^{1 \times \text{m}}, \rho, \tilde{\text{SK}}_\text{i}),$ $\text{Help}(\text{MSK})>$: The Verifier and the Issuer run together this algorithm (they are assumed to be able to communicate, e.g. through a simple request/response interaction). The Verifier chooses a random vector $\boldsymbol{v} = (s, y_2, \ldots, y_m)$ in Z_p^n, computes $\lambda_k = M_k \cdot \boldsymbol{v}$ and, helped by the Issuer for the exponentiation, produces the ciphertext: $C' = (\bar{K}_i^s)^{\sum_{j \in V} \gamma^{n+1-j}}$, $C_k = (\bar{L}_i^{\lambda_k})^{a \sum_{j \in V} \gamma^{n+1-j}} (\bar{L}_i^{-s})^{a_k}$, $((\bar{K}_{i,k})^s)^{\frac{1}{\beta}} = \bar{K}_{i,k}^{\frac{s}{\beta}}$, $(\bar{W}_i^s)^{\frac{1}{\beta}} = \bar{W}_i^{\frac{s}{\beta}}$. Similarly, it computes the secret $(\tilde{g}^{\gamma^{n+1}})^s$ and keeps it private.
- $\mu \leftarrow \text{Decrypt}(\text{SK}_\text{i}, \text{C})$: For each k such that $\rho_k \in S$ the algorithm computes ω_k such that $\sum_k \omega_k \lambda_k = s$ and

$$\mu = \left(\frac{C'}{\prod_k [C_k \bar{K}_{i,\rho_k}^{\frac{s}{\beta}}]^{\omega_k} \bar{W}_i^{\frac{s}{\beta}}} \right)^{\frac{1}{e}}$$

Using a technique similar to that in Appendix A, we can prove (chosen plaintext) security of the above construction. We can then apply the Fujisaki-Okamoto transformation as in Sect. 2.4 to make it CCA-IND - in particular, ensuring that $\mu == (\tilde{g}^{\gamma^{n+1}})^s$ - and thus proving correctness, unforgeability and anonymity when used in conjunction with the credential verification protocol. Finally, to prove possession of the credential, using the same technique described in [6], the Prover - instead of sending μ - can send a signature over $(\mu; \tilde{g}^{et})$ with the randomized key et. We observe that this final formulation is particularly light for the Prover. In Fig. 1 we report our performance evaluation for the algorithms

Randomize and Decrypt, noting that the Prover may also precompute values by running Randomize in batch mode before any interaction with the Verifier.

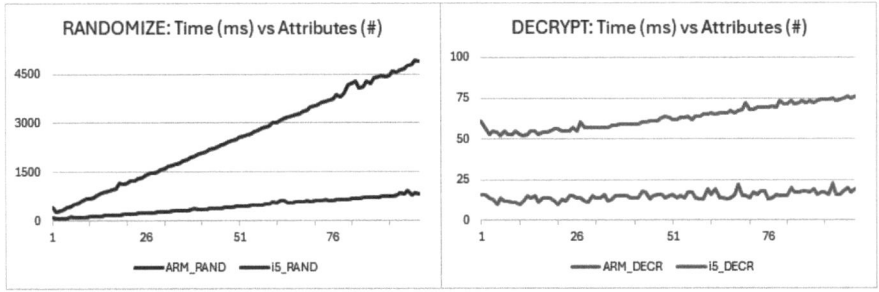

Fig. 1. Performance evaluation of Prover's algorithms Randomize and Decrypt, in terms of time (ms) vs number of attributes *actually used* by the Prover to satisfy a policy. Testbed: JavaScript running on Chrome v.135 over ARM Cortex A-53 and Intel i5 platforms, implementing the two algorithms using NIST standard secp256r1 curve.

6 Conclusion

We are witnessing renewed interest for Anonymous Credentials due to the raising of mDL and the EUDIW. However, the lack of standardization and regulatory approval hinders their adoption. Relying on well-understood and easy-to-implement cryptographic primitives may be a first step toward their effective adoption. In this paper, we shown that a Functional credential system with anonymous proof of predicates can be implemented on top of the well-known Water's 2008 Ciphertext Policy ABE scheme. Furthermore, we shown it is possible to achieve efficient revocation by combining Water's scheme with a dynamic accumulator. Finally, inspired by the ongoing work on the BBS signature, we presented a pairing-free, Holder-bound version of the resulting protocol. To the best of our knowledge, our work is the first one to combine rich policy expressiveness, revocation, and anonymous proof of predicates over attributes into a single framework. More efficient (multi-authority) ABE scheme and (universal) accumulators may be considered in future works.

A Proof of Theorem in Section 3.3

Theorem 2. *Under the General Decisional Diffie-Hellman Exponent hardness assumption [2], chosen an access structure* A^* *and a set of non-revoked credentials* V^*, *no polynomial-time adversary can selectively break our system, provided all credentials satisfying* A^* *are not in* V^*.

Proof. Consider an adversary A with non-negligible advantage $\epsilon = Adv_A$ that plays a security game against our construction. We build the following simulator:

- *Init.* The adversary chooses $\mathbb{A}^* = (M^*, \rho^*)$ and V^* (i.e. the set of keys not satisfying the access structure that will eventually stay in V just before the challenge) and gives it to the challenger.
- *Setup.* Given a group G of prime order p and generator g and a bilinear pairing e such that $e \colon G \times G \to G_T$, the simulator takes in:
  - the terms $g^a, g^b, g^{ab}, g^{bs^*}$
  - for each $i \in V^*$, the terms $g^{s^* \gamma^{n+1-i}}$
  - for each i the sequence $g^{\frac{b\gamma^i}{a}}, g^{\frac{b\gamma^i}{a^2}}, \ldots, g^{\frac{b\gamma^i}{a^{m^*}}}$, but not $g^{b\gamma^i}$
  - the sequence $g, g^\gamma, \ldots, g^{\gamma^n}, g^{\gamma^{n+2}}, \ldots, g^{\gamma^{2n}}$, but not $g^{\gamma^{n+1}}$
  - the sequence $g, g^{a^j\gamma}, \ldots, g^{a^j\gamma^n}, g^{a^j\gamma^{n+1}}, \ldots, g^{a^j\gamma^{2n}}$ including $g^{a^j\gamma^{n+1}}$, for each a^j with $j \in [-m^*, m^*]/\{0\}$
  - T which is either a random element in G_T or $e(g,g)^{bs^*\gamma^{n+1}}$.

Note that from the above given terms, the simulator is not able to compute $g^{\gamma^{n+1}}$ in polynomial time and therefore cannot directly compute $e(g,g)^{bs^*\gamma^{n+1}}$ as $e(g^{bs^*}, g^{\gamma^{n+1}})$. The challenger chooses random group elements $h_1, h_2, \ldots, h_u$ where u is the maximum number of system attributes.

The simulator creates an empty accumulator $acc_V = acc_0 = 1$, and two empty public sets: $V = \{\}$ and $U = \{\}$.

Chosen $z_x \in Z_p$, for each x, if $\rho^*(k) = x$, h_x is computed as

$$h_x = acc_{V^*}^{z_x} \cdot acc_{V^*}^{aM^*_{k,1}} \cdot acc_{V^*}^{a^2 M^*_{k,2}} \cdot \ldots \cdot acc_{V^*}^{a^{m^*} M^*_{k,m^*}} =$$

$$(\prod_{j \in V^*} g^{\gamma^{n+1-j}})^{z_x} \prod_{l=1}^{m^*} (\prod_{j \in V^*} g^{a^l \gamma^{n+1-j}})^{M^*_{k,l}}$$

otherwise let $h_x = acc_{V^*}^{z_x}$

The challenger releases the public key MPK: $g, g^b, h_1, h_2, \ldots, h_u$, $acc_V = \prod_{j \in V} g^{\gamma^{n+1-j}}$, $acc_V^a = \prod_{j \in V} g^{a\gamma^{n+1-j}}$, and the sequence $g^\gamma, \ldots, g^{\gamma^n}$, $g^{\gamma^{n+2}}, \ldots, g^{\gamma^{2n}}$ (but not $g^{\gamma^{n+1}}$).

The challenger also releases

$$e(g,g)^{b\gamma^{n+1}} = e(g^{\frac{b}{a^j}\gamma^i}, g^{a^j\gamma^{n+1-i}})$$

- *Phase 1.* The adversary makes repeated private key queries corresponding to sets of attributes that either not satisfy the access structure or satisfy it but will not be eventually in V^*:
  - chosen $r_i \in Z_p$, $t_i = r_i + (w_1 a^{-1} + w_2 a^{-2} + \cdots + w_{m^*} a^{-m^*})\gamma^i$ where $\boldsymbol{w} = (w_1, \ldots, w_{m^*}) \in Z_p^{m^*}$ and $w_1 = -1$:

$$K_i = g^{abt_i + b\gamma^i} =$$

$$g^{abr_i - b\gamma^i + \frac{w_2}{a} b\gamma^i + \frac{w_3}{a^2} b\gamma^i + \cdots + \frac{w_{m^*}}{a^{m^*-1}} b\gamma^i + b\gamma^i} =$$

$$g^{abr_i}(\prod_{j=2}^{m^*} g^{\frac{b\gamma^i}{a^{j-1}}})^{w_j}$$

$$L_i = (g^{t_i})^b =$$

$$g^{br_i + b(w_1 a^{-1} + w_2 a^{-2} + \cdots + w_{m^*} a^{-m^*})\gamma^i} =$$

$$g^{br_i} \prod_{j=1}^{m^*} (g^{\frac{b\gamma^i}{a^j}})^{w_j}$$

Note that the factor $g^{b\gamma^i}$ is not needed to compute K_i nor L_i.

- For each $x_k \in S_i$ where $\rho^*(k) = x_k$, K_{i,x_k} is computed as:

$$K_{i,x_k} = h_{x_k}^{t_i} =$$

$$(acc_{V^*}^{z_x} \cdot acc_{V^*}^{aM_{k,1}^*} \cdot acc_{V^*}^{a^2 M_{k,2}^*} \cdot$$

$$\cdots \cdot acc_{V^*}^{a^{m^*} M_{k,m^*}^*})^{r_i + (w_1 a^{-1} + w_2 a^{-2} + \cdots + w_{m^*} a^{-m^*})\gamma^i} =$$

$$acc_{V^*}^{(z_x + aM_{k,1}^* + a^2 M_{k,2}^* + \cdots + a^{m^*} M_{k,m^*}^*)(r_i + (w_1 a^{-1} + w_2 a^{-2} + \cdots + w_{m^*} a^{-m^*})\gamma^i)} =$$

$$(\prod_{j \in V^*} g^{\gamma^{n+1-j}})^{r_i z_x} \prod_{l=1}^{m^*} (\prod_{j \in V^*} g^{a^l \gamma^{n+1-j}})^{r_i M_{k,l}^*} \cdot$$

$$\prod_{l=1}^{m^*} (\prod_{j \in V^*} g^{\frac{(\gamma^{n+1-j})\gamma^i}{a^l}})^{w_l z_x} \prod_{o=1}^{m^*} \prod_{l \neq o}^{m^*} (\prod_{j \in V^*} g^{a^{o-l}(\gamma^{n+1-j})\gamma^i})^{w_l M_{k,o}^*} \cdot$$

$$\prod_{l=1}^{m^*} (\prod_{j \in V^*} g^{\gamma^{n+1-j}\gamma^i})^{w_l M_{k,l}^*}$$

The last term apparently requires $g^{\gamma^{n+1}}$ when $i \in V^*$. However, we note that for those keys not satisfying the access structure, for any row k of M^* where $\rho^*(k) = x_k$ (i.e., the attribute $x_k \in S_i$ is used in the access structure) we can choose $w_2 \ldots w_{m^*}$ so that the equation $\boldsymbol{w} M_k^* = 0$ holds, and

$$\prod_{l=1}^{m^*} (\prod_{j \in V^*} g^{\gamma^{n+1-j}\gamma^i})^{w_l M_{k,l}^*} = 1$$

Therefore, computing K_{i,x_k}, for each $i \in V^*$ not satisfying the access structure does need terms like $g^{a^l(\gamma^{n+1-i})\gamma^i} = g^{a^l \gamma^{n+1}}, l \neq 0$, but never uses $g^{\gamma^{n+1}}$. For those keys satisfying the access structure (where $\boldsymbol{w} M_k^* = 0$ does not hold), but not in V^* we note that in the above term $\gamma^{n+1-j}\gamma^i \neq \gamma^{n+1}$. Therefore, we do not use $g^{\gamma^{n+1}}$ to compute K_{i,x_k}.

- For each $x_k \in S_i$ where x_k is not used in the access structure, K_{i,x_k} is computed as:
$$K_{i,x_k} = h_{x_k}^{t_i} =$$
$$acc_{V^*}^{z_x(r_i + w_1 a^{-1} + w_2 a^{-2} + \cdots + w_{m^*} a^{-m^*})} =$$
$$(\prod_{j \in V^*} g^{\gamma^{n+1-j}})^{z_x r_i} \prod_{l=1}^{m^*} (\prod_{j \in V^*} g^{\frac{\gamma^{n+1-j}}{a^l}})^{w_l}$$

- The witness is computed as: $W_i = \prod_{j \neq i} g^{\gamma^{n+1+i-j}}$
- The simulator includes i in the set V and U: $V = V_{old} \cup \{i\}, U = U_{old} \cup \{i\}$ and updates $acc_V = \prod_{j \in V} g^{\gamma^{n+1-j}}$ and $acc_V^a = \prod_{j \in V} g^{a \gamma^{n+1-j}}$.

– *Revocation.* The simulator revokes any key K_i which is asked by removing i from set V. Each key owner updates her witnesses as usual (except for witnesses of removed keys). The public parameters are updated as usual. *Phase 1* and *Revocation* are repeated (even interleaved with each other) so that any key satisfying the access structure is removed. Hence, V^* is the final set of keys in the accumulator.

– *Challenge.* Finally the adversary submits two equal length messages M_0 and M_1. The challenger flips a random coin β, and encrypts M_β. The challenger gives to the adversary the ciphertext:
$$\{M_\beta\}_{A^*} = M_\beta e(g,g)^{bs\gamma^{n+1}} = M_\beta T$$

and the terms:
$$C'^* = g^{bs^*}$$
$$C''^* = acc_{V^*}^{s^*} = \prod_{j \in V^*} g^{s^* \gamma^{n+1-j}}$$

Chosen $v = (s^*, s^*a + y'_2, \ldots, s^*a^{m^*-1} + y'_{m^*})$ with randomly sampled $y'_2, \ldots, y'_{m^*}$ from Z_p and $\lambda_k = M_k^* \cdot v = M_{k,1}^* s^* + M_{k,2}^*(s^*a + y'_2) + \cdots + M_{k,m^*}^*(s^*a^{m^*-1} + y'_{m^*})$ and given

$$h_{\rho_k}^{-s^*} =$$
$$(acc_{V^*}^{s^*})^{-z_{\rho_k}} acc_{V^*}^{-as^* M_{k,1}^*} \cdot acc_{V^*}^{-a^2 s^* M_{k,2}^*} \cdot \ldots \cdot acc_{V^*}^{-a^{m^*} s^* M_{k,m^*}^*}$$

The term C_k^* can be finally computed as
$$C_k^* = acc_{V^*}^{a\lambda_k} h_{\rho_k}^{-s^*} =$$
$$(acc_{V^*}^{s^*})^{-z_{\rho_k}} \prod_{l=2}^{m^*} (acc_{V^*})^{aM_{k,l}^* y'_l} =$$
$$\frac{\prod_{l=2}^{m^*} (\prod_{j \in V^*} g^{a\gamma^{n+1-j}})^{M_{k,l}^* y'_l}}{(\prod_{j \in V^*} g^{s^* \gamma^{n+1-j}})^{z_{\rho_k}}}$$

- *Phase 2.* Phase 1 is repeated with the restriction that none of the sets of attributes for which a key is requested satisfies the access structure $\mathbf{A}^*$. Revocation may also occur in this phase.
- *Guess.* After querying for at most q keys, the adversary outputs a guess β' of β with probability $Pr[A(\beta' == \beta)]$. When T is a tuple, the adversary's advantage in guessing $e(g,g)^{bs^*\gamma^{n+1}}$ is $\epsilon = Pr[A(\beta' == \beta)] - \frac{1}{2}$.

Using the terminology of the generic proof template by Boneh, Boyen, and Goh (introduced in Sect. 3.3), we observe that the monomial $f^* = bs^*\gamma^{n+1}$ is independent of the two sets of terms

$$Q = \{1\}$$

$$P = \{1, a, b, ab, bs^*,$$

$$\forall_{i \neq n+1} \gamma^i,$$

$$\forall_{i \in [1,2n], j \in [1,m^*]} \frac{b}{a^j}\gamma^i,$$

$$\forall_{i \in V^*} s^*\gamma^{n+1-i},$$

$$\forall_{i \in [1,2n], j \in [-m^*,m^*]/\{0\}} a^j \gamma^i\}$$

Also, using a new generator $g' : g' = g^{a^{m^*}}$ it is easy to transform each term in P into monomials where the maximum degree between $f^* = bs^*\gamma^{n+1}$ and any of them is $d = 2m^* + 2n - 1$. Therefore, if the advantage would ϵ exceeded the negligible quantity $\frac{(q+2\sigma+2)^2 \cdot d}{2p}$ (with σ being the (variable) number of monomials in P), as in the hypothesis, then the General Decisional Diffie-Hellman Exponent assumption would be broken. □

References

1. Ambrona, M., Barthe, G., Schmidt, B.: Generic transformations of predicate encodings: constructions and applications. In: Katz, J., Shacham, H. (eds.) CRYPTO 2017. LNCS, vol. 10401, pp. 36–66. Springer, Cham (2017). https://doi.org/10.1007/978-3-319-63688-7_2
2. Boneh, D., Boyen, X., Goh, E.J.: Hierarchical identity based encryption with constant size ciphertext. Cryptology ePrint Archive, Paper 2005/015 (2005). https://eprint.iacr.org/2005/015
3. Camenisch, J., Kohlweiss, M., Soriente, C.: An accumulator based on bilinear maps and efficient revocation for anonymous credentials. In: Jarecki, S., Tsudik, G. (eds.) PKC 2009. LNCS, vol. 5443, pp. 481–500. Springer, Heidelberg (2009). https://doi.org/10.1007/978-3-642-00468-1_27
4. Chase, M., Meiklejohn, S., Zaverucha, G.: Algebraic macs and keyed-verification anonymous credentials. In: Proceedings of the 2014 ACM SIGSAC Conference on Computer and Communications Security, CCS 2014, pp. 1205–1216. Association for Computing Machinery, New York (2014). https://doi.org/10.1145/2660267.2660328

5. Derler, D., Hanser, C., Slamanig, D.: A new approach to efficient revocable attribute-based anonymous credentials. In: Groth, J. (ed.) Cryptography and Coding, pp. 57–74. Springer, Cham (2015)
6. Desmoulins, N., Dumanois, A., Kane, S., Traoré, J.: Making BBS anonymous credentials eIDAS 2.0 compliant. Cryptology ePrint Archive, Paper 2025/619 (2025). https://eprint.iacr.org/2025/619
7. Deuber, D., Maffei, M., Malavolta, G., Schröder, M.R.D., Simkin, M.: Functional credentials. Proc. Privacy Enhancing Technol. **2018** (2018). https://doi.org/10.1515/popets-2018-0013
8. Flamini, A., Sciarretta, G., Scuro, M., Sharif, A., Tomasi, A., Ranise, S.: On cryptographic mechanisms for the selective disclosure of verifiable credentials. J. Inf. Secur. Appl. **83**(C) (2024). https://doi.org/10.1016/j.jisa.2024.103789
9. Frigo, M., Shelat, A.: Anonymous credentials from ECDSA. Cryptology ePrint Archive, Paper 2024/2010 (2024). https://eprint.iacr.org/2024/2010
10. Fujisaki, E., Okamoto, T.: Secure integration of asymmetric and symmetric encryption schemes. In: Wiener, M. (ed.) CRYPTO 1999. LNCS, vol. 1666, pp. 537–554. Springer, Heidelberg (1999). https://doi.org/10.1007/3-540-48405-1_34
11. Hanser, C., Slamanig, D.: Structure-preserving signatures on equivalence classes and their application to anonymous credentials. In: Sarkar, P., Iwata, T. (eds.) ASIACRYPT 2014. LNCS, vol. 8873, pp. 491–511. Springer, Heidelberg (2014). https://doi.org/10.1007/978-3-662-45611-8_26
12. Lapon, J., Kohlweiss, M., Decker, B., Naessens, V.: Analysis of revocation strategies for anonymous idemix credentials. In: De Decker, B., Lapon, J., Naessens, V., Uhl, A. (eds.) CMS 2011. LNCS, vol. 7025, pp. 3–17. Springer, Heidelberg (2011). https://doi.org/10.1007/978-3-642-24712-5_1
13. Orrù, M., Tessaro, S., Zaverucha, G., Zhu, C.: Oblivious issuance of proofs. In: Reyzin, L., Stebila, D. (eds.) CRYPTO 2024. LNCS, vol. 14928, pp. 254–287. Springer, Cham (2024). https://doi.org/10.1007/978-3-031-68400-5_8
14. Paquin, C., Policharla, G.V., Zaverucha, G.: Crescent: stronger privacy for existing credentials. Cryptology ePrint Archive, Paper 2024/2013 (2024). https://eprint.iacr.org/2024/2013
15. Schul-Ganz, G., Segev, G.: Generic-group identity-based encryption: a tight impossibility result. Cryptology ePrint Archive, Paper 2021/745 (2021). https://eprint.iacr.org/2021/745
16. Song, D.X.: Practical forward secure group signature schemes. In: Proceedings of the 8th ACM Conference on Computer and Communications Security, CCS 2001 pp. 225–234. Association for Computing Machinery, New York (2001). https://doi.org/10.1145/501983.502015
17. Tessaro, S., Zhu, C.: Revisiting BBS signatures. In: Hazay, C., Stam, M. (eds.) EUROCRYPT 2023. LNCS, vol. 14008, pp. 691–721. Springer, Cham (2023). https://doi.org/10.1007/978-3-031-30589-4_24
18. Waters, B.: Ciphertext-policy attribute-based encryption: an expressive, efficient, and provably secure realization. In: Catalano, D., Fazio, N., Gennaro, R., Nicolosi, A. (eds.) PKC 2011. LNCS, vol. 6571, pp. 53–70. Springer, Heidelberg (2011). https://doi.org/10.1007/978-3-642-19379-8_4
19. Waters, B., Green, M.: The openabe design document. Technical report, Zeutro LLC Encryption and Data Security (2018). https://github.com/zeutro/openabe/blob/master/docs/libopenabe-v1.0.0-design-doc.pdf

Privacy-Preserving k-Nearest Neighbor Query: Faster and More Secure

Jialin Chi[1], Cheng Hong[2], Axin Wu[3], Tianqi Sun[4], ZheChen Li[2], Min Zhang[1(✉)], and Dengguo Feng[1]

[1] TCA Lab, Institute of Software, Chinese Academy of Sciences, Beijing, China
{jialin,zhangmin,fengdg}@iscas.ac.cn
[2] Ant Group, Hangzhou, China
{vince.hc,lizhechen.lzc}@antgroup.com
[3] State Key Laboratory of Cryptology, Beijing, China
waxinsec@163.com
[4] School of Cryptology, University of Chinese Academy of Sciences, Beijing, China
suntianqi21@mails.ucas.ac.cn

Abstract. The k-nearest neighbor query is widely used in various applications. Due to security and privacy concerns, it is important to protect the confidentiality of sensitive information. However, existing solutions either violate the privacy requirements (i.e., data, query, result or indirect privacy) or scale badly with the data size. We first highlight the vulnerabilities of additive homomorphic encryption-based approaches. We then conduct in-depth research on the **P**rivacy-**P**reserving k-**N**earest **N**eighbor (PPkNN) query to simultaneously address the aforementioned concerns. Using the secret sharing technique and a model of two non-colluding servers, we design a Basic PPkNN (BPPkNN) protocol for arbitrary dimensional datasets. BPPkNN obliviously rearranges the dataset in a divide-and-conquer manner, reducing interaction rounds from linear to sublinear. We further propose a Voronoi-based PPkNN (VPPkNN) protocol for geo-location datasets, which uses the Voronoi diagram for index construction and a greedy algorithm for index compression. By obliviously accessing only a small portion of the dataset, VPPkNN significantly reduces expensive operations. We prove that our protocols simultaneously preserve data, query, result, and indirect privacy. Experimental results demonstrate that our protocols outperform existing approaches by at least an order of magnitude in query response time and, for the first time, scale to datasets with one million points.

1 Introduction

The k-Nearest Neighbor (kNN) query plays an important role in various applications, such as data mining and information retrieval. The kNN query identifies the top-k nearest points to a specified query within a dataset. Considering the vital importance of security and privacy, it is imperative to guarantee the confidentiality of datasets, queries and results. Extensive research has focused on addressing the privacy concerns surrounding kNN queries over encrypted data, such as the methods based on transformation [1], privacy homomorphism [2], standard encryption [3], Order-Preserving Encryption (OPE) [4], projection [5], prefix membership testing [6,7], etc. Despite their efficiency, there is still a need for further enhancement in terms of indirect information protection [19]. Particularly, these methods expose access patterns to servers, which can be exploited by attacks [17,18] to infer or partially recover datasets and queries.

Related works aiming at kNN access pattern hiding [8–14] commonly adopt Additive Homomorphic Encryption (AHE) primitives (e.g., Paillier cryptosystem) and perform secure computations through the interaction between two non-colluding servers. Since these methods require a significant number of encryption, decryption and exponential operations, they incur substantial computational overhead. The performance problem becomes more severe as the key size increases. For instance, according to NIST recommendations, the Paillier key size K should be at least 2048 bits [31]. Our experimental tests show that, when $K = 2048$ and $k = 5$, the running times for [13] and [14] over 2^{14} points are > 24 hours and 1.6 hours, respectively, which is hardly acceptable in practice.

Security concerns are more significant. Although the above methods successfully hide access patterns, they suffer from varying degrees of information leakage. Some [8–12] leak statistical information about data and queries, such as the frequency of accesses to index rows and the percentile of the pivot, which allows the servers or clients to infer the positional relationships between data and queries. Other schemes [13,14] use weak basic security protocols. For example, [19] shows that the secure minimum protocol in [13] exposes whether two values are equal. We demonstrate in this paper that [14] and other AHE-based methods [10–12] have flaws in the random numbers chosen for secure division and comparison protocols. Based on practical tests of our proposed decomposition-based attack, there is a non-trivial probability that [14] allows the servers to recover sensitive values with high accuracy.

In this paper, we propose a Basic PPkNN (BPPkNN) protocol to improve the efficiency and security of **P**rivacy-**P**reserving k-**N**earest **N**eighbor (PPkNN) queries. In terms of efficiency, BPPkNN is built on the more efficient secret sharing technique instead of the expensive AHE primitives, replacing encryption/decryption operations with multiplicative operations. Both datasets and queries are secret shared between two non-colluding servers, and the queries are performed under secure two-party computation protocols. Top-k sorting over secret shared data consumes most of the query response time (more than 97% of the total time). An intuitive method is to perform k rounds of bubble sort (as presented in [25]), which requires $O(kN)$ communication rounds and executes $O(kN)$ times the secure comparison protocol, where N is the data size.

We improve efficiency in two different ways. In BPPkNN, we employ the Secure Sort (SecSort) protocol in a hierarchical divide-and-conquer fashion, reducing the interaction rounds from $O(kN)$ to $O(k\log_2 N)$. To address scenarios with large values of k, we then propose a variant of BPPkNN, called BPPkNN-bitonic. This variant replaces the divide-and-conquer technique with bitonic sort, a classical and widely used oblivious sorting algorithm with $O(N\log_2^2 N)$ comparison operations and $O(\log_2^2 N)$ interaction rounds. Our experimental results show that as k approaches N, BPPkNN-bitonic outperforms BPPkNN more.

For geo-location datasets, we propose a more efficient protocol called Voronoi-based PPkNN (VPPkNN), which employs the Voronoi diagram and our BPPkNN protocol. In VPPkNN, we compress the index by partitioning the dataset into t groups and separately storing the adjacent generators of points within each group. As a result, we reduce the complexity of index traversal from $O(NT)$ to $O(tT)$, where $t \ll N$. By designing several secure protocols to obliviously access the Voronoi index, nearest neighbors can be computed using BPPkNN from a small portion of the entire dataset. Consequently, the number of secure comparison operations is reduced from $O(kN)$ to $O(m + M + k^2 T)$, where $m, M, T \ll N$.

The main contributions of this paper are as follows.

- We develop a decomposition-based attack on AHE-based protocols and provide a comprehensive evaluation through both theoretical analysis and experiments, demonstrating the effectiveness of our attack.
- To enhance both security and efficiency, we propose BPPkNN, which uses the secret sharing technique and is designed to support arbitrary dimensional datasets. We design the SecSort protocol to obliviously rearrange the dataset and implement several optimizations for the core oblivious top-k sorting problem.
- For geo-location datasets, we propose an optimized protocol, called VPPkNN, which combines BPPkNN with the Voronoi diagram. We use a greedy algorithm to compress the Voronoi index and introduce the SecVC, SecAG and SecDedup protocols to enable oblivious access to the compressed index. VPPkNN reduces the number of points that need to be searched by BPPkNN from the entire dataset to a small subset.
- Our PPkNN protocols return accurate results while simultaneously preserving data, query, result, and indirect privacy. Our experiments under real network conditions demonstrate that our protocols yield at least an order of magnitude improvement in query response time compared to existing works [13,14,25], making them well-suited for querying large datasets. For instance, in NN queries on 1 million points, VPPkNN requires only 10.45 s/22.35 s under the fast/slow network.

The paper is organized as follows. Section 2 introduces the preliminaries. Section 3 presents the problem formulation. Section 4 describes vulnerabilities of AHE-based methods. Section 5 and Sect. 6 detail BPPkNN and VPPkNN, respectively. Security and performance are discussed in Sect. 7 and Sect. 8. Section 9 reviews related works. Finally, Sect. 10 concludes this paper.

2 Preliminaries

2.1 Additive Secret Sharing

Let p be a prime and l be the bit length of p. $\mathbb{Z}_p$ is a prime field. The sharing $[x]$ of an integer $x \in \mathbb{Z}_p$ is a pair $([x]_1, [x]_2)$ of random integers subject to $[x]_1 + [x]_2 = x \pmod{p}$. Party $\mathcal{C}_\alpha$ holds the share $[x]_\alpha$.

Secure Multiplication (SecMul). To facilitate the multiplication of $[x]$ and $[y]$, a Beaver triple [24] is needed, which is secret shared between $\mathcal{C}_1$ and $\mathcal{C}_2$. For simplicity, the secure multiplication of $[x]$ and $[y]$ is denoted by $[x] \cdot [y]$.

Secure Distance Computation (SecDist). SecDist [25] takes as input the secret shares of two points $\mathbf{p}$ and $\mathbf{q}$, and outputs the secret shares of the squared Euclidean distance between $\mathbf{p}$ and $\mathbf{q}$, denoted by $[\text{Dist}(\mathbf{p}, \mathbf{q})^2]$.

Secure Comparison (SecComp). SecComp [26] takes as input $[x]$ and $[y]$, and outputs the secret shares of the boolean result $\text{Bool}(x < y) \in \{0, 1\}$.

Secure Equality Test (SecEq). SecEq [26] takes as input $[x]$ and $[y]$, and outputs the secret shares of the boolean result $\text{Bool}(x = y) \in \{0, 1\}$.

Both inputs and outputs of these protocols are secret shared over $\mathbb{Z}_p$. The random values (e.g., Beaver triple) are generated offline using Oblivious Transfer [27], Homomorphic Encryption [28] or a trusted third party [29]. These protocols are used in a black-box manner and can be replaced with more efficient alternatives. Common notations used extensively in this paper are given in Table 1.

Table 1. The Summary of Notations.

Notation	Definition
$\mathbf{p}_i, p_{i,j}$	a data point and the j-th dimension of the point
id_i	identifier of data point $\mathbf{p}_i$
$\mathbf{q}, q_i$	a query point and the i-th dimension of the query
N, d	number of data points and number of dimensions in dataset $\mathcal{D}$
$\mathbb{Z}_p, l$	the secret sharing domain and the bit length of p
$[x]$	additive secret sharing of value x
$\text{VC}(\mathbf{p}_i), \text{AG}(\mathbf{p}_i)$	Voronoi cell and adjacent generators of $\mathbf{p}_i$
$\mathcal{AG}_i, \mathcal{VC}_i$	i-th rows of table $\mathcal{AG}$ and $\mathcal{VC}$
$\mathbf{rect}_i, \mathcal{BP}_i$	a rectangle and data points whose Voronoi cells overlap with $\mathbf{rect}_i$
t, T	number of rows in table $\mathcal{AG}$ and number of tuples in each row
m, M	number of rows in table $\mathcal{VC}$ and number of tuples in each row

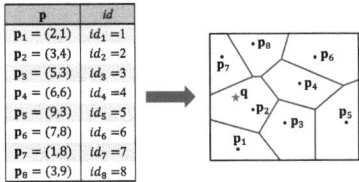

Fig. 1. An Example of Voronoi Diagram.

2.2 Voronoi Diagram

As shown in Fig. 1, given the dataset $\mathcal{D} = \{(\mathbf{p}_i, id_i) | 1 \leq i \leq N\}$, the Voronoi diagram divides $\mathcal{D}$ into N disjoint Voronoi cells and each Voronoi cell belongs to a unique point. Any point lying in the Voronoi cell of point $\mathbf{p}_i$ (denoted as $\text{VC}(\mathbf{p}_i)$) is closer to $\mathbf{p}_i$ than to any other point in $\mathcal{D}$. Here, $\mathbf{p}_i$ is called the generator of $\text{VC}(\mathbf{p}_i)$. The Voronoi cells that share the same edges are called adjacent cells and their generators are called adjacent generators. The adjacent generators of $\mathbf{p}_i$ is denoted as $\text{AG}(\mathbf{p}_i)$. The Voronoi diagram exhibits two properties: 1) If and only if the query point $\mathbf{q}$ falls into $\text{VC}(\mathbf{p}_i)$, $\mathbf{p}_i$ is the nearest neighbor to $\mathbf{q}$; 2) If $\mathbf{p}'_1, ..., \mathbf{p}'_k$ are the first k nearest neighbors of the query point $\mathbf{q}$, then $\mathbf{p}'_k$ is among the adjacent generators of $\mathbf{p}'_1, ..., \mathbf{p}'_{k-1}$, i.e., $\mathbf{p}'_k \in \text{AG}(\mathbf{p}'_1) \cup ... \cup \text{AG}(\mathbf{p}'_{k-1})$.

3 Problem Formulation

3.1 System Architecture

Our system architecture depicted in Fig. 2 consists of five parties: Trusted Third Party ($\mathcal{TTP}$), Data Owner ($\mathcal{DO}$), Data User ($\mathcal{DU}$) and two Cloud Servers ($\mathcal{C}_1$ and $\mathcal{C}_2$). Specifically, the system works as follows.

Preprocessing: $\mathcal{DO}$ first creates the index $\mathcal{I}$ for his/her d-dimensional dataset $\mathcal{D} = \{(\mathbf{p}_i, id_i) | 1 \leq i \leq N\}$, where $\mathbf{p}_i = (p_{i,1}, ..., p_{i,d})$ represents a data point and id_i is its identifier. Then, $\mathcal{DO}$ generates the secret shares $[\mathcal{I}]_1$ and $[\mathcal{I}]_2$, and sends them to $\mathcal{C}_1$ and $\mathcal{C}_2$ respectively. $\mathcal{TTP}$ periodically generates the secret shared random values (e.g., Beaver triple) used during the online phase.

Query Processing: $\mathcal{DU}$ splits the query $\mathbf{q} = (q_1, ..., q_d)$ into two secret shares $[\mathbf{q}]_1$ and $[\mathbf{q}]_2$, and uploads them to the servers. Here, $[\mathbf{q}]_\alpha = ([q_1]_\alpha, ..., [q_d]_\alpha)$. Then, $\mathcal{C}_1$ and $\mathcal{C}_2$ process the kNN query over $[\mathcal{I}]$ and return the secret shared result set $[\mathcal{R}]$ to $\mathcal{DU}$. At the end, $\mathcal{DU}$ recovers the final result $\mathcal{R}$.

3.2 Security Model

We mainly consider the semi-honest model. Specifically, all parties are scrupulous in following the protocol specification, yet attempt to learn additional information by inferring and analyzing the transcripts received during the execution. Furthermore, we assume that the two servers are non-colluding, which is a widely adopted assumption in prior works [9–14, 25].

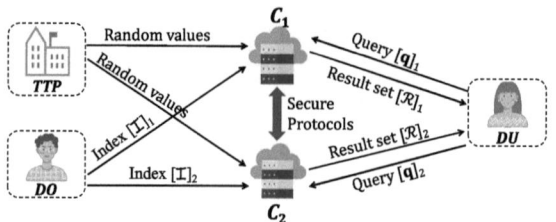

Fig. 2. Overview of System Architecture.

4 Insecurity of AHE-Based Methods

This section focuses on the Secure Division Computation (SDC) and Secure Minimum Computation (SMC) protocols described in [14] to illustrate how adversaries can recover sensitive input from intermediate decrypted values. The method [14] adopts the Paillier cryptosystem and two non-colluding servers, where $\mathcal{C}_1$ holds Paillier's public key pk and $\mathcal{C}_2$ holds Paillier's private/public key pair (sk, pk). Let $E(\cdot)$ be the encryption function with pk, $\mathbb{Z}_P$ be the plaintext space of Paillier, and $\|\cdot\|$ be the bit length of "$\cdot$". The main ideas of SDC and SMC are as follows. We refer to Algorithm 1 and Algorithm 3 of [14] for more details.

The SDC protocol considers $\mathcal{C}_1$ with input $(E(x), E(\Delta))$ and outputs $E(x/\Delta)$ to $\mathcal{C}_1$, where x and Δ are not known to $\mathcal{C}_1$ and $\mathcal{C}_2$. First, $\mathcal{C}_1$ sends $E(x') = E(x)^{r_1} \cdot E(\Delta)^{r_1 \cdot r_2}$ and $E(\Delta') = E(\Delta)^{r_1}$ to $\mathcal{C}_2$, where r_1 and r_2 are two random numbers. After decryption, $\mathcal{C}_2$ computes $h = x'/\Delta'$, and returns $E(h)$ to $\mathcal{C}_1$. Finally, $\mathcal{C}_1$ eliminates r_2 from $E(h)$. The correctness of SDC relies on the equation:

$$x/\Delta = x'/\Delta' - r_2 = (x \cdot r_1 + \Delta \cdot r_1 \cdot r_2)/(\Delta \cdot r_1) - r_2 \qquad (1)$$

To ensure the correctness, it is essential that the values of x' and Δ' do not overflow, i.e., $x', \Delta' < P$. Assuming the bit length of x and Δ is L, and the bit length of r_1 and r_2 is κ, then $\kappa < (\|P\| - 1 - L)/2$.

The SMC protocol considers $\mathcal{C}_1$ with input $(E(x), E(y))$ and outputs $E(\min(x, y))$ to $\mathcal{C}_1$, where x and y are not known to $\mathcal{C}_1$ and $\mathcal{C}_2$. SMC requires $\mathcal{C}_1$ to send $E(\alpha) = E(x - y)^{r_1}$ or $E(\alpha) = E(y - x)^{r_1}$ to $\mathcal{C}_2$, according to a random function $F \in \{0, 1\}$. After decryption, $\mathcal{C}_2$ obtains $\epsilon = \text{Bool}(\alpha < 0)$ and returns $E(\epsilon)$ to $\mathcal{C}_1$. The correctness of SMC depends on α preserving the magnitude relationship between x and y, necessitating that $|x - y| * r_1$ does not overflow. Assuming the bit length of x and y is L, and the bit length of r_1 is κ, then $\kappa < \|P\| - 1 - L$.

Our Decomposition-Based Attack. During SDC and SMC, $\mathcal{C}_1$ ensures that the values of sensitive data remain hidden from $\mathcal{C}_2$ by multiplying them by random numbers. However, to maintain the correctness of the computation, these random numbers are not randomly chosen from $\mathbb{Z}_P$, thus they cannot perfectly disguise the sensitive data. Indeed, $\mathcal{C}_2$ can potentially identify a small set of "legal" values for the sensitive data by exhaustively testing all possible values. Let's examine

SDC as a concrete example. Given that the range of Δ is significantly smaller than that of r_1, $\mathcal{C}_2$ sequentially sets Δ to integers from 1 to $2^L - 1$ and computes $r_1 = \Delta'/\Delta$. If r_1 is an integer and falls within the valid range $0 < r_1 \leq 2^\kappa - 1$, then (Δ, r_1) forms a pair of legal values. By substituting these legal values into the equation for x', $\mathcal{C}_2$ can further identify the possible values for x and r_2 similarly. Furthermore, the following proposition provides an upper bound on the size of the set of all legal values. Here, $g(x) = \sharp\{d \in \mathbb{N}_+ \cap [2, U_a] : d \mid x\}$. The proofs of the propositions are given in Appendix A.

Proposition 1. *Let $U_a, U_b \in \mathbb{N}_+$ be two positive constants. Suppose that a and b are chosen uniformly at random from $\mathbb{N}_+ \cap [2, U_a]$ and $\mathbb{N}_+ \cap [2, U_b]$, respectively. Then, $\mathbb{P}\left[g(a \cdot b) \leqslant O(\log U_a)\right] = \Omega\left(\frac{1}{\log U_a}\right)$.*

According to Proposition 1, the number of legal values of Δ is at most $O(\log \hat{\Delta})$ with a probability of $\Omega(\frac{1}{\log \hat{\Delta}})$, where $\hat{\Delta}$ denotes the upper bound of Δ. Since the range of Δ is relatively small, we conclude that $\mathcal{C}_2$ can efficiently recover the values of Δ and x with a non-trivial probability. Further, the following propositions illustrate the lower bounds of the probability that the number of legal Δs is extremely small.

Proposition 2. *Let $U_a, U_b \in \mathbb{N}_+$ be two positive constants. Suppose that a and b are chosen uniformly at random from $\mathbb{N}_+ \cap [2, U_a]$ and $\mathbb{N}_+ \cap [2, U_b]$, respectively. Then, $\mathbb{P}\left[g(a \cdot b) = 1\right] = \Omega\left(\frac{1}{\log^2 U_a}\right)$.*

Proposition 3. *Let $U_a, U_b \in \mathbb{N}_+$ be two positive constants. Suppose that a and b are chosen uniformly at random from $\mathbb{N}_+ \cap [2, U_a]$ and $\mathbb{N}_+ \cap [2, U_b]$, respectively. Then, $\mathbb{P}\left[g(a \cdot b) \leqslant 3\right] = \Omega\left(\frac{\log \log U_a}{\log^2 U_a}\right)$.*

Propositions 2–3 demonstrate that there is a non-trivial probability that $\mathcal{C}_2$ can recover the values of Δ and x with high accuracy. Further, we verify the effectiveness of our attack on SDC and SMC through experiments. Specifically, we perform experiments with sensitive data following both uniform and normal distributions. We randomly select sensitive input and use our attack to identify the legal values of Δ and x in SDC, as well as the legal values of $|x - y|$ in SMC. We repeat the experiment 1000 times and calculate the percentage of instances where the number of legal values is no more than 3. As depicted in Fig. 3(a)–(b), for normally distributed data, approximately 34% $\sim$ 39% of the instances in SDC and 23% $\sim$ 28% of the instances in SMC have no more than 3 legal values. For uniformly distributed data, the results are much more positive, as shown in Fig. 3(c)–(d). Additionally, L and $\|P\|$ have a negligible effect on the results.

5 Basic PP*k*NN Protocol

This section presents BPP*k*NN and its variant, BPP*k*NN-bitonic. The index construction of BPP*k*NN is straightforward. $\mathcal{DO}$ splits each point into secret shares attribute-wise, and then outsources the secret shared index $[\mathcal{I}] = \{([\mathbf{p}_i], [id_i]) | 1 \leq i \leq N\}$ to the servers. Next, we focus on the query processing phase.

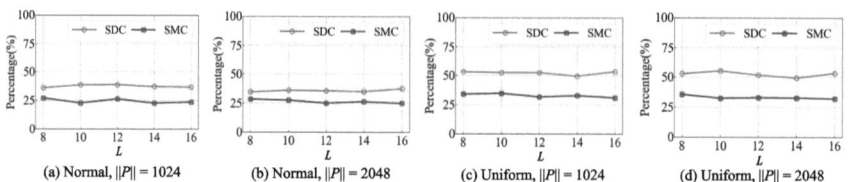

Fig. 3. Performance of Our Attack.

5.1 Query Processing

The servers first execute SecDist to compute the secret shared distance between each data point and the query. Then, they obliviously rearrange the points using the Secure Sort (SecSort) protocol. After the rearrangement, the point in the first position is identified as the nearest neighbor. During this process, no sensitive information, such as the identifiers of nearest neighbors, is revealed to the servers. The overall steps of BPPkNN are highlighted in Algorithm 1.

Step 1: Secure Distance Computation (lines 2–5). For each point $([\mathbf{p}_i], [id_i])$, $\mathcal{C}_1$ and $\mathcal{C}_2$ compute the secret shared distance $[\delta_i] = [\text{Dist}(\mathbf{p}_i, \mathbf{q})^2]$ using SecDist, construct the tuple $[\mathbf{e}_i] = ([\mathbf{p}_i], [id_i], [\delta_i])$, and add it to the temporary set $[\mathcal{T}]$.

Step 2: Secure kNN Computation (lines 6–21). $\mathcal{C}_1$ and $\mathcal{C}_2$ first divide $[\mathcal{T}]$ into $a = |\mathcal{T}|$ sequences, with each sequence $[\mathcal{S}_{0,i}]$ containing one tuple $[\mathbf{e}_i]$. Then, they iteratively merge two adjacent sequences using SecSort until a single sequence $[\mathcal{S}_{\lceil \log_2 a \rceil, 1}]$ is obtained. $[\mathcal{T}]$ is updated to $[\mathcal{S}_{\lceil \log_2 a \rceil, 1}]$. During this process, the first tuple of each sequence always holds the closest point within that sequence. Finally, the first tuple of $[\mathcal{T}]$ is added to the result set $[\mathcal{R}]$ and removed from $[\mathcal{T}]$. This process repeats until k nearest neighbors are found.

Step 3: Result Recovery (lines 22–23). $\mathcal{DU}$ recovers the final result $\mathcal{R}$.

Secure Sort (SecSort). SecSort takes as input a secret shared sequence $[\mathcal{S}] = \{[\mathbf{e}_1], ..., [\mathbf{e}_a]\}$, the indices α, β of the two tuples to be sorted, and a boolean value θ, where $\alpha < \beta$ and $\theta \in \{0, 1\}$ indicates the sorting order. The protocol outputs an updated secret shared sequence $[\mathcal{S}] = \{[\mathbf{e}_1], ..., [\mathbf{e}_a]\}$, where $\mathbf{e}_\alpha$ and $\mathbf{e}_\beta$ are sorted in ascending ($\theta = 0$) or descending ($\theta = 1$) order, while other tuples remain unchanged. The main idea of SecSort is to obliviously "compare-swap" the two tuples. Given $[\mathbf{e}_\alpha] = ([\mathbf{p}_\alpha], [id_\alpha], [\delta_\alpha])$ and $[\mathbf{e}_\beta] = ([\mathbf{p}_\beta], [id_\beta], [\delta_\beta])$, the servers securely compute the comparison bit $[\phi] = [\text{Bool}(\delta_\alpha < \delta_\beta)]$ using SecComp. We first consider the case where $\theta = 0$ (ascending order). If $\phi = 0$, the two tuples are swapped; otherwise, they remain unchanged. More specifically, the servers store $[\mathbf{e}_\alpha]$ in a temporary tuple $[\mathbf{e}']$. Then $[\mathbf{e}_\alpha]$ is updated to $[\mathbf{e}_\beta] + [\phi] \cdot ([\mathbf{e}'] - [\mathbf{e}_\beta])$ and $[\mathbf{e}_\beta]$ is updated to $[\mathbf{e}'] + [\mathbf{e}_\beta] - [\mathbf{e}_\alpha]$. When $\theta = 1$ (descending order), the operation is the opposite of when $\theta = 0$.

Example 1. As shown in Fig. 4, $\mathcal{C}_1$ and $\mathcal{C}_2$ first compute the distance for each point using SecDist. Then, $\mathcal{C}_1$ and $\mathcal{C}_2$ generate four sequences $[\mathcal{S}_{0,1}] \sim [\mathcal{S}_{0,4}]$, and merge them layer by layer using SecSort. Finally, a single sequence $[\mathcal{S}_{2,1}]$ is obtained. The servers find the nearest point $[\mathbf{p}_2]$ from the first tuple of $[\mathcal{S}_{2,1}]$.

Algorithm 1: Basic PPkNN (BPPkNN) Protocol.

Input: Secret shared index $[\mathcal{I}]$ and secret shared query point $[\mathbf{q}]$.
Output: Result set $\mathcal{R}$.
// $\mathcal{C}_1$ & $\mathcal{C}_2$
1 initialize the temporary set $[\mathcal{T}] = \emptyset$ and the result set $[\mathcal{R}] = \emptyset$;
2 **for** $i = 1$ to N **do**
3 $\quad$ $[\delta_i] \leftarrow$ SecDist$([\mathbf{p}_i], [\mathbf{q}])$;
4 $\quad$ construct the tuple $[\mathbf{e}_i] = ([\mathbf{p}_i], [id_i], [\delta_i])$ and add it to $[\mathcal{T}]$;
5 **end**
6 **while** $|\mathcal{R}| < k$ **do**
7 $\quad$ int $a = |\mathcal{T}|$;
8 $\quad$ **for** $[\mathbf{e}_i] \in [\mathcal{T}]$ **do**
9 $\quad\quad$ construct a sequence $[\mathcal{S}_{0,i}] = \{[\mathbf{e}_i]\}$;
10 $\quad$ **end**
11 $\quad$ **for** $j = 1$ to $\lceil \log_2 a \rceil$ **do**
12 $\quad\quad$ **for** $i = 1$ to $\lceil a/2^j \rceil$ **do**
13 $\quad\quad\quad$ int $a = |\mathcal{S}_{j-1,2i-1}|$, $b = |\mathcal{S}_{j-1,2i}|$, $c = a + b$;
14 $\quad\quad\quad$ construct a new sequence $[\mathcal{S}_{j,i}] = \{[\mathbf{e}''_1], ..., [\mathbf{e}''_c]\}$;
15 $\quad\quad\quad$ copy $[\mathcal{S}_{j-1,2i-1}]$ and $[\mathcal{S}_{j-1,2i}]$ to $[\mathbf{e}''_1], ..., [\mathbf{e}''_c]$ in order;
16 $\quad\quad\quad$ $[\mathcal{S}_{j,i}] \leftarrow$ SecSort$([\mathcal{S}_{j,i}], 1, a+1, 0)$;
17 $\quad\quad$ **end**
18 $\quad$ **end**
19 $\quad$ update $[\mathcal{T}] = [\mathcal{S}_{\lceil \log_2 a \rceil, 1}]$;
20 $\quad$ add the first tuple of $[\mathcal{T}]$ to the result set $[\mathcal{R}]$ and remove it from $[\mathcal{T}]$;
21 **end**
22 $\mathcal{C}_\alpha$ returns $[\mathcal{R}]_\alpha$ to $\mathcal{DU}$;
// $\mathcal{DU}$
23 recovers $\mathcal{R}$ locally;

5.2 Extension

BPPkNN-bitonic. When k is large, we can apply bitonic sort to further reduce the round complexity from $O(k\log_2 N)$ to $O(\log_2^2 N)$. Bitonic sort relies on bitonic sequences, i.e., concatenations of two subsequences sorted in opposite directions. The key operation in bitonic sort is to "compare-swap" a pair of tuples, which can be securely implemented by SecSort. However, since bitonic sort requires sorting all points, BPPkNN-bitonic only supports efficient queries on small datasets.

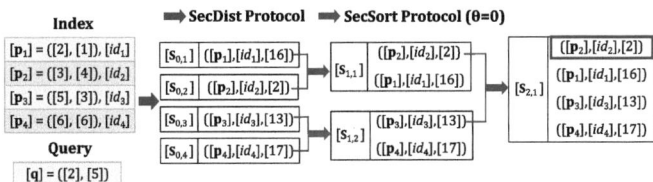

Fig. 4. An Example of BPPkNN.

Queries on Non-Numerical Data. BPPkNN can support other data types (textual, categorical, etc.) by replacing SecDist with appropriate protocols.

Textual Data. The difficulty of Cosine similarity (CosDist) computation lies in the division operation over shared values. To avoid division operations, $\mathcal{DO}$ first computes the least common multiple π of all text vectors $\|\mathbf{v}_1\|, ..., \|\mathbf{v}_N\|$, where $\|\cdot\|$ denotes the Euclidean norm. Then, $\mathcal{DO}$ computes $\mathbf{p}_i = \frac{\pi}{\|\mathbf{v}_i\|}\mathbf{v}_i$ and outsources $[\mathbf{p}_i]$ to servers. Given the query $[\mathbf{q}]$, the servers compute $[\pi\|\mathbf{q}\|\text{CosDist}(\mathbf{v}_i,\mathbf{q})] = [\mathbf{p}_i \cdot \mathbf{q}]$ by SecMul, and then sort the data based on these values.

Categorical Data. The Hamming distance (HamDist) is commonly used to measure the number of attributes that have different values between two vectors. Given the secret shares of two vectors $[\mathbf{p}]$ and $[\mathbf{q}]$, SecEq is executed d times to determine whether each attribute of the two vectors is the same. Then, the Hamming distance is computed as $[\text{HamDist}(\mathbf{p},\mathbf{q})] = \Sigma_{i=1}^{d}[1 - \text{Bool}(p_i = q_i)]$.

6 Voronoi-Based PPkNN Protocol

In BPPkNN, the servers need to scan the entire dataset, and SecComp is executed $O(kN)$ times. In this section, we propose VPPkNN which involves only $O(m + M + k^2T)$ times SecComp, where $m, M, T \ll N$. Specifically, the first nearest neighbor $\mathbf{p}'_1$ is identified based on Property 1 of the Voronoi diagram, i.e., the query $\mathbf{q}$ falls into the Voronoi cell of $\mathbf{p}'_1$. According to Property 2, to find the i-th nearest neighbor $\mathbf{p}'_i$ (for $i > 1$), we retrieve the adjacent generators of the first $i - 1$ nearest neighbors, delete duplicates, and find $\mathbf{p}'_i$ from the remaining points. To avoid leaking privacy, there exist three key technical challenges.

Challenge 1: How to obliviously find $\mathbf{p}'_1$? Due to the irregular shape of Voronoi cells, securely determining whether $\mathbf{q}$ falls into VC($\mathbf{p}_i$) is challenging. To overcome this, we partition the data space into non-overlapping rectangles, and create a table $\mathcal{VC}$ to store the points whose Voronoi cells overlap with each rectangle, separately. This transforms the polygonal inclusion problem into the rectangular inclusion problem. We propose the Secure VC Read (SecVC) protocol to obliviously find the rectangle containing $\mathbf{q}$ and retrieve its corresponding points. BPPkNN is then used to find $\mathbf{p}'_1$ among these points.

Challenge 2: How to obliviously get the adjacent generators of a given point? Since the number of adjacent generators varies greatly among different points, we use a greedy algorithm to group data points for index compression. A table $\mathcal{AG}$ is created to store the adjacent generators of points in each group separately. Additionally, we propose the Secure AG Read (SecAG) protocol to obliviously read the adjacent generators of a given point from $\mathcal{AG}$.

Challenge 3: How to obliviously delete duplicates from the adjacent generators? Already found nearest neighbors need to be deleted from the adjacent generators for subsequent searches. To prevent revealing which points are deleted, we propose the Secure Deduplication (SecDedup) protocol to obliviously "delete" duplicates. SecDedup adds a large value to the duplicates, ensuring they will not be retrieved as nearest neighbors in subsequent steps. Note that we do not physically remove points, so the servers know nothing about the operation.

6.1 Index Construction

The index $\mathcal{I} = \{\mathcal{AG}, \mathcal{VC}\}$ consists of two tables. $\mathcal{DO}$ splits $\mathcal{I}$ into secret shares attribute-wise and outsources the shared index $[\mathcal{I}]$ to the servers.

Table $\mathcal{AG}$. Given the Voronoi diagram, we partition the points into multiple groups using a greedy algorithm. Let T be the maximum number of adjacent generators, i.e., $T = \max(|\mathrm{AG}(\mathbf{p}_1)|, ..., |\mathrm{AG}(\mathbf{p}_N)|)$. Points are initially sorted in descending order based on the number of adjacent generators. For each point $\mathbf{p}_i$, we assign it to an existing group if the total number of adjacent generators of points within that group does not exceed T; otherwise, we create a new group. This yields t groups $\mathcal{G}_1, ..., \mathcal{G}_t$, where $\mathcal{G}_i = \{\mathbf{p}_{i,1}, ..., \mathbf{p}_{i,s_i}\}$ and $\sum_{j=1}^{s_i} |\mathrm{AG}(\mathbf{p}_{i,j})| \leq T$. Next, we construct the table $\mathcal{AG}$ and store the adjacent generators of the points within $\mathcal{G}_i$ in the i-th row of $\mathcal{AG}$ (denoted as $\mathcal{AG}_i$). Specifically, for each adjacent generator $\mathbf{p}'$ of $\mathbf{p}_{i,j} \in \mathcal{G}_i$, we generate a tuple $(\mathbf{p}', id', \varphi')$ and add it to $\mathcal{AG}_i$, where $\mathbf{p}' \in \mathcal{G}_{\varphi'}$. Finally, we ensure each row of $\mathcal{AG}$ has the same size T by padding with dummy points, which are randomly chosen from $\mathcal{D}$.

Example 2. Figure 5(a) shows an example of table $[\mathcal{AG}]$, where $T = 5$. Since $\mathbf{p}_1$ and $\mathbf{p}_5$ have 2 and 3 adjacent generators respectively, they can be assigned to the same group $\mathcal{G}_5$. Then $\mathrm{AG}(\mathbf{p}_1)$ and $\mathrm{AG}(\mathbf{p}_5)$ are stored in row $\mathcal{AG}_5$.

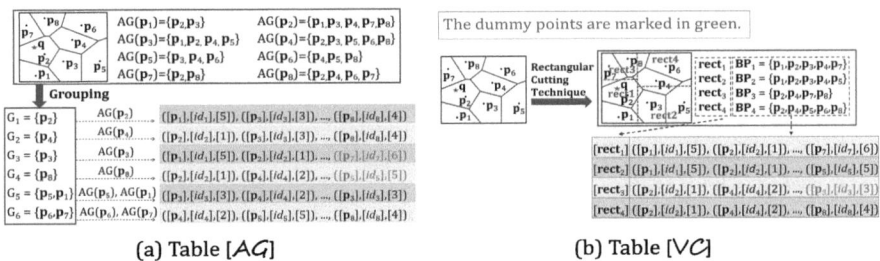

Fig. 5. An Example of the Secret Shared Index.

Table $\mathcal{VC}$. We first apply the rectangular cutting technique [7] to partition the data space into m non-overlapping rectangles. The main idea is to choose a dimension and cut the rectangle **rect** into two rectangles (**rect**$_1$, **rect**$_2$) so that the maximum number of the Voronoi cells that **rect**$_i$ overlaps is minimized. The points whose Voronoi cells overlap with **rect**$_i$ is represented as $\mathcal{BP}_i$. Then, we construct the table $\mathcal{VC}$ which contains two columns, and store **rect**$_i$ and $\mathcal{BP}_i$ in the i-th row of $\mathcal{VC}$ (denoted as $\mathcal{VC}_i$). More specifically, the boundary values $(l_{i,1}, l_{i,2}, u_{i,1}, u_{i,2})$ of **rect**$_i$ is stored in the first column, where $(l_{i,1}, l_{i,2})$ and $(u_{i,1}, u_{i,2})$ are the lower left and upper right vertices respectively. For each point $\mathbf{p}_{i,j} \in \mathcal{BP}_i$, we generate a tuple $(\mathbf{p}_{i,j}, id_{i,j}, \varphi_{i,j})$ and add it to the second column, where $\mathbf{p}_{i,j} \in \mathcal{G}_{\varphi_{i,j}}$. Similarly, we pad each row to a fixed size $M = \max(|\mathcal{BP}_1|, ..., |\mathcal{BP}_m|)$ using dummy points.

Example 3. Figure 5(b) illustrates an example of table $[\mathcal{VC}]$. The Voronoi diagram is partitioned into four parts and $M = 5$. The rectangle **rect**$_1$ and the points $\mathcal{BP}_1$ whose Voronoi cells overlap with **rect**$_1$ are stored in $\mathcal{VC}_1$.

6.2 Query Processing

The servers first use SecVC to obliviously identify the rectangle in $[\mathcal{VC}]$ that contains the query and retrieve the corresponding secret shared points $[\mathcal{BP}_i]$. Then, BPPkNN is applied to compute the first nearest neighbor from $[\mathcal{BP}_i]$. To find the i-th nearest neighbor $(i > 1)$, the servers fetch the secret shared adjacent generators of the first $i-1$ nearest neighbors from $[\mathcal{AG}]$ using SecAG. Then, SecDedup is executed to "delete" duplicates, and BPPkNN is executed to compute the next nearest neighbor from the updated set. During this process, no sensitive information, such as the access patterns of tables, is revealed to the servers. The main steps involved in VPPkNN are shown in Algorithm 2.

Algorithm 2: Voronoi-Based PPkNN (VPPkNN) Protocol.

Input: Secret shared index $[\mathcal{I}] = \{[\mathcal{AG}], [\mathcal{VC}]\}$ and secret shared query $[\mathbf{q}]$.
Output: Result set $\mathcal{R}$.
// $\mathcal{C}_1$ & $\mathcal{C}_2$
1 initialize the result set $[\mathcal{R}] = \emptyset$;
2 $[\mathcal{BP}_i] \leftarrow$ SecVC($[\mathcal{VC}], [\mathbf{q}]$);
3 $([\mathbf{p}'_1], [id'_1], [\varphi'_1]) \leftarrow$ BPPkNN($[\mathcal{BP}_i], [\mathbf{q}]$);
4 add $([\mathbf{p}'_1], [id'_1])$ to $[\mathcal{R}]$;
5 int $i = 2$;
6 while $i \leq k$ do
7 $\quad [\mathcal{AG}_{\varphi'_{i-1}}] \leftarrow$ SecAG($[\mathcal{AG}], [\varphi'_{i-1}]$);
8 $\quad \{[\mathcal{AG}_{\varphi'_1}], ..., [\mathcal{AG}_{\varphi'_{i-1}}]\} \leftarrow$ SecDedup($\{[\mathcal{AG}_{\varphi'_1}], ..., [\mathcal{AG}_{\varphi'_{i-1}}]\}, [\mathcal{R}]$);
9 $\quad ([\mathbf{p}'_i], [id'_i], [\varphi'_i]) \leftarrow$ BPPkNN($\{[\mathcal{AG}_{\varphi'_1}], ..., [\mathcal{AG}_{\varphi'_{i-1}}]\}, [\mathbf{q}]$);
10 $\quad$ add $([\mathbf{p}'_i], [id'_i])$ to $[\mathcal{R}]$;
11 $\quad i++$;
12 end
13 $\mathcal{C}_\alpha$ returns $[\mathcal{R}]_\alpha$ to $\mathcal{DU}$;
// $\mathcal{DU}$
14 recovers $\mathcal{R}$ locally;

Step 1: Secure first NN Computation (lines 2–4). The servers use SecVC to obliviously read $[\mathcal{BP}_i]$ from $[\mathcal{VC}]$ such that $\mathbf{q} \in \mathbf{rect}_i$. They then apply BPP$k$NN to $[\mathcal{BP}_i]$ to compute the first nearest neighbor, denoted as $([\mathbf{p}'_1], [id'_1], [\varphi'_1])$.

Step 2: Secure i-th NN Computation (lines 5–12). To find the i-th nearest neighbor, the servers first use SecAG to obliviously read the adjacent generators of the $(i-1)$-th nearest neighbor from $[\mathcal{AG}]$. Then, SecDedup is executed to "delete" the already identified nearest neighbors from their adjacent generators. Finally, $\mathcal{C}_1$ and $\mathcal{C}_2$ apply BPPkNN to the remaining adjacent generators to compute the i-th nearest neighbor $([\mathbf{p}'_i], [id'_i], [\varphi'_i])$.

Step 3: Result Recovery (lines 13–14). $\mathcal{DU}$ recovers the final result $\mathcal{R}$.

Secure VC Read (SecVC). SecVC takes as input the secret shares of table $[\mathcal{VC}]$ and query $[\mathbf{q}]$, and outputs the secret shared points $[\mathcal{BP}']$ such that $\mathbf{q} \in \mathbf{rect}'$. The core idea of SecVC is to first locate the rectangle containing $\mathbf{q}$, and then traverse the entire table to compute the corresponding points. For each rectangle $\mathbf{rect}_i$, the servers compare its boundary values $([l_{i,1}], [l_{i,2}], [u_{i,1}], [u_{i,2}])$ with $[\mathbf{q}]$

using SecComp. Specifically, $[\mu_i] = [\text{Bool}(l_{i,1} < q_1)]$, $[\nu_i] = [\text{Bool}(l_{i,2} < q_2)]$, $[\upsilon_i] = [\text{Bool}(q_1 < u_{i,1})]$ and $[\omega_i] = [\text{Bool}(q_2 < u_{i,2})]$. Then, $\mathcal{C}_1$ and $\mathcal{C}_2$ compute the indicator $[\gamma_i] = [\mu_i] \cdot [\nu_i] \cdot [\upsilon_i] \cdot [\omega_i]$. If $\mathbf{q} \in \mathbf{rect}_i$, then $\gamma_i = 1$; otherwise, $\gamma_i = 0$. After this, the j-th point $\mathbf{p}'_j$ in $\mathcal{BP}'$ is computed as $[\mathbf{p}'_j] = \sum_{i=1}^{m}[\gamma_i] \cdot [\mathbf{p}_{i,j}]$. The correctness relies on the fact that if $\mathbf{q} \notin \mathbf{rect}_i$, then $\gamma_i \cdot \mathbf{p}_{i,j}$ is equal to (0,0), effectively excluding points from other rectangles. The values of $[id'_j]$ and $[\varphi'_j]$ are computed similarly.

Secure AG Read (SecAG). SecAG takes as input the secret shares of table $[\mathcal{AG}]$ and index $[\varphi]$ of the targeted row, and outputs $[\mathcal{AG}_\varphi]$. First, the servers locate the targeted row by comparing φ with each row index $1 \le i \le t$ using SecEq, obtaining indicators $[\gamma_1], ..., [\gamma_t]$, where $[\gamma_i] = [\text{Bool}(\varphi = i)]$. Similar to SecVC, the servers then traverse the entire table to obliviously compute the secret shares of the targeted row.

Secure Deduplication (SecDedup). After computing the s-th nearest neighbor $(\mathbf{p}'_s, id'_s, \varphi'_s)$ and reading its adjacent generators $\mathcal{AG}_{\varphi'_s}$, we consider two cases: (1) obliviously "deleting" the first $s - 1$ nearest neighbors from $\mathcal{AG}_{\varphi'_s}$; and (2) obliviously "deleting" $\mathbf{p}'_s$ from the adjacent generators of the first $s - 1$ nearest neighbors. SecDedup takes as input the already identified nearest neighbors and their sets of adjacent generators, and outputs the updated sets. Here, we focus on the first case, as the second is addressed in a similar way. For each tuple $([\mathbf{p}''_i], [id''_i], [\varphi''_i]) \in [\mathcal{AG}_{\varphi'_s}]$, the servers compare $[id''_i]$ with the identifiers of the first $s - 1$ nearest neighbors $[id'_1], ..., [id'_{s-1}]$ using SecEq, and obtain the comparison bits $[v_{i,1}], ..., [v_{i,s-1}]$, where $[v_{i,j}] = [\text{Bool}(id'_j = id''_i)]$. Then, $\mathcal{C}_1$ and $\mathcal{C}_2$ compute the indicator $[\gamma_i] = \sum_{j=1}^{s-1}[v_{i,j}]$. If any id'_j matches id''_i, then $\gamma_i = 1$ and $\mathbf{p}''_i$ needs to be deleted; otherwise, $\gamma_i = 0$. After this, the servers locally update $[\mathbf{p}''_i]$ by adding MAX $\cdot [\gamma_i]$, effectively preventing duplicate points from being selected in subsequent computations. Here, MAX is a large constant.

7 Complexity and Security Analysis

7.1 Round, Computational and Communication Complexities

In this paper, we define three types of costs: 1) *Operation cost*, given by the number of local multiplication operations; 2) *Synchronization cost*, which is determined by the number of communication rounds across parties; and 3) *Communication cost*, measured by the number of messages exchanged between parties. Table 2 provides the complexities of our proposed protocols.

7.2 Security Analysis

We adopt the **Ideal/Real** simulation paradigm [32], which has been widely applied in related works [11,14–16,19,25]. In the real world, the protocol follows the PPkNN protocol, while in the ideal world, two probabilistic polynomial time simulators try to simulate the real-world execution. A protocol is considered secure if the two worlds are computationally indistinguishable. We define the

Table 2. Complexity Analysis.

Protocol	Operation	Synchronization	Communication
SecSort	$O(l+d)$	$O(1)$	$O(l+d)$
SecVC	$O(lm+mM)$	$O(1)$	$O(lm+mM)$
SecAG	$O(lt+tT)$	$O(1)$	$O(lt+tT)$
SecDedup	$O(lkT)$	$O(1)$	$O(lkT)$
BPPkNN	$O(kNl+kNd)$	$O(k\log_2 N)$	$O(kNl+kNd)$
BPPkNN-bitonic	$O((l+d)N\log_2^2 N)$	$O(\log_2^2 N)$	$O((l+d)N\log_2^2 N)$
VPPkNN	$O(lm+lM+mM+ktl+ktT+k^2lT)$	$O(\log_2 M + k\log_2 kT)$	$O(lm+lM+mM+ktl+ktT+k^2lT)$

ideal functionalities $\mathcal{F}_{\text{BPP}k\text{NN}}$ and $\mathcal{F}_{\text{VPP}k\text{NN}}$ that our PPkNN protocols achieve as follows. The security proofs are given in Appendix B (Fig. 6 and 7).

Parameters: $N, d, k, \mathbb{Z}_p$.
- On input $[\mathcal{I}]_\alpha$ and $[\mathbf{q}]_\alpha$ from $\mathcal{C}_\alpha$, store $[\mathcal{I}]_\alpha$ and $[\mathbf{q}]_\alpha$.
- When both inputs are received, recover $\mathcal{I}$ and $\mathbf{q}$. Compute the distance between each data point and $\mathbf{q}$. Sort the data points in ascending order according to their distances. Add the first k data points to the result set $\mathcal{R}$. Output $\mathcal{R}$ to client.

Fig. 6. Ideal functionality $\mathcal{F}_{\text{BPP}k\text{NN}}$.

Parameters: $m, M, t, T, k, \mathbb{Z}_p$.
- On input $[\mathcal{I}]_\alpha$ and $[\mathbf{q}]_\alpha$ from $\mathcal{C}_\alpha$, store $[\mathcal{I}]_\alpha$ and $[\mathbf{q}]_\alpha$.
- When both inputs are received, recover $\mathcal{I}$ and $\mathbf{q}$. Compute $\mathbf{rect}_i$ that contains $\mathbf{q}$ and add the first nearest point $(\mathbf{p}'_1, id'_1, \varphi'_1)$ in $\mathcal{BP}_i$ to the result set $\mathcal{R}$. For $2 \leq s \leq k$, compute the s-th nearest point $(\mathbf{p}'_s, id'_s, \varphi'_s)$ in $\mathcal{AG}_{\varphi'_1} \cup \ldots \cup \mathcal{AG}_{\varphi'_{s-1}} - \mathcal{R}$ and add it to $\mathcal{R}$. Output $\mathcal{R}$ to client.

Fig. 7. Ideal functionality $\mathcal{F}_{\text{VPP}k\text{NN}}$.

Theorem 1. *If SecDist and SecSort are secure under the semi-honest model, then BPPkNN and BPPkNN-bitonic securely implement the functionality $\mathcal{F}_{\text{BPP}k\text{NN}}$.*

Theorem 2. *If SecVC, SecAG, SecDedup and BPPkNN are secure under the semi-honest model, then VPPkNN securely implements the functionality $\mathcal{F}_{\text{VPP}k\text{NN}}$.*

8 Performance Evaluation

8.1 Experiment Setup

We compare our PPkNN protocols with three methods: 1) **SkNNm** [13], which uses Paillier and requires comparing the entire dataset k times; 2) **SVkNN**

[14] (without verification), which uses Paillier with the Voronoi diagram; and 3) BSkNN [25], which applies the secret sharing technique combined with bubble sort. As discussed in Sect. 1, SkNNm and SVkNN are the closest to ours in terms of security among the AHE-based methods, while BSkNN is the most up-to-date secret sharing-based solution.

Setup. The servers $\mathcal{C}_1$, $\mathcal{C}_2$ and other parties ($\mathcal{TTP}$, $\mathcal{DO}$ and $\mathcal{DU}$) are set up on three Amazon EC2 m5d.2xlarge instances with 8 vCPU and 32.0 GB RAM each. The baseline/maximum bandwidth is 2.5/10.0 Gbps. We have two sets of experiments: (1) *fast network*, where all instances are in the "us-east-2" availability zone (latency $<$ 1 ms); (2) *slow network*, where $\mathcal{C}_2$ is hosted in "us-west-2" and others are in "us-east-2" (latency 49 ms). Our implementation is in Java.[1]

Dataset. We adopt a real geo-location dataset (Gowalla) [30] and a synthetic dataset (SYN). The synthetic dataset is randomly generated with attributes following a uniform distribution. All values are normalized to 12-bit integers.

Parameter Setting. We measure the performance of the protocols by varying the number of points N, the query parameter k and the number of dimensions d. For the Paillier-based methods, the key size K is set to 2048 as recommended in [31]. The parameter m in VPPkNN is set to 128 or 256 by default. For each protocol, we measure its average execution time over 20 random queries.

8.2 Experimental Results

Performance of Query Processing Phase. The running times of our protocols involve both computational and communication costs. The results show that our protocols yield at least an order of magnitude improvement in query response time and our protocols facilitate efficient queries on 1 million points.

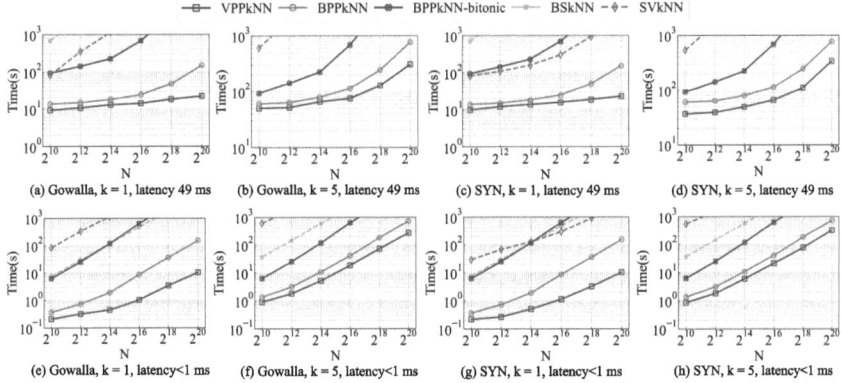

Fig. 8. Impact of N on Running Time ($d = 2$).

---

[1] Code available at https://github.com/suntq123/PPkNN.

Impact of N. Figure 8 (e)–(h) illustrates the performance of the protocols with varying N on the fast network. Results exceeding 1,000 s (e.g., SkNNm) are omitted. Compared to BSkNN, BPPkNN achieves an order of magnitude improvement in performance, while VPPkNN shows an improvement of 1 to 2 orders of magnitude. Both BPPkNN and VPPkNN outperform AHE-based methods by 2 orders of magnitude, with VPPkNN even achieving up to 3 orders of magnitude in some cases. For Gowalla NN queries with $N = 2^{12}$ points, VPPkNN, BPPkNN, BSkNN, SVkNN, and SkNNm take 0.32 s, 0.74 s, 29.41 s, 332.96 s, and over 2 hours, respectively. As shown in Fig. 8 (a)–(d), our protocols exhibit similar trends under the slow network. We also evaluate the number of rounds and the communication size of our protocols, which grow almost linearly with N, as illustrated in Fig. 9 and Fig. 10.

Impact of k. Figure 11 shows the performance of our protocols with varying k on the fast network. BPPkNN-bitonic is more suitable for scenarios with large values of k, and the closer k is to N, the more BPPkNN-bitonic outperforms BPPkNN and VPPkNN, due to the lower communication cost. The time costs of BPPkNN and VPPkNN increase almost linearly, whereas that of BPPkNN-bitonic remains independent of k, as bitonic sort requires sorting all points.

Impact of d. As shown in Fig. 12, the time costs of BPPkNN and BPPkNN-bitonic increase slightly with d increasing, since d mainly affects SecDist.

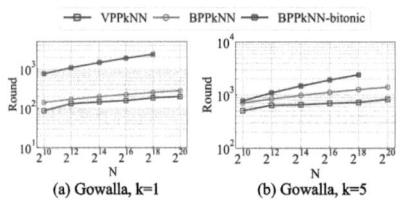

Fig. 9. Impact of N on Number of Rounds ($d = 2$)

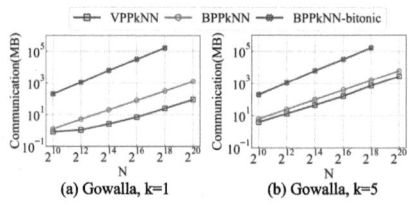

Fig. 10. Impact of N on Communication Size ($d = 2$)

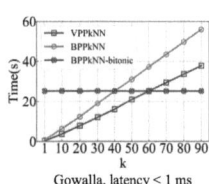

Fig. 11. Impact of k ($N = 2^{12}, d = 2$)

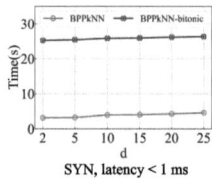

Fig. 12. Impact of d ($N = 2^{12}, k = 5$)

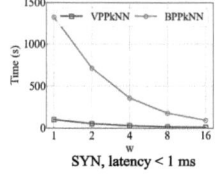

Fig. 13. Parallel Implementation ($N = 10^7, k = 1$)

Parallel Implementation. To further demonstrate the scalability of our protocols, we implement a distributed version using a manager-worker model: $\mathcal{C}_{1,1}, \mathcal{C}_{2,1}$ act as managers, and $\mathcal{C}_{i,2},...,\mathcal{C}_{i,w}$ are the workers of $\mathcal{C}_{i,1}$. The secret shared index is divided into w sub-indices, each handled by a server pair ($\mathcal{C}_{1,j}, \mathcal{C}_{2,j}$). Each pair processes its assigned sub-index and sends the intermediate results to the managers for final computation. Figure 13 shows the time costs of parallelized protocols on 10 million points with varying w. The near-linear speedup demonstrates that our distributed version effectively reduces response time.

Table 3. Preprocessing Cost of Varying N on Gowalla ($d = 2, k = 1$, latency 49 ms). Each cell contains the total time for computation and communication, as well as the communication size.

N	VPPkNN		BPPkNN		BPPkNN-bitonic		BSkNN		SVkNN	SkNNm
	one time	per query	one time	per query	one time	per query	one time	per query	one time	one time
2^{10}	11.19 s 0.11 MB	5.23 s 2.16 MB	0.01 s 0.01 MB	5.44 s 4.03 MB	0.01 s 0.01 MB	18.58 s 93.72 MB	0.01 s 0.01 MB	5.69 s 4.22 MB	30.78 s 1.53 MB	87.78 s 1.51 MB
2^{12}	29.51 s 0.41 MB	5.12 s 2.42 MB	0.03 s 0.04 MB	10.78 s 16.16 MB	0.03 s 0.04 MB	52.43 s 531.64 MB	0.03 s 0.04 MB	10.01 s 15.82 MB	202.17 s 6.11 MB	337.13 s 5.99 MB
2^{14}	104.2 s 1.58 MB	5.35 s 3.57 MB	0.05 s 0.16 MB	16.98 s 64.65 MB	0.05 s 0.16 MB	52.43 s 2.79 GB	0.05 s 0.16 MB	16.13 s 64.82 MB	505.03 s 24.43 MB	1390.11 s 23.99 MB
2^{16}	486.11 s 5.97 MB	5.32 s 7.07 MB	1.56 s 0.63 MB	34.43 s 258.61 MB	1.56 s 0.63 MB	691.05 s 14.48 GB	1.56 s 0.63 MB	32.94 s 257.97 MB	2306.07 s 97.89 MB	5318.88 s 95.98 MB
2^{18}	2814.67 s 23.46 MB	5.44 s 21.08 MB	3.21 s 2.53 MB	66.76 s 1.01 GB	3.21 s 2.53 MB	1212.31 s 72.84 GB	3.21 s 2.53 MB	81.02 1.02 GB	8954.54 s 391.03 MB	21425.69 s 383.99 MB
2^{20}	19184.15 s 96.21 MB	6.53 s 63.24 MB	5.56 s 10.13 MB	287.05 s 4.04 GB	5.56 s 10.13 MB	–	5.56 s 10.13 MB	290.31 s 4.03 GB	35304.28 s 1.55 GB	81521.23 s 1.49 GB

Performance of Preprocessing Phase. The preprocessing cost consists of two parts: 1) the one-time cost on $\mathcal{DO}$ for index construction; and 2) the per-query cost on $\mathcal{TTP}$ for generating random numbers. Table 3 presents the preprocessing cost on Gowalla under the slow network. The one-time costs of BPPkNN and BSkNN are the same, with both being more efficient and having smaller index sizes than AHE-based methods. Due to the Voronoi diagram, VPPkNN requires more time for index construction and results in a larger index size than BPPkNN and BSkNN. For the per-query cost, BPPkNN and BSkNN have similar costs, while VPPkNN incurs a lower cost due to fewer secure comparison operations.

9 Related Work

Methods based on transformation [1], privacy homomorphism [2], standard encryption [3], OPE [4], projection [5], and prefix membership testing [6,7] expose access patterns, which allows attackers to infer sensitive information with some prior knowledge [17,18]. By adopting AHE and two non-colluding servers, Elmehdwi et al. [13] introduce the first kNN method that hides access patterns by obliviously scanning the entire dataset. Following the framework of [13], Cui et al. [14] adopt the Voronoi diagram for data filtering and introduce a secure scheme for location-based kNN queries. The works [8–12] further optimize these frameworks. However, these solutions are not suitable for practical applications in terms of security and efficiency. Specifically, the basic security protocols in [10–12,14] are vulnerable to our decomposition-based attack. The method in [8] reveals the percentile of the pivot to both servers and clients, and it also requires clients to participate in the query process. The scheme in [9] exposes the number of points related to the query, allowing adversaries to infer the query distribution. In [10], the servers can determine whether the targeted record has been visited. The method in [11] discloses the distances between points and the query. The approach in [12] enables adversaries to determine whether the same row is accessed in two different queries. Additionally, the running times of the AHE-based methods are not acceptable due to heavy cryptographic operations. Recent works [15,16] study the private approximate kNN problem for high-dimensional data, which differs from our goal of returning accurate results.

10 Conclusion

In this paper, we investigate the problem of PPkNN queries. We first devise a decomposition-based attack that exposes vulnerabilities in AHE-based protocols. We then propose BPPkNN applicable to arbitrary dimensional data, and VPPkNN designed for geo-location data. Experimental results demonstrate that our protocols significantly outperform existing works. To our knowledge, this is the first work to scale to datasets of 1 million points while simultaneously preserving data, query, result, and indirect privacy. In future work, we plan to extend our protocols to support PPkNN queries under the malicious model.

Acknowledgments. This work is supported by National Key R&D Program of China (2022YFB4501500, 2022YFB4501503), and the China Postdoctoral Science Foundation under Grant Number 2024T170080.

A Proofs of Propositions

A.1 Proof of Proposition 1

Proof. In fact, for any $a \in \mathbb{N}_+ \cap [2, U_a]$ and $b \in \mathbb{N}_+ \cap [2, U_b]$, if $g(b) = 0$, $g(a \cdot b)$ will be fully determined by $g(a)$. In other words, for any $n \in \mathbb{N}_+$, we have $\mathbb{P}[g(a \cdot b) = n] \geq \mathbb{P}[g(a) = n] \cdot \mathbb{P}[g(b) = 0]$. According to Theorem 3.3 in [20], for any $x \in \mathbb{N}_+$, we have

$$\sum_{n \leq x} d(n) = x \log x + (2\gamma - 1)x + O(\sqrt{x}), \tag{2}$$

which indicates that when $n = O(\log U_a)$, $\mathbb{P}[g(a) = n] = \mathbb{P}[d(a) = n] = \Theta(1)$. Therefore,

$$\mathbb{P}[g(a \cdot b) \leq O(\log n)] \geq \Theta(1) \cdot \mathbb{P}[g(b) = 0]. \tag{3}$$

Further, applying the trivial sieve method on $\mathbb{N}_+ \cap [2, U_b]$, we have

$$\mathbb{P}[g(b) = 0] = \frac{1}{U_b - 1} \cdot \sum_{p_1, p_2, \ldots, p_k \in \mathcal{P} \cap [2, U_a]} (-1)^k \cdot \left\lfloor \frac{U_b - 1}{p_1 \cdot p_2 \cdots p_k} \right\rfloor \geq \prod_{p \in \mathcal{P} \cap [2, U_a]} \left(1 - \frac{1}{p}\right), \quad (4)$$

where $\mathcal{P}$ denotes the set of all prime numbers. By Mertens' Theorem [21], we have

$$\mathbb{P}[g(b) = 0] \geq \prod_{p \in \mathcal{P} \cap [2, U_a]} \left(1 - \frac{1}{p}\right) = \frac{e^\gamma}{\log U_a} + O\left(\frac{1}{\log^2 U_a}\right). \quad (5)$$

Combining inequalities (3) and (5), we have

$$\mathbb{P}[g(a \cdot b) \leq O(\log U_a)] \geq \Theta(1) \cdot \Theta\left(\frac{1}{\log U_a}\right), \quad (6)$$

which completes the proof.

A.2 Proof of Proposition 2

Proof. By the prime number theorem [22], there are totally $\Theta(\frac{U_a}{\log U_a})$ prime numbers in $\mathbb{N}_+ \cap [2, U_a]$, which indicates that

$$\mathbb{P}[g(a) = 1] = \frac{1}{U_a - 1} \cdot \Theta\left(\frac{U_a}{\log U_a}\right) = \Theta\left(\frac{1}{\log U_a}\right). \quad (7)$$

Therefore, by inequality (5), we have

$$\mathbb{P}[g(a \cdot b) = 1] \geq \mathbb{P}[g(a) = 1] \cdot \mathbb{P}[g(b) = 0] = \Omega\left(\frac{1}{\log^2 U_a}\right), \quad (8)$$

which completes the proof.

A.3 Proof of Proposition 3

Proof. First of all, it is worth noting that when a is semiprime (there exists prime numbers p, q that $a = p \cdot q$), we have $g(a) = 3$. Additionally, if $g(b) = 0$ holds, we have $g(a \cdot b) = 3$. In other words, $\mathbb{P}[g(a \cdot b) \leq 3] \geq \mathbb{P}[a \text{ is semiprime}] \cdot \mathbb{P}[g(b) = 0]$. According to [23], the number of semiprime numbers in $\mathbb{N}_+ \cap [2, x]$ is

$$\pi_2(x) = \frac{x \log \log x}{\log x} + 0.265 \cdot \frac{x}{\log x} + O\left(\frac{x}{\log^2 x}\right) \geq \frac{x \log \log x}{\log x}. \quad (9)$$

Since a is uniformly chosen at random from $\mathbb{N}_+ \cap [2, U_a]$, we have

$$\mathbb{P}[a \text{ is semiprime}] \geq \frac{1}{U_a - 1} \cdot \frac{U_a \cdot \log \log U_a}{\log U_a} = \Theta\left(\frac{\log \log U_a}{\log U_a}\right). \quad (10)$$

Further, by inequality (5),

$$\mathbb{P}[g(a \cdot b) \leq 3] \geq \Theta\left(\frac{\log \log U_a}{\log U_a}\right) \cdot \Theta\left(\frac{1}{\log U_a}\right) = \Theta\left(\frac{\log \log U_a}{\log^2 U_a}\right), \quad (11)$$

which completes the proof.

Parameters: $a = |\mathcal{S}|, \alpha, \beta, \theta, \mathbb{Z}_p$.
- On input $[\mathcal{S}]_i$ from $\mathcal{C}_i$, store $[\mathcal{S}]_i$.
- When both inputs are received, recover $\mathcal{S} = \{\mathbf{e}_1, ..., \mathbf{e}_a\}$. If $\theta = 0$, then sort $\mathbf{e}_\alpha$ and $\mathbf{e}_\beta$ in ascending order; otherwise, sort $\mathbf{e}_\alpha$ and $\mathbf{e}_\beta$ in descending order. Compute the secret shares of $\mathcal{S}$ over $\mathbb{Z}_p$. Output $[\mathcal{S}]_i$ to $\mathcal{C}_i$.

Fig. 14. Ideal functionality $\mathcal{F}_{\text{SecSort}}$.

Parameters: $m, M, \mathbb{Z}_p$.
- On input $[\mathcal{VC}]_\alpha$ and $[\mathbf{q}]_\alpha$ from $\mathcal{C}_\alpha$, store $[\mathcal{VC}]_\alpha$ and $[\mathbf{q}]_\alpha$.
- When both inputs are received, recover $\mathcal{VC}$ and $\mathbf{q}$. Find the rectangle $\mathbf{rect}_i$ that contains $\mathbf{q}$. Compute the secret shares of $\mathcal{BP}_i$ over $\mathbb{Z}_p$. Output $[\mathcal{BP}_i]_\alpha$ to $\mathcal{C}_\alpha$.

Fig. 15. Ideal functionality $\mathcal{F}_{\text{SecVC}}$.

B Security Proofs

B.1 Security of Subprotocols

The ideal functionalities $\mathcal{F}_{\text{SecSort}}$, $\mathcal{F}_{\text{SecVC}}$, $\mathcal{F}_{\text{SecAG}}$ and $\mathcal{F}_{\text{SecDedup}}$ that our subprotocols SecSort, SecVC, SecAG and SecDedup achieve are defined as follows (Fig. 14, 15, 16 and 17).

Theorem 3. *If SecMul, SecComp and SecEq are secure under the semi-honest model, then SecSort, SecVC, SecAG and SecDedup securely implement the functionalities $\mathcal{F}_{\text{SecSort}}$, $\mathcal{F}_{\text{SecVC}}$, $\mathcal{F}_{\text{SecAG}}$ and $\mathcal{F}_{\text{SecDedup}}$, respectively.*

Proof. According to the composition theorem [32], the security of SecSort is subject to the security of SecMul and SecComp which are proved secure in [24, 26]. The simulator for $\mathcal{C}_1$ feeds random secret shares to SecComp and gets back the secret shares of the boolean result. Then, it feeds the boolean result and two tuples to SecMul, and gets back the secret shares of the updated tuples. All intermediate values are uniformly random in $\mathbb{Z}_p$. The view generated from simulator is indistinguishable from the real view, and the same holds for $\mathcal{C}_2$. Therefore, SecSort is secure under the semi-honest model. Similarly, we can prove that SecVC, SecAG and SecDedup are secure.

B.2 Proof of Theorem 1

Proof. According to the composition theorem [32], the security of BPPkNN depends on SecDist and SecSort, which have been proved secure in [25] and Theorem 3. The simulator for $\mathcal{C}_1$ feeds the secret shares of random data points and query to SecDist, and gets back the secret shares of the distances. Then,

---
Parameters: $t, T, \mathbb{Z}_p$.
- On input $[\mathcal{AG}]_\alpha$ and $[\varphi]_\alpha$ from $\mathcal{C}_\alpha$, store $[\mathcal{AG}]_\alpha$ and $[\varphi]_\alpha$.
- When both inputs are received, recover $\mathcal{AG}$ and φ. Compute the secret shares of $\mathcal{AG}_\varphi$ over $\mathbb{Z}_p$. Output $[\mathcal{AG}_\varphi]_\alpha$ to $\mathcal{C}_\alpha$.

Fig. 16. Ideal functionality $\mathcal{F}_{\text{SecAG}}$.

Parameters: s, T, MAX, $\mathbb{Z}_p$.
- On input $[\mathcal{AG}_{\varphi'_1}]_\alpha, ..., [\mathcal{AG}_{\varphi'_s}]_\alpha$ and $[\mathcal{R}]_\alpha$ from $\mathcal{C}_\alpha$, store $[\mathcal{AG}_{\varphi'_1}]_\alpha, ..., [\mathcal{AG}_{\varphi'_s}]_\alpha$ and $[\mathcal{R}]_\alpha$.
- When both inputs are received, recover $\mathcal{AG}_{\varphi'_1}, ..., \mathcal{AG}_{\varphi'_s}$ and $\mathcal{R}$. For each point in $\mathcal{AG}_{\varphi'_1}, ..., \mathcal{AG}_{\varphi'_s}$, if it belongs to $\mathcal{R}$, then add MAX to each dimension of the point. Compute the secret shares of $\mathcal{AG}_{\varphi'_1}, ..., \mathcal{AG}_{\varphi'_s}$ over $\mathbb{Z}_p$. Output $[\mathcal{AG}_{\varphi'_1}]_\alpha, ..., [\mathcal{AG}_{\varphi'_s}]_\alpha$ to $\mathcal{C}_\alpha$.

Fig. 17. Ideal functionality $\mathcal{F}_{\text{SecDedup}}$.

the secret shares of points and their distances are fed to SecSort, and gets back the secret shares of the top-k nearest points. The view generated from simulator is indistinguishable from the real view, and the same applies to $\mathcal{C}_2$. In addition, $\mathcal{DU}$ only receives the query result and learns nothing about other points. Thus, BPPkNN securely implements the functionality $\mathcal{F}_{\text{BPP}k\text{NN}}$. Similarly, we can prove that BPPkNN-bitonic is also secure.

B.3 Proof of Theorem 2

Proof. According to the composition theorem [32], the security of VPPkNN is subject to the security of SecVC, SecAG, SecDedup and BPPkNN which are proved secure in Theorem 3 and Theorem 1. The simulator for $\mathcal{C}_1$ feeds the secret shares of random index and query to SecVC, and forwards the output with the query to BPPkNN. Then, the simulator gets back the secret shares of the first nearest neighbor. To compute the s-th nearest neighbor ($2 \leq s \leq k$), the simulator first feeds the secret shares of index and targeted row number to SecAG, and gets back the secret shares of adjacent generators. Then, the simulator sends the secret shares of adjacent generators and result set to SecDedup, and forwards the output with the query to BPPkNN. The view generated from simulator is indistinguishable from the real view. The simulator for $\mathcal{C}_2$ works in the same fashion. In addition, $\mathcal{DU}$ only obtains the query result. Thus, VPPkNN securely implements the functionality $\mathcal{F}_{\text{VPP}k\text{NN}}$.

References

1. Wong, W. K., Cheung, D. W. L., Kao, B., et al.: Secure KNN computation on encrypted databases. In: SIGMOD, pp. 139–152 (2009)
2. Hu, H., Xu, J., Ren, C., et al.: Processing private queries over untrusted data cloud through privacy homomorphism. In: ICDE, pp. 601–612 (2011)
3. Yao, B., Li, F., Xiao, X.: Secure nearest neighbor revisited. In: ICDE, pp. 733–744 (2013)
4. Wang, B., Hou, Y., Li, M.: Practical and secure nearest neighbor search on encrypted large-scale data. In: INFOCOM, pp. 1–9 (2016)
5. Lei, X., Liu, A. X., Li, R., et al.: SecEQP: a secure and efficient scheme for SkNN query problem over encrypted geodata on cloud. In: ICDE, pp. 662–673 (2019)
6. Lei, X., Tu, G. H., Liu, A. X., et al.: Fast and secure KNN query processing in cloud computing. In: CNS, pp. 1–9 (2020)

7. Li, R., Liu, A.X., Xu, H., et al.: Adaptive secure nearest neighbor query processing over encrypted data. IEEE Trans. Dependable Secure Comput. **19**(1), 91–106 (2020)
8. Asif, H., Vaidya, J., Shafiq, B., et al.: Secure and efficient k-NN queries. In: IFIPAICT, pp. 155–170 (2017). https://doi.org/10.1007/978-3-319-58469-0_11
9. Kim, H.I., Kim, H.J., Chang, J.W.: A secure KNN query processing algorithm using homomorphic encryption on outsourced database. Data Knowl. Eng. **123**, 1–20 (2017)
10. Li, Z., Tian, G., Tan, S.: Secure and efficient k-nearest neighbor query with privacy-preserving authentication. In: SocialSec, pp. 175–198 (2022)
11. Cui, N., Qian, K., Cai, T., et al.: Towards multi-user, secure, and verifiable kNN query in cloud database. IEEE Trans. Knowl. Data Eng. (2023)
12. Ghunaim, T., Kamel, I., Al Aghbari, Z.: Secure kNN query of outsourced spatial data using two-cloud architecture. J. Supercomput. **79**(18), 21310–21345 (2023). https://doi.org/10.1007/s11227-023-05495-7
13. Elmehdwi, Y., Samanthula, B. K., Jiang, W.: Secure k-nearest neighbor query over encrypted data in outsourced environments. In: ICDE, pp. 664–675 (2014)
14. Cui, N., Yang, X., Wang, B., et al.: Svknn: efficient secure and verifiable k-nearest neighbor query on the cloud platform. In: ICDE, pp. 253–264 (2020)
15. Servan-Schreiber, S., Langowski, S., Devadas, S.: Private approximate nearest neighbor search with sublinear communication. In: S&P, pp. 911–929 (2022)
16. Chen, H., Chillotti, I., Dong, Y., et al.: SANNS: scaling up secure approximate k-nearest neighbors search. In: USENIX Security, pp. 2111–2128 (2020)
17. Kellaris, G., Kollios, G., Nissim, K., et al.: Generic attacks on secure outsourced databases. In: CCS, pp. 1329–1340 (2016)
18. Kornaropoulos, E. M., Papamanthou, C., Tamassia, R.: Data recovery on encrypted databases with k-nearest neighbor query leakage. In: S&P, pp. 1033–1050 (2019)
19. Liu, J., Yang, J., Xiong, L., et al.: Secure skyline queries on cloud platform. In: ICDE, pp. 633–644 (2017)
20. Apostol, T.: Introduction to Analytic Number Theory. Springer, Heidelberg (2013)
21. Mertens, F.: Ein beitrag zur analytischen zahlentheorie. Journal für die reine und angewandte Mathematik **78**, 46–62 (1874)
22. Hadamard, J.: Sur la distribution des zéros de la fonction $\zeta(s)$ et ses conséquences arithmétiques. Bulletin de la Societé mathematique de France **24**, 199–220 (1896)
23. Ishmukhametov, S.T., Sharifullina, F.F.: On distribution of semiprime numbers. Russ. Math. **58**(8), 43–48 (2014). https://doi.org/10.3103/S1066369X14080052
24. Beaver, D.: Efficient multiparty protocols using circuit randomization. In: CRYPTO, pp. 420–432 (1991). https://doi.org/10.1007/3-540-46766-1_34
25. Liu, L., Su, J., Liu, X., et al.: Toward highly secure yet efficient KNN classification scheme on outsourced cloud data. IEEE Internet Things J. **6**(6), 9841–9852 (2019)
26. Nishide, T., Ohta, K.: Multiparty computation for interval, equality, and comparison without bit-decomposition protocol. In: PKC, pp. 343–360 (2007)
27. Schneider, T., Zohner, M.: GMW vs. Yao? Efficient secure two-party computation with low depth circuits. In: FC, pp. 275–292 (2013)
28. Rathee, D., Schneider, T., Shukla, K. K.: Improved multiplication triple generation over rings via RLWE-based AHE. In: CANS, pp. 347–359 (2019)
29. Knott, B., Venkataraman, S., Hannun, A., et al.: Crypten: secure multi-party computation meets machine learning. Adv. Neural. Inf. Process. Syst. **34**, 4961–4973 (2021)

30. Cho, E., Myers, S. A., Leskovec, J.: Friendship and mobility: User movement in location-based social networks. In: KDD, pp. 1082–1090 (2011)
31. NIST: Recommendation for key management. Special Publication 800-57 Part 1 Revision 5 (2020)
32. Goldreich, O.: Foundations of Cryptography: Volume 2, Basic Applications. Cambridge university press, vol. 2 (2009)

Breaking Verifiability and Vote Privacy in CHVote

Véronique Cortier, Alexandre Debant[✉], and Pierrick Gaudry

Université de Lorraine, LORIA, INRIA, CNRS, Nancy, France
{veronique.cortier,alexandre.debant,pierrick.gaudry}@loria.fr

Abstract. CHVote is one of the two main electronic voting systems developed in the context of political elections in Switzerland, where the regulation requires a specific setting and specific trust assumptions.

We show that actually, CHVote fails to achieve vote secrecy and individual verifiability (here, recorded-as-intended), as soon as one of the online components is dishonest, contradicting the security claims of CHVote. In total, we found 9 attacks or variants against CHVote, 2 of them being based on a bug in the reference implementation. We confirmed our findings through a proof-of-concept implementation of our attacks.

1 Introduction

Several countries use Internet voting for politically binding elections, at least in trials. This often comes with the discovery of flaws, such as in Australia [21], Estonia [24], Switzerland [14], United States [28], or France [15]. One of the most demanding countries in terms of regulation is Switzerland. The requirements are provided in an ordinance of the Swiss Federal Chancellery [26] and include:

- *vote secrecy*: no one should know how a voter voted;
- *individual verifiability*: when a voter successfully completes their voting session, they must be guaranteed that their vote will be counted, as intended;
- *universal verifiability*: the result corresponds to the recorded ballots.

The ordinance comes with a demanding trust model: trust must be split between different components; some of them being online, others offline. Security goals must be met even if all but one online component are compromised. Moreover, for individual verifiability, the ordinance requires to leverage verification codes to protect against corrupted voting devices. Voters (securely) receive a voting sheet, with a verification code for each candidate. They confirm their ballot only if their voting device is able to display the right verification code, which guarantees that it has encrypted the right vote. This property is called cast-as-intended.

To improve confidence in the system, the Chancellery also asks for a public specification and a public code. Public scrutiny is encouraged through a bug

---

This work benefited from funding managed by the French National Research Agency under the France 2030 programme with the reference ANR-22-PECY-0006.

bounty program and regular intrusion tests. A symbolic and a cryptographic proofs of the protocol are needed before its deployment.

CHVote. Since the last major flaw found in 2019 [14] against a protocol proposed by Scytl, the only system used in practice is the one developed by SwissPost, that is an evolution of the Scytl system. However, in the Swiss landscape, there is a second major proposed protocol, CHVote, the main competitor to the SwissPost protocol. The Canton of Geneva has been developing a voting system since 2003, and it has been used by 125 000 voters in 4 cantons [1]. A second generation of their system, much more secure, has been developed since 2016 [19]. This is the system we refer to when we talk about CHVote. While the funding from the Canton of Geneva has been discontinued in 2018 [2], CHVote is still under continuous development both in terms of specification (20 versions from 2017 to 2024) and reference code (last release of OpenCHVote is 2.3.1 on December 2024), with new funding from the Federal Chancellery in 2024 [20].

The CHVote protocol relies on Oblivious Transfer (OT) [17] in order to achieve cast-as-intended. The idea is natural: the online system as a whole must return the verification code corresponding to the candidate A when receiving an encryption of A, *without learning* A, which is exactly the principle of OT. CHVote then builds upon this idea and extends it in order to distribute the trust among the online components (only one is trusted) and to allow for k-out-of-n OT, in order to cover elections where voters may select up to k candidates among n. CHVote is claimed to fully satisfy the Chancellery requirements.

Our Contributions. We conduct a systematic review of the CHVote protocol and we discovered that it satisfies neither vote secrecy nor individual verifiability, as soon as one online component is dishonest. On the first side, our attack on vote secrecy relies on an issue on the OT primitive used in CHVote. Indeed, it does not protect against *selective failure attack* [10]. Hence a dishonest component may selectively modify one of their (shared) verification codes and see whether the voter can still proceed. If yes, the voter did not vote for the candidate corresponding to the modified code. We show that this attack can be made completely silent (when the voter did not vote for the modified option) in the subsequent phases of the protocol, and undetected by the other (honest) components of the system, including the external auditor.

On the other side, our verifiability attack relies on the fact that CHVote misses an agreement procedure between the online components: they each answer independently, even if they do not share the same view. This can be exploited by a malicious component, collaborating with a dishonest voting device, to register a ballot for B while the voter has selected A and received the corresponding verification code for A. The dishonest component will be able to pretend that it has only seen a ballot for B, and the honest components will silently accept a confirmation phase made of mixed contributions (from ballots for A and B). The inconsistency between the views of the honest and dishonest components will be caught only after the tally, by the external auditor, with no way of distinguishing between the honest and dishonest behaviors.

Moreover, we discovered that the reference implementation of CHVote [3] fails to perform some of the checks mentioned in the specification of the components of the system. We exploit this implementation bug to show that the (first) online component of the system can fully manipulate the received ballots, replacing them by any vote of its choice, without being detected by the other online components of the system. This attack will, again, be detected after the tally, by the external auditor. However, the Chancellery does not assume any honest auditor for the individual verifiability property.

We also considered the case where all online components are dishonest for vote secrecy, as prescribed by the Chancellery when all the online components are operated by the same private company (which is the case in practice). CHVote does not claim any security in this case and, actually, vote secrecy completely collapses in this case since we show that honest but curious online components fully learn who voted what, although they do not have the entirety of the decryption key. Since they do not need to behave maliciously, the attack is undetectable. It simply relies on the fact that the last decryption step, performed by an external offline authority, is missing a round of shuffling, probably due to organizational constraints.

We implemented our main attacks against the reference implementation and confirmed our findings. The attacks that are in the original threat model of CHVote have also been privately acknowledged by the authors and the implementation bug has been corrected accordingly in version 2.4.2. In the last part of this paper, we discuss possible directions on how to fix the CHVote protocol.

Related Work. An attack against individual verifiability was found in 2017 [9], due to the fact that the oblivious transfer primitive did not achieve sender privacy. Hence a dishonest voting device could actually obtain the verification code corresponding to candidate A while encrypting a vote for B. This flaw was fixed in a later version of the specification. Up to our knowledge, no other attack was found against CHVote since then. A symbolic and a cryptographic security proofs have been proposed [8], for verifiability only (no proof for vote secrecy). These proofs fail to catch our verifiability attacks due to the fact that they considered that the counted ballots are the ones registered by the honest online component. This issue however is that it is impossible to identify which component is honest.

2 Overview of CHVote and Trust Model

2.1 Presentation of the Protocol

In the work, we refer to the latest version of the specification at the time of writing, namely the 20-th revision of [20], corresponding to version 4.3. The full protocol supports a wide variety of possibilities, including multiple questions, multiple answers, several counting circles, and even write-ins. To illustrate our attacks, we concentrate on a minimalistic situation, where there is only one question, and the voter must select exactly one voting option among n possibilities.

Cryptography and Notations. We loosely follow the notation system of the specification. Let G be a cyclic group generated by g of prime order q. The protocol relies on ElGamal encryptions in G. If m is a group element, then the encryption of m with public key pk and randomness r is $\mathsf{Enc}^r_{\mathsf{pk}}(m) = (\mathsf{pk}^r m, g^r)$. A list of group elements $p_1, p_2, \ldots, p_n$ encode the n voting options: if the option number s is selected by the voter, the voting client encrypts $m = p_s$.

Various zero-knowledge proofs are used. They are classical proofs of knowledge based on Sigma protocols. In this paper, we denote by π_X a proof of knowledge of X. We use hash as a notation for a cryptographic hash function, and we write short_hash when the output is small, due to usability considerations, and can be brute-forced. We always use the notation $X^{(j)}$ for some data X related to the j-th authority. We denote $[X^{(j)}]_j$ or $[X_j]_j$ a vector of data indexed by j.

Participants. The protocol relies on several authorities:

- **Election administrator (Admin).** It defines the general setting (electoral roll, questions, etc.), and holds a share of the decryption key.
- **Election authorities (EA).** They produce voting material to be sent to voters by postal mail; during the voting phase, they collect the encrypted ballots, and send the verification codes to the voters; each EA also holds a share of the decryption key.
- **Printing authority (Printer).** During the setup, it collects the data from the election authorities, prints them, and sends them to voters by post.
- **Verifier.** This group of third-parties checks that the data at the end of the election is consistent.

Finally, in order to study the cast-as-intended property, it is important to separate the **Voter** from their **Voting client**.

In a typical Swiss situation, the number of Election authorities is 4, but this is not at all fixed in the protocol.

Setup. First, Admin defines the setting, including the n possible voting options, and, together with the EAs, collectively generates a public key pk. Then, for each voter, the j-th EA picks a set of partial verification codes $[M_i^{(j)}]_{1 \leq i \leq n}$, one for each voting option. Upon reception of these, for all i, the Printer hashes each $M_i^{(j)}$ to a short bit string $V_i^{(j)}$, and aggregate them with a xor to produce a verification code vc_i printed on the voter's voting sheet. The EAs also collectively produce the eligibility data $\hat{x} = g^X$, where $X = \sum_j X^{(j)}$ (called voting code in the specification), the confirmation data $\hat{y} = g^Y$, where $Y = \sum_j Y^{(j)}$, and the vote validity data $\hat{z} = g^Z$, where Z can be deduced from the $[M_s^{(j)}]_j$, for any selection s (more details about Z will be given when describing the verifiability attack). The values X and Y are computed by the Printer by aggregating contributions of all the EAs, and printed on the voter's sheet. The EAs know $\hat{x}, \hat{y}$ and $\hat{z}$ for each voter.

Voting Phase. This is a 2-round protocol between the Voter and the EAs, via the Voting client, summarized in Fig. 1. During this phase, the EAs do not communicate with each other. First, the voter gives their eligibility data X and their selected voting option to their Voting client, which encrypts it with pk

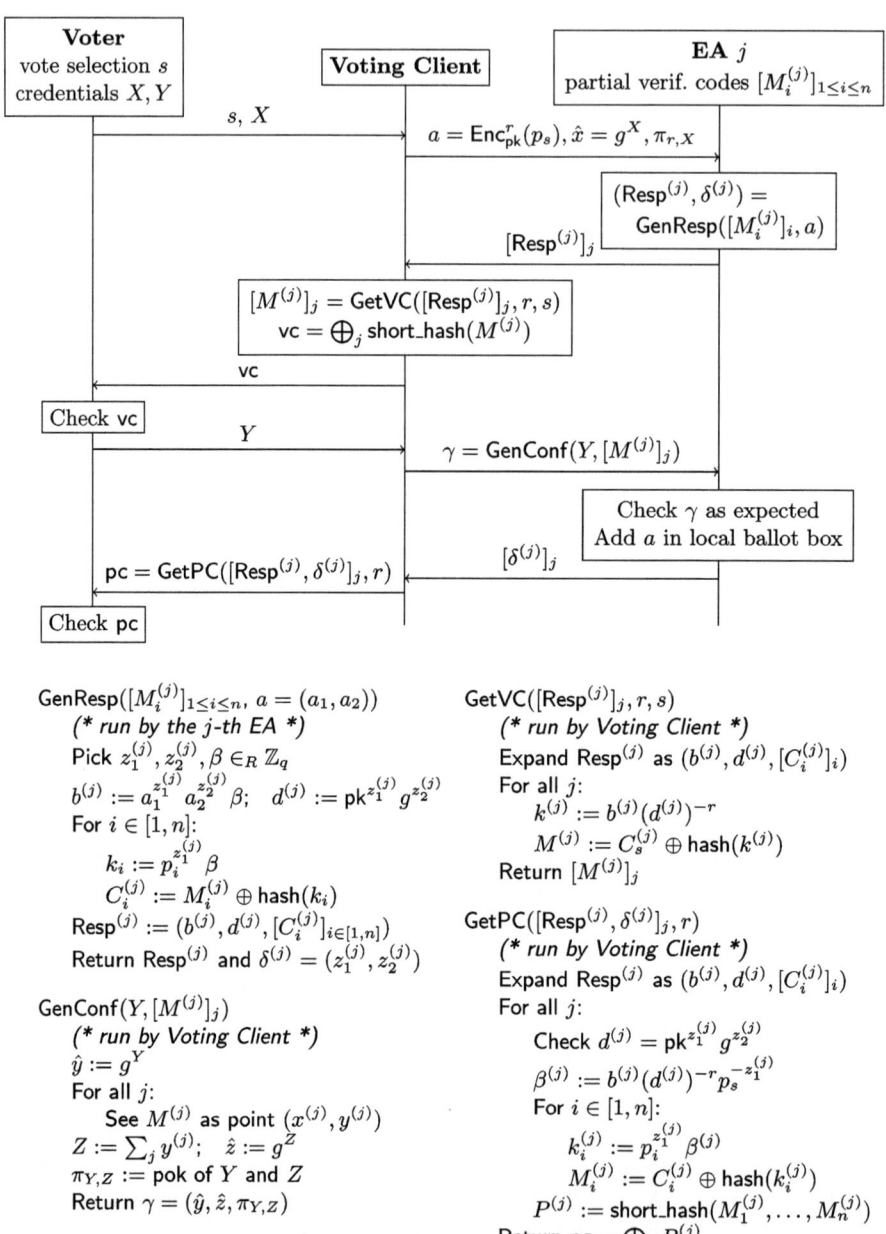

Fig. 1. Overview of the voting phase of the CHVote protocol. This is a simplified version of Protocols 7.6 and 7.7 in [20]. The four algorithms are simplified versions of Algorithms 8.27 to 8.38

and sends it to all the EAs, together with $\hat{x} = g^X$ and a ZKP. The j-th EA does its "sender" part of the OT protocol, and produces n values $[C_i^{(j)}]_{1 \leq i \leq n}$. The tricky part is that the ElGamal ciphertext sent by the Voting client is seen as the "query" part of the OT. From the $[C_i^{(j)}]_i$ and other opening data, the Voting client can compute $[M_s^{(j)}]_j$, and then follow the same procedure as the printer to produce the verification code vc, shown to the Voter.

The Voter checks that the code corresponds to the one printed on paper, and if this is the case, it initiates the second round by giving its confirmation code Y to the Voting client, which can deduce $\hat{y}$ and $\hat{z}$ from it and previously received information. Together with a ZKP, this form γ that is sent to the EAs. Each authority checks that γ corresponds to the values committed during the setup phase. If this is the case, they record the ballot in their (local) ballot box, and then send additional data, so that the Voting client can compute all the partial verification codes, and not only the one corresponding to s. From these, the Voting client deduces a participation code pc, that the Voter can compare to what is printed on their sheet.

Tally Phase. The EAs perform one round of verifiable mixnets, and then one round of partial decryption. Finally, Admin completes its partial decryption, and publishes the result. The Verifier checks that all the data is consistent.

2.2 Trust Model and Security Claims

Security Properties. Like most e-voting protocols, CHVote aims at preserving vote secrecy and verifiability. Verifiability can be defined as three properties:

- *recorded-as-intended*: if a voter has successfully performed all their checks, then they are guaranteed that their ballot is correctly recorded, for the vote they intended.
- *universal verifiability*: the result of the election corresponds to the recorded ballots.
- *eligibility*: recorded ballots only come from voters who have effectively voted.

Recorded-as-intended combines cast-as-intended (the cast ballot corresponds to the voter's intent) and recorded-as-cast (the recorded ballot is the cast one). It is often called individual verifiability in the literature. However, in the Chancellery terminology [26], individual verifiability stands for the combination of recorded-as-intended and eligibility, hence we avoid here the terminology "individual verifiability" to avoid confusion.

Trust Model. In the trust model considered by the Swiss Chancellery, the adversary controls all communications over the Internet. Moreover it controls several authorities depending on the security property.

- One-out-of-4 EAs is assumed to be honest for all properties (privacy and verifiability), except if all EAs are operated by a private company. In the second case, none are trusted for privacy but one-out-of-4 remains trusted for verifiability.

- The Voting client is trusted for vote privacy (since the vote is entered in clear) but untrusted for verifiability.
- The Election administrator is trusted (their share of the decryption key remains secret).
- The Verifier is always trusted as a whole, except for recorded-as-intended. It means that the Swiss Chancellery almost always assumes that at least one third-party will behave honestly and do the expected checks (others can be dishonest; it is of interest in particular for vote privacy). Regarding recorded-as-intended, the Swiss Chancellery considers that the property must hold relying on the voter's checks and the behaviour of the honest trusted authority only.

Discussion on the Trust Model. CHVote is claimed to be secure for the trust model of the Swiss Chancellery ([20], page 13). However, this claim comes with the strong assumption that at least one EA is honest. While this made sense in the original version of the Ordinance, this no longer matches the current state of the Ordinance nor the recent deployments of e-voting in Switzerland, in which a single company (SwissPost) is operating the elections (with distinct servers administered by distinct teams for each EA). In this context, the Chancellery requires that none of the EAs is trusted for vote secrecy.

For verifiability, it is assumed that at least one EA is honest. There is no other choice for recorded-as-intended. Indeed, when all EAs are corrupted, they can collaborate with the Voting client to compute the verification code of any candidate and hence, they can register a ballot for a candidate B while the voter will be convinced to have voted for A. Similarly for universal verifiability, since there is no public bulletin board, colluding malicious EAs can easily drop any ballot they wish. The trust assumption is more questionable for eligibility. Indeed, the voter could have some private data generated during the Setup, used to "sign" a ballot, which would prevent ballot stuffing even if all EAs are dishonest. For example, the protocol developed by SwissPost [27] guarantees eligibility even when the 4 online authorities are compromised. We therefore consider additionally the scenario where all EAs are dishonest for eligibility.

Security Claims and Attacks. We summarize on Table 1 the security claims of the CHVote protocol, namely, both vote secrecy and all three verifiability properties should be satisfied as soon as one EA is honest.

In the remaining of the paper, we show that, actually, both vote secrecy and recorded-as-intended are broken as soon as one EA is dishonest. We provide several variants of our attack against vote secrecy and we propose a fix to make all our vote secrecy attacks detectable. However, our fix no longer works if all EAs are dishonest, which is the trust model considered in actual deployments. Moreover, we show that CHVote is subject to ballot stuffing when all EAs are compromised. While outside the trust model considered by CHVote and the Chancellery, we believe that this is flaw since it could be avoided.

Table 1. Trust model of the Chancellery and attacks on CHVote. In gray : outside the trust model of the Chancellery. D stands for dishonest, H for honest. ≥ 1 means that 1 out 4 authorities is honest and < 4 means that there is at least one dishonest authority. ✘^{I}: attack on the implementation only, not the specification

	CHVote claims			Our findings		
	VD	EAs		VD	EAs	
Vote secrecy						
• base case	H	≥ 1 H	✓	H	< 4 H	1. weak Oblivious Transfer ✘ attack by complaint (Section 3.1) ✘ undetectable attack (Section 3.2) ✘ variant using OT malleability (Section 3.3)
				H	EA$_1$ D	2. missing check for EA_1 ✘^{I} secrecy breach by drop (Section 3.5)
• single priv. comp.	H	all D	–	H	all D	1. + 2. + ✘ full vote disclosure, undetectable (Section 3.6)
Recorded-as-intended	D	≥ 1 H	✓	D	< 4 H	✘ missing consensus algorithm (Section 4.1)
				H	EA$_1$ D	✘^{I} missing check by honest EAs (Section 4.2)
Universal verifiability	D	≥ 1 H	✓	–	–	–
Eligibility						
• base case	H	≥ 1 H	✓	–	–	–
• single priv. comp.	H	all D	–	H	all D	✘ ballot stuffing (Section 4.3) ✘ ballot stuffing, online only (Section 4.3)

3 Vote Secrecy Attacks

3.1 Attack by Complaint

The idea of the attack against vote secrecy is very simple. We assume that one EA is dishonest (say EA$_1$ w.l.o.g.) and wishes to learn how Alice voted. During setup, EA$_1$ has generated partial verification codes $[M_i^{(1)}]_{1 \leq i \leq n}$, for Alice, one for each voting option. EA$_1$ simply modifies one partial verification code, e.g., $M_1^{(1)}$, and observes the behaviour of the voter under attack:

- if Alice did not vote for candidate 1, her voting device will compute the expected verification code and she will be able to proceed, entering her confirmation code.
- if Alice did vote for candidate 1, then her voting device won't produce a valid verification code and Alice will stop voting and will report the incident.

Hence, EA$_1$ can deduce if Alice voted for candidate 1. EA$_1$ can also choose to modify all partial verification codes but $M_1^{(1)}$ if it prefers that Alice does not complain when her vote is guessed correctly. More generally, EA$_1$ can modify any number of its partial verification codes depending on the information it wants to learn.

A protection against this kind of attack is discussed in an early version of CHVote [19]. The goal is to make this attack detectable not only to voters (they complain) but also to the (honest) EAs. This idea relies on a centralized bulletin board and the fact that each EA reveals z_1, z_2 to the bulletin board when sending their contribution to the participation code. However, this approach has not been fully explored in CHVote, that has no central bulletin board.

3.2 Privacy Attack Without Detection

A drawback of the attack explained in the previous section is that, even when the voter receives a correct verification code, they won't be able to complete the voting phase. Indeed, the participation code pc computed by their voting device is a function of the list of the partial verification codes $[M_i^{(1)}]_{1 \leq i \leq n}$ received during the first phase. Hence, if a malicious EA tampered with their partial verification codes, pc will be modified. We show that if a malicious EA (say EA_1) correctly guessed Alice's vote so that she did not complain while EA_1 modified some of the $[M_i^{(1)}]$ then it is possible to improve the attack so that Alice successfully completes her voting session, while she has lost vote secrecy.

Pre-image. The attack relies on the fact that the contribution of each EA is hashed to a short element *before* being xor-ed together. Indeed, the participation code pc equals $\bigoplus_j P^{(j)}$ where each $P^{(j)}$ is a contribution of EA_j: $P^{(j)} := \mathsf{short\_hash}(M_1^{(j)}, \ldots, M_n^{(j)})$. Since short_hash outputs a string with an entropy up to 24 bits according to the specification, it is very easy to perform a brute-force search and find a second pre-image with another value of $M_1^{(1)}$ giving the same code.

Hence a malicious EA_1 can modify $M_1^{(1)}$ into M_1', to conduct the attack explained in the previous section, in such a way that

$$\mathsf{short\_hash}(M_1^{(1)}, M_2^{(1)}, \ldots, M_n^{(1)}) = \mathsf{short\_hash}(M_1', M_2^{(1)}, \ldots, M_n^{(1)}) \quad (1)$$

This lets pc unchanged, hence neither Alice nor her voting device can detect the manipulation. None of the honest EAs will detect the manipulation either, which leads to a secrecy loss, without any detection. A more detailed explanation of the attack can be found in Appendix (Fig. 3).

Collision. One advantage of the previous attack is that it is sufficient to corrupt the dishonest authority during the voting phase, hence when it is an online server, offering a large attack surface. However, if the dishonest authority is corrupted from the setup phase, then it is possible to speed-up the search for collisions using the Birthday paradox: EA_1 will search for two values $M_1^{(1)}$ and M_1', such that Eq. (1) holds. This way, a collision will be found in an (asymptotic) expected number of trials $\sqrt{\pi \ell / 2}$ instead of ℓ, where ℓ is the number of possible participation codes. This can be useful to attack many voters, and also shows that mitigations based on enlarging the length of the code are probably unrealistic.

3.3 Attack Variants

We provide a variant of our attack that exploits the malleability of the OT primitive. This variant does not provide a more powerful attack but shows that the OT primitive would require an in-depth modification to prevent our attack.

Harmless Malleability. We first notice that a malicious authority EA_j can apply a different algorithm for GenResp, without any change in the protocol behavior. In particular, it can chose $z_1 = z_2$ and, for any m_{att}, replace a_1 by $a'_1 = a_1 m_{\mathsf{att}}^{-1}$ and a_2 by $a'_2 = a_2 m_{\mathsf{att}}$ without any noticeable change. Indeed, in the second line of GenResp, the normal computation is $b^{(j)} := a_1^{z_1} a_2^{z_2} \beta$. If instead, the dishonest EA computes $b^{(j)}$ as $b^{(j)} := a'^{z_1}_1 a'^{z_2}_2 \beta = a_1^{z_1} a_2^{z_2} \beta (m_{\mathsf{att}})^{z_2 - z_1} = a_1^{z_1} a_2^{z_2} \beta$ if $z_1 = z_2$.

This does not lead to any attack but it highlights the fact that a security proof would require to characterize complex harmless adversarial behaviors.

Harmful Malleability. This malleability can be turned into an effective attack against secrecy. A dishonest EA may use the following algorithm to generate its response, where we highlight the changes in yellow :

GenResp$'([M_i^{(j)}]_{1 \leq i \leq n}, a = (a_1, a_2))$
  Pick $z_1, z_2, \beta \in_R \mathbb{Z}_q$
  $b^{(j)} := (a_1 \, p_{\mathsf{att}}^{-1})^{z_1} (a_2 \, p_{\mathsf{att}})^{z_2} \beta; \quad d^{(j)} := \mathsf{pk}^{z_1} g^{z_2}$ (* p_{att} *chosen by EA* *)
  For $i \in [1, n]$:
    $k_i := p_i^{z_2} \beta$ (* *instead of* $k_i := p_i^{z_1} \beta$ *)
    $C_i^{(j)} := M_i^{(j)} \oplus \mathsf{hash}(k_i)$
  Resp$^{(j)} := (b^{(j)}, d^{(j)}, [C_i^{(j)}]_{i \in [1, n]})$
  Return Resp$^{(j)}$ and $\delta^{(j)} = (z_1, z_2)$

Then, when the voting client computes the verification code corresponding to the sent ballot $(a_1, a_2) = (\mathsf{pk}^r p_s, g^r)$, it computes in particular:

$$k^{(j)} := b^{(j)} (d^{(j)})^{-r} = (a_1 p_{\mathsf{att}}^{-1})^{z_1} (a_2 p_{\mathsf{att}})^{z_2} \beta \mathsf{pk}^{-rz_1} g^{-rz_2}$$
$$= \mathsf{pk}^{-rz_1} p_s^{z_1} g^{rz_2} p_{\mathsf{att}}^{z_2 - z_1} \beta \mathsf{pk}^{-rz_1} g^{-rz_2}$$
$$= p_s^{z_1} p_{\mathsf{att}}^{z_2 - z_1} \beta.$$

– Either the voter voted for the candidate att guessed by the attacker, in which case $k^{(j)} = p_{\mathsf{att}}^{z_2} \beta$, as computed by the dishonest EA;
– or the voter voted for another candidate and $k^{(j)}$ computed by the voter won't correspond to the one used by EA and the vc will be an arbitrary random value.

We hence retrieve the same kind of attack than the one in Sect. 3.1.

3.4 Mitigation

An obvious mitigation is to compute the short_hash only at the end, that is, $\mathsf{pc} = \mathsf{short\_hash}(\bigoplus_j Q^{(j)})$ where $Q^{(j)} := \mathsf{hash}(M_1^{(j)}, \ldots, M_n^{(j)})$. This does not fix the vote secrecy attack explained in Sect. 3.1, but at least, all voters under attack will detect an issue during the confirmation phase.

We note however that this mitigation is insufficient when all EAs are dishonest since they could again find collisions that let pc unchanged. The only counter-measure to keep this mitigation is to increase the size of pc to 256 bits (to avoid the square root attacks relying on the Birthday paradox). This would however cause usability issues.

3.5 Attack by Drop

In the reference implementation [3], we noticed an implementation bug that offers another type of vote secrecy attack, namely, the proof of shuffle performed by EA_1 (specifically) is never verified by the other EAs. The specification somehow assumes that an EA receives the shuffle information from the others in the correct order, but the implementation has to take care of the fact that they can be re-ordered. Therefore the code uses the following greedy strategy: when receiving a shuffle from EA number j, then it checks whether data number $j-1$ is available and if so, checks the ZKP, and it does the same with data number $j+1$. This typically leads to off-by-one issues that must be carefully addressed. In the present case, when checking data number $j-1$, it was also checking whether the ZKP number $j-1$ was available, instead of of the ZKP number j (i.e. the one that relates a shuffle between $j-1$ and j). Concretely, in file S400.java, in the first test get_bold_pi_tilde().isPresent(k - 1), the value $k-1$ should be replaced by k. And actually, testing the presence of the ZKP is maybe useless.

Since the shuffle of EA_1 is not verified, EA_1 may actually drop some of the ballots, reducing the anonymity set. For example, in an extreme case, it could remove all ballots except Alice's ballot, wait for decryption, and learn Alice's vote. Even when EA_1 only remove some of the ballots, this forms a theoretical attack since it would learn another information than the expected tally. This attack would in particular break existing definitions of vote secrecy [6,7,16] and hence forbid a security proof. Note that this attack will be detected by the Verifier but too late, since the ballots are already decrypted when the Verifier checks the election data.

We describe a more dramatic exploit of this bug in Sect. 4.2.

Discussion. When the Chancellery has introduced the requirement that the system remains secure even when all EAs are dishonest, in case they are operated by a single private company, they have also excluded the attack by drop we just described (see 2.7.2 of [26]). Indeed, this attack is unavoidable when all EAs are dishonest, since they may always drop ballot. We see however no reason to tolerate such attacks when at least one EA is honest.

3.6 Full Vote Disclosure

When the EAs are operated by a single company, which corresponds to "real-world setting within the Swiss context" according to the CHVote specification ([27], page 59), then the Chancellery requires that vote secrecy still holds when the EAs are all dishonest.

Unfortunately, vote secrecy completely collapses in CHVote in this threat model. Indeed, each EA holds a share of the decryption key, while the last share is owned by the Administrator, operated by another entity (typically, a Canton). However, the Administrator decrypts the ballots *without shuffling them*. Hence, the EAs learn exactly who voted what, for all voters, in a honest but curious setting. They simply need to remember how they shuffled the ballots. Since they do not even need to conduct any active attack, the loss of vote secrecy (for the entire set of voters) is undetectable.

4 Verifiability Attacks

4.1 Breaking Recorded-as-Intended

One dishonest EA collaborating with a dishonest voting client is actually sufficient to break recorded-as-intended. More precisely, a voter can successfully complete their voting procedure for a candidate s while their vote will not be counted. This contradicts the security claim that "the voter is given proofs [...] to confirm that no attacker has altered any partial vote before the vote has been registered as cast in conformity with the system" [26].

The attack relies on the fact that there is no consensus between the EAs: they respond independently, even if they do not receive the same encrypted vote. Moreover, we realized that the confirmation phase is completely independent of the vote of the voter.

The idea of the attack is simple and is depicted in Fig. 2. When the voter selects candidate s, the (dishonest) voting client actually prepares two ballots: $a = \text{Enc}_{\text{pk}}^{r}(p_s)$ and $a' = \text{Enc}_{\text{pk}}^{r'}(p_{s'})$ where s' is the candidate chosen by the attacker. The honest EAs are given a, while the dishonest EA gets both a and a'. The honest EAs respond normally. The dishonest EA provides 2 responses: one computed from a, such that the voting client can compute the expected verification code vc. But it also computes the response from a'. This way, the dishonest authority will behave "honestly" (e.g., regarding its logs), as if it had only received the ballot a'. We then notice that γ computed by the voting client and the δ^j sent by the EAs do not depend on the ballot a, as explained in Appendix B. Hence, the rest of the confirmation procedure continues normally and the voter successfully receives their participation code.

At the end of the voting phase, the EAs have inconsistent views: the honest EAs have seen a while the dishonest EA will claim to have seen a'. But their transcript are made of purely honestly computed data so it is impossible to detect who misbehaved. Since CHVote does not provide any agreement procedure, the system simply crashes in this case, so our attack is detectable. Yet, it breaches the security claim since it results in a "manipulation [of the vote] that goes undetected by the voter but not by the system" (explanation of the rewarded attacks in the bug bounty program [4] organized for the Swiss Post protocol).

4.2 Full Vote Manipulation, Due to a Missing Check

There is actually a simpler attack, due to the implementation bug explained in Sect. 3.5. Indeed, since the shuffle performed by the first EA is never verified, EA_1

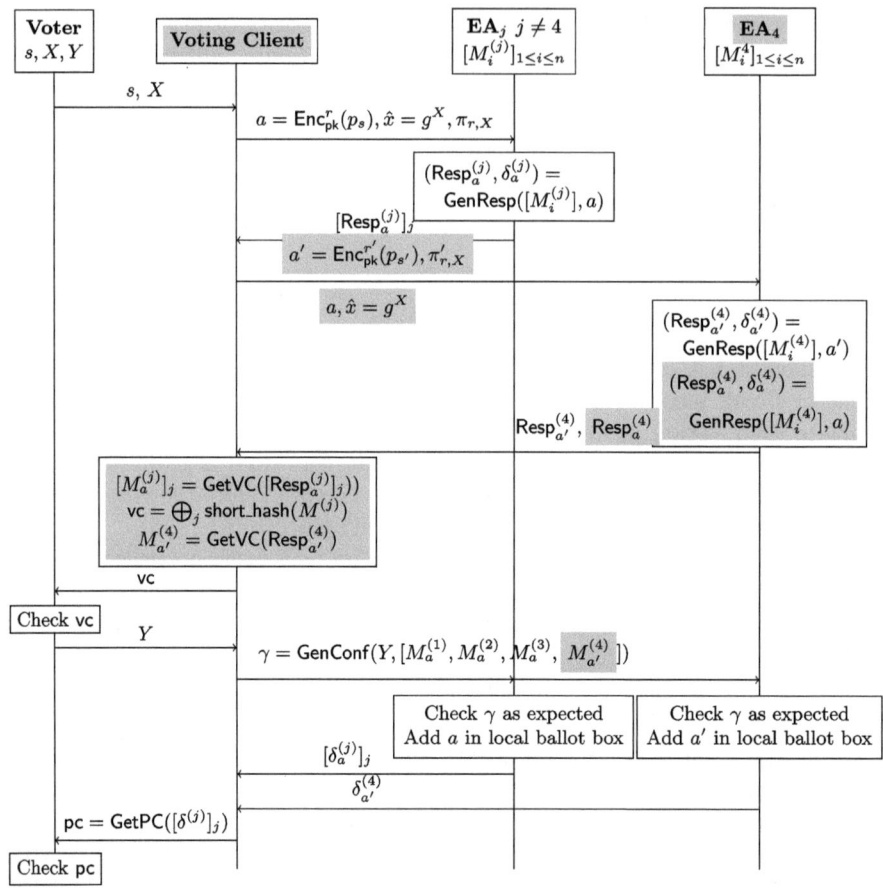

Fig. 2. Attack against individual verifiability (recorded-as-intended). We arbitrarily assign the dishonest authority to EA_4. Dishonest steps are written in yellow (Color figure online)

does not even need to collaborate with corrupted voting devices to change the votes. The attack works as follows:

- during the voting phase, EA_1 behaves normally,
- during the tally, instead of shuffling, EA_1 produces a novel list of ElGamal ciphertexts, for candidates of their choice, with an empty proof of shuffling,
- this manipulation is undetected by the other three (honest) EAs.

This attack will be detected, after the publication of the result, by the Verifier. However, the Chancellery does not assume an honest Verifier for the recorded-as-intended property. This attack is very easy to fix, by forcing the EAs to check all the proofs of shuffle.

4.3 Ballot Stuffing

Each voter needs two secret credentials X and Y to cast a vote. The EAs have collectively computed these secret credentials and stored the corresponding public credentials $\hat{x} = g^X$ and $\hat{y} = g^Y$. Obviously, if they are all compromised, they can cast a vote on behalf of a voter using X and Y. Such an attack is outside the security model in Switzerland because eligibility is part of a larger set of properties (called universal verifiability) and hence they assume that at least one EA is honest. We believe that this assumption is too strong for eligibility and can be avoided, as it is done in the SwissPost protocol [27].

In the rest of this section, we show that actually, the online components can break eligibility, that is, can add ballots, even if the (offline) setup phase is run honestly and the secret shares of X and Y are erased. This leads to a more powerful attack since online components are more vulnerable to attacks. Even if outside the official security model, we believe that such a weakness should be avoided. Moreover, our attacks reveal some missing checks in the verification algorithm, that could be easily added.

Our attack assumes a dishonest voter and all dishonest EAs. Given the credentials X and Y of one dishonest voter, the EAs can forge several ballots $b_1, \ldots, b_k$ corresponding to this voter. When providing the audit data to the Verifier, the EA are supposed to give the list of public credentials $\hat{x}_1, \ldots, \hat{x}_n$ and $\hat{y}_1, \ldots, \hat{y}_n$ of the n voters. Instead, they can replace the credentials of absentee voters (say $\hat{x}_1, \ldots, \hat{x}_k$) by $\hat{x}, \ldots, \hat{x}$ replicated k times and similarly for the credentials $\hat{y}$. They can then add $b_1, \ldots, b_k$ as the first k ballots of the election.

This attack is not caught by the Verifier due to two shortcomings:

- The online EAs share their views of the protocol with the Verifier only once, at the very end of the protocol (see [20, Section 7.5]). Instead, authorities should commit to their data as soon as possible: once after the setup (with the public credentials), once after the voting phase, and once after tally.
- The Verifier does not check that the credentials are pairwise distinct (see [20, Algorithm 8.54]).

5 Experiments

The CHVote designers provide OpenCHVote [3], a reference implementation of the protocol. For our experiments, we used the latest release 2.3.1. This project also contains a simulator to easily set-up test elections and run experiments. We leveraged this implementation to demonstrate the validity of our attacks.

OpenCHVote. OpenCHVote is a Java project organised as a multimodule Maven project to ease its compilation. Even if it is a large project made of dozens of thousands of lines of code, it was easy to navigate between the different modules, packages, files, and identify the key classes that implement the algorithms of interest. Indeed, the code is perfectly aligned with the protocol specification [20]:

there is one module per role, one class per task (i.e. atomic step of the protocol identified in the flow charts), and one class per algorithm or sub-algorithm.

Instrumentation. We instrumented the source code to test the validity of our main attacks, i.e. Sections 3.1, 3.2, 4.1, 4.2. The instrumented source code is available at [5] for reproducibility. Our changes are twofold: first, we implemented the Byzantine behaviours of the dishonest parties in the different attack scenarios as variants of the different algorithms and sub-algorithms. Second, we relaxed the checks done by the different parties to prevent early aborts in attack scenarios for which the attack is known to be detectable. Instead of aborting, we extended the output of the simulator to precisely identify which check fails. Finally, we provide a script that can be used to run our different attacks and observe the behaviour of the system. We also observed that fixing the off-by-one bug made the corresponding attacks disappear.

Results. We managed to reproduce the attacks and confirm the undetectability of the claimed ones. The compilation and the simulations run in a few minutes on a standard laptop (i.e. Apple M2 Pro with 32GB RAM). Computationally-wise, the most critical parts lie in the privacy attack described in Sect. 3.2. Indeed, this requires to compute a collision for the short_hash($\cdot$) function. In our experiments, the code performs about 10,000 iterations per second, where an iteration prepares a sequence of $[M_i]_i$ and computes the short_hash. The attack based on second preimage requires about 65500 iterations, hence 6.5 s, (avg. on 10,000 tests) which remains reasonable to be computed on the fly. As expected, looking for a collision is more efficient and requires only 319 iterations, hence 0.032s, (avg. on 10,000 tests). These numbers are consistent with the theoretical estimates based on the security parameter: this last was set to Level_1 during our experiments meaning that the participation code pc was a 5-digits long code (i.e. belongs to $\{0,\ldots,9\}^5$). This would correspond to an entropy of 16.66 bits, but due to byte-level rounding in the implementation, this is just 16 bits, which is consistent with our experimental measurements.

6 Discussion

We have shown a variety of serious attacks against CHVote. According to the bug bounty program [4] organized for the Swiss Post protocol (which, of course, does not apply to CHVote), our two attacks against recorded-as-intended would have been rewarded between 50 to 70 kE each, while our family of attacks against vote secrecy would be valued between 40 to 50kE. Some of our attacks are easily fixable, others require more in-depth modifications that we discuss here.

Missing Agreement Procedure. As shown in Sect. 4.1, the system may reach a state in which the different EAs do not agree on the list of the ballots to be included in the tally. Since the views of each EA look like honest ones, it seems impossible to define an agreement procedure to solve this inconsistency without changing the protocol. SwissPost encountered the exact same problem in 2022 and updated their protocol to solve it. A similar idea could be re-used in CHVote.

Informally, the fix consists in adding a round of "commitments" during the voting phase to ensure that the EAs agree on the ballot that will be eventually counted during the tally for each voter. Then an EA can convince a third-party that a ballot must be included in the tally by proving the knowledge of a commitment from all EAs. Of course, such a change in the protocol deserves a formal analysis of its effectiveness and impact on the security of the protocol.

Fixing Oblivious Transfer. We already discussed some possible mitigations to make our attack detectable for vote privacy, although it does not suffice when all EAs are dishonest. However, a detectable attack against vote secrecy remains an attack: if voters complain when they receive an incorrect verification code, their vote may be leaked to a malicious EA, which is not acceptable in the current threat model. Note that CHVote does not provide a mechanism to (provably) identify the misbehaving entity and this is a tricky issue since a voter may also make mistakes or intentionally complain without any reasons.

The discovered vulnerability on CHVote is known as a *selective failure attack* in OT literature [10]. Fixing the protocol would require an in-depth modification of the protocol. The first idea is to use *committed oblivious transfer* [12,13] so that an EA cannot later modify their M_j. The idea of committed oblivious transfer is that the sender (each EA in our protocol) commits their secrets commit(M_1, r_1), ..., commit(M_n, r_n), the receiver (the voter) commits to their choice i with commit(i, r) and at the end of the protocol, it obtains a commitment commit(M_i, u) with the opening u, where each party proves that they behaved as expected. The first proposals by Crépeau [12,13] were inefficient but several more efficient protocols have been proposed later on [18,22,23]. However, the setting in evoting is particular since the voter is not present during the setup. For example, [22,23] assume that the receiver (i.e. voter here) has a private key, which may be difficult to establish in the evoting context. Moreover, since the voters may choose k-out-of-n candidates, the 1-out-of-2 oblivious transfer protocol needs to be turned into k-out-of-n [25], as already done in CHVote but not for committed oblivious transfer. In addition, there is not a single sender but it needs to be distributed over the 4 Election authorities, among which 3 are fully dishonest (and not semi-dishonest as incorrectly assumed in CHVote [11]). To summarize, all the needed building blocks seem to be available in the literature but the design of an OT protocol suitable in the evoting context will require a careful design and may affect the overall efficiency of the protocol.

Security Proof. The OT primitive used in CHVote has been modified after a first attack against cast-as-intended [9]. Our attack against recorded-as-cast shows that the verifiability proof published in 2018 [8] does not cover the agreement phase that should tell which ballots are tallied. Indeed, the proof assumes that the honest EA is known *a priori* by the system. More importantly, no privacy proof has ever been conducted on CHVote, while this protocol uses an OT primitive in a crafted way (not blackbox). For example, it embeds an ElGamal encryption inside the OT. Moreover, it extends the OT with subsequent exchanges (confirmation code and participation code) that have an impact on the security. For example, our vote secrecy attack could be detectable with longer codes.

Therefore, a proof of vote secrecy appears to be critical to assess the security of future versions of CHVote. A challenging aspect of the proof will be to identify if the usual security property of OT (here receiver privacy) is indeed sufficient for vote secrecy as a whole.

Conflict of Interest. The authors are collaborating with SwissPost through research contracts between the company and their (academic) research laboratory. SwissPost is a Swiss company developing and selling the evoting system currently in use in Switzerland for local and federal elections. This work has been performed outside the time dedicated to these contracts; the results, views and opinions presented in the paper are those of the authors alone.

A Privacy Attack

We provide a detailed description of our attack in Fig. 3.

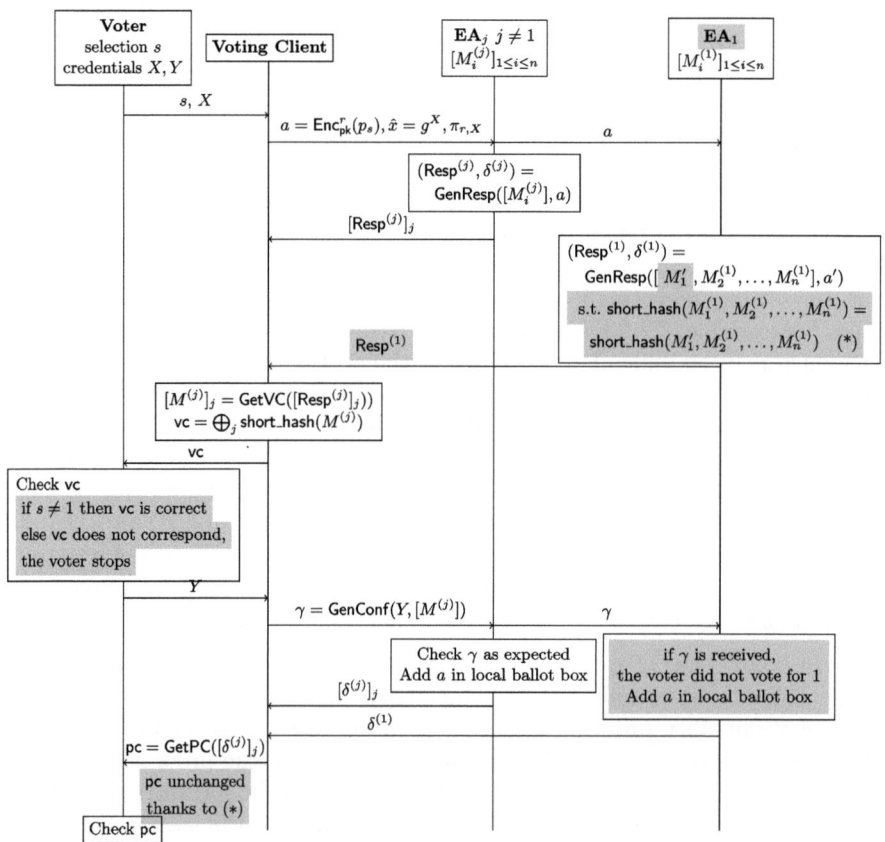

Fig. 3. Privacy attack by (non) complaint, undetectable

B Recorded-as-Intended Attack for an Arbitrary Number k of Selections

For the sake of clarity, we have presented CHVote in the simple case where voters select $k = 1$ candidate among n possible choices. We now explain the general case, with an arbitrary number of selections $k \leq n$. The corresponding algorithms, in a simplified version, are displayed in Fig. 4. This leaves our attack against recorded-as-intended, presented in Sect. 4.1, unchanged.

Setup. Each EA generates partial verification codes $[M_i^{(j)}]_{1 \leq i \leq n}$ as follows: for each voter they first pick some random polynomial $A^{(j)}$ of degree $k - 1$ and then generate n random points $M_i^{(j)} = (x_i, y_i)$ where x_i is a random value and $y_i = A^{(j)}(x_i)$. This corresponds to Algorithm GenPoints (Algorithm 8.11 of [20]).

The EAs also collectively compute $Z_v = \prod_j g^{A^{(j)}(0)}$, used during the confirmation phase to check that it corresponds to the second component Z of γ.

Confirmation Phase. During the confirmation phase, the voting client obtains k partial verification codes, hence k points of each polynomial $A^{(j)}$. It then uses a Lagrange interpolation to compute $A^{(j)}(0)$ and can deduce $Z = g^{\sum_j A^{(j)}(0)}$. The resulting GenConf algorithm is displayed in Fig. 4, it corresponds to Algorithms 8.32 and 8.33 of [20].

The interesting point for our attack is that $A^{(j)}(0)$ does not depend on the exact points received during the first step of the voting phase. In particular $A^{(j)}(0)$ remains identical whether it has been computed thanks to the ballot a or a' (using the notations of Sect. 4.1).

GenPoints(n, k) (* run by the j-th EA *)
  Pick $A^{(j)} \in_R \mathbb{Z}_q[X]$ random polynomial of degree $k - 1$
  For $i \in [1, n]$:
    $x_i \in_R \mathbb{Z}_q$
    $y_i := A^{(j)}(x_i)$
    $M_i^{(j)} := (x_i, y_i)$
  Return $[M_i^{(j)}]_j$ and $y_0 := A^{(j)}(0)$

GenConf$(Y, [M^{(j)}]_j)$ (* run by Voting Client *)
  $\hat{y} := g^Y$
  For all j:
    See the k codes $M_i^{(j)}$ as point (x_i, y_i) $z^{(j)} := \sum_{i=1}^{k} y_i \prod_{j=1, j \neq i}^{k} \frac{x_j}{x_j - x_i}$
    (* ie $z^{(j)} := A^{(j)}(0)$ *)
  $Z := \sum_j z^{(j)}$; $\hat{z} := g^Z$
  $\pi_{Y,Z} :=$ pok of Y and Z
  Return $\gamma = (\hat{y}, \hat{z}, \pi_{Y,Z})$

Fig. 4. Generation of the partial verification codes and of the confirmation response for an arbitrary number k of selections

References

1. E-voting system - CHVote - Canton de Genève. https://republique-et-canton-de-geneve.github.io/chvote-1-0/index-fr.html. Accessed Dec 2024
2. Point presse du conseil d'etat du 28 novembre 2018 (2018). https://www.ge.ch/document/point-presse-du-conseil-etat-du-28-novembre-2018#extrait-12897
3. OpenCHVote. Version 2.3.1 (2024). https://gitlab.com/openchvote
4. Policy for the Swiss Post E-Voting public bug bounty programme (2024). https://yeswehack.com/programs/swiss-post-evoting
5. Source code artefact for reproducibility (2025). https://homepages.loria.fr/PGaudry/openchvote-2.3.1-attacks.zip. Instrumented version of OpenCHVote 2.3.1
6. Benaloh, J.: Verifiable secret-ballot elections. Ph.D. thesis, Yale University (1987)
7. Bernhard, D., Cortier, V., Galindo, D., Pereira, O., Warinschi, B.: A comprehensive analysis of game-based ballot privacy definitions. In: 36th IEEE Symposium on Security and Privacy (S&P 2015) (2015)
8. Bernhard, D., Cortier, V., Gaudry, P., Turuani, M., Warinschi, B.: Verifiability analysis of CHVote. Cryptology ePrint Archive, Paper 2018/1052 (2018)
9. Brelle, A., Truderung, T.: Cast-as-intended mechanism with return codes based on PETs. In: E-Vote-ID 2017 (2017)
10. Camenisch, J., Neven, G., Shelat, A.: Simulatable adaptive oblivious transfer. In: Naor, M. (ed.) EUROCRYPT 2007. LNCS, vol. 4515, pp. 573–590. Springer, Heidelberg (2007). https://doi.org/10.1007/978-3-540-72540-4_33
11. Chu, C.-K., Tzeng, W.-G.: Efficient k-out-of-n oblivious transfer schemes with adaptive and non-adaptive queries. In: Vaudenay, S. (ed.) PKC 2005. LNCS, vol. 3386, pp. 172–183. Springer, Heidelberg (2005). https://doi.org/10.1007/978-3-540-30580-4_12
12. Crépeau, C.: Verifiable disclosure of secrets and applications (abstract). In: Quisquater, J.-J., Vandewalle, J. (eds.) EUROCRYPT 1989. LNCS, vol. 434, pp. 150–154. Springer, Heidelberg (1990). https://doi.org/10.1007/3-540-46885-4_17
13. Crépeau, C., Graaf, J., Tapp, A.: Committed oblivious transfer and private multi-party computation. In: Coppersmith, D. (ed.) CRYPTO 1995. LNCS, vol. 963, pp. 110–123. Springer, Heidelberg (1995). https://doi.org/10.1007/3-540-44750-4_9
14. Culnane, C., Essex, A., Lewis, S.J., Pereira, O., Teague, V.: Knights and knaves run elections: internet voting and undetectable electoral fraud. IEEE Secur. Priv. (2019)
15. Debant, A., Hirschi, L.: Reversing, breaking, and fixing the French legislative election e-voting protocol. In: USENIX Security Symposium 2023 (2023)
16. Delaune, S., Kremer, S., Ryan, M.: Verifying privacy-type properties of electronic voting protocols. J. Comput. Secur. **17** (2009)
17. Even, S., Goldreich, O., Lempel, A.: A randomized protocol for signing contracts. Commun. ACM **28**(6), 637–647 (1985)
18. Garay, J.A.: Efficient and universally composable committed oblivious transfer and applications. In: First Theory of Cryptography Conference, TCC (2004)
19. Haenni, R., Koenig, R.E., Dubuis, E.: Cast-as-intended verification in electronic elections based on oblivious transfer. In: Electronic Voting - First International Joint Conference, E-Vote-ID (2016)
20. Haenni, R., Koenig, R.E., Locher, P., Dubuis, E.: CHVote protocol specification. Cryptology ePrint Archive, Paper 2017/325 (2017). Version 4.3, 13 December 2024

21. Halderman, J.A., Teague, V.: The New South Wales iVote system: security failures and verification flaws in a live online election. In: Haenni, R., Koenig, R.E., Wikström, D. (eds.) VOTELID 2015. LNCS, vol. 9269, pp. 35–53. Springer, Cham (2015). https://doi.org/10.1007/978-3-319-22270-7_3
22. Jarecki, S., Shmatikov, V.: Efficient two-party secure computation on committed inputs. In: Naor, M. (ed.) EUROCRYPT 2007. LNCS, vol. 4515, pp. 97–114. Springer, Heidelberg (2007). https://doi.org/10.1007/978-3-540-72540-4_6
23. Kiraz, M.S., Schoenmakers, B., Villegas, J.: Efficient committed oblivious transfer of bit strings. In: Garay, J.A., Lenstra, A.K., Mambo, M., Peralta, R. (eds.) ISC 2007. LNCS, vol. 4779, pp. 130–144. Springer, Heidelberg (2007). https://doi.org/10.1007/978-3-540-75496-1_9
24. Mueller, J.: Breaking and fixing vote privacy of the Estonian e-voting protocol IVXV. In: Workshop on Advances in Secure Electronic Voting (2022)
25. Naor, M., Pinkas, B.: Oblivious transfer with adaptive queries. In: Wiener, M. (ed.) CRYPTO 1999. LNCS, vol. 1666, pp. 573–590. Springer, Heidelberg (1999). https://doi.org/10.1007/3-540-48405-1_36
26. Swiss Federal Chancellery: Federal Chancellery Ordinance on Electronic Voting (OEV) (2022). https://www.fedlex.admin.ch/eli/cc/2022/336/en
27. Swiss Post: Swiss Post voting system: System specification. version 1.4.0. Technical report, Swiss Post, February 2024
28. Wolchok, S., Wustrow, E., Isabel, D., Halderman, J.A.: Attacking the Washington, D.C. internet voting system. In: Keromytis, A.D. (ed.) FC 2012. LNCS, vol. 7397, pp. 114–128. Springer, Heidelberg (2012). https://doi.org/10.1007/978-3-642-32946-3_10

Zero-Click SnailLoad: From Minimal to No User Interaction

Stefan Gast[1(✉)], Nora Puntigam[1], Simone Franza[1],
Sudheendra Raghav Neela[1], Daniel Gruss[1], and Johanna Ullrich[2]

[1] Graz University of Technology, Graz, Austria
{stefan.gast,sudheendra.neela,daniel.gruss}@tugraz.at,
{nora.puntigam,simone.franza}@student.tugraz.at
[2] University of Vienna, Vienna, Austria
johanna.ullrich@univie.ac.at

Abstract. Network side channel often rely on privileged attacker positions, e.g., physical proximity, person-in-the-middle scenarios, or code on the victim machine. Recent fully remote attacks without a privileged position are either easily mitigated (e.g., ICMP pings) or require minimal user interaction (e.g., SnailLoad).

In this paper, we reduce user interaction in fully remote network side-channel attacks in two directions: First, we analyze 21 communication tools that automatically establish connections without user interaction with external references. We identify privacy-concerning automated behavior for 4 out of 11 messengers and 6 out of 10 email clients, leaking victim IP addresses without user interaction, undermining end-to-end encryption, and even enabling remote SnailLoad attacks without user interaction. Second, we show that even without any specific client software, merely processing TCP packets can already enable zero-click attacks. We introduce a novel latency measurement method based on TCP SYN packets, exploiting that TCP SYN packets to a closed port either lead to a timeout or, in our experiments about once per second, an ICMP-based response. Timing these responses yields a coarse SnailLoad trace, sufficient to mount a video fingerprinting attack with an F_1 score of 56% compared to 89% on a similar Internet connection and the same number of videos as prior work. Thus, our findings confirm in both directions that fully automated side-channel attacks without user interaction are feasible and posing a relevant privacy threat.

Keywords: Network side channel · Video fingerprinting · Timing

1 Introduction

Network side channels exploit observable features such as packet timings, sizes, the number of transmitted packets, and other metadata [2,17,19,22,28,36,37,39, 50,60,61,67], inferring sensitive information, including streamed videos [20,57] or accessed websites [3,10,20,21,47,58,62,66,73], content from voice communications [76], or sensitive personal details such as medical and financial information [14]. Traditionally, most attacks have relied on passive monitoring from within the same network or through attacker-controlled infrastructure along the communication path.

Only recently, some works have considered fully remote attack scenarios, where attackers measure latency exclusively from their own network packets [20,46,48]. For example, Murdoch and Danezis [48] demonstrated that network latency variations could reveal activities of a Tor relay node, while Gast et al. [20] showed how attackers could deduce victim website and video accesses solely from observed latency traces between attacker and victim. Fully remote attacks represent a significantly greater threat, as they require minimal attacker resources, can easily be scaled, and may be disguised within benign web content such as advertisements, enabling potentially widespread exploitation.

Despite being a greater threat, fully remote attacks typically still require some user interaction, e.g., clicking a link or visiting a webpage with attacker-controlled content. This limits realistic attack scenarios to e.g., malicious advertisements or some form of user interaction. Without the requirement of user interaction, attacks would be significantly easier to scale and mount in practice. Given many other contexts where remote resources are loaded, e.g., messenger and email programs, and some protocols requiring interaction with remote clients without initiating a connection, we ask the following research question: *Does system and software behavior enable fully remote network side-channel attacks like SnailLoad* **without the need for user interaction?**

In this paper, we systematically investigate the possibility of fully remote network side-channel attacks ("zero-click") in two directions: the behavior of software and the network stack. **First**, we analyze realistic scenarios involving popular client-side software such as messenger platforms and email clients. Specifically, we examine whether such widely used applications automatically initiate external network connections upon receiving content, without explicit user interaction with the content (e.g., the message or email). In our experiments, we observe privacy- and confidentiality-compromising behaviors in 4 out of 11 messenger platforms and 6 out of 10 tested email clients. These applications automatically establish external connections, revealing victim IP addresses without any user interaction, undermining end-to-end encryption, and enabling zero-click remote SnailLoad-style attacks in practice.

Second, we consider an even more generic threat scenario. Even in absence of privacy- and confidentiality-compromising client software, the basic behavior of network stacks in common operating systems may enable zero-click attacks. To explore this, we develop a novel latency measurement method based solely on unsolicited TCP SYN packets sent from the attacker to a closed port on the victim's home gateway (*i.e.*, router). Unsolicited TCP SYN packets to closed ports trigger a *TCP RST* or an *ICMP Destination Unreachable* response, yielding a measurable latency for a SnailLoad-style attack. However, we observe that these requests often do not reach target systems or time out due to highly restrictive rate limiting. Still, on 9 connections in our experiments, we are able to obtain a response to our unsolicited TCP SYN packets.

By distinguishing timings and ICMP responses of timed-out packets, we generate latency traces analogous to SnailLoad. However, our trace is significantly coarser, given the infrequent response rate of only one packet per second. While we expected this coarse granularity to be a hindrance for practical attacks, we discover that these sparse traces are in fact still sufficient to mount practical side-channel attacks. In a video fingerprinting attack with 10 videos, we achieve an F_1 score of 56%, demonstrating the practicality of our zero-click method compared to SnailLoad's original F_1 score of 89% on a similar Internet connection.

Our results clearly demonstrate that zero-click fully remote network side-channel attacks are not only theoretically possible but practical, highlighting significant privacy threats in everyday software and standard network behaviors. This expands the threat model of SnailLoad substantially beyond previous scenarios. Given that the vast majority of client systems use TCP/IP as well as messenger and email software today, this reveals a fundamental risk overlooked in prior work. Consequently, our work indicates that further mitigations need to be researched and deployed against fully remote network side-channel attacks, especially zero-click variants.

Contributions. We make the following key contributions:

1. We systematically analyze automated external resource handling across 11 messengers and 10 widely-used email clients. Our results reveal unsolicited connections in all 11 messengers, and 8 email clients, with 4 messengers and 6 email clients leaking the victim IP address.
2. We perform in-depth case studies for the affected messengers and 8 email clients. We identify 3 email clients vulnerable to single-click attacks and 4 messengers vulnerable to implicit attacks (triggered implicitly by other user actions), and 1 email client and 1 messenger to zero-click attacks.
3. We introduce a novel zero-click latency measurement approach based solely on unsolicited TCP SYN packets sent to closed ports on the victim gateway. Our experiments show that highly restrictive rate-limiting on the gateway typically only leads to a single response per second, which is orders of magnitude lower than the resolution from prior work.
4. We show that despite the coarse granularity of our latency measurements, our approach still suffices to mount practical video-fingerprinting attacks, reaching an F_1 score of 56%, with zero user interaction.

Outline. Section 2 provides background. Section 3 systematically analyzes external reference handling in messenger and email clients. Section 4 introduces a novel TCP SYN-based measurement method for SnailLoad-style attacks. Section 5 discusses implications, mitigations, and limitations. Section 6 concludes.

2 Background

In this section, we provide background on network side channels including fully remote attacks, as well as automated behaviors in applications and protocols.

Network Side-Channel Attacks. Side-channel attacks exploit information leaking through measurable physical or behavioral characteristics of systems. Network side channels exploit packet timing [19,80], packet sizes [17,27,58], transmission directions [5,16,34,52,74], packet data [8,40,79], or a combination thereof [1,4,10–12,14,22–24,36,39,42,50,51,54–57,59,64,65,67,72,75–77]. Without needing direct access to the target, this allows adversaries to make inferences about the system state [8,40,79], a user [1,4,55,75,80], or their activities [14,28,67,76].

Network side channels have been used to infer websites visited by a user [5,10,16,19,24,26,27,34,39,50,51,56,58,59,61,64,65,74], videos streamed [2,17,23,37,52,57,72], applications used [39], and even sensitive data like medical records and voice conversations [14,76]. Typically, these attacks operate in person-in-the-middle (PITM) scenarios, which require a significant degree of access or control over the victim's network infrastructure, such as being on the same (wireless) network or having access to a compromised router along the traffic path. Additionally, many attacks assume that the attacker can either capture packets directly or induce traffic on the victim's system through some form of code execution (e.g., JavaScript in a browser [1,4,57] or a native application [1,75]). These assumptions restrict the practicality of deploying such attacks at scale, particularly against arbitrary victims on the open Internet.

Fully Remote Network Side-Channel Attacks. In contrast to traditional network side channels, fully remote variants do not rely on traffic interception or victim-side code execution [7,9,20,21,29,35,44,45,68]. With these, an off-path attacker exchanges network packets with a victim system, inferring sensitive data from observed responses. Eliminating the need for proximity or privilege, they are easier to mount and scale. While most of these attacks reconstruct properties of remote systems, e.g., their operating system or uptime, only two attacks focus, like the more powerful PITM-based attacks, on the identification of the accessed content by solely observing packet timing [20,21]. Gong et al. [21] and Gast et al. [20] exploited contention at the bottleneck of standard internet connections – typically the last-mile link – where traffic queues cause measurable delays. Gong et al. [21] mounted a website-fingerprinting attack through round-trip times of ICMP Echo (*i.e.*, ping) messages to a victim's home router. Gast et al. [20] mounted website- and video-fingerprinting attacks through a TCP connection with the victim and measuring round-trip times of acknowledgments.

Unlike PITM attacks, fully remote network side-channel attacks require no special position or victim-side execution environment, aside from the requirement that the victim loads some asset from the attacker, e.g., an image or a background transfer. Many active hosts do not reply to ICMP requests [6,29]. This mitigates the attack by Gong et al. [21], albeit at the expense of network diagnosis. Gast et al. [20] rely on TCP and cannot be mitigated in the same way. While powerful, the attack requires that the victim initiates a connection and loads some asset from the attacker, limiting deployment scenarios to content embedding or social engineering.

Security Risks of External Resources. Modern client applications, e.g., email and messenger platforms, and web browsers, routinely render external content, including images, style sheets, or fonts, fetched from third-party servers. In particular, email clients can fetch external resources referred to in HTML emails. Similarly, messenger applications often follow external links embedded into messages to display previews (e.g., for direct image links) or additional information (e.g., Open Graph [49] data for websites). This, however, introduces several security and privacy risks: First, accessing external resources may leak that a particular message has been read, e.g., tracking pixels or web bugs [18]. Second, additional metadata might be leaked such as the user's IP address, operating system and device behavior [71,79]. Third, it enables attackers to inject or serve malicious content under the guise of legitimate-looking resources [25, 43,69,70].

For mitigation, applications employ proxy servers, sandboxing techniques, or prompt users before loading external content. However, these defenses are inconsistently applied and often disabled by users. For example, users might enable external content in their email client if mails render improperly otherwise. Moreover, even timing and volume of traffic via a proxy can still carry identifying information or enable fingerprinting [27,78]. Attackers can deliver carefully crafted external references via email or messaging content, inducing connections to their own infrastructure without user consent. Kirchner et al. [38] found that 21 of 36 instant-messaging mobile apps and 20 of 41 web-based instant-messaging platforms analyze messages, visiting unique URLs and potentially leaking such side-channel information without user consent.

Such mechanisms can also activate background network interactions that serve as the basis for side-channel measurements. If external resources are fetched automatically upon message reception or preview, attackers may observe latency variations caused by concurrent victim activity. These behaviors, while subtle, introduce a broad attack surface for remote adversaries, especially when combined with fully remote side-channel techniques.

Automated Responses in Network Protocols. Network protocols such as TCP and ICMP include built-in mechanisms for responding to unsolicited packets. These behaviors are crucial for the proper functioning of the internet, yet they also represent a potential side-channel vector. In particular, responses to malformed, unexpected, or incomplete packets can expose timing information that reveals network congestion, bandwidth bottlenecks, or the presence of specific services [29]. For example, TCP initiates connections using a three-way handshake beginning with a SYN packet [33]. If a SYN is sent to an open port, a SYN-ACK is returned; if the port is closed, the system may respond with a TCP RST or an ICMP *Destination Unreachable* message. ICMP itself is designed as a diagnostic protocol, with messages such as *Echo Reply*, *Time Exceeded*, and *Port Unreachable* intended to inform senders of network conditions [30,31].

Modern operating systems implement rate-limiting and filtering to restrict volume and frequency of responses. For example, ICMP Echo (*i.e.*, ping), which sends a ping request to check if a host is reachable, is often disabled for security [13,41,63]. Additionally, ICMP rate limiting may suppress replies to other repeated probes, and firewalls may drop unsolicited packets altogether. However, in practice, many devices still emit rate-limited responses, e.g., on home internet gateways (*i.e.*, home routers), given their verbose default configurations [29].

3 Exploiting Embedding of External Elements

Gast et al. [20] achieved client connections to an attacker-controlled server via an external reference embedded in a benign website the victim user visits. While requiring no elevated attacker privileges or code execution, this model still depends on user interaction, e.g., clicking a link or loading a webpage.

In this section, we systematically analyze how far user interaction can be eliminated with default-configured native and web-based messenger and email applications. We evaluate whether these applications automatically initiate network connections upon receiving, processing, or displaying references to external references. Such behavior would allow a fully automated version of SnailLoad, bypassing the user entirely, which we call *Zero-Click SnailLoad*.

Threat Model. We assume an attacker able to legitimately send messages or emails to the victim. The attacker has no further access to the victim's system, no ability to execute code, and no control over the underlying network infrastructure. The attacker-controlled server hosts a file or image referenced via a URL. The victim receives a message or email referencing the attacker's server. The attacker aims to mount a SnailLoad attack, without any interaction by the victim. We consider two attack vectors: The first attack vector is link previews, message rendering, or other background processing in **messenger clients**. The second attack vector is external references in HTML emails in **email clients**.

For completeness, we also investigate the possibility of attacking the sender of a message: In a scenario where the sender forwards a link to a benign-looking image (e.g., a meme), that actually attacks the sender using SnailLoad. In this scenario, the victim does not click or open the link but only forwards it. This also undermines end-to-end encryption as parts of the message are used to trigger a request to a remote server of either the attacker or the platform provider.

3.1 Evaluation Methodology

We deploy a SnailLoad-style server that records information of the potential unsolicited network connections. The server logs the following information for each incoming connection: (1) the source IP address, to determine whether it is the victim's client connecting, a proxy or a web cache by the messenger platform and (2) whether the external resource is loaded or the connection aborts. To the outside, the external resource appears as a static file. We embed the external reference into each message or email, e.g., in the form of a simple image tag: `<img src="http://atta.ck/plot.jpg">`. The image may or may not be visible on the client, e.g., a legitimate-looking image or a small tracking pixel.

Table 1. Observed behavior of messenger platforms with embedded external references

Messenger	Victim Role	Trigger	Image Previews	Link Website Previews	Link Previews	Client / Server Connection	Caching	Latencies	Observable	Implicit Attack
Discord	Sender	Send	✓	✓[1]		Server	✓[2]	✓[3]	✗	
	Receiver	–	✓[4]	✓[4]		–	✓[2]	✗	✗	
Facebook Mes.	Sender	Send	✓	✓[1]		Server	✓[5]	✓[3]	✗	
	Receiver	–	✓[4]	✓[4]		–	✓[5]	✗	✗	
Google Chat	Sender	Type, Send	✓	✓[1]		Server	✓[5]	✓[3]	✗	
	Receiver	–	✓[4]	✓[4]		–	✓[5]	✗	✗	
iMessage[6]	Sender	Type, Send	✓	✓[1]		Server	✗	✓[3]	✗	
	Receiver	–	✓[4]	✓[4]		–	✗	✗	✗	
iMessage[7]	Sender	Type, Send	✓	✓[1]		Client	✗	✓	✓	
	Receiver	–	✓[4]	✓[4]		–	✗	✗	✗	
Instagram	Sender	Send	✓	✓[1]		Server	✓[5]	✓[3]	✗	
	Receiver	–	✓[4]	✓[4]		–	✗	✗	✗	
Microsoft Teams	Sender	Send	✓	✓[1]		Server	✓[5]	✓[3]	✗	
	Receiver	Open Chat	✓	✓[1]		Server	✓[5]	✓[3]	✗	
Signal	Sender	Type	✗	✓[1]		Client	✗	✓	✓	
	Receiver	–	✗	✓[4]		–	✗	✗	✗	
Snapchat	Sender	Send	✓	✓[1]		Server	✓[5]	✓[3]	✗	
	Receiver	–	✓[4]	✓[4]		–	✗	✗	✗	
Telegram	Sender	Type, Sending	✓	✓[1]		Server	✓[2]	✓[3]	✗	
	Receiver	–	✓[4]	✓[4]		–	✓[2]	✗	✗	
Viber	Sender	Send	✓	✓[1]		Client	✓[8]	✓	✓	
	Receiver	Open Chat	✓[9]	✓[1,9]		Client[9]	✓[8,9]	✓[9]	✓[9]	
Whatsapp	Sender	Type	✓	✓[1]		Client	✓[8]	✓	✓	
	Receiver	–	✓[4]	✓[4]		–	✓	✗	✗	

[1] also follows `og:image` Open Graph meta tag, [2] server-side, only main link cached, `og:image` is followed every time, [3] only server-side latencies, [4] same preview as sender, [5] server-side, [6] iCloud Private Relay enabled, [7] iCloud Private Relay disabled, [8] client-side, until app is closed, [9] only if sender is in contact list

We evaluate whether the client opens a connection (1) immediately upon message receipt, e.g., email delivery on the client; (2) when there is interaction with other messages, e.g., scrolling or hovering over the malicious message; (3) when clicking the message and it is being rendered; and for completeness also (4) when entering or sending a link. Each test is repeated multiple times per platform to ensure reproducibility and to assess caching behavior.

3.2 Messenger Platforms

Messenger platforms are an attractive target for remote side-channel attacks due to their ubiquity, always-on behavior, and support for rich message content, including embedded links. To assess their vulnerability to zero-click SnailLoad-style attacks, we systematically analyzed 11 popular messengers: Discord, Facebook Messenger, Google Chat, iMessage, Instagram Direct Messenger, Microsoft Teams, Signal, Snapchat, Telegram, Viber, and WhatsApp. Each platform is tested using its default configuration across desktop, web, and mobile variants (if they exist). For iMessage, we measure two configurations, one with iCloud Private Relay enabled and one without. We largely find the same behavior across platforms, with similar backend handling of messages (e.g., through a CDN).

For each platform, we examine two types of referencing an attacker-controlled server: a direct link to an image (e.g., http://atta.ck/plot.jpg) and a link to a website (e.g., http://atta.ck). The website also has an Open Graph og:image meta tag, used by all messengers to retrieve website preview images, potentially also enabling attacks. This allows us to observe the connection behavior for both types of links, and potential differences, in various usage scenarios. More specifically, we test whether a connection is established when composing a message, sending it, interacting with the app but not the conversation, opening the conversation, or interacting with the embedded link. We record whether a client-side or server-side connection occurred, whether the user's IP address was exposed, whether repeated interactions triggered additional requests (indicating lack of caching), and whether a link preview was rendered. Finally, we determined whether these conditions suffice to enable a zero-click or implicit variants of SnailLoad, which we only found in 4 messengers.

The results, summarized in Table 1, show that all messengers perform some form of automatic interaction with external links, establishing unsolicited connections, typically through server-side proxies. Concretely, 8 out of 11 platforms initiate server-side connections when messages are sent or received. Note that this undermines end-to-end encryption as parts of the message, *i.e.*, the URL, are exposed to the platform provider without user consent.

We observe that 4 messengers, Whatsapp, Signal, iMessage and Viber, expose user IP addresses through direct client-side connections. For these messengers, a connection is triggered immediately upon typing the link or when sending the final message, and is made directly from the sender's device. This exposes not only when a link is sent but also enables an attacker to target a victim forwarding a benign-looking image to others. While caching may limit the effect, unique links can be sufficient to identify users. For iMessage, the connection behavior is more nuanced: The user's IP address is exposed when sending a link to an external resource but only upon receiving a message if iCloud Private Relay is disabled. Otherwise, the IP address is not exposed but also no manual interaction is required for the proxy to access the resource. Thus, iMessage enables an implicit SnailLoad attack, *i.e.*, no user interaction with the external resource, on the sender and, in some configurations, also on the receiver. For Viber, we found the behavior even more security- and privacy-concerning: In addition to opening a client-side connection when sending the message, we also observed it to open a client-side connection when the receiving user opens the chat window and has the sender in the contact list, enabling targeted SnailLoad attacks.

We conclude that exploiting unsolicited link interactions for SnailLoad-type attacks is a feasible attack vector for some messengers. Most messengers use proxy servers for interaction with the remote server, which still leaks side-channel information and in particular undermines the confidentiality of the communication channel through out-of-band requests to the platform provider, e.g., undermining end-to-end encryption. However, messengers vulnerable to zero-click and implicit attacks using no proxy server enable full SnailLoad attacks, *i.e.*, they raise stronger privacy concerns.

3.3 Email Clients

Email clients are also an attractive target for remote side-channel attacks. They are widely used, run most of the time, and support embedding of external resources, e.g., pictures. To assess their vulnerability to zero-click SnailLoad-style attacks, we systematically analyze 10 email clients: Apple Mail (macOS, iPhone, Watch), BlueMail, eM Client, Gmail, GMX, Mailbird, Microsoft Outlook, Proton Mail, Spark Mail, and Thunderbird. Each platform is tested using its default configuration across desktop, web, and mobile variants (if they exist). For Apple Mail, we explicitly test different configurations of *Protect Mail Activity* and *iCloud Private Relay* to assess privacy-relevant differences. We specify when applications are found to expose different behavior on different platforms.

We embed a static reference to an image on an attacker-controlled server into an HTML email and observe connection behavior in various usage scenarios. We focus only on the receiver side as the client email was crafted by the attacker. We record whether external references are loaded automatically, what kind of connection is established (client-side or via a proxy), whether the user's IP address is exposed, and which user actions (if any) triggers the connection. We record whether a client-side connection occurs and whether the image is automatically rendered. Finally, we determine whether these conditions suffice for zero-click SnailLoad, which we found in the Spark Mail email client.

Table 2 summarizes the connection behavior of all tested email clients. Compared to messengers, where most platforms use a proxy to access the image, we observe a much higher rate of direct client-side IP exposure in email clients. Across all tested clients, **6 out of 10** establish client-side connections. In *BlueMail*, the connection is made automatically upon opening the email, in *Spark Mail* even upon just hovering the email. In particular the behavior of *Spark Mail* is critical as it enables an end-to-end zero-click SnailLoad attack. Apple Mail shows different behavior across devices. On macOS and iPhone with *Protect Mail Activity* and *iCloud Private Relay* enabled, external content is retrieved through proxies, e.g., Cloudflare. In contrast, Apple Mail on the Apple Watch establishes a direct connection if the email has previously been opened on another device, making it vulnerable to a time-delayed attack scenario. This inconsistency in behavior can introduce privacy compromises that may go unnoticed by users

Table 2. Observed behavior of email clients with embedded external references

Client	Trigger	Client Conn.	Server Conn.	Autom. Display	Caching	Single-Click Att.	Zero-Click Att.
Apple Mail (macOS)	Open	✗	✓	✓	✓	✗	✗
Apple Mail (iPhone)	Open	✗	✓	✓	✓	✗	✗
Apple Mail (Watch)	Open	✓	✗	✓	✓	✓	✗
BlueMail	Open	✓	✗	✓	✗	✓	✗
eM Client	Manual Click	✓	✗	✗	✓	✗	✗
Gmail (Web/iPhone)	Open	✗	✓	✓	✓	✗	✗
GMX (Web)	None	✗	✗	-	-	-	-
Mailbird	Manual Click	✓	✗	✗	✓	✗	✗
Microsoft Outlook	Manual Click	✗	✓	✗	✓	✗	✗
Proton Mail (Web)	None	✗	✗	-	-	-	-
Spark Mail	Hover Inbox	✓	✗	✗	✗	✓	✓
Thunderbird	Manual Click	✓	✗	✗	✓	✗	✗

who assume Apple Mail behaves uniformly across devices. BlueMail exposes similar behavior in all scenarios when opening an email. Web-based clients expose less side-channel information in our attack. Proton Mail and GMX block all unsolicited external connections and require explicit interaction for the remote resource to load. Gmail, while automatically loading external references, consistently uses proxy infrastructure. While this masks the user's IP address, it still leaks when the user opens an email, which can be a privacy concern. Similarly, Microsoft Outlook relies on user-initiated clicks and proxy loading, exposing similar information as Gmail albeit upon a user click.

In summary, web-based clients behave more similar to messengers, where server-side connections are the default, whereas native email clients and apps frequently expose user metadata to remote servers via client-side connections. BlueMail and Apple Mail on the Apple Watch require the user to open the email to run a SnailLoad attack. Spark Mail enables reliable zero-click SnailLoad attacks without even opening the email.

4 Eliminating User Interaction with TCP SYNs

In the previous section, we minimized user interaction significantly, yet some level of interaction remained unavoidable. This leads to the continued exploration of the paper's central question: Can user interaction be entirely eliminated?

To address this, the threat model pivots from a direct TCP connection with the victim to an attacker interacting with the victim's home gateway. As ICMP

Table 3. Requirements for the TCP SYN attack. The victim needs to have a public IP address (without carrier-grade NAT), with the home gateway responding to incoming TCP SYN packets on the closed port. Rate limits on the home gateway only reduce the attacker's effective sample rate, but cannot prevent the attack.

Carrier-Grade NAT	●	●	●	●	○	○	○	○
Home Gateway Responding	●	●	○	○	●	●	○	○
Rate Limit	●	○	●	○	●	○	●	○
Attack feasible	✗	✗	✗	✗	✓	✓	✗	✗

Echo Replies are frequently disabled and TCP ports closed, we explore whether the router's responses to unsolicited TCP SYNs are another source of network latency leakage. Even if a connection cannot be established, the router may respond with a TCP RST or an ICMP Destination Unreachable that can be leveraged to gather network activity patterns. First, we examine 4 different internet connection and home gateway combinations to analyze under which conditions their response behavior can be exploited. Second, we mount a video fingerprinting attack, achieving an F_1 score of 56% for 10 YouTube videos, showing that such attacks are feasible even without user interaction. Third and finally, to assess the practicality on other connections, we perform a user study with the internet connections of 102 participants, revealing that 9 of the examined connections are potentially exploitable.

4.1 Examining TCP SYN Response Behavior

In this section, we investigate whether closed port TCP SYN response timings can be generally used to infer a victim's network activity. Therefore, we initially observe the behavior of 4 Internet connection and home gateway combinations. From the observed behavior, we derive the prerequisites for an attack.

Measurement Setup. We send TCP SYN packets with a specific destination port, to the gateway's public IP address and record the round-trip times between the sent TCP SYN and the received response (or an encountered timeout). For each tested Internet connection and gateway, two sets of measurements are performed. First, latency traces are recorded while the network remains idle to establish a baseline. Then, we record traces while a video stream is playing on YouTube to observe potential differences in response behavior. We repeat each test multiple times with varying TCP SYN intervals ranging from 50ms to 100ms, on multiple ports to ensure the observed effects are not port-specific.

Results and Key Observations. We examine 4 connection and gateway combinations at two different ISPs. We observe different behaviors across the four tested connections, revealing varying levels of susceptibility to the attack:

For both cable connections from *ISP A*, we did not receive any responses from both of the two tested routers. This behavior suggests that these routers do not

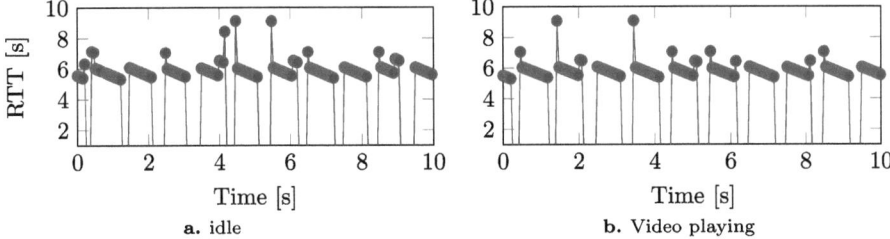

Fig. 1. TCP SYN response times of a 120 Mbit/s cable connection, idle and with a video playing, with a 10 s timeout for responses. We only receive responses after sending multiple TCP SYN packets, which then are replied to in rapid succession, causing a sawtooth pattern. Additionally, packets are silently dropped in periodic intervals, indicating a rate-limit. The traces for an idle and a busy connection look very similar, as the TCP SYN packets are handled by the carrier-grade NAT and therefore do not travel over the last-mile bottleneck.

respond in a way that could reveal network activity and that the attack is not feasible for these routers. For the cable connection from *ISP B*, we receive responses to our TCP SYN packets, see Fig. 1. Interestingly, the router only replies after receiving multiple TCP SYN packets, answering the packets accumulated until that point in rapid succession, causing rather large baseline response delays. Instead of consistently receiving responses, the results show a mix of refusals and timeouts occurring in evenly spaced intervals, suggesting a token bucket-based rate limiter. Comparing Figs. 1a and 1b, the pattern is consistent for the idle network and during video streaming. This pinpoints the presence of carrier-grade NAT [32], *i.e.*, multiple home gateways share a public IPv4 address. As a result, TCP SYN packets sent to the victim's external IP address do not reach their home gateway but are instead handled at the ISP level. Consequently, the attack is not applicable in this scenario.

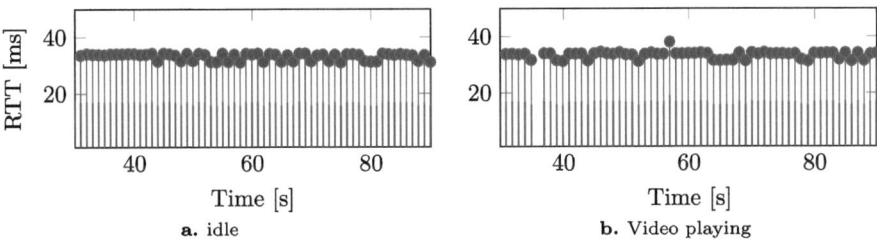

Fig. 2. TCP SYN response times of a 50 Mbit/s ADSL connection, idle and with a video playing, with a 50 ms timeout for responses. When idle, we receive a response once per second within approximately 35 ms. When a video is playing, we observe increased response times and additional timeouts when the client is buffering a video segment.

In contrast, the DSL connection from *ISP B* exhibits two clearly distinct and reproducible patterns, depending on whether the network is idle or actively streaming a video. As shown in Fig. 2, the latency traces for an idle network follow a stable pattern, whereas measurements taken during video streaming display a unique and consistently observable fluctuation. This effect is present across all measurement variations, confirming that the attack successfully detects network activity.

Evaluation. Our results demonstrate that closed port TCP SYN responses can indeed be exploited to measure network latencies and to capture distinct patterns of network activity. This offers a potential solution to eliminate the user interaction element in SnailLoad. However, it is evident that the attack is not universally applicable to all routers or ISPs. In particular, two conditions must be met for the attack to be successful: First, the victim's gateway must have a public IP address, without relying on carrier-grade Network Address Translation. Otherwise, the requests are handled by the victim's ISP and do not reach the internet connection's last mile, a prerequisite of the attack. Second, the victim's home gateway has to respond to incoming TCP SYNs designated to a closed port. These responses often are rate-limited, yet, in Sect. 4.2 we show that this does not prevent attacks. Table 3 summarizes these prerequisites.

4.2 Video Fingerprinting with TCP SYNs

In this section, we mount an end-to-end video fingerprinting attack, exploiting gateway responses to TCP SYN packets sent to a closed port. While the victim user streams a video, the attacker repeatedly sends TCP SYN packets and records the latencies of the corresponding ICMP Destination Unreachable messages sent by the gateway. We demonstrate our attack on a set of 10 videos trending on YouTube. For each video, we record 50 latency traces of 180 s length in Full HD. We then train a CNN on 40 of the traces collected for each video and evaluate the attack on the remaining 10 traces. Our attack achieves an F_1 score of 56%, significantly higher than the random guessing accuracy of $F_1 = 10\%$.

Threat Model. Like in Sect. 3, the attacker is unable to intercept any traffic and cannot run any code on the victim's system. We assume the victim's gateway does not respond to ICMP echo messages. However, we assume the router responds to incoming TCP SYN packets destined to closed ports with either TCP RST or ICMP Destination Unreachable messages. Additionally, we consider the victim's gateway to have a public IP address without carrier-grade NAT (cf. Sect. 4.1), and that the attacker knows the victim's IP address.

Trace Recording. Our setup consists of the victim clien, playing the YouTube videos, and an attacker-controlled virtual server in the cloud, recording the latency traces. The client is connected to the home gateway, which is connected to the Internet via a 50 Mbit/s ADSL connection. The home gateway is in its default configuration, rate limiting ICMP to 1 packet per second. A script on the victim client controls the automated recording of the individual traces. We record 50 traces per video, *i.e.*, 500 traces in total, recorded in random order to prevent order-related effects. For each trace, the script signals the start of a new trace to the server, waits for 1 s to 3 s and starts playing the video in Firefox 136.0.3. While the video is playing, the server repeatedly sends TCP SYN packets to a closed port on the victim's gateway, in 50 ms intervals. For each TCP SYN packet, the server records the latency of the corresponding response. For unresponded TCP SYNs, the server records a latency of 50 ms. After 180 s, the script signals the end of the trace to the server and stops the video.

Training the CNN. Like prior work [15,20,53], we apply a Short-Time Fourier Transform (STFT) to each trace and train a Convolutional Neural Network (CNN) on the results. Due to the ICMP rate limit, we choose a rather large window size of 256 samples for the STFT, *i.e.*, 12.8 s with a sampling interval of 50 ms. Our CNN consists of 3 convolutional layers, each of which followed by a max pooling layer and a dropout layer. These 3 blocks are followed by a flatten layer and another dropout layer. This dropout layer is followed by 2 blocks, each consisting of a dense layer and a dropout layer. These blocks are followed by a final dense layer, yielding the estimated likelihoods that the input corresponds to the specific label for each possible label. Out of the 50 traces for each video, we use 36 traces as a training set to fit the model, 4 traces as a validation set to evaluate the model during training and 10 traces as a test set for the evaluation of the trained model. We empirically choose the hyperparameters for the CNN to achieve good generalization against the validation set and apply early-stopping to reduce overfitting.

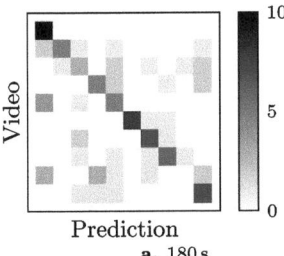
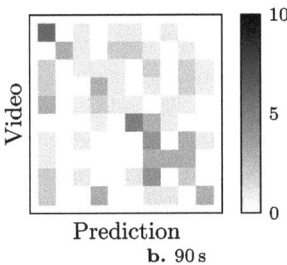

Fig. 3. Confusion matrices of the video-fingerprinting attack based on TCP SYN packets. On a 50 Mbit/s ADSL connection, we achieve an F_1-score of 56%, with 50 traces per video and a recording time of 180 s per trace. For comparison, if we reduce the recording time to 90 s, the F_1-score drops to 31%

Results. We evaluate the trained model on the test set, consisting of the remaining 10 traces per video. Despite the rate-limit imposed by the victim's gateway, we achieve an F_1-score of 56%, significantly higher than random guessing (which would be $F_1 = 10\%$). On a similar ADSL connection, Gast et al. [20] reported a higher accuracy of $F_1 = 89\%$ for their attack based on TCP ACKs, with a recording time of only 90 s per trace. However, their video-fingerprinting attack worked with a sample rate of 20 Hz, while we are effectively restricted to only 1 Hz by the ICMP rate-limit. For comparison, we also evaluate our attack with the recorded traces truncated to 90 s. With this, the accuracy drops to only $F_1 = 31\%$. Figure 3 shows the confusion matrices for both 180 s and 90 s traces. Our results show that rate-limiting is not sufficient to mitigate leakage from response timings. Even with a relatively strict rate-limit of only 1 response per second, video-fingerprinting attacks are still feasible.

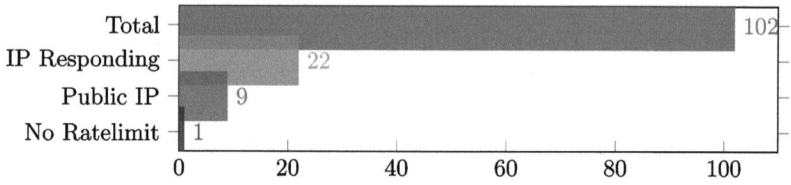

Fig. 4. User study results on internet connections with 102 participants. For 22 connections responded to TCP SYN requests to closed ports. Of these 22 connections, 9 had a public IP without carrier-grade NAT, making them potentially vulnerable to our attack. 1 of the vulnerable connections did not even rate limit the responses

4.3 User Study

For an estimate of the general applicability of this attack, we conducted a user-study with 102 computer science students. With their consent, we collected their IP addresses and examined the response behavior of the IP addresses with regard to Sect. 4.1. We also asked the participants about the type of Internet connection they have and whether they have a true public IP address, without a carrier-grade NAT. Figure 4 summarizes the results of our study, finding 9 out of 102 (i.e., 8.8%) of the examined connections to be potentially vulnerable. 7 of them responded with ICMP Destination Unreachable messages, all of them rate-limited to 1 response per second. 1 home gateway responded with TCP RST messages, delayed in a similar way as the responses from the cable connection in Sect. 4.1. 1 home gateway responded with TCP RST messages and did not even rate-limit them.

5 Discussion

The feasibility of fully automated, zero-click network side-channel attacks depends strongly on the behavior of applications and the network. Our work shows that there is a significant variance across messengers and email clients in their default behavior and with how little interaction they expose users to this threat, e.g., single- or zero-click. Still, our results are sufficient to show that it is not necessary for the victim to initiate a connection through user interaction, such as opening an email or opening a website. This does not only make the attack by Gast et al. [20] more scalable, with little to no user interaction, it also exposes victim timing information and IP addresses. Surprisingly, we also found that both client-side proxied server-side accesses pose a separate privacy risk as these accesses undermine end-to-end encryption by exposing message parts, *i.e.*, text looking like a URL, to out-of-band provider APIs, e.g., to generate previews. There is an abundance of applications beyond the ones we investigated that could similarly serve as targets of our attacks.

Similarly, our TCP SYN-based measurements depend on the handling of TCP SYN requests. As described in Sect. 4, many networks simply ignore these requests and, thus, do not expose themselves to zero-click SnailLoad-style attacks. Still, a significant number of users is affected, rendering our attack a real-world threat. With increasing adoption of IPv6 for private internet connections, the need for NAT decreases, exposing more devices behind the last-mile bottleneck as potential targets. Furthermore, other protocols may expose similar behavior that leaks round-trip time information. In essence, with our work, the SnailLoad attack surface has shifted from attacks depending on *some* user activity to unknowingly initiate the attack to attacks where the user does not initiate the attack, cannot see that an attack is going on, nor interfere with the attack. Consequently, SnailLoad-style attacks must be taken more seriously and mitigations are needed for commodity systems.

6 Conclusion

In this paper, we systematically investigated realistic scenarios for fully remote network side-channel attacks requiring no user interaction. We analyzed software-induced and network-level vectors, showing that attackers can eliminate the need for explicit user action while still mounting practical attacks.

First, we examined the handling of external references in widely-used software. Our analysis of 10 email clients and 11 messenger platforms revealed privacy- and confidentiality-compromising behavior in 6 email clients and 4 messengers. 4 messengers and 1 email client automatically initiate external connections from the client machine, undermining end-to-end encryption, enabling attackers to exfiltrate victim IP addresses and to perform SnailLoad-style attacks.

Second, we introduced a novel TCP SYN-based latency measurement approach that bypasses software-specific behavior entirely. By sending TCP SYN packets to closed ports, we observe a low-rate but consistent signal of ICMP responses (about 1 packet per second). Despite this coarseness, we demonstrate the feasibility of video fingerprinting attacks. This shows that even fundamental behaviors of the network stack enable zero-click remote attacks, independent of specific application-level functionality.

Taken together, our results show that zero-click fully remote side-channel attacks are not only theoretically possible but practically feasible. They expose a previously underestimated attack surface, arising from both common software practices and inherent network behavior. This highlights an urgent need for reconsidering assumptions in the design of secure systems and network stacks.

Acknowledgments. We thank our anonymous reviewers for their valuable feedback. This research is supported in part by the European Research Council (ERC project FSSec 101076409), the Austrian Science Fund (FWF SFB project SPyCoDe 10.55776/F85 and FWF project NeRAM 10.55776/I6054), and SBA-K1 NGC, a COMET Center within the COMET - Competence Centers for Excellent Technologies Programme, funded by BMIMI, BMWET, and the federal state of Vienna. Additional funding was provided by a generous gift from Intel. Any opinions, findings, and conclusions or recommendations expressed in this paper are those of the authors and do not necessarily reflect the views of the funding parties.

References

1. Abbot, T., Lai, K., Lieberman, M., Price, E.: Browser-based attacks on tor. In: PET (2007)
2. Afandi, W., Bukhari, S.M.A.H., Khan, M.U.S., Maqsood, T., Khan, S.U.: Fingerprinting technique for YouTube videos identification in network traffic. IEEE Access **10**, 76731–76741 (2022)
3. Apthorpe, N., Reisman, D., Sundaresan, S., Narayanan, A., Feamster, N.: Spying on the smart home: privacy attacks and defenses on encrypted IoT traffic. arXiv:1708.05044 (2017)
4. Arp, D., Yamaguchi, F., Rieck, K.: Torben: a practical side-channel attack for deanonymizing tor communication. In: ASIA CCS (2015)
5. Bahramali, A., Bozorgi, A., Houmansadr, A.: Realistic website fingerprinting by augmenting network traces. In: CCS (2023)
6. Bano, S., et al.: Scanning the internet for liveness. In: Computer Communications Review (2018)
7. Bender, A., Sherwood, R., Spring, N.: Fixing ally's growing pains with velocity modeling. In: SIGCOMM (2008)
8. Beverly, R.: A robust classifier for passive TCP/IP fingerprinting. In: PAM (2004)
9. Beverly, R., Luckie, M., Mosley, L., Claffy, K.: Measuring and characterizing ipv6 router availability. In: PAM (2015)
10. Bhat, S., Lu, D., Kwon, A., Devadas, S.: Var-CNN: a data-efficient website fingerprinting attack based on deep learning. PoPETS **4**, 292–310 (2019)
11. Bissias, G.D., Liberatore, M., Jensen, D., Levine, B.N.: Privacy vulnerabilities in encrypted HTTP streams. In: PET (2006)
12. Bushart, J., Rossow, C.: Padding Ain't enough: assessing the privacy guarantees of encrypted DNS. In: USENIX FOCI (2020)
13. Chaba, Y., Singh, Y., Aneja, P.: Performance analysis of disable IP broadcast technique for prevention of flooding-based DDoS attack in MANET. J. Networks **4**(3), 178–183 (2009)
14. Chen, S., Wang, R., Wang, X., Zhang, K.: Side-channel leaks in web applications: a reality today, a challenge tomorrow. In: S&P (2010)
15. Chen, Z., Xu, Y.Q., Wang, H., Guo, D.: Deep STFT-CNN for spectrum sensing in cognitive radio. IEEE Commun. Lett. (2020)

16. Deng, X., et al.: Robust multi-tab website fingerprinting attacks in the wild. In: S&P (2023)
17. Dubin, R., Dvir, A., Pele, O., Hadar, O.: I know what you saw last minute-encrypted HTTP adaptive video streaming title classification. IEEE Trans. Inf. Forensics Secur. **12**(12), 3039–3049 (2017)
18. Englehardt, S., Han, J., Narayanan, A.: I never signed up for this! Privacy implications of email tracking. In: PETS (2018)
19. Feghhi, S., Leith, D.J.: A web traffic analysis attack using only timing information. IEEE Trans. Inf. Foren. Secur. (2016)
20. Gast, S., Czerny, R., Juffinger, J., Rauscher, F., Franza, S., Gruss, D.: SnailLoad: exploiting remote network latency measurements without JavaScript. In: USENIX Security (2024)
21. Gong, X., Borisov, N., Kiyavash, N., Schear, N.: Website detection using remote traffic analysis. In: PETS (2012)
22. Gu, J., Wang, J., Yu, Z., Shen, K.: Walls have ears: traffic-based side-channel attack in video streaming. In: INFOCOM (2018)
23. Hasselquist, D., Witwer, E., Carlson, A., Johansson, N., Carlsson, N.: Raising the bar: improved fingerprinting attacks and defenses for video streaming traffic. In: PoPETS (2024)
24. Hayes, J., Danezis, G.: k-fingerprinting: a robust scalable website fingerprinting technique. In: USENIX Security (2016)
25. Heiderich, M., Niemietz, M., Schuster, F., Holz, T., Schwenk, J.: Scriptless attacks: stealing the pie without touching the sill. In: CCS (2012)
26. Herrmann, D., Wendolsky, R., Federrath, H.: Website fingerprinting: attacking popular privacy enhancing technologies with the multinomial Naïve-Bayes classifier. In: CCSW (2009)
27. Hintz, A.: Fingerprinting websites using traffic analysis. In: PET (2003)
28. Hogye, M.A., Hughes, C.T., Sarfaty, J.M., Wolf, J.D.: Analysis of the Feasibility of Keystroke Timing Attacks over SSH Connections. Technical report, School of Engineering and Applied Science University of Virginia (2001)
29. Holzbauer, F., Maier, M., Ullrich, J.: Destination reachable: what ICMPv6 error messages reveal about their sources. In: IMC (2024)
30. Internet Engineering Task Force: RFC 792: internet control message protocol (1981). https://datatracker.ietf.org/doc/html/rfc792
31. Internet Engineering Task Force: RFC 4443: Internet Control Message Protocol (ICMPv6) for the Internet Protocol Version 6 (IPv6) Specification (2006). https://datatracker.ietf.org/doc/html/rfc4443
32. Internet Engineering Task Force: Common Requirements for Carrier-Grade NATs (CGNs) (2013). https://datatracker.ietf.org/doc/rfc6888/
33. Internet Engineering Task Force: RFC 9293: Transmission Control Protocol (TCP) (2022). https://datatracker.ietf.org/doc/html/rfc9293
34. Jin, Z., Lu, T., Luo, S., Shang, J.: Transformer-based model for multi-tab website fingerprinting attack. In: CCS (2023)
35. Kadloor, S., Gong, X., Tezcan, T., Borisov, N.: Low-cost side channel remote traffic analysis attack in packet networks. In: IEEE ICC (2010)
36. Khan, M.U.S., Bukhari, S.M.A.H., Maqsood, T., Fayyaz, M.A.B., Dancey, D., Nawaz, R.: SCNN-attack: a side-channel attack to identify YouTube videos in a VPN and non-VPN network traffic. Electronics **11**(3) (1 2022)
37. Khan, M.U., Bukhari, S.M., Khan, S.A., Maqsood, T.: ISP can identify YouTube videos that you just watched. In: IEEE FIT (2021)

38. Kirchner, R., Koch, S., Kamangar, N., Klein, D., Johns, M.: A black-box privacy analysis of messaging service providers' chat message processing. Privacy Enhancing Technol. (2024)
39. Korczyński, M., Duda, A.: Markov chain fingerprinting to classify encrypted traffic. In: IEEE Conference on Computer Communications (2014)
40. Lastovicka, M., Jirsik, T., Celeda, P., Spacek, S., Filakovsky, D.: Passive OS fingerprinting methods in the jungle of wireless networks. In: NOMS (2018)
41. Lau, F., Rubin, S.H., Smith, M.H., Trajkovic, L.: Distributed denial of service attacks. In: International Conference on Systems, Man and Cybernetics (2000)
42. Lescisin, M., Mahmoud, Q.: Tools for active and passive network side-channel detection for web applications. In: WOOT (2018)
43. Liang, B., You, W., Liu, L., Shi, W., Heiderich, M.: Scriptless timing attacks on web browser privacy. In: Annual IEEE/IFIP International Conference on Dependable Systems and Networks (2014)
44. Luckie, M., Beverly, R., Brinkmeyer, W., Claffy, K.: Speedtrap: internet-scale IPv6 alias resolution. In: IMC (2013)
45. Lyon, G.: Nmap network scanning: the official Nmap project guide to network discovery and security scanning. Insecure (2009)
46. Mittal, P., Khurshid, A., Juen, J., Caesar, M., Borisov, N.: Stealthy traffic analysis of low-latency anonymous communication using throughput fingerprinting. In: CCS (2011)
47. Msadek, N., Soua, R., Engel, T.: IoT device fingerprinting: machine learning based encrypted traffic analysis. In: Wireless Communications and Networking Conference (WCNC) (2019)
48. Murdoch, S.J., Danezis, G.: Low-cost traffic analysis of Tor. In: S&P (2005)
49. Open Graph: The Open Graph protocol (2025). https://ogp.me/
50. Panchenko, A., et al.: Website fingerprinting at internet scale. In: NDSS (2016)
51. Panchenko, A., Niessen, L., Zinnen, A., Engel, T.: Website fingerprinting in onion routing based anonymization networks. In: WPES (2011)
52. Rahman, M.S., Mathews, N., Wright, M.: Video fingerprinting in tor. In: CCS (2019)
53. Rauscher, F., Kogler, A., Juffinger, J., Gruss, D.: IdleLeak: exploiting idle state side effects for information leakage. In: NDSS (2024)
54. Reed, A., Kranch, M.: Identifying HTTPS-protected Netflix videos in real-time. In: CODASPY (2017)
55. Reed, M., Syverson, P., Goldschlag, D.: Anonymous connections and onion routing. J. Sel. Areas Commun. **16**(4), 482–494 (1998)
56. Rimmer, V., Preuveneers, D., Juarez, M., Van Goethem, T., Joosen, W.: Automated website fingerprinting through deep learning. In: NDSS (2017)
57. Schuster, R., Shmatikov, V., Tromer, E.: Beauty and the burst: remote identification of encrypted video streams. In: USENIX Security (2017)
58. Shen, M., Gao, Z., Zhu, L., Xu, K.: Efficient fine-grained website fingerprinting via encrypted traffic analysis with deep learning. In: International Symposium on Quality of Service (IWQOS) (2021)
59. Shen, M., Ji, K., Gao, Z., Li, Q., Zhu, L., Xu, K.: Subverting website fingerprinting defenses with robust traffic representation. In: USENIX Security (2023)
60. Shen, M., Liu, Y., Zhu, L., Du, X., Hu, J.: Fine-grained webpage fingerprinting using only packet length information of encrypted traffic. TIFS **16**, 2046–2059 (2020)

61. Shen, M., Wei, M., Zhu, L., Wang, M.: Classification of encrypted traffic with second-order Markov chains and application attribute bigrams. TIFS **12**(8), 1830–1843 (2017)
62. Shintre, S., Gligor, V., Barros, J.: Optimal strategies for side-channel leakage in FCFS packet schedulers. In: International Symposium on Information Theory (ISIT) (2015)
63. Singh, A., Nordström, O., Lu, C., Dos Santos, A.L.: Malicious ICMP tunneling: Defense against the vulnerability. In: Australasian Conference on Information Security and Privacy (ACISP) (2003)
64. Sirinam, P., Imani, M., Juarez, M., Wright, M.: Deep fingerprinting: undermining website fingerprinting defenses with deep learning. In: CCS (2018)
65. Sirinam, P., Mathews, N., Rahman, M., Wright, M.: Triplet fingerprinting: more practical and portable website fingerprinting with N-shot learning. In: CCS (2019)
66. Skowron, M., Janicki, A., Mazurczyk, W.: Traffic fingerprinting attacks on internet of things using machine learning. IEEE Access **8**, 20386–20400 (2020)
67. Song, D.X., Wagner, D., Tian, X.: Timing analysis of keystrokes and timing attacks on SSH. In: USENIX Security (2001)
68. Spring, N., Mahajan, R., Wetherall, D.: Measuring ISP topologies with rocketfuel. In: SIGCOMM (2002)
69. Stivala, G., Pellegrino, G.: deceptive previews: a study of the link preview trustworthiness in social platforms. In: NDSS (2020)
70. Trampert, L., Schwarz, M.: Hidden in plain sight: scriptless microarchitectural attacks via truetype font hinting. In: uASC (2025)
71. Trampert, L., Weber, D., Gerlach, L., Rossow, C., Schwarz, M.: Cascading spy sheets: exploiting the complexity of modern CSS for email and browser fingerprinting. In: NDSS (2025)
72. Walsh, T., Thomas, T., Barton, A.: Exploring the capabilities and limitations of video stream fingerprinting. In: S&P Workshops (2024)
73. Wang, T., Cai, X., Nithyanand, R., Johnson, R., Goldberg, I.: Effective attacks and provable defenses for website fingerprinting. In: USENIX Security (2014)
74. Wang, T., Goldberg, I.: Improved website fingerprinting on Tor. In: WPES (2013)
75. Wang, X., Luo, J., Yang, M., Ling, Z.: A potential HTTP-based application-level attack against Tor. Future Gen. Comput. Syst. (2011)
76. White, A., Matthews, A., Snow, K., Monrose, F.: phonotactic reconstruction of encrypted VoIP conversations: Hookt on Fon-iks. In: S&P (2011)
77. Wright, C., Bellard, L., Monrose, F., Masson, G.: Language identification of encrypted VoIP traffic: Alejandra y Roberto or Alice and Bob? In: USENIX Security (2007)
78. Xue, D., Kallitsis, M., Houmansadr, A., Ensafi, R.: Fingerprinting obfuscated proxy traffic with encapsulated TLS handshakes. In: USENIX Security (2024)
79. Zalewski, M.: p0f v3 (3.09b) (2014). https://lcamtuf.coredump.cx/p0f3/
80. Zhu, Y., Graham, B., Bettati, R., Zhao, W.: Correlation-based traffic analysis attacks on anonymity networks. IEEE Trans. Parallel Distributed Syst. (2010)

Analysis of Input-Output Mappings in Coinjoin Transactions with Arbitrary Values

Jiri Gavenda(✉)[iD], Petr Svenda[iD], Stanislav Bobon, and Vladimir Sedlacek[iD]

Masaryk University, Brno, Czechia
{gavenda,xsvenda,xbobon,vlada.sedlacek}@mail.muni.cz

Abstract. A coinjoin protocol aims to increase transactional privacy for Bitcoin and Bitcoin-like blockchains via collaborative transactions, by violating assumptions behind common analysis heuristics. Estimating the resulting privacy gain is a crucial yet unsolved problem due to a range of influencing factors and large computational complexity.

We adapt the BlockSci on-chain analysis software to coinjoin transactions, demonstrating a significant (10–50%) average post-mix anonymity set size decrease for all three major designs with a central coordinator: Whirlpool, Wasabi 1.x, and Wasabi 2.x. The decrease is highest during the first day and negligible after one year from a coinjoin creation.

Moreover, we design a precise, parallelizable privacy estimation method, which takes into account coinjoin fees, implementation-specific limitations and users' post-mix behavior. We evaluate our method in detail on a set of emulated and real-world Wasabi 2.x coinjoins and extrapolate to its largest real-world coinjoins with hundreds of inputs and outputs. We conclude that despite the users' undesirable post-mix behavior, correctly attributing the coins to their owners is still very difficult, even with our improved analysis algorithm.

Keywords: Bitcoin · CoinJoin · Anonymity · Privacy

1 Introduction

A coinjoin is a collaborative cryptocurrency transaction attempting to improve the users' privacy. A good estimation of the resulting level of anonymity is crucial for multiple parties. The users need a metric to decide when their funds are sufficiently mixed to stop participating, as every iteration incurs a non-zero cost paid in mining and coordination fees. Meanwhile, chain analysts – such as law enforcement agencies (LEAs) – need data to interpret digital evidence in case of tracking stolen funds or funds coming from a criminal activity. In both of these scenarios, anonymity is typically computed based on a suite of heuristics with no proper data-supported evidence, partially due to the inherently missing ground truth for real coinjoin transactions.

One option to estimate anonymity is to enumerate all possible input-output mappings, as done in [2,16]. However, all currently published approaches suffer from potentially false assumptions (e.g., number of inputs coming from one wallet) and imprecisions (e.g., oversimplification of fees). We believe this methodology needs to be adapted to the design and implementation of the specific coinjoin in question.

Additionally, the privacy depends not only on the transaction on its own, but also on the subsequent on-chain behavior of all participating users. Even if a given output initially "hides" within a set of outputs of the same denomination, subsequent transactions often reveal its owner – due to consolidations (joining multiple outputs into one) or linking with real-world identities (e.g., sending an output to a regulated exchange).

Research Questions. To investigate the privacy properties of real coinjoins, we ask the following research questions:

RQ1: What is the post-mix behavior of users participating in Wasabi 1.x, 2.x and Whirlpool coinjoin designs, and how does it affect the initially obtained anonymity of mixed outputs?

RQ2: How to algorithmically evaluate the anonymity obtained from coinjoin participation when additional information about the users' on-chain behavior and client implementation is available?

Contributions. To answer our research questions, we contribute the following:

- We extend the major open-source BlockSci project [13] for detection and analysis of coinjoins with extraction of behavioral consolidation patterns of real on-chain users, highlighting eventual stabilization of the anonymity set loss over time (Sect. 3).
- We design a precise generic method to compute all possible mappings between sets of coinjoin inputs and outputs. It incorporates hard limitations of client software implementation, participation fees, and consolidation behavior observed for on-chain users (Sect. 4).
- We evaluate the method on real coinjoins, showing privacy gains with practical implications both for the users as well as forensic analysts interpreting past transactions (Sect. 5).

The extended BlockSci project is available at https://github.com/crocs-muni/blocksci. Data processing scripts and all results are available under a permissive license at https://github.com/crocs-muni/coinjoin-mappings.

2 Coinjoin Transactions and Mappings

A *coinjoin transaction* (or just a *coinjoin*) [17] is created collaboratively by multiple users with the goal of gaining privacy by obfuscating the link between the addresses of their inputs and outputs. In a typical coinjoin, each user owns multiple inputs and multiple outputs. Repeating values and multiple possibilities of decomposing the input sum then create uncertainty about which inputs and outputs are linked together. Figure 1a shows a simple example (omitting fees).

2.1 Our Coinjoin Model

We use a notation partially compatible with [16] but modify it to consider fees. We denote the set of input and output coins by I and O, respectively, and fix a mapping $v : I \cup O \to \mathbb{N}$ that assigns numerical values[1] to coins[2]. A *coinjoin* is then a triple $T = (I, O, v)$. For a user $u \in U$, we let $\epsilon_u \geq 0$, χ_u be their mining and coordination[3] fees, respectively.

Definition 1. *For $u \in U$, $I_u \subseteq I$, $O_u \subseteq O$, we call (I_u, O_u) a sub-mapping if*

$$\sum_{i \in I_u} v(i) = \sum_{o \in O_u} v(o) + \epsilon_u + \chi_u. \tag{1}$$

Definition 2. *A* mapping *is a set of sub-mappings $\{(I_1, O_1), \ldots, (I_k, O_k)\}$ such that for each $u, u' \in U$, $u \neq u'$, we have $I_u \subseteq I$, $O_u \subseteq O$, $I_u \cap I_{u'} = \emptyset$, $O_u \cap O_{u'} = \emptyset$.*

In this paper, we study the different mappings admissible for a given coinjoin T. We denote the set of all such mappings by $\mathcal{M}_T$, or just $\mathcal{M}$ when T is clear from the context. Note that while T is public information, $\mathcal{M}_T$ is typically difficult to compute, and the number of users is not even constant across the mappings. Figure 1b shows 4 out of the 24 mappings for the example coinjoin.

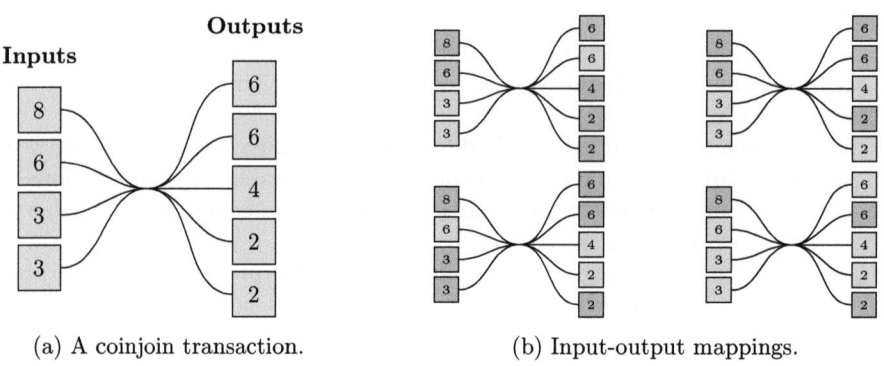

(a) A coinjoin transaction.   (b) Input-output mappings.

Fig. 1. An example of a coinjoin with arbitrary output denominations, without fees and with 4 of 24 possible input-output mappings visualized.

---

[1] These are written as fractions of BTC, but correspond to integer amounts of satoshis.
[2] By abuse of language, we sometimes do not distinguish between a coin and its value.
[3] This fee could be negative if the user receives money from others. In particular, there can be a special user c called a *coordinator* with $\epsilon_c = 0$ and $\chi_c = -\sum_{u \in U \setminus \{c\}} \chi_u$.

2.2 Coinjoin Implementations

On a very high level, a coinjoin generally consists of several phases:

- Input selection: each user registers coins that they would like to mix (typically done by the wallet).
- Output selection: each wallet determines how to decompose the sum of user's inputs into outputs of feasible denominations (either fixed or arbitrary).
- Signing: each user confirms that they agree with the result.

A typical example of a coinjoin implementation with fixed values is Samourai Whirlpool [22] based on the ZeroLink protocol [9]. Coinjoins created with Whirlpool have the same number (typically 5 or 8) of inputs and outputs of the same denomination (0.5, 0.05, 0.01, or 0.001 BTC), except for some of the inputs having a slightly higher value to pay the mining fees.

Wasabi 1.0 [28] is also based on Zerolink. Its inputs can have any value, but each user has a single output of a fixed size and possibly a second output for a leftover value ("change"). From version 1.1, each transaction can have multiple mixed denominations, and each user can have one output per denomination.

Wasabi 2.x [27] is based on the WabiSabi protocol [10], allowing coinjoins with arbitrary values. Users can register any values as inputs and outputs, but their wallets compute possible output denominations using a predefined algorithm. Limiting the number of output denominations assures a high probability of multiple users registering the same output values.

Another example of an implementation with arbitrary values is JoinMarket [12]. While the previous implementations have a coordinator facilitating the creation of the transaction, JoinMarket instead features users of two kinds – makers and takers. Takers are the ones who want to gain anonymity by mixing, while makers provide their coins for mixing for a fee. A taker selects multiple makers, then creates the transaction and asks the makers to sign it. Thus, the taker knows the mapping of the transaction, while the makers do not.

Fee Structures. These implementations differ in their fee structure. The fees are not only economically relevant to the users, but also impact the reconstruction of mappings, as a user's output values may not always match their input values.

Typically, there are two types of fees:

1. Mining fees paid to miners of the block in which the transaction is included.
2. Coordination fees paid to the transaction coordinator or other users.

In Samourai Whirlpool, the coordination fee is paid in a special transaction TX0 preceding the actual mixing. TX0 serves to split the original values into the standard values used in Whirlpool. The coordination fee is a percentage of the standard denomination, typically around 5% of the value, but tens of such outputs can be obtained from a single TX0. The outputs of TX0 are slightly higher than the standard value to pay for mining fees. To allow repeated mixing, mining fees are paid in full by the inputs coming directly from TX0, while the inputs coming from previous coinjoins do not incur any fees.

Both Wasabi 1.x and Wasabi 2.x split the cost of mining fees fairly between the users based on the number of inputs and outputs they register. In Wasabi 1.x, the coordination fee depends on the size of the standard outputs and the number of outputs with the same value (typically about 0.15% of the standard output value). In Wasabi 2.x, until version 2.2.0, a coordinator could charge a fee as a percentage of the input value. The default coordinator charged 0.3%, but let inputs of less than 0.01 BTC and inputs coming from a previous coinjoin mix for free. All Wasabi 2.x versions have to deal with decomposition leftover: since a precise decomposition of the input sum into a set of output values is not always possible, and due to mining fees, it may not be economically reasonable for the user to get the leftover value ("change"). The coordinator can claim this change if enough users leave them in a given round; otherwise, it is left for miners.

A JoinMarket's taker pays a fee to the makers as a reward for letting him use their funds. The fee currently averages at around 0.001% of the value provided by a maker. The taker typically also pays the mining fee for the whole transaction.

2.3 Previous Work

A major privacy concern of Bitcoin is the possibility of clustering addresses based on their ownership. Finding the owner of one of the addresses reveals the owner of the whole cluster. Many papers were dedicated to simple yet efficient heuristics for such address clustering and on-chain activity analysis [1,13,15,18,20,21].

As the adoption of coinjoins started growing, so did the need to adapt the on-chain clustering heuristics. Most attempts in this area focused simply on the detection and avoidance of coinjoins and gathering statistical data about these transactions [7,19,23–26]. We show how the on-chain heuristics can be used to facilitate the analysis of the post-mix behavior of coinjoin users.

Goldfeder et al. [11] analyzed the possibility of linking addresses to user identities using cookies on merchants' websites. They further proposed an intersection attack allowing the linking of inputs and outputs of coinjoins. However, this attack assumes a perfect clustering of the transaction inputs.

Two works [2,16] have analyzed input-output ownership in coinjoins by looking at the possible mappings. In both of these works, the entropy and probability computation works only under the assumption that all the mappings have the same likelihood of occurrence. This assumption does not hold in practice, as some mappings never occur, and some are more likely than others due to the implementations' limits and users' behavior.

Maurer et al. [16] additionally analyzed the upper bound of the complexity of the enumeration of all coinjoin mappings in a case without fees. They describe how such an enumeration can be used to compute the Shannon entropy of the transaction and the probability that the same user owns an input-output pair.

The same entropy and input-output link probability are also computed by the Boltzmann tool [2], which can work with real transactions with mining fees as well as with the fee structure of JoinMarket. It does not work explicitly with the individual mappings, but speeds up the computation by computing only a matrix of the link probabilities.

We follow up and show how to enumerate mappings with a more precise fee computation and considering properties of real coinjoins, without assuming that all mappings have equal probability.

2.4 Attacker Model

We assume an observer performing analysis of all the information recorded on the public blockchain, as well as private information obtained by actively participating in transactions and interacting with public APIs of the discussed coinjoin implementations. A typical example is a chain analysis company providing anti-money laundering checks for regulated financial institutions or support for law enforcement investigations.

2.5 Anonymity

Notions of anonymity can differ and choosing the "correct" one can lead to fundamental philosophical questions. We use a pragmatic definition: The anonymity of a coinjoin output is the entropy (amount of uncertainty) that an attacker has regarding correctly attributing this output to its true owner. Clearly, this depends on the attacker's knowledge; when not specified otherwise, we will assume they only have public knowledge.

3 Analysis of Post-Mix Anonymity Set Loss

A passive attacker (analyst) can retrospectively obtain all past coinjoins recorded on the blockchain. If analyzed in separation, the basic source of uncertainty is the *anonymity set* of an output o, defined as $A(o) := \{o' \in O \mid v(o') = v(o)\}$. In this section, we extend the on-chain analysis tool BlockSci [13] to detect post-mix merges (consolidations) of coinjoin outputs using common ownership heuristics. Then we use the consolidations to quantify the decrease in the effective anonymity set size of each coinjoin, which impacts privacy not only for the owner of the consolidated outputs, but also for all other users. The detected consolidations serve as an input to our mappings enumeration algorithm (Sect. 5).

BlockSci Project and Its Limitations. BlockSci [13] is an open-source project by researchers at Princeton University that allows on-chain analysis of Bitcoin and Bitcoin-like blockchains. It provides efficient and easy-to-use programmatic access to all blockchain data without being tailored to a specific use, using two interfaces: a Python API and a C++ API. The Python API is designed for simpler and intuitive exploration using a Jupyter Notebook, while the C++ API is designed for performance-heavy and highly parallelizable tasks. The parallelization utilizes the *MapReduce* framework [5] and always-in-RAM placement of crucial data structures to perform fast and large-scale analysis over a direct acyclic graph (DAG) and related transaction metadata extracted from on-chain as well as off-chain sources. The *Map* function is parallelized on input data segments and performs detection of coinjoins or address clustering using multiple CPUs. The *Reduce* function combines the *Map*'s outputs, e.g., collating detected clusters of addresses.

The original version of BlockSci suffers from three main limitations:

- it does not analyze the context of coinjoin-related transactions,
- its address clusterer is insufficient for coinjoin analysis,
- it is no longer actively maintained (since 2020) and uses outdated heuristic algorithms, limiting its utility.

We address all these limitations and present an updated BlockSci project with added coinjoin detection algorithms, coinjoin context analyses, and deployment scripts at https://github.com/crocs-muni/blocksci[4].

3.1 An Improved Coinjoin Detection Algorithm

The original BlockSci already contained a simplistic coinjoin detection algorithm used to *avoid* processing the coinjoins in subsequent address clustering analyses. While the algorithm might have been sufficient in 2019, it fails to properly classify many coinjoins created by later designs, resulting in a massive number of both false positives and false negatives.

We extended BlockSci with three algorithms for improved coinjoin detection based on the work of Stütz et al. [24]. For Wasabi 2.x, we applied two more rules:

- the inputs and outputs must belong to at least five different addresses,
- for transactions executed after May 1st, 2024, there are at least 20 inputs (unlike 50 before) – to account for the emergence of new, smaller coordinators after the official Wasabi 2.x coordinator (zkSNACKs) was stopped.

The decreased threshold for a number of inputs naturally resulted in an increased number of false positives, which we mitigated by detecting candidates with a missing connection to any other coinjoin and/or exhibiting a level of address reuse higher than 70%. We manually verified the candidate false positives and placed them on the continuously maintained exclusion list.

The final detection accuracy was verified against the Dumplings project [7] as well as a list of all finished coinjoins obtained by actively querying running coinjoin coordinators. We obtained a perfect match for Whirlpool transactions and a near-perfect match for Wasabi 1.x and Wasabi 2.x transactions, with differences identified manually as misclassifications by the Dumplings project.

---

[4] The original upstream repository is not accepting any new pull requests.

3.2 Anonymity Degradation over Time

The initial anonymity of an output obtained at the time of participation in a coinjoin is not permanent. Depending on the actions carried out by the owner as well as other users, it will likely degrade over time. For example, if a user consolidates two (or more) outputs from one coinjoin, the *common input ownership* heuristic links both outputs together into the same address cluster, decreasing their anonymity. Crucially, this also decreases the anonymity of all outputs with the same denomination, as the number of indistinguishable outputs decreases.

A significant obstacle to determining the exact anonymity of outputs in real coinjoins is the lack of knowledge about the post-mix behavior of each separate user, which is exactly the information the user wants to hide by using a coinjoin. However, we can still study the statistical patterns of users' behavior by using post-mix consolidation heuristics.

For a coinjoin output o, we define its anonymity set loss after d days as

$$A_d(o) := \frac{|\{o \in A(o) \mid o \text{ has been consolidated within } d \text{ days after the coinjoin}\}|}{|A(o)|},$$

and extend this to the whole transaction by averaging over all outputs[5]:

$$A_d := \frac{1}{|O|} \sum_{o \in O} A_d(o).$$

By a consolidation, we mean a non-coinjoin transaction that includes at least two inputs incoming from (not necessarily distinct) coinjoin transactions. (We disregard transactions with only a single coinjoin input, as these are not linking mixed outputs of the same user).

The initial $A_0 = 0$ represents anonymity set loss when no future user actions are considered yet, while A_∞ considers all consolidation transactions to present[6]. As we show on real coinjoin data in Sect. 3.3, the consolidation patterns vary significantly in time and among different coinjoin designs.

Our Algorithm 1 first computes the dictionary by linking specific output denominations to the number of their occurrences for each coinjoin. Then, we search for any transaction (up to d days after the initial coinjoin for computing A_d) that has ≥ 2 inputs from any of the detected coinjoins and lower the corresponding number of occurrences in the dictionary. Outputs mixed again by a future coinjoin are automatically excluded from consolidations as assumptions for common input heuristics are trivially invalidated. We optimize our analysis by avoiding repeated iteration over huge DAG structures and parallelize it using the *MapReduce* paradigm.

Algorithm 1 is *conservative* and will typically *overestimate* A_d due to two factors. Firstly, we assume that any consolidation transaction provides an actionable anonymity set loss – i.e., an analyst can attribute the merged outputs to

---
[5] This is the same as a weighted average over all denominations.
[6] As of 6 April 2025.

Algorithm 1. Anonymity set loss due to coinjoin outputs consolidation.

>**function** GET_CONSOLIDATED_OUTPUTS(cj, t, CJ) ▷ cj, t: txs, CJ: all coinjoins
>　**if** |OUTPUTS(CJ) ∩ INPUTS(t)| ≥ 2 **then**
>　　**return** OUTPUTS(cj) ∩ INPUTS(t) ▷ All consolidated cj's outputs
>　**else**
>　　**return** ∅ ▷ No consolidation detected
>**function** COMPUTE_LOSS(d, CJ) ▷ d: days interval, CJ: all coinjoins
>　$H \leftarrow \{\}$ ▷ Initialize dictionary of losses
>　**for all** $cj \in CJ$ **do**
>　　$X \leftarrow \emptyset$ ▷ Initialize set of detected consolidations
>　　**for all** $t \in$ GET_TXS_IN_TIMEFRAME$(time(cj), d)$ **do**
>　　　$O \leftarrow$ GET_CONSOLIDATED_OUTPUTS(cj, t, CJ)
>　　　X.APPEND(O)
>　　$H[cj] \leftarrow |X|/|$OUTPUTS$(cj)|$ ▷ Ratio of consolidated to all cj's outputs
>　**return** H

a specific user from a set of known coinjoin inputs owners. In practice, the analyst will be able to do so only for some fraction of all consolidation transactions, resulting in a smaller anonymity set loss than computed. Secondly, the inclusion of any misclassified consolidation transaction (e.g., structurally different coinjoin designs) will also artificially increase the computed A_d, despite not providing truly actionable information to the analyst. However, the occasional inclusions of coinjoins with a small number of outputs only have a small impact on the aggregate statistics for the anonymity set loss presented in Sect. 3.3. If the number of these false consolidations starts to rise in the future (e.g., due to a new coinjoin design with a large number of inputs), the coinjoin detection and consolidation detection algorithms will need to be updated. The *overestimation* of anonymity set loss is favorable from the point of view of mixing users, who will, in reality, obtain higher privacy than implied by our conservative algorithm.

Deployment Setup. Our analyses were performed on a machine with two 64-core AMD EPYC 7713 2.0 GHz processors, providing 256 threads in total, 2TB DDR4 3200 Mhz RAM (typically around 400 GB was utilized), and Red Hat Enterprise Linux host OS, using Bitcoin blockchain state till date 2025-04-06 (block height 891137). As the direct compilation of the original code for a current OS is difficult due to dependency on outdated packages, we opted for a Podman-based containerization using a Ubuntu 20.04 image.

3.3 Results for Whirlpool, Wasabi 1.x and Wasabi 2.x

We computed A_d for days $d \in \{1, 7, 31, 365, \infty\}$ using Algorithm 1. For all coinjoin designs, the biggest anonymity set degradation, caused by the post-mix behavior of users, usually happens within the very first day after the coinjoin creation, as visible in Fig. 2. Conversely, any degradation after one year is usually negligible.

For coinjoins with arbitrary values (Wasabi 1.1 and Wasabi 2.x), the anonymity set loss may differ across output denominations as discussed in Appendix A. The general trend is that smaller denominations are consolidated more frequently than the larger ones, with average results presented in Fig. 2 being close to smaller denominations due to their higher relative frequency in real coinjoins.

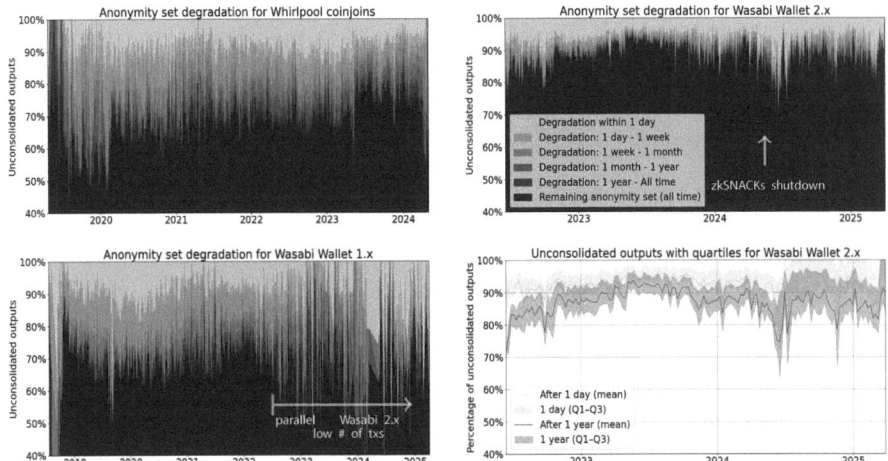

Fig. 2. Anonymity set loss over time for Whirlpool, Wasabi 1.x, and Wasabi 2.x as a result of users' post-mix actions within a specific time interval. The darkest part marks the remaining fraction of the initial anonymity set. For Wasabi 2.x, the last sub-figure also shows the Q1 and Q3 quartiles. The anonymity set loss is averaged over all output denominations of coinjoins created at a given time.

Averaging over all Whirlpool's pools, we observed a relatively stable A_∞ – between 30% to 50% (later coinjoins tend to have a lower loss), as shown in the first sub-figure of Fig. 2. The 0.001, 0.01, and 0.05 BTC pools exhibit a roughly comparable loss (Fig. 5 in Appendix A). The largest 0.5 BTC pool has a smaller anonymity set loss overall, which might be explained by a lower need for any consolidation given an already large output.

For Wasabi 1.x, the anonymity set loss is around 25–40% soon after its start until the first quarter of 2023, when it decreases significantly. However, the results from the later period are less representative as the number of Wasabi 1.x coinjoins significantly decreased from more than a thousand to smaller tens per month, in favor of the parallelly available operation of the superseding Wasabi 2.x design operated by the same coordinator.

For Wasabi 2.x, the anonymity set loss is below 20%, with a larger loss from June to August 2024 due to several contesting coordinators after the shutdown of the zkSNACKs coordinator. Afterwards, the *kruw.io* coordinator became dominant, and its size of coinjoins, as well as the anonymity set loss returned to the values comparable to the (now defunct) zkSNACKs coordinator. The last sub-figure in Fig. 2 also shows first and third quartiles for anonymity set loss for Wasabi 2.x, exhibiting higher fluctuation for the post-zkSNACKs period, especially for the loss within a single day after a conjoin. Percentage-wise, the post-mix consolidations with a negative impact on the anonymity set loss happen significantly less for Wasabi 2.x due to the very high rate of remixes. Whirlpool and Wasabi 1.x have roughly comparable losses.

4 Coinjoin Mappings Enumeration Algorithm

In this section, we discuss how to compute a coinjoin's privacy metrics in detail. The three main steps are as follows:

1. enumerate all coinjoin mappings,
2. compute the probability of each individual mapping,
3. use results from steps 1 and 2 to compute privacy metrics for the whole coinjoin, as well as for individual users.

4.1 Enumeration of Possible Mappings

The problem of enumerating all possible mappings of a coinjoin is super-exponential by its nature, as already enumerating all possible input partitions is super-exponential [4]. The algorithm that we use to enumerate the mappings consists of the following steps:

1. fee preprocessing,
2. additional knowledge preprocessing,
3. computation of sub-mappings,
4. sub-mapping filtering,
5. enumeration of valid sub-mapping combinations into mappings.

First, we describe the general parallelizable algorithmic approach for steps 3 and 5 without considering fees. Then, we discuss how to implement Step 1 for different fee structures and the changes needed in Step 3 to accommodate for fees. Next, we explore specific implementation properties to filter out sub-mappings (Step 4) that cannot occur. Finally, we describe how to use additional knowledge (Step 2) that an attacker can potentially have. In Appendix D, we outline how to generalize this approach to multiple consecutive coinjoins.

Algorithmic Approach. The core of our mapping enumeration is the computation of sub-mappings and their combination into mappings. The computation of sub-mappings can be transformed into computing all solutions of a subset sum problem (SSP) [14]. In SSP for a given set of values S and a target value t, the goal is to find a subset of S that sums to t. Finding sub-mappings of a coinjoin without fees can be transformed to an SSP instance by setting $t = 0$ and using the inputs and negated outputs as the elements of S. To solve the SSP, we opt for a backtracking approach. Similarly, we use backtracking to find compatible combinations of sub-mappings. Notice that backtracking is easily parallelizable, allowing for a fast multi-core implementation. Since we need to precompute all the sub-mappings, the worst-case memory complexity is exponential.

A naive approach is to enumerate all the mappings. However, coinjoins typically contain groups of the same-valued inputs and outputs. Therefore, such an enumeration would lead to a large number of mappings that are distinct only by a permutation of coins of the same value. To use this knowledge, we can enumerate only mappings up to a permutation of the same-valued coins. We call such mappings *numeric*. It is possible to compute all the mappings corresponding to a numeric one. However, typically, it is sufficient to know just the number of the corresponding mappings for the computation of coinjoin-relevant privacy metrics. The number of numeric mappings, therefore, gives us a lower bound on the complexity of mapping-enumeration-based analysis of coinjoins.

Fees. For each fee structure described in Sect. 2, the enumeration algorithm needs a slightly different modification. If the coinjoin contains only predictable mining fees (Whirlpool) or predictable mining and coordination fees (Wasabi 1.x), we can remove the fees during transaction preprocessing and analyze the coinjoin as if it contained none.

However, if there is an unpredictable component to any of the fees (e.g., decomposition fees in Wasabi 2.x), the enumeration needs to be modified. If we can estimate a lower bound on the fees, we can subtract it from the input and output values. Then, the difference δ between the upper and lower bound on the fees is a tolerance that needs to be added to the enumeration algorithm. Any sub-mapping where the difference between inputs and outputs is lower than δ needs to be considered for the possible mappings.

Similarly, if the transaction can contain fees paid between users (JoinMarket), the sum of inputs and outputs of sub-mappings does not need to be exactly equal. In this case, the difference between inputs and outputs can be negative if the user gets paid to provide his funds for mixing. The number of sub-mappings with a positive or negative input-output difference can be considered when combining sub-mappings into mappings, as there could be a constraint on this property, e.g., JoinMarket has at most one sub-mapping with a positive difference.

Implementation Restrictions on Mappings. If we assume that all the parties participating in the creation of a coinjoin use an unmodified implementation of the client wallet for the specific coinjoin protocol, we can limit the space of possible mappings based on the wallet's behavior.

The coinjoins often follow some structure, e.g., Whirlpool allows only a fixed number of inputs and outputs in a transaction, and each user with a single client wallet has exactly one input and output. In other cases, the rules are more relaxed, but often, there is some limit on the number of inputs and outputs of each user or on the possible combinations of sub-mappings into mappings.

These limitations can typically be adhered to by filtering the discovered sub-mappings. Alternatively, for faster computation, some of the rules can be implemented already as pruning rules in the backtracking search for sub-mappings.

Additional Attacker's Knowledge. So far, the analysis uses solely information directly available from the coinjoin or the protocol used to create it, which can typically be assessed based on the structure of the transaction. However, the attacker can obtain additional information about the transaction's inputs and outputs as described in Sect. 3.

If the attacker knows that some inputs (or outputs) belong to the same user, during the preprocessing of the transaction, he can sum their values and merge them into a single input (output). When enumerating all mappings (not just numerical ones), the attacker can also use the information that some inputs or outputs belong to different users, filtering out any sub-mappings that attribute them to the same user.

If the attacker knows that an input-output pair is owned by a single user, he can replace the higher one with the difference of their values and remove the lower one. These operations reduce the coinjoin size, making it easier to analyze.

4.2 Mapping Probability

To estimate each user's privacy in a coinjoin, we need to know how likely individual mappings are to occur. This depends on multiple factors:

- the distribution and privacy level of coins that the users want to mix,
- the input selection of a coinjoin,
- the output selection of a coinjoin.

We will take a Bayesian standpoint, treating unknowns as random variables. Then we can compute the probability $p(M)$ of the mapping M occurring as $p(M) = p(M|A) \cdot p(A)$, where $A : I \rightarrow U$ assigns the inputs to their owners.

The probability $p(A)$ depends on the first two out of the three factors above. In some cases, this probability is fully determined by the input coin selection implemented in the wallet software. For example, the Samourai wallet (for Whirlpool coinjoin) always selects just a single input regardless of the number of coins in the wallet. The opposite extreme would be a wallet always registering all its coins to a coinjoin; $p(A)$ would then be fully determined by the probability distribution of coins among users.

The probability $p(M|A)$ depends solely on the wallet's output selection implementation. In many cases, this process is deterministic; therefore, given the input attribution to users, all but one numeric mapping has a probability of zero. However, some implementations, including Wasabi 2.x, randomize this process, making the analysis more difficult as discussed in Sect. 5.2.

4.3 New Privacy Metric

Previous works [2,16] computed the entropy as $E(T) = \log_2(|\mathcal{M}_T|)$, a special case of the Shannon entropy when all the mappings have the same probability $1/|\mathcal{M}_T|$ of occurring. We consider the more general case

$$E(T) := - \sum_{M \in \mathcal{M}_T} p(M) \cdot \log(p(M)).$$

This entropy captures how unpredictable the whole coinjoin is, and allows comparing different coinjoin designs. However, from the user's perspective, it is more important to asses the unpredictability of their specific sub-mapping. We could directly compute the probability of the user's actual sub-mapping S as

$$p(S) := \sum_{M \in \{M' \in \mathcal{M} | S \in M'\}} p(M).$$

In practice, though, the anonymity of different outputs within a sub-mapping can vary dramatically (e.g., depending on the number of times the same value is present), so $p(S)$ might not be a fine enough metric.

The usual measure adopted by previous work [2,16] is the probability $p(i,o)$ that a given input-output pair is linked, with the additional information about mappings' probability computed as

$$p(i,o) := \sum_{M \in \{M' \in \mathcal{M} | \exists (I,O) \in M': i \in I, o \in O\}} p(M).$$

This can be useful for analysing the transaction, but not so much for a regular user. We propose a new metric providing a conservative estimate of how well a user's output o is mixed, using the knowledge of their set of inputs I. We compute it as

$$p(I,o) := \max_{i \in I} p(i,o).$$

Clearly $p(i',o) \leq p(I,o)$ for any $i' \in I$, so if an attacker finds out that this user owns i', our metric bounds the information gained. While computing $p(M)$ is typically still not feasible for real-world coinjoins, it entails a more detailed description than the practically used metrics based on anonymity sets.

5 Evaluation of Wasabi 2.x Coinjoins

In this section, we evaluate our approach on coinjoins created by Wasabi 2.x. We chose Wasabi 2.x over Wasabi 1.x and Samourai Whirlpool as these two are no longer active (shutdown in 2024) and have very strict limitations on sub-mappings, making the enumeration trivial. While JoinMarket is actively used and allows non-trivial mappings, the taker in this protocol has complete control over the final transaction, allowing him to estimate his privacy better. Thus, we preferred Wasabi 2.x, where no single entity knows the complete mapping.

We also employ the anonymity set loss observed for real coinjoins in Sect. 3 as one of the inputs for practical computations of the mapping enumeration. Firstly, we utilize concrete consolidations for a given coinjoin to decrease the effective number of outputs by merging ones consolidated under the same transaction into a single one. Secondly, we use the average anonymity set loss to lower the expected size of larger coinjoins during complexity extrapolation.

5.1 Mapping Enumeration

The necessary modifications of the enumeration algorithm for Wasabi 2.x are described in Appendix B. To obtain data for the evaluation, we used a Wasabi 2.x emulator [6] with coins randomly assigned to wallets so that the resulting transactions have a small number of inputs and outputs. Emulations provide us with a large number of small coinjoins where we know the ground truth mappings, allowing us to validate our approach by checking that the emulated mapping is among the enumerated numeric mappings.

We evaluated 220 transactions in total. In all cases, the real mapping from the emulation was among the enumerated mappings, indicating that our method does not omit possible mappings. Figure 3 shows the number of mappings for different coinjoin sizes, where the size is defined as the sum of the number of inputs and outputs.

While the variance in the number of numeric mappings for the same size is high, we can see a clear exponential growth for the average case. We can extrapolate this trend to larger coinjoin sizes to evaluate the expected number of numeric mappings for real-world coinjoins. The graph shows the expected average number of numeric mappings for a median coinjoin produced under the zkSNACKs coordinator (2022–2024) and the kruw.io coordinator in 2025. Their size is lowered by the percentage of consolidations observed in Sect. 3. In both cases, the enumeration of all numeric mappings would be infeasible, suggesting that users get sufficient privacy unless an attacker obtains additional information to be able to analyze the transaction properly.

We further found five small real Wasabi 2.x coinjoins and enumerated the possible numeric mappings for them. For real transactions, we were able to use the output consolidations. However, unlike in the Sect. 3, we linked together only the outputs that are almost certainly owned by a single entity to avoid potentially falsely assumed consolidations. A table with the transaction IDs and their number of numeric mappings is available in Apppendix E.

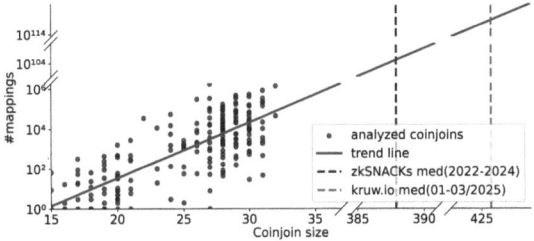
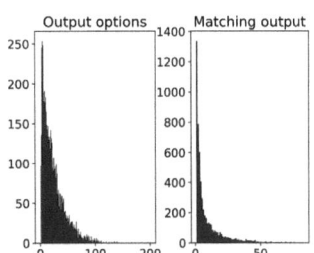
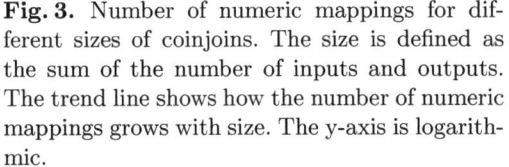

Fig. 3. Number of numeric mappings for different sizes of coinjoins. The size is defined as the sum of the number of inputs and outputs. The trend line shows how the number of numeric mappings grows with size. The y-axis is logarithmic.

Fig. 4. Distribution of the number of possible output selections and the order of the matching output.

5.2 Mapping Probability

Computing $p(M)$ consists of computing $p(A)$ and $p(M|A)$ separately. We do not know A, but from a privacy perspective, it is better to assume that the attacker knows $p(A)$, or even worse, knows which assignment A really occurred. With such an assumption, $p(M)$ depends only on the output selection of Wasabi 2.x. A direct way to obtain the probability of a coinjoin mapping would be to repeatedly simulate the output selection for all the wallets in the given coinjoin. Then, from the observed results, we would filter the mappings that have the same resulting set of output values as the original coinjoin, and assess their probability based on the number of their occurrences. However, such a simulation would likely produce an extreme number of different outcomes, making it infeasible to simulate the process enough times to obtain the probabilities. Therefore, we propose to simulate wallets individually and assign probabilities to sub-mappings, which is more efficient. Then, based on the probabilities of sub-mappings, compute the probability of a whole mapping.

To provide statistics on the output selection, we used 100 emulated coinjoins of realistic size – with hundreds of inputs and outputs. Then, we modified the Wasabi 2.x output-selection simulator Sake [8] and used it to simulate the output selection. When simulating all the wallets, we obtained the exact matching sub-mapping on the first try for 29% of the wallets, showing relatively low entropy in the output selection. Furthermore, we modified the simulator to return all the sub-mappings for a given user, from which it selects randomly in the last step of output selection. We ran it 100 times for each wallet, as the set of possible outputs can differ. Figure 4 shows the distribution of the number of obtained sub-mappings for individual wallets and the distribution of indices of matching decompositions when ordered by their estimated probability. In 3% of cases, the emulated mapping did not occur among the simulated ones, suggesting that either more iterations would be needed or that the Sake simulator and the real

Wasabi 2.x wallets behave differently. An additional mismatch between Sake and Wasabi 2.x led us to discover bugs in the Wasabi 2.x described in Appendix C.

6 Conclusions

The paper tackles an open question of accurate anonymity estimation of privacy-enhancing trustless coinjoins with a centralized coordinator. We first show that despite frequent post-mix consolidations by participating users, the anonymity set loss for coinjoin outputs stabilizes and does not deteriorate significantly after the first year of coinjoin creation. Together with an exact fee computation and implementation-specific limits, we propose an improved algorithm to enumerate input-output mappings suitable especially for Wasabi 2.x coinjoins, practical enough to fully enumerate real coinjoins of smaller coordinators and provide extrapolated complexity estimations for the large ones. We conclude that large real Wasabi 2.x coinjoins still provide sufficient privacy even against improved analytical methods utilizing information extractable from the public blockchain.

Acknowledgments. The work was supported by EU CHESS grant #101087529.

A Anonymity Set Loss Results

The anonymity set loss is not the same for different output denominations, as shown for all three investigated coinjoin designs in Fig. 5. The general trend is that smaller denominations are consolidated more frequently, resulting in higher anonymity set loss. Such observed behavior is logical – the larger denominations have a higher chance of being alone enough for a subsequent payment, while smaller ones require joining multiple outputs to pay the desired amount.

B Wasabi 2.x Mappings Enumeration

Wasabi 2.x Fees. Wasabi 2.x has 3 types of fees – mining fees, coordination fees, and fees paid because of imprecise decomposition of inputs into outputs (paid to miners or the coordinator). The coordination fees of 0.3% can be easily subtracted from the relevant inputs. If we have a precise mining fee rate for a given transaction, we can also easily remove the mining fees. The decomposition fees cannot be removed as they are unpredictable. Therefore, we need to allow the sub-mappings to have the sum of inputs higher than the sum of outputs by this amount, plus some small margin to cover a possible error in mining fee computation. The upper limit on the decomposition fee is the minimal registrable output amount defined by the coordinator or the minimal value that is economical for the user, if it is higher.

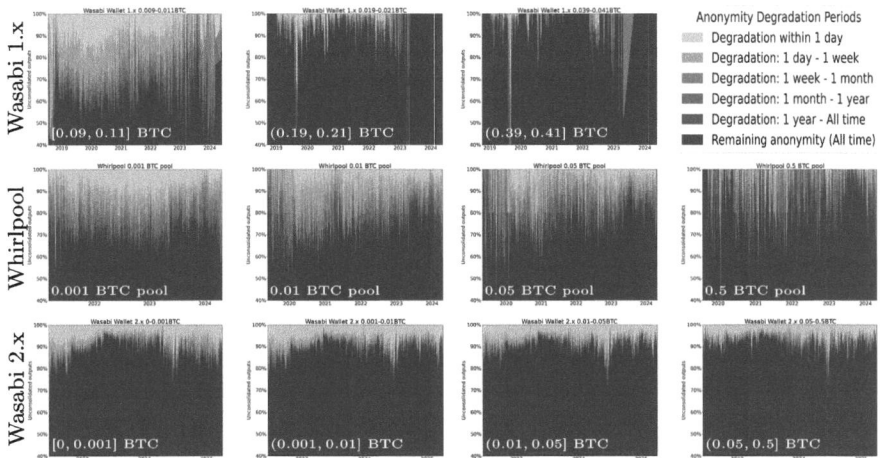

Fig. 5. Anonymity set loss for Wasabi 1.x, Whirlpool and Wasabi 2.x for different output denominations. All graphs have a y-axis range from 40% to 100%.

Wasabi 2.x Mapping Restrictions. If we assume that all users follow the protocol as implemented in Wasabi 2.x, then there are some limitations on the potential mappings of the resulting coinjoins. By analyzing the implementation of Wasabi 2.x, we identified the following restrictions on potential mappings.

Each user can register at most 10 inputs and 10 outputs. BTCPay [3] has a coinjoin implementation compatible with Wasabi 2.x, which allows users to register up to 30 inputs. Therefore, we consider a limit of 30 inputs per user.

Another factor limiting possible sub-mappings is that each wallet registers at most one change output, i.e., output that is not among the common denominations for a given coinjoin round. However, this restriction was recently loosened by the introduction of payments in coinjoins. As one user can have up to 4 payments in one coinjoin, there can be up to 5 outputs with values different from common denominations. Since we analyze only very small transactions, we decided not to implement this mapping restriction.

C Discovered Wasabi 2.x Implementation Bugs

When using Sake, we discovered that in some cases, the simulator never reproduces the same outputs for a wallet as observed in the emulation. We discovered that the simulator computes the common output denominations for all wallets at the same time, as it is assumed that all wallets should come up to the same values. However, the computation in Wasabi 2.x can sometimes produce different denominations for different wallets due to incorrect handling of coordination fees. This bug can lead to the linking of inputs to outputs if an attacker can find which combination of inputs could trigger such an incorrect computation of output denominations and observe such denominations in the outputs.

D Multiple Coinjoin Mappings Enumeration

In practice, it is common to participate in multiple consecutive coinjoins. Our approach to mapping enumeration can be extended to analyze multiple interconnected transactions at once. To analyze a set of transactions $\mathcal{T}$, we can create a new artificial transaction for which the mappings will then be enumerated. The artificial transaction will inherit all inputs/outputs of transactions that are not coming directly from/to another transaction in $\mathcal{T}$. For each pair of transactions from $\mathcal{T}$, we also need to know their order and the capacity of their link, i.e., the sum of outputs going from the first transaction to the second one.

The enumeration then proceeds as usual, just filtering out the (sub-)mappings where the transfer of value between a pair of transactions would be higher than the capacity of their link.

E Mappings of Real Coinjoins

We chose 5 small Wasabi 2.x coinjoins produced in 2024 by one of the currently running coordinators to test if the enumeration is practically applicable to real transactions. Table 1 shows the number of numeric mappings for these transactions. The coordination fee charged by the coordinator was 0%, and we used a range of possible mining fee rates as the mining fee rate used by wallets when choosing the output values can be different from the final fee rate of the whole transaction. However, it is possible to obtain the precise mining fee rate used in the transaction by regularly querying the coordinator's public API and logging this information. Note that the reported runtime of the mappings enumeration

Table 1. Number of numeric mappings and execution time (T) in seconds and peak memory usage (PMU) in MBs for real Wasabi 2.x coinjoins by the *opencoordinator.org* coordinator.

Transaction ID	#Mappings	T	PMU
7e875be692881180ed3f322831615c280daf077bfd14bc120fb3c03dc6d381f6	6565	35.5	33
f5f4fbf79355c777b9a83aef9202e85d4af83ffaf4b7f14e5ff6fd1b163eb3b0	38	0.07	36
c92a6046249fd613019e5dccb0f6c188e4d607eade2738250a10b7e1da2a0489	2575	3.3	38
a0ddfff8b16eaa9c461a15a2b70d174530b649426ac0472464b62f4a5ef02d6a	34301	402	35
ad5ad29922ab3067ecfcc608eba03c3d0aef08ce80a75e563ba8904875648743	17935	15998	42

---

[7] https://github.com/WalletWasabi/WalletWasabi/pull/13598.

algorithm varies significantly (observed also for emulated coinjoins in Sect. 5.1) and is not directly proportional to the coinjoin size, nor the number of mappings found.

References

1. Androulaki, E., Karame, G.O., Roeschlin, M., Scherer, T., Capkun, S.: Evaluating user privacy in bitcoin. In: Financial Cryptography and Data Security, pp. 34–51. Springer, Berlin, Heidelberg (2013)
2. Boltzmann authors: Boltzmann (2016), https://github.com/Samourai-Wallet/boltzmann, Accessed 28 Apr 2025
3. BTCPay server: BTCPay server, https://btcpayserver.org/, Accessed 28 Apr 2025
4. De Bruijn, N.G.: Asymptotic Methods in Analysis. Courier Corporation (2014)
5. Dean, J., Ghemawat, S.: MapReduce: simplified data processing on large clusters. Commun. ACM **51**(1), 107–113 (2008). Jan
6. Dufka, A., Rýpar, D.: EmuCoinJoin: a container-based setup for the emulation of CoinJoin transactions on RegTest network, https://github.com/crocs-muni/coinjoin-emulator, Accessed 03 Nov 2025
7. Ficsor, A.: Dumplings (2020), https://github.com/nopara73/Dumplings, Accessed 28 Apr 2025
8. Ficsor, A.: Sake (2021), https://github.com/nopara73/Sake, Accessed 28 Apr 2025
9. Ficsor, A.: ZeroLink: the bitcoin fungibility framework (2022), https://nopara73.medium.com/introducing-zerolink-the-bitcoin-fungibility-framework-dc5338086198, Accessed 28 Apr 2025
10. Ficsor, A., Seres, I.A., Kogman, Y., Ontivero, L.: Wabisabi: centrally coordinated coinjoins with variable amounts (2021)
11. Goldfeder, S., Kalodner, H.A., Reisman, D., Narayanan, A.: When the cookie meets the blockchain: privacy risks of web payments via cryptocurrencies. Proc. Priv. Enhancing Technol. **2018**(4), 179–199 (2018)
12. JoinMarket authors: JoinMarket, https://github.com/JoinMarket-Org/joinmarket-clientserver, Accessed 28 Apr 2025
13. Kalodner, H., et al.: BlockSci: design and applications of a blockchain analysis platform. In: USENIX Security 2020, pp. 2721–2738, August 2020
14. Kellerer, H., Pferschy, U., Pisinger, D.: The subset sum problem, pp. 73–115. Springer, Berlin, Heidelberg (2004)
15. Maesa, D.D.F., Marino, A., Ricci, L.: Uncovering the bitcoin blockchain: an analysis of the full users graph. In: IEEE International Conference on Data Science and Advanced Analytics (DSAA), pp. 537–546 (2016)
16. Maurer, F.K., Neudecker, T., Florian, M.: Anonymous CoinJoin transactions with arbitrary values. In: IEEE Trustcom/Bigdatase/Icess, pp. 522–529 (2017)
17. Maxwell, G.: CoinJoin: bitcoin privacy for the real world (2013), https://bitcointalk.org/index.php?topic=279249.0, Accessed 28 Apr 2025
18. Meiklejohn, S., et al.: A fistful of bitcoins: characterizing payments among men with no names. In: Internet Measurement Conference, pp. 127–140 (2013)
19. Möser, M., Böhme, R.: The price of anonymity: empirical evidence from a market for bitcoin anonymization. J. Cybersecur. **3**(2), 127–135 (2017)
20. Reid, F., Harrigan, M.: An analysis of anonymity in the bitcoin system, pp. 197–223. Springer, New York (2013)

21. Ron, D., Shamir, A.: Quantitative analysis of the full bitcoin transaction graph. In: Financial Cryptography and Data Security, pp. 6–24. Springer, Berlin, Heidelberg (2013)
22. Samourai authors: Samourai wallet - whirlpool, https://web.archive.org/web/20240417214653/, https://www.samouraiwallet.com/whirlpool, Accessed 28 Apr 2025
23. Schnoering, H., Vazirgiannis, M.: Heuristics for detecting coinjoin transactions on the bitcoin blockchain. arXiv:2311.12491 (2023)
24. Stütz, R., Stockinger, J., Moreno-Sanchez, P., Haslhofer, B., Maffei, M.: Adoption and actual privacy of decentralized CoinJoin implementations in bitcoin. In: AFT 2022, pp. 254–267. ACM, New York, USA (2023)
25. Tironsakkul, T., Maarek, M., Eross, A., Just, M.: The unique dressing of transactions: wasabi CoinJoin transaction detection. In: EICC 2022, pp. 21–28. ACM, New York, USA (2022)
26. Wahrstätter, A., Taudes, A., Svetinovic, D.: Reducing privacy of coinjoin transactions: quantitative bitcoin network analysis. IEEE Trans. Dependable Secure Comput. **21**(5) (2024)
27. Wasabi Wallet authors: wasabi wallet - bitcoin privacy wallet with coinjoin, https://wasabiwallet.io/, Accessed 28 Apr 2025
28. zkSNACKs: wasabi wallet, https://github.com/WalletWasabi/WalletWasabi/tree/v1.98.4.0, Accessed 28 Apr 2025

Email Cloaking: Deceiving Users and Spam Email Detectors with Invisible HTML Settings

Bingyang Guo[1], Mingxuan Liu[2], Yihui Ma[3], Ruixuan Li[3], Fan Shi[1], Min Zhang[1(✉)], Baojun Liu[2,3(✉)], Chengxi Xu[1], Haixin Duan[2,3], Geng Hong[4], Min Yang[4], and Qingfeng Pan[5]

[1] National University of Defense Technology, Hefei, China
zhangmindy@nudt.edu.cn
[2] Zhongguancun Laboratory, Beijing, China
[3] Tsinghua University, Beijing, China
lbj@tsinghua.edu.cn
[4] Fudan University, Shanghai, China
[5] Coremail, Guangzhou, China

Abstract. Development of HTML emails increases parsing complexity and discrepancies. Owing to parsing and rendering differences, email systems expose a new attack surface: Cloaked Spam Email (CSE). CSE exploits the legitimate functions of HTML and Cascading Style Sheets (CSS) to build invisible content for cloaking. It can stealthily bypass spam engines and deceive users. However, there is a lack of the understanding of this novel email cloaking threat, let alone a systematic assessment of its threat impacts, leaving a defense gap.

To fill the understanding gap of CSE risk, this paper reveals its threat impacts via empirical analysis and real-world measurements. First, through systematic analysis of CSS rendering features and their applicability to email clients, we identified 16 invisible configurations. Based on these findings, we conducted a comprehensive evaluation of 14 well-known email services. Our results reveal 12 services vulnerable to CSE, with our constructed spam samples successfully bypassing their detection and reaching victim inboxes, including Gmail, Fastmail, and QQ. To systematically assess the impact of CSEs in the wild, we developed a detection framework and applied it to two real-world spam datasets: an open-source spam dataset and the actual logs from a renowned email service provider. Through analyzing a combined total of 8,816,785 emails, we successfully detected 102,156 CSE attacks, highlighting the presence of such threats in the email ecosystem. Finally, we responsibly disclosed these vulnerabilities to affected email providers and provided mitigation recommendations against CSE threat.

Keywords: Abusive Content · Email Cloaking · Spam Detection Bypass

---

B. Guo and M. Liu—Both are first authors.

1 Introduction

Email services have become one of the most popular communication platforms, attracting numerous spammers to disseminate deceptive content via email services. Statistics indicate that the average number of spam emails sent per day is 85 billion [45], resulting in potential financial losses of up to 1.026 trillion dollars [16]. Spam filtering relies on multiple factors, including sender verification (e.g., SPF) [27] and content detection [7,19,20,37]. Given spam's need for malicious content, content-based detection is the primary defense against it [17,46]. However, the development of HTML emails has brought content-parsing issues, creating new attack surfaces for traditional content-based detection methods.

We uncovered a novel email cloaking technique, which is termed as **Cloaked Spam Email (CSE)**. CSE can covertly bypass spam detection engines. As shown in Fig. 1, it utilizes the CSS configuration in HTML emails that can create invisible effects, inserting interfering text content into the emails. This interferes with the judgment of spam detection engines, thus achieving the goal of bypassing detection. Specifically, since clients parse and render emails strictly according to the configuration for the purpose of displaying them, the content embedded by attackers is invisible in the recipient's email client. However, as detection engines do not need to display emails, they will read all the text content without any rendering, making the embedded content visible to spam detection engines. These embedded texts (usually legitimate) change the semantic meaning of spam emails, enabling them to stealthily bypass spam detection engines. Moreover, CSE can also increase the likelihood of users clicking on spam emails. As shown in Fig. 2, attackers utilize the differences between the email preview interface and the main text interface. By using invisible tags, they embed normal content at the beginning of the email, ensuring that normal email content is seen in the email summary, thereby inducing users to click on spam emails.

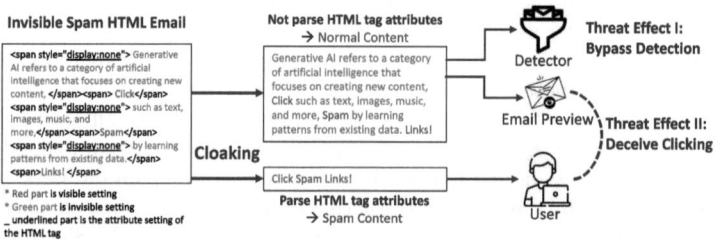

Fig. 1. Threat example of Cloaked Spam Email (CSE).

Research Gap. Significant efforts have been made to enhance the security of email services, such as SPF [27], DKIM [2], and DMARC [31], which verify the integrity and confidentiality of senders and emails, numerous studies have investigated efficient spam detection based on email headers [29], sending behavior

[24], and email content [7,19,20,37]. However, these defense mechanisms have not recognized the impact of email cloaking techniques that utilize invisible attribute CSS properties. Although Betts et al. [5] recognized the potential risks of text content hiding, it did not conduct a systematic analysis of email cloaking, thus still lacking a systematical understanding of novel CSE threat. Therefore, a comprehensive assessment of CSE risks is crucial for enhancing email providers' defense capabilities against this stealthy bypassing action.

Threat Impact of CSE. To assess CSE threat, we conducted systematic tests on 14 major email providers. First, by thoroughly analyzing HTML implementation standards[1] and validating them in email clients, we identified 16 invisible configurations that can render text content invisible. We categorized them into five groups: 1) visibility control; 2) color-related; 3) size-related; 4) layout-related; and 5) content manipulation. To test whether the use of invisible CSS configurations could bypass spam detection engines, we collected test samples from open-source spam datasets and selected 14 email providers. We embedded 16 invisible CSS properties within these spam samples separately to interfere with the detection systems' judgment of email content while ensuring user readability, resulting in a total of 2,240 test samples. Finally, we sent these spam test samples to the controlled test accounts of the 14 email providers (ensuring no impact on regular users) and recorded whether these emails were identified as spam. The results revealed that 12 email providers, e.g., Gmail and iCloud, were vulnerable to CSE risks, with test samples successfully bypassing detection engines and reaching users' inboxes.

Real-World Impact of CSE. Additionally, we conducted a large-scale assessment of CSE impact using two real-world spam datasets: an open-source spam dataset and the actual logs from a leading email service provider. Specifically, we developed CSEMiner for identifying CSE and applied it to the two real-world spam datasets. Through analyzing a total of 8,816,785 emails, CSEMiner successfully identified 102,156 CSE attacks, involving 73,202 distinct spam senders. In addition, among the 170,260 suspicious emails provided by the partner email providers, we found that 8,561 (5.03%) employed CSE techniques, from which we identified 324 distinct spam campaigns.

Contributions. The paper makes the following contributions:

- We systematically unveil a novel email cloaking technique, termed Cloaked Spam Email (CSE), which exploits invisible CSS property configurations. CSE not only circumvents spam detection mechanisms but also enhances the deceptive impact on users. Our evaluation code and partial results are open-sourced at https://github.com/MingxuanLiu/Cloaked_Spam_Email-ESORICS25.

---

[1] https://html.spec.whatwg.org/multipage/.

- We comprehensively evaluate the threat impact of CSE on 14 mainstream email providers. Our threat assessment reveals that 12 email providers are vulnerable to CSE threat. We have responsibly disclosed this risk to all affected vendors, receiving positive responses.
- Threat impact measurements carried out on two real-world datasets reveal that Cloaked Spam Email (CSE) technology has been misused to create spam emails. Empirical assessments indicate that these techniques pose a threat to the current email systems.

2 Background and Threat Model of CSE

In this section, we illustrate the preliminary information of email service and the detailed threat description of CSE.

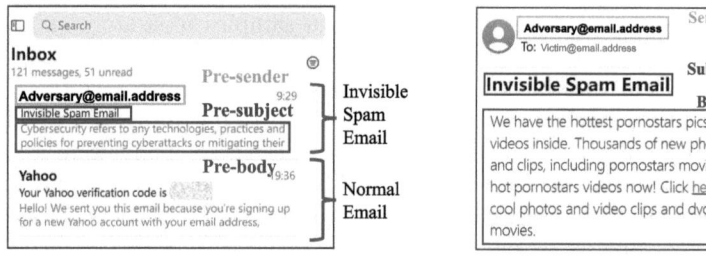

(a) Email Preview Interface. (b) Full Email View of CSE.

Fig. 2. Example of email preview interface and full email view.

2.1 Background

Email services, utilizing the Simple Mail Transfer Protocol (SMTP) [36], operate through a multi-step process: 1) Sender's mail user agent (MUA) transmits email to mail transfer agent (MTA) via SMTP or HTTP; 2) Sender's MTA forwards to receiver's MTA via SMTP; 3) Receiver's MTA delivers to receiver's MUA via HTTP, IMAP, or POP3 [28]; 4) Receiver's MUA parses and displays the email content to users. Driven by demand for more complex content presentation (e.g., image), email communication evolved from simple plain text in the early internet era to HTML-based formats [13]. Similar to HTML parsing and rendering of websites, email terminals must adhere to various HTML configurations, such as font and font size, when displaying emails on the User Interface (UI). However, email clients' limited HTML rendering capabilities and security concerns led to the adoption of a restricted HTML subset for emails [33]. Specifically, HTML email excludes certain HTML tags (like <iframe>) and JavaScript (JS) support, balancing enhanced visual presentation with compatibility and security considerations across diverse email platforms.

As HTML format is introduced into email content, the rendering and display of email clients have become increasingly complex, also introducing some rendering discrepancies between different components. This parsing difference mainly stems from the functional disparities among different components, that is, those components that require UI display and those that do not. For example, the following two sets of parsing differences.

Parsing Difference I: Between Spam Detector and Full Email View for Users. The email content is a key feature for spam detection [39], so many vendors' detectors aim for comprehensive content processing. Additionally, due to the lack of complex UI display requirements and performance limitations in handling large volumes of emails, spam detectors typically do not render emails but instead extract the content of interest from semi-structured email files for analysis. Specifically, they usually directly extract all the text content within emails, not performing any rendering process. This leads to a difference where detectors can see text set as invisible, while users cannot view that portion from the email UI interface (i.e., full email view).

Parsing Difference II: Between Preview Interface and Full Email View. The email preview is the first UI displayed to users in the MUA (as shown in Fig. 2a). Users can only see the complete email content after clicking on a specific email (as shown in Fig. 2b). The email preview typically consists of three parts: pre-sender (sender name or email address), pre-subject (email subject) and pre-body (email summary). The purpose of the email preview is to provide users with a summary before opening the email, significantly enhancing processing efficiency. The pre-body reflects the summary of the full email content, which is typically a limited number of initial characters as the summary (e.g., Gmail allows summaries from 0 to 5 lines) [12]. Since pre-body only displays text, lacking strong rendering requirements, and thus often does not adhere to CSS properties. This results in a rendering discrepancy between the pre-body and body, where the pre-body can show text set as invisible, but the body cannot.

2.2 Threat Exploitation of CSE

CSE exploits the rendering discrepancies to create email cloaking threat, allowing it to bypass spam detection (threat effect I), but also deceiving users into clicking on spam emails (threat effect II).

Threat Effect I: Bypass Spam Detection. Parsing difference I of email content seen between spam detectors and users' full email view allows CSE to evade detection. Because spam detectors do not render CSS properties, they process both invisible and visible text together. As shown in Fig. 1, adversaries embed "normal" distracting text within CSS properties with invisible attributes. This distracting text truncates the malicious content in spam, undermining its original harmful semantics and making it difficult for spam detectors to identify malicious features, thereby bypassing detection. However, since users see content rendered according to HTML attributes, they do not view the "normal" text used for truncation, allowing the carefully crafted spam content to be fully conveyed to the victim, while bypassing detection, as shown in Fig. 1.

Threat Effect II: Deceive Victim Clicking. Parsing difference II between the pre-body in the email preview and the body in the full view allows CSE to deceive victims into clicking on spam. Since the pre-body displays only email content, it does not strictly adhere to HTML rendering. Due to the space-constrained, preview interface lacking complex-format display needs, pre-body usually neither needs nor adheres to HTML configurations when extracting text. Adversaries embed "normal" content at the beginning of the email, ensuring that the pre-body shows legitimate content to users, thereby reducing victims' suspicion towards CSE emails and increasing the likelihood of clicks, as shown in Fig. 2.

Threat Model. CSE has two main objectives. To ensure the success of spam email attacks, adversaries need to ensure that the emails can successfully reach the recipients' inboxes, that is, bypass spam detection engines. Regarding enhancing the success rate of spam email attacks, adversaries need to deceive victims into opening the emails in the email preview interface as much as possible. Implementing CSE is straightforward for adversaries, as they need to meet two conditions to attempt sending CSE to any victim's email and evade spam detection: 1) a server or email account capable of sending emails without being blocked by the target email system; 2) knowledge of CSS properties with invisible configurations. Victims can be threatened by CSE as long as they have an email account for receiving emails and a MUA for checking them.

3 Evaluation of CSE Threat Impact

To evaluate the threat impact of CSE, we conducted tests on popular email services. Initialized by the selection of target email services, we first systematically examined CSS properties which could cause invisible parsing effect. Then, we tested the target email services by constructing a series of test samples with invisible settings to evaluate whether they could bypass spam detection engines.

3.1 Selection of Target Email Services

To conduct the tests, we need accounts from target email service providers. Based on market popularity, we selected dominant email service providers, most of which have over 1 billion users. Among them, we chose 25 email service providers that allow public registration, which were also testing targets in prior studies [22, 38].

Considering that the attack goal of CSE is primarily to bypass the spam detection engine, it is necessary to simultaneously identify a batch of spam samples and email providers, ensuring that spam samples without CSE technology can be stably identified as spam by the spam detection engines of email providers. We conducted a pre-experiment based on the open-source spam email datasets (detailed in Sect. 3.3). Specifically, we randomly sampled 60 spam emails from these three datasets and sent plain spam text (without hidden configurations) to test email accounts of selected providers, observing whether the emails reached the spam folders of their users. Table 7 shows the results. Four email providers produced inconsistent results in two consecutive tests on the same spam sample, making it difficult to determine their performance to detect the test sample. Seven email providers only classified a few (fewer than 10) spam emails, including Tutamail.com and Rambler.ru, and Five providers did not classify any test emails as spam (e.g., Naver.com). Finally, we ultimately selected 14 email providers with stable detection performance in tests of 60 spam emails—those showing no inconsistent results and identifying at least 10 spam emails.

Table 1. CSS properties and invisible configurations.

Category	Invisible Configurations
Visibility control	(A1) display: none;
	(A2) visibility: hidden;
	(A3) visibility: collapse;
Color control	(B1) color: transparent;
	(B2) opacity: x^*;
	(B3) blur: x^*;
	(B4) text-to-background contrast: $y^\#$;
	(B5) mix-blend-mode: x^*
Size control	(C) font-size: x^*;
Layout control	(D1) position: absolute; margin/padding: x^*
	(D2) position: absolute; left/top/right/bottom: x^*
	(D3) transform: translate[X|Y] (x^*)
	(D4) line-height/text-indent:x^*
Content Manipulation	(E1) position & z-index
	(E2) mask/-webkit-mask
	(E3) clip: rect(x^*)/ clip-path

x^*: A constructed value based on the effect of the corresponding CSS property
$y^\#$: The degree of difference between font color and background color

3.2 Identification of Invisible CSS Properties

To comprehensively identify CSS properties with invisible configurations suitable for constructing CSE, we employed a combination of static and dynamic analysis.

Static Analysis. First, we identify CSS properties with invisible potential from statically analyzing standard documents, as they may pose CSE risks. Specifically, two security researchers manually reviewed HTML standards[2], identifying 16 CSS properties capable of creating invisible effects and categorizing them into five strategic groups. Table 1 summarizes the principles and implementations of these 5 classes of CSS properties.

- *Visibility control.* To enhance dynamic control and rendering performance, HTML provides 3 CSS properties that can directly hide elements on the screen, such as "(A1) `display:none`".
- *Color Control.* To enhance visual richness in emails, HTML allows the adjustment of opacity and color of text and background. On one hand, text transparency makes it invisible. On the other hand, a low text-background color contrast makes text blend into the background, achieving an invisible effect.
- *Size Control.* In HTML, "`font-size`" specifies text size, which influences user attention. Text that is too small can be nearly invisible. Particularly, setting the font size to zero means the text won't be displayed on the screen, effectively being totally hidden.
- *Layout Control.* Due to screen size limitations, email clients can only display content within specific dimensions. The space limitation causes users to be unable to directly read content that exceeds this range, thereby creating an indirect hiding effect. Although users can scroll to view it, most may not realize this, making the hiding effect valid.
- *Content Manipulation.* HTML allows elements to stack, enabling top content to cover bottom content. Additionally, elements can be clipped, and if the clipping area is large enough, it can hide all content. Thus, using other content to overlay or clip text can effectively conceal target text.

Dynamic Analysis. Subsequently, we conducted dynamic analysis on the 16 HTML CSS properties to verify their actual rendering in email clients and tested the rendering of email summaries across different providers. Specifically, we added benign test text (as shown in green in Fig. 1) to these CSS properties, constructed HTML emails, and sent them to test accounts of 14 target email providers. By manually observing the hiding effects in the email clients, we confirmed the effectiveness of these properties. As depicted in Table 8, we found that all 16 properties successfully created hiding effects, indicating their potential for constructing CSE.

---

[2] https://html.spec.whatwg.org/multipage/.

3.3 Evaluation Setup

In this study, we aimed to assess the impact of CSE risks on 14 target email providers. We modified samples originally identified as spam to create CSE and observed whether they could bypass spam detection. Specifically, a successful threat is indicated by CSE reaching the user's inbox instead of the spam folder within that email provider.

Spam Email Text. To assess the bypass capability of CSE, we first needed a set of spam data that could be successfully recognized by target spam detection engines. We obtained relevant data from three public spam detection competitions. Two datasets were sourced from Kaggle's spam detection datasets[3], both comprising English spam data with classification labels. We randomly selected 30 emails marked as spam from these datasets as candidate samples. Additionally, considering some target email providers are based in China, we also selected a Chinese spam dataset from the DataFontain competition[4], which includes various user-reported Chinese spam texts with manually labeled types, primarily involving scams and underground industries. From this dataset, we randomly sampled 30 spam emails as Chinese candidate samples. *Ultimately, our spam dataset contains 30 English samples and 30 Chinese samples.*

Testing Case Construction. As described in Sect. 3.1, we sent original spam emails to the candidate providers, which led to the selection of 14 providers. Based on the test results, we randomly selected 10 emails marked as spam from each provider and extracted their body content as malicious text samples. Using these samples, we designed test cases to systematically evaluate CSE's bypass capability across different email services. Specifically, we added benign text (interference text) to truncate the malicious text. We sourced a large number of normal sentences from two public projects[5] as interference text and randomly inserted them into the malicious text at word-level positions. To ensure the interference text remained invisible to users, we used one unique invisible configuration (Table 1) for each test case. Thus, we obtained a total of 160 CSE test samples for each email service, calculated as 10 (malicious text samples) × 16 (invisible configurations).

3.4 Evaluation Results of CSE Threat Impact

We sequentially sent test samples to each email provider and recorded the bypass status, where a test email appearing in the user's inbox (rather than the spam folder) indicated a successful bypass. Table 2 presents the evaluation

---

[3] https://www.kaggle.com/datasets/mfaisalqureshi/spam-email/data and https://www.kaggle.com/datasets/ashfakyeafi/spam-email-classification.
[4] https://www.datafountain.cn/competitions/508/datasets.
[5] https://github.com/hitokoto-osc/sentences-bundle?tab=readme-ov-file and https://github.com/Armanidrisi/quote-generator-api.

Table 2. CSE bypass experiment results on 14 target email services.

Email Services	A1	A2	A3	B1	B2	B3	B4	B5	C	D1	D2	D3	D4	E1	E2	E3
Gmail.com	●	◐	◐	◐	◐	◐	◐	◐	●	◐	◐	◐	◐	◐	◐	◐
iCloud.com	●	●	●	●	●	●	◐	◐	●	◐	◐	●	●	◐	●	●
Yahoo.com	●	◐		◐	◐	◐	◐	◐		◐	◐	◐	◐	◐	◐	◐
Yandex.com																
Aol.com	●			◐		◐										
Fastmail.com				●	●		◐	◐		●	●	●	●	●	●	●
Onet.pl	●	●	●	●	●	●	●	●	●	●	●	●	●	●	●	●
163.com	●	●	●	●	●	●	●	●	●	●	●	◐	●	●	●	●
126.com	●	●	●	●	●	●	●	●	●	●	●	◐	●	●	●	●
139.com	●	●		◐		◐				◐	◐			◐	◐	
QQ.com	●	●		●			◐	●	◐	◐	●		◐	●	●	
Sina.com	◐	◐	◐	◐	◐	◐	◐	◐	◐	◐	◐	◐	◐	◐	◐	◐
Sohu.com																
Yeah.net	●	●	●	●	●	●	●	●	●	●	●	●	◐	●	●	●

● means that CSE can bypass spam detection and render according to the configuration, not displaying the interference text.

◐ means that CSE can bypass spam detection, while the client does not render according to the configuration but displays interference texts.

results for 14 email providers. Notably, except for Sohu.com and Yandex.com, the other 12 providers (85.71%) were all affected by CSE to varying degrees. Seven providers, including Gmail.com, iCloud.com, Onet.pl, and 163.com, struggled to handle CSE risks, with all test samples bypassing security measures. Importantly, Onet.pl effectively bypassed all tested configurations due to robust support for the CSS properties proposed. This highlights the significant threat posed by CSE. Additionally, we found that not all email providers adhered to all HTML configurations, resulting in limited impact for 39.6% of bypassed spam cases due to rendering issues, which allowed users to see the interference text. For example, Sina.com did not render any of the proposed CSS properties; while CSE emails reached the inbox, the interference text was also visible to users. Despite the rendering flaws that allowed interference text to be shown to victims, the malicious text successfully bypassed spam detection, still indicating a significant threat. This underscores the vulnerability of the spam detection engines of affected providers when confronted with complex HTML configurations.

Furthermore, we conducted fine-grained experiments on Sohu and Yandex, two providers seemingly immune to CSE, to infer their countermeasures. Specifically, we designed four control groups: sending benign content only, benign content with hidden configuration interference text, spam content only, and malicious content with hidden configuration interference text. Each group sent 20 emails to both providers. Sohu identified all emails with invisible configurations as spam, while some without invisible configurations reached users' inboxes—indicating Sohu may employ defenses against invisible configurations. Yandex classified all control group emails as spam, likely due to strict filtering policies. These results explain their CSE resistance, which inspires our CSE defense strategies discussed in Sect. 5.

4 Real-World Impact of Cloaked Spam Email

To comprehensively understand and characterize the landscape of CSE in the wild, we designed and implemented CSEMiner, a framework to automatically detects email cloaking. Subsequently, we applied CSEMiner to two real spam datasets and measured real-world CSE threat impact.

4.1 CSEMiner Design

Figure 3 depicts the overall design of the CSEMiner architecture, composed of 3 steps. First, *Pre-processing* parses the spam emails to filter out unparsable emails due to non-compliance and non-HTML emails. Second, *Feature Extraction* uses an HTML path analyzer to analyze the final style of each piece of text, forming sentence-attribute pairs. Finally, *Cloaking Detection* analyzes the attribute features corresponding to each sentence to determine if cloaking exists.

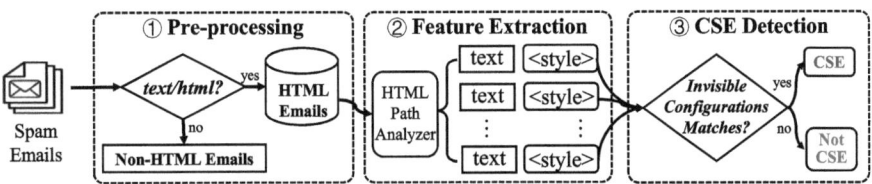

Fig. 3. CSEMiner architecture.

Dataset. In our evaluation, we use two real-world datasets, as shown in Table 3.

- *Spam Archive dataset* [18]. It collects over 8 million spam emails from March 1998 to the present. The dataset collects spam emails using a series of honeypot email addresses, each of which stores the full message header and body as a file. We collected 8,646,525 spam emails between January 2000 and December 2024.

- *Real-world Suspicious emails dataset.* We collaborated with Coremail[6], a leading China email provider serving many universities and businesses, and deployed a powerful automated analytics engine as well as human analytics to protect customers from spam. We obtained 170,260 suspicious HTML emails from its security gateway for a total of 31 days (from July 22, 2024 to August 21, 2024). Each message log is a complete email, including its metadata and contents.

4.2 CSEMiner Implement and Evaluation

Pre-processing. Since invisible configurations for CSE threat only occur in HTML emails, to improve efficiency, we filter out HTML emails during the pre-processing stage. Specifically, for emails with a single content type, CSEMiner excludes emails whose Content-Type is "`text/plain`". For MIME-multipart emails, CSEMiner determine whether the email contains a "`text/html`" part.

Feature Extraction. To facilitate identifying the existence of CSE, CSEMiner extracts text and corresponding rendering style from each candidate email to form text-style pairs. Initially, CSEMiner leverages BeautifulSoup to parse HTML documents. It reads the HTML document and converts it into a Document Object Model (DOM) tree. Subsequently, CSEMiner traverses the DOM tree. For each path from the root node to a leaf node that contains text, it meticulously records the style sets. As it moves along each path, the style are sequentially updated until reaching the leaf node. At this point, the text and the updated style are saved together, giving rise to a text-attribute pair. Ultimately, this comprehensive process successfully assembles a collection of text-attribute pairs, laying a solid foundation for further cloaking analysis.

Cloaking Detection. CSEMiner examines whether the style of each text contains invisible configurations to detect CSE. For each text-style pair, CSEMiner checks whether the style meets the invisible configurations in Table 1. If they do, the text is marked as invisible. Otherwise, the text is marked as visible. Finally, to exclude interference from misconfigurations (e.g., minimal hidden text that cannot semantically perturb emails to bypass spam detectors), we define emails satisfying both 1) *invisible text characters length > 10* and 2) *the proportion of inbvisible text > 10* as CSE. Emails failing these criteria are not CSE.

Detection and Evaluation. In our dataset of 8,816,785 spam emails, CSEMiner first excluded 5,178,482 non-HTML emails and discovered 102,156 CSEs in the remaining 3,638,303 HTML emails. Due to the limitations of the ground-truth, we manually examined the detection results. We randomly sampled 2,000

---

[6] https://www.coremail.cn/.

emails from the suspected CSEs, extracted their HTML source codes, and manually reviewed their contents. We confirmed that 1,973 were indeed CSEs, resulting in a false positive rate of only 1.35% (27). Subsequently, we randomly selected 2,000 emails without hidden text for a manual inspection. It was found that only 12 of them were misidentified, with a false negative rate of only 0.6%. We further examined the misclassified data, and the errors originated from two aspects. First, for some incomplete configurations, browsers will perform specific optimizations, and CSEMiner does not modify the content of the files. For example, some invalid emails set bgcolor="000000", while the standard representation should be bgcolor="#000000". Second, our method lacks support for some uncommon styles. For example, multi-layer table nesting causes confusion in parsing background colors. These two reasons lead to errors in the parsing of the final styles, thus resulting in misclassification.

4.3 Measurement of CSE

Overall Results. Table 3 presents the overall detection results, including their senders and associated domains. Totally, we discovered 102,156 CSEs in 3,638,303 HTML emails. In particular, 5.03% of spam emails employ CSE techniques in the real-world Suspicious email dataset. These CSE emails originated from 73,202 distinct senders, averaging 1.40 CSE messages per sender. This demonstrates that CSE technology has been exploited in the real-world to construct spam emails. Furthermore, we checked domains from CSE senders and found CSE activities show domain-level dynamism. In our measurements, many domains had only one email address (86.32% in Spam Archive, 86.60% in Suspicious emails). Analysis showed they're self-hosted, suggesting attackers use domain-registration flexibility for continuous CSE spam attacks.

Table 3. Overall statistics of datasets and detection results.

Dataset	Emials	HTML Emails	CSE	Precentage	CSE Sender	CSE Domain
Spam Archive	8,646,525	3,468,043	93,595	2.70%	72,613	45,920
Suspicious emails	170,260	170,260	8,561	5.03%	589	470
Total	8,816,785	3,638,303	102,156	2.81%	73,202	46,390

Invisible Configuration Categories. We conducted a systematic investigation into the typological distribution and prevalence of invisible configuration. CSEMiner automatically traces the ultimately rendered CSS properties for each email, enabling precise categorization of cloaked content according to the taxonomic classes enumerated in Table 1. We further records the adoption frequency of each category across distinct CSE attack instances. Table 4 shows the adoption of each invisible configuration category. Our findings reveal that color control and size control-the most straightforward text style configuration technique-constitute the predominant invisibility methods. In contrast, layout control techniques were deployed in fewer than 1% of CSEs due to implementation complexity. In a similar vein, we did not identify content manipulation techniques in our dataset. Notably, 24,683 CSEs (23.14%) employed multiple complementary invisibility techniques, with hybrid configurations combining at least two distinct evasion strategies. This combination of techniques suggests that spammers are leveraging diverse methods to enhance the effectiveness of their CSEs, making defense of CSE threat for email providers more challenging.

Table 4. The usage of invisible configures.

Invisible Configure	# CSE in Spam Archive(%)	# CSE in Suspicious email(%)	# CSE in Two dataset(%)
Visibility control	6,147(6.57%)	7,535 (88.02%)	13,682 (13.39%)
Color control	76,467 (81.70%)	8,000 (93.45%)	84,467 (82.68%)
Size control	20,369 (21.76%)	769 (8.98%)	21,138 (20.69%)
Layout control	116 (0.12%)	209 (2.44%)	325 (0.32%)
Content manipulation	0 (0.00%)	0 (0.00%)	0 (0.00%)

Invisible Text Embedding Strategy. Subsequently, we investigated the general way in which hidden content is embedded. We used three categories to describe the invisible text embedding strategy: 1) *Add paragraph*: large portions of invisible text were introduced to the extent that the semantics of the original text were changed. 2) *Disrupt word*: single or multiple invisible characters were added to truncate keywords and thus disrupt the original semantics. 3) *Insert word*: entire words were inserted into the email to disrupt the sentence flow. The key difference between 2) and 3) lies in whether keywords are disrupted. For Chinese texts, if a word is split into individual Chinese characters, it is considered that the keyword has been disrupted, and it is thus classified as a disrupt word. Due to the limitations of the ground-truth, we randomly selected 1,000 samples from each of the two datasets and carried out a manual annotation. Table 5 shows the embedding strategies in the 2,000 samples. We found that "Add paragraph" was widely applied. At the same time, "Insert word" was the least common (only 30 instances in Spam archive, and none were detected in the Suspicious emails. This is most likely because a large number of Chinese emails are included.). In addition, we also observed that 863 (43.15%) CSEs contain at least 2 different invisible text embedding strategies.

CSE Campaigns. To ascertain diversified adversarial strategies, we aggregated the collected CSEs into CSE campaigns. We define a CSE campaign as a set of CSEs that contain the same sender address or similar content. First, emails sharing identical sender addresses are clustered. Subsequently, we leverage TF-IDF

Table 5. The usage of 3 obfuscation text types.

Obfuscation Text Type	# CSE in Spam Archive(%)	# CSE in Suspicious email(%)	# CSE in Two dataset(%)
Add paragraph	938 (93.80%)	994 (99.40%)	1,932 (96.60%)
Disrupt word	91 (9.10%)	810 (81.00%)	901 (45.05%)
Insert word	30 (3.00%)	0 (0.00%)	30 (1.5%)

(Term Frequency-Inverse Document Frequency) vectorization with cosine similarity thresholds to group emails with isomorphic semantic patterns of subjects and visible body content. Specifically, the thresholds are determined based on our experience, with $\theta = 0.8$ for subjects, $\theta = 0.6$ for visible body content. Finally, we identified 324 campaigns and Table 6 shows three representative campaigns.

Table 6. Examples of three typical campaigns.

Subject	Count	CSE Tech.*	Sender	Type
About the third quarter XXXX process	6,687	A, B	91 senders 91 domains	phishing
International express export	142	B	1 senders 1 domains	spam (ad)
Additional information is required to protect your account from unauthorized use.	27	B, C	27 senders 27 domains	phishing

*: CSE Tech. means the CSE hiding techniques used by this campaign: A for Visibility control, B for Color control, C for Size control, D for Layout control, and E for Content Manipulation.

The first CSE campaign was a phishing attempt targeting corporate employees. Attackers impersonated human resources and admin departments, sending emails demanding employees complete urgent statistical tasks by day's end. These emails contained a link to a document, which VirusTotal flagged as malicious. To obscure their malicious intent, the attackers inserted random characters and symbols into the message and hid the obfuscating text using the "display: none" property. Additionally, these emails ended with a proverb, hidden by setting color as white, further diluting their maliciousness. This technique helped the emails bypass spam detection more effectively while maintaining high readability for the recipient. The second campaign comprises promotional emails originating from the transportation sector. These messages embed semantically disordered paragraphs within their advertising content while employing CSS obfuscation techniques via "background-color: white" and "color=white" to conceal the injected text passages. The third campaign is also a phishing activity. In this campaign, the attacker claimed that there were abnormalities in the user's bank account and asked the user to click on the given link to log in to the account. However, the given link was identified as malicious by VirusTotal. In this activity, the attacker inserted large chunks of text and meaningless strings into the text for semantic obfuscation, and used "`font-size: 1px`" and "`color: #ffffff`" on the interfering text to hide them.

5 Discussion

Ethics. All experiments in this work adhered to ethical guidelines, specifically the Belmont Report [6] and the Menlo Report [25]. First, for the threat impact testing of 14 email providers, we employed temporarily registered controlled email accounts and ensured that the experiment did not affect any legitimate users. Second, the sending process for CSE test emails was strictly controlled, maintaining a frequency of one email every five seconds to prevent any disruption to the normal operations of the email providers. Third, assessing the real-world threat impact of CSE requires processing email content, which is extremely private. To address ethical concerns around real user data, we used honeypot data from "non-real users" for evaluation (i.e., honeypot data). Finally, to mitigate CSE risks, we responsibly disclosed this risk to 12 affected email providers and offered them defense recommendations. To date, we have received confirmation from four providers and are actively assisting them in resolving the issue.

Limitation. Despite our best efforts to evaluate the real-world impact of CSE from two dataset. There still have certain limitations. For ethical reasons, the real-world evaluation focused on a limited dataset (i.e., honeypot data) of this email provider rather than the entire email log. Therefore, this evaluation represents a low-bound of its actual threat impact. However, we identified over 6k real exploitation cases in this dataset, indicating the threat's existence. Furthermore, the results obtained on a large-scale open-source dataset, also demonstrate the influence of CSE. Besides, in our threat assessment of 14 email providers, we found that 12 were affected by CSE, further highlighting its significant impact. Second, we evaluated CSE risk impacts based on character length and ratio in invisible configurations. To minimize false positives interfering with evaluation results, we set stringent judgment thresholds based on observations. While acknowledging potential false negatives—meaning our results may represent only the lower bound of CSE impact—we believe our findings sufficiently demonstrate CSE risks, given both datasets derive from real-world email traffic.

Mitigation. Spam detection engines can identify CSE by comparing discrepancies between visible and invisible content. Email clients could add risk warning features for messages with hidden content—for example, displaying prompts in the inbox and body text: "This email may contain hidden text; please screen carefully". Such alerts enhance user vigilance and mitigate fraud risks. As a first step, our work systematically reveals and evaluates the risk. Leveraging insights from this research, detecting such risks will form part of our future work. Furthermore, we publicly shared our threat assessment code and results to assist the email community in mitigating CSE risks.

6 Related Works

As a widely used communication methods, email security has garnered significant attention. First, numerous studies focus on defensive technologies against sender spoofing attacks that bypass email authentication systems, proposing a range of security and encryption protocols for email authentication. These include STARTTLS [21,34,35], Sender Policy Framework (SPF) [9,27], DomainKeys Identified Mail (DKIM) [8,42], Domain-based Message Authentication, Reporting and Conformance (DMARC) [3,30], DANE [10,32], and PGP [40].

Additionally, spam content detection depends on several key features of spam detection include three aspects. First, the email's metadata reflects the sender's credibility, including the sender's email address and IP address [11,20,29]. Second, the text content of the email (including the subject and body) indicates its primary purpose, making it a crucial feature for spam detection [26,37]. Moreover, some studies detect spam based on links embedded in the email [20]. Besides, spam often embeds malicious content in attachments, so some methods detect spam based on both the body content and attachments [43]. Finally, the behavior patterns of email sending can reveal abnormal user behavior [7,19,20,23,41], such as significant changes in sending patterns after a legitimate account is compromised. These features are not used in isolation, which are typically combined for detection [1,4,14,15,44].

However, current defense and detection systems overlook the impact of email parsing, as most spam detection engines do not assess the parsing effects of HTML emails, relying solely on plain text content detection. Consequently, these defense mechanisms struggle to address the CSE cloaking risk, providing adversaries with significant opportunities to bypass spam detection engines.

7 Conclusion

Spam detection systems' oversight of email client rendering of HTML emails allows adversaries to exploit email cloaking. This paper presents Cloaked Spam Email (CSE), a novel technique using HTML invisible attributes to hide content from users. Through analysis HTML standard, we identified 16 invisible attributes. Subsequently, we generated a set of spam emails containing invisible configurations. After sending these test emails to email accounts of 14 mainstream email providers, we assessed whether the emails successfully bypassed spam detection and reached users' inboxes rather than their spam folders. Our evaluation revealed that 12 email providers were affected by CSE risks, e.g., Gmail and iCloud. Moreover, we evaluated the real-world risk impacts of CSE on a open-source spam dataset and the real data from a Chinese email service provider. In total, we discovered 102k CSEs, which demonstrates the real-world exploitation impact of CSE. Finally, we responsibly disclosed these risks to the affected providers, receiving confirmation from four of them and actively assisting in the remediation of the vulnerabilities.

Acknowledgement. This work was supported by the National Key Research and Development Program of China (Grant No. 2022YFB3102902). Haixin Duan is supported by the Taishan Scholars Program.

A Pre-measure spam detection Results

Table 7 illustrates the spam detection results of 25 email providers.

Table 7. Spam detection result on 25 email service.

Email Service	#Inbox/#Spam	Email Service	#Inbox/#Spam
Gmail.com	2/58	Fastmail.com	50/10
Outlook.com	✕	Cock.li	✕
iCloud.com	2/58	Onet.pl	8/52
Yahoo.com	0/60	163.com	10/50
Mail.ru	✕	126.com	6/54
Protonmail.com	60/0	139.com	7/53
Yandex.com	0/60	189.com	60/0
GMX.com	✕	QQ.com	0/60
Naver.com	60/0	Sina.com	0/60
Tutamail.com	57/3	Sohu.com	6/54
Rambler.ru	54/6	Tom.com	60/0
Daum.net	60/0	Yeah.net	5/55
Aol.com	0/60		

✕   inconsistent results.

B Email Rendering Evaluation Results

Table 8 illustrates the rendering results of target email providers.

Table 8. Email rendering in different email clients.

Category	Client Name	Pre-body	Body (Supported CSS conf.)
Web	Gmail.com, Yahoo.com, Yandex.com, Aol.com	Unrendered HTML	A1, C1
	iCloud.com	Unrendered HTML	A1, A2, A3, B1, B2, B3, B5, C, D3, D4, E2, E3
	Fastmail.com	Unrendered HTML	A1, A2, A3, B1, B2, B3, C, D1, D2, D3, D4, E1, E2, E3
	Onet.pl	Unrendered HTML	A1, A2, A3, B1, B2, B3, B5, C, D3, D4, E1, E2, E3
	163.com, 126.com, Yeah.com	None	A1, A2, A3, B1, B2, B3, B4, B5, C, D1, D2, D3, E1, E2, E3
	139.com	None	A1, A2, A3, B3, C1, D4
	qq.com	Unrendered HTML	A1, A2, A3, B1, B2, B3, B4, C, D3, E2, E3
	sina.com, sohu.com	None	None
Application	Gmail, Yandex Mail	Unrendered HTML	A1, C1
	Fastmail	Unrendered HTML	A1, A2, A3, B1, B2, B3, C, D1, D2, D3, D4, E1, E2, E3
	Onet Poczta	Unrendered HTML	All
	NetEase Mail Master (163, 126, Yeah)	Unrendered HTML	A1, A2, A3, B1, B2, B3, B4, C, D3, D4, E1, E2, E3
	139 Mail	Unrendered HTML	A1, A2, A3, B3, C1, D4
	QQ Mail	Unrendered HTML	A1, A2, A3, B1, B2, B3, C, D3, D4, E2, E3
	Yahoo Mail, Sina Mail, Sohu Mail	Unrendered HTML	None

References

1. Abu-Nimeh, S., Nappa, D., Wang, X., Nair, S.: A comparison of machine learning techniques for phishing detection. In: Cranor, L.F. (ed.) Proceedings of the Anti-Phishing Working Groups 2nd Annual eCrime Researchers Summit 2007, Pittsburgh, Pennsylvania, USA, 4–5 October 2007. ACM International Conference Proceeding Series, ACM (2007)
2. Allman, E., Callas, J., Delany, M., Libbey, M., Fenton, J., Thomas, M.: Domainkeys identified mail (DKIM) signatures. RFC **4871**, 1–71 (2007)
3. Ashiq, M.I., Li, W., Fiebig, T., Chung, T.: You've got report: measurement and security implications of {DMARC} reporting. In: 32nd USENIX Security Symposium (USENIX Security 23), pp. 4123–4137 (2023)
4. Bergholz, A., Chang, J.H., Paass, G., Reichartz, F., Strobel, S.: Improved phishing detection using model-based features. In: CEAS 2008 - The Fifth Conference on Email and Anti-Spam, Mountain View, California, USA, 21–22 August 2008 (2008)

5. Betts, L., Biddle, R., Lottridge, D., Russello, G.: Exploring content concealment in email. In: 2024 APWG Symposium on Electronic Crime Research (eCrime) (2024)
6. for the Protection of Human Subjects of Biomedical, U.S.N.C., Research, B.: The Belmont report: ethical principles and guidelines for the protection of human subjects of research. Department of Health, Education and Welfare (1979)
7. Cidon, A., Gavish, L., Bleier, I., Korshun, N., Schweighauser, M., Tsitkin, A.: High precision detection of business email compromise. In: Heninger, N., Traynor, P. (eds.) 28th USENIX Security Symposium, USENIX Security 2019, Santa Clara, CA, USA, 14–16 August 2019, pp. 1291–1307. USENIX Association (2019)
8. Crocker, D., Hansen, T., Kucherawy, M.: Domainkeys identified mail (dkim) signatures. Technical report (2011)
9. Czybik, S., Horlboge, M., Rieck, K.: Lazy gatekeepers: a large-scale study on SPF configuration in the wild. In: Montpetit, M., Leivadeas, A., Uhlig, S., Javed, M. (eds.) Proceedings of the 2023 ACM on Internet Measurement Conference, IMC 2023, Montreal, QC, Canada, 24–26 October 2023, pp. 344–355. ACM (2023)
10. Dukhovni, V., Hardaker, W.: The dns-based authentication of named entities (DANE) protocol: updates and operational guidance. RFC **7671**, 1–33 (2015)
11. Duman, S., Kalkan-Cakmakci, K., Egele, M., Robertson, W.K., Kirda, E.: Emailprofiler: spearphishing filtering with header and stylometric features of emails. In: 40th IEEE Annual Computer Software and Applications Conference, COMPSAC 2016, Atlanta, USA, 10–14 June 2016, pp. 408–416. IEEE Computer Society
12. Elias, B.: What is an email preheader and how can it increase email open rates? (2023). https://www.activecampaign.com/blog/email-preheader
13. EmailLabs: Email marketing statistics and metrics (2007). http://www.emaillabs.com/tools/email-marketing-statistics.html
14. Fette, I., Sadeh, N.M., Tomasic, A.: Learning to detect phishing emails. In: Williamson, C.L., Zurko, M.E., Patel-Schneider, P.F., Shenoy, P.J. (eds.) Proceedings of the 16th International Conference on World Wide Web, WWW 2007, Banff, Alberta, Canada, 8–12 May 2007, pp. 649–656. ACM (2007)
15. Garera, S., Provos, N., Chew, M., Rubin, A.D.: A framework for detection and measurement of phishing attacks. In: Proceedings of the 2007 ACM Workshop on Recurring Malcode, pp. 1–8 (2007)
16. Global Anti-Scam Alliance (GASA): The global state of scams - 2023 (2023). https://www.gasa.org/_files/ugd/7bdaac_b0d2ac61904941aeb4cbf0217aa355d2.pdf
17. Google: Understanding Gmail's spam filters (2022). https://workspace.google.com/blog/identity-and-security/an-overview-of-gmails-spam-filters
18. Guenter, B.: Spam archive. https://untroubled.org/spam/
19. Ho, G., et al.: Detecting and characterizing lateral phishing at scale. In: Heninger, N., Traynor, P. (eds.) 28th USENIX Security Symposium 2019, Santa Clara, CA, USA, 14–16 August 2019, pp. 1273–1290. USENIX Association (2019)
20. Ho, G., Sharma, A., Javed, M., Paxson, V., Wagner, D.A.: Detecting credential spearphishing in enterprise settings. In: Kirda, E., Ristenpart, T. (eds.) 26th USENIX Security Symposium 2017, Vancouver, BC, Canada, 16–18 August 2017, pp. 469–485. USENIX Association (2017)
21. Hoffman, P.E.: SMTP service extension for secure SMTP over transport layer security. RFC **3207**, 1–9 (2002)
22. Hu, H., Wang, G.: End-to-end measurements of email spoofing attacks. In: Enck, W., Felt, A.P. (eds.) 27th USENIX Security Symposium, USENIX Security 2018, Baltimore, MD, USA, 15–17 August 2018, pp. 1095–1112. USENIX Association (2018)

23. Hu, X., Li, B., Zhang, Y., Zhou, C., Ma, H.: Detecting compromised email accounts from the perspective of graph topology. In: Proceedings of the 11th International Conference on Future Internet Technologies, CFI, Nanjing, China, 15–17 June 2016. ACM
24. Jáñez-Martino, F., Alaíz-Rodríguez, R., González-Castro, V., Fidalgo, E., Alegre, E.: A review of spam email detection: analysis of spammer strategies and the dataset shift problem. Artif. Intell. Rev. **56**(2), 1145–1173 (2023)
25. Kenneally, E., Dittrich, D.: The menlo report: ethical principles guiding information and communication technology research. Available at SSRN 2445102 (2012)
26. Khonji, M., Iraqi, Y., Jones, A.: Mitigation of spear phishing attacks: a content-based authorship identification framework. In: 6th International Conference for Internet Technology and Secured Transactions, ICITST 2011, Abu Dhabi, UAE, 11–14 December 2011. pp. 416–421. IEEE (2011)
27. Kitterman, S.: Sender policy framework (SPF) for authorizing use of domains in email, version 1. RFC **7208**, 1–64 (2014)
28. Klensin, J.C., Catoe, R., Krumviede, P.: IMAP/POP authorize extension for simple challenge/response. RFC **2095**, 1–5 (1997). https://doi.org/10.17487/RFC2095
29. Krause, T., Uetz, R., Kretschmann, T.: Recognizing email spam from meta data only. In: 7th IEEE Conference on Communications and Network Security, CNS 2019, Washington, DC, USA, 10–12 June 2019, pp. 178–186. IEEE (2019)
30. Kucherawy, M., Zwicky, E.: Domain-based message authentication, reporting, and conformance (dmarc). Technical report (2015)
31. Kucherawy, M.S., Zwicky, E.D.: Domain-based message authentication, reporting, and conformance (DMARC). RFC **7489**, 1–73 (2015). https://doi.org/10.17487/RFC7489
32. Lee, H., Ashiq, M.I., Müller, M., van Rijswijk-Deij, R., Kwon, T.T., Chung, T.: Under the hood of DANE mismanagement in SMTP. In: 31st USENIX Security Symposium (USENIX Security 22), pp. 1–16. USENIX Association, Boston (2022)
33. mailchimp: Limitations of html email. https://mailchimp.com/help/limitations-of-html-email/
34. Mayer, W., Zauner, A., Schmiedecker, M., Huber, M.: No need for black chambers: testing TLS in the e-mail ecosystem at large. In: 11th International Conference on Availability, Reliability and Security, ARES 2016, Salzburg, Austria, 31 August–2 September 2016, pp. 10–20. IEEE Computer Society (2016)
35. Poddebniak, D., Ising, F., Böck, H., Schinzel, S.: Why TLS is better without STARTTLS: a security analysis of STARTTLS in the email context. In: Bailey, M.D., Greenstadt, R. (eds.) 30th USENIX Security Symposium, USENIX Security 2021, 11–13 August 2021, pp. 4365–4382. USENIX Association (2021)
36. Postel, J.: Simple mail transfer protocol. RFC **821**, 1–72 (1982)
37. Saidani, N., Adi, K., Allili, M.S.: A semantic-based classification approach for an enhanced spam detection. Comput. Secur. **94**, 101716 (2020)
38. Shen, K., et al.: Weak links in authentication chains: a large-scale analysis of email sender spoofing attacks. In: Bailey, M.D., Greenstadt, R. (eds.) 30th USENIX Security Symposium, USENIX Security 2021, 11–13 August 2021. USENIX Association (2021)
39. Standardization Administration of the People's Republic of China: Information security technology—technical specification for anti-spam products(gb/t 30282-2023) (2023). https://std.samr.gov.cn/gb/search/gbDetailed?id=FC816D04FF0A62EBE05397BE0A0AD5FA

40. Stransky, C., Wiese, O., Roth, V., Acar, Y., Fahl, S.: 27 years and 81 million opportunities later: investigating the use of email encryption for an entire university. In: 2022 IEEE Symposium on Security and Privacy (SP), pp. 860–875. IEEE (2022)
41. Stringhini, G., Thonnard, O.: That ain't you: blocking spearphishing through behavioral modelling. In: Almgren, M., Gulisano, V., Maggi, F. (eds.) DIMVA 2015. LNCS, vol. 9148, pp. 78–97. Springer, Cham (2015). https://doi.org/10.1007/978-3-319-20550-2_5
42. Wang, C., et al.: A large-scale and longitudinal measurement study of DKIM deployment. In: 31st USENIX Security Symposium (USENIX Security 22), pp. 1185–1201. USENIX Association, Boston (2022)
43. Wang, J., Katagishi, K.: Image content-based "email spam image" filtering. J. Adv. Comput. Netw. **2**(2), 110–114 (2014)
44. Whittaker, C., Ryner, B., Nazif, M.: Large-scale automatic classification of phishing pages. In: Proceedings of the Network and Distributed System Security Symposium NDSS, San Diego, USA, 28 February–3 March 2010. The Internet Society (2010)
45. WORLDMETRICS.ORG: Global email traffic dominated by spam, accounting for 58.5% (2024). https://worldmetrics.org/spam-statistics/
46. Yahoo: Manage spam and mailing lists in new yahoo mail. https://help.yahoo.com/kb/SLN28056.html?guccounter=1

BlowPrint: Blow-Based Multi-factor Biometrics for Smartphone User Authentication

Howard Halim, Eyasu Getahun Chekole[✉], Daniël Reijsbergen, and Jianying Zhou

Singapore University of Technology and Design, Singapore, Singapore
{howard_halim,eyasu_chekole,daniel_reijsbergen,jianying_zhou}@sutd.edu.sg

Abstract. Biometric authentication is a widely used security mechanism that leverages unique physiological or behavioral characteristics to authenticate users. In multi-factor biometrics (MFB), multiple biometric modalities, e.g., physiological and behavioral biometrics, are integrated to mitigate the limitations inherent in single-factor biometric systems. The primary research challenge within MFB lies in identifying novel behavioral techniques capable of meeting critical criteria, including high accuracy, high usability, non-invasiveness, resilience against spoofing and other known attacks, and low use of computational resources. Despite ongoing advancements, current behavioral biometric techniques often fall short of fulfilling one or more of these requirements. In this work, we propose *BlowPrint*, a novel behavioral biometric technique that allows us to authenticate users based on their phone blowing behaviors. In brief, we assume that the way users blow on a phone screen can produce distinctive acoustic patterns, which can serve as a unique behavioral biometric identifier for effective user identification or authentication. The acoustic features of blowing, such as differences in pattern, intensity, frequency, and timing, are unique to each person, making this technique highly accurate, non-invasive, and exceedingly robust against spoofing and other attacks. Moreover, it can be concurrently performed and seamlessly integrated with other physiological techniques, such as facial recognition, thereby enhancing usability. To assess BlowPrint's effectiveness, we conduct an empirical study involving 50 participants from whom we collect blow-acoustic and facial feature data in both sitting and standing modes. Subsequently, we compute the similarity scores of the blow-acoustic data using various time-series similarity algorithms, while we use a pretrained FaceNet-512 model for the facial recognition features. Finally, we combine the similarity scores of the two modalities through score-level fusion and compute the accuracy using a machine learning-based classifier. As a result, the proposed method demonstrates an accuracy of 99.35% for blow acoustics, 99.96% for facial recognition, and 99.82% for the combined approach. The experimental results demonstrate BlowPrint's high effectiveness in terms of authentication accuracy, spoofing attack resilience, usability, non-invasiveness, and other aspects.

Keywords: Blow-Acoustic · Facial Recognition · Biometric Authentication · Behavioral Biometrics · Physiological Biometrics · Multi-Factor Biometrics

1 Introduction

The increasing reliance on digital services has necessitated robust authentication mechanisms to protect user data. Traditional password, PIN or key-based authentication systems are vulnerable to a wide range of attacks, including phishing, brute-force, social engineering, and side-channel attacks [8,14]. Biometric authentication, which leverages physiological (e.g., fingerprints, face, iris and retina) or behavioral (e.g., gait, voice and keystroke dynamics) traits, offers a more secure alternative [15]. It is increasingly used as a secure and convenient method for identity verification, replacing or complementing traditional password-based systems. However, single-factor biometric authentication methods have several limitations and are often insufficient to address the growing sophistication of modern cyberattacks. For example, physiological biometric methods are vulnerable to a wide range of attacks, such as spoofing, forging and deepfaking [29,52]. On the other hand, behavioral biometric methods offer resilience against these attacks. However, accuracy and stability remains a major challenge in behavioral biometric due to variations in user behavior, environmental sensitivity, and temporal instability, leading to lower accuracy and reliability problems [10]. For instance, voice-based authentication is highly susceptible to background noise, while gait recognition can be influenced by changes in footwear or walking surfaces.

To alleviate the shortcomings in single-factor biometrics, multi-factor biometrics (MFB) have been increasingly adopted. MFB can enhance the security, resilience, and robustness of the authentication process by integrating and utilizing complementary data derived from multiple biometric factors, typically through a combination of physiological and behavioral traits. The main challenge in MFB lies in the design of novel behavioral biometric techniques that satisfy several critical criteria, including high accuracy, resilience against known attacks (e.g., spoofing resistance), usability (e.g., non-intrusive and seamless integration with other modalities), non-invasiveness, and minimal computational resource requirements, among others.

To overcome these challenges, we propose a novel behavioral biometric technique that effectively authenticates users based on their phone blowing behaviors. In brief, we hypothesize that the manner in which individuals blow on their phone screen produces distinctive and unobtrusive acoustic patterns, which can serve as a unique behavioral biometric for effective user authentication. The blow-acoustic signals are captured in audio waveform by the phone's built-in microphone and constitute a novel modality for user authentication and verification. This novel approach offers a distinctive set of salient features and significant advantages over existing behavioral biometric techniques:

- *Enhanced accuracy*: The acoustic characteristics of blowing, defined by variations in pattern, intensity, frequency, and timing, is unique to each individual, which renders the modality highly accurate and exceedingly difficult for adversaries to replicate.
- *Resistance to known attacks*: Unlike voice-based biometrics, which are susceptible to being recorded and replayed, blow acoustics are inherently less prone to such spoofing or replicating attempts, thereby offering greater security.
- *High usability and seamless integration*: This modality can be effortlessly incorporated alongside certain physiological biometric techniques, such as facial recognition, enhancing overall system usability without compromising functionality.
- *Non-invasive nature*: The blow-acoustic process is entirely contactless and touch-free, ensuring a non-intrusive user experience that aligns with modern expectations for hygiene, convenience, and user privacy.
- *Rapid execution with minimal resource requirements*: The authentication process is swift, requiring only a few brief blowing samples, and operates solely using the device's native microphone—eliminating the need for additional hardware.

To establish a robust MFB system, we seamlessly integrate the blow-acoustic behavioral biometric technique with a facial recognition physiological biometric technique, which leverages the uniqueness of facial features for user identification and authentication. The unique patterns in a person's blow-acoustic behavior and facial recognition features can be captured simultaneously using the phone's built-in microphone and camera, respectively, to offer a more accurate and robust user authentication system. These modalities are also seamlessly integrated using score-level fusion [36]. This significantly enhances usability, mitigates integration complexity and reduces processing times in MFB.

As a proof-of-concept, we have implemented the BlowPrint application and collected time-series data comprising blow-acoustic signals and facial features from 50 participants. Each participant performed 10 sessions in sitting and standing modes. We then evaluated the accuracy of the proposed technique using multiple metrics from the literature, e.g., the false acceptance and rejection rates. To this end, we first compute the similarity score across different blow-acoustic patterns collected from various users and sessions. This is achieved using a range of widely recognized similarity algorithms, such as Euclidean Distance (ED) [19], Dynamic Time Warping (DTW) [22,37], Shape Dynamic Time Warping (shapeDTW) [48,55], DTW+S, [43,44], Shape-Based Distance (SBD) [33,39], and Time Warp Edit Distance (TWED) [32]. The resulting similarity scores are also compared to determine the most effective similarity algorithm for the proposed technique. Furthermore, we employ a pretrained FaceNet-512 model [42] to compute the similarity scores across different facial features collected from the participants. Finally, we combined the similarity scores of the two techniques through score-level fusion and compute the accuracy using the k-Nearest Neighbors (kNN) algorithm [26], a machine learning-based classifier. Overall, the blow-acoustic technique achieves an accuracy of 99.35% and a false acceptance rate of 0.42% in our dataset, while the facial recognition technique achieved an accuracy of 99.96%, with a false acceptance rate of 0.04%. Furthermore, the score-level fusion of both techniques yielded an accuracy of 99.82%, with a false acceptance rate of 0.18%.

Overall, this work offers the following main contributions.

- We introduce a novel behavioral biometric technique based on phone blowing acoustics, which provides numerous advantages over most existing techniques. This includes high accuracy, resilience against replication and spoofing attacks, enhanced usability, seamless integration with other modalities, non-invasiveness, high robustness in different postural modes, rapid execution, and minimal resource requirements.
- The seamless integration of the proposed phone blowing acoustics technique with facial recognition enhances overall security by complementing the robust security capabilities of the latter, which is grounded in physiological biometrics.
- We conducted a comprehensive evaluation of the proposed MFB technique by developing a prototype application, BlowPrint, and collecting empirical data from 50 participants. The technique demonstrated high effectiveness, achieving an accuracy of 99.59% for the blow acoustics, 99.96% for the facial recognition, and 99.82% for the combined approach through score-level fusion.

2 Related Work

Recent works in biometric authentication systems have explored a variety of modalities, with the main categories being physiological biometrics, behavioral biometrics or a combination of the two.

2.1 Physiological Biometrics

Physiological biometrics, also known as biological biometrics refer to the use of inherent physical characteristics of individuals for identity authentication and recognition. Common physiological biometrics modalities include the face [50], iris [16,53], fingerprint [31], ear [1], and hand geometry [38]. These biometrics are unique to each individuals, which has led to their long-standing use in authentication system [12].

Despite their reliability and widespread adoption, these type of biometrics have several limitations. Some modalities, such as fingerprint scanning, may be considered invasive or raise hygiene concerns. Others like face recognition, are vulnerable to spoofing attacks using photographs. Furthermore, advances in artificial intelligence and machine learning enabled the creation of deepfake attakcs [5]. Hence, systems that lack robust liveness detection mechanisms are particularly vulnerable to such attacks, emphasizing the need for enhanced security measures in biometric authentication.

2.2 Behavioral Biometrics

Behavioral biometrics have gained increasing attention as a non-intrusive and user-friendly means of authentication. These modalities leverage unique patterns in user behavior such as breathing [13], touch interactions [17], and keystroke dynamics [56].

De Luca et al. [17] proposed a touch-based behavioral biometric authentication system layered on top of the traditional pattern password mechanism in smartphones. The system utilizes the speed, pressure, and rhythm of touch input for user authentication. Similarly, Zheng et al. [56] proposed a tapping-based behavioral biometric authentication system for smartphone. It captures the acceleration, pressure, size, and time of the keystroke, and uses a one-class machine learning algorithm for authentication. However, both approaches are inherently invaise, as they require direct physical interaction with the smartphone screen, which may not be suitable for all scenarios or user preferences. Chauhan et al. [13] analyzes breathing patterns to identify users based on three types of breathing behavior: sniffing, normal, and deep breathing. The study demonstrates that breathing behavior is unique, achieving a true positive rate (TPR) as high as 94'%'. However, its evaluation is limited to only these 3 breathing patterns, raising questions about its scalability and adaptability in addition to the low accuracy rate achieved.

Despite the promise of unimodal behavioral biometrics, they suffer from several inherent limitations. These include reduced robustness, as accuracy can degrade in the presence of noise, environmental variations, or changes in user behavior, and increased susceptibility to spoofing or imitation attacks [21,47,51].

2.3 Multi-factor Biometrics

Recent studies have explored the combination of multiple biometric modalities to improve authentication accuracy. Multi-factor biometric authentication systems can offer enhanced security and robustness by leveraging complementary information from different biometric traits. Most existing multimodal biometric systems predominantly rely on physiological traits, such as facial features, irises, touch, and fingerprint.

Al-Wasy et al. [3] proposed a multimodal biometric system using a deep learning approach that integrates facial features and both left and right irises, employing a fusion module at the score and rank levels. Aizi et al. [2] implemented a score-level fusion strategy based on fingerprint and iris as its multimodal biometric. Srivastava et al. [45] also proposed a multimodal biometric system combining finger-knuckle print and iris data, then applying a neuro-fuzzy classifier at the match level. However, these proposed system exclusively relies on physiological biometrics, without incorporating behavioral modalities, limiting its adaptability in scenarios where physical traits may be unavailable or compromised. Moreover, [2,45] biometrics modalities do not share the same anatomical region which can be awkward in practical use [25], and with the absence of behavioral biometrics may further reduce resilience against sophisticated attacks.

Mahfouz et al. [30], a multimodal behavioral biometric authentication system that leverages feature-level fusion of various behavioral modalities, including touch gestures, dynamic keystroke, and accelerometer data. While it reduces reliance on physical traits, systems that depend solely on behavioral biometrics may suffer from variability due to a user's mood, health, or environmental distractions, potentially affecting accuracy, robustness and usability.

El Rahman et al. [20] proposed a hybrid approach combining ECG and fingerprint biometrics using multiple fusion strategies. While the combination of physiological and behavioral modalities aims to enhance security and robustness, the system remains somewhat invasive, requiring users to directly scan the fingerprint while additional equipment outside smartphone is required to capture the ECG signals.

Lee et al. [27] developed an authentication method for IoT devices that processes both touch and motion data using sensors from a smartphone and smartwatch. While effective in concurrent data acquisition, the method requires users to wear a smartwatch, limiting convenience and applicability in scenarios where such smartwatches are unavailable.

Wu et al. [54] proposed an authentication system that utilizes hand geometry features and acoustic sensing technique. While Zhou et al. [57] proposed an authentication system that utilizes facial landmarks and acoustic sensing. Both system utilizes echoes as an acoustic features. However, the accuracy and equal error rate (EER) presented in these systems are not as high as those achieved by our approach, as shown in Sect. 5.2.

Despite these advancements, existing multimodal systems still face notable limitation. As highlighted by Koffi et al. [25], among the various biometrics modality combinations, voice and face biometrics stand out for their balance of robustness, security, and usability. Particularly due to their inherent support for liveness detection and minimal of intrusiveness. Building upon these insights, our proposed implementation addresses the aforementioned challenges by introducing a novel fusion of physiological and behavioral modalities that ensures improved security, usability, while maintaining high accuracy. A qualitative and quantitative comparison of the relevant related works and that of our proposed technique is presented in Table 3.

3 Threat Model and System Requirements

3.1 Threat Model

In our threat model, we consider various types of attacks that specifically target biometric systems. In particular, we assume the following capabilities of the adversary.

- Sensors are not compromised by the adversary and can produce the expected biometric data.
- Biometric data (i.e., blow-acoustic and facial image data) is stored securely, and can not be read or manipulated by the adversary.

- Spoofing attacks may use synthetic biometric samples (e.g., deepfake face images, recorded blow sound, and replicated blow-acoustic patterns) to bypass authentication.
- Biometric duplication attacks may exploit residual physiological biometrics such as facial images publicly available online.
- Replay attacks can use previously recorded blow sounds or static images to spoof the system, but the current blow pattern cannot be known to the adversary.

3.2 System Requirements

In the following, we outline the key aspects that we consider as essential requirements within the context of behavioral or multi-factor biometrics. These requirements also serve as our evaluation criteria to evaluate both existing and proposed biometric techniques.

Accuracy. A behavioral biometric technique should demonstrate high accuracy to effectively minimize the risk of impersonation attacks (i.e., by having a low false positive rate), while also enhancing user convenience by lowering the authentication attempts (i.e., by having a low false negatives).

Resilience Against Known Attacks. A behavioral biometric technique should demonstrate high resilience against certain known attacks, including the following:

- *Spoofing attacks*: Attacks that may use synthetic biometric samples (e.g., deepfake face images, recorded voice) to bypass authentication.
- *Replication attacks*: Attacks that attempt to replicate biometric traits through brute-forcing or other techniques.
- *Privacy leakage*: Unauthorized data collection and misuse of biometric information.

Usability. One of the primary challenges in behavioral biometrics and MFB is usability. In this regard, the key usability factors include:

- *User convenience*: The system should be intuitive and non-intrusive.
- *Response time*: Authentication should be fast and seamless.
- *Seamless integration*: Combining multiple biometric techniques in a single authentication attempt (one-shot authentication) improves user experience by minimizing the need for separate actions and reducing processing time. For instance, face and voice recognition can be conducted concurrently, thereby eliminating the requirement for sequential authentication steps.

Non-invasiveness. To address hygiene-related concerns, behavioral biometric techniques should be performed in a touchless manner. Moreover, data collection should be limited to brief durations (typically no more than a few seconds) and must not occur without the user's awareness that their behavior is being monitored.

MFB Support. In light of the inherent limitations of single-factor biometric systems, it is imperative that biometric authentication techniques incorporate multiple biometric modalities, typically through the integration of both behavioral and physiological factors.

Low Resource Requirements. Behavioral biometric authentication should be conducted using minimal resources, i.e., the computational resources and sensors available on a regular smartphone, without requiring additional hardware or software tools.

4 BlowPrint: Proposed Technique

4.1 Overview

This section presents a detailed description of *BlowPrint*, a novel behavioral biometric technique that effectively authenticates users based on their phone blowing behaviors. It is also seamlessly integrated with a facial recognition physiological biometric technique to form a robust and effective MFB, Using the BlowPrint application, the phone blowing acoustic signals are recorded using the phone's built-in microphone, while facial features are captured using the front camera of the phone. The phone is positioned at a fixed distance d to ensure uniformity in blow sound and facial image captures. This is achieved by letting the user position her face inside an oval shape indicator. The process is illustrated in Fig. 1.

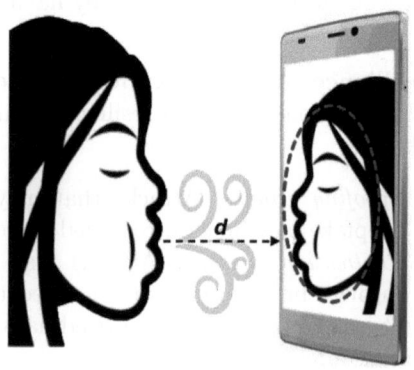

Fig. 1. Illustration of BlowPrint

4.2 Workflow

This section outlines the workflow of BlowPrint, detailing the main activities and phases involved in the proposed authentication procedure. A high-level architecture of the workflow is illustrated in Fig. 2. The process begins with users interacting with the BlowPrint application on a running mobile device, which concurrently captures the blow-acoustic and facial feature data.

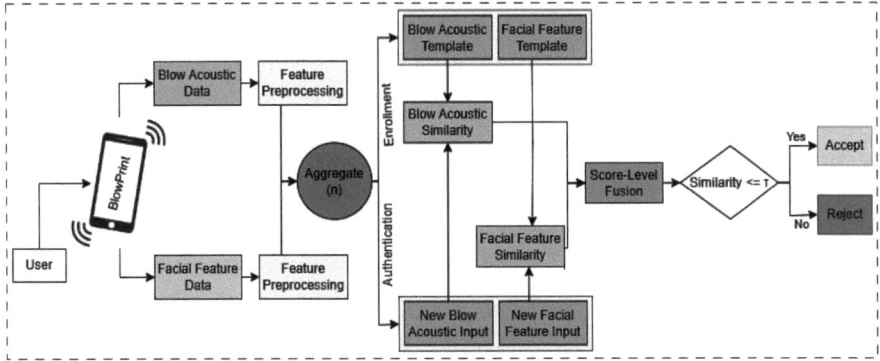

Fig. 2. A high-level workflow of BlowPrint

Data Collection. To evaluate the effectiveness of the proposed biometric technique, the blow-acoustic and facial feature data were collected from several users using the BlowPrint application. A standard smartphone model with a built-in microphone and front-facing camera were used to collect the blow-acoustic and facial feature data, respectively. Since the intensity and consistency of the blow-acoustic data as well as quality of the face image can be affected by the distance between the user and the phone, we set a fixed distance d between the user and the phone while performing data collection. This is achieved by designing an appropriate oval-shaped indicator in the application where the users need to positioned their face in it before data collection is activated. When the position is validated, the camera captures facial features and the microphone records blow-acoustic signals. Users are required to blow into the microphone while facing the camera, ensuring that both modalities are captured in one shot.

Feature Preprocessing. These raw biometrics data undergo dedicated preprocessing stages to extract suitable features for matching. In the blow-acoustic modality, the system captures the raw audio signal (amplitude) at a sampling rate of 48 kHz, recording every 0.02 s, which yields 960 samples per window. Each sample window is reduced to a single value using the Root Mean Square (RMS) operation to represent its intensity. The resulting 5-second RMS signal is then refined using a Simple Moving Average (SMA) filter [28] to suppress noise and smooth short-term fluctuations.

For the facial modality, the application utilizes the Google ML Kit Android Face Detection Library [23] to detect and crop facial regions. The cropped facial images are subsequently passed through a deep learning model which generates a facial embeddings used for the facial similarity computation

Following feature preprocessing, the systems proceed with a parallel biometric authentication pipeline for blow-acoustic and facial recognition modalities, each performing similarity computation before being combined via score-level fusion and compared against the threshold (τ).

4.3 Similarity Computation

Blow-Acoustic Similarity Computation. The similarity computation for the blow-acoustic modality was conducted by leveraging a series of time-series similarity algorithms. These algorithms serve as the foundation for measuring the similarity between enrolled and query signals, which are then compared using a decision threshold to determine whether an authentication attempt is accepted or rejected. This similarity-based decision process forms the basis for evaluating the overall accuracy of the system. The algorithms employed include the following.

- **ED** [19]: A point-to-point similarity measure used to compute distance between 2 time-series by directly comparing corresponding elements.
- **DTW** [22,37]: A time-series similarity measure that allows non-linear alignments by compares each point to the closest matching point in the other sequence while preserving temporal order.
- **shapeDTW** [48,55]: An extension of the DTW algorithm that incorporates local shape descriptors to align segments with similar structural patterns. In this experiment, the compound shape descriptor, combining raw values and their first-order derivatives, was used to enhance local structure matching.
- **DTW+S** [43,44]: A DTW-based technique that captures similarity using a shapelet representation matrix, enhancing alignment through discriminative local patterns.
- **SBD** [33,39]: A similarity measure based on normalized cross-correlation that aligns time-series based on the most correlated subsequences.
- **TWED** [32]: A time-series similarity measure that combines edit distance with time-lag penalties, allowing flexible alignment by accounting the temporal distortions and magnitude differences.

Facial Similarity Computation. Various deep learning models have been developed for facial recognition, including FaceNet [40], VGG-Face [34], DeepFace [49], ArcFace [18], and others. While each model has its own characteristics, such as different embedding sizes, loss functions, and backbone architectures, Serengil et al. [41] provide a comprehensive benchmark comparing the performance of these models on the same dataset. The results show that FaceNet-512 consistently achieves the highest accuracy among the evaluated models.

Based on these findings, the similarity computation for the facial modality in our system was conducted using a pretrained FaceNet-512 model [42]. This model maps cropped facial images into 512-dimensional embeddings, where facial similarity is computed using cosine similarity [46] between the embeddings of enrolled and query images.

Aggregated Similarity Computation. To compute the overall accuracy of the proposed technique, we aggregate the similarity scores of the two modalities using the score-level fusion technique [36]. Although various fusion methods are available, we employ score-level fusion in our approach, as it demonstrates superior performance compared to alternative techniques. In this method, the matching scores derived from both blow-acoustic and facial recognition modalities are first normalized using the min-max normalization technique [24] and subsequently combined using the weighted summation method with equal weights [9]. The resulting fused score is subsequently evaluated using the kNN algorithm. For a given value of k, the k closest similarities to the enrolled templates are identified and compared against a predefined threshold, τ. If the similarity falls below τ, the user is authenticated; otherwise, access is denied. For each user, τ is dynamically determined according to the k and targeted recall value q, as outlined in Sect. 5.2.

4.4 Enrollment and Authentication Phases

As in any conventional biometric systems, the proposed biometric technique involves the usual enrollment and authentication phases. During the enrollment phase, a biometric template is generated for each user based on preprocessed and fused blow-acoustic and facial feature data collected over multiple sessions. This template is securely stored and serves as the user's unique biometric identifier. During the authentication phase, the system receives new blow-acoustic and facial feature inputs from a user. Like in the enrollment phase, these inputs undergo the preprocessing stage before computing the similarity scores of each modalities by comparing the resulting data with the enrolled biometric template. These scores are then combined using score-level fusion. If the fusion similarity score falls within a predefined threshold τ, i.e., $Similarity \leq \tau$, the user is successfully authenticated; otherwise, it is rejected.

4.5 Implementation Details

To validate the proposed technique, a proof-of-concept application, BlowPrint, was implemented on the Android platform. This application allows the capture of users' phone blowing acoustic signals and facial features for both the enrollment and authentication phases. It leverages Android's native APIs for real-time media processing. Specifically, audio signals are captured using the `android.media` package [7], which provides access to the raw audio recording. For facial images, the `android.hardware.camera2` package [6] is used, along with Google ML Kit Android Face Detection Library [23] to identify and crop suitable regions for facial preprocessing.

Furthermore, an automated evaluation framework using R and Python was implemented, enabling the end-to-end processing pipeline, from data collection to performance evaluation, to be conducted seamlessly. The main evaluation logic is developed in R, with support from several Python libraries integrated via the `reticulate` package [4], which allows calling Python code directly within the R environment. The evaluation framework comprises a set of modules that utilize the similarity algorithms discussed in Sect. 4.3 to compute the accuracy of each biometric modality and their fusion.

5 Evaluation and Discussion

In this section, we evaluate the effectiveness of BlowPrint through an empirical study involving acoustic and facial feature data from human participants. We investigate the accuracy achieved by the various similarity computation techniques from Sect. 4.3 and use the score-level fusion method to combine the blow-acoustic and facial feature datasets.

5.1 Data Collection and Extraction

We conducted an empirical study consisting of 50 participants, including 40 males and 10 females. The participants were randomly chosen from various demographic groups with an approximate age range of 22 to 65 years. Each participant performed 10 sessions which each lasted 5 s. To ensure robustness of the proposed technique in different postures and contexts, two types of data collection modes – sitting and standing – were used: each participant performed 5 sessions while sitting and 5 sessions while standing. The collected blow-acoustic signals and facial features were stored in CSV format for further processing.

For illustration purposes, we depict the raw blow-acoustic data of four participants in Fig. 3, demonstrating different blow patterns of different users performed in 10 sessions for a span of 5 s each. The raw blow-acoustic data was captured using the `android.media` library [7], specifically the `AudioRecord` class, which leverages the ENCODING_PCM_FLOAT format to represent the audio intensity. In the figures, the red dotted line (i.e., "Signature") represents an aggregated data of the 10 sessions, generated using the DBA algorithm [35] – this is for illustration purposes only and not for authentication.

The collected raw acoustic data are further refined to suppress noise and other short-term fluctuations. This data refinement is carried out using the Moving Average technique [28], specifically the Simple Moving Average (SMA) with a window size of 8 time slots. For illustration purposes, the refined acoustic data of the four participants are depicted in Fig. 4. The dataset collected for our experimental evaluation can be found online [11] (participants' facial images are excluded due to privacy reason).

5.2 Accuracy Evaluation

Evaluation Methodology. We evaluate the performance of BlowPrint in terms of its resilience to an attacker who has gained access to the device running BlowPrint, but who has no knowledge of the user's blow-acoustic pattern. We use the other users' blow patterns as proxies for the pattern produced by an attacker: successful attempts are recorded as a true positive (TP), and as a false negative (FN) otherwise. Next, we test all of the 490 sessions by other users in the dataset against each user's base readings – if the user is authenticated, then this is recorded as a false positive (FP) and as a true negative (TN) otherwise.

Our main accuracy metric is the false acceptance rate (FAR), which is defined as $\frac{FP}{FP+TN}$. Similarly, the false rejection rate (FRR) is defined as $\frac{FN}{FN+TP}$. We

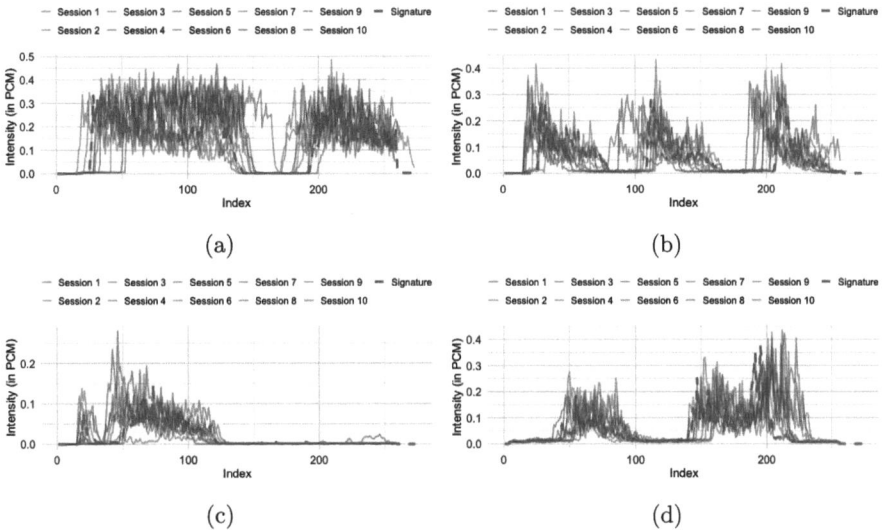

Fig. 3. Sample raw blow-acoustic data of (a) Participant 1 (b) Participant 2 (c) Participant 3 (d) Participant 4, where "Signature" is the DBA-based aggregated data of the 10 sessions

define the overall accuracy as $\frac{\text{TP}+\text{TN}}{\text{TP}+\text{TN}+\text{FP}+\text{FN}}$. Finally, we consider the effective error rate (EER), which is the minimal achievable maximum of the FAR and FRR. We do note that there is an inherent asymmetry in our setting between a false positive (in which the attacker gains unauthorized access) and a false negative (in which the user needs to retry) because of the relatively low cost of retrying a blow attempt after a failed login. For example, if we consider the following two settings (both from Table 1), 1) FPR=1.81%, FNR=0% and 2) FPR=0.27% and FNR=20%, then the first setting has more than a 10× lower maximum error rate than the second (1.81% vs. 20%), whereas the second has an FPR that is 6.7% lower than the first. Since the user may prefer the second setting if she values security over convenience, the "best" achievable maximum error rate is not necessarily the most appropriate metric in our setting. As such, we focus on the FAR over the EER as our main accuracy metric.

To compute the accuracy of BlowPrint, we use a range of k values (e.g., $k = 1$ to $k = 4$) and target recall values (e.g., $q = 10$, $q = 9$ and $q = 8$). The authentication threshold τ for each user is dynamically determined based on the specified k value and target recall value q such that q of her total n sessions would result in successful authentication. Higher values of q lead to higher thresholds, which makes it more likely that the user succeeds in authentication, but also easier for the attacker to succeed. Having set a threshold, we compute and compare BlowPrint's accuracy using multiple baseline and state-of-the-art similarity algorithms from the literature, including the ED, DTW, shapeDTW, DTW+S, SBD, and TWED as discussed in Sect. 4.3.

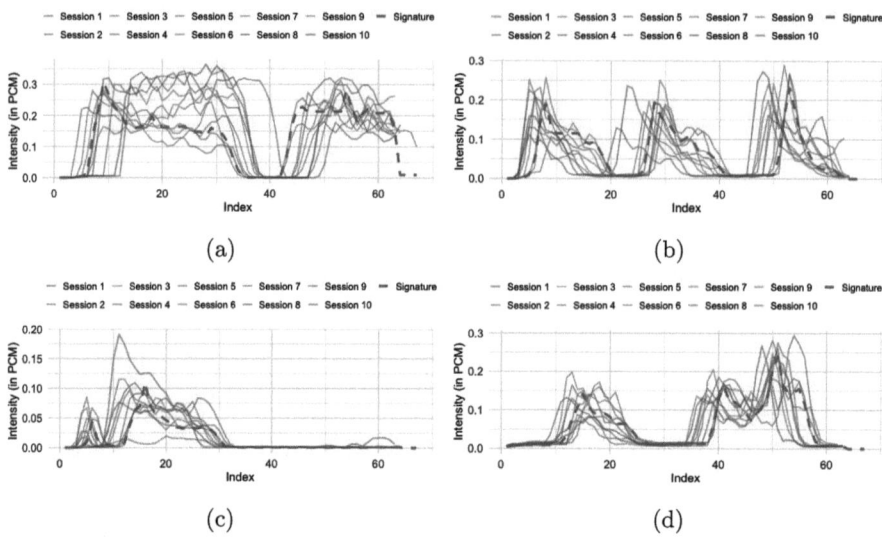

Fig. 4. Sample refined blow-acoustic data of (a) Participant 1 (b) Participant 2 (c) Participant 3 (d) Participant 4, where "Signature" is the DBA-based aggregated data of the 10 sessions

Evaluation Results. The observed EER, accuracy, FAR, and FRR as described previously are displayed in Table 1. We evaluate three distinct scenarios: using only the sitting data, only the standing data, and the combined dataset. As highlighted above, we also consider different values of k (e.g., $k = 1, 2, 3, 4$) and q (e.g., $q = 10, 9, 8$) to compute the accuracy of BlowPrint. The authentication threshold τ is automatically determined based on these parameters. We observe that the accuracy remains relatively stable for k values ranging from 1 to 4, exhibiting only minor fluctuations between 0.01% and 0.2% across different q values. Due to space limitation, we present below only the accuracy of BlowPrint for $k = 1$ across different q values, computed using the different similarity algorithms mentioned above. Among the different algorithms, DTW demonstrates the highest accuracy in most cases. The lowest FAR in our experiments is achieved by DTW with a target recall of 8 out of 10 sessions. Under this configuration, users may be required to re-record 20% of login attempts, but with a lower FAR (0.27%) as a result.

We observe that the accuracy tends to be higher for data collected in the standing mode than in the sitting mode. This discrepancy may be attributed to the fact that participants recorded the sitting data prior to the standing data, thereby gaining familiarity and improved consistency during the latter sessions. Nonetheless, the observed difference in accuracy is relatively minor (smaller than the variations observed across different time series similarity methods),

Table 1. Observed EER, accuracy, FAR, and FRR for a variety of time series analysis techniques, and for various target recall values. Bold values indicate the best FAR results in each category.

Series	Mode	EER	q = 5 (Sit & Stand)			q = 10 (Both)			q = 4 (Sit & Stand)			q = 9 (Both)			q = 8 (Both)		
			accuracy	FAR	FRR				accuracy	FAR	FRR				accuracy	FAR	FRR
ED	Sit	0.1115	0.8907	0.1115	0.000				0.9498	0.0476	0.1760				-	-	-
	Stand	0.0754	0.9261	0.0754	0.000				0.9729	0.0240	0.1800				-	-	-
	Both	0.0920	0.8748	0.1278	0.000				0.9521	0.0470	0.0920				0.9726	0.0241	0.1880
DTW	Sit	0.0178	0.9826	**0.0178**	0.000				0.9934	**0.0029**	0.1840				-	-	-
	Stand	0.0042	0.9959	**0.0042**	0.000				0.9948	**0.0016**	0.1840				-	-	-
	Both	0.0181	0.9822	**0.0181**	0.000				0.9924	**0.0058**	0.1000				0.9935	**0.0027**	0.1920
shapeDTW	Sit	0.0274	0.9731	0.0274	0.000				0.9894	0.0073	0.1760				-	-	-
	Stand	0.0155	0.9848	0.0155	0.000				0.9900	0.0066	0.1760				-	-	-
	Both	0.0370	0.9638	0.0370	0.000				0.9825	0.0160	0.0940				0.9886	0.0077	0.1900
DTW+S	Sit	0.0207	0.9798	0.0207	0.000				0.9882	0.0082	0.1880				-	-	-
	Stand	0.0165	0.9838	0.0165	0.000				0.9872	0.0095	0.1760				-	-	-
	Both	0.0334	0.9672	0.0334	0.000				0.9862	0.0121	0.0960				0.9885	0.0079	0.1860
SBD	Sit	0.0504	0.9506	0.0504	0.000				0.9883	0.0082	0.1840				-	-	-
	Stand	0.0224	0.9780	0.0224	0.000				0.9886	0.0081	0.1720				-	-	-
	Both	0.0384	0.9624	0.0384	0.000				0.9849	0.0138	0.0980				0.9881	0.0082	0.1900
TWED	Sit	0.0752	0.9263	0.0752	0.000				0.9661	0.0311	0.1720				-	-	-
	Stand	0.0502	0.9508	0.0502	0.000				0.9874	0.0094	0.1680				-	-	-
	Both	0.0866	0.9151	0.0866	0.000				0.9650	0.0339	0.0900				0.9851	0.0113	0.1900

demonstrating the robustness of the proposed technique across different postural modes. Table 2 presents the observed EER, accuracy, FAR, and FRR after combining the best blow-acoustic and facial recognition techniques using score-level fusion. Notably, this fusion approach yields a FAR of 0, indicating that no false positives were detected in our experimental evaluation.

Table 2. Observed EER, accuracy, FAR, and FRR for the best blow-acoustic and face recognition techniques, and after combining them using score-level fusion.

Biometrics Features	EER	q = 10			q = 9			q = 8		
		accuracy	FAR	FRR	accuracy	FAR	FRR	accuracy	FAR	FRR
blow-acoustic	0.0181	0.9822	0.0181	0.000	0.9924	0.0058	0.1000	0.9935	0.0027	0.192
Facial Recognition	0.0004	0.9996	0.0004	0.000	0.9980	0.0000	0.098	0.9960	0.0000	0.198
Score-level fusion	0.0018	0.9982	0.0018	0.000	0.9981	0.0000	0.094	0.9960	0.0000	0.198

5.3 Usability Evaluation

User Convenience. The proposed blow-acoustic technique is user-friendly and convenient for authentication. A simple blow on the phone enables the user to complete the authentication process. As such, it is an easy-to-use, intuitive, non-intrusive and highly practical behavioral biometric technique.

Seamless Integration. The proposed blow-acoustic behavioral biometric technique is seamlessly integrated with the facial recognition physiological method. Data from both modalities are captured simultaneously, and the authentication decision is made using a score-level fusion. Consequently, the blow-acoustic technique demonstrates strong compatibility for integration with other biometric modalities.

5.4 Non-invasiveness Evaluation

The proposed blow-acoustic technique is entirely contactless and touch-free, requiring to perform only a simple blow directed at the phone screen. The procedure is also conducted within a matter of few seconds. Consequently, this technique is highly non-invasive and significantly reduces hygiene-related concerns and the risk of privacy violations associated with physical contact.

5.5 Low Resource Requirements

The proposed biometric technique does not require any additional or specialized hardware or software. It is compatible even with low-specification smartphones equipped solely with a camera and microphone. As such, it represents a highly cost-effective solution that is accessible to users with standard or budget-friendly mobile devices.

5.6 Comparison with Related Works

In Table 3, we summarize the comparison between BlowPrint and the most closely related work discussed in Sect. 2. For each work, we present the best reported accuracy in terms of the metrics discussed in this section. Furthermore, we indicate whether they meet the other requirements discussed in Sect. 3.2: attack resistance, usability, non-invasiveness, MFB support, and low resource requirements. We observe that BlowPrint achieves the highest accuracy and is one of only three works to satisfy all requirements.

Table 3. Qualitative and quantitative comparison of related works

Related work	Evaluation Criteria								
	EC1				EC2	EC3	EC4	EC5	EC6
	Acc.	FAR	FRR	EER					
Chauhan et al. [13]	—	2%	6%	—	✓	✓	✓	✗	✓
De Luca et al. [17]	77%	21%	19%	—	✓	✓	✗	✗	✓
Zheng et al. [56]	—	—	—	3.65%	✓	✓	✗	✗	✓
Al-Waisy et al. [3]	99%	—	—	—	✗	✓	✓	✓	✓
Aizi et al. [2]	95%	3.89%	1.5%	—	✗	✓	✗	✓	✓
Srivastava et al. [45]	99.7%	—	—	20%	✗	✗	✗	✓	✗
Mahfouz et al. [30]	—	—	—	0.84%	✗	✓	✗	✓	✓
El Rahman et al. [20]	—	—	—	—	✓	✓	✗	✓	✗
Lee et al. [27]	83%	1–7%	—	—	✓	✓	✗	✓	✗
Wu et al. [54]	—	—	—	2–3%	✓	✓	✓	✓	✓
Zhou et al. [57]	93.75%	—	10%	—	✓	✓	✓	✓	✓
Ours	99.82%	0.18%	0%	0.18%	✓	✓	✓	✓	✓

Description of notations: EC1: Accuracy, EC2: Resilience against known attacks, EC3: Usability, EC4: Non-Invasiveness, EC5: MFB Support, EC6: Low Resource Requirements. ✓: Achieved, ✗: Not Achieved, —: Not Reported

6 Conclusion

This paper presents a novel behavioral biometric authentication technique, called BlowPrint, that utilizes the phone blowing behavior of users to uniquely identify or authenticate them. To enhance its robustness and reliability, the technique was also seamlessly integrated with a facial recognition-based physiological biometric technique, forming a more effective multi-factor biometrics for a more secure and convenient user authentication.

We employed various distance similarity algorithms alongside a machine learning-based classifier to compute the similarity scores of different blow-acoustic patterns, while we used a pretrained FaceNet-512 model for facial recognition. Subsequently, the similarity scores of the two modalities were combined using score-level fusion and the overall accuracy was computed using the kNN algorithm. The experimental results demonstrate that the proposed biometric technique offers high accuracy when compared to related works. Furthermore, it demonstrates several other advantages, such as high usability, non-invasiveness, and resilience against known attacks (e.g., spoofing attack) with minimal resource requirements.

The proposed protocol has significant applications in user authentication for online banking, smartphone unlocking, access control systems, and more. Future work will focus on improving the system's robustness and scalability in real-world applications, particularly in dynamic environments. In addition, its robustness and resilience can be further improved by leveraging machine learning-based techniques.

Acknowledgement. This research is supported by the National Research Foundation, Singapore and Infocomm Media Development Authority under its Trust Tech Funding Initiative (DTC-T2FI-CFP-0002). Any opinions, findings and conclusions or recommendations expressed in this material are those of the author(s) and do not reflect the views of National Research Foundation, Singapore and Infocomm Media Development Authority.

References

1. Abaza, A., Ross, A., Hebert, C., Harrison, M.A.F., Nixon, M.S.: A survey on ear biometrics. ACM Comput. Surv. (CSUR) **45**(2), 1–35 (2013)
2. Aizi, K., Ouslim, M.: Score level fusion in multi-biometric identification based on zones of interest. J. King Saud Univ.-Comput. Inf. Sci. **34**(1), 1498–1509 (2022)
3. Al-Waisy, A.S., Qahwaji, R., Ipson, S., Al-Fahdawi, S.: A multimodal biometric system for personal identification based on deep learning approaches. In: 2017 Seventh International Conference on Emerging Security Technologies (EST), pp. 163–168. IEEE (2017)
4. Allaire, J., Ushey, K., Tang, Y.: Reticulate: interface to python (2024). https://CRAN.R-project.org/package=reticulate
5. Alrawili, R., AlQahtani, A.A.S., Khan, M.K.: Comprehensive survey: biometric user authentication application, evaluation, and discussion. Comput. Electr. Eng. **119**, 109485 (2024)
6. Android Developers: android.hardware.camera2 - android developers (2024). https://developer.android.com/reference/android/hardware/camera2/package-summary
7. Android Developers: android.media - android developers (2024). https://developer.android.com/reference/android/media/package-summary
8. Ang, K.W., Chekole, E.G., Zhou, J.: Unveiling the covert vulnerabilities in multi-factor authentication protocols: a systematic review and security analysis. ACM Comput. Surv. **57**(11) (2025). https://doi.org/10.1145/3734864
9. Ayan, B., Abacıoğlu, S., Basilio, M.P.: A comprehensive review of the novel weighting methods for multi-criteria decision-making. Information **14**(5), 285 (2023)
10. Ayeswarya, S., Singh, K.J.: A comprehensive review on secure biometric-based continuous authentication and user profiling. IEEE Access (2024)
11. BlowPrint-Authors: BlowPrint Dataset (2025). https://github.com/eyaget/Biometrics/tree/main/BlowPrint-Dataset
12. Chaudhari, R.D., Pawar, A.A., Deore, R.S.: The historical development of biometric authentication techniques: a recent overview. Int. J. Eng. Res. Technol. (IJERT) **2**(10) (2013)
13. Chauhan, J., Hu, Y., Seneviratne, S., Misra, A., Seneviratne, A., Lee, Y.: Breathprint: breathing acoustics-based user authentication. In: Proceedings of the 15th Annual International Conference on Mobile Systems, Applications, and Services, pp. 278–291 (2017)

14. Chimuco, F.T., Sequeiros, J.B., Lopes, C.G., Simões, T.M., Freire, M.M., Inácio, P.R.: Secure cloud-based mobile apps: attack taxonomy, requirements, mechanisms, tests and automation. Int. J. Inf. Secur. **22**(4), 833–867 (2023)
15. Dargan, S., Kumar, M.: A comprehensive survey on the biometric recognition systems based on physiological and behavioral modalities. Expert Syst. Appl. **143**, 113114 (2020)
16. Daugman, J.: How iris recognition works. In: The Essential Guide to Image Processing, pp. 715–739. Elsevier (2009)
17. De Luca, A., Hang, A., Brudy, F., Lindner, C., Hussmann, H.: Touch me once and I know it's you! implicit authentication based on touch screen patterns. In: Proceedings of the SIGCHI Conference on Human Factors in Computing Systems, pp. 987–996 (2012)
18. Deng, J., Guo, J., Xue, N., Zafeiriou, S.: Arcface: additive angular margin loss for deep face recognition. In: Proceedings of the IEEE/CVF Conference on Computer Vision and Pattern Recognition, pp. 4690–4699 (2019)
19. Elmore, K.L., Richman, M.B.: Euclidean distance as a similarity metric for principal component analysis. Mon. Weather Rev. **129**(3), 540–549 (2001)
20. El_Rahman, S.A.: Multimodal biometric systems based on different fusion levels of ECG and fingerprint using different classifiers. Soft Comput. **24**, 12599–12632 (2020)
21. Galbally, J., Marcel, S., Fierrez, J.: Biometric antispoofing methods: a survey in face recognition. IEEE Access **2**, 1530–1552 (2014)
22. Giorgino, T.: DTW: dynamic time warping algorithms (2009). https://CRAN.R-project.org/package=dtw. R package version 1.22-3
23. Google Developers: ML Kit: Face Detection on Android. https://developers.google.com/ml-kit/vision/face-detection/android. Accessed 14 Jan 2025
24. Kiran, A., Vasumathi, D.: Data mining: min–max normalization based data perturbation technique for privacy preservation. In: Proceedings of the Third International Conference on Computational Intelligence and Informatics: ICCII 2018, pp. 723–734. Springer (2020)
25. Koffi, E.: Voice biometrics fusion for enhanced security and speaker recognition: a comprehensive review. Linguist. Portfolios **12**(1), 6 (2023)
26. Kramer, O., Kramer, O.: K-nearest neighbors. In: Dimensionality Reduction with Unsupervised Nearest Neighbors, pp. 13–23 (2013)
27. Lee, J., Park, S., Kim, Y.G., Lee, E.K., Jo, J.: Advanced authentication method by geometric data analysis based on user behavior and biometrics for IoT device with touchscreen. Electronics **10**(21), 2583 (2021)
28. Macaulay, F.R.: Introduction to "the smoothing of time series". In: The Smoothing of Time Series, pp. 17–30. NBER (1931)
29. Madan, D., Hosseini, S.E., Pervez, S.: The effect of vulnerability in facial biometric authentication. In: 2023 16th International Conference on Developments in eSystems Engineering (DeSE), pp. 726–730. IEEE (2023)
30. Mahfouz, A., Mostafa, H., Mahmoud, T.M., Sharaf Eldin, A.: M2auth: a multimodal behavioral biometric authentication using feature-level fusion. Neural Comput. Appl. **36**(34), 21781–21799 (2024)
31. Maltoni, D., Maio, D., Jain, A.K., Prabhakar, S., et al.: Handbook of Fingerprint Recognition, vol. 2. Springer (2009)
32. Marteau, P.F.: Time warp edit distance with stiffness adjustment for time series matching. IEEE Trans. Pattern Anal. Mach. Intell. **31**(2), 306–318 (2008)

33. Paparrizos, J., Gravano, L.: k-shape: efficient and accurate clustering of time series. In: Proceedings of the 2015 ACM SIGMOD International Conference on Management of Data, pp. 1855–1870 (2015)
34. Parkhi, O., Vedaldi, A., Zisserman, A.: Deep face recognition. In: BMVC 2015- Proceedings of the British Machine Vision Conference 2015. British Machine Vision Association (2015)
35. Petitjean, F., Ketterlin, A., Gançarski, P.: A global averaging method for dynamic time warping, with applications to clustering. Pattern Recogn. **44**(3), 678–693 (2011)
36. Rasool, R.A.: Feature-level vs. score-level fusion in the human identification system. Appl. Comput. Intell. Soft Comput. **2021**(1), 6621772 (2021)
37. Sakoe, H., Chiba, S.: Dynamic programming algorithm optimization for spoken word recognition. IEEE Trans. Acoust. Speech Signal Process. **26**(1), 43–49 (1978)
38. Sanchez-Reillo, R., Sanchez-Avila, C., Gonzalez-Marcos, A.: Biometric identification through hand geometry measurements. IEEE Trans. Pattern Anal. Mach. Intell. **22**(10), 1168–1171 (2000)
39. Sardá-Espinosa, A.: dtwclust: time series clustering along with optimizations for the dynamic time warping distance (2019). https://CRAN.R-project.org/package=dtwclust. R package version 5.5.7
40. Schroff, F., Kalenichenko, D., Philbin, J.: Facenet: a unified embedding for face recognition and clustering. In: Proceedings of the IEEE Conference on Computer Vision and Pattern Recognition, pp. 815–823 (2015)
41. Serengil, S., Özpınar, A.: A benchmark of facial recognition pipelines and co-usability performances of modules. Bilişim Teknolojileri Dergisi **17**(2), 95–107 (2024)
42. Shubham0204: Face Recognition With FaceNet on Android (FaceNet_512). https://github.com/shubham0204/FaceRecognition_With_FaceNet_Android. Accessed 15 Jan 2025. Model file used: facenet_512.tflite from the repository assets
43. Srivastava, A.: DTW+S: Shape-based comparison of time-series with ordered local trend. arXiv preprint arXiv:2309.03579 (2023). Code available at https://github.com/scc-usc/DTW_S_apps
44. Srivastava, A.: DTW_S_apps: Applications of DTW+S (2023). https://github.com/scc-usc/DTW_S_apps
45. Srivastava, R., et al.: Match-level fusion of finger-knuckle print and iris for human identity validation using neuro-fuzzy classifier. Sensors **22**(10), 3620 (2022)
46. Steck, H., Ekanadham, C., Kallus, N.: Is cosine-similarity of embeddings really about similarity? In: ACM Web Conference, pp. 887–890 (2024)
47. Sumalatha, U., Prakasha, K.K., Prabhu, S., Nayak, V.C.: A comprehensive review of unimodal and multimodal fingerprint biometric authentication systems: fusion, attacks, and template protection. IEEE Access (2024)
48. Szafraniec, M.: shapeDTW python implementation. https://github.com/MikolajSzafraniecUPDS/shapedtw-python. gitHub Repository
49. Taigman, Y., Yang, M., Ranzato, M., Wolf, L.: Deepface: closing the gap to human-level performance in face verification. In: Proceedings of the IEEE Conference on Computer Vision and Pattern Recognition, pp. 1701–1708 (2014)
50. Tolba, A., El-Baz, A., El-Harby, A., et al.: Face recognition: a literature review. Int. J. Signal Process. **2**(2), 88–103 (2006)
51. Tolosana, R., Vera-Rodriguez, R., Fierrez, J., Morales, A., Ortega-Garcia, J.: Deepfakes and beyond: a survey of face manipulation and fake detection. Inf. Fusion **64**, 131–148 (2020)

52. Wang, T., Liao, X., Chow, K.P., Lin, X., Wang, Y.: Deepfake detection: a comprehensive survey from the reliability perspective. ACM Comput. Surv. **57**(3), 1–35 (2024)
53. Wildes, R.P.: Iris recognition: an emerging biometric technology. Proc. IEEE **85**(9), 1348–1363 (1997)
54. Wu, C., Chen, J., He, K., Zhao, Z., Du, R., Zhang, C.: Echohand: high accuracy and presentation attack resistant hand authentication on commodity mobile devices. In: Proceedings of the 2022 ACM SIGSAC Conference on Computer and Communications Security, pp. 2931–2945 (2022)
55. Zhao, J., Itti, L.: shapeDTW: shape dynamic time warping. Pattern Recogn. **74**, 171–184 (2018)
56. Zheng, N., Bai, K., Huang, H., Wang, H.: You are how you touch: user verification on smartphones via tapping behaviors. In: 2014 IEEE 22nd International Conference on Network Protocols, pp. 221–232. IEEE (2014)
57. Zhou, B., Lohokare, J., Gao, R., Ye, F.: Echoprint: two-factor authentication using acoustics and vision on smartphones. In: Proceedings of the 24th Annual International Conference on Mobile Computing and Networking, pp. 321–336 (2018)

GET-AID: Graph-Enhanced Transformer for Provenance-Based Advanced Persistent Threats Investigation and Detection

Zhicheng Huang[1], Fengyuan Xu[1], Jiahong Yang[1], Wenting Li[3(✉)], Zonghua Zhang[2(✉)], Chenbin Zhang[1], Meng Ma[1], and Ping Wang[1(✉)]

[1] Peking University, Beijing, China
{zhichengh,jahoo,zcbin,mameng,pwang}@pku.edu.cn,
fengyuanxu@stu.pku.edu.cn
[2] CRSC R&D Institute, Beijing, China
zonghua.zhang@ieee.org
[3] Beijing Institute of Graphic Communication, Beijing, China
wentingli@pku.edu.cn

Abstract. Advanced Persistent Threats (APTs) pose a serious threat to the security of critical infrastructure and increase the risk of sensitive data leakage. They employ sophisticated techniques to evade detection and thus may bypass defense mechanisms. Current provenance-based methods have yielded promising results in APT detection and investigation, but they still face significant challenges. They rely heavily on prior knowledge, struggle to accurately trace the long-duration propagation of malicious events, and are deficient in attack scenario analysis. To address these challenges, we propose GET-AID, a Graph-Enhanced Transformer for provenance-based Attack Investigation and Detection, which requires no prior knowledge. First, we construct subgraphs from event sequences based on their temporal relationships to enable long-duration node-level tracking. Second, we introduce a two-stage graph encoder that leverages node-level and event-level attention mechanisms to capture the relationships across the subgraphs. Finally, GET-AID identifies anomalous events and generate attack scenarios across subgraphs by tracing associated nodes across subgraphs. Experimental results on multiple real-world APT datasets demonstrate the effectiveness of the proposed GET-AID, achieving precision, recall, and F1-scores of 100% in open-source datasets and approaching 100% in others. Furthermore, results from attack scenario reconstruction, performance overhead analysis, and continuous training validate the end-to-end usability and attack analysis capabilities of the GET-AID framework.

Keywords: network security · APT attack · attack detection · attack scenario · graph attention

1 Introduction

Advanced Persistent Threats (APTs) are coordinated cyberattacks in which adversaries infiltrate a network and move stealthily through multiple purposeful stages (such as initial intrusion, internal network movement, and data exfiltration) [1]. APT attack can bypass traditional defense systems because they exploit novel or unique vulnerabilities (e.g. 0-day). In this way, as the primary targets, large institutions and corporations usually suffer from severe threats of sensitive data leakage or key infrastructure damage. For example, Sandworm disabled domain controllers in the 2018 Winter Olympics IT backbone [2]; in 2023, Lazarus breached VoIP provider 3CX's supply chain [3]; and they infiltrated two major energy infrastructures in the US and Europe [4].

APT attackers can execute multiple attack chains at every stage, i.e. sequences of actions such as exploiting a vulnerability or stealing credentials. Provenance graph-based methods have become a mainstream approach for detecting malicious action and analyzing these chains [5,6]. Generated from system (audit) logs, a *provenance graph* is a directed acyclic graph (DAG) with rich contextual information. *Nodes* in the graph represent system entities (processes, files, network sockets) and *edges* denote causal dependencies (e.g. "`process A read file B`", "`process A send to IP X.X.X.X`"). Analysts or automated tools can use provenance graph to pinpoint alerts or anomalies to system entities and trace the attacker's actions, reconstructing the attack chain into a coherent scenario.

Provenance graph-based methods are categorized into rule-based and anomaly-based approaches. Rule-based methods [7-10] heavily rely on manually defined rules or attack signatures provided by Cyber Threat Intelligence (CTI) to perform matching against the provenance graph. They struggle to cope with evolving APT attack patterns, such as zero-day attacks. Anomaly-based methods construct behavioral models using techniques like statistical analysis [11,12] and machine learning [13-16] to identify deviations from normal behavior as potential attacks. Insufficient training data or the lack of labels for malicious samples can lead to poor performance in anomaly detection methods. Recent provenance-based graph-learning methods have achieved promising results in identifying anomalies [17-19], or utilizing fewer predefined rules [20]. However, to detect and analyze APT attacks, they still face one or more of the following challenges:

(1) Knowledge reliance. Some graph learning approaches still rely on expert knowledge to label the training data [14] or manual intervention to pinpoint the attack nodes [20]. The knowledge reliance restricts the scalability and adaptability of these methods to emerging threats.

(2) Limited long-duration tracking. Precise, fine-grained detection and tracking help to infer causal relationships for critical attack behaviors. Existing learning methods struggle to capture the malicious events during their long-term propagation [21,22]. They may focus primarily on intrusion alerts [13] or specific relationships [23], potentially failing to extract correlations between complex activities that are separated by long time intervals in the logs.

(3) Deficiency in attack scenario reconstruction. While numerous learning-based techniques reduce the reliance on predefined rules [15] and enhance detection performance [18,19], they often fall short in explaining how individual alerts coalesce into a coherent, end-to-end attack scenario. However, security analysts require insights into how detection results are used to reconstruct the attack scenario. Particularly during runtime detection, alerts must be contextualized within an evolving attack scenario to support real-time response requirements.

Our Solution and Contribution. Our key observation is that simultaneously addressing the aforementioned three challenges requires overcoming the context loss caused by the *locality problem* [20]. In provenance graph learning, nodes and their surroundings are often represented by decomposing the graph into fixed-size K-hop local neighborhoods. When representations derived from these overlapping neighborhoods are aggregated, interactions with neighbors beyond the K-hop boundary and their associated context are inherently lost. This context loss significantly hinders models aiming to operate without **knowledge reliance**. Correlations between nodes will become implicit as models can extract and transfer features deeply. The less models know about these correlations, the more external knowledge is required to understand the features. Meanwhile, attackers intentionally design attack paths spanning multiple hops; the fixed-hop decomposition disrupts the ability to **track the long-distance interactions**. Furthermore, given that APT actions are typically sparse events distributed across the graph, local aggregation methods struggle to connect these sparse steps, thereby hard to **reconstruct the attack scenario**.

To address these three challenges, we propose GET-AID, a novel framework overcoming the *locality problem*, enabling accurate detection of critical APT events and comprehensive analysis of attack scenarios. GET-AID expands the exploration of each node's neighbors beyond fixed distances to capture richer local features. Then a global attention mechanism is employed to mitigate context loss during graph neighborhood aggregation. As a self-supervised anomaly detection method, GET-AID uses long-range context from local features to predict anomalous edges without need of external knowledge. GET-AID integrates the Transformer-based architecture involving local node attention and global event attention to track node features in a long run. GET-AID detects anomalies both from event-level and graph-level, enabling merging malicious activities from high-level to reconstruct attack scenarios.

Experimental evaluation on StreamSpot [24], ATLAS [14], and the DARPA TC E5 dataset [25] demonstrates that GET-AID outperforms state-of-the-art methods in detection and exhibits end-to-end usability. Code is publicly available at Github[1]. In summary, this paper makes the following contributions:

- Overcomes the locality problem by integrating expanded neighbor exploration with global attention, capturing rich local dependencies while preserving global context.

---

[1] https://github.com/rpybd/GET-AID.

- Employs a self-supervised Transformer architecture with attention for robust, precise tracking and detection of long-duration malicious activities, reducing dependence on external knowledge.
- Achieves fine-grained anomaly detection at both edge and graph levels, enables interpretable attack scenario reconstruction, and demonstrates end-to-end usability.

2 Background and Related Work

Description of APT Attacks. The essence of APT detection is to find the attack events and values involved in an attack campaign from the system logs. Formally, set E represents all attack events in an APT attack campaign, and an APT attack event $E_i \in E$ can be described in a six tuple:

$$E_i = \langle Time, sIP, dIP, sPort, dPort, action \rangle \tag{1}$$

where $Time$ denotes attack time, sIP and dIP refer to source IP address and destination IP address respectively, $sPort$ and $dPort$ respectively represent source port and destination port, and $action$ often means malicious behaviors in network such as `connect`, `write`, or `execute`. As a description of the deterministic APT attackers exploit vulnerabilities in the target network to progressively invade, an attack scenario can be represented by $\mathcal{A} = \langle V, E \rangle$, where set E represents all attack events and V is the set of attack and network entities. Based on the detected attack events and their causal relationships in a provenance graph, $\mathcal{A}$ can be reconstructed.

Provenance-Based Graph-Learning Methods. Due to their strong representational learning capabilities, graph learning techniques are particularly well-suited for anomaly-based APT detection. They can generalize beyond predefined rules or labeled samples. Sequence-based and NLP-based methods such as ATLAS [14] and Extractor [26] employ causal modeling and semantic role labeling on provenance patterns, while GNN-based techniques - KAIROS [17], DeepHunter [21], HINTI [23], Unicorn [13], MAGIC [18], THREATRACE [15] - use attention, masking, and GraphSAGE sampling to detect anomalies on dynamic graphs. These approaches mitigate the need for manual rules and address local receptive-field constraints through neighbor sampling and hierarchical pooling [5], offering adaptive intrusion detection capabilities.

APT Analysis. Post-incident APT attribution analysis (threat hunting) uses collected provenance graphs to identify attacker origins and potential targets. Meanwhile, real-time analysis and reconstruction of ongoing attack scenarios are more valuable for enabling timely intervention. Reconstructing APT scenarios often relies on audit logs and alerts from IDS, SIEM, or EDR platforms [27–29], which can suffer from alert fatigue and fragmented data lacking high-level phase context [7,30]. Recent interpretation tools-such as encrypted traffic feature learning [31], integrate graph embeddings and attention mechanisms [32] to visualize and explain causal event sequences. These tools enhance analysts' understanding of multi-stage APT campaigns.

3 Our GET-AID Architecture

We develop a GNN-based Transformer framework to investigate APT attacks without relying on *prior* knowledge, termed GET-AID for easier reference. Compared to existing methods [13,17], the key innovation of GET-AID is its temporally-aware neighbor selection in provenance graphs, coupled with a Transformer to preserve long-range dependencies among the selected nodes. Specifically, GET-AID consists of four operational modules that work systematically to characterize attack activities in the provenance graph. The overall architecture and key operations are illustrated in Fig. 1.

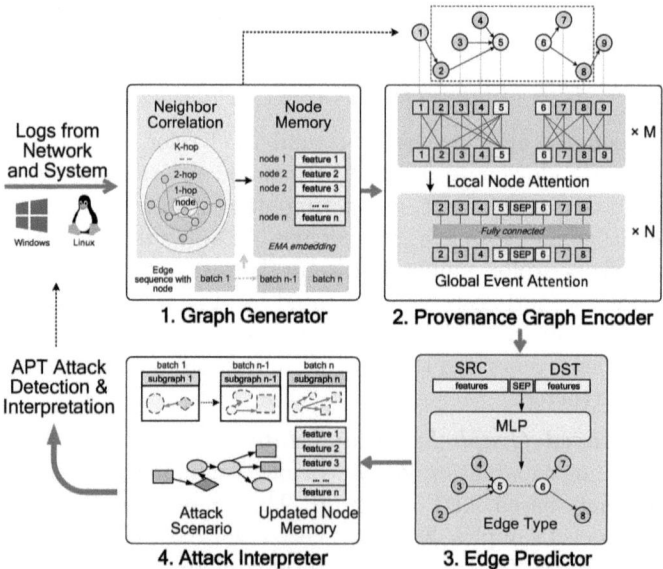

Fig. 1. Architectural overview of GET-AID: raw data is transformed into provenance graphs after the Graph Generator; attack information is extracted via the Provenance Graph Encoder and Edge Predictor; after detection, attack scenarios are reconstructed by the Attack Interpreter.

- **Graph Generator**: ingests raw audit logs and, through the Neighbor Correlation process, constructs minute-level subgraphs incorporating multi-hop dependencies to expand each node's local view. The Node Memory mechanism then carries forward contextual embeddings across successive windows, reducing long-duration context loss.
- **Provenance Graph Encoder**: combines a Local Node Attention layer with a Global Event Attention layer. Local Node Attention aggregates recent temporary neighbor features in a subgraph, and Global Event Attention preserves contextual information across the subgraphs over a longer range. This dual-attention design directly addresses fixed-hop limitations, fusing both local detail and global topology into the node representations.

– **Edge Predictor**: leverages the enriched embeddings from the encoder to perform masked edge reconstruction using an MLP, using cross-entropy loss adjusted for rarity. By scoring edges within the extended receptive field, it reduces sensitivity to local reconstruction errors and captures anomalies spanning multiple hops.
– **Attack Interpreter**: traces the sequence of detected anomalous edges using the accumulated Node Memory to reconstruct complete, multi-stage attack graphs. By merging subgraphs over time, it enables end-to-end scenario reconstruction with less context loss.

3.1 Graph Generator

The Graph Generator module takes network logs and audit logs from platforms such as Windows and Linux platform as inputs. It maintains a database that stores source nodes, target nodes, timestamps, and message information using edges as the primary key. Through the Neighbor Correlation process, the Graph Generator selects the n nearest-in-time edges within a predefined hop limit between nodes to construct a subgraph for training. This process reduces the provenance graph size, generates an appropriate number of subgraphs, and accelerates processing while retaining sufficient node information. Therefore, the edges in the provenance graph are divided into sequences and segmented by fixed lengths.

To preserve sufficient context, Graph Generator incorporates a node memory management mechanism that handles dynamic updates of node embeddings and timestamps in temporal graphs. Specifically, it leverages dictionary structures to store memory vectors and timestamps for each node in Node Memory process. To ensure stability and continuity in dynamic environments, embeddings are updated using an Exponential Moving Average (EMA) approach. This method smooths embedding updates while mitigating fluctuations caused by rapid changes in graph states. Timestamp updates are computed using median values, which enhance the system's robustness against potential outliers in temporal data. Given a timestamp T, the EMA of the node feature for v_i in a subgraph can be computed as follows:

$$EMA_T = \alpha \cdot X_T^{v_i} + (1 - \alpha) \cdot EMA_{T-1} \tag{2}$$

where EMA_T represents the Exponential Moving Average at timestamp T, $X_T^{v_i}$ is the node feature value at timestamp $T-1$, and EMA_{T-1} is the Exponential Moving Average at the previous timestamp $T-1$. α is the smoothing factor, typically between 0 and 1. A higher α gives more weight to recent values. This method allows EMA to smooth the feature values, giving more importance to the most recent observations while still retaining the influence of previous values.

3.2 Provenance Graph Encoder

The Provenance Graph Encoder is designed to model the temporal and structural relationships within graph-based APT attack data. It incorporates two critical layers Local Node Attention layer and Global Event Attention layer to encode local and global contextual information for APT detection without reliance on expert intervention. This enables attack events to be detected and attributed to specific subgraphs at fine granular levels such as specific times and individual nodes, enhancing the fine-grained detection capability. The Provenance Graph Encoder takes edge sequence according to the settled size in each batch. The Local Node Attention layer computes the embedding representation of each node based on timestamps and message information. The Global Event Attention layer generates neighbor features for source and target nodes and performs sequence modeling using the Transformer.

(1) Local attention layer. To obtain information of direct neighbors, this layer generates node embeddings a two-layer graph convolution neural network using graph attention mechanism, which can be expressed as formula below:

$$\text{Attention}(Q, K, V, M) = \text{softmax}\left(\frac{QK^T}{\sqrt{d_k}} + M\right)V \quad (3)$$

where $Q \in \mathbb{R}^{n \times d_k}$ is the query matrix, $K \in \mathbb{R}^{n \times d_k}$ is the key matrix, $V \in \mathbb{R}^{n \times d_k}$ is the value matrix, and $M \in \mathbb{R}^{n \times n}$ is the mask matrix. d_k is the dimension of key, and n represent sequence length of query, key, and value. The value of the mask matrix is 0 to indicate that the position should be masked, and the value is 1 to indicate that the position can participate in the computation. The purpose of the mask is to add a sufficiently small negative number (e.g., $-\infty$) to the attention scores (i.e., QK^T), making the corresponding position's softmax value 0, thereby preventing these positions from participating in the computation. Each layer applies attention to capture high-order dependencies and interactions among nodes. During initialization, a time encoder is integrated to embed relative time differences, which are concatenated with message features to define edge features.

In the forward pass, the relative time differences between each edge's source node's last update and the current time are calculated. These time differences are encoded and combined with message features to form the edge features. These features pass through the first graph convolution layer, which applies ReLU activation to extract complex patterns. The second graph convolution layer further refines the output, producing final embeddings that capture rich temporal and structural information. We use the node tokens generated by Node Memory as input (Q, K, V), where n is the number of nodes in the subgraph. As the $v_{source} - e - v_{destination}$ is the basic unit, we use the mask mechanism to ensure that only linked nodes of v_{source} and $v_{destination}$ can participate in the attention calculation. By setting the mask coefficients of unlinked nodes to -100, the attention coefficients can be seen as 0.

(2) Global event attention layer. The Global event attention layer is based on Transformer Encoder, and employs sequence embedding to focus on relevant portions of the graph. This module starts by projecting input node features into an embedding space using a linear layer. The embeddings are then processed by the layered Transformer Encoder, each of which layer integrates multi-head self-attention as in Eq. 3 and feedforward networks to learn deep contextual patterns. The output of the converter is divided into SEP feature (which represents the separation feature of the abnormal event) and node embeddings. This output also are used to update the memory module and predict the edge class respectively.

For each source node and target node, the adjacent node features are extracted and the sequence is filled, which is input into the converter for sequence modeling. The forward pass uses a masking mechanism to selectively focus attention on critical nodes and edges, ensuring the model captures important causal relationships. Additionally, the positional encoding process introduces position information into the sequence, preserving order sensitivity for temporal graph data. The model uses cross entropy loss to calculate classification errors, and back-propagation to optimize graph embedding and edge prediction performance. During the training process, the model dynamically updates node memory and adjacency loading state to adapt to continuous time evolution and new information injection. The attention mechanism of the Global Event Attention Layer is similar to that of the Local Attention Layer, with the key difference being the removal of masking. Mask matrix $M \in \mathbb{R}^{n \times n}$ in Eq. 3 is set to all 1, allowing all nodes to participate in the attention computation to capture global features.

3.3 Attack Detection and Interpretation

The detection process is completed by Edge Predictor, and reports the detected attack events (abnormal edges) and corresponding malicious nodes with the

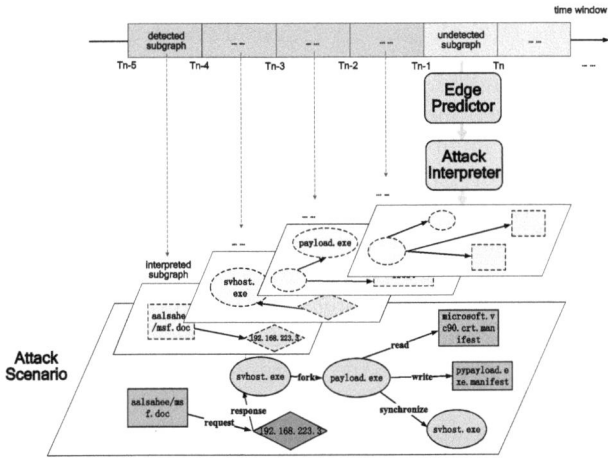

Fig. 2. The process of incremental merging of subgraphs after Edge Predictor and Attack Interpreter: from malicious file msf.doc to malware pypayload.exe. The case is from the ATLAS S4 dataset.

information. As shown in Fig. 2, the Attack Interpreter can illustrate attack scenarios of the subgraphs in small time steps.

As an anomaly-based attack detection method, GET-AID do not requies any attack signatures or signals known a priori. More importantly, our approach enables fine-grained detection by performing edge-level anomaly inspection and minute-level subgraph analysis across both spatial and temporal dimensions. Since each batch generates subgraphs on an edge-by-edge basis, the duration represented by each subgraph can be as short as a few minutes, while the number of included nodes remains within a manageable range. Edge Predictor predicts edge state and report anomalies based on the prediction process. It focuses on processing the features of the source node (SRC) and destination node (DST) to infer the type of edge that connects them. The module follows a structured workflow to determine edge types, such as interactions or relationships within the graph. Input features from the SRC and DST nodes are concatenated with a separator token (SEP) to form the complete input representation. This combined feature vector serves as the input for the predictive model. The core of the Edge Predictor is a MLP, which performs the following operations: (1) processing concatenated node features through a series of dense layers, and (2) learning patterns and relationships between SRC and DST nodes to infer the type of edge that connects them. The final output of the Edge Predictor is the predicted edge type, enabling the model to label the connections between nodes based on their learned relationships.

After the prediction process, we can get the loss $\mathcal{L}$. We use $\mathcal{L}$ and the rareness to determine whether an edge is abnormal.

The loss function $\mathcal{L}$ is the cross-entropy loss and can be computed as:

$$\mathcal{L} = -\frac{1}{N} \sum_{i=1}^{N} \log \left(\frac{\exp(y_{\text{pred},i,y_i})}{\sum_{c=1}^{C} \exp(y_{\text{pred},i,c})} \right) \tag{4}$$

where for each edge sample i, y_i is the index of the true class label, and $y_{\text{pred},i,c}$ is the raw logit predicted for class c. N is the number of edge samples in the subgraph, and C is the number of classes.

A node is rare if its corresponding system entity does not appear frequently in a benign execution. We use the Inverse Document Frequency (IDF) [33] same to compute rareness of nodes linked to the edge. For edge e_i, we justify its anomaly state S_i as positive when $loss > threshold \vee IDF > threshold$.

The ability to generate and interpret fine-grained yet concise attack scenarios is particularly critical for anomaly detection systems like GET-AID. The Attack Interpreter is designed to improve the interpretability of the model and provide transparent, actionable insights to security analysts by visualizing the detection, association, and localization of malicious nodes. Specifically, the Attack Interpreter takes in subgraphs containing malicious events and incrementally merges related attack events involving anomalous nodes using the Louvain community detection algorithm, similar to the approach adopted in KAIROS [17]. This module identifies abnormal nodes connected by anomalous edges and compares them with those in subsequent subgraphs. By interpreting these subgraphs step by step, GET-AID constructs a coherent and progressive view of the attack scenario.

4 Evaluation

We evaluate our method to answer the following questions:
Q1. Can GET-AID accurately detect anomalies caused by APT attacks? How does its performance compare to existing methods? (Sect. 4.2)
Q2. In what ways do the modules targeting the locality issue in provenance graph learning enhance the performance of GET-AID? (Sect. 4.3)
Q3. Can the attack scenario be accurately reconstructed using only the detected anomalies? (Sect. 4.4)
Q4. How does GET-AID perform end-to-end when deployed within practical workflows, particularly in long-running systems? (Sect. 4.5)

4.1 Experimental Settings

Datasets. We use total 830G of publicly available datasets StreamSpot, DARPR TC E5, and ATLAS. They are widely used in provenance-based systems to compare the performance of different models [13,15,17,18,20]. The three datasets record whole system behaviors from platforms including Linux, FreeBSD, Android, and Windows. ATLAS has event-level and node-level ground-truth, while StreamSpot and E5 provide graph-level ground-truth. Each dataset will be used in its corresponding evaluation experiments. *ATLAS* [14] contains attack scenarios exploiting 6 CVE vulnerabilities in controlled Windows systems. Alsaheel et al. executed 10 real-world APT campaigns (four single-host and six multi-host scenarios) and simulated benign activities to collect this dataset. With fine-grained ground-truth, ATLAS supports the demonstration of attack scenario across similar exploit cases. *StreamSpot* [24] is a simulated dataset created by Manzoor et al. in a controlled Linux environment. It includes 5 benign scenarios and 1 attack scenario of 6*100 graphs. As one of the earliest datasets for online graph anomaly detection, it features short, well-defined attack paths, making it a standard benchmark for evaluating detection responsiveness and false positive control. *DARPA TC E5* [25] stems from the fifth APT simulation under the DARPA Transparent Computing program on enterprise networks. The dataset includes multi-host logs collected over several days via provenance systems (e.g., CADETS, ClearScope, THEIA) and exhibits distinct time windows linked to benign or attack behaviors. E5 contains a larger number of advanced attack activities than the former E3 dataset. It presents significant challenges due to its scale (over 800 GB) and extreme class imbalance, where malicious samples can constitute as little as 0.003% (e.g., in DARPA TC E5-CADETS).

Comparison Methods. Similar to our approach, KAIROS [17], ThreatTrace [15], and Unicorn [13], are run-time, anomaly-based, open-source, and do not rely on predefined attack patterns. KAIROS can discover APT attacks events and abnormal subgraphs. THREATRACE may generate false positives by misclassifying nearby benign nodes. Unicorn is incapable of precise event detection. So in event-level, we compare with KAIROS, the *state-of-the-art* method in APT detection, to evaluate the ability to comprehensively track malicious events. In terms of the graph level, we compare all methods.

4.2 Attack Detection Results

Typical indicators for classification problem are used as evaluation metrics, including Precision, Accuracy, F1-Score, Recall, and Area Under Curve(AUC). We focus on false positives (FP) and false negatives (FN), representing benign samples misclassified as threats and missed malicious samples, respectively. These reflect the detection system's false alarm and miss alarm rates. Following their experimental settings (as in Appendix A.3) such as dataset split, we fairly compare the reproduced detection results of them with GET-AID.

Event-Level Detection. On the mixed benign-malicious Windows CVE scenarios, GET-AID consistently outperforms KAIROS across key metrics in Table 1. For instance, in CVE-2017-11882, precision rises from 0.4135 to 0.7267 and recall from 0.6081 to 0.8810, substantially reducing both false positives and false negatives. Even the minimum precision improvement across tasks exceeds 6% (observed in CVE-2015-5119). The CVE-2017-11882 scenario involves an attacker exploiting an Office vulnerability using files to redirect users to a malicious software. Compared to other scenarios, this one features fewer attack events but involves more attack nodes and longer attack paths. GET-AID demonstrates a superior ability to track this complex process compared to KAIROS.

Table 1. Comparison Between GET-AID and KAIROS on ATLAS (Event-level)

Dataset	Method	FN	FP	Precision	Accuracy	F1-Score	Recall	AUC
CVE 2015-5122	KAIROS	680	2560	0.4746	0.9544	0.5856	0.7701	0.9369
	GET-AID	43	1044	**0.7618**	**0.9858**	**0.8496**	**0.9857**	**0.9896**
CVE 2015-3105	KAIROS	1926	9909	0.5731	0.9500	0.6510	0.8247	0.9584
	GET-AID	36	7720	**0.6828**	**0.9967**	**0.7796**	**0.9969**	**0.9908**
CVE 2017-11882	KAIROS	1518	3362	0.4135	0.9485	0.4920	0.6081	0.8714
	GET-AID	463	1316	**0.7267**	**0.9815**	**0.7959**	**0.8810**	**0.9555**
CVE 2017-0199	KAIROS	2052	28306	0.4518	0.9001	0.5324	0.8203	0.9025
	GET-AID	380	35872	**0.5168**	0.8964	**0.5861**	**0.9669**	**0.9630**
CVE 2015-5119	KAIROS	751	3481	0.7574	0.9550	0.8370	0.9354	0.9846
	GET-AID	285	1720	**0.8682**	**0.9787**	**0.9187**	**0.9755**	**0.9943**
CVE 2018-8174	KAIROS	718	3233	0.4082	0.9583	0.5303	0.7564	0.9096
	GET-AID	155	1611	**0.6342**	**0.9813**	**0.7598**	**0.9474**	**0.9631**

While GET-AID demonstrates reduced false negative and false positive rates across most scenarios, it exhibits an elevated false positive rate in the case of CVE-2017-0199. Performance on the single-host version of this task was strong, but false positives increased so the accuracy decreases (while false negatives remained low) in the multi-host setting (see Table 4 in Appendix). This particular multi-host scenario contains less data but has the highest volume of benign events. The attack utilizes msf.doc to deliver a malicious file. We hypothesize that GET-AID might be overly sensitive to similar benign document transfer behaviors in the test data, leading to difficulty in fully distinguishing benign activity in this specific case.

However, the model does not rely solely on individual event analysis; it correlates events with nodes and subgraphs. Subtle event variations are merged and mapped to node interactions, mitigating the impact of event-level false positives. Subsequent graph-level detection validates GET-AID's ability to manage these false positives and track node interactions effectively, thereby improving overall performance.

Graph-Level Detection. Compared all baseline methods on StreamSpot, GET-AID captures each provenance graph without any context truncation, achieving flawless detection (FN = 0, FP = 0) and exceeding StreamSpot itself, Unicorn and THREATRACE methods in Table 2. StreamSpot has concise and deterministic attack sequences. Our focused neighbor sampling combined with localized self-attention effectively captures these clear attack features, leading to strong performance. Other baseline methods also achieve good results on this dataset. Note that due to differing time window partitioning strategies among methods, the datasets are processed into varying numbers of subgraphs.

Table 2. Comparison of Graph-level Detection Results on Streamspot

Method	FN	FP	TP	TN	Precision	Accuracy	F1-Score	Recall
StreamSpot	2	8	23	117	0.7419	0.9333	0.8214	0.9200
Unicorn	1	1	24	124	0.9600	0.9867	0.9600	0.9600
THREATRACE	0	1	25	125	0.9615	0.9933	0.9804	1.0000
KAIROS	0	0	100	375	1.0000	1.0000	1.0000	1.0000
GET-AID (**Ours**)	0	0	100	375	1.0000	1.0000	1.0000	1.0000

Since Unicorn was not originally evaluated on E5, our comparison on the E5 dataset was limited to Kairos and ThreaTrace. KAIROS uses manual correction to enhance precision. As we prioritize the reliability of the dataset's ground truth, we adopted the adjusted KAIROS results, which are consistent with those from our reproduction efforts. The experimental results in Table 3 on the multi-stage APT attacks with varied path lengths demonstrate GET-AID's consistent superiority over other methods. GET-AID maintains extremely low false-negative and false-positive rates. In contrast, KAIROS's limited context aggregation yields residual false positives, especially under high benign variability. Consequently, GET-AID achieves perfect detection in the Theia scenario and records zero misses in the Cadets and Clearscope scenarios.

Our neighbor-sampling strategy directs attention toward the most active edges, minimizing missed detections of multi-hop lateral movements, and preventing the model from mislabeling non-malicious entities that remain active post-compromise (e.g., an Nginx process continuing legitimate requests in Cadets). Nevertheless, because global attention does not uniformly penalize all rare benign behaviors, a small number of false positives persist (Cadets.FP = 1; Clearscope.FP = 3), indicating that unusual benign events such as irregular screenshot can slightly reduce precision. Experimental results on the StreamSpot and E5 datasets demonstrate the effectiveness of our model, GET-AID, particularly when working with **imbalanced data**. The results on StreamSpot, which contains mixed benign and malicious behaviors, validate GET-AID's robustness to potential reconstruction errors. Furthermore, the results on the E5 dataset showcase GET-AID's generalization capability, successfully identifying anomalous samples even when trained solely on benign data.

Table 3. Comparison of Graph-level Detection Results on DARPA E5 (Graph-level)

Dataset	Method	FN	FP	TP	TN	Precision	Accuracy	F1-Score	Recall	AUC
clearscope	THREATRACE	2	4	8	218	0.6667	0.9741	0.7273	0.8000	0.9503
	KAIROS	1	3	9	219	0.7500	0.9828	0.8182	0.9000	0.9432
	GET-AID	0	3	11	253	**0.7857**	**0.9888**	**0.8800**	**1.0000**	**0.9941**
theia	THREATRACE	1	1	1	173	0.5000	0.9886	0.5000	0.5000	0.9083
	KAIROS	0	1	2	173	0.6667	0.9594	0.8024	1.0000	0.9821
	GET-AID	0	0	2	174	**1.0000**	**1.0000**	**1.0000**	**1.0000**	**1.0000**
cadets	THREATRACE	1	4	6	243	0.6000	0.9803	0.7059	0.8571	0.9205
	KAIROS	0	9	7	238	0.4380	0.9650	0.6090	1.0000	0.9820
	GET-AID	0	1	16	237	**0.9412**	**0.9961**	**0.9697**	**1.0000**	**0.9979**

4.3 Ablation Study

To pinpoint how individual modules contribute to GET-AID's performance, we conduct experiments using the CADETS and CVE-2017-0199 datasets. These studies show the results of different neighbor selection strategies on the locality issue, and isolate the impact of GNN, neighbor selection, and Transformer components.

Modules Impact on Performance. To quantify the contribution of each core module in GET-AID, we evaluate three ablated variants on both CADETS and CVE-2017-0199: (1) without the GNN embedding module, (2) with random neighbor selection, and (3) without the Transformer layer. Figure 3 summarizes the results. Overall, removing either the GNN or the neighbor-selection strategy causes the largest performance drop, since these components capture the most critical local patterns. The Transformer's attention to these relationships further enhances anomaly detection. Specifically, on both datasets, disabling the GNN or replacing its learned neighbors with random ones leads to a significant decline in Precision and F1 Score, as fine-grained local anomalies can no longer be detected. In the CVE-2017-0199 multi-host scenario, this ablation also fragments local dependency chains and dramatically reduces Recall for lateral-movement events. Removing the Transformer—which applies global self-attention to link distant events—yields a smaller but noticeable degradation: although self-attention can introduce extra noise, slightly lowering event-level Accuracy and Precision on CVE-2017-0199, it remains crucial for modeling long-range dependencies and identifying graph-level anomalies, as evidenced by drops in F1 and AUC on CADETS when it is disabled. This capability is particularly valuable for security practitioners engaged in incident analysis and attack forensics.

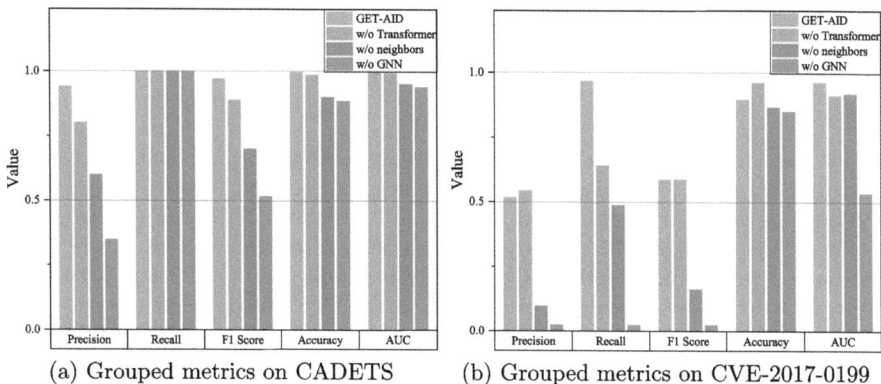

Fig. 3. Ablation analysis on CADETS and CVE-2015-0199 datasets. Subfigures (a) and (b) illustrate the result of four ablation cases (without GNN, random neighbors, without Transformer, and GET-AID) on CADETS and CVE-2017-0199.

Selection of Neighbors. To more comprehensively study the impact of neighbor selection, we choose different neighbor depth (the maximum neighborhood depth K-hop) and the number of selected neighbors on CADETS CVE-2017-0199. The results in Fig. 4 show that 2-hop and neighbors = 20 are appropriate to capture the locality. On CADETS, grouped metrics by hop depth reveals a clear peak at two hops: a 2-hop neighborhood delivers the most balanced, consistently high scores, indicating that extending the receptive field just far enough to encompass key lateral movements—while avoiding superfluous distant nodes—best mitigates context loss. On CVE-2017-0199, the 3D surface of hop depth versus neighbor sample size shows that the combination of 2 hops an'd 20 sampled neighbors attains uniformly superior metrics. Common operations are usually paired (e.g., I/O, request and response), so 2-hop may effectively expand context to capture multi-stage exploit chains without introducing excess odd-hop noise. Interestingly, varying the neighbor sample size does not significantly affect performance, and larger sizes incur additional computational overhead; therefore, a size of 20 provides is a good option.

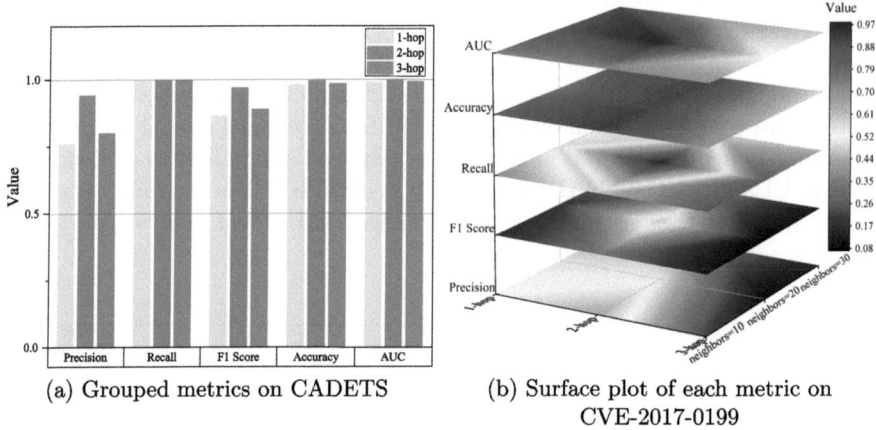

(a) Grouped metrics on CADETS

(b) Surface plot of each metric on CVE-2017-0199

Fig. 4. Impact of neighbor selection strategies on performance. Subfigure (a) presents a grouped bar chart illustrating the impact of neighbor selection depths (13) on model performance across five metrics on the CADETS dataset. Subfigure (b) shows the results on the CVE-2017-0199 dataset using a 3D stacked surface plot, where the x- and y-axes represent hop depths (13) and neighbor sample sizes (10, 20, and 30), respectively, and the z-axis indicates metric values across five surfaces. The color gradient from red to blue visualizes the magnitude of each metric. (Color figure online)

4.4 Attack Scenarios Reconstruction

After studying the detection performance on CVE-2015-0199 (S4 and M5), we select the S4 part to illustrate the attack scenario reconstruction result from GET-AID, which describes how the attacker exploited the CVE 2017-0199 vulnerability on the Windows platform to perform a leaked file attack. The attacker initiated the attack from IP 192.168.223.3, using a phishing email attachment to establish an entry point. The graph depicts a CVE-2017-0199 exploitation in which the victim host 192.168.223.128 issues an HTTP request to 0xalsaheel.com and retrieves the malicious RTF document msf.doc delivered to the user directory. The document msf.doc then connects to 192.168.223.3 to download the secondary payload pypayload.exe. Upon execution by svchost.exe, pypayload.exe launches cmd.exe to perform command operations, reads and writes the system file. Figure 5 display results from the consecutive attack subgraphs. GET-AID detects the anomalies in event-level first (red-edges), and merges the events by malicious nodes (red-noes) to determine the status of subgraphs. Once detected, malicious subgraphs will be merged according to the relevant malicious nodes former and later. From the reconstructed scenario, we can pinpoint the origin of msf.doc: 0xalsaheel.com.

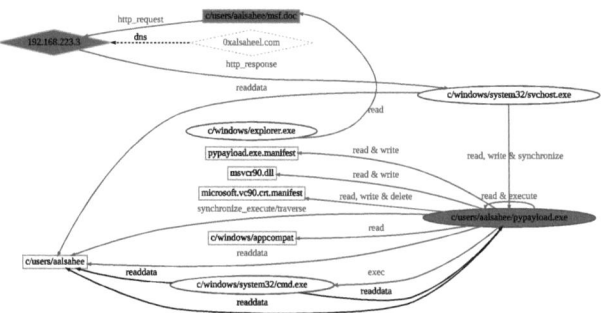

Fig. 5. Reconstructed attack scenario in ATLAS S-4 scenario. An attack initiated from IP 192.168.223.3, leveraging msf.doc and pypayload.exe to compromise the host.

4.5 End-to-End Usability

We evaluated GET-AID's ability to learn and update across time windows with various trainingtesting regimes: training on a single benign window and testing on a malicious one, training and testing on benign windows, and training on a mix of one benign and 0.2 malicious windows, followed by testing on the remaining malicious data. The model incrementally ingests new time windows, incorporating false positives to counter concept drift and avoid errors. Periodic retraining ensures stable and accurate detection performance as benign behavior evolves. We also assessed the runtime overhead on the CADETS dataset. Data were processed in batches of 256 edges, with a temporal span exceeding 10 s per batch. Despite this, processing time per batch remained under 1 s during both training and inference (durations and processing time are provided in Sect. A.2.). Given GET-AID's support for streaming graph processing and incremental learning, the system can handle real-time log data without delays.

5 Conclusion and Discussion

GET-AID addresses the locality problem and enables APT detection and attack scenario reconstruction without external knowledge. GET-AID outperforms state-of-the-art APT detection methods on three open-source datasets, and extensive experimental results confirm GET-AID's effectiveness for real-time security solutions. Nevertheless, GET-AID is subject to certain limitations that pave the way for future research. The generalization of hyperparameters (such as hop-depth and neighbor count) for unseen data and dynamic environments warrants further investigation. Moreover, a more rigorous experimental and formal analysis is required for adversarial behaviors that mimic benign patterns (i.e., evasion attacks). Finally, establishing a robust quantitative measure for scene reconstruction is an unresolved issue. Addressing these challenges will be our primary focus moving forward.

Acknowledgments. This work is funded by the CRSC R&D Institute, the Foundation of Intelligent Parallel Technology Laboratory (2024JK15), the National Key Research and Development Project of China (2020YFB1805400), and the National Natural Science Foundation of China (62072006, 92167104).

A Appendix

A.1 Full Event-Level Detetcion Results of GET-AID and KAIROS on ATLAS's Ten Scenarios in Table 4

Table 4. Comparison Between GET-AID and KAIROS on ATLAS (Event-level)

Dataset	Method	Precision	Accuracy	F1 Score	Recall	AUC	TP	TN	FN	FP
S1-CVE-2015-5122	KAIROS	0.5337	0.9546	0.6342	0.7815	0.9432	2464	57308	689	2153
	GET-AID	**0.9231**	**0.9950**	**0.9518**	**0.9822**	**0.9924**	3097	59203	56	258
S2-CVE-2015-3105	KAIROS	0.3141	0.9379	0.4458	0.7679	0.9475	8112	296535	2452	17717
	GET-AID	**0.4157**	**0.9543**	**0.5870**	**0.9982**	**0.9961**	10545	299433	19	14819
S3-CVE-2017-11882	KAIROS	0.4255	0.9478	0.4975	0.5988	0.8921	2204	78721	1477	2976
	GET-AID	**0.7731**	**0.9839**	**0.8264**	**0.8875**	**0.9660**	3267	80738	414	959
S4-CVE-2017-0199	KAIROS	0.7723	0.9511	0.8431	0.9281	0.9572	10959	68322	849	3231
	GET-AID	**0.9008**	**0.9820**	**0.9391**	**0.9808**	**0.9867**	11581	70278	227	1275
M1-CVE-2015-5122	KAIROS	0.4155	0.9541	0.5369	0.7586	0.9305	2109	73508	671	2967
	GET-AID	**0.6004**	**0.9765**	**0.7473**	**0.9892**	**0.9868**	2750	74645	30	1830
M2-CVE-2015-5119	KAIROS	0.7574	0.9550	0.8370	0.9354	0.9846	10867	78888	751	3481
	GET-AID	**0.8682**	**0.9787**	**0.9187**	**0.9755**	**0.9943**	11333	80649	285	1720
M3-CVE-2015-3105	KAIROS	0.8321	0.9621	0.8561	0.8815	0.9692	10416	78361	1400	2101
	GET-AID	**0.9499**	**0.9927**	**0.9722**	**0.9956**	**0.9972**	11764	79842	52	620
M4-CVE-2018-8174	KAIROS	0.4082	0.9583	0.5303	0.7564	0.9096	2230	88489	718	3233
	GET-AID	**0.6342**	**0.9813**	**0.7598**	**0.9474**	**0.9631**	2793	90111	155	1611
M5-CVE-2017-0199	KAIROS	0.1313	0.8490	0.2217	0.7125	0.8477	8066	310382	3254	53381
	GET-AID	**0.1328**	0.8107	**0.2330**	**0.9529**	**0.9392**	10787	293295	533	70468
M6-CVE-2017-11882	KAIROS	0.4014	0.9491	0.4865	0.6173	0.8507	2513	96376	1558	3747
	GET-AID	**0.6803**	**0.9790**	**0.7653**	**0.8745**	**0.9450**	3560	98450	511	1673

A.2 The Duration Time and Cost Time of Each Batch on CADETS on Figure 6

A.3 Experiments Details

The proposed model is implemented in Python 3.7.16, using PyTorch 1.9.1 for neural network construction and TransformerConv, and Graphviz is used for graph visualization. All experiments were conducted with Intel CPU E5-2699, 256 GB, and NVIDIA RTX 2080 Ti GPU in CUDA 12.8 environment. The model was trained with a batch size of 128, 1024 edges seperately. The Adam optimizer was employed with a learning rate of $5*10^{-5}$, epsilon set to $1*10^{-8}$, and a weight decay of 0.01 to ensure stable convergence and mitigate overfitting.

In both single-host and multi-host settings, models were trained on ATLAS data from all scenarios excluding the specific one designated for testing. Compare the average results per CVE scenario (where multi-host data available). For both StreamSpot and DARPA E5, we used a 50% split for training and the remaining 50% for testing. Notably, the StreamSpot training data included malicious samples, whereas the DARPA E5 training utilized only benign samples. Both datasets were partitioned into subgraphs based on time windows, with the task being graph-level classification (benign/malicious). The model was trained

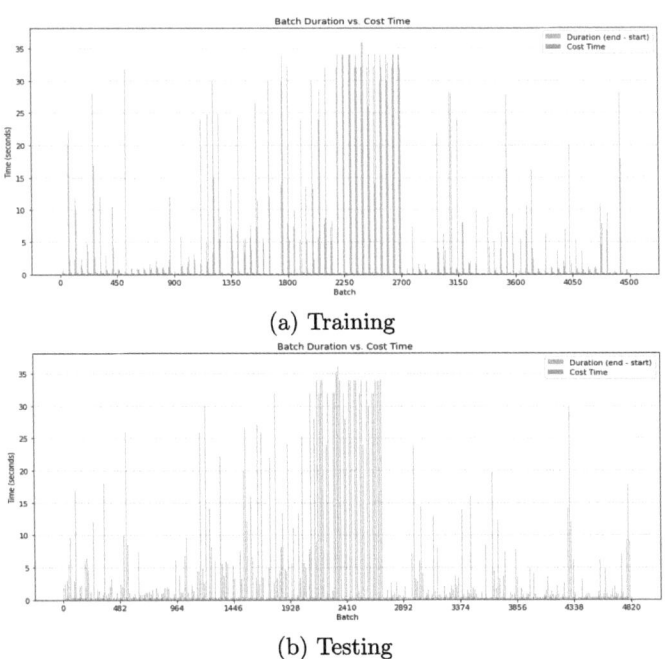

(a) Training

(b) Testing

Fig. 6. Batch duration and cost time on CADETS.

for 30 epochs. The use of exact training/test splits ensures no data leakage. Furthermore, by comparing the convergence trends and final values of the training and test errors, we verified that no significant overfitting occurred.

References

1. MANDIANT: Mandiant: Exposing one of china's cyber espionage units (2016). https://www.fireeye.com/content/dam/fireeye-www/services/pdfs/mandiant-apt1-report.pdf/
2. Archive, N.S.: Cyber brief: Russian apts and the olympics (2019). https://nsarchive.gwu.edu/news/cyber-vault/2019-08-05/cyber-brief-russian-apts-olympics
3. Cloud, G.: 3cx software supply chain compromise (2023). https://cloud.google.com/blog/topics/threat-intelligence/3cx-software-supply-chain-compromise/
4. Security.com: X_trader affects critical infrastructure organizations in U.S. and Europe (2023). https://www.security.com/threat-intelligence/xtrader-3cx-supply-chain
5. Stojanović, B., Hofer-Schmitz, K., Kleb, U.: Apt datasets and attack modeling for automated detection methods: a review. Comput. Secur. **92**, 101734 (2020)
6. Cybersecurity, (CISA), I.S.A.: Incident detection, response, and prevention (2025). https://www.cisa.gov/topics/cyber-threats-and-advisories/incident-detection-response-and-prevention
7. Hossain, M.N., et al.: Sleuth: real-time attack scenario reconstruction from cots audit data. In: Proceedings of the 26th USENIX Security Symposium (USENIX Security 17), pp. 487–504 (2017)
8. Milajerdi, S.M., Eshete, B., Gjomemo, R., Venkatakrishnan, V.: Poirot: aligning attack behavior with kernel audit records for cyber threat hunting. In: Proceedings of the 2019 ACM SIGSAC Conference on Computer and Communications Security (CCS), pp. 1795–1812 (2019)
9. Milajerdi, S.M., Gjomemo, R., Eshete, B., Sekar, R., Venkatakrishnan, V.: Holmes: real-time apt detection through correlation of suspicious information flows. In: Proceedings of the 2019 IEEE Symposium on Security and Privacy (S&P), pp. 1137–1152 (2019)
10. Hossain, M.N., Sheikhi, S., Sekar, R.: Combating dependence explosion in forensic analysis using alternative tag propagation semantics. In: Proceedings of the 2020 IEEE Symposium on Security and Privacy (S&P), pp. 1139–1155 (2020)
11. Hassan, W.U., et al.: Nodoze: combatting threat alert fatigue with automated provenance triage. In: Proceedings of the Symposium on Network and Distributed System Security (NDSS 19) (2019). https://doi.org/10.14722/ndss.2019.23349
12. Wang, Q., et al.: You are what you do: Hunting stealthy malware via data provenance analysis. In: Proceedings of the Symposium on Network and Distributed System Security (NDSS 20) (2020). https://doi.org/10.14722/ndss.2020.24167
13. Han, X., Pasquier, T., Bates, A., Mickens, J., Seltzer, M.: Unicorn: runtime provenanunicorce-based detector for advanced persistent threats. In: Proceedings of the Symposium on Network and Distributed System Security (NDSS 20), pp. 1–18 (2020)
14. Alsaheel, A., et al.: Atlas: a sequence-based learning approach for attack investigation. In: Proceedings of the 30th USENIX Security Symposium (USENIX Security 21), pp. 3005–3022 (2021)

15. Wang, S., et al.: Threatrace: detecting and tracing host-based threats in node level through provenance graph learning. IEEE Trans. Inf. Forensics Secur. **17**, 3972–3987 (2022)
16. Zeyi, L., Pan, W., Zixuan, W.: Flowgananomaly: flow-based anomaly network intrusion detection with adversarial learning. Chin. J. Electron. **33**(1), 58–71 (2024). https://doi.org/10.23919/cje.2022.00.173
17. Cheng, Z., et al.: Kairos: practical intrusion detection and investigation using whole-system provenance. In: Proceedings of the 2024 IEEE Symposium on Security and Privacy (S&P), pp. 3533–3551. IEEE (2024)
18. Jia, Z., Xiong, Y., Nan, Y., Zhang, Y., Zhao, J., Wen, M.: Magic: detecting advanced persistent threats via masked graph representation learning. In: Proceedings of the 33rd USENIX Security Symposium (USENIX Security 24), pp. 5197–5214 (2024)
19. Ur Rehman, M., Ahmadi, H., Ul Hassan, W.: Flash: a comprehensive approach to intrusion detection via provenance graph representation learning. In: Proceedings of the 2024 IEEE Symposium on Security and Privacy (S&P), pp. 3552–3570 (2024)
20. Goyal, A., Wang, G., Bates, A.: R-caid: embedding root cause analysis within provenance-based intrusion detection. In: Proceedings of the 2024 IEEE Symposium on Security and Privacy (S&P), pp. 3515–3532. IEEE (2024)
21. Wei, R., Cai, L., Zhao, L., Yu, A., Meng, D.: Deephunter: a graph neural network based approach for robust cyber threat hunting. In: Proceedings of the 2021 Security and Privacy in Communication Networks, pp. 3–24 (2021)
22. Li, Z., Cheng, X., Sun, L., Zhang, J., Chen, B.: A hierarchical approach for advanced persistent threat detection with attention-based graph neural networks. Secur. Commun. Netw. **2021**, 1939–0114 (2021)
23. Zhao, J., Yan, Q., Liu, X., Li, B., Zuo, G.: Cyber threat intelligence modeling based on heterogeneous graph convolutional network. In: Proceedings of the 23rd International Symposium on Research in Attacks, Intrusions and Defenses (RAID 20), pp. 241–256 (2020)
24. Manzoor, E., Momeni, S., Venkatakrishnan, V., Akoglu, L.: Streamspot code and data (2016). https://sbustreamspot.github.io/
25. Torrey, J.: Transparent computing engagement 5 data release (2020). https://github.com/darpa-i2o/Transparent-Computing
26. Satvat, K., Gjomemo, R., Venkatakrishnan, V.: Extractor: extracting attack behavior from threat reports. In: Proceedings of the 2021 IEEE European Symposium on Security and Privacy (EuroS&P), pp. 598–615 (2021)
27. Alshamrani, A., Myneni, S., Chowdhary, A., Huang, D.: A survey on advanced persistent threats: techniques, solutions, challenges, and research opportunities. IEEE Commun. Surv. Tutorials **21**(2), 1851–1877 (2019)
28. Kaspersky: Kaspersky endpoint detection and response expert (2023). https://www.kaspersky.com/enterprise-security/endpoint-detection-response-edr/
29. Gartner: Endpoint detection and response (EDR) solutions reviews and ratings (2023). https://www.gartner.com/reviews/market/endpoint-detection-and-response-solutions/
30. Pei, K., et al.: Hercule: attack story reconstruction via community discovery on correlated log graph. In: Proceedings of the 32rd Annual Conference on Computer Security Applications (ACSAC 16), pp. 583–595 (2016)
31. Fu, Z., et al.: Encrypted malware traffic detection via graph-based network analysis. In: Proceedings of the 25th International Symposium on Research in Attacks, Intrusions and Defenses (RAID 22), pp. 495–509 (2022)

32. Kapoor, M., Melton, J., Ridenhour, M., Krishnan, S., Moyer, T.: Prov-gem: automated provenance analysis framework using graph embeddings. In: Proceedings of the 20th IEEE International Conference on Machine Learning and Applications (ICMLA 21), pp. 1720–1727 (2021)
33. Church, K., Gale, W.: Inverse document frequency (IDF): a measure of deviations from poisson. In: Natural Language Processing Using Very Large Corpora, pp. 283–295. Springer, Cham (1999)

The Economics of Deception: Structural Patterns of Rug Pull Across DeFi Blockchains

Bhavani Kalal[1], Abdulrahman Alhaidari[2(✉)], Balaji Palanisamy[2], and Shamik Sural[1]

[1] Indian Institute of Technology Kharagpur, Kharagpur, India
monu223@kgpian.iitkgp.ac.in, shamik@cse.iitkgp.ac.in
[2] University of Pittsburgh, Pittsburgh, PA, USA
{aba70,bpalan}@pitt.edu

Abstract. Rug pull schemes vary structurally in their methods and in how blockchains shape their economic profiles. We measure how rug pulls operate across six blockchains: *Solana, Polygon, Arbitrum, Avalanche, Ethereum, and BNB Smart Chain*. Each chain shows distinct execution patterns, not just in scam rate but in how capital enters and exits. Solana records the highest rug pull density (55% of all tokens flagged) and the shortest liquidity lifespans. Most pools live for less than an hour, yet 71% yield net gains for their creators. The remove-to-add liquidity ratios in Solana exceed 1.0, compared to other chains. Avalanche shows fewer scams but deeper capital engagement, averaging 227 liquidity additions per rug-pulled token. Ethereum anchors cross-chain flows but exhibits the lowest attacker profitability. Post-removal traces reveal structured use of bridges like Wormhole and Stargate. Stablecoins (USDC, USDT) dominate bridge activity, enabling fast, high-liquidity exits. Solana tokens show bridged values exceeding one quadrillion USD, signaling pricing anomalies absent in legitimate pools. We define ten observed patterns, including atomic drains, fake-volume deployments, non-interactive exits, and bridge laundering. Our analysis relies on data from thousands of tokens and pools without external labels, exposing execution-layer asymmetries shaped by liquidity management design, gas friction, and interoperability channels.

Keywords: Rug pull · Decentralized finance (DeFi) · Rug pull detection · Decentralized exchanges (DEXs)

1 Introduction

Rug pulls in Blockchain platforms are not just scams, they are structured financial exploits shaped by execution platform architecture (i.e., decentralized

---

B. Kalal and A. Alhaidari—Contributed equally.

© The Author(s), under exclusive license to Springer Nature Switzerland AG 2026
V. Nicomette et al. (Eds.): ESORICS 2025, LNCS 16056, pp. 211–232, 2026.
https://doi.org/10.1007/978-3-032-07901-5_11

exchange (DEX) design). While typically framed as social deception or contract abuse, their mechanics follow patterns tied to liquidity and DEX design, gas costs, and cross-chain tooling. In 2021 alone, rug pulls caused over $2.8 billion in losses [9], yet detection systems are still narrowly scoped, often focusing on Ethereum heuristics or token labeling [8,29]. Emerging blockchains such as Solana [37], Arbitrum [18], and Avalanche [31] introduce new risk surfaces because they enable faster exits, lower-cost attacks, and hidden laundering routes through bridges. These conditions yield unique exploit geometries not captured in prior studies.

Our work presents a cross-chain measurement of rug pull behavior and liquidity operations across six blockchain networks: *Solana, Polygon, Arbitrum, Avalanche, Ethereum, and BNB Smart Chain (BSC)*. We extensively analyze token-level liquidity, trace the lifecycle of scam tokens across chains, and identify ecosystem-specific dynamics. Execution environments vary widely. Chains differ in throughput, fee models, and interoperability support, each influencing how rug pulls are deployed, concealed, and completed. Our focus is on structural profiling of how rug pulls are architected, how long liquidity persists, how remove-to-add ratios evolve, and how funds disperse after withdrawal, especially in cross-chain contexts.

We report three main findings. First, scam frequency does not align with profitability. Solana accounts for the highest number of rug pulls but features the shortest liquidity lifetimes and relatively low returns per token. In contrast, Avalanche and Polygon exhibit fewer scams but yield higher add volumes, longer durations, and greater per-token returns. Second, the ratio between removed and added liquidity, especially on a log scale, serves as a strong behavioral signal. For legitimate tokens, this ratio tends to remain near one, reflecting organic market activity. Rug pulls deviate from this pattern: some remove liquidity immediately, while others front-load adds before a coordinated exit. These patterns appear as distinct clusters in distribution plots and are consistent across blockchains. Third, we observe that exit strategies are often shaped by bridge availability. Arbitrum-based scams frequently route to Polygon or Optimism, while Avalanche scams prefer bridges like Celer and Wormhole. These patterns suggest that attackers optimize for speed, cost, and anonymity, not merely network conditions. Notable examples such as AnubisDAO ($60M) illustrate how short-duration liquidity schemes can result in substantial capital loss within hours [13].

These results offer a taxonomy of rug pull behaviors across blockchain ecosystems. Rather than limiting detection to Ethereum-centric patterns, we provide a broader empirical analysis for understanding how different platforms influence the structure and success of these scams. Our findings suggest that both frequency and magnitude must be considered in order to develop effective defenses.

Our Contributions. Our paper makes the following contributions to empirically characterizing rug pulls across DeFi blockchains. (i) We build a standardized methodology to compare liquidity behaviors across six blockchains for

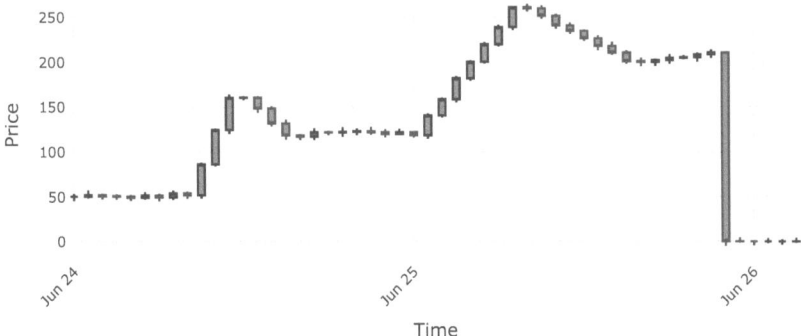

Fig. 1. Classic rug pull example pattern where token price surges gradually, then stabilizes with minor fluctuations, and finally collapses in a near-vertical drop

consistent detection of structural rug pull patterns. (ii) We empirically characterize blockchain-specific differences in rug pull execution methods such as liquidity duration, add/remove ratios, profitability profiles, and exit methods, which inform detection models. (iii) We trace post-liquidity removal fund flows through bridges to identify anomalous bridged token values. (iv) We define a taxonomy of ten liquidity exploitation strategies based on observed economic behaviors to show how AMM designs and cross-chain tools shape rug pull methods. (v) We collect and analyze a large-scale token and liquidity dataset (2021–2024) to measure rug pull prevalence, attacker success rates, and fund movements via cross-chain bridges.

The rest of this paper is organized as follows. Section 2 provides background on blockchain architectures and DEXs. Section 3 introduces our taxonomy of rug pull dynamics based on cross-chain behavioral patterns. Section 4 presents our data collection, token profiling framework, and measurement methodology. Section 5 reports empirical results from our cross-chain analysis. Next, we present our main findings and their implications for detection and defense strategies.

2 Background

EVM and Non-EVM. Ethereum and its derivatives (e.g., BNB Smart Chain, Avalanche, Polygon, Arbitrum) share a common execution standard — the Ethereum Virtual Machine (EVM), allowing code portability via bytecode compatibility [6]. Solana, in contrast, adopts a distinct runtime and consensus stack [32]. Its custom virtual machine, coupled with a dual consensus model (Proof of History and Proof of Stake), produces differentiated execution semantics, resource metering, and runtime behaviors.

Tokens and Accounts. Tokens in EVM-based systems follow standards such as ERC-20 [5], which define balance tracking, transfer logic, and event emis-

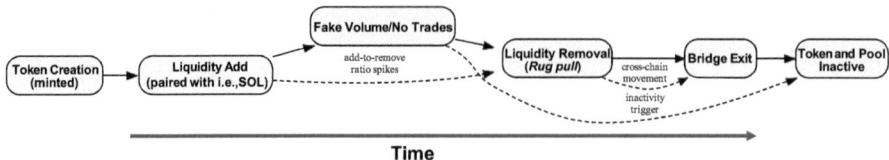

Fig. 2. Execution timeline of a rug pull token. It shows main lifecycle events and behavioral annotations such as add-to-remove ratio spikes, inactivity, and cross-chain fund exit bridge.

sions [28]. Solana's tokens, instantiated via mint addresses, diverge in instantiation paths and do not rely on contract interfaces. Our framework tracks token minting, provisioning, and withdrawal activity across these heterogenous environments.

Transactions and Gas Fees. All state changes are recorded via transactions. EVM chains impose gas fees proportional to computational cost and network congestion [34,38]. Solana decouples transaction execution from fee predictability through fixed costs and parallelism, enabling sub-cent micro-transactions with higher throughput.

Blockchains in Our Study. Ethereum and BNB Smart Chain represent mature, EVM-compatible systems with dense user activity and established DEX protocols. Solana introduces an alternate execution environment with higher throughput and negligible fees. Arbitrum and Polygon serve as rollup and sidechain solutions, respectively, reducing L1 costs. Avalanche incorporates its own consensus and fee model while maintaining Solidity support [4,23,25]. Each blockchain has a different liquidity management mechanism, and they rely on automated market makers (AMMs) in decentralized exchanges (DEXs) [36].

AMMs, DEXs, and Liquidity Pools. AMMS replace traditional order books by executing deterministic swaps via invariant pricing curves. Liquidity pools lock asset pairs and facilitate swaps by adjusting internal balances based on constant-product (or variant) rules [7,33]. Pools are not passive vaults; they expose patterns based on frequency, volume, and asymmetry of capital flows [1].

3 Rug Pull Taxonomy and Dynamics

Rug pulls do not typically exploit code vulnerabilities [39]. The smart contracts often look normal but the deception happens from how and when liquidity is removed. Our measurement study reveals a reproducible spectrum of behaviors shaped by chain constraints, AMM logic, and attacker objectives. These patterns vary across blockchains in execution timeline, interaction model, and liquidity footprint. Figure 1 presents an example of how users identify a rug pull using the token price chart, and Fig. 2 shows the typical execution timeline.

Prior studies categorize rug pulls based on their visible outcome or contract logic. For instance, in liquidity removal [30], developers pair a worthless token with a legitimate asset (e.g., ETH), attract user capital, then withdraw the valuable side. Token dumping [22] involves large creator-held supplies sold post-hype to crash the token price. More evasive patterns include honeypots [10], where sell functions are restricted for everyone but the creator, and limiting sell orders [21], which hardcode permissions to block user exits. These approaches are distinct from soft rug pulls [30], where abandonment is gradual, and hard rug pulls [29], where liquidity is drained instantly and all channels disappear.

These classical types, however, overlook the structural liquidity behaviors we observe on-chain. From over 20,000 flagged liquidity pools across six blockchains, we identify ten execution-level patterns:

1-Hour Exit. Tokens on Solana frequently exit in less than one hour. Pools are provisioned, capital is added, and immediately withdrawn, before user interactions begin.

Large-Scale Single Withdrawal. Avalanche and Polygon show tokens with large cumulative liquidity adds but a single removal. On average, rug-pulled tokens on Avalanche accumulate 227 liquidity additions before being drained, the highest of any chain. These exits extract substantial capital in one event, maximizing per-token loss.

Reverse Liquidity. On Solana, removed liquidity often exceeds total added value (average remove-to-add ratio >1.0). This indicates structural asymmetry, often via internal provisioning.

Delayed Exit Strategy. Some tokens mimic legitimate activity for weeks or months. On Polygon and Ethereum, average rug pull durations exceed 9,000 h, with exits delayed until capital peaks.

Non-interactive Rug Pull. Some pools show add and remove events but no swaps. These are likely scripted, avoiding user transactions and mimicking DEX liquidity without actual trading.

Unprofitable Rug Pulls. Not all rug pulls succeed. On Ethereum, Arbitrum, and BNB Smart Chain, most removed values are lower than added, indicating attacker loss or failed execution. On Arbitrum, only 17.65% of classified rug pulls resulted in a net profit for the attacker, the lowest of any chain. In contrast, Solana stands out as the only ecosystem where the majority of rug pulls (71.38%) are profitable, which highlights a vastly different risk-reward landscape for attackers.

Gradual Drain. Liquidity is removed in staggered intervals instead of a single event. This tactic avoids triggering heuristics that detect abrupt full exits.

AMM-Driven Execution. Attackers exploit AMMs with low friction, such as Raydium or TraderJoe, which permit instant pool creation and flexible provisioning.

Bridge Exit. On Arbitrum and Avalanche, rug pulls are often followed by outbound transfers via Wormhole or Stargate. These bridge flows occur within minutes of liquidity exit, reducing traceability.

Artificial Inflation. On Solana, some tokens show bridged values exceeding 1 quadrillion, orders of magnitude beyond their swap history. These are not seen in legitimate tokens and suggest manipulated pricing or fake supply.

These patterns form a taxonomy of execution-layer rug pulls that complements and extends prior classification. While traditional heuristics focus on token logic or social cues, our structure captures how capital behavior reveals intent. Lifecycle phases also align with this framing, such as token creation [15], hype amplification [35], liquidity accumulation [26], timed withdrawal [19], and disappearance [9] remain integral, but the mechanisms vary by chain and AMM design.

Cross-chain protocols further complicate the fund attribution [24]. Extracted rug pull funds are routed through bridge networks. They appear as legitimate on the target blockchain (where the fund is bridged), which is similar to money laundering schemes. Platforms used like Stargate [17], Wormhole, and Celer enable anonymized value transfer. These flows are visible in our dataset: attacker-controlled wallets initiate bridge transactions shortly after final liquidity removal, suggesting a laundering step rather than post-exit fund migration.

This taxonomy integrates existing classifications with new empirically observed patterns. Instead of relying on hardcoded signatures, it grounds rug pull detection in measurable liquidity asymmetries, irregular timing behaviors, and the specific mechanisms used to exit liquidity.

The taxonomy uncovers structural anomalies not captured by prior work. On Solana, removed liquidity often exceeds added value, showing simulated depth through internal provisioning. Bridge interactions reach implausible magnitudes, pointing to artificial token inflation. Despite minimal lifespans, most Solana rug pulls yield net profit, unlike Ethereum and BNB Smart Chain, where attackers have a higher chance of incurring losses. Several pools show scripted behavior with no external interaction. Exit events are followed almost immediately by cross-chain transfers, suggesting preconfigured laundering strategies. These patterns reflect adaptive exploitation shaped by execution cost, AMM logic, and bridge availability.

4 Token, Liquidity Data and Measurement

To conduct a comprehensive cross-blockchain analysis of rug pull dynamics, we leveraged Flipside, a blockchain analytics platform that provides standardized access to on-chain data across multiple blockchains. This approach allowed us to maintain consistency in our data collection methodology while accounting for blockchain-specific nuances across Ethereum, BNB Smart Chain, Solana, Polygon, Avalanche, and Arbitrum.

4.1 The Token and Liquidity Pools Dataset

We developed extensive custom SQL queries through Flipside's [11] analytics platform to extract standardized datasets for each blockchain. Flipside's comprehensive blockchain coverage enabled us to access transaction data, liquidity events, token metrics, and cross-chain activities in a consistent format. This approach eliminated the need for multiple data sources and ensured data consistency across all six blockchains. Between January 2021 and November 2024, we assembled standardized token-level datasets for six blockchains using Flipside's analytics platform.

EVM Blockchains. For EVM-compatible chains such as Ethereum, BNB Smart Chain, Polygon, Avalanche, and Arbitrum, our dataset includes contract address, token symbols, cumulative liquidity metrics (added and removed), counts of liquidity events, computed add-to-remove ratios, and timestamps corresponding to key lifecycle moments such as the first pool activity, last pool activity, and most recent swap. We also recorded the transaction ID associated with the last swap, the aggregate liquidity removed in the final five withdrawals, gas usage (measured in ETH-equivalent), and two derived labels: inactivity status and rug pull classification.

Non-Evm Blockchains. Solana, as a non-EVM chain with a distinct architectural model, required a parallel schema. Instead of contract addresses and token symbols, we indexed data by token mint addresses. The Solana-specific dataset mirrors the EVM fields conceptually, including total added and removed liquidity, event counts, add-to-remove ratios, and timestamps for pool activity and swaps. Since Solana does not expose gas usage in the same manner, this feature is omitted. Additionally, the field summarizing the final removal events reflects the raw withdrawn amount rather than a liquidity token sum.

Cross-Chain Data. To analyze cross-chain activity, we extracted bridge transaction records for all six blockchains. For EVM chains, we tracked the token address, symbol, bridge platform, origin and destination chains, and the total USD-equivalent value bridged. On Solana, we recorded the same bridge attributes keyed by token mint, excluding token symbol where unavailable.

These raw data points enabled several computed metrics. For each token, we derived liquidity ratios to capture disproportionate extraction, token lifespan measured by the interval between initial and final pool activity, and a remove-pattern signal based on the last five withdrawal operations. For EVM-based tokens, we also quantified total gas expenditure as a proxy for economic commitment. Lastly, we linked post-removal bridge flows to the token's liquidity exit to analyze how funds were routed cross-chain following suspected rug pulls.

4.2 Rug Pull Classification

We implemented a systematic approach to classify tokens as rug pulls based on *inactivity status* and *liquidity withdrawal pattern*. A token is considered inactive if no swap transactions have occurred for an extended period of time (i.e., at least a week). On the other hand, for liquidity withdrawal pattern, we classified a token as a potential rug pull if more than 50% of the total withdrawn liquidity was removed in the last 5 withdrawal transactions. These thresholds were determined empirically based on our analysis of a preliminary labeled dataset. We observed that tokens confirmed as rug pulls consistently saw over 50% of their liquidity drained in a very small number of final transactions. This pattern is different from the more gradual liquidity changes in legitimate, even dormant projects. The one-week inactivity period was chosen as a conservative measure to filter out tokens that are merely experiencing low trading volume.

This classification approach allowed us to identify rug pulls across different blockchain ecosystems using consistent criteria while accounting for blockchain-specific characteristics.

4.3 Challenges and Limitations of Data

Despite the comprehensive coverage provided by Flipside, several limitations should be acknowledged:

i. **Data Completeness**: While Flipside provides extensive coverage, some transactions may not be captured, particularly for newer or less popular tokens.
ii. **Architectural Differences**: The fundamental differences between Solana and EVM-compatible chains required slightly different data structures and analysis approaches.
iii. **Historical Data Availability**: For some blockchains, particularly newer ones like Arbitrum, historical data availability was more limited.
iv. **Smart Contract Verification**: Flipside data does not always include smart contract verification status, limiting some aspects of code analysis.

The combined signal identifies rug pulls: tokens that exit and disappear fit this pattern, while dormant but honest projects typically retain their liquidity. However, the heuristic may still flag benign events like migrations or upgrades that briefly empty the pool. This heuristic may flag benign events like upgrades. False positives can be reduced by using off-chain data such as developer announcements on social media or community forums.

4.4 Rug Pull Measurement Framework

To enable meaningful cross-blockchain comparisons, we developed a unified measurement framework that accounts for blockchain-specific characteristics while maintaining consistent metrics across all ecosystems.

Metrics for Comparison. Our framework incorporates several key metrics for cross-chain analysis, summarized in Table 1.

Table 1. Key Metrics for Rug Pull Analysis

Category	Metrics
Liquidity Dynamics	- Total added and removed liquidity
	- Add-to-remove ratio
	- Number of liquidity addition and removal events
	- Patterns in the last 5 liquidity removal transactions
Token Lifecycle Metrics	- Token lifespan (first to last pool activity)
	- Time to rug pull (creation to major removal)
	- Inactive period duration (since last swap)
Economic Indicators	- Gas fees used (for EVM chains)
	- Bridged value across chains
	- Bridge platform usage patterns
Cross-Chain Activity	- Origin and destination chains for bridged funds
	- Total value bridged
	- Bridge platform preferences

Cross-Chain Standardization and Comparison. To enable fair comparisons across different blockchain architectures, we implemented several standardization techniques:

i *Value Normalization*: We normalized monetary values to USD to account for different native tokens and their price fluctuations.
ii *Time Period Alignment*: We aligned analysis periods across all blockchains to ensure temporal comparability, focusing on the period from January 2021 to November 2024.

iii **Metric Standardization**: We standardized metrics like liquidity ratios and token lifespans to enable direct cross-chain comparisons despite architectural differences.

5 Empirical Results from Cross-Chain Rug Pulls

Our analysis of liquidity duration across tokens on multiple blockchains reveals significant variations in how long tokens maintain liquidity (Table 2). The data shows substantial differences between blockchains, with some ecosystems supporting longer-lived tokens than others.

Table 2. Liquidity Duration Statistics (in hours)

Blockchain	Avg Duration	Min Duration	Max Duration
Polygon	17532.93	0.11	33598.95
Arbitrum	10611.22	0.02	28118.48
Avalanche	14647.41	0.01	32816.83
Solana	1339.27	0.00	32528.53
Ethereum	14559.37	0.03	33599.91
BNB Smart Chain	12352.03	0.03	33599.95

When converted to more intuitive time units, Polygon shows the longest average liquidity duration at approximately 24.4 months, while Solana exhibits the shortest at just 55.8 days. Notably, all blockchains have instances of extremely short-lived tokens (minimum durations near zero), indicating the presence of tokens that lose liquidity almost immediately after creation.

5.1 1-Hour Exit and Delayed Exit Strategy

Solana shows the shortest average rug pull lifetime (620.10 h or approximately 25.8 days), suggesting that fraudulent actors may operate more quickly on this chain (Fig. 3).

The minimum lifetimes across all chains are strikingly short (under 1 h in some cases), indicating that some rug pulls are executed almost immediately after token launch, which is consistent with *pump and dump* schemes (Table. 3).

Rug pull tokens on Polygon have the longest average lifetime (9203.23 h or approximately 383.5 days), potentially reflecting a more patient approach by fraudulent actors on this blockchain.

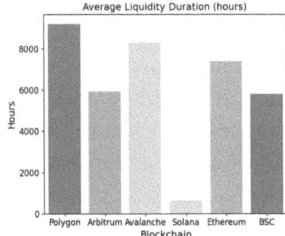 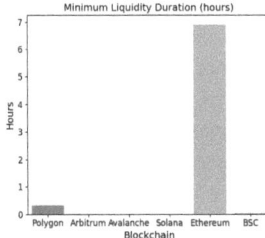 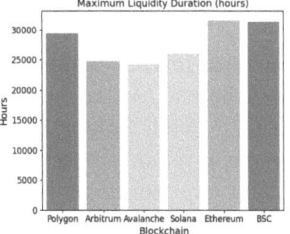

Fig. 3. Average, Minimum, and Maximum Liquidity Duration for Rug pull Tokens.

Table 3. Percentage of Profitable Rug Pulls by Blockchain

Blockchain	Positive Profit %	Negative Profit %
Polygon	26.71%	73.29%
Arbitrum	17.65%	80.39%
Avalanche	40.45%	59.55%
Solana	71.38%	27.00%
Ethereum	27.91%	72.09%
BNB Smart Chain	47.27%	52.73%

5.2 Unprofitable Rug Pulls

The majority of rug pull tokens on most blockchains actually show negative profitability, suggesting that many attempted rug pulls may not be financially successful for their perpetrators (Table. 4).

Solana is a notable exception, with 71.38% of rug pull tokens showing positive profits. This aligns with Solana's higher percentage of rug pull tokens overall and suggests that rug pull operations on Solana may be more financially successful than on other chains. BNB Smart Chain, Ethereum, and Polygon show success rates below 50%, with Polygon at just 26.71% (Table. 5).

Table 4. Percentage of Rug pull Tokens by Blockchain

Blockchain	Rug pull Percentage
Solana	55.05%
Polygon	14.34%
Arbitrum	15.84%
Avalanche	19.47%
Ethereum	21.75%
BNB Smart Chain	18.21%

5.3 Reverse Liquidity

The data reveals significant differences in liquidity management patterns across blockchains. Avalanche shows the highest mean number of liquidity additions (227.10), while Solana has the lowest (5.77). Solana is the only blockchain where the mean remove-to-add ratio exceeds 1.0, indicating that on average, tokens on Solana experience more liquidity removals than additions, which is a possible alarming sign for users (Fig. 4).

Table 5. Liquidity Events Statistics

Blockchain	Mean Adds	Median Adds	Mean Removes	Median Removes	Mean Remove/Add Ratio	Median Remove/Add Ratio
Solana	5.77	2	4.35	3	1.15	1.00
Polygon	172.03	10	14.75	4	0.95	0.36
Arbitrum	127.73	20	5.31	3	0.50	0.21
Avalanche	227.10	29	15.21	4	0.52	0.20
Ethereum	52.92	14	5.29	3	0.60	0.26
BNB Smart Chain	56.79	12	5.41	4	0.52	0.30

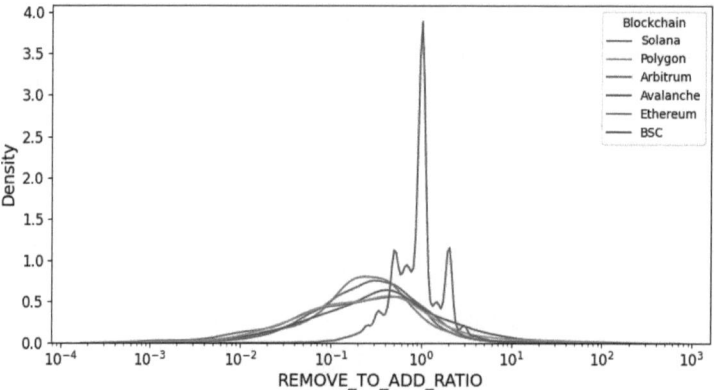

Fig. 4. Distribution of Remove-to-Add Ratio (Log Scale).

We observe that the liquidity of many rug pull tokens is withdrawn shortly after being created, especially where the token lifetime is extremely short (i.e., 1 h exit) and bridging may follow rapidly.

Our analysis reveals that rug pull tokens on Polygon have the longest average lifetime (9203.23 h or approximately 383.5 days), potentially reflecting a more patient approach by fraudulent actors on this blockchain. In contrast, Solana shows the shortest average rug pull lifetime (620.10 h or approximately 25.8 days), suggesting that fraudulent actors may operate more quickly on this chain (Fig. 5) (Table. 6).

Table 6. Rug pull Token Lifetime Statistics (in hours)

Blockchain	Avg Duration	Min Duration	Max Duration
Polygon	9203.23	0.32	24745.19
Arbitrum	5912.12	0.02	24745.19
Avalanche	8322.40	0.01	24745.19
Solana	620.10	0.00	26002.41
Ethereum	7398.40	6.90	31553.77
BNB Smart Chain	5792.62	0.03	31291.03

5.4 Cross-Chain Bridge Exits

Bridge volumes on Solana reach values in the quadrillions of USD (Table 7), far exceeding possible economic activity. These anomalies, absent in legitimate tokens, suggest either unit misconversion, oracle pricing errors, or exploitation of bridge infrastructure. The distribution across platforms is visualized in (Fig. 6).

The values observed for Solana bridge activity are in the quadrillions of dollars, exceeding the entire global financial system's value by orders of magnitude. This suggests token valuation anomalies specific to Solana, or potential exploitation of bridge mechanisms for artificial value inflation.

For both all tokens and rug pull tokens, the same anomalous mint addresses on Solana show extremely high bridged values (Table 8). The distribution of these top bridged tokens is shown in Fig. 7. This suggests that these specific tokens may be central to the observed anomalies and potentially represent sophisticated mechanisms for value manipulation or fraudulent activity.

The observation of quadrillion-dollar bridged values on Solana highlights critical instability in cross-chain infrastructure. Whether due to a price oracle bug or a smart contract exploit, the root cause warrants a security audit. In our study, such anomalies appear only in tokens linked to rug pulls and never in legitimate assets. These impossible valuations thus serve as high-confidence indicators of fraud and expose a vulnerability that attackers may actively be exploiting.

5.5 Main Findings

Our cross-chain analysis shows substantial variation in liquidity dynamics across DeFi blockchains. Polygon exhibits the longest average liquidity duration (24.4

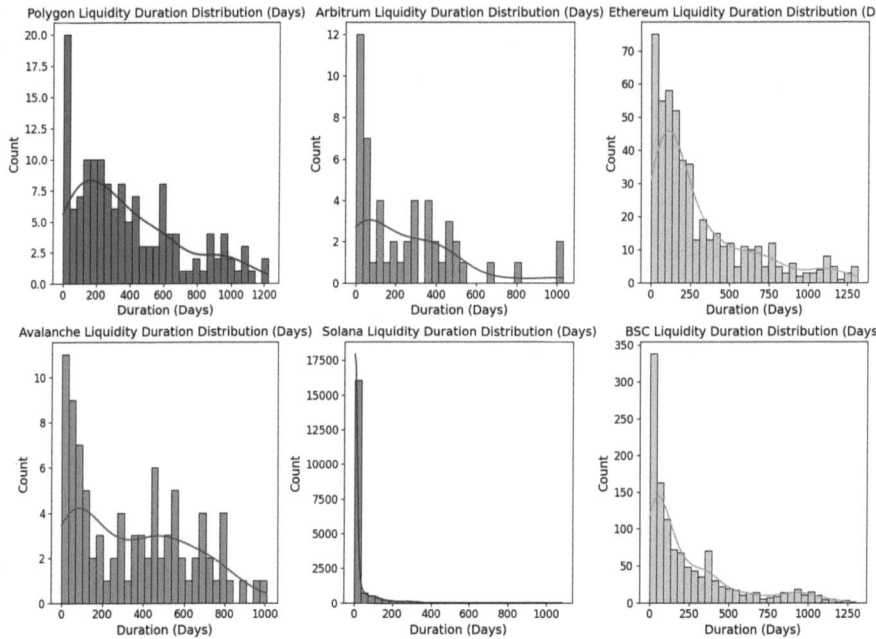

Fig. 5. Distribution of Liquidity Duration for Rug pull Tokens.

Table 7. Bridge Platforms from Solana (by Bridged Value)

Platform	Total Bridged Value (USD)
Wormhole	$3,356,889,881,143,329.00
deBridge	$148,418,389,194,951.00
Mayan Finance	$3,097,191,892,145.19

months), while Solana shows the shortest (55.8 days). Solana also records the highest percentage of rug pull tokens (55.05%), more than double the rate observed on any other blockchain. Rug pull tokens generally have shorter lifespans than legitimate tokens across all blockchains, with Solana's rug pulls averaging only 25.8 days in liquidity duration.

Liquidity patterns suggest additional differences. On Solana, the remove-to-add liquidity ratio exceeds 100% on average, meaning tokens often experience more liquidity removals than additions, a strong structural warning sign. Avalanche, in contrast, exhibits the highest mean number of liquidity additions for rug pull tokens (227.10).

Profitability patterns split across chains, which is contrary to common expectations. Most rug pull attempts on blockchains overall result in negative returns for attackers. However, Solana again stands out, with 71.38% of rug pulls achiev-

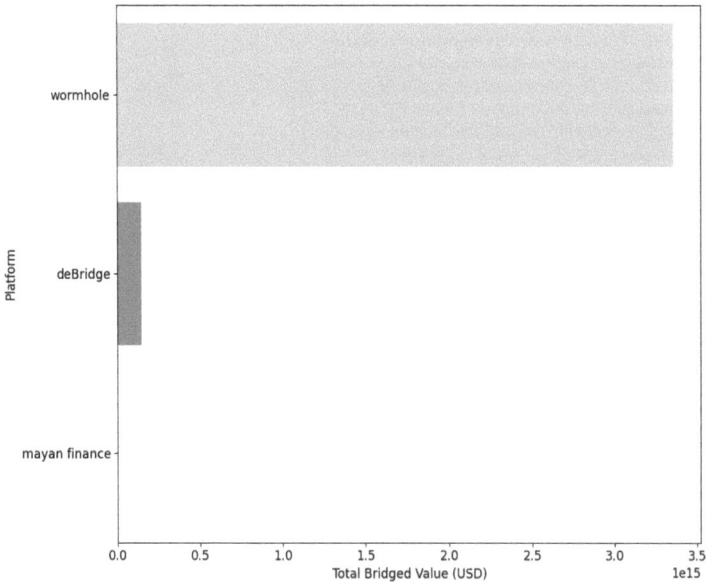

Fig. 6. Bridge Platforms from Solana

Table 8. Top Tokens Bridged from Solana (by Mint (token) Address)

Mint Address	Total Bridged Value (USD)
3K9HBbAviWBx7CQZ3dTWxfE5XzU8bYGm9tUhjN2t7QoQ	$1,174,101,004,349,780.00
BYj4B3kUPdHjQNM2tLW5iwq2QcVQkvTmmJ8qA3mmiSM	$1,000,000,000,000,000.00
DF75DjaQ1nJn2GkSVYq5coC6wTqcRsyv4Sjkk2rrMuPZ	$1,000,000,000,000,000.00
3KigWBTxtP51T8fgjZLK3ZvXhNQzABytHKpxrRdDpgab	$108,329,221,233,060.00
7ZCm8WBN9aLa3o47SoYctU6iLdj7wkGG5SV2hE5CgtD5	$64,047,764,251,204.74

ing positive profits. Short-lived rug pulls (under one hour from token launch to liquidity exit) are observed across all blockchains.

Bridge activity shows Ethereum is the main source of cross-chain liquidity, with $41.9 billion bridged to Polygon, $36.4 billion to Avalanche, and $19.9 billion to Arbitrum. Stablecoins (especially USDC and USDT) and wrapped assets (WETH, WBTC) dominate cross-chain transfers.

However, Solana exhibits extraordinary anomalies in bridge activity, as bridged token values are in the quadrillions of dollars. This far exceeds possible financial activity. These anomalies persist even when focusing exclusively on rug pull tokens and suggest a strong association between fraudulent liquidity schemes and anomalous cross-chain fund flows. Bridge platform preferences also vary by chain, with Ethereum favoring native bridges, while Solana, Avalanche,

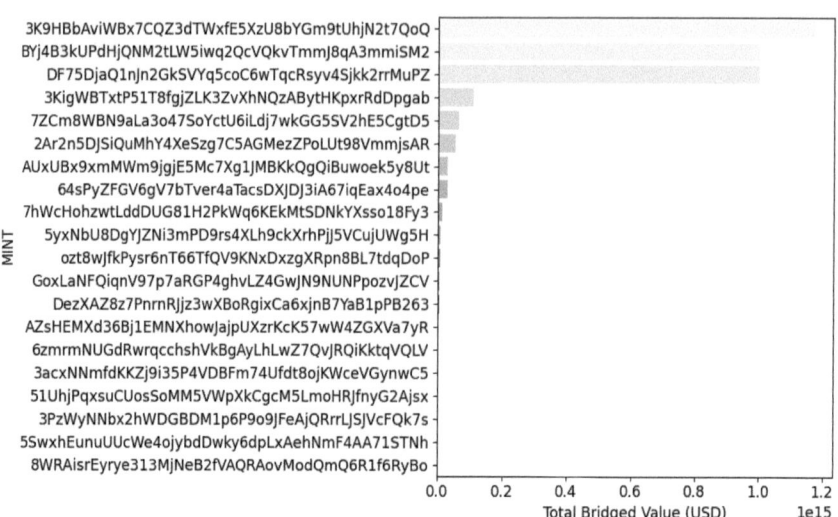

Fig. 7. Top 20 Tokens Bridged from Solana.

and Arbitrum rely more heavily on third-party protocols like Stargate, Wormhole, and Celer cBridge.

5.6 Implications for Rug Pull Detection

The observed patterns in liquidity exits and bridge activity provide valuable insights for rug pull detection and prevention. We outline them below:

i. Extremely high bridge values that significantly deviate from realistic economic activity should be flagged as potential indicators of fraudulent token manipulation.
ii. Blockchains with both high rug pull percentages and anomalous bridge activity (particularly Solana) warrant enhanced scrutiny and potentially more stringent regulatory frameworks.
iii. The consistent use of stablecoins in both legitimate and fraudulent bridge activity suggests that monitoring unusual stablecoin flows across bridges could help identify potential rug pull preparations.
iv. The similar bridge platform usage between all tokens and rug pull tokens indicates that detection mechanisms should focus on token-specific behaviors rather than bridge platform selection.

The extreme anomalies observed in Solana's bridge activity, combined with its high rug pull percentage, suggest that this blockchain may face unique challenges in ensuring cross-chain security and preventing fraudulent token activities. Further investigation into the specific mechanisms behind these anomalous values is warranted to develop more effective detection and prevention strategies.

6 Related Work

Research on rug pulls has expanded significantly in recent years, yet comprehensive cross-blockchain comparative analyses remain scarce. Current datasets and research efforts exhibit several limitations that constrain their generalizability and diagnostic power. In our previous work, we developed SolRPDS[1] (Solana Rug Pull Dataset) [2], the first specialized dataset for analyzing rug pulls within the Solana blockchain ecosystem. SolRPDS encompasses approximately four years of DeFi data spanning from February 2021 to November 2024, capturing both suspected and confirmed tokens exhibiting rug pull patterns. The dataset is derived from 3.69 billion transactions across the Solana network, identifying 62,895 suspicious liquidity pools and 22,195 tokens that demonstrate patterns consistent with rug pulls. SolRPDS includes several critical attributes that facilitate the identification and analysis of rug pull activities, including liquidity activities (additions, removals, and ratios), temporal data such as timestamps for first pool activity, last pool activity, and last swap, as well as inactivity status annotations and transaction details including withdrawn token amounts and transaction IDs. Our experiments with SolRPDS demonstrated its utility for developing automated detection systems, with machine learning classifiers achieving up to 97.6% accuracy in classifying token activity status. While SolRPDS provided valuable insights into Solana-specific rug pulls, it highlighted the need for extending this approach to multiple blockchain ecosystems.

Other available datasets also suffer from significant limitations. CryptoScamDB [12] contains information on various cryptocurrency scams, including rug pulls, but lacks detailed technical analysis of the mechanisms employed. Rug Pull Finder [27] is a community-driven database focused primarily on Ethereum-based rug pulls, with limited coverage of other blockchains. The DeFiLlama [14] Rug Pull List tracks major DeFi rug pulls but focuses primarily on high-value incidents. Chain Analysis Reports provide aggregate data on rug pulls but often lack granular details on individual incidents. The Uniswap [16] dataset is a comprehensive collection of tokens launched on Uniswap, with research indicating that 97.7% of these tokens were identified as rug pulls. This dataset expanded to include 27,588 tokens, with 26,957 labeled as scams or rug pulls and only 631 as non-malicious.

Recent research has identified 34 distinct root causes for rug pulls, yet existing datasets document only 7 of these causes across 2,448 instances. Current detection tools can identify 25 of these 34 root causes, achieving 73.5% coverage, but 9 root causes remain undetectable by existing tools.

Several critical gaps remain in the research landscape. First, most studies focus on a single blockchain, typically Ethereum or BNB Smart Chain, with limited comparative analysis across multiple chains [19]. Second, there is limited understanding of how blockchain-specific architectural features influence rug pull dynamics [6]. Third, insufficient research has been conducted on how different AMM designs across blockchains affect vulnerability to rug pulls [3]. Fourth,

---
[1] https://github.com/DeFiLabX/SolRPDS

there is limited research on how economic factors like gas fees influence rug pull frequency and profitability [26]. Fifth, there is inadequate tracking and analysis of how rug pullers move funds across different blockchains [20]. Lastly, the field lacks a unified methodology for measuring and comparing rug pull characteristics across blockchains [8].

Our work overcomes the critical limitations of prior research. While incident databases like CryptoScamDB [12] and Rug Pull Finder [27] serve as useful catalogs, they are limited in the number of rug pull tokens and lack the granular on-chain data, such as liquidity add/remove ratios, that is essential for building a behavioral understanding of these exploits. Furthermore, the vast majority of previous work and detection tools have been narrowly focused on Ethereum and BSC heuristics [8]. Our framework creates a standardized, cross-chain methodology that directly compares EVM and non-EVM chains, revealing how fundamental differences in architecture and cost between platforms like Ethereum and Solana shape the execution and economics of these scams.

7 Conclusion

Rug pull behaviors are shaped by execution cost, AMM logic, and bridge infrastructure. The cross-chain analysis shows consistent liquidity asymmetries, patterned exits, and platform-specific attack strategies. Solana shows the highest fraud prevalence and anomalous bridge values. These structural differences emphasize the need for detection methods grounded in liquidity behavior and supported by a taxonomy of execution patterns, with sensitivity to each platform. Future work may explore the causes of the quadrillion-dollar bridge values observed on Solana. Also, combining on-chain liquidity data with off-chain sources like social media can improve detection. For example, correlating the timing of liquidity additions with social media hype campaigns, a factor known to influence rug pull success, could provide a multi-modal signal for earlier and more accurate detection.

Acknowledgement. This material is based upon work supported by the National Science Foundation under Grant #2020071. Any opinions, findings, and conclusions or recommendations expressed in this material are those of the authors and do not necessarily reflect the views of the National Science Foundation.

A Appendix

The following figures were excluded from the main body of the paper for brevity. They expand on the liquidity lifecycle and remove/add ratios discussed in the main text.

A. Liquidity Duration Patterns

In Figure 8, Polygon shows the highest average liquidity duration (17,533 h), while Solana has the lowest (1,339 h). Minimum durations are near zero for

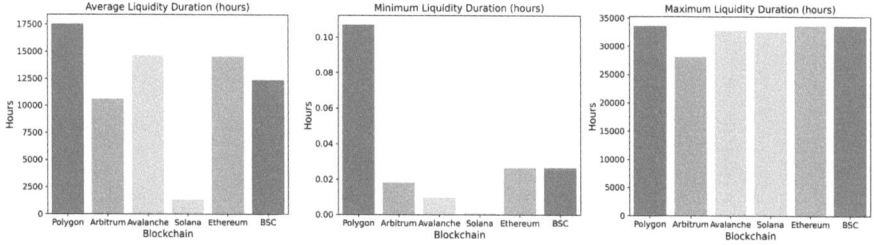

Fig. 8. Liquidity Duration Summary Across Blockchains

Solana, compared to ≈ 0.11 hours on Polygon. Maximum durations are similar across all chains, with Polygon slightly ahead at 33,599 h.

Polygon and Ethereum (Fig. 9) show the longest median liquidity durations (≈ 800 and ≈ 500 days). Solana has the shortest median (≈ 20 days) and a dense cluster of outliers, reflecting large-scale short-lived tokens. All chains exhibit wide variability, with Polygon and Avalanche reaching up to 1,400 days.

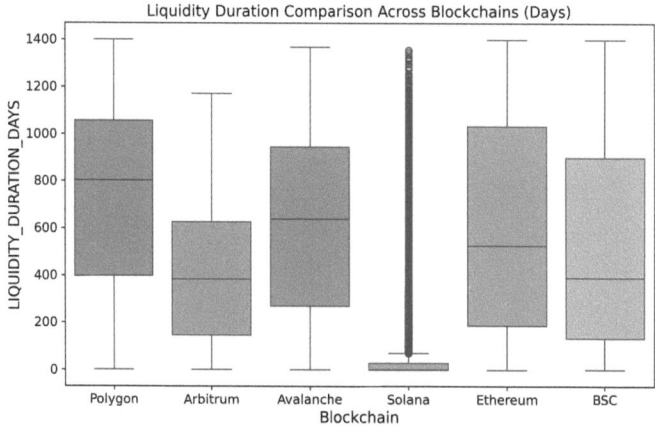

Fig. 9. Boxplot Comparison of Liquidity Duration Across Blockchains.

B. Liquidity Adds and Removes

Polygon and Arbitrum (in Fig. 10) have the highest average liquidity additions (≈ 12,000 and ≈ 11,500), while Solana has the lowest (≈ 5,000). In contrast, Solana leads in average removals (≈ 3,400), which exceeds all other blockchains. Ethereum, on the other hand, shows the lowest average removals (≈ 300). The distribution of liquidity adds and removes is shown in Fig. 11, and the distribution of the remove-to-add ratio is shown in Fig. 12.

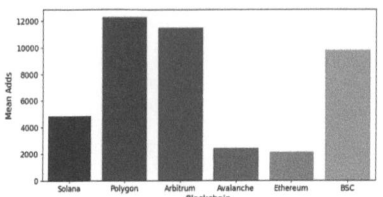 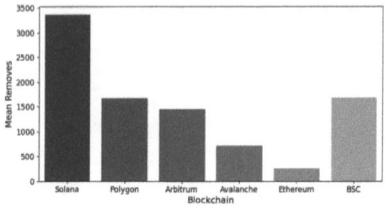

(a) Average Liquidity Adds per Blockchain   (b) Average Liquidity Removed per Blockchain

Fig. 10. Liquidity activity comparison across blockchains.

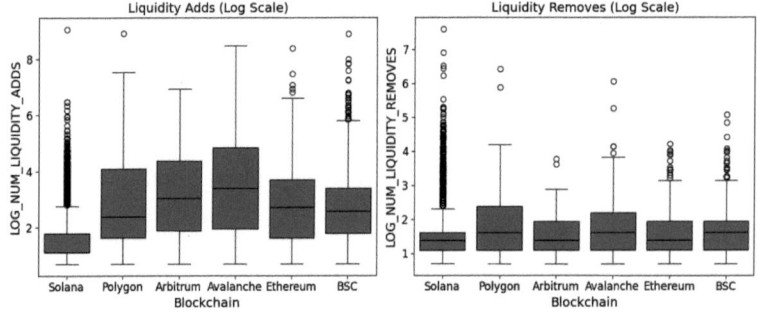

Fig. 11. Distribution of Liquidity Adds and Removes for Rug pull Tokens (Log Scale).

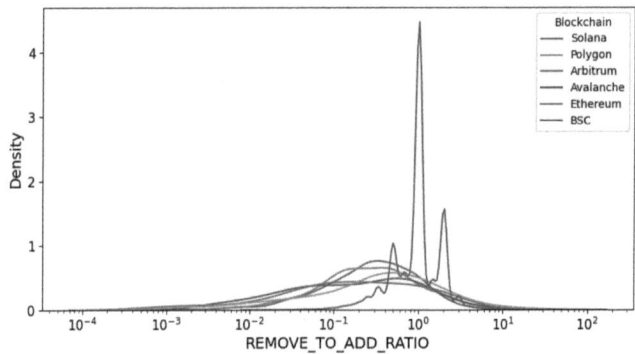

Fig. 12. Distribution of Remove-to-Add Ratio for Rug pull Tokens.

References

1. Adaramola, O.: The dark arts of crypto laundering and the nigerian financial ecosystem: examining regulatory perspectives of virtual assets and virtual asset providers in mitigating money laundering risks in Nigeria. J. Econ. Criminol. **7**, 100117 (2025)

2. Alhaidari, A., Kalal, B., Palanisamy, B., Sural, S.: Solrpds: a dataset for analyzing rug pulls in solana decentralized finance. In: Proceedings of the Fifteenth ACM Conference on Data and Application Security and Privacy, pp. 293–298 (2025)
3. Angeris, G., Chitra, T.: Improved price oracles: constant function market makers. In: Proceedings of the 2nd ACM Conference on Advances in Financial Technologies, pp. 80–91 (2020)
4. Avalabs: Avalanche whitepaper (2021). https://www.avalabs.org/whitepapers
5. Bauer, D.P.: Erc-20: fungible tokens. In: Getting Started with Ethereum: a Step-by-Step Guide to Becoming a Blockchain Developer, pp. 17–48. Springer (2022)
6. Buterin, V., et al.: A next-generation smart contract and decentralized application platform. White Paper **3**(37), 2–1 (2014)
7. Capponi, A., Jia, R.: Liquidity provision on blockchain-based decentralized exchanges. Available at SSRN 3805095 (2021)
8. Cernera, F., La Morgia, M., Mei, A., Sassi, F.: Token spammers, rug pulls, and sniper bots: An analysis of the ecosystem of tokens in ethereum and in the binance smart chain (BNB). In: 32nd USENIX Security Symposium (USENIX security 23), pp. 3349–3366 (2023)
9. Chainalysis: The 2022 crypto crime report (2022). https://www.chainalysis.com/reports/2022-crypto-crime-report, chainalysis Research Report
10. Chen, W., Guo, X., Chen, Z., Zheng, Z., Lu, Y., Li, Y.: Honeypot contract risk warning on ethereum smart contracts. In: 2020 IEEE International Conference on Joint Cloud Computing, pp. 1–8. IEEE (2020)
11. Crypto, F.: Flipside — the platform for intelligent blockchain growth (2025). https://flipsidecrypto.xyz/
12. CryptoScamDB: CryptoScamDB: Cryptocurrency Scam Database (2025). https://cryptoscamdb.org/
13. DeFi Watch: Anubisdao rug pull explained (2022). https://defiwatch.org/anubisdao-rug
14. DeFiLlama: DeFi Dashboard (2024). https://defillama.com . accessed: 2024-05-14
15. Freni, P., Ferro, E., Moncada, R.: Tokenomics and blockchain tokens: a design-oriented morphological framework. Blockchain: Res. Appl. **3**(1), 100069 (2022)
16. Heimbach, L., Schertenleib, E., Wattenhofer, R.: Risks and returns of uniswap v3 liquidity providers. In: Proceedings of the 4th ACM Conference on Advances in Financial Technologies, pp. 89–101 (2022)
17. Huang, C., Yan, T., Tessone, C.J.: Seamlessly transferring assets through layer-0 bridges: An empirical analysis of stargate bridge's architecture and dynamics. In: Companion Proceedings of the ACM Web Conference 2024, pp. 1776–1784 (2024)
18. Kalodner, H., Goldfeder, S., Chen, X., Weinberg, S.M., Felten, E.W.: Arbitrum: scalable, private smart contracts. In: 27th USENIX Security Symposium (USENIX Security 18), pp. 1353–1370 (2018)
19. Lin, Z., Chen, J., Wu, J., Zhang, W., Wang, Y., Zheng, Z.: Crpwarner: warning the risk of contract-related rug pull in defi smart contracts. IEEE Trans. Softw. Eng. (2024)
20. Mao, H., Nie, T., Sun, H., Shen, D., Yu, G.: A survey on cross-chain technology: challenges, development, and prospect. IEEE Access **11**, 45527–45546 (2022)
21. Mohan, V.: Automated market makers and decentralized exchanges: a defi primer. Financ. Innov. **8**(1), 20 (2022)
22. Nguyen, M.H., Huynh, P.D., Dau, S.H., Li, X.: Rug-pull malicious token detection on blockchain using supervised learning with feature engineering. In: Proceedings of the 2023 Australasian Computer Science Week, pp. 72–81 (2023)

23. Offchain Labs: Arbitrum Technical Overview (2022). https://docs.arbitrum.io/
24. Ou, W., Huang, S., Zheng, J., Zhang, Q., Zeng, G., Han, W.: An overview on cross-chain: Mechanism, platforms, challenges and advances. Comput. Netw. **218**, 109378 (2022)
25. Polygon: polygon developer documentation (2022). https://polygon.io/docs
26. Qin, K., Zhou, L., Gervais, A.: Quantifying blockchain extractable value: how dark is the forest? In: 2022 IEEE Symposium on Security and Privacy (SP), pp. 198–214. IEEE (2022)
27. Rug Pull Finder: Rug Pull Finder — Crunchbase (2025). https://www.crunchbase.com/organization/rug-pull-finder. Accessed: 2025-03-20
28. Schär, F.: Decentralized finance: on blockchain and smart contract-based financial markets. Rev. Fed. Reserve Bank St Louis **103**(2), 153–174 (2021)
29. Sharma, T., Agarwal, R., Shukla, S.K.: Understanding rug pulls: an in-depth behavioral analysis of fraudulent NFT creators. ACM Trans. Web **18**(1), 1–39 (2023)
30. Sun, D., Ma, W., Nie, L., Liu, Y.: Sok: Comprehensive analysis of rug pull causes, datasets, and detection tools in defi. arXiv preprint arXiv:2403.16082 (2024)
31. Tanana, D.: Avalanche blockchain protocol for distributed computing security. In: 2019 IEEE International Black Sea Conference on Communications and Networking (BlackSeaCom), pp. 1–3. IEEE (2019)
32. Thompson, P.: Solana sees first rug pull: Luna yield disappears with $6.7m in digital currency. https://coingeek.com/solana-sees-first-rug-pull-luna-yield-disappears-with-6-7m-in-digital-currency/ (2021). coinGeek
33. Tran, T., Tran, D.A., Nguyen, T.: Order book inspired automated market making. IEEE Access (2024)
34. Wood, G., et al.: Ethereum: A secure decentralised generalised transaction ledger. Ethereum project yellow paper **151**(2014), 1–32 (2014)
35. Wu, H., et al.: Your token becomes worthless: unveiling rug pull schemes in crypto token via code-and-transaction fusion analysis. arXiv preprint arXiv:2506.18398 (2025)
36. Xu, J., Paruch, K., Cousaert, S., Feng, Y.: Sok: Decentralized exchanges (DEX) with automated market maker (AMM) protocols. ACM Comput. Surv. **55**(11), 1–50 (2023)
37. Yakovenko, A.: Solana: A new architecture for a high performance blockchain v0.8.13 (2018)
38. Yang, R., Murray, T., Rimba, P., Parampalli, U.: Empirically analyzing ethereum's gas mechanism. In: 2019 IEEE European Symposium on Security and Privacy Workshops (EuroS & PW), pp. 310–319. IEEE (2019)
39. Zhou, Y., Sun, J., Ma, F., Chen, Y., Yan, Z., Jiang, Y.: Stop pulling my rug: exposing rug pull risks in crypto token to investors. In: Proceedings of the 46th International Conference on Software Engineering: Software Engineering in Practice, pp. 228–239 (2024)

Privacy-Preserving Trajectory Data Publication Via Differentially-Private Representation Learning

Youcef Korichi[1](✉), Josée Desharnais[1], Sébastien Gambs[2], and Nadia Tawbi[1]

[1] Université Laval, Québec, Canada
{youcef.korichi.1,josee.desharnais,nadia.tawbi}@ulaval.ca
[2] Université du Québec à Montréal, Montréal, Canada
gambs.sebastien@uqam.ca

Abstract. In recent years, a huge amount of mobility data has been collected from multiple sources, which has shown increasing utility in various domains such as transportation optimization, disease spread prediction and location-based services. However, trajectory data, a specific type of mobility data, raises substantial privacy concerns due to its high inference potential with respect to the personal information of users. To address this issue, we propose a new privacy-preserving trajectory data publication mechanism based on representation learning and differential privacy. Our approach is based on an effective and scalable trajectory-to-vector encoder that is based on a transformer neural architecture. First, we demonstrate that directly using such an encoder does not suffice to protect the original raw data, as the encoder can still expose information that may reflect individual characteristics of the underlying data, thus raising privacy concerns similar to those associated with directly sharing this data. More precisely, we show that an adversary that has access to the encoder can exploit it to conduct a successful Trajectory-User Linking (TUL) attack. Afterwards to address this issue, we introduce an efficient privacy-preserving trajectory-to-vector encoder, combining PATE (Private Aggregation of Teacher Ensemble) framework and Domain-Adaptive Pre-Training (DAPT), which provides a satisfying privacy-utility trade-off. In particular, the learned encoder can be employed as a building block for other mobility-related downstream tasks.

1 Introduction

In our modern digital era, the importance of mobility data, which captures the movements of persons and vehicles over time from one location to another is recognized across various domains [11]. For instance, the analysis of mobility data has demonstrated significant utility by enabling public health authorities to investigate the spread of diseases, identify regions with elevated exposure risk and assess the effectiveness of public health interventions [4]. Additionally, it can facilitate city planners' understanding of global movement patterns and enable the optimization of transportation infrastructure [38], enable traffic engineers and local authorities to identify congested areas or routes to be able to design more efficient traffic management strategies [16]. Finally, it allows the development of Location-based Service (LBS) such as navigation and mapping, social networking, fleet management and local recommendations [15].

A trajectory is a special type of mobility data, composed of an ordered sequence of timestamped locations. In recent years, a massive amount of trajectory data has been collected from a wide range of sources, such as GPS devices, mobile phones, connected vehicles and public transportation systems, just to name a few. This vast amount of trajectory data is highly correlated with individuals' private information, thus raising significant privacy concerns. For instance, Trajectory-User Linking (TUL) is a specific type of attack that aims at determining the identity to whom belongs a given anonymized trajectory [25]. TUL can be used as a basis to conduct other privacy attacks due to the inference potential of mobility data and the insights that can be derived from it such as:

- **Identity exposure** [10]: TUL can lead to the identification of individuals based on their movement patterns. Even when trajectory data is anonymized, linking the data to a specific user can reveal their identity, especially in conjunction with other data sources.
- **Sensitive location disclosure** [40]: TUL can expose visits to sensitive locations, such as medical facilities, political gatherings or personal residences. This can lead to unintended disclosures about an individual's health status, political affiliations or personal habits.
- **Behavioral profiling** [28]: By analyzing movement patterns, TUL can enable detailed behavioral profiling. This can include predicting future movements, understanding personal preferences or inferring socio-economic status, which can be used for targeted advertising or discriminatory purposes.

The reliance of classical trajectory data mining on handcrafted feature extraction limits its adaptability to large-scale data. To address this, methods based on machine learning have emerged as the go-to methods for a wide variety of mobility-related tasks such as database storage [21], trajectory data querying [13], similarity measurement [36], travel mode identification [17] and travel time estimation [34]. Furthermore, numerous state-of-the-art approaches for trajectory data mining rely on Deep Learning (DL) algorithms [33]. In particular, Representation Learning [2] is a foundational concept in DL, whose primary goal is to employ learned encoders to transform raw, often high-dimensional data into lower-dimensional, structured representations that are useful for downstream tasks, such as classification, regression, clustering or data synthesis. These encoders are trained using DL models that extract meaningful features from data while addressing challenges like efficiency and scalability.

In this work, our main objective is to preserve the privacy of individuals in trajectory data publication. More precisely, the main contributions of our work can be summarized as follows.

- We propose an effective TUL attack that exploits a small dataset of non-anonymized trajectories and the trajectory-to-vector trained on private data to showcase the need to employ a more advanced approach to obtain a privacy-preserving encoder. In particular, our attack outperforms state-of-the-art models for TUL in the setting in which the adversary has a limited access to private non-anonymized trajectories.
- We designed an end-to-end machine learning pipeline for privacy-preserving trajectory data publication based on PATE and DAPT (Domain-Adaptive Pre-Training) [12] mitigating the vulnerability of trajectory-to-vector encoders while keeping a good privacy utility trade-off. In a nutshell, PATE is a differentially-private framework for training machine learning models while preserving the privacy of individual data points in the training dataset. To realize this, PATE leverages an ensemble of teacher models to provide labels to a student model in a privacy-preserving manner. Thus, the student learns from aggregated knowledge of the teacher's models rather than directly from the sensitive data. DAPT refers to the process of further specializing a pre-trained model on a domain-specific corpus to improve its performance.
- We have conducted an experimental comparison between our approach and related models for privacy-preserving trajectory data publication, namely Priv-STEO [20] and Mo-PAE [39].

This paper is organized as follows. In Sect. 2, we introduce the relevant background on differential privacy and PATE and review the relevant literature on TUL as well as adversarial approaches for privacy-preserving mobility data publication. In Sect. 3, we formally describe the considered problem, our model architecture, and our end-to-end pipeline for privacy-preserving trajectory-to-vector encoder learning. Afterwards in Sect. 4, we present the experimental evaluation, comparing in particular our approach to other state-of-the-art learning-based methods employed for privacy-preserving trajectory data publication under different scenarios. Finally, we conclude in Sect. 5 by discussing possible future works.

2 Background and Related Work

2.1 Differential Privacy and PATE

Differential Privacy (DP) [5] is a framework that provides strong, mathematically proven privacy guarantees, ensuring that the inclusion or exclusion of a single individual's data in a dataset does not significantly affect the outcome of any analysis, thus making it practically impossible to infer anything about any individual within the dataset. More precisely, considering that two datasets D and D' are said to be adjacent if they differ by a single element, DP can be defined as follows.

Definition 1. *((ϵ, δ) -Differential Privacy [5])* Assume a randomized mechanism $\mathcal{M}$ and positive real numbers ϵ and δ. The mechanism $\mathcal{M}$ is said to provide

(ϵ, δ)-differential privacy if, for any adjacent datasets D and D', and arbitrary output $S \subseteq \text{Range}(\mathcal{M})$

$$P[\mathcal{M}(D) \in S] \leq e^\varepsilon \times P[\mathcal{M}(D') \in S] + \delta.$$

Let $\mathcal{M}_1, \ldots, \mathcal{M}_k$ be randomized algorithms, each satisfying (ε, δ)-differential privacy. Then, for any $\delta' > 0$, the composition of these k mechanisms satisfies (ε', δ')-differential privacy, where:

$$\varepsilon' = \sqrt{2k \ln(1/\delta')} \cdot \varepsilon + k\varepsilon(e^\varepsilon - 1), \quad \delta_{\text{total}} = k\delta + \delta'$$

Let $\mathcal{M}$ be a randomized mechanism that satisfies (ε, δ)-differential privacy. Let $f : \mathcal{R} \to \mathcal{R}'$ be any (possibly randomized) function that does not depend on the input dataset. Then the composition $f \circ \mathcal{M}$ also satisfies (ε, δ)-differential privacy.

The Private Aggregation of Teacher Ensembles (PATE) framework, introduced in [26], is a differentially-private learning paradigm that leverages an ensemble of teacher models trained independently on disjoint subsets of sensitive data and transfers knowledge to a student model. The main advantage of PATE compared to similar frameworks like DP-SGD [1] and learning on synthetic data [19] is its genericity and the relative easiness to be integrated into existing trajectory encoding models. More precisely, let $\mathcal{D}_{\text{priv}} = \bigcup_{i=1}^{n} \mathcal{D}_i$ be a sensitive dataset partitioned into n disjoint subsets, in which each $\mathcal{D}_i$ is used to train a teacher model f_i. Let $\mathcal{X}_{\text{unlabeled}}$ denote a set of public unlabeled inputs drawn from a similar distribution. Each teacher model $f_i : \mathcal{X} \to \mathcal{Y}$ is trained on its private subset $\mathcal{D}_i$. For any unlabeled input $x \in \mathcal{X}_{\text{unlabeled}}$, the ensemble produces a vote count vector:

$$\mathbf{v}(x) = (v_1(x), v_2(x), \ldots, v_k(x)) \in \mathbb{N}^k$$

in which $v_j(x)$ is the number of teachers predicting class j. To ensure differential privacy, noise is added to the counts:

$$\tilde{v}_j(x) = v_j(x) + \mathcal{N}(0, \sigma^2) \quad \text{or} \quad \tilde{v}_j(x) = v_j(x) + \text{Lap}(1/\epsilon).$$

The final aggregated label is obtained via:

$$\hat{y}(x) = \arg\max_j \tilde{v}_j(x)$$

Finally, a student model f_{student} is trained on the pseudo-labeled dataset:

$$\mathcal{D}_{\text{student}} = \{(x, \hat{y}(x)) \mid x \in \mathcal{X}_{\text{unlabeled}}\}$$

This training does not expose the student to the private dataset $\mathcal{D}_{\text{priv}}$. The privacy loss due to querying the teacher ensemble is measured using privacy accounting technique such as the moments accountant, which provide tight bounds on the cumulative privacy budget over multiple queries.

2.2 Trajectory-User Linking (TUL)

TUL [10] is a trajectory classification task that aims at linking an anonymized trajectory to the user to whom it belongs [28]. Multiple recent TUL methods rely on machine learning approaches to learn accurate associations between a trajectory's features and the identity of its owner. In particular, machine learning models tailored for learning on sequential data, such as Recurrent Neural Networks (RNNs) [10] and Transformers [6], have shown high performance in extracting complex mobility patterns.

For instance, VAE for TUL [41] is a representation learning approach to solve the TUL problem using a Variational Auto Encoder (VAE), which has demonstrated improvements in efficiency and linking performance on real geo-tagged social media datasets. Adversarial Attentive TUL [9] leverages an attention mechanism to dynamically capture complex relationships in user check-ins from trajectory data. Additionally, it uses a Generative Adversarial Network (GAN) to approximate the data distribution of human trajectories.

TUL approach via RNN (TULER) [10] relies on RNNs to extract sequential transition patterns in trajectories and associate them with specific users. It implements word embedding techniques to learn representations for different locations within the trajectories, which are then processed through an RNN model to discern mobility patterns relevant to the TUL task. However, standard RNN models are unable to digest large contextual windows, which are necessary to capture long-range dependencies. This limits their capacity to extract semantically rich representations of trajectories.

Mutual Distillation Learning for TUL (MainTUL) [3] has been proposed to address the TUL problem for sparse check-in mobility data. It uses an RNN trajectory encoder and a temporal-aware transformer trajectory encoder to capture long-term time dependencies and achieves superior performance compared to former methods on real-world check-in mobility datasets. Siamese Network for TUL [37], a Siamese network-based model, captures semantic information in the trajectory and requires only a few labeled trajectories per user for identification.

Finally, TUL-STEO [20] leverages the transformer architecture for handling trajectory data efficiently by exploiting rich and informative characteristics of trajectories useful for TUL. More precisely, it employs a similar approach to [8] but adapt it to the objective of carrying a TUL attack with less cumbersome handcrafted feature extraction and with a scalable ML pipeline.

2.3 Privacy-Aware Adversarial Networks in Human Mobility

The concept of privacy-aware adversarial networks in human mobility prediction focuses on addressing the challenges of maintaining user privacy while leveraging trajectory data for understanding human mobility patterns [22]. For example, in [7], the authors have introduced a privacy-aware approach using GANs for predicting next-week trajectories. This approach maintains privacy by generating synthetic trajectories that are similar to real ones but sufficiently different to safeguard privacy. To measure privacy, they rely on the TUL accuracy, while to quantify utility a function called *TrajLoss* has been defined that measures the difference between the actual trajectory and the corresponding synthetic trajectory data in spatial, temporal and semantic dimensions, with *TrajLoss* being used as a loss function to train the generator.

In [29], the authors have introduced a novel DL model to generate synthetic trajectories that preserve privacy while retaining essential spatial, temporal and semantic characteristics of real trajectory data. This end-to-end model, named LSTM-TrajGAN, incorporates Long Short-Term Memory (LSTM) networks within a GAN framework to effectively address privacy concerns associated with the sharing and publication of individual-level trajectory data. The authors used the same metrics as [7] for utility and privacy. In [39], the authors have developed a novel LSTM-based adversarial mechanism (Mo-PAE) with representation learning to achieve privacy-preserving feature representation of original trajectory data for sharing purposes. The proposed model quantifies the privacy-utility trade-off of mobility datasets in terms of trajectory reconstruction risk, user re-identification risk and mobility predictability.

Finally, even more recently in [20], the authors employed the BERT (Bidirectional Encoder Representations from Transformers) model to solve the TUL task. Their model, TUL-STEO, employs the MLM (Masked Language Model) objective to learn rich and useful representations from trajectories. In a nutshell, MLM is a pretraining objective used in Natural Language Processing (NLP) models, such as BERT, for unsupervised learning of contextualized word representations. In MLM, a portion of the input text is masked and the model learns to predict the masked tokens based on the surrounding context. In addition, they introduced a privacy-preserving mechanism, named Priv-STEO, for trajectory obfuscation, based on adversarial training in which they combine TUL-STEO classifier and MLM to learn private trajectory representations while preserving utility. In the experiments, we will compare our approach to Mo-PAE and Priv-STEO, which we consider to be the closest works to ours.

3 Trajectory-To-Vector Encoder Learning Approach

In this section, we first review the problem statement and adversary model that we consider before describing in detail the different steps of our framework.

3.1 Problem Statement and Adversary Model

Trajectory data are modeled as a set of irregular and unaligned time series, which are sequences of timestamped instances of tuples of the form

$$T_{k,m} = \langle (t_1, x_1, y_1, \text{tid}_k, \text{uid}_m), \ldots, (t_n, x_n, y_n, \text{tid}_k, \text{uid}_m) \rangle$$

in which t_i is a timestamp, x_i and y_i are GPS or Cartesian coordinates, tid_k is a trajectory (or session) identifier and uid_m is a user identifier. Basically, $T_{k,m}$ denotes the k-th trajectory of the m-th user, which means that (t_n, x_n, y_n) refers to the n-th timestamped location in the k-th trajectory of the m-th user.

We assume that the adversary has access to a historical dataset of non-anonymized trajectories as well as the pre-trained trajectory-to-vector encoder. The adversary's objective is to re-identify anonymized trajectories contained in published dataset by retrieving the identity of users to whom they belong. Hence, following the previous formulation, the adversary's objective is to infer the user's identifier *uid* for trajectories in the anonymized dataset. In contrast, the data curator's objective is to defend against the adversary's attack without causing significant degradation of the published trajectory-to-vector encoder utility.

3.2 Overview of Our Approach

Preprocessing Steps. Preparing raw trajectory data for input into transformer-based models involves several critical pre-processing steps. These steps aim to clean, simplify and adapt spatio-temporal sequences into a format compatible with token-based models.

Filtering and Discretization. Filtering trajectory data is a crucial process for preparing these data for analysis and ensuring their quality. Basically, we have applied to our data *spatial filtering*, which removes points that fall outside a specified geographical area. In addition, for the experiments reported in Sect. 4, we have filtered out all trajectories outside the pre-training public dataset region. Additionally, we rely on *local pooling* to reduce the number of points in the trajectories while preserving their general geometries, which means that locations with close timestamps are averaged. We also employ geohash-based location encoding [24], which is a hierarchical spatial data structure that divides the earth into a grid of rectangles, each encoded with a short string of characters. Trajectories can be discretized by converting each location point into its corresponding Geohash code. In addition, Geohash allows for adjustable precision.

Tokenization. Tokenization is the process of breaking down text into smaller units called tokens, which can be words, subwords or characters. In general, transformer models can only process data belonging to a finite vocabulary. In our case, our initial vocabulary is composed of all geohashes present in our pre-training datasets. More precisely, we rely on Byte Pair Encoding (BPE) [31] to reduce the size of our dataset vocabulary, which is a subword tokenization method widely used in natural language processing tasks, especially in transformer-based models such as GPT and BERT. BPE starts by breaking the input text into individual characters and iteratively merges the most frequent adjacent character pairs to form subwords. This process continues until a predefined vocabulary size is reached, capturing common word fragments and entire words efficiently. The BPE strikes a balance between character-level and word-level representations, enabling it to handle rare and out-of-vocabulary words by splitting them into meaningful subword units. The adaptive nature of BPE means that the encoding reflects relevant spatial distribution patterns in the data, such as areas of high traffic or important spatial clusters without explicitly predefining spatial scales.

Time Encoder. Time2Vec [18] is a representation learning technique designed to capture temporal patterns in time series data by providing a more expressive representation of time compared to traditional linear time features, allowing models to better understand complex temporal relationships. The key idea behind Time2Vec is to represent a point in time by a vector that encodes both linear and periodic components, allowing the model to capture patterns that repeat over time as well as trends. More precisely, the Time2Vec representation typically consists of a vector with two parts: the first contains a linear representation of time, similar to traditional time features while the second part encodes periodic components, using a set of sinusoidal functions with different frequencies. Formally given a time point t, the Time2Vec vector $T(t)$ can be mathematically defined as follows:

$$T(t) = [(\omega_0 t + \phi_0), \sin(\omega_1 t + \phi_1), \ldots, \sin(\omega_q t + \phi_q)] \qquad (1)$$

in which $\omega_0 t + \phi_0$ represents the linear component of time, with ω_0 being the weight and ϕ_0 the bias, $\sin(\omega_i t + \phi_i)$ for $i = 1, \ldots, q$ denote the periodic components, each with its own weight ω_i and bias ϕ_i and $q + 1$ is the total number of components in the Time2Vec vector, capturing various periodic patterns at different frequencies.

In our approach, we implemented Time2Vec as a learnable layer in the trajectory-to-vector encoder, in which the weights ω_i and biases ϕ_i are parameters learned during training, which enables the model to adapt the Time2Vec representation to the specific temporal patterns present in the trajectory data it is trained on. In particular, a peculiar property of trajectory data is the irregularity of sampling as locations are not always taken in regularly spaced temporal intervals. Moreover, the time gaps carry information about the moving entity.

Trajectory-to-Vector Encoder. In this subsection we describe the architecture of our trajectory-to-vector encoder and its training procedure. Encoder-only transformers are widely used to create dense vector representation of sequences, which can then be used for tasks like semantic similarity, clustering, sequence classification or as input features for other machine learning models. Our encoder architecture is based on BERT (Bidirectional Encoder Representations from Transformers) [30,32], RoBERTa (Robustly optimized BERT Pre-training approach) [23], DeBERTa [14] and ModernBert [35]. A high-level description is given in Fig. 1.

Hereafter, we describe our procedure for fine-tuning the trajectory-to-vector encoder, which is pre-trained on public data. More precisely, we have adapted it to the characteristics of the private data, while providing (ϵ, δ)-differential privacy guarantee. Our procedure is based on PATE, with adaptation to MLM and trajectory data with the details of this procedure being given in Algorithm 1. A high-level description of the process is also illustrated in Fig. 2.

In summary, a query set $\mathcal{Q}$ is sampled from the public dataset and some of its tokens are masked. Teacher and student models are initialized from the

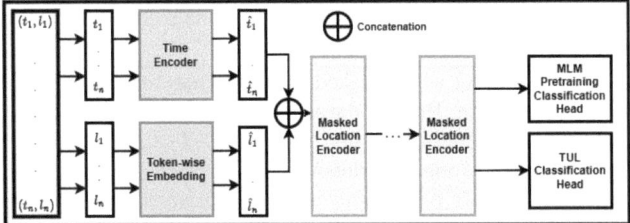

Fig. 1. Trajectory-to-vector encoder architecture.

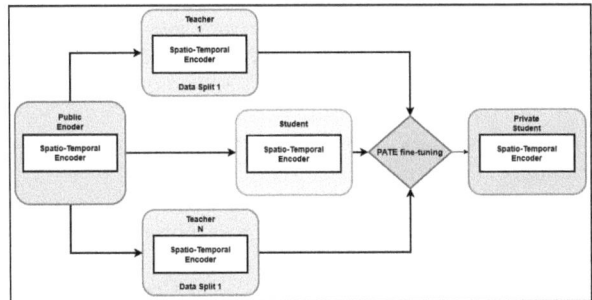

Fig. 2. Privacy-preserving trajectory-to-vector encoder DAPT.

trajectory-to-vector encoder, which was pre-trained on the public dataset. Teachers are fine-tuned on their respective splits, with each teacher predicting the masked token and votes are counted for each token of the vocabulary. A Gaussian noise is applied to each count and the token with the majority noisy vote replaces the masked token. Finally, the student is fine-tuned on the unmasked query set. In addition, if there is a consensus, the collectively predicted token is used to replace the masked token while if the disagreement is large, the token from the public data is used instead to replace the masked token. Given the predicted distributions $(\hat{y}^{(1)}, \ldots, \hat{y}^{(n)})$ for masked tokens and the actual one-hot encoded distributions $(y^{(1)}, \ldots, y^{(n)})$, the MLM loss for a single trajectory is:

$$L_{MLM}((y^{(1)}, \ldots, y^{(n)}), (\hat{y}^{(1)}, \ldots, \hat{y}^{(n)})) = -\sum_j \sum_i y_i^{(j)} \log(\hat{y}_i^{(j)}),$$

in which n is the number of masked tokens, j is over masked tokens and i is over the vocabulary. The student is (ϵ, δ)-differentially private with $\epsilon = \left(\frac{k(\lambda+1)}{2\sigma^2}\right)$ and $\delta = \exp(-\lambda\epsilon)$ in which k is the number of queries, σ is the noise level and λ is the considered moment order used in the moment accountant method. The composability property of (ϵ, δ)-differential privacy guarantees that any post-processing of the output, as long as it does not access the private data, does not increase the privacy loss and preserves the same privacy parameters (ϵ, δ)

Algorithm 1. PATE with Public Queries and Disagreement Threshold for privacy preserving trajectory-to-vector encoder

Require: Public query set $\mathcal{Q}$ with masked tokens, trajectory-to-vector encoder Enc, pre-trained on public data, Private dataset $\mathcal{D}$ split into n subsets $\{\mathcal{D}_1, \mathcal{D}_2, \ldots, \mathcal{D}_n\}$ with disjoint users' identifiers, Teacher models $\{T_1, T_2, \ldots, T_n\}$, Noise scale σ, Disagreement threshold θ, Moment order λ

Ensure: Differentially private predictions and (ϵ, δ) privacy guarantee for the student model

1: Initialize each teacher model T_i from Enc
2: Fine-tune each teacher model T_i on its respective dataset $\mathcal{D}_i$
3: Initialize the student model S from Enc
4: Initialize moment accountant $\mathcal{M}$ to track privacy loss
5: **for** each query sequence $q \in \mathcal{Q}$ with masked tokens **do**
6:   Obtain predictions for the masked token(s) from each teacher T_i: $\{y_1, y_2, \ldots, y_n\}$
7:   For each class (vocabulary token c), count teacher votes: $V[c]$ = Count of $y_i = c$ for $c \in$ Vocabulary
8:   Compute the maximum votes: MaxVotes $= \max_c V[c]$
9:   Compute disagreement as the proportion of non-max votes: Disagreement $= 1 - \frac{\text{MaxVotes}}{n}$
10: **if** Disagreement $\leq \theta$ **then** ▷ Consensus or low disagreement
11:    **if** MaxVotes $= n$ (all teachers agree) **then**
12:      Assign the consensus token: $y^* \leftarrow \arg\max_c V[c]$
13:    **else**
14:      Add Gaussian noise to each vote count: $\tilde{V}[c] = V[c] + \mathcal{N}(0, \sigma^2)$
15:      Determine the predicted token by selecting the class with the highest noisy vote count: $y^* = \arg\max_c \tilde{V}[c]$
16:      Update moment accountant $\mathcal{M}$ for the Gaussian mechanism used:
$$\alpha_\mathcal{M}(\lambda) \leftarrow \frac{\lambda(\lambda+1)}{2\sigma^2}$$
17:    **end if**
18: **else** ▷ High disagreement exceeds threshold
19:    Return the original token from the input query (public data): $y^* \leftarrow q_{\text{original}}$
20: **end if**
21: Assign the label y^* to the masked token in query q
22: **end for**
23: Compute (ϵ, δ) privacy guarantee using the moments:
24: $\epsilon = \left(\frac{k(\lambda+1)}{2\sigma^2}\right)$ and $\delta = \exp(-\lambda\epsilon)$ ▷ k is the number of queries
25: Train the student model S using the labeled sequences $\mathcal{Q}$
26: Return the student model S and the (ϵ, δ) privacy guarantee

4 Experimental Evaluation

Hereafter, we describe the datasets, evaluation metrics and the baseline models for comparative evaluation, before presenting our findings including model performance and limitations.

Baselines for TUL Attacks and Defenses. The first baseline that we consider is MainTUL model [3], which integrates two core components: an RNN trajectory encoder and a temporal-aware transformer trajectory encoder. We also use as a second baseline TULAR [10] (Trajectory-User Link with Attention Recurrent Networks), an end-to-end attention RNN framework. TULAR is designed to selectively focus on parts of the source trajectories when linking, using the Trajectory Semantic Vector (TSV) through unsupervised location representation learning and recurrent neural networks. Finally, the third baseline is TUL-STEO [20], which leverages the transformer architecture for handling efficiently characteristics of trajectories useful for TUL.

Additionally, in terms of defense we compare ourselves to MO-PAE [39] an LSTM-based adversarial mechanism with representation learning to achieve privacy-preserving feature representation of original mobility data. The second baseline for defense is Priv-STEO [20], a privacy-preserving machine learning pipeline designed to mitigate TUL attacks on mobility data building on the STEO architecture mentioned previously.

Datasets and Evaluation Metrics. For our experiments, we have used two publicly available mobility datasets that we describe hereafter. The Geolife dataset[1], published by Microsoft, consists of trajectories of user movements collected over several years from a large number of participants using GPS devices. More precisely, it contains 17,621 trajectories of 182 users, accounting overall for 24,876,978 positions (we have only kept the locations in Beijing). The Gowalla dataset[2] originates from a social networking service whose users shared their locations through check-ins, including geographic coordinates, timestamps and occasionally location names. We have filtered the positions to keep only locations in Beijing for Gowalla dataset and remove users with less than 10 locations by trajectory and less than 10 daily trajectories in the dataset. This leads to 48244 trajectories of 416 users in Beijing, with overall 2 285 414 positions.

Following the related work, we chose the following metrics to assess the success of our attack in our experiments: *Acc@1, Acc@5, Macro-P, Macro-R* and *Macro-F1*. These metrics are detailed below and *Macro-F1* is the harmonic mean of the precision (*i.e., Macro-P*) and recall (*i.e. Macro-R*), averaged across all classes (*i.e.*, users in TUL):

$$Acc@N = \frac{\#\text{true class in } n\text{first predicted classes}}{\#\text{number classes}}, \quad Macro\text{-}P = \frac{1}{M}\sum_{j=1}^{M} P_j$$

$$Macro\text{-}R = \frac{1}{M}\sum_{j=1}^{M} R_j, \quad Macro\text{-}F1 = 2 \times \frac{Macro\text{-}P \times Macro\text{-}R}{Macro\text{-}P + Macro\text{-}R}$$

---

[1] https://www.microsoft.com/en-us/research/publication/geolife-gps-trajectory-dataset-user-guide/.
[2] https://snap.stanford.edu/data/loc-Gowalla.html.

Experimental Setting. In all our experiments, we consider Geolife as a public dataset and Gowalla as the private dataset. By filtering Gowalla dataset, we keep only the 226 users with locations in Beijing. Each location was encoded as a geohash with precision equal to 8, which represents a region of 19 m X 10 m. A lagged sliding window was considered for trajectory slicing, in which the window represents 6 h and the lag represents 10 min. We consider a context window of 512 tokens, in which the geohash, which represents a location, is split into multiple tokens.

We use the entirety of the public dataset (Geolife) for pre-training while 90% of the private dataset (Gowalla) was used as the data to be published. The remaining 10% of the private dataset is considered as the data collected by the adversary, which is used to conduct the TUL attack. The hyper-parameters of the trajectory-to-vector encoder are the number of attention blocks (6), the number of attention heads (12), the maximum sequence length (514), the vocabulary size (52000), the token embedding size (768), the fully-connected network size (3072) and the output vector size (768). We have run a grid search by varying the mentioned hyperparameters in the following ranges 'Attention blocks: {2, 6, 12}, attention heads: {2, 4, 6, 12}, the ones chosen give the best performances.

We analyze the TUL attack's effectiveness against the private dataset under various scenarios, focusing on how different pre-training configurations of the trajectory-to-vector model influence the vulnerability to TUL. For each configuration, we take into account the data utility degradation as well as the privacy loss. For utility, the trajectory-to-vector encoder is used to predict masked token in a trajectory. More precisely, it computes the top-N predictions for each masked position and evaluates the encoder's performance using reconstruction top-N accuracy, comparing predictions against the ground truth tokens. The reconstruction error directly measures how well the encoder-decoder reconstructs the original input sequence from its latent representation, which is the core objective during pretraining with MLM. Thus, it reflects the model's ability to capture and reproduce the underlying structure and semantics of the trajectory data. In contrast, the average Haversine distance only considers the spatial distance between corresponding points, ignoring sequence structure, temporal dependencies and other contextual information that the encoder is designed to capture. For privacy, the adversary builds its attack model by adding a classification head to the trajectory-to-vector encoder. This model is fine-tuned on the collected private data to map trajectories to the corresponding user's identifiers. Thus, top-N privacy loss is defined as the top-N accuracy of the attack model. More precisely the loss function for TUL is defined as follows: Given the predicted distribution $\hat{u}$ for a user identifier and the actual one-hot encoded distribution u, the TUL loss for a single trajectory is:

$$L_{TUL}(u, \hat{u}) = -\sum_i u_i \log(\hat{u}_i), \text{ with } i \text{ over user identifiers.}$$

We have used a k-fold cross validation with $k = 10$, which is a robust statistical method used to evaluate the performance and generalizability of machine learning models. By systematically partitioning the dataset and rotating the roles of training, validation and test data, it enables a more reliable and statistically significant assessments of model performance compared to a single train-test split.

Experiment I (without Pre-training). Our goal, in this experiment is to provide a baseline, to assess the impact of pre-training on the accuracy of TUL attack. The attack model (**Model I**) is trained directly on the private data, collected by the adversary, without exploiting a pre-trained trajectory-to-vector encoder. Table 1 as well as Figs. 3a and 3b demonstrate the feasibility level of a TUL attack with limited data.

Table 1. Results TUL.

Models	Metrics				
	Acc@1	Acc@5	Macro-P	Macro-R	Macro-F1
Baselines					
MainTUL	34.20%	38.06%	36.73%	31.63%	24.02%
TULAR	27.78%	37.74%	32.84%	36.46%	22.64%
TUL-STEO	30.78%	41.68%	38.06%	28.01%	17.71%
Experiment I					
Model I	44.60%	64.28%	37.15 %	44.61%	41.43%
Experiment II					
Model II	52.75%	73.80%	45.06 %	52.75%	57.71%
Experiment III					
Model III	64.76%	85.00%	60.87 %	64.76%	60.13%

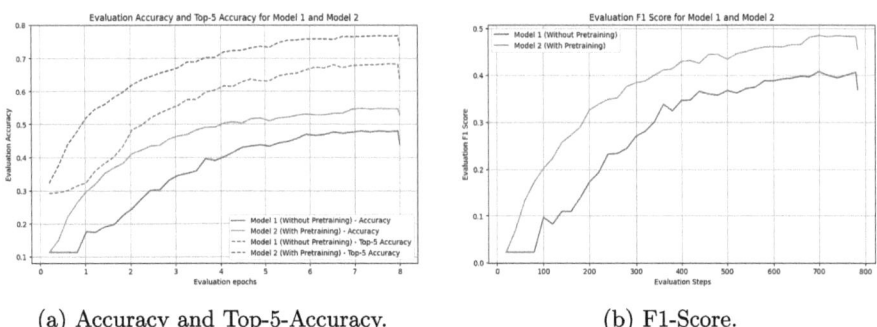

(a) Accuracy and Top-5-Accuracy.   (b) F1-Score.

Fig. 3. Exp II: TUL results - Pre-training only on public data.

Experiment II (pre-training on public data). In this experiment, our objective is to assess the impact of pre-training trajectory-to-vector encoder on the accuracy of TUL attack. The trajectory-to-vector encoder is pre-trained on the entirety of the public dataset (*i.e.*, Geolife) while the attack model (**Model II**) fine-tunes the pre-trained encoder on the TUL task. More precisely, this model is trained on 8% of the private data (Gowalla) and validated on 2%, while the remaining 90% of the private data are used to assess this approach. Table 1 as well as Figures 3a and 3b showcase an 18% increase in accuracy compared the non pre-trained model in Experiment I. Figure 6a displays an example of a trajectory sampled from the private data and its reconstruction, indicating that while the reconstruction retains the general geometry of the sampled trajectory, it fails to capture its specificities.

Furthermore, Fig. 4a displays some attention score matrices from the first and the last layers. On the first layer, an anti-diagonal pattern can be observed, which indicates that each token attends only to itself. In contrast, the more complex patterns on the last layer, demonstrate that the encoder learned to exploit a larger context in order to predict the masked token. Finally, Fig. 4b displays some attention score matrices from the first and the last layers, associated with the special token "<s>". This token has a triple use. First, it is used to indicate the starting of a trajectory. Second, it is used as a pooling token, which means the information extracted from the whole context is accumulated in this token's embedding. Finally, the embedding of "<s>" is used for predicting the masked token and, for user identifier prediction after TUL fine-tuning. These attention scores show that mostly only symbols at positions 3 to 6 in a geohash are used for user identification. The two first symbols represent the region of Beijing and as all localizations are in these same region the classifier does not use them for user identification. The symbols from 3 to 6 represent a region of 470 m X 610 m, beyond this precision symbols are rarely used for identification.

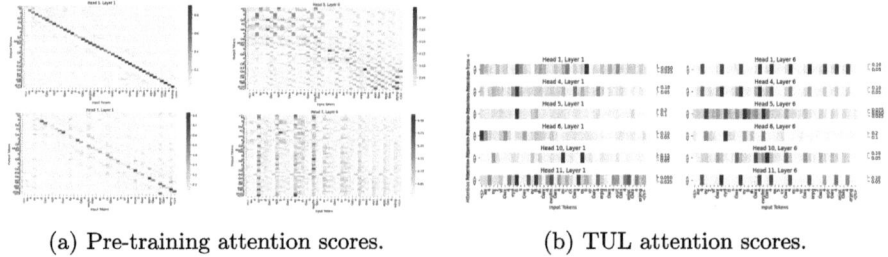

(a) Pre-training attention scores.   (b) TUL attention scores.

Fig. 4. Exp II: Attention scores during pre-training and TUL fine-tuning.

Experiment III (pre-training on public and private data). This experiment aims at assessing the impact of fine-tuning a trajectory-to-vector encoder on the accuracy of TUL attack, while the fine-tuning is done on the private data. Trajectory-to-vector encoder is pre-trained on the totality of public dataset (Geolife) and fine-tuned on 80% of the private data (Gowalla). The attack model (**Model II**) fine-tunes the pre-trained encoder on the TUL task. More precisely, this model is trained on 8% of the private data (Gowalla) and validated on 2% while the 20% of the private data is used to test it. Table 1 as well as Figs. 5a and 5b show a 45% increase in accuracy. Furthermore, Fig. 6b displays an example of a trajectory sampled from the private data and its reconstruction. The encoder captured, almost perfectly, the specificities of the sampled trajectory. Moreover, this experiment indicates the need for a privacy-preserving approach to encoder adaptation to the private dataset.

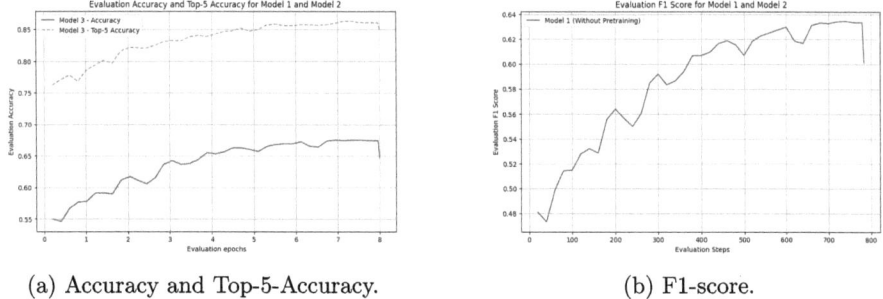

(a) Accuracy and Top-5-Accuracy. (b) F1-score.

Fig. 5. Exp III: TUL results - Pre-training on public and private data.

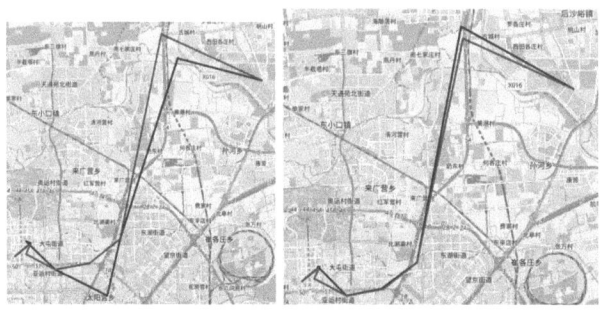

(a) Exp II: Pre-training on public data. (b) Exp III: Pre-training on public and private data.

Fig. 6. Trajectory Reconstruction Results in which the original trajectory is in red and the reconstructed one in blue. (Color figure online)

Experiment IV (privacy-preserving DAPT with PATE). Our goal in this experiment is to demonstrate the effectiveness of our privacy-preserving fine-tuning approach. To realize this, the trajectory-to-vector encoder is pre-trained on the entirety of the public dataset (Geolife). Afterwards, two teachers and a student encoder are initialized from the pre-trained encoder, with each teacher being fine-tuned on a share of the private dataset (Gowalla) (each of these two shares represent trajectories of disjoint subsets of users). A query subset is sampled from the public dataset and then 15% of tokens in each trajectory of the query subset are masked. For each masked token, the two teachers vote for a token to replace the masked token and then votes are aggregated and a Gaussian noise is added. Finally, the token with the highest noisy vote is selected to replace the masked token and the unmasked query dataset is used to fine-tune the student. The privacy guarantees provided by the Private Aggregation of Teacher Ensembles (PATE) framework do not depend on the number of teacher models [27]. While increasing the number of teachers can lead to more stable and reliable voting outcomes, this approach also results in smaller data splits for each teacher. In turn, smaller splits limit the amount of data available to each teacher, which can hinder their ability to learn meaningful patterns from the data. As a consequence, the overall utility of the aggregated query dataset may be reduced, even though the privacy level remains unaffected by the teacher count itself. Our datasets have a limited size and we have tried experiments with an additional number of teachers but observed that this leads to a decreased utility

The results in Table 2 show that, with a "moderate" noise level, our student encoder provides performances close to Priv-STEO [20], which is the state-of-the-art model. Furthermore, we point out that our model provides a formal guarantee of privacy, while the baseline models provide no such guarantee. Figure 7a displays a situation in which each teacher votes on a masked private trajectory. In Figs. 7b and 7c showcase the impact of the noise level on the quality of the reconstructed trajectory.

Table 2. Results Utility vs Privacy

Models	Utility		Privacy Loss	
	Acc@1	Acc@5	Acc@1	Acc@5
Experiment IV: Baselines				
Mo-PAE	34.21%	47.15%	24.24%	35.34%
Priv-STEO ($\lambda = 0.5$)	68.57%	81.63%	17.50%	21.13%
Experiment IV	$\sigma = 10$	$\epsilon = 3$	$\delta = 0.05$	
Model IV.1	55.62%	75.27%	18.50%	24.46%
Experiment IV	$\sigma = 100$	$\epsilon = 0.03$	$\delta = 0.97$	
Model IV.2	17.46%	24.67%	4.75%	13.35%

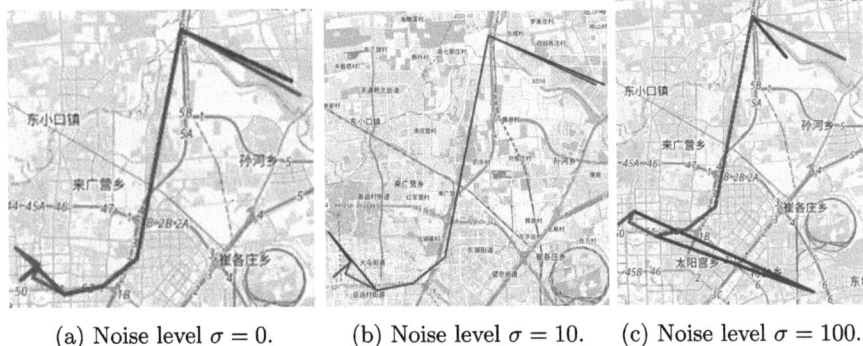

Fig. 7. Exp III: Trajectory reconstruction using PATE aggregation with two teachers and different noise levels. (a) Blue: teacher 1 predictions, green: teacher 2 predictions. (b) and (c) Red: original trajectory. Blue: reconstructed trajectory. (Color figure online)

5 Conclusion

In this work, we presented a trajectory-to-vector encoder, which is an improvement of STEO [20]. More precisely, the trajectory-to-vector encoder that we designed is a transformer neural network that maps trajectories to dense and informative vectors. This encoder can be employed as building block in various downstream machine learning tasks or as a standalone feature extractor. In particular, the improvements proposed in our approach to encoder learning, combining a set of regularization techniques and a robustness-motivated masking strategy, have enabled our encoder to outperform baselines accuracy, in TUL attack, by more than 10%. Furthermore, we showcased that, although the direct use of DAPT on private data increases our encoder's utility, it leaks information about the users in this data. This motivated us to develop a more advanced approach to DAPT, that preserves privacy, while limiting utility degradation. The proposed privacy-preserving approach for DAPT combines MLM and PATE to obtain a differentially-private encoder preserving a high level of utility, with the noisy aggregation of teachers' votes being used to augment a subset of the public data. This augmented data is used to fine-tune a student encoder, thus infusing it with private data patterns without compromising privacy. Our experiments show that this approach has an utility comparable to baselines while providing formal guarantees, which is not the case of the baselines.[3]

Acknowledgments. This work is supported by the DEEL Project CRDPJ 537462-18 funded by the Natural Sciences and Engineering Research Council of Canada (NSERC) and the Consortium for Research and Innovation in Aerospace in Québec (CRIAQ). Josée Desharnais, Sébastien Gambs and Nadia Tawbi acknowledge the support of NSERC, Sébastien Gambs is also supported by the Canada Research Chair program.

---

[3] https://deel.quebec.

References

1. Abadi, M., et al.: Deep learning with differential privacy. In: Proceedings of the ACM Conference on Computer and Communications Security. vol. 24–28-October-2016 (2016). https://doi.org/10.1145/2976749.2978318
2. Bengio, Y., Courville, A., Vincent, P.: Representation learning: a review and new perspectives. IEEE Trans. Pattern Anal. Mach. Intell. **35**(8) (2013). https://doi.org/10.1109/TPAMI.2013.50
3. Chen, W., Li, S., Huang, C., Yu, Y., Jiang, Y., Dong, J.: Mutual distillation learning network for trajectory-user linking. In: IJCAI International Joint Conference on Artificial Intelligence (2022). https://doi.org/10.24963/ijcai.2022/274
4. Colizza, V., Barrat, A., Barthelemy, M., Valleron, A.J., Vespignani, A.: Modeling the worldwide spread of pandemic influenza: baseline case and containment interventions. PLoS Medicine **4**(1) (2007). https://doi.org/10.1371/journal.pmed.0040013
5. Dwork, C.: Differential Privacy. In: Bugliesi, M., Preneel, B., Sassone, V., Wegener, I. (eds.) Automata, Languages and Programming, pp. 1–12. Springer Berlin Heidelberg, Berlin, Heidelberg (2006). https://doi.org/10.1007/11787006_1
6. Feng, J., et al.: DeepMove: predicting human mobility with attentional recurrent networks. In: The Web Conference 2018 - Proceedings of the World Wide Web Conference, WWW 2018 (2018). https://doi.org/10.1145/3178876.3186058
7. Fontana, I., Langheinrich, M., Gjoreski, M.: GANs for privacy-aware mobility modeling. IEEE Access **11** (2023). https://doi.org/10.1109/ACCESS.2023.3260981
8. Franco, L., Placidi, L., Giuliari, F., Hasan, I., Cristani, M., Galasso, F.: Under the hood of transformer networks for trajectory forecasting. Pattern Recogn. **138** (2023). https://doi.org/10.1016/j.patcog.2023.109372
9. Gao, Q., Zhang, F., Yao, F., Li, A., Mei, L., Zhou, F.: Adversarial mobility learning for human trajectory classification. IEEE Access **8** (2020). https://doi.org/10.1109/ACCESS.2020.2968935
10. Gao, Q., Zhou, F., Zhang, K., Trajcevski, G., Luo, X., Zhang, F.: Identifying human mobility via trajectory embeddings. In: IJCAI International Joint Conference on Artificial Intelligence. vol. 0 (2017). https://doi.org/10.24963/ijcai.2017/234
11. González, M.C., Hidalgo, C.A., Barabási, A.L.: Understanding individual human mobility patterns. Nature **458**(7235) (2009). https://doi.org/10.1038/nature07850
12. Gururangan, S., et al.: Don't stop pretraining: adapt language models to domains and tasks. In: Proceedings of the Annual Meeting of the Association for Computational Linguistics (2020). https://doi.org/10.18653/v1/2020.acl-main.740
13. He, H., et al.: TraSS: efficient trajectory similarity search based on key-value data stores. In: Proceedings - International Conference on Data Engineering, vol. 2022-May (2022). https://doi.org/10.1109/ICDE53745.2022.00218
14. He, P., Liu, X., Gao, J., Chen, W.: Deberta: decoding-enhanced BERT with disentangled attention. In: ICLR 2021 - 9th International Conference on Learning Representations (2021)
15. Huang, H., Gartner, G., Krisp, J.M., Raubal, M., Van de Weghe, N.: Location based services: ongoing evolution and research agenda. J. Location Based Serv. **12**(2) (2018). https://doi.org/10.1080/17489725.2018.1508763
16. Janssens, D., Yasar, A.U.H., Knapen, L.: Data science and simulation in transportation research (2013). https://doi.org/10.4018/978-1-4666-4920-0
17. Jiang, X., de Souza, E.N., Pesaranghader, A., Hu, B., Silver, D.L., Matwin, S.: TrajectoryNet: an Embedded GPS Trajectory Representation for Point-based Classification Using Recurrent Neural Networks. In: Proceedings of the 27th Annual

International Conference on Computer Science and Software Engineering, CASCON 2017 (2020)
18. Kazemi, S.M., et al.: Time2Vec: Learning a Vector Representation of Time (7 2019)
19. Kim, J.W., Jang, B.: Deep learning-based privacy-preserving framework for synthetic trajectory generation. J. Netw. Comput. Appl. **206** (2022). 10.1016/j.jnca.2022.103459
20. Korichi, Y., Desharnais, J., Gambs, S., Tawbi, N.: Leveraging transformer architecture for effective Trajectory-User Linking (TUL) attack and its mitigation, pp. 271–290 (2024). https://doi.org/10.1007/978-3-031-70903-6_14
21. Li, R., et al.: TrajMesa: a distributed NoSQL-based trajectory data management system. IEEE Trans. Knowl. Data Eng. **35**(1) (2023). https://doi.org/10.1109/TKDE.2021.3079880
22. Liu, S., Du, J., Shrivastava, A., Zhong, L.: Privacy adversarial network: representation learning for mobile data privacy. In: Proceedings of the ACM on Interactive, Mobile, Wearable and Ubiquitous Technologies **3**(4) (2019). https://doi.org/10.1145/3369816
23. Liu, Y., et al.: RoBERTa: a robustly optimized bert pretraining approach (7 2019)
24. May Petry, L., Leite Da Silva, C., Esuli, A., Renso, C., Bogorny, V.: MARC: a robust method for multiple-aspect trajectory classification via space, time, and semantic embeddings. Int. J. Geograph. Inform. Sci. **34**(7) (2020). https://doi.org/10.1080/13658816.2019.1707835
25. Murakami, T., et al.: Designing a location trace anonymization contest. Proc. Priv. Enhanc. Technol. **2023**(1) (2023). https://doi.org/10.56553/popets-2023-0014
26. Papernot, N., Goodfellow, I., Abadi, M., Talwar, K., Erlingsson, U.: Semi-supervised knowledge transfer for deep learning from private training data. In: 5th International Conference on Learning Representations, ICLR 2017 - Conference Track Proceedings (2017)
27. Papernot, N., McDaniel, P., Goodfellow, I., Jha, S., Celik, Z.B., Swami, A.: Practical black-box attacks against machine learning. In: ASIA CCS 2017 - Proceedings of the 2017 ACM Asia Conference on Computer and Communications Security (2017). https://doi.org/10.1145/3052973.3053009
28. Pellungrini, R., Pappalardo, L., Pratesi, F., Monreale, A.: A data mining approach to assess privacy risk in human mobility data. ACM Trans. Intell. Syst. Technol. **9**(3) (2017). https://doi.org/10.1145/3106774
29. Rao, J., Gao, S., Kang, Y., Huang, Q.: LSTM-TrajGAN: a deep learning approach to trajectory privacy protection. In: Leibniz International Proceedings in Informatics, LIPIcs, vol. 177 (2020). https://doi.org/10.4230/LIPIcs.GIScience.2021.I.12
30. Rogers, A., Kovaleva, O., Rumshisky, A.: A primer in bertology: what we know about how bert works. Trans. Assoc. Comput. Linguist. **8** (2020). 10.1162/tacl_a_00349
31. Sennrich, R., Haddow, B., Birch, A.: Neural machine translation of rare words with subword units. In: 54th Annual Meeting of the Association for Computational Linguistics, ACL 2016 - Long Papers, vol. 3 (2016). https://doi.org/10.18653/v1/p16-1162
32. Sun, C., Qiu, X., Xu, Y., Huang, X.: How to fine-Tune BERT for text classification? In: Lecture Notes in Computer Science (including subseries Lecture Notes in Artificial Intelligence and Lecture Notes in Bioinformatics), vol. 11856 LNAI (2019). https://doi.org/10.1007/978-3-030-32381-3_16
33. Tom Mitchell: Machine Learning textbook (1997)

34. Wang, D., Zhang, J., Cao, W., Li, J., Zheng, Y.: When will you arrive? Estimating travel time based on deep neural networks. In: 32nd AAAI Conference on Artificial Intelligence, AAAI 2018 (2018). https://doi.org/10.1609/aaai.v32i1.11877
35. Warner, B., et al.: Smarter, better, faster, longer: a modern bidirectional encoder for fast, memory efficient, and long context finetuning and inference (12 2024)
36. Yao, D., Cong, G., Zhang, C., Bi, J.: Computing trajectory similarity in linear time: a generic seed-guided neural metric learning approach. In: Proceedings - International Conference on Data Engineering, vol. 2019-April (2019). https://doi.org/10.1109/ICDE.2019.00123
37. Yu, Y., et al.: TULSN: Siamese network for trajectory-user linking. In: Proceedings of the International Joint Conference on Neural Networks (2020). https://doi.org/10.1109/IJCNN48605.2020.9206609
38. Yuan, J., Zheng, Y., Xie, X.: Discovering regions of different functions in a city using human mobility and POIs. In: Proceedings of the ACM SIGKDD International Conference on Knowledge Discovery and Data Mining (2012). https://doi.org/10.1145/2339530.2339561
39. Zhan, Y., Haddadi, H., Kyllo, A., Mashhadi, A.: Privacy-aware human mobility prediction via adversarial networks. In: Proceedings - 2nd International Workshop on Cyber-Physical-Human System Design and Implementation, CPHS 2022 (2022). https://doi.org/10.1109/CPHS56133.2022.9804533
40. Zhao, Q., Zuo, C., Pellegrino, G., Lin, Z.: Geo-locating drivers: a study of sensitive data leakage in ride-hailing services. In: 26th Annual Network and Distributed System Security Symposium, NDSS 2019 (2019). https://doi.org/10.14722/ndss.2019.23052
41. Zhou, F., Gao, Q., Trajcevski, G., Zhang, K., Zhong, T., Zhang, F.: Trajectory-user linking via variational autoencoder. In: IJCAI International Joint Conference on Artificial Intelligence, vol. 2018-July (2018). https://doi.org/10.24963/ijcai.2018/446

Fine-Grained, Privacy-Augmenting LI-Compliance in the LAKE Standard

Pascal Lafourcade[1], Elsa López Pérez[2], Charles Olivier-Anclin[1], Cristina Onete[3], Clément Papon[3(✉)], and Mališa Vučinić[2]

[1] LIMOS, Université Clermont Auvergne, Clermont-Ferrand, France
[2] Inria, 48 Rue Barrault, 75013 Paris, France
[3] XLIM, Université de Limoges, Limoges, France
clement.papon@unilim.fr

Abstract. The Internet Engineering Task Force and its LAKE working group standardized the Ephemeral Diffie-Hellman over COSE (EDHOC) authenticated key-exchange protocol for use in constrained Internet of Things deployments. The use cases include cellular networks, such as NB-IoT, but also non-cellular networks such as 6TiSCH, and LoRaWAN. As a result of its use in cellular networks, EDHOC will be subject to Lawful Interception (LI), which allows a group of authorities to break, if equipped with a warrant, the end-to-end (E2E) security of the channel established through EDHOC. Current implementations of EDHOC would only allow lawful interception by using the cellular network operator as a legitimate endpoint, essentially running a Person-in-the-Middle attack against the protocol. In this work, we focus on a privacy-preserving, fine-grained LI-compliant modification of EDHOC for all four authentication methods that this protocol currently supports. We achieve this via a careful white-box composition of EDHOC with the Lawful Interception Key-Exchange approach of Arfaoui et al. (ESORICS 2021) and Bultel and Onete (SAC 2022). Our resulting construction not only achieves strong key-security, but also non-frameability, and LI-compliance, without breaking the identity-protection property of EDHOC. Our implementation results show that, while LIKE adds an overhead to a standard EDHOC implementation in Rust, the resulting protocol remains practical while achieving much better privacy and LI-compliance.

1 Introduction

Privacy is a human right. The Universal Declaration for Human Rights[1], states: *"No one shall be subjected to arbitrary interference with his privacy [...] or correspondence [...]. Everyone has the right to the protection of the law against such [...] attacks.* "The United Nations describes privacy as a cornerstone of other basic human rights, like *"the free development and expression of an individual's*

---

[1] https://www.un.org/en/universal-declaration-human-rights/.

personality, identity, and beliefs, and their ability to participate in political, economic, social and cultural life"[2].

Edward Snowden's 2013 revelations of widespread mass surveillance engendered public outcry. Advocates for sacrificing privacy for the sake of (inter-)national security clashed with privacy supporters warning of censorship and autocracy. Examples of illegal mass-surveillance abound today. The NSA once collected call data from all Verizon customers, and data pertaining to calls in the Bahamas and Afghanistan [11]. During the COVID-19 pandemic, contact-tracing data was used in order to facilitate criminal investigations [10]. A recently-proposed EU regulation on moderating child sexual abuse material (CSAM) in encrypted communications enables mass client-side scanning, in spite of outspread criticism from both scientists [24] and socio-economical entities [6].

Mass-surveillance is a threat to basic human rights. Yet, even strong privacy advocates agree that investigations *limited in scope and motivation* (by lawfully-obtained warrants) can be legitimate [1]. This is the type of limited Lawful Interception (LI) that the *EU resolution on security through encryption and security despite encryption* supports [9].

Lawful Interception (LI) has been a legal and technical requirement for over 30 years in mobile communications, featuring prominently in 3GPP specifications[3]. Every operator that provides end-to-end encrypted user communication is subject to such requirements.

LAKE. The Lightweight Authenticated Key Exchange (LAKE) working group of the Internet Engineering Task Force (IETF) standardized a lightweight secure-channel establishment for use in NB-IoT, 6TiSCH, and LoRaWAN. Since it will be used in mobile environments, LAKE must comply with LI.

The solution proposed by LAKE is EDHOC [25]: a mutually-authenticated lightweight secure-channel establishment scheme, guaranteeing identity-protection as a form of privacy. The Initiator and Responder may choose to authenticate either through signatures or by using static DH-keys. As described in Sect. 3, the protocol completes in 1.5, optionally 2, round trips. Starting from the 2nd message, communications may be authenticated and/or encrypted using intermediate secrets.

EDHOC is not LI-compliant by design. Naïvely, this can be achieved by turning mobile infrastructure nodes into endpoints – as is the case for other protocols, like AKA; this comes, however, at the cost of an *unnecessary loss of privacy*, making mobile network operators complicit to mass surveillance.

In this paper, we aim to render the EDHOC protocol LI-compliant without this massive loss of privacy. Ideally, our LI-EDHOC scheme must guarantee the security of exchanged messages except with respect to their sender, the receiver, and the collaborative efforts of *all* the Lawful Interception authorities[4] permitted

---

[2] UNO, https://www.ohchr.org/en/special-procedures/.
[3] See technical specifications TS33126; TS33127; TS33128.
[4] LI is performed differently from one country to another. For instance in France, Lawful Interception requires the technical cooperation of the operator, the legislative branch, and law-enforcement. We model each participant that requires a cryp-

to intercept. Moreover, interception should be fine-grained, limited only to one session at a time.

We use the pairing-free Lawful-Interception Key-Exchange (LIKE) approach [5] described in Sect. 2. Applying LIKE to a real-world protocol such as EDHOC, which features four methods of authentication and complex key schedules, while also preserving EDHOC's lightweight character and identity-protection, is far from trivial. An important challenge, for instance, stems from the fact that EDHOC features two types of authentication, which can be combined arbitrarily. While signature-based authentication is compatible with past LIKE approaches, it is not clear that MAC-based authentication will provide provable non-frameability. Another important challenge is combining LIKE with the complex key-schedule of the EDHOC protocol.

Our Contribution. We describe LI-compliant extensions for EDHOC's four authentication methods, and guarantee:

- **Key-secrecy:** session traffic keys are indistinguishable from random except for that session's Initiator, Responder, and the collusion of all the authorities allowed to perform LI for that session.
- **Non-Frameability:** it is impossible to falsely accuse a user of taking part in a session that it did not run.
- **LI Compliance:** the mobile infrastructure nodes (proxies) forwarding the communication can prove keys computed in accepting sessions are lawfully-interceptable by the correct set of LI authorities.
- **Identity-protection:** an attacker (active for Initiator and passive for Responder) cannot learn the identities of the two endpoints.

Each property provably holds in the LIKE models of [2,5], and a (modified) identity-protection model of [8]. Moreover, we provide an open-source implementation of our scheme in Rust optimized for constrained devices. We demonstrate the feasibility of our scheme by evaluating it on two hardware platforms that are typical examples of hardware used in the LAKE use cases.

Related Work. Lawful Interception initially relied on Key-Escrow: the idea of entrusting communication to a managing trusted third party (TTP), which could learn the session key. Unfortunately, Key-Escrow often requires the online presence of authorities and can easily be pushed to mass surveillance. In spite of new LI techniques [3], current LI still relies on Key Escrow [16,26].

Our work comes closest to a different approach [2] called LIKE, which aimed to achieve fine-grained LI-compliant Authenticated Key-Exchange (AKE) with better privacy. A first pairing-based instantiation [2] was rendered more efficient,

---

tographic key as an authority – which allows us to construct our protocol in an elegant manner. In other countries, potentially more authorities might be required. Our system is flexible and can address all such scenarios. Our protocol is designed to allow parties to be aware of potential LI (as we believe transparency should be reinforced) – but this could be technically adjusted to allow proxies to indicate, in a prior message, the authorities that must be used for each exchange.

pairing-free, and usable in roaming scenarios by Bultel and Onete [5]. One property provided by LIKE is non-frameability, which is also underlined by recent related work [4] in the context of 5G (and beyond) network architectures.

Some techniques for connection-monitoring and data-encryption [13,15] could be extended to the LI scenario, though this is not their original goal. As they rely on pairings, they are incompatible with lightweight AKE, however. Finally, a worthwhile privacy-preserving alternative for LI is provided by CRUMPLE [27], which provides LI through a proof of work. This interesting approach is, unfortunately, not sufficiently efficient to comply with current LI requirements (which demand that interception yield "timely" results).

Finally note that throughout the standardization process of EDHOC [25], the protocol was analysed in various versions. A formal analysis using SAPIC+ identified weaknesses and proposed modifications in EDHOC version 12 [17]; later, the authors verified draft 14, showing that many previously identified issues had been addressed. Cottier and Pointcheval then provided an analysis of EDHOC draft 15 [7,8] and suggested further improvements. In 2023, Günther and Mukendi [12] analyzed draft 17 and proposed changes to the key schedule and to the construction of transcript hashes.

2 The LIKE Framework and Further Primitives

Originally introduced in the context of mobile authenticated key-exchange protocols, Lawful Interception Key Exchange (LIKE) is a two-party AKE scheme featuring two proxies, representing the serving networks of the two endpoints [2]. The system also features a number of authorities, which need not be online for the duration of each protocol session. Each handshake is lawfully-interceptable by the collaboration of all the members of an authority set, whose size and composition depend on current legislations.

Formally, LIKE is defined as LIKE = (Setup, UKeyGen, OpKeyGen, AKeyGen, AKE, Verify, TDGen, Open). Setup provides a global setup for the choice of universal parameters. The next three algorithms allow mobile users, operators, and authorities to generate long-term public keys. The LIKE protocol is run in sessions via the AKE algorithm. The verification algorithm allows for the verification of the soundness of the handshake and for the validation of the participants, whereas the last two algorithms provide mechanisms for LI.

LIKE assumes a scenario in which the two endpoints can only communicate through the proxies, and the protocol guarantees: key-security, non-frameability, and LI compliance (also called "honest-operator" in [2,5]). Key-security is ensured by essentially ensuring that only the legitimate owners of keys associated with authorities can retrieve meaningful trapdoor information for the session keys – and even then, only the composition of all the required trapdoors yields and the session key. Non-frameability requires, in LIKE, the use of signatures for both endpoints. The Honest-operator property is achieved by providing the proxy a means of verifying the LI-compliance of a protocol transcript, while not providing the proxy any information about the session key. In this paper, we

Table 1. Current authentication methods registered by IANA (0-1-2-3)

ID	Initiator	Credential I	Responder	Credential R
0	Signature	$(\mathsf{ssk}_\mathsf{I}, \mathsf{spk}_\mathsf{I})$	Signature	$(\mathsf{ssk}_\mathsf{R}, \mathsf{spk}_\mathsf{R})$
1	Signature	$(\mathsf{ssk}_\mathsf{I}, \mathsf{spk}_\mathsf{I})$	Static Diffie-Hellman	(r, g^r)
2	Static Diffie-Hellman	(i, g^i)	Signature	$(\mathsf{ssk}_\mathsf{R}, \mathsf{spk}_\mathsf{R})$
3	Static Diffie-Hellman	(i, g^i)	Static Diffie-Hellman	(r, g^r)

start from [5], a follow-up work of [2] which achieved pairing-free LIKE in the roaming scenario, by using an Elgamal-like encryption of the session secret.

Our approach carefully combines this second LIKE approach, and makes use of both Non-Interactive Proofs of Knowledges (NIPoK) and Signatures of Knowledge (SoK). Let $\mathcal{R}$ be a binary relation and let $\mathcal{L}$ be a language such that $s \in \mathcal{L} \iff (\exists w, (s, w) \in \mathcal{R})$. We denote by $\nu := \mathsf{NIPoK}\{w : (w, s) \in \mathcal{R}\}$ the proof of knowledge of a witness w for a statement s, and by $\sigma := \mathsf{SoK}_m\{w : (w, s) \in \mathcal{R}\}$ the signature of knowledge on message m using witness w. Both NIPoKs and SoKs must be complete, extractable, and zero-knowledge.

3 The EDHOC Protocol

EDHOC is a two-party mutually-authenticated Diffie-Hellman-based AKE scheme relying on Krawczyk's SIGMA-I protocol [19]. It features three mandatory messages and an optional fourth. The handshake is run in sessions between an Initiator I and a Responder R, which can choose how they want to authenticate: either by using signature schemes, or by using a certified static Diffie-Hellman (DH) key. The four combinations of authentication mechanisms are called methods 0, 1, 2, and 3, as described in Table 1. We denote by $(\mathsf{ssk}_\mathsf{P}, \mathsf{spk}_\mathsf{P})$ the private/public signature keys of party P, and by (p, g^p) party P's long-term static DH private/public keys. The parties indicate their preferred means of authentication method in message_1.

Protocol Outline. Figure 1 depicts the EDHOC message flow. The first message, always sent unencrypted, consists of parameters METHOD and SUITES_I, indicating the authentication method and desired cipher suite, a *connection identifier* C_I which acts as a session identifier for peers running multiple sessions, some additional information called external authorization data EAD_1, and a fresh ephemeral public key g^x (we denote the corresponding private key as x).

If the Responder supports the method and cipher suite, it computes message_2, which consists of an ephemeral DH element g^y sent in clear (the private key is denoted as y) and a ciphertext, encrypted with a key denoted as sk2, derived from g^x and g^y. The plaintext consists of: a connection identifier C_R, an identifier indicating the Responder's long-term authentication credential, some additional data EAD_2, and an authentication by the Responder, consisting of either a signature (methods 1 and 3) or a MAC (methods 0 and 2). The

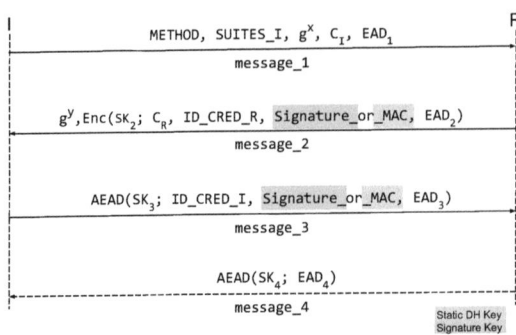

Fig. 1. The EDHOC message flow [22]

signature is computed with the Responder's private key ssk_R over the credential identifier ID_CRED_R, a transcript hash TH_2 detailed in Fig. 2, the public key spk_R, and EAD_2. If the Responder uses static-DH authentication, then the MAC key is derived from both the ephemeral DH product of g^x and g^y and from the semi-static DH product of g^x and the static element g^r.

The Initiator decrypts the ciphertext in message_2 with the key sk2, derived from g^x and g^y (the latter is sent in clear). Then, it recovers and verifies the Responder's authentication, according to the authentication method. message_3 is somewhat similar to message_2, except that it is AEAD-encrypted using a key derived either solely from the ephemeral DH values g^x and g^y (methods 0 and 2) or from both the ephemeral DH product of g^x and g^y, and the semi-static DH product of g^x and g^r (methods 1 and 3).

The optional message_4 provides explicit key-confirmation and is an AEAD-encryption on additional data EAD_4. The encryption key is derived from the previously computed ephemeral (and potentially semi-static) DH products, and additionally, for methods 2 or 3, a new semi-static DH product between the ephemeral value g^y and the Initiator's static DH element g^i.

The full key-schedule of the protocol is depicted in Fig. 2. EDHOC uses two functions, EDHOC_Expand and EDHOC_Extract, with the EDHOC hash algorithm in the selected cipher suite to derive keys used in message processing. EDHOC_Extract is used to derive fixed-length uniformly pseudorandom keys (PRKs) from Elliptic Curve DIFFIE-HELLMAN (ECDH) shared secrets.
EDHOC_Expand is used to define a key derivation function, EDHOC_KDF, for generating MACs and for deriving output keying material (OKM) from PRKs.

There are three main secret values that are computed, labelled, respectively PRK_{2e}, PRK_{3e2m} and PRK_{4e3m}. The notations indicate the purposes of these secrets: the 2e subscript indicates the key is used to encrypt message_2 content. The 3e2m subscript indicates the value is used to encrypt message_3 and (depending on the authentication method) compute the MAC in message_2. Note that in case of signature-only authentication (method 0), the entire key-

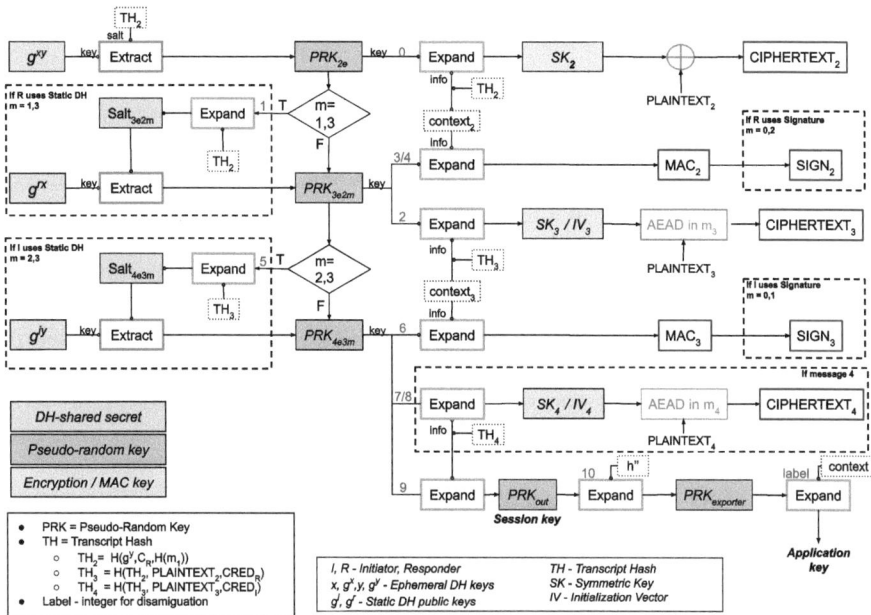

Fig. 2. EDHOC's key scheduling. The figure shows how keys are derived for all four authentication methods [23]

schedule is derived from the ephemeral DH values g^x and g^y. If both parties use static DH authentication, the key schedule resembles X3DH[5], using the ephemeral DH product and two semi-static ones.

EDHOC Primitives. While EDHOC can be instantiated with different primitives, currently its implementations use elliptic-curve cryptography [23]. We will require the hardness of both the Decisional Diffie-Hellman (DDH) and the Gap Diffie-Hellman (GDH) problems in the groups selected in protocol sessions. Key-derivation for EDHOC employs HKDF [20]. In this paper, we idealise both extraction and expansion as a random oracle. Once expanded, keys are used in two fundamental ways: 1) for stream-cipher encryption (XOR-ing key-bits with plaintext-bits, which we require to be injective [8,21]), and 2) for AEAD-encryption (which we require to be AEAD-secure), both IND − CPA-secure. Key-derivation steps also rely on updated session hashes. We idealise the hash function $\mathcal{H}$ as a random oracle (in practice, instantiated as SHA256). Finally, signature-based authentication requires the use of an EUF-CMA-secure signature scheme DS = (DS.Gen, DS.Sign, DS.Verif) (usually instantiated as EdDSA or ES256), while static-DH-based authentication is combined with a MAC scheme, implemented in EDHOC as EDHOC_Expand.

---

[5] https://signal.org/docs/specifications/x3dh/.

4 LI-Compliant EDHOC

In order to empower Mobile Network Operators (MNOs) with the ability to provide privacy-preserving LI-compliant secure-channel establishment, we encrypt session secrets in the session state, such that only the collaboration of the entire authority-set will be able to decrypt these values. For that purpose, we essentially combine the LIKE approach and the EDHOC protocol (Sect. 3).

The composition is not black-box, for several important reasons. The first is our wish to preserve as many of the EDHOC properties as possible, including identity-protection. The latter requires that network adversaries (passive, for Responders, active, for Initiators) are unable to distinguish the endpoint's identity (Initiator or Responder). As a result, some of the LIKE messages will need to be incorporated in EDHOC's encrypted messages, modifying them in a non-trivial fashion. As a result, we prefer to use different notations for the two protocols, referring to EDHOC's first and second messages as message_1 and message_2 (as in Sect. 3), as opposed to M_1 and M_2 for our protocol LI-EDHOC. Another problem is verifying the consistency of the elements input in the key-computation, which we discuss below. Finally, we choose white-box composition for the sake of efficiency – since some LIKE elements are already present in EDHOC.

An important modification we make to the original LIKE [2,5] is that the session keys take as input an additional nonce n_r (and we use the exporter keys featured in EDHOC). This artifice of our construction is necessary in order to enforce LI-compliance on the Initiator's side. Thus, we include the nonce n_r in the context of the exporter PRK expansion (bottom right of Fig. 2). Encrypting part of the handshake also raises a serious concern with respect to LI-compliance, in which proxies must be able to prove that the elements required to compute the key are consistent with the encrypted secrets and the ciphertexts. A naïve solution would be to send the entire messages unencrypted (thus nullifying the identity-protection afforded by EDHOC). Our solution tries to reconcile both LI requirements and identity-protection. We make endpoints send their encryption keys (not secrets) for handshake messages, encrypted with a key shared between the endpoint and the proxy[6], which allows the latter to verify the consistency of the transcript[7].

In order to provide LI-recovery of session keys, we essentially encrypt some component session secrets. This could be done naïvely by running the protocol of [5] for each secret in parallel; that, however, would be suboptimal and could

---

[6] This is not a strong assumption, as the mobile protocol stack feature a hierarchy of keys usable to that effect.
[7] We considered two alternative approaches. The key under which the keys are encrypted could be negotiated during the handshake, at the expense of additional complexity. We discarded this alternative since a shared key is already present in the 5G stack. A second cleaner alternative would be to encrypt handshake messages with a different key, which is computable by the proxies and endpoints. Unfortunately this would require modifying the key schedule of EDHOC (already standardized) and introducing cumbersome key-computation tools including pairings.

Fine-Grained, Privacy-Augmenting LI-Compliance in the LAKE Standard   261

Initiator		Proxy P_I		Proxy P_R		Responder
InitRun1(ID_I)	$\xrightarrow{M_1}$	$Prox_I Run1(M_1)$	$\xrightarrow{M_1}$	$Prox_R Run1(M_1)$	$\xrightarrow{M_1}$	
						RespRun1(ID_R, M_1)
	$\xleftarrow{M_2}$	$Prox_I Run2(M_2)$	$\xleftarrow{M_2}$	$Prox_R Run2(M_2)$	$\xleftarrow{M_2}$	
InitRun2(ID_I, M_2)						
	$\xrightarrow{M_3}$	$Prox_I Run3(M_3)$	$\xrightarrow{M_3'}$		$\xrightarrow{M_3'}$	
						RespRun2(ID_R, M_3')
InitRun3(ID_I, M_4'')	$\xleftarrow{M_4''}$	$Prox_I Run4(M_4')$	$\xleftarrow{M_4'}$	$Prox_R Run3(M_4)$	$\xleftarrow{M_4}$	

Fig. 3. Message flow of the LI-EDHOC handshake protocols. Algorithms for the **Static-Sign** (ID = 2) instances are provided in Figs. 4 and 5.

potentially break the LI-compliance guarantee, since EDHOC features an interdependence between the ephemeral and semi-static secrets. Each secret will be recovered by the authorities from an ElGamal-like encryption of it under the product of the authorities' keys. During the protocol, each authority derives a trapdoor (essentially a local decryption with just its own private key) – and by using the homomorphic properties of ElGamal, the combination of all trapdoors yields the session's secret. Crucially, if even one authority withholds its trapdoor, the secret remains hidden – even from a collusion of all other authorities.

We proceed to describe our protocol, whose handshake is also depicted in Figs. 3, 4 and 5. Due to space restrictions, we only detail LI-EDHOC for authentication method 2 (**Static-Sign**). The other 3 methods are included in our full version [21].

Setup and Key Generation. Endpoints (Initiators and Responders), proxies, and authorities will all generate long-term keys. Endpoints generate signature keypairs (ssk_U, spk_U) for authentication, using the algorithm $DS.Gen(1^\lambda)$ (for signature-based authentication) and DH pairs (p, g^p) with $p \in \{i, r\}$ (for static authentication). Proxies generate signature keys (ssk_{Prox}, spk_{Prox}) which authenticate LI material. Authorities generate DH keys for LI $\{\Lambda.SK, \Lambda.pk = g^{\Lambda.SK}\}$, for which they prove knowledge of the private key: $\Lambda.ni \leftarrow NIPoK\{\Lambda.SK : \Lambda.pk = g^{\Lambda.SK}\}$. We set $\Lambda.PK \leftarrow (\Lambda.pk, \Lambda.ni)$. Formal descriptions are provided in [21].

Precomputation. Handshakes are preceded by a precomputation phase, during which users and proxies verify all authorities' public keys and proofs. Note that due to roaming, LI can take place for an independent set of authorities at each end (Initiator and Responder). In addition, at this point we assume that, if the proxy does not already have a shared key pcsk, then we assume both the proxy and the endpoint generate this common key[8].

Let $(\Lambda_j^I.PK)_{j=1}^{n_I}$ denote the vector of the authority public keys involved in the interception (with Λ_j^I an authority for all $j \in [\![1, n_I]\!]$, and with each $\Lambda_j^I.PK = (\Lambda_j^I.pk, \Lambda_j^I.ni)$). The Initiator and its proxy $Prox_I$ verify the proofs as $NIPoKver(\Lambda_j^I.pk, \Lambda_j^I.ni)$ and proceeds if all verifications pass. They set $h_I \leftarrow \prod_{j=1}^{n_I} \Lambda_j^I.pk$, and

---
[8] This would be done at the beginning of each handshake anyway, within the 5G protocol stack.

InitRun1(ID$_I$)
─────────────────────────
1 : $(x \twoheadleftarrow_\$ \mathbb{Z}_p^*, g^x), \mathsf{C}_I \twoheadleftarrow_\$ \{0,1\}^{l_c}$
2 : return $M_1 \leftarrow (\mathsf{MCS} \| g^x \| \mathsf{C}_I \| \mathsf{EAD}_1)$

InitRun2(ID$_I$, M_2)
─────────────────────────
1 : Parse M_2 as $(g^y \| c_2), g^{xy} \leftarrow (g^y)^x, g^{yi} \leftarrow (g^y)^i$
  // Compute sk$_2$, decrypt c_2
2 : Compute TH$_2$, PRK$_{2e}$, sk$_2$ as in RespRun1, lines 4,5,9
3 : $m_2 \leftarrow \mathsf{Dec}(\mathsf{sk}_2, c_2)$, parse m_2 as $(\mathsf{C}_R \| \mathsf{ID}_R \| \sigma_2 \| \mathsf{EAD}_2)$
4 : sid $\leftarrow (\mathsf{C}_I, \mathsf{C}_R, g^x, g^y)$
5 : Compute CTX$_2$, t_2' as in RespRun1, lines 6,7
  // Verify Responder authentication
6 : $\boxed{\text{if DS.Verif}(\mathsf{spk}_R, (l_{\mathsf{sig}} \| \mathsf{CTX}_2 \| t_2'), \sigma_2) \neq 1}$
7 :   then return $\perp$
  // Compute key-schedule for 3rd message
8 : TH$_3 \leftarrow \mathcal{H}(\mathsf{TH}_2, m_2, \mathsf{ID}_R)$, CTX$_3 \leftarrow (\mathsf{ID}_I \| \mathsf{TH}_3 \| g^i \| \mathsf{EAD}_3)$
9 : sk$_3 \leftarrow$ HKDF_Expand(PRK$_{2e}$, 3$\|$TH$_3\|l_{\mathsf{key}}, l_{\mathsf{key}}$)
10: IV$_3 \leftarrow$ HKDF_Expand(PRK$_{2e}$, 4$\|$TH$_3\|l_{\mathsf{iv}}, l_{\mathsf{iv}}$)
11: ad$_3 \leftarrow (l_{\mathsf{aead}} \| \text{``''} \| \mathsf{TH}_3)$
12: salt$_{4e3m} \leftarrow$ HKDF_Expand(PRK$_{2e}$, 5$\|$TH$_3\|l_{\mathsf{hash}}, l_{\mathsf{hash}}$)
13: PRK$_{4e3m} \leftarrow$ HKDF_Extract(salt$_{4e3m}, g^{yi}$)
  // Authenticate (static DH in method 2)
14: $\boxed{t_3 \leftarrow \text{HKDF\_Expand}(\mathsf{PRK}_{4e3m}, 6 \| \mathsf{CTX}_3 \| l_{\mathsf{mac}}, l_{\mathsf{mac}})}$
  // Ensure LI-compliance and assemble M_3
15: $m_3 \leftarrow (\mathsf{ID}_I \| t_3 \| \mathsf{EAD}_3), c_3 \leftarrow \mathsf{Enc}'(\mathsf{sk}_3, \mathsf{IV}_3, \mathsf{ad}_3, m_3)$
16: TH$_4 \leftarrow \mathcal{H}(\mathsf{TH}_3, m_3, \mathsf{ID}_I)$
17: ⌐ H$_I \leftarrow (h_I g^y)^x$, H$_I^1 \leftarrow (h_I g^y)^i$ ¬
18: ⌐ stm$_I \leftarrow [X = g^x \wedge \mathsf{H}_I = (h_I g^y)^x \wedge X_1 = g^i$
        $\wedge \mathsf{H}_I^1 = (h_I g^y)^i]$ ¬
19: ⌐ ni$_I \leftarrow$ SoK$_{\omega_I \| \mathsf{ID}_R \| \mathsf{TH}_3 \| \mathsf{TH}_4}\{(x, i) : \mathsf{stm}_I\}$ ¬
20: ⌐ $K_I \leftarrow (\mathsf{sk}_2 \| \mathsf{sk}_3 \| \mathsf{IV}_3 \| t_2), S_I \leftarrow \mathsf{Enc}''(\mathsf{pcsk}_{I, \mathsf{Prox}_I}, K_I)$ ¬
21: return $M_3 \leftarrow (c_3 \| \mathsf{H}_I \| \mathsf{H}_I^1 \| \mathsf{ni}_I \| S_I)$

InitRun3(ID$_I$, M_4'')
─────────────────────────
1 : Parse M_4'' as $(c_4 \| n_r \| \mathsf{val} \| \mathsf{TH}_5)$, if $c_4 = \perp$ then return $\perp$
2 : if TH$_5 \neq \mathcal{H}(\mathsf{TH}_4, \mathsf{val}, n_r)$ then return $\perp$
3 : Compute sk$_4$, IV$_4$, ad$_4$ as in RespRun2, lines 7-9
4 : $m_4 \leftarrow \mathsf{Dec}'(\mathsf{sk}_4, \mathsf{IV}_4, \mathsf{ad}_4, c_4)$, parse m_4 as EAD$_4$
5 : if $m_4 = \perp$ then return $\perp$
6 : PRK$_{\mathsf{out}} \leftarrow$ HKDF_Expand(PRK$_{4e3m}, 7\|$TH$_4\|$⌐n_r¬$\|l_{\mathsf{hash}}, l_{\mathsf{hash}}$)
7 : terminated $\leftarrow 1$

RespRun1(ID$_R$, M_1)
─────────────────────────
1 : $(y \twoheadleftarrow_\$ \mathbb{Z}_p^*), \mathsf{C}_R \twoheadleftarrow_\$ \{0,1\}^{l_c}$
2 : Parse M_1 as (MCS$\|g^x\|\mathsf{C}_I\|\mathsf{EAD}_1$)
  // Compute key-schedule for 2nd message
3 : $g^{xy} \leftarrow (g^x)^y$, sid $\leftarrow (\mathsf{C}_I, \mathsf{C}_R, g^x, g^y)$
4 : TH$_2 \leftarrow \mathcal{H}(g^y, \mathcal{H}(M_1))$
5 : PRK$_{2e} \leftarrow$ HKDF_Extract(TH$_2, g^{xy}$)
6 : sk$_2 \leftarrow$ HKDF_Expand(PRK$_{2e}, 0\|$TH$_2\|l_2, l_2$)
7 : CTX$_2 \leftarrow (\mathsf{C}_R \| \mathsf{ID}_R \| \mathsf{TH}_2 \| \mathsf{EAD}_2)$
8 : $t_2 \leftarrow$ HKDF_Expand(PRK$_{2e}, 2\|$CTX$_2\|l_{\mathsf{mac}}, l_{\mathsf{mac}}$)
  // Authenticate (signature in method 2)
9 : $\boxed{\sigma_2 \leftarrow \mathsf{DS.Sign}(\mathsf{ssk}_R, (l_{\mathsf{sig}} \| \mathsf{CTX}_2 \| t_2))}$
  // Assemble M_2
10: $m_2 \leftarrow (\mathsf{C}_R \| \mathsf{ID}_R \| \sigma_2 \| \mathsf{EAD}_2), c_2 \leftarrow \mathsf{Enc}(\mathsf{sk}_2, m_2)$
11: return $M_2 \leftarrow (g^y \| c_2)$

RespRun2(ID$_R$, M_3')
─────────────────────────
1 : Parse M_3' as c_3
  // Compute sk$_3$ and decrypt c_3
2 : Compute TH$_3$, sk$_3$, IV$_3$, ad$_3$ as in InitRun2, lines 8-11
3 : $m_3 \leftarrow \mathsf{Dec}'(\mathsf{sk}_3, \mathsf{IV}_3, \mathsf{ad}_3, c_3)$, parse m_3 as $(\mathsf{ID}_I \| t_3 \| \mathsf{EAD}_3)$
4 : Get g^i from ID$_I, g^{yi} \leftarrow (g^i)^y$
  // Compute key-schedule for 4th message
5 : Compute CTX$_3$, salt$_{4e3m}$, PRK$_{4e3m}$ as in InitRun2, lines 8,12,13
6 : TH$_4 \leftarrow \mathcal{H}(\mathsf{TH}_3, m_3, \mathsf{ID}_I)$, ad$_4 \leftarrow (l_{\mathsf{aead}}, \text{``''} \| \mathsf{TH}_4)$
7 : sk$_4 \leftarrow$ HKDF_Expand(PRK$_{4e3m}, 8\|$TH$_4\|l_{\mathsf{key}}, l_{\mathsf{key}}$)
8 : IV$_4 \leftarrow$ HKDF_Expand(PRK$_{4e3m}, 9\|$TH$_4\|l_{\mathsf{key}}, l_{\mathsf{key}}$)
  // Verify Initiator authentication
9 : $t_3' \leftarrow$ HKDF_Expand(PRK$_{4e3m}, 6\|$CTX$_3\|l_{\mathsf{mac}}, l_{\mathsf{mac}}$)
10: $\boxed{\text{if } t_3 \neq t_3' \text{ then return } \perp}$
  // Ensure LI-compliance and assemble M_4
11: ⌐ H$_R \leftarrow (h_R g^x)^y$, H$_R^1 \leftarrow (h_R g^i)^y$ ¬
12: ⌐ stm$_R \leftarrow [Y = g^y \wedge \mathsf{H}_R = (h_R g^x)^y \wedge \mathsf{H}_R^1 = (h_R g^i)^y]$ ¬
13: ⌐ ni$_R \leftarrow$ SoK$_{\omega_R \| \mathsf{ID}_I \| \mathsf{TH}_2 \| \mathsf{TH}_3 \| \mathsf{TH}_4}\{y : \mathsf{stm}_R\}$ ¬
14: ⌐ $K_R \leftarrow (\mathsf{sk}_2 \| \mathsf{sk}_3 \| \mathsf{IV}_3 \| t_2), S_R \leftarrow \mathsf{Enc}''(\mathsf{pcsk}_{R, \mathsf{Prox}_R}, K_R)$ ¬
15: $m_4 \leftarrow \mathsf{EAD}_4, c_4 \leftarrow \mathsf{Enc}'(\mathsf{sk}_4, \mathsf{IV}_4, \mathsf{ad}_4, m_4)$
16: ⌐ $n_r \twoheadleftarrow_\$ \{0,1\}^{l_{\mathsf{rand}}}$, val $\leftarrow \mathcal{H}(g^{xy}, \text{``''}, n_r)$ ¬
17: PRK$_{\mathsf{out}} \leftarrow$ HKDF_Expand(PRK$_{4e3m}, 7\|$TH$_4\|$⌐n_r¬$\|l_{\mathsf{hash}}, l_{\mathsf{hash}}$)
18: terminated $\leftarrow 1$, TH$_5 \leftarrow \mathcal{H}(\mathsf{TH}_4, \mathsf{val}, n_r)$
19: return $M_4 \leftarrow (c_4 \| n_r \| \mathsf{val} \| \mathsf{TH}_5 \| \mathsf{H}_R \| \mathsf{H}_R^1 \| \mathsf{ni}_R \| S_R)$

Fig. 4. The LI-EDHOC protocol for authentication method 2. Dashed boxes represent operations associated with LI. The notation MCS denotes the method and the cipher suite that the Initiator wants to use

$\omega_I \leftarrow (\Lambda_j^I)_{j=1}^{n_I} \| \mathsf{ID}_I$, returning (h_I, ω_I). This is analogous on the Responder side and its associated proxy Prox$_R$.

The values (h_I, ω_I) and pcsk$_{I, \mathsf{Prox}_I}$ (for the Initiator), and (h_R, ω_R) and pcsk$_{R, \mathsf{Prox}_R}$ (for the Responder), are shared between the proxies and the endpoints, and both entities check (h, ω) to ensure that neither of them is cheating. We assume moreover that the proxies know the identity of the endpoints (as is already the case following an initial AKA/Handshake). This stage can be done once and then reused for multiple sessions (for the same set of authorities of an endpoint).

Handshake. We assume all precomputations are done. The handshake is run as described in Fig. 3, with details provided in Figs. 4 (endpoint computations) and 5 (for the proxies, in Appendix C).

The first message sent by the Initiator is unchanged compared to EDHOC and contains the Initiator's ephemeral secret g^x. This message is faithfully forwarded by both proxies, which store g^x and ω_I (for the Initiator's proxy), respectively ω_R (on the Responder side). The Responder follows EDHOC and generates the ephemeral secret g^y, then follows the key-schedule in order to obtain the secret PRK_{2e} and the derived key sk2. In method 2, the Responder computes a signature using its long-term signing key[9]. The computed message is the same as in EDHOC (line 10 of the `RespRun1` routine in Fig. 4), and it is XOR-encrypted with sk2. The Responder proxy stores g^y and the message. On the Initiator side, the proxy forwards the message faithfully, but stores g^y.

LI elements start being added from the third message onward. In method 2, keys are computed based on two DH products g^{xy} and g^{iy} (the Initiator contributes its static long-term DH key g^i as well as the ephemeral g^x). The Initiator computes trapdoor messages H_I and H_I^1 (line 17 of `InitRun2` in Fig. 4), which essentially encrypt g^{xy} and g^{iy} under the product h_I of the authorities' public keys. In order to prevent the Initiator from cheating, the latter has to compute a signature of knowledge proving that the exponents of the ephemeral g^x, the static g^i and both H_I and H_I^1 are the same (line 18). The message that is signed consists of the set of identities ω_I, as well as the Responder's identity and the concatenation of the transcript hashes used to compute the keys. Finally, in order to prevent cheating, the Initiator encrypts the tag t_2 and the keys used to encrypt/AE-encrypt messages m_2, m_3 with the key $\mathsf{pcsk}_{\mathsf{I},\mathsf{Prox}_\mathsf{I}}$ it shares with its proxy as S_I. Thus M_3 is composed of ciphertexts c_3 and S_I, and LI elements H_I, H_I^1 and ni_I. The ciphertext S_I allows the proxy to decrypt/AE-decrypt the received second- and third-message ciphertexts, and verify the correctness of both transcript-hash values and the signature σ_2 (aborting if the endpoint misbehaves). Then it will store the transcript hashes, long-term static Initiator DH key, the two trapdoors, the signature of knowledge, the Responder identifier, and the HMAC, forwarding only the EDHOC ciphertext c_3 to the Responder's proxy.

The procedure is analogous for the preparation of the fourth message on the Responder's side after receiving and analyzing the third message as in the original protocol. Note that this message is compulsory in LI-EDHOC, as opposed to the original protocol. The final ingredient for Lawful Interception is an added nonce n_r generated by the Responder and input in the key-generation step in `RespRun2` lines 19-20 in Fig. 4.

The reason we must add n_r in the key-computation step is as follows: unlike in [2,5], the Responder's signature of knowledge is verified only after the lat-

---

[9] This correspond to the authentication method provided in the original EDHOC protocol. In method 2, the Responder authenticates by signing t_2, and the Initiator authenticates thanks to t_3 partially computed with its static DH share.

ter computed the final key. Thus, if the Initiator computed the key before the Responder, the Initiator's proxy might not be able to provide LI-interceptable communication. The nonce n_r is sent unencrypted in the fourth mandatory message to the Initiator, which can now compute the same session key. In order to ensure that this nonce also arrives securely at the proxies and the Initiator, the Responder sends the nonce n_r, a verification value val and $\mathsf{TH}_5 = \mathcal{H}(\mathsf{TH}_4, \mathsf{val}, n_r)$, so that every party may check the validity of the nonce (using TH_4 they all computed themselves). In addition, the proxy Prox_R also verifies the signature σ_2 with the tag t_2. Finally each proxy stores in the session state the nonce n_r, the tag t_2 and the value val, for a potential verification from the authorities.

Verification of sst. The session state sst consists of: $\omega\|\mathsf{MCS}\|g^x\|g^y\|g^i\| \mathsf{TH}_2\|\mathsf{TH}_3\|\mathsf{TH}_4\|M_1\|m_2\|m_3\|\mathsf{H}\|\mathsf{H}^1\|\mathsf{ni}\|\mathsf{pid}\|t_2\|n_r\|\mathsf{val}\|\sigma$. The plaintext messages m_2, m_3 allow for the verification of the transcript hashes and the authentication of both parties (through signatures of knowledge). The verification algorithm also extracts, from ω the public keys of the authorities, for which the proofs of knowledge of the discrete logarithm must be verified. Subsequently the signature of knowledge is verified with respect to both the signed message and to the equality of the discrete logarithm used to compute H and H^1. Since method **Static-Sign** only requires the Responder to use signature-based authentication, the verification algorithm obtains, from m_2 and t_2 all the necessary information to verify the signatures σ_2. Finally, parsing sst as $\tau\|\sigma$, the signature σ generated by the proxy is verified with respect to the message τ.

Lawful Interception. Given an sst, authorities invariably must first verify it (using the process described above). If sst is correct, each authority Λ^d first derives individual trapdoors for each of the two secrets: compute $\mathsf{A}_I \leftarrow g^x$, $\mathsf{A}_R \leftarrow g^y$, $\Lambda^d.\mathsf{td}_1 \leftarrow \mathsf{A}_d^{\Lambda^d.\mathsf{SK}}$, $\Lambda^d.\mathsf{td}_2 \leftarrow g^{i\Lambda^d.\mathsf{SK}}$ ($d \in \{I, R\}$) and prove

$$\Lambda^d.\mathsf{td}_0 \leftarrow \mathsf{NIPoK}\{\Lambda^d.\mathsf{SK} : \Lambda^d.\mathsf{pk} = g^{\Lambda^d.\mathsf{SK}} \wedge \Lambda^d.\mathsf{td}_1 = \mathsf{A}_d^{\Lambda^d.\mathsf{SK}} \wedge \Lambda^d.\mathsf{td}_2 = g^{i\Lambda^d.\mathsf{SK}}\}.$$

Finally, set and return $\Lambda^d.\mathsf{td} \leftarrow (\Lambda^d.\mathsf{td}_0, \Lambda^d.\mathsf{td}_1, \Lambda^d.\mathsf{td}_2)$. Once all trapdoors are available, all parties verify the proofs $\Lambda^d.\mathsf{td}_0$ and reconstitute the secrets g^{xy} and g^{iy}. The calculations, e.g., on the Initiator's side for g^{xy}, are as follows:

$$\frac{\mathsf{H}_I}{\prod_{j=1}^{n_I} \Lambda_j^I.\mathsf{td}_1} = \frac{(h_I g^y)^x}{\prod_{j=1}^{n_I} g^{x\Lambda_j^I.\mathsf{SK}}} = \frac{\left(\prod_{j=1}^{n_I} g^{\Lambda_j^I.\mathsf{SK}}\right)^x g^{xy}}{\prod_{j=1}^{n_I} g^{x\Lambda_j^I.\mathsf{SK}}} = \frac{\prod_{j=1}^{n_I} g^{x\Lambda_j^I.\mathsf{SK}} g^{xy}}{\prod_{j=1}^{n_I} g^{x\Lambda_j^I.\mathsf{SK}}} = g^{xy}.$$

To retrieve g^{iy}, we proceed in the same way, using H^1, and either $\Lambda^d.\mathsf{td}_1$ or $\Lambda^d.\mathsf{td}_2$ depending on the point of view (Initiator or Responder).

At this point, authorities check the validity of the last unverified element of the sst: n_r. To do this they simply compute $\mathcal{H}(g^{xy}, \text{" "}, n_r)$ and compare this value to the provided val value in sst. This verification ensures that this n_r, transmitted by the proxy, is indeed the one used by the endpoints to compute their session key $\mathsf{PRK}_{\mathsf{out}}$. Finally, with the two secrets g^{xy} and g^{iy}, the authorities, using the verified additional data TH_2, TH_3, TH_4 and n_r, are now able to recompute the original EDHOC's key derivation schedule to derive the original session key $\mathsf{PRK}_{\mathsf{out}}$ (which coincides with the one computed by the endpoints).

5 Security Analysis in the Random Oracle Model

Our LI-EDHOC protocol guarantees the key-security, non-frameability, and LI-compliance security properties from LIKE [2,5], but also a stronger property of EDHOC: identity protection. We provide here only a high-level description of the security model. A complete formalization is in the full version [21].

Execution Environment. LIKE includes three types of participants: endpoints belonging to a set ESet, proxies from a set PROXSet, and authorities in a set AUTHSet. Each party has private and public parameters (P.$\overline{\text{SK}}$, P.$\overline{\text{PK}}$) – which for EDHOC are in fact private/public *keysets* instead of just *one key*. We also make endpoints and proxies store a set of symmetric keys shared between them in an attribute P.PCSK = $\{(Q, \text{pcsk}_{P,Q})\}$, Q $\in$ ShareSet (if P $\in$ ESet, then ShareSet = PROXSet and vice-versa). Any party may be corrupted, yielding to the adversary one element of the private keyset. The party stores a corruption bit P.SK.γ for each key SK $\in$ P.$\overline{\text{SK}}$.

Protocol sessions are always run by *instances* of four parties: two endpoints, playing the parts of Initiator and Responder; and two proxies. We denote by π_P^q the qth instance of P. Each endpoint/proxy instance keeps track of *attributes*, including: the session identifier π_P^q.sid; the computed session key π_P^q.PRK$_{\text{out}}$; a session state π_P^q.sst; partner identifiers AID for the authorities chosen by that party as legitimate for Lawful Interception, PNID for the partnering endpoint (or endpoints if this is a proxy instance), and ProxID for the partnering proxies; a flag indicating authentication acceptance (denoted $\pi_P^q.\alpha$); and π_P^q.role (the role role $\in$ {Initiator, Responder, Proxy$_I$, Proxy$_R$} of P in the handshake).

To better capture EDHOC, endpoint party instances require several additional values: π_P^q.meth (the method that will be used for a session involving this instance); π_P^q.SK (the private key used by P to authenticate); π_P^q.pid.PK (the public key that P expects its partner to use for authentication), a flag indicating the corruption of the long-term private key used by that instance (denoted π_P^q.SK.γ); a flag indicating the revelation of the session key (denoted $\pi_P^q.\rho$); and π_P^q.ProxID (the identity ProxID $\in$ PROXSet of the party's proxy). Both proxy and endpoint instances also store the current symmetric encryption key π_P^q.pcsk $\in$ P.PCSK used during the handshake. Finally proxy instances store two specific values : π_P^q.sst (the session state built during the protocol session run) and π_P^q.tr (the transcript of the protocol session run).

Following [2,5] we define the notion of instances *have matching conversation*.

Definition 1. *Let* (P, Q) *be two endpoints with* P $\neq$ Q *and let* q, j *be two natural integers. We say that* π_P^q *has matching conversation with* π_Q^j *(or that* π_P^q *matches* π_Q^j*) if* π_P^q.sid $\neq \perp$, π_P^q.sid $= \pi_Q^j$.sid, Q $= \pi_P^q$.PNID *and* P $= \pi_Q^j$.PNID.

For *correctness*, accepting endpoint instances that have matching conversation compute the same session key; accepting endpoint instance keys are lawfully-interceptable by the collaboration of all the authorities in the instance's AID.

Oracles. Similarly to [2,5], we use game-based security notions and give the adversary access to oracles, such as: oRegister(P, type, P.$\overline{\text{PK}}$) ($\mathcal{A}$ can register either honest parties, or malicious parties, with malicious $P.\overline{PK}$); $\mathsf{oSend}(\pi_P^q, m)$ ($\mathcal{A}$ can send a message to an endpoint instance $\pi_{P'}^j$); $\mathsf{oReveal}(\pi_P^q)$ ($\mathcal{A}$ learns the session key of endpoint instance π_P^q); $\mathsf{oTest}_b(\pi_P^q)$ – which can only be queried once, and returns either the real session key computed by endpoint instance π_P^q or a random key, depending on the value of a bit b; and $\mathsf{oRevealTD}(\mathsf{sst}, \mathsf{I}, \mathsf{R}, \mathsf{Prox}, \mathsf{AID}, \ell)$ ($\mathcal{A}$ learns the trapdoor of authority Λ_ℓ registered in authority set AID for a session with state sst). We need to modify two oracles in our work, extending them to capture multiple authentication modes and credentials:

- $\mathsf{oNewSession}(\mathsf{P}, \mathsf{role}, \mathsf{PNID}, \mathsf{PK}_\mathsf{I}, \mathsf{PK}_\mathsf{R}, \mathsf{ProxID}, \mathsf{AID})$ – which creates endpoint/proxy instances of an endpoint/proxy P with role role = Initiator or role = Responder, or role = Proxy, with Initiator authentication using the Initiator's public credential PK_I and Responder authentication using Responder credential PK_R. This allows to create an instance using a specific method (either 0, 1, 2 or 3);
- $\mathsf{oCorrupt}(\mathsf{P}, \ell)$ – which allows the adversary to corrupt the ℓth long-term key of party P.

Key Security. In the key-security game, the adversary uses all the oracles presented above in order to learn the value of the bit b used for the single oTest query. The adversary wins if, and only if, it guarantees the soundness property (*i.e.*, two honest instances having matching conversation and running a protocol session derive the same session key), it guesses b correctly and if its oTest query targets *fresh* instances (*i.e.*, for which the long-term authentication credential used by both endpoints in that instance is uncorrupted at the time of the test query, the session key has not been revealed, and at least one authority in AID is honest and its trapdoor has not been revealed). This is fully detailed in [21].

Non-frameability. In this game, the adversary may query all but the oTest oracle, and wins if it ties an honest endpoint P to a session with state sst, in which P did not end in an accepting state.

LI-compliance. In LI-compliance, the adversary may query all but the oTest oracle, and must output a proxy session in which the key retrieved by LI differs from the key that can be extracted from the session transcript.

The security of LI-EDHOC. We state the security theorems of LI-EDHOC for all the four authentication methods and prove them in the full version [21]. Interestingly, allowing both static-DH-based and signature-based authentication yields both a positive and a negative outcome. On the plus side, if one credential is lost or corrupted, the endpoint need not immediately re-initialize its public keys. Moreover, note that EDHOC's static-DH authentication mode is still forward-secure, since it is combined with an ephemeral secret. On the downside, however, the use of static-DH authentication renders non-frameability difficult to prove, requiring either heavier computations (which we present in the full version, for completeness), or a slight modification of the standard Discrete Logarithm problem (we will require access to a CDH oracle, akin to how GDH requires DDH oracle access). We dub this new problem *Oracle-DLog*[10].

Definition 2 (Oracle-DLog). Let $\mathbb{G}$ be a cyclic group of prime order p generated by $g \in \mathbb{G}$. Let $x \leftarrow \$\mathbb{Z}_p^*$ and $X \leftarrow g^x$. The *Oracle-DLog* problem challenges an adversary in possession of $(g, p, \mathbb{G}, X)$, with oracle access to $\mathcal{O}_{\mathsf{CDH}}(\cdot)$ – returning, on input $Y = g^y \in \mathbb{G}$, the value $g^{xy} \in \mathbb{G}$ – to retrieve x.

Theorem 1. *If LI-EDHOC is instantiated with an* EUF − CMA*-secure signature scheme; zero-knowledge and extractable proofs and signatures of knowledge; IND-CPA and injective encryption schemes; and if DDH and GDH problems are hard in* $\mathbb{G}$*, then LI-EDHOC (methods 0,1,2,3) achieve key security, LI-compliance, and (*Initiator *and* Responder*) identity protection. Moreover, LI-EDHOC method 0 also achieves non-frameability. If, in addition, the Oracle DLog problem is hard in* $\mathbb{G}$*, LI-EDHOC (methods 1,2,3) also guarantee non-frameability.*

6 Implementation and Evaluation

As method 3 (**static-static**) of authentication is likely to be the most expensive, we implement LI-EDHOC in this particular setting (which appears in the full version). We complement the `lakers` implementation of EDHOC in Rust, with bindings for C and Python. As an online addition to this article, we release the LIKE implementation as open source[11].

Our implementation transports LIKE elements within the External Authorization Data (EAD) fields of EDHOC. This allows for selective activation of lawful interception maintaining EDHOC's base structure. There are two main additions to the lakers implementation of EDHOC: (1) the cryptographic primitives supporting the generation and verification of the Signature of Knowledge. We instantiate the SoK as described in Appendix A. (2) dedicated EAD handlers that generate and process LIKE elements during the EDHOC handshake. These handlers populate the EAD field of the message with the necessary additional elements of LIKE. The implementation includes the pre-computation phase performed once for a given set of peers and authorities, during which the values (h_I, ω_I) are computed.

We evaluate the implementation on two typical constrained platforms, based on the ARM Cortex-M core[12]: (1) nRF52840 development board featuring an ARM Cortex-M4F processor running at 64 MHz with 256 kB RAM and 1 MB flash memory, and (2) STM32WBA55CG development board featuring an ARM Cortex-M33 processor running at 32 MHz with 128 kB RAM and 512 kB flash memory. We measure both overhead and execution time. To measure the later,

---
[10] This problem is similar to the *Q-One-More DiffieHellman* problem defined in [18].
[11] https://github.com/ElsaLopez133/lakers.git.
[12] Note that we are not making a comparison here, but simply presenting implementation results on commonly used platforms.

we used the Saleae Logic 8 logic analyzer connected to specific GPIO pins on both development boards, that are toggled at the beginning and end of given code sections (Fig. 6, Appendix C). The sampling frequency is set to 40 MS/s (Mega Samples per second). For the evaluation, the Initiator and the Responder are located on the same physical device, which removes the network communication overhead and allows us to focus on computational performance. Note that the evaluation does not include the proxies which run on non-constrained devices.

We made a comparison of the message overhead for the Initiator (messages 1 and 3) running EDHOC authenticated with DH Static Keys, with and without implementing LIKE. With LIKE, a total of 152 bytes (37 for the first message, and 115 for the third) are carried out for the Initiator, while without, only 56 bytes (37 for the first message, and 19 for the third) are carried out. The extra bytes compared to the standard EDHOC implementation in the third message come from the additional signature of knowledge.

Table 2, in Appendix C, shows the time measurements for both microcontrollers. "Software LIKE" corresponds to a software-based implementation, with all cryptographic operations performed in software, without any hardware acceleration. "Hardware LIKE" corresponds to a hardware-accelerated implementation where elliptic curve operations (point addition and point multiplication), field operations (modular multiplication and modular addition) and hash operations are performed using hardware acceleration.

Table 2 shows that the implementation of LIKE comes with a significant overhead, mainly due to the expensive ECC point multiplications and additions which figure in the SoK. We note an (expected) effect of the clock frequency and processor architecture on performance: the software-based implementation on Cortex M4F is comparable with the hardware-based implementation on Cortex M33. Finally, we observe that hardware acceleration substantially reduces the execution time differences observed between base EDHOC and LI-EDHOC for the Cortex M33 device, making lawful-interception more practical for deployment in constrained devices. Future iterations of this implementation could implement hardware acceleration as well in the nRF52840 (Cortex M4F) to further improve performance and reduce computation times.

Moreover, it would be interesting to run future experiments on hardware dedicated for ECC computations, such as [14]. Finally note that, whereas static authentication requires a lengthy signature of knowledge, complexity drops for authentication methods relying only on ephemeral secrets (*i.e.,* where peers use signatures to authenticate).

7 Conclusion

Mobile environments come with a compulsory Lawful Interception (LI) clause for mobile network operators (MNOs). Naïve LI, however, is intrusive, essentially forcing the operator to eavesdrop on all communications. Our work provides *fine-grained, session-specific* LI for the complex EDHOC protocol, which is being standardized for mobile use in the LAKE IETF working group. Our

LI-EDHOC scheme provably guarantees key-security, non-frameability, and a proof of LI key-recovery for EDHOC's 4 authentication methods, while preserving identity-protection and explicit authentication. Evaluations on two different ARM Cortex-M platforms, show that our protocol remains efficient in constrained environments, especially when the signatures of knowledge benefit from hardware acceleration. Even better performances are likely to be obtained for signature-based authentication methods, or if the processor was optimized for ECC computations.

Acknowledgments. This work has been partially supported by the French National Research Agency under the France 2030 label (NF-HiSec ANR-22-PEFT-0009) and through the PRIvacy-preserving tools for the VAliation and SecurIty of Queries (PRIVASIQ) project (ANR-23-CE39-0008). The views reflected herein do not necessarily reflect the opinion of the French government.

A NIPoK/SoK Instantiation

We present here the instantiation of the SoK used in method 3, *i.e.*, the one we implemented, and describe how to adapt it to method 2 (presented in the core of the paper). LI-EDHOC in method 3 requires, for the SoK, a proof of knowledge of the equality of three discrete logarithms, and of the equality of two other discrete logarithms, in order to certify that the elements H_d, H_d^1 and H_d^2 are well formed. We consider a hash function $\mathcal{H}_{\mathsf{SoK}} : \mathbb{G} \times \{0,1\}^* \to \mathbb{Z}_p^*$ modeled as a random oracle. We use the following instantiation for the Initiator SoK. The Initiator has witnesses x and i to the statement $\mathsf{stm}_\mathsf{I} = \big[X = g^x \wedge H_\mathsf{I} = (h_\mathsf{I} g^y)^x \wedge H_\mathsf{I}^1 = (h_\mathsf{I} g^r)^x \wedge X_1 = g^i \wedge H_\mathsf{I}^2 = (h_\mathsf{I} g^y)^i\big]$, and will sign message $m_\mathsf{I} = \omega_\mathsf{I} \| \mathsf{ID}_\mathsf{R} \| \mathsf{TH}_2 \| \mathsf{TH}_3 \| \mathsf{TH}_4$. The Initiator runs the SoK algorithm as follows and when he checks ni_I, the proxy Prox_I runs the SoKver algorithm.

$\mathsf{SoK}(m_\mathsf{I}, (x,i), \mathsf{stm}_\mathsf{I})$: Pick random $r_\mathsf{I}, s_\mathsf{I} \leftarrow \$ \mathbb{Z}_p^*$. Compute $I_1 \leftarrow g^{r_\mathsf{I}}$, $I_2 \leftarrow (h_\mathsf{I} g^y)^{r_\mathsf{I}}$, $I_3 \leftarrow (h_\mathsf{I} g^r)^{r_\mathsf{I}}$, $I_4 \leftarrow g^{s_\mathsf{I}}$, $I_5 \leftarrow (h_\mathsf{I} g^y)^{s_\mathsf{I}}$, $\alpha_\mathsf{I} \leftarrow \mathcal{H}_{\mathsf{SoK}}(I_1 I_2 I_3 I_4 I_5, m_\mathsf{I})$, $\beta_\mathsf{I} \leftarrow r_\mathsf{I} - \alpha_\mathsf{I} x \pmod{p}$ and $\gamma_\mathsf{I} \leftarrow s_\mathsf{I} - \alpha_\mathsf{I} i \pmod{p}$. Return $\mathsf{ni}_\mathsf{I} = (\alpha_\mathsf{I}, \beta_\mathsf{I}, \gamma_\mathsf{I})$.

$\mathsf{SoKver}(m_\mathsf{I}, \mathsf{stm}_\mathsf{I}, \mathsf{ni}_\mathsf{I})$: Compute $I_1' \leftarrow g^{\beta_\mathsf{I}}(g^x)^{\alpha_\mathsf{I}}$, $I_2' \leftarrow (h_\mathsf{I} g^y)^{\beta_\mathsf{I}}(h_\mathsf{I}^x g^{xy})^{\alpha_\mathsf{I}} = (h_\mathsf{I} g^y)^{\beta_\mathsf{I}}(H_\mathsf{I})^{\alpha_\mathsf{I}}$, $I_3' \leftarrow (h_\mathsf{I} g^r)^{\beta_\mathsf{I}}(h_\mathsf{I}^x g^{xr})^{\alpha_\mathsf{I}} = (h_\mathsf{I} g^r)^{\beta_\mathsf{I}}(H_\mathsf{I}^1)^{\alpha_\mathsf{I}}$, $I_4' \leftarrow g^{\gamma_\mathsf{I}}(g^i)^{\alpha_\mathsf{I}}$ and $I_5' \leftarrow (h_\mathsf{I} g^y)^{\gamma_\mathsf{I}}(h_\mathsf{I}^i g^{iy})^{\alpha_\mathsf{I}} = (h_\mathsf{I} g^y)^{\gamma_\mathsf{I}}(H_\mathsf{I}^2)^{\alpha_\mathsf{I}}$. Return 1 if $\alpha_\mathsf{I} = \mathcal{H}_{\mathsf{SoK}}(I_1' I_2' I_3' I_4' I_5', \omega_\mathsf{I})$, else return 0.

On their side, the Responder and his proxy Prox_R work with the statement $\mathsf{stm}_\mathsf{R} = \big[Y = g^y \wedge H_\mathsf{R} = (h_\mathsf{R} g^x)^y \wedge H_\mathsf{R}^1 = (h_\mathsf{R} g^i)^y \wedge Y_1 = g^r \wedge H_\mathsf{R}^2 = (h_\mathsf{R} g^x)^r\big]$, the witnesses y and r, and the message $m_\mathsf{R} = \omega_\mathsf{R} \| \mathsf{ID}_\mathsf{I} \| \mathsf{TH}_2 \| \mathsf{TH}_3 \| \mathsf{TH}_4$. The SoK and SoKver algorithms work in the same way.

In authentication method 2, this SoK is the same on the Initiator side, see Fig. 4. On the Responder side, however, the SoK is less computationally expensive, as the Responder proves the equality of two discrete logarithms instead of three, omitting thus the Responder-side equivalents of I_4 and I_5.

B Further Properties: Identity-Protection

Identity-Protection was defined in [8] and tailored to the EDHOC protocol. We slightly modify this game in order to tailor it to our modification of EDHOC. We prove that our protocol preserves the following two properties also achieved by the original scheme: that the Initiator's identity is hidden by encryption against an active attacker; and that the Responder's identity is also hidden by encryption against a passive attacker.

C Additional Figures and Tables

$\text{Prox}_{I/R}\text{Run1}(M_1)$

1 : Parse M_1 as $(\text{MCS}\|g^x\|\text{C}_{\text{I}}\|\text{EAD}_1)$
2 : $\tau_{I/R} \leftarrow \omega_{I/R}\|\text{MCS}\|g^x$ // Initialize τ_I/τ_R
3 : return M_1

$\text{Prox}_I\text{Run3}(M_3)$

1 : Parse M_3 as $(c_3\|\text{H}_{\text{I}}\|\text{H}_{\text{I}}^1\|\text{ni}_{\text{I}}\|S_{\text{I}})$
   // Decipher S_I and verify transcript hashes
2 : $K_{\text{I}} \leftarrow \text{Dec}''(\text{pcsk}_{\text{I},\text{Prox}_{\text{I}}}, S_{\text{I}})$, parse K_{I} as $(\text{sk}_2\|\text{sk}_3\|\text{IV}_3\|t_2)$
3 : $m_2 \leftarrow \text{Dec}(\text{sk}_2, c_2)$, get $\text{ID}_{\text{R}}, \sigma_2$ from m_2
4 : $\text{TH}_2 \leftarrow \mathcal{H}(g^y, \mathcal{H}(M_1))$, $\text{TH}_3 \leftarrow \mathcal{H}(\text{TH}_2, m_2, \text{ID}_{\text{R}})$
5 : $\text{ad}_3 \leftarrow (l_{\text{aead}}\|\text{" "}\|\text{TH}_3)$, $m_3 \leftarrow \text{Dec}'(\text{sk}_3, \text{IV}_3, \text{ad}_3, c_3)$
6 : $\text{TH}_4 \leftarrow \mathcal{H}(\text{TH}_3, m_3, \text{ID}_{\text{I}})$
   // Verify SoK and HMAC, update τ_I
7 : if $\text{SoKver}(\omega_{\text{I}}\|\text{ID}_{\text{R}}\|\text{TH}_2\|\text{TH}_3\|\text{TH}_4, \text{stm}_{\text{I}}, \text{ni}_{\text{I}}) \neq 1$
8 :   or if $\text{DS.Verif}(\text{spk}_{\text{R}}, (l_{\text{sig}}\|\text{CTX}_2\|t_2), \sigma_2) \neq 1$
9 :   then return $\bot$
10 : $\tau_{\text{I}} \leftarrow \tau_{\text{I}}\|g^y\|\text{TH}_2\|\text{TH}_3\|\text{TH}_4\|M_1\|m_2\|m_3\|\text{H}_{\text{I}}\|\text{H}_{\text{I}}^1\|\text{ni}_{\text{I}}\|\text{ID}_{\text{R}}\|t_2$
11 : return $M_3' \leftarrow c_3$

$\text{Prox}_I\text{Run4}(M_4')$

1 : Parse M_4' as $(c_4\|n_r\|\text{val}\|\text{TH}_5)$
2 : if $\text{TH}_5 = \mathcal{H}(\text{TH}_4, \text{val}, n_r)$ then return $\bot$
   // Update and sign τ_I
3 : $\tau_{\text{I}} \leftarrow \tau_{\text{I}}\|n_r\|\text{val}, \sigma_{\text{I}} \leftarrow \text{DS.Sign}(\text{ssk}_{\text{Prox}_{\text{I}}}, \tau_{\text{I}})$
4 : $\text{sst}_{\text{I}} \leftarrow \tau_{\text{I}}\|\sigma_{\text{I}}$, return $M_4'' \leftarrow M_4'$

$\text{Prox}_{I/R}\text{Run2}(M_2)$

1 : Parse M_2 as $(g^y\|c_2)$
2 : $\tau_{I/R} \leftarrow \tau_{I/R}\|g^y$ // Update τ_I/τ_R
3 : return M_2

$\text{Prox}_R\text{Run3}(M_4)$

1 : Parse M_4 as $(c_4\|n_r\|\text{val}\|\text{TH}_5\|\text{H}_{\text{R}}\|\text{H}_{\text{R}}^1\|\text{ni}_{\text{R}}\|S_{\text{R}})$
   // Decipher S_R and verify transcript hashes
2 : $K_{\text{R}} \leftarrow \text{Dec}''(\text{pcsk}_{\text{R},\text{Prox}_{\text{R}}}, S_{\text{R}})$
3 : Parse K_{R} as $(\text{sk}_2\|\text{sk}_3\|\text{IV}_3\|t_2)$
4 : $m_2 \leftarrow \text{Dec}(\text{sk}_2, c_2)$, $\text{TH}_2 \leftarrow \mathcal{H}(g^y, \mathcal{H}(M_1))$
5 : $\text{TH}_3 \leftarrow \mathcal{H}(\text{TH}_2, m_2, \text{ID}_{\text{R}})$, $\text{ad}_3 \leftarrow (l_{\text{aead}}\|\text{" "}\|\text{TH}_3)$
6 : $m_3 \leftarrow \text{Dec}'(\text{sk}_3, \text{IV}_3, \text{ad}_3, c_3)$, get ID_{I} from m_3
7 : $\text{TH}_4 \leftarrow \mathcal{H}(\text{TH}_3, m_3, \text{ID}_{\text{I}})$
   // Verify SoK and HMAC, update and sign τ_R
8 : if $\text{DS.Verif}(\text{spk}_{\text{R}}, (l_{\text{sig}}\|\text{CTX}_2\|t_2), \sigma_2) \neq 1$
9 :   then return $\bot$
10 : if $\text{SoKver}(\omega_{\text{R}}\|\text{ID}_{\text{I}}\|\text{TH}_2\|\text{TH}_3\|\text{TH}_4, \text{stm}_{\text{R}}, \text{ni}_{\text{R}}) \neq 1$
11 :   then return $\bot$
12 : if $\text{TH}_5 \neq \mathcal{H}(\text{TH}_4, \text{val}, n_r)$ then return $\bot$
13 : $\tau_{\text{R}} \leftarrow \tau_{\text{R}}\|g^i\|\text{TH}_2\|\text{TH}_3\|\text{TH}_4\|M_1\|m_2\|m_3\|$
       $\text{H}_{\text{R}}\|\text{H}_{\text{R}}^1\|\text{ni}_{\text{R}}\|\text{ID}_{\text{I}}\|t_2\|n_r\|\text{val}$
14 : $\sigma_{\text{R}} \leftarrow \text{DS.Sign}(\text{ssk}_{\text{Prox}_{\text{R}}}, \tau_{\text{R}})$, $\text{sst}_{\text{R}} \leftarrow \tau_{\text{R}}\|\sigma_{\text{R}}$
15 : return $M_4' \leftarrow (c_4\|n_r\|\text{val}\|\text{TH}_5)$

Fig. 5. Proxies instantiation of the LI-EDHOC protocol with ID = 2

Table 2. LI-EDHOC handshake (LIKE) vs. EDHOC (base) runtime evaluation (in seconds), for implementations fully run in software (SW) or featuring ECC, field operations, and hashes that are hardware accelerated (HW)

Operation	Cortex M4F @ 64 MHz		Cortex M33 @ 32 MHz			
	SW LIKE	SW base	SW LIKE	SW base	HW LIKE	HW base
Precomputation Phase						
Precomputation (vok_log_auth)	1.8095	–	7.1282	–	0.5798	–
Precomputation (h)	0.0015	–	0.0057	–	0.00005	–
Precomputation (w)	0.0015	–	0.0055	–	0.0009	–
Subtotal	**1.8125**	–	**7.1394**	–	**0.5808**	–
Initiator						
Message_1	0.0016	0.0016	0.0062	0.0062	0.0016	0.0016
Message_3	9.1231	2.8495	35.9294	11.2157	4.1256	1.2649
(SoK)	(6.2477)	–	(24.6097)	–	(2.8484)	–
Subtotal	**9.1247**	**2.8511**	**35.9356**	**11.2219**	**4.1272**	**1.2665**

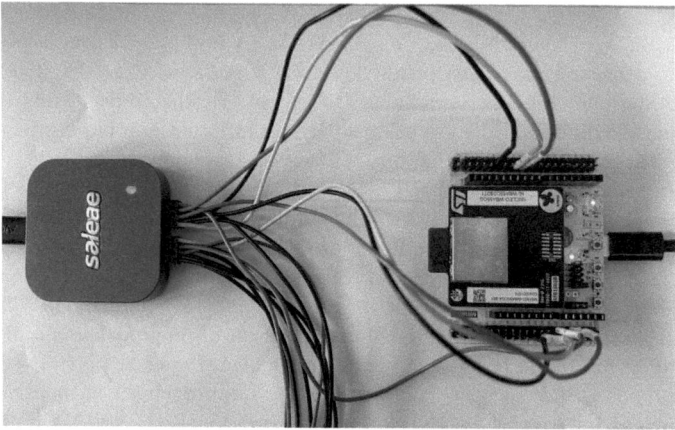

Fig. 6. Our evaluation setup for the embedded evaluation board STM32WBA55CG (to the right). We toggle General Purpose Input/Output pins and record execution times using a logic analyzer (to the left) which runs on a PC

References

1. Abelson, H., et al.: Keys under doormats. Comms. ACM **58**(10), 24–26 (2015)
2. Arfaoui, G., et al.: How to (legally) keep secrets from mobile operators. In: Proceedings of ESORICS, pp. 23–43 (2021)

3. Bellare, M., Rivest, R.L.: Translucent cryptography - an alternative to key escrow, and its implementation via fractional oblivious transfer. J. Cryptol. **12**(2), 117–139 (1999)
4. Boeira, F., Asplund, M., Barcellos, M.: Provable non-frameability for 5G lawful interception. In: Proceedings of WiSec, pp. 109 – 120 (2023)
5. Bultel, X., Onete, C.: Pairing-free secure-channel establishment in mobile networks with fine-grained lawful interception. In: Proceedings of ACM SAC, pp. 968–970 (2022)
6. Global Encryption Coalition. Joint statement on the dangers of the may 2024 council of the EU comrpomise proposal on EU CSAM (2024)
7. Cottier, B., Pointcheval, D.: Security analysis of the edhoc protocol (2022)
8. Cottier, B., Pointcheval, D.: Security analysis of improved edhoc protocol. In: Foundations and Practice of Security (2023)
9. EU Council. Resolution on security through encryption and security despite encryption (2020)
10. FairTrials. Short update: Police in germany defend the use of contact tracing for criminal investigations (2020)
11. Franceschi-Bicchierai, L.:The 10 biggest revelations from edward snowden's leaks (2014)
12. Günther, F., Mukendi, M.L.T.: Careful with mac-then-sign: A computational analysis of the edhoc lightweight authenticated key exchange protocol. In: IEEE (EuroS&P), pp. 773–796 (2023)
13. He, X., Li, L., Peng, H.: A key escrow-free kp-abe scheme and its application in standalone authentication in iot. IEEE Internet Things J. **11**(7), 11381–11394 (2024)
14. Hu, X., Li, X., Zheng, X., Liu, Y., Xiong, X.: A high speed processor for elliptic curve cryptography over nist prime field. IET Circ. Dev. Syst. **16**, 350–359 (2022)
15. Huang, Meijuan, Liu, Yutian, Yang, Bo., Zhao, Yanqi, Zhang, Mingrui: Efficient revocable attribute-based encryption with data integrity and key escrow-free. Information **15**, 32 (2024)
16. Huso, I., Olivieri, M., Galgano, L., Rashid, A., Piro, G., Boggia, G.: Design and implementation of a looking-forward lawful interception architecture for future mobile communication systems. Comput. Netw. **249**, 110518 (2024)
17. Jacomme, C., Klein, E., Kremer, S., Racouchot, M.: A comprehensive, formal and automated analysis of the EDHOC protocol. USENIX Sec. **23**, 5881–5898 (2023)
18. Januzelli, J., Xu, J.: A complete characterization of one-more assumptions in the algebraic group model. Cryptology ePrint Archive, Paper 2024/1954 (2024)
19. Krawczyk, H.: SIGMA: the "SIGn-and-MAc" approach to authenticated diffie-hellman and its use in the IKE protocols. In: Boneh, D. (ed.) CRYPTO 2003. LNCS, vol. 2729, pp. 400–425. Springer, Heidelberg (2003). https://doi.org/10.1007/978-3-540-45146-4_24
20. Krawczyk, H., Eronen, P.: HMAC-based Extract-and-Expand Key Derivation Function (HKDF). RFC 5869 (May 2010)
21. Lafourcade, P., et al.:Fine-grained, privacy-augmenting li-compliance in the lake standard (full version) (2025). https://hal.science/hal-05126079
22. López Pérez, E., Watteyne, T., Marin-Lopez, R., Onete, C., Vučinić, M.: Pre-shared key authentication with edhoc: The security-performance tradeoff. awaiting for publication (2025)
23. López Pérez, E., Selander, I.G., Mattsson, J.P., Watteyne, T., Vučinić, M.: An overview of security analysis, Edhoc is a new security handshake standard (2024)

24. 379 scientists and researchers from 36 countries. Open letter on the position of scientists and researchers on the updated version of the EU's proposed Child Sexual Abuse Regulation (2024)
25. Selander, G.., Preuss Mattsson, J., Palombini, F.: Ephemeral Diffie-Hellman over COSE (EDHOC). RFC 9528 (2024)
26. Ungaro, G., Ricchitelli, F., Huso, I., Piro, G., Boggia, G.: Design and implementation of a lawful interception architecture for b5g systems based on key escrow. In: IEEE CSCN, pp. 207–207 (2022)
27. Wright, C., Varia, M.: Crypto crumple zones: enabling limited access without mass surveillance. In: Proceedings of EuroS&P, pp. 288–306 (2018)

RIPOST: Two-Phase Private Decomposition for Multidimensional Data

Ala Eddine Laouir[✉] and Abdessamad Imine

Université de Lorraine, CNRS, Inria, LORIA, 54000 Nancy, France
ala-eddine.laouir@loria.fr

Abstract. In this paper, we focus on the problem of publishing multidimensional data under differential privacy (DP), particularly on how to construct privacy-preserving views using a domain decomposition approach. The core idea is to recursively split the domain into sub-domains until convergence, then perturb and publish them. The result is a tree structure that enables efficient indexing and fast approximation processing of queries, while ensuring privacy. Existing decomposition-based methods face two main challenges: (i) efficiently managing the privacy budget over an indefinite decomposition depth h, and (ii) designing a data-dependent splitting strategy that minimizes the error while limiting the subdomain size. We propose RIPOST, a multidimensional decomposition algorithm with bounded and flexible budget allocation that eliminates the need for a predefined depth h and exploits a data-aware splitting strategy with a good trade-off between privacy and utility. RIPOST follows a two-phase process: it first isolates non-empty sub-domains from empty ones, and then refines the decomposition using the mean function to minimize inaccuracies. Through extensive experiments, RIPOST consistently outperforms state-of-the-art methods in terms of data utility and accuracy across various datasets and scenarios.

Keywords: Differential Privacy · Hierarchical Decompositions

1 Introduction

Releasing a privacy-preserving view of data, under differential privacy, has attracted strong interest from researchers and major corporations. Differential privacy has become the de facto standard for data protection [1,22,23], guaranteeing that the presence or absence of any individual does not significantly impact the released view, thus preserving plausible deniability for membership. Such views can be used for OLAP queries, multi-dimensional histograms, and data mining tasks such as clustering [27], encouraging research in this area.

A naive approach [5] would be to add noise to all data points, but this results in a significant loss of data utility. Therefore, more sophisticated mechanisms and techniques have been proposed in the literature. Some use generative models to produce synthetic differentially private data [2,9,11,21,24,26,29], focusing primarily on image data or regular tabular data. Others [16–18] propose workload-dependent algorithms that aim to release answers to a predefined batch of queries rather than the full data view. The generative-based solutions are generally designed as general-purpose algorithms (especially those utilizing deep learning models) without a specific focus on multidimensional data or tensors. On the other hand, workload-dependent approaches are constrained by their reliance on the query workload, which limits their usability. Moreover, these methods often have high computational complexity, making them less scalable for multidimensional data.

Another set of solutions focuses on decomposition-based algorithms, which are ideal for multidimensional data, and allows data indexing by a *tree structure* for faster and more efficient tasks such as OLAP queries. These methods are also the most used for spatial data compared to the other approaches. Several differentially private decomposition approaches have been proposed [3,12,14,19,27,28], but they face two main challenges:

- **Dependence on decomposition depth** h : Many methods [3,14,19,28] pre-estimate h to manage the privacy budget, with only [12,27] overcoming this limitation to varying extents. Note that the noise will be injected proportionally to h. However, a small h makes the resulting tree nodes too coarse, while a large h leads to excessive noise in the tree leaves.
- **Data-aware splitting**: Approaches like [27] use data-independent splitting, while [12] applies data-aware splitting only partially throughout the decomposition. An efficient data-aware splitting reduces both unnecessary decomposition and errors, but it inevitably reintroduces the issue of budget management over any arbitrary h as it must be differentially private.

All existing domain decomposition methods fail to successfully address both challenges. In contrast, our proposed method, RIPOST (p**R**ivate v**I**ew by two-**P**hase decomp**O**sition for multidimen**S**ional da**T**a), effectively overcomes these limitations, providing a high-accuracy view compared to other approaches.

Contributions. Our proposed solution RIPOST, eliminates the need for a predefined decomposition depth h through a novel privacy budget distribution strategy, which relies on a convergent series. This strategy allows for a flexible and refined private decomposition. Additionally, RIPOST uses a novel two-phase data-aware splitting strategy. The first phase identifies and separates empty sub-domains from populated ones, thus avoiding unnecessary decompositions. The populated sub-domains with large aggregation errors are then passed to the second phase, where further decomposition reduces the error. The decomposition results in a tree structure that accelerates query processing, with evaluations occurring at the leaf nodes, similar to existing methods such as [12,27]. Extensive experiments show that RIPOST outperforms existing methods in terms of utility.

Roadmap. The paper is structured as follows: Sect. 2 reviews related work. Section 3 introduces the key concepts and notation. Section 4 describes the decomposition problem under DP. Section 5 presents in details RIPOST. The extensive evaluation is provided in Sect. 6. Section 7 discusses potential improvements and extensions, and we conclude in Sect. 8 by outlining key results and contributions.

2 Related Work

Data publication under Differential Privacy (DP) is a key research topic. The naive approach *'Identity'*, injects noise into each tensor cell [4,5], causing excessive perturbation and inaccuracy. To address this, methods for publishing high-dimensional data under DP have been developed. In this section, we present state-of-the-art solutions for this problem.

Partitioning Approaches. Rather than perturbing data, [16,28] proposed algorithms that partition data into bins. In [16], the Laplace mechanism is applied after minimizing *aggregation error*, but this is limited to small-domain data due to the difficulty of finding optimal partitions. Other approaches, such as [20,27], recursively decompose the domain, using a quadtree method. Partitioning continues until convergence, with blocks storing perturbed(DP) representative values. The challenge in domain decomposition is setting the depth limit, h, for budget distribution. Some methods [3,14,19] use heuristics, while [27] avoids this to prevent performance loss. HDPView [12] improves upon [27] with a data-dependent strategy, but is still partially limited by h.

Workload-Based Approaches. Some methods focus on releasing a subset of data based on predefined queries, called *Workload*. [17] introduces a matrix mechanism (MM) for optimizing queries, and [18] extends this for high-dimensional data. HDMM improves [16], but suffers from workload dependency and computationally expensive matrix operations. PrivateSQL [13] considers relational data where computing the sensitivity is a major issue, then uses [16,18] to create the view. [15] uses random sampling to create a data synopsis and a perturbation table, introducing a hybrid system between data publishing and query answering.

Private Generative Models. Generative models are used to create synthetic private data. [26] trained a Bayesian network with DP guarantees, [29] used Marginals, and [2,8,9,11,21] used deep learning models for data synthesis. These models excel in certain classification tasks but are less effective for tabular data compared to [26]. Limitations include: (1) They are not optimized for tensor structures or OLAP tasks, and (2) They are computationally expensive, especially for large or frequently updated datasets.

In our work, we propose a new algorithm `RIPOST`, a workload-independent domain decomposition-based approach. `RIPOST` addresses the limitations and inefficiencies of existing methods such as [3,12,27] and provides a better quality view in terms of *accuracy* while ensuring *data privacy and utility*.

3 Preliminaries

In this section, we introduce the concepts and notation used throughout the paper.

Database. Let $\mathcal{B}$ be a database with a set of tuples defined over $|D|$ dimensions (or attributes), with $D = \{d_1, \ldots, d_{|D|}\}$ and $|D|$ is the number of dimensions of $\mathcal{B}$. Each dimension $d \in D$ is associated with a domain (or range) $\Omega_d = [d_s, d_e]$, containing $|\Omega_d| = d_e - d_s + 1$ discrete and totally ordered values. The overall domain size of $\mathcal{B}$ is $|\Omega_D| = \prod_{d \in D} |\Omega_d|$. For instance, in Fig. 1, the database "Fact Table" is shown with $D = \{Age, Service, Patient\}$ and $\Omega_{Service} = [0, 10]$.

Tensor. A tensor $\mathcal{T}$ is a *multidimensional* data structure created by aggregating $\mathcal{B}$ based on a subset of $m \leq |D|$ dimensions in D. Such aggregation could be done using a SQL "group-by" query such as:

SELECT $(d_1, \ldots, d_m,$ aggreg(.) AS measure) FROM B GROUP BY $(d_1, \ldots, d_m)$

Here, $d_1, \ldots, d_m \in D$ are dimensions and aggreg(.) is an aggregate function such as COUNT, SUM, AVG, etc., which takes an attribute (or dimension) as a parameter. Using COUNT to build a tensor $\mathcal{T}$, the measure attribute contains the number of rows that have the same values (or coordinates) on the dimensions $d_1, \ldots, d_m$. In this case, $\mathcal{T}$ is called a *count tensor*. In this work, we will focus on count tensors[1]. For simplicity, we will refer to "count tensor" simply as "tensor."

In *Fact Table* of Fig. 1, the dimensions *Patient* and *Age* have been aggregated to create a tensor, which can be represented either as a *multidimensional array* or as a *tabular*. The first representation visualizes (and stores) the entire domain (e.g. tensor on $\Omega_{Service}$ in Fig. 1), while the second stores only the non-empty($\neq$ 0) cells of the domain. Since our goal is to protect the entire data (empty and non-empty cells), we therefore consider the entire domain.

Count Range Queries. We consider a special class of queries, namely *count range queries*. A count range query Q is defined on k dimensions ($k \leq |D|$) with

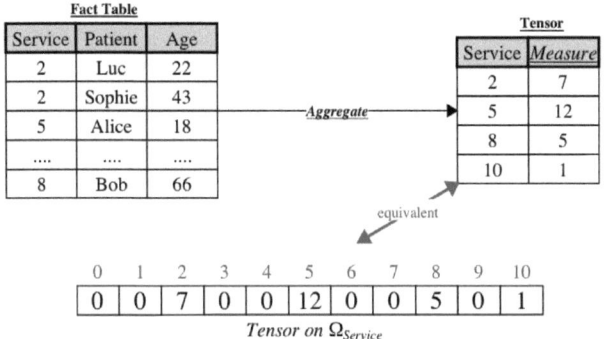

Fig. 1. Data Model.

---

[1] Note that our work can be generalized to any aggregation function.

subranges $Q = \{\tau_1^Q \subseteq \Omega_{d_1}, \ldots, \tau_k^Q \subseteq \Omega_{d_k}\}$, and it computes the *sum* of the cells within those ranges. Given the tensor in Fig. 1, a query $Q = \{\texttt{Service} \in [7,10]\}$ will return 6.

Differential Privacy (DP). DP is a privacy model that provides formal guarantees of *indistinguishability*, ensuring that query results do not reveal significant information about the presence or absence of any particular individual. Consequently, it hides information about which of the *neighbouring tensor* was used to answer the query [6].

Definition 1 (Neighbouring Tensors [6]**).** *Two tensors T and T' are neighbouring if we can obtain one of them by incrementing the value of a cell in the other by 1. We denote this distance as $Dist(T, T') = 1$.*

Let M be a randomized data publishing algorithm. M is *differentially private*, when it is insensitive to the presence or absence of any individual in T.

Definition 2 (ϵ-Differential privacy [6]**).** *An algorithm M satisfies ϵ-differential privacy (or ϵ-DP) if for any neighbouring tensors T and T', and all possible sets of outputs S:*

$$\frac{Pr[M(T) \in S]}{Pr[M(T') \in S]} \le e^{\epsilon}$$

The parameter ϵ is called the privacy budget.

Let f be a query on a tensor T whose its answer $f(T)$ returns a number. The *sensitivity* of f is the maximum amount by which the output of f changes for any neighbouring tensors.

Definition 3 (Sensitivity [6]**).** *The sensitivity of a query f for any two neighboring tensors T, T' is:*

$$\Delta_f = \max_{T,T'} \|f(T) - f(T')\|_1$$

where $\|.\|_1$ is the L_1 norm.

For instance, if f is a count range query then Δ_f is 1. To achieve DP for a query f, we need to add random noise to its answer $f(T)$. To inject adequate noise, some fundamental mechanisms have been developed for DP, such as the *Laplace Mechanism* [6].

Definition 4 (Laplace Mechanism [6]**).** *The* Laplace mechanism *adds noise to $f(T)$ as:*

$$f(T) + Lap\left(\frac{\Delta_f}{\epsilon}\right)$$

where Δ_f is the sensitivity of f, and $Lap(\alpha)$ denotes sampling from the Laplace distribution with center 0 and scale α.

For example, if f is a count range query then the noise is sampled from the distribution $Lap(1/\epsilon)$.

Unlike the Laplace Mechanism (based on noisy numerical answers), the *Exponential mechanism* allows for selecting the "best" element (according to a scoring function) in a set while preserving DP [6].

Definition 5 (Exponential Mechanism [6]**).** *Given a set of values V extracted from a tensor $\mathcal{T}$ and a real scoring function u to select values in V. The* Exponential Mechanism *randomly samples v from V with probability proportional to:*

$$\exp\left(\frac{\epsilon \times u(\mathcal{T}, v)}{2 \times \Delta_u}\right)$$

where Δ_u is the sensitivity of u.

The Exponential Mechanism satisfies DP by approximately maximizing the score of the value it returns, while sometimes returning a value from the set that does not have the highest score.

The combination of several DP mechanisms is possible and privacy accounting is handled using DP's sequential and parallel composition properties. Let $M_1, ..., M_n$ be mechanisms satisfying $\epsilon_1, ..., \epsilon_n$ -DP.

Theorem 1 (Sequential Composition [6]**).** *An algorithm sequentially applying $M_1, ..., M_n$ satisfies $\left(\sum_{j=1}^{n} \epsilon_j\right)$-DP.*

Theorem 2 (Parallel Composition[6]**).** *An algorithm applying $M_1, \ldots, M_n$ to n disjoint datasets in parallel satisfies ($max_{j=1}^{n}\epsilon_j$)-DP.*

4 Problem Statement

Given a tensor $\mathcal{T}$, the spatial decomposition problem consists of dividing its domain into disjoint sub-domains (or sub-blocks) such that cells within each block are approximated by their mean $\bar{x}$ with minimal error, called *Aggregation Error* (AE). AE quantifies the deviation of cells from uniformity: $AE = \sum_{c \in b} |\bar{x} - c|$, where c represents a cell in block b. Range queries are then estimated on the basis of block intersections. Minimizing AE is crucial to maximize the utility of decomposition. A decomposition algorithm has two main components: (i) Convergence Condition (**CC**), which decides if further partitioning is needed. (ii) Splitting Strategy (**SS**), which defines how to divide a domain into sub-domains. The result is a tree structure (i.e. spatial index) in which each node contains a smaller domain and traversing paths from the root allows efficient computations for range queries [3]. Inspired from [12], Fig. 2 describes a decomposition tree (without DP) of a one-dimensional tensor with domain $[0, 10]$, where: (i) **CC** bounds the subdomain aggregation error, $AE \leq \theta$ with $\theta = 10$ in our example. (ii) **SS** splits a domain into two sub-domains and selects the splitting point that minimizes $AE(\text{left}) + AE(\text{right})$.

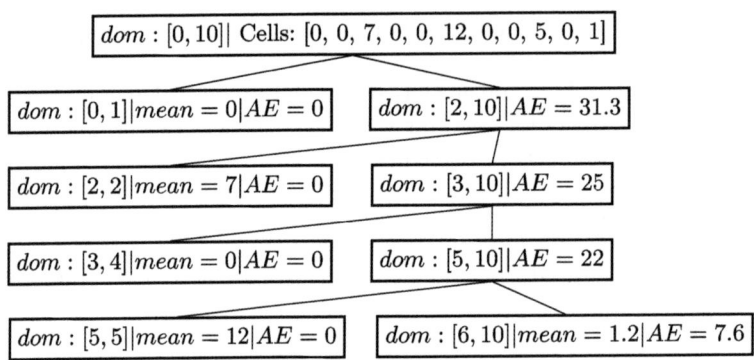

Fig. 2. Example of a decomposition Tree.

The mean is assigned only to each leaf node (ln), and only the set of leaves TL is considered for the query approximation. For a count range query $Q = \{\text{Service} \in [7, 10]\}$, the approximation is computed by: $A(Q) = \sum_{ln \in TL} (ln_{\text{dom}} \cap Q_{\text{dom}}) \times ln_{\text{mean}}$, resulting in $A(Q) = 4.8$. When the decomposition is DP, each block (leaf) must be noised, introducing another error called *Perturbation Error* (PE). The two errors, AE and PE, are inversely related: more blocks reduce AE but increase PE, and vice versa.

First Challenge. Creating a DP decomposition algorithm requires determining the max depth h to bound number of the convergence condition **CC** tests. Since **CC** is data dependent, it is necessary to limit and distribute the privacy budget ϵ. Indeed, using the sequential composition of DP, the noise will be proportional to h. Defining the maximum depth h independently simplifies budget management but may not optimize AE and PE [3,10]. Using a heuristic to determine h is impractical because (1) it must be DP, and (2) finding the optimal h is computationally expensive and often results in approximations [14,19].

PrivTree [27] bypasses the dependency on h by introducing a *Biased Convergence Condition (BCC)*. Given two positive thresholds θ and δ, the key observation of [27] is that budget consumption is limited to the privacy budget ϵ if two conditions hold: (1) $M(b) \gg \theta$ for each intermediate node b (where M is a monotonic metric such as the count of a empty cells) in order to continue the decomposition, and (2) $M(b_p) - M(b_c) \geq \delta$ for parent/child pairs. To ensure the second condition for all datasets, the BCC replaces $M(b)$ with $\hat{M}(b) = \max\{\theta - \delta, M(b) - \text{depth}(b) \times \delta\}$, where $\text{depth}(b)$ is the distance from the root to node b. The budget remains constant at ϵ, ensuring DP regardless of h. While the BCC eliminates the need for a fixed depth, its main drawback is the deterministic bias term "$M(b) - \text{depth}(b) \times \delta$" which can become negative (in addition to Laplace noise) even in the presence of a block b still requiring decomposition. This can lead to *early convergence*, when the decomposition stops prematurely, before reaching an optimal balance between AE and PE.

Second Challenge. How does the splitting strategy (**SS**) balance the errors AE and PE? A data-independent **SS**, like splitting block b into $2^{|D|}$ sub-blocks (e.g. the *quad-tree* [3]), can create excessive blocks, increasing PE without reducing AE. A data-dependent **SS** leverages the domain content to choose the best split point that leads to the best convergence with the fewest generated blocks. To achieve this convergence we must: (1) use a DP mechanism dependent on h (as illustrated in [12]), and (2) make sure that **SS** leads to convergence based on the metric M in **CC**. Moreover, using AE alone for splitting ignores other tensor features, such as sparsity, that could improve the strategy.

Our proposed solution RIPOST addresses both of these challenges by using dynamic budget allocation to bypass the need for predefined h and by leveraging tensor sparsity for a data-aware splitting strategy.

5 Proposed Algorithm

5.1 Overview of RIPOST

RIPOST addresses the key challenges outlined in Sect. 4. It introduces a novel budget management strategy independent of h, a splitting strategy that operates in two phases: first, it separates empty cells from non-empty cells, and then it minimizes **AE** in each block. The overall algorithm of RIPOST is described in Algorithm 1. It operates as follows:

- RIPOST takes as input a tensor $\mathcal{T}$, a total budget ϵ, and hyper-parameters α, β, γ for dividing the budget over the first and second phases (Lines 1-4).
- In the first phase, the algorithm checks if $sum \leq \theta_1$ in the current block (Line 9). If *Secure_cc* is **False**, the block is split into two sub-blocks to minimize the mix of empty and non-empty cells (Line 12).
- If *Secure_cc* is **True**, the block is added to **converged_blocks** (Line 10). This process repeats until there are no non-converged blocks (Line 7).
- In the second phase, all blocks from the first phase are tested and split again to minimize **AE** (Lines 17-18). Each block with minimal **AE** is added to **converged_blocks** (Line 22); otherwise, it is split (Line 24). The process repeats until all blocks converge (Line 19).
- Finally, the average of each block in **converged_blocks** is perturbed and the **secure_view** is returned (Line 29).

Regarding the budget distribution (Lines 1-4): α splits the total privacy budget ϵ between the decomposition budget ϵ_d and the perturbation budget ϵ_p. The parameter β then splits ϵ_d over both phases of RIPOST, namely ϵ_1 and ϵ_2. Lastly, γ divides ϵ_1 and ϵ_2 between the convergence and splitting components. The entire budget for *Secure_cc* (resp. *Secure_ss*) in the current phase is passed as a parameter (Lines 9, 12, 21, 24). Each iteration consumes only a portion of the budget. Section 5.2 explains budget distribution, while Sect. 5.3 provides the implementation of *Secure_cc* and *Secure_ss*.

Algorithm 1. Our decomposition algorithm RIPOST

Require: $\mathcal{T}$: Tensor; ϵ:budget; α, β, γ: hyperparameters
1: $\epsilon_p, \epsilon_d \leftarrow \epsilon \times (1 - \alpha), \epsilon \times \alpha$
2: $\epsilon_1, \epsilon_2 \leftarrow \epsilon_d \times \beta, \epsilon_d \times (1 - \beta)$
3: $\epsilon_{cc}^1, \epsilon_{ss}^1 \leftarrow \epsilon_1 \times \gamma, \epsilon_1 \times (1 - \gamma)$
4: $\epsilon_{cc}^2, \epsilon_{ss}^2 \leftarrow \epsilon_2 \times \gamma, \epsilon_2 \times (1 - \gamma)$
5: converged_blocks $\leftarrow$ []
6: non_converged_blocks $\leftarrow [\mathcal{T}]$
7: **while** non_converged_blocks $\neq \emptyset$ **do** ▷ First phase
8:     $block \leftarrow$ non_converged_blocks.pop()
9:     **if** $Secure\_cc(block, Sum, \leq, \theta_1, \epsilon_{cc}^1)$ **then**
10:         $converged\_blocks.add(block)$
11:     **else**
12:         $left\_block, right\_block \leftarrow Secure\_ss(Min, block, \epsilon_{ss}^1)$
13:         non_converged_blocks.push(left_block)
14:         non_converged_blocks.push(right_block)
15:     **end if**
16: **end while**
17: non_converged_blocks $\leftarrow converged\_blocks$
18: converged_blocks $\leftarrow$ []
19: **while** $non\_converged\_blocks \neq \emptyset$ **do** ▷ second phase
20:     $block \leftarrow non\_converged\_blocks.pop()$
21:     **if** $Secure\_cc(block, AE, \leq, \theta_2, \epsilon_{cc}^2)$ **then**
22:         converged_blocks.push(block)
23:     **else**
24:         $left\_block, right\_block \leftarrow Secure\_ss(AE, block, \epsilon_{ss}^2)$
25:         non_converged_blocks.push(left_block)
26:         non_converged_blocks.push(right_block)
27:     **end if**
28: **end while**
29: $secure\_view \leftarrow perturb(converged\_blocks)$
30: **return secure_view**

5.2 Privacy Budget Distribution

To ensure RIPOST satisfies ϵ-DP, we must introduce randomness while keeping the total budget under ϵ. As discussed in Sect. 4, limiting depth often leads to challenges and tradeoffs. To avoid this, we define a function that distributes any given budget ϵ across any arbitrary depth h such that:

$$\epsilon \geq \sum_{i=1}^{h} \epsilon_i = \sum_{i=1}^{h} \epsilon \times \omega_i \quad \text{where} \quad \omega_i \in]0,1[, \quad \text{and} \quad 1 \geq \sum_{i=1}^{h} \omega_i \quad (1)$$

To define a weight ω_i distribution according to the constraint in Eq. 1, we use the convergent series [25] S to be:

$$\omega_i = \frac{1}{i(i+1)} \quad \text{for positive integers } i, \quad \sum_{i=1}^{\infty} \omega_i = 1 \quad (2)$$

However, the series places most of the budget on the first few levels, leading to large weights early in the decomposition (consumes most of ϵ). This can result in excessive noise injection early on and cause the *Early Convergence*(Section 4).

Simply using a slower series may not be enough. To slow down the weight distribution, we sum multiple instances of the series term by term. For example, with $S = \frac{1}{i(i+1)}$, we define $S^2 = \frac{2}{i(i+1)}$, which decays slower but doesn't satisfy Eq. 1. However, the first term of S^2, $S_1^2 = 1$, allows us to adjust the remaining terms so that their sum equals 1. This adjustment, or offset os, ensures the series decays slower while still satisfying the constraint in Eq. 1.

For $S = \frac{1}{i(i+1)}$, we use a series $S^k = \frac{k}{i(i+1)}$ with a given offset os to define the weight w_i as: $w_i = S^k_{(i+os)}$. With this, we define a function $get\_weight(.)$, used by the $Secure\_cc$ and $Secure\_ss$ functions in Algorithm 1, to allocate the appropriate budget for each operation based on the block's b depth h_b at each phase: $get\_weight(h_b) := S^k_{(h_b+os)}$.

Setting the appropriate offset os depends on the choice of S. In our work, we considered $S = \frac{1}{i(i+1)}$, though other convergent series can also be used. Given S, we know that:

$$\sum_{i=1}^{n} \frac{1}{i(i+1)} \leq 1 - \frac{1}{n+1} \implies \sum_{i=1}^{n} \frac{k}{i(i+1)} \leq k\left(1 - \frac{1}{n+1}\right) \leq k$$

Thus, we define os such as:

$$\sum_{i=1}^{os-1} \frac{k}{i(i+1)} \geq k-1 \text{ and } \sum_{i=os}^{n} \frac{k}{i(i+1)} \leq 1$$

The first sum $\sum_{i=1}^{os-1} \frac{k}{i(i+1)}$ represents the terms we ignore, while the second sum $\sum_{i=os}^{n} \frac{k}{i(i+1)}$ represents the terms we use in function $get\_weight(.)$. Based on this, we get:

$$\sum_{i=1}^{os-1} \frac{k}{i(i+1)} \geq k-1 \implies k\left(1 - \frac{1}{(os-1)+1}\right) \geq k-1 \implies os \geq k$$

Figure 3 shows the S and its variants S^k, with w_i values at each depth. Notice how S^k distribute the budget slower than S, thus reducing the noise injected at the early levels.

Other alternatives, like uniform budget distribution, are impractical since h is unknown. While a growing series could be useful [3], it also requires a predefined h, making it difficult to ensure the constraint in Eq. 1.

5.3 Secure Convergence and Partitioning

In Algorithm 1, both phases use the same functions for convergence and splitting, differing only in the parameters, suggesting they follow the same logic. In this section we presents this two function and how they ensure DP.

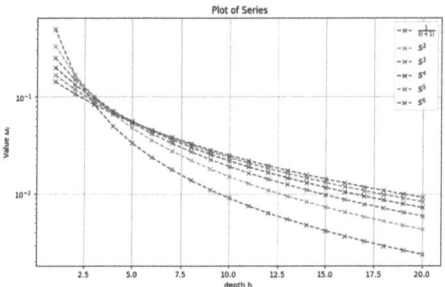

Fig. 3. ω_i for each level of depth h using S^k.

Secure Convergence Condition *Secure_cc*: Algorithm 2 describes the function *Secure_cc*, which takes a block B, a convergence metric M, a threshold θ, and the privacy budget ϵ for the current phase (ϵ_{cc}^1 or ϵ_{cc}^2 in Algorithm 1).

Algorithm 2 computes the budget ϵ_i for the current iteration using *get_weight*(.) function and the block's depth (Lines 1-2). The function *depth*(.) returns the block's depth in the current phase, resetting to 1 when B transitions from phase 1 to phase 2 of Algorithm 1. *Secure_cc* perturbs the metric (Line 3) and returns True or False based on whether it's $\leq \theta$. Since θ has little impact on the output [27], it's set to 0 by default.

Algorithm 2. Secure_cc

Require: B: block, M:metric, ϵ, θ
1: $\omega_i \leftarrow get\_weight(depth(B))$
2: $\epsilon_i \leftarrow \omega_i \times \epsilon$
3: $value \leftarrow M(B) + Lap(\Delta_M/\epsilon_i)$
4: **return** $value \leq \theta$

Algorithm 3. Secure_ss

Require: B: block, M:metric, ϵ
1: $\omega_i \leftarrow get\_weight(depth(B))$
2: $\epsilon_i \leftarrow \omega_i \times \epsilon$
3: **for** $i \in \Omega_B$ **do**
4:     $prob[i] \leftarrow exp\left(\frac{\epsilon_i \times score(B,M,i)}{4 \times \Delta_M}\right)$
5: **end for**
6: $point \leftarrow random\_choice(\Omega_B, prob)$
7: $B_L, B_R \leftarrow split(B, point)$
8: **return** B_L, B_R

Secure_cc uses the *Laplace mechanism* (Line 3) to ensure DP, with noise scale depending on Δ_M, the metric's sensitivity.

Theorem 3 (Sensitivity Δ_M of Min, Sum, and AE). *For neighboring tensors T and T': $\Delta_{Min} = 1$, $\Delta_{Sum} = 1$, and $\Delta_{AE} = 2$.*

(For proof see appendix A)

Secure Splitting Strategy *Secure_ss*: Algorithm 3 shows the steps of *Secure_ss*, which takes a block, metric, and budget ϵ (ϵ_{ss}^1 or ϵ_{ss}^2) for the current phase of Algorithm 1. It computes the budget for the current iteration (Lines 1-2), like *Secure_cc*, and then calculates a sampling probability for each cutting point (Lines 3-5) using the *Exponential mechanism* (Definition 5).

The function $score$ takes a block B, a metric, and a cutting point i. It treats B as if it is split at i into two halves, B_L and B_R, and assigns a score based on the metric and the phase of Algorithm 1:

1. **If metric is 'Min'** : $Score_i = -\min\{\min_{B_L}, \min_{B_R}\}$, where $\min_{B_L}$ and $\min_{B_R}$ represent the minimum between number of empty and nonempty cells in the left and right blocks, respectively. A cutting point with $\min \approx 0$ gets the highest score, as it has the minimum mix of cells.
2. **If metric is 'AE'** : $score_i = -(AE_{B_L} + AE_{B_R})$, favoring the cutting point with the minimal AE.

Since the measure is computed twice (on B_L and B_R), the score's sensitivity is set as $\Delta_{score} = 2 \times \Delta_M$ (Theorem 3). Then, **unequal probability sampling** (Line 6) selects a random cutting point, splitting B into B_L and B_R, which are returned as results.

5.4 Privacy Budget

In the produced decomposition tree (Sect. 4) each path from the root to leaf operates on disjoint domain of the data, so we track consumption on one path and use parallel composition (Theorem 2) for the full decomposition budget consumption. Each leaf node ln is produced after k and p iterations through two decomposition phases (Algorithm 1) and final perturbation. By sequential composition, the accumulated budget must satisfy:

$$\frac{Pr[ln \mid T]}{Pr[ln \mid T']} \leq e^\epsilon \tag{3}$$

Given the budget allocation in Sect. 5.2 and definitions 4, 5, $Secure\_cc$ and $Secure\_ss$ consume at most their respective budgets, ensuring (Full details in Appendix B):

$$\frac{Pr[ln \mid T]}{Pr[ln \mid T']} \leq e^{\epsilon^1_{cc}+\epsilon^1_{ss}+\epsilon^2_{cc}+\epsilon^2_{ss}+\epsilon_p} \leq e^\epsilon$$

Thus, the algorithm respects ϵ for any branch depth h.

6 Experiments

To evaluate RIPOST, we conducted extensive comparative experiments with existing algorithms. This section discusses the main results and observations.

6.1 Experiments Setup

Datasets. In our experiments, we used the following well-known datasets: (i) **Census Adult**[2] is a benchmark dataset containing demographic information about individuals and their income. (ii) **Fire Department and Emergency Medical Services Dispatched Calls for Service (Fire)**[3] contains records of emergency calls made to the fire department in San Francisco. (iii) **Gowalla-2D**[4] is a geo-location check-in dataset. (iv) **Jm1**[5] is a dataset containing static source code analysis data for defect detection. For each dataset we generated a several tensors and thousands of queries, the Table 1 shows the different stats on each dataset. In the remainder of this section, we will emphasize how we used each dataset/workload.

Table 1. Dataset and workload statistics

Datasets	#Dimensions	#Workloads	#Queries	Domain
Adult	15	119 + 8	(5 + 8) × 3000	8.9×10^{18}
Fire	35	119 + 8	(5 + 8) × 3000	2.291×10^{57}
Gowalla	2	1	3000	10^6
Jm1	21	456	5 × 3000	2×10^{21}

Evaluation Metrics. To measure query error, we used RMSE (Root-Mean-Square Error) defined as: $\text{RMSE} = \sqrt{\frac{1}{n}\sum_{Q \in W}(Q(\mathcal{T}) - Q(\dot{\mathcal{T}}))^2}$ where W is the workload, and $\mathcal{T}$, $\dot{\mathcal{T}}$ are the original and private views of the tensor, respectively. To compare results across algorithms, we calculated the relative RMSE (**R-RMSE**) by dividing the RMSE of each approach on a workload W by the RMSE of our approach on the same workload. If R-RMSE > 1, our approach outperforms the others, with **R-RMSE** indicating the scale difference. If R-RMSE < 1, our approach under-performs, and **R-RMSE** shows the fraction of the RMSE of the other approach relative to ours.

Competitors. We compared RIPOST with several recent solutions (in addition to *Identity* [5]) from the literature (see Sect. 2), namely:(i) HDPView [12] and PrivTree [27] for domain decomposition approaches; (ii) HDMM [18] and DAWA [16] for workload-dependent approaches; (iii) PrivBayes [26] and P3GM [21] for generative models creating DP datasets.

---

[2] http://archive.ics.uci.edu/ml/datasets/Adult.
[3] https://data.sfgov.org/Public-Safety/Fire-Department-and-Emergency-Medical-Services-Dis/nuek-vuh3/data.
[4] http://snap.stanford.edu/data/loc-Gowalla.html.
[5] https://www.openml.org/search?type=data&sort=runs&id=1053&status=active.

Hyperparameters. We set $\epsilon = 0.1$. For RIPOST, we set $\alpha = 0.3$, $\gamma = 0.9$, and $\beta = 0.4$ (we will show the effect of each in the experiments). For the competitors[6], we used the same hyperparameter values as those reported in their original paper

Source Code: The code[7], and additional experiments can be found in the GitHub repository (due to space limitations).

6.2 RIPOST performances analysis

Partitioning and Generative Approaches. In the first part of the experiments, we compared RIPOST with HDPView, PrivTree, PrivBayes, and P3GM using the Adult and Fire datasets. For each, we created 2-, 3-, ..., 6-dimensional tensors, each with its own workloads. Table 2 shows the number of distinct tensors/workloads generated for each dimensionality. These different tensors/workloads are used to ensure a thorough and robust evaluation.

Table 2. Number of Tensors/Workloads per Number of Dimensions

# Dimensions	2	3	4	5	6
# Tensors/Workloads	21	35	35	21	7

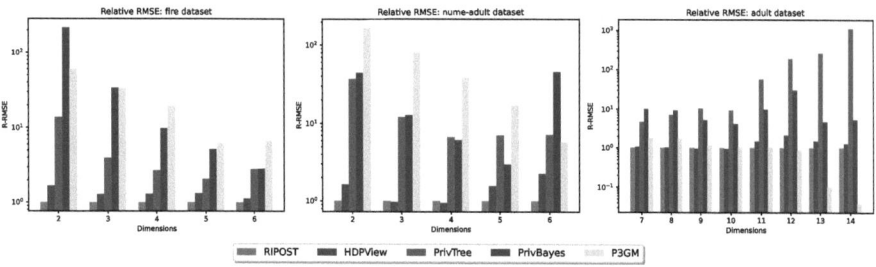

Fig. 4. R-RMSE results based on Adult dataset.

Figures 4 show the average R-RMSE for each approach on the Adult and Fire datasets. Our approach outperforms all others in the tests. In Fig. 4, HDPView is our closest competitor, but its performance drops as the number of dimensions increases, due to its inability to calibrate PE and AE at high-dimensional tensors. Additionally, in both figures, PrivTree performs worse than RIPOST and

---

[6] A disclaimer: The model in [21] computes the privacy budget based on data size and training sample, making it difficult to tune ϵ for all tensors in our tests with minimal changes to the original setup. To ensure fairness, [21] was allocated a larger budget within the range [0.1, 1], depending on the tensor.

[7] https://github.com/AlaEddineLaouir/RIPOST.git.

HDPView, as noted in Sect. 4, due to limitations like data-independent SS. For the generative approaches, PrivBayes and P3GM, improve with higher dimensions due to more training data but never outperform our approach (at best 10× bigger RMSE), as they are not optimized for tensors and OLAP range queries. Notably, they neglect the *measure* attribute created by aggregation (Sect. 3). To test performance further, we scaled the tests to higher dimensions using the Adult dataset, creating tensors from 7 to 14 dimensions, each with a workload of 3000 queries to assess view quality. Figure 4 (3rd plot) shows that our approach scales better and remains consistent compared to others. HDPView is a close competitor, but generative approaches, especially P3GM, also improve. P3GM benefited from (i) minimal aggregation in the 14-dimensional *Adult* tensor, reducing the effect of neglecting the *measure* attribute, and (ii) higher budget consumption, leading to less noise[8].

Spatial Data. Another important use case is publishing spatial data, where decomposition algorithms are commonly used. To highlight RIPOST's performance, we compared it on the Gowalla dataset with HDPView and PrivTree, generating 3000 queries to assess view quality.

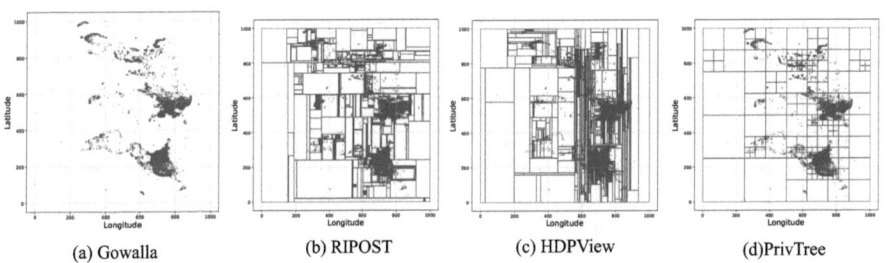

(a) Gowalla (b) RIPOST (c) HDPView (d) PrivTree

Fig. 5. Gowalla-2D Partitioning

Figure 5 shows the spatial decomposition of the Gowalla dataset by RIPOST, HDPView, and PrivTree. PrivTree generated the fewest blocks, converging early, supporting the critiques in Sect. 4, and resulting in an RMSE ×25 larger than ours. Comparing RIPOST to HDPView in Fig. 5, RIPOST detected larger empty blocks during the first partitioning phase and focused deeper partitioning on dense regions in the second phase. In contrast, HDPView applied more partitioning across a wider domain, incorrectly partitioning empty regions and mixing blocks, which affected its performance. Based on our test queries, HDPView had an RMSE 27% larger than RIPOST.

---

[8] A disclaimer: The model in [21] computes the privacy budget based on data size and training sample, making it difficult to tune ϵ for all tensors in our tests with minimal changes to the original setup. To ensure fairness, [21] was allocated a larger budget within the range [0.1, 1], depending on the tensor.

Workload Dependent Approaches. To compare RIPOST with HDMM, DAWA, and Identity, we used smaller tensors due to the high complexity of HDMM/DAWA and the memory requirements of Identity. We tested on the Adult dataset (*Small-Adult*) and the Jm dataset, increasing dimensions and creating 3000 test queries at each step.

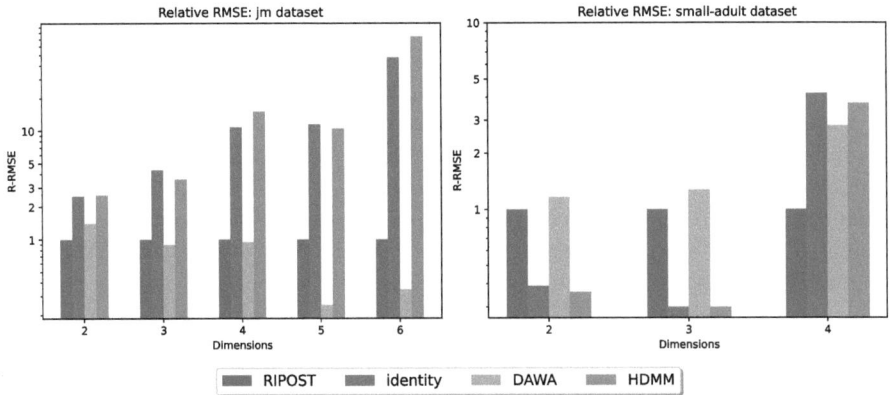

Fig. 6. R-RMSE results based on small-adult dataset.

Figure 6 show the R-RMSE results for the Small-Adult and Jm datasets. DAWA and HDMM struggle as dimensions/domain size increase due to suboptimal workload strategies. In contrast, RIPOST outperforms them in most tests. For Identity (in both plots), noise accumulates with increasing domain size and the RMSE grows.

Sensitivity analysis of hyperparameters We evaluate RIPOST by varying one hyperparameter at a time, using a 2D tensor from the *Adult* dataset and a random workload and measured the RMSE and the number of leaves (blocks).

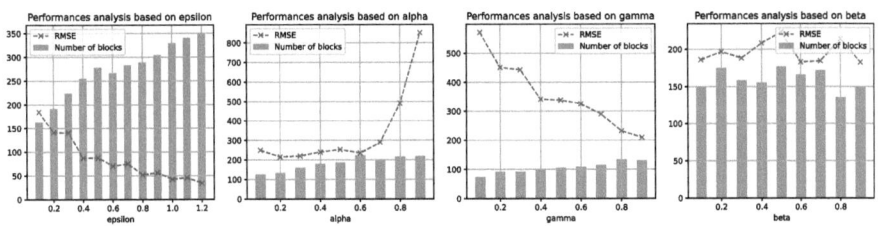

Fig. 7. Analysis of hyperparameters.

Privacy Budget. ϵ: We evaluated RIPOST with varying ϵ. Smaller ϵ strengthens privacy but increases noise. Figure 7 shows that as ϵ increases, RMSE decreases, and the number of blocks grows, with $Secure\_cc$ becoming more accurate. Perturbation error (PE) had minimal impact as noise in the leaf blocks becomes smaller also. **Parameter** α: In Algorithm 1, RIPOST uses α to allocate the privacy budget between leaf perturbation (ϵ_p) and decomposition (ϵ_d). A smaller α favors leaf perturbation. From Fig. 7 (second plot), we see that as α increases, more blocks are generated, but RMSE also rises due to higher perturbation error (PE). The best performance occurs when α is between 0.2 and 0.4, balancing decomposition accuracy and PE. **Parameter** γ: In Algorithm 1, RIPOST uses γ to allocate the decomposition budget between $Secure_{cc}$ and $Secure_{ss}$ for each phase. A smaller γ favors $Secure_{ss}$ over $Secure_{cc}$. From Fig. 7 (third plot), we see that RMSE decreases and the number of blocks increases as γ gets bigger, indicating that $Secure_{cc}$ in both phases plays important role to avoid *Early Convergence* issue. **Parameter** β: In Algorithm 1, RIPOST uses β to allocate the budget ϵ_d between the two decomposition phases: phase 1 (ϵ_1) and phase 2 (ϵ_2). A smaller β favors phase 2. From Fig. 7 (fourth plot), we see that RMSE and the number of blocks fluctuate with β, indicating that both phases are equally crucial for optimal performance. Highlighting the importance of phase 1, one of RIPOST's key features(Section 4).

7 Discussion

In this section, we discuss possible extensions to improve RIPOST. First, since $Secure_{cc}$ and $Secure_{ss}$ never consume their full budgets (Sect. 5.2), unused budget could be reallocated to ϵ_p to reduce perturbation error (PE). Second, applying $Secure_{cc}$ every k steps could similarly save budget for ϵ_p. Another improvement could be random sampling cutting points in Algorithm 3 (line 3) could enforce privacy, save budget [7], and speed up computation, though possibly at a cost to partition quality. Finally, while RIPOST uses the generated tree for faster queries, it could be extended to also boost query accuracy [3,27].

8 Conclusion

In this work, we addressed the challenge of releasing privacy-preserving view of multidimensional data using a domain decomposition-based method. We introduced RIPOST, which overcomes the limitations of previous solutions, particularly in data-aware splitting and independence from decomposition depth h. Through extensive experiments, we showed that RIPOST outperforms existing methods in terms of utility. These positive results motivate us to explore future extensions, particularly in tighter budget management and reducing computational costs.

A Proof Sensitivity of Metrics Used

For *Sum* (**and** *Min*): Since *Sum* (or *Min*) sum the count in each cell (counts the number of empty or nonempty cells), the change between two neighbouring tensors is at most 1, so $\Delta_{Sum} = 1$ ($\Delta_{Min} = 1$).

For AE: Consider tensors $\mathcal{T}$ and $\mathcal{T}'$. If c_l in $\mathcal{T}'$ changes by $+1$, the AE is computed as follows:

$$AE(T) = \sum_{c \in \Omega_D} |\bar{x} - c| \text{ and } \quad \bar{x} = \frac{Sum(T)}{|\Omega_D|},$$
$$AE(T') = \sum_{c \in \Omega_D, c \neq c_l} |\bar{x}' - c| + |\bar{x}' - c_l| \text{ and } \bar{x}' = \frac{Sum(T)+1}{|\Omega_D|}. \quad (4)$$

From Eq. 4, $AE(T') \leq \sum_{c \in \Omega_D} |\bar{x} - c| + 2 \times \frac{n-1}{n}$, leading to $\Delta_{AE} = |AE(T) - AE(T')| \leq 2 \times \frac{n-1}{n} \leq 2$.

B Proof of Privacy Accounting

To compute the privacy budget, we track consumption along one path from root $\mathcal{T}$ to a leaf, since each branch handles a distinct portion of $\mathcal{T}$ (Sect. 4), and deduce total consumption via parallel composition. Each leaf node comes from a branch through two decomposition phases (Algorithm 1). With k iterations in phase one and p in phase two, the algorithm perturbs the leaves before publishing. The total privacy budget is computed using sequential composition, accumulating the budget from each iteration.

So, to ensure that the budget consumption by the algorithm is in bound of the total budget ϵ given as input to Algorithm 1, means proving that for any given leaf block B_l this equation holds:

$$\frac{Pr[B_l|T]}{Pr[B_l|T']} \leq e^{\epsilon} \quad (5)$$

Let B_l^i be the i'th predecessor of B_l along the path from the root to B_l. According to Algorithm 1, for *Secure_cc* in the first phase, the budget consumption is:

$$\left| \prod_{i=1}^{k-1} \frac{Pr[Sum(B_l^i) + Lap(\lambda_i) > \theta_1]}{Pr[Sum(B_l'^i) + Lap(\lambda_i) > \theta_1]} \right| \times \frac{Pr[Sum(B_l^k) + Lap(\lambda_k) \leq \theta_1]}{Pr[Sum(B_l'^k) + Lap(\lambda_k) \leq \theta_1]}$$

For *Secure_ss* in the first phase:

$$\prod_{i=1}^{k} \frac{Pr[point_j|B_l^i, Min]}{Pr[point_j|B_l'^i, Min]}$$

In the second phase, for *Secure_cc*:

$$\left| \prod_{i=k}^{p-1} \frac{Pr[AE(B_l^i) + Lap(\lambda_i) > \theta_2]}{Pr[AE(B_l'^i) + Lap(\lambda_i) > \theta_2]} \right| \times \frac{Pr[AE(B_l^p) + Lap(\lambda_p) \leq \theta_2]}{Pr[AE(B_l'^p) + Lap(\lambda_p) \leq \theta_2]}$$

For *Secure_ss* in the second phase:

$$\prod_{i=k}^{p} \frac{Pr[point_i|B_l^i, AE]}{Pr[point_i|B_l'^i, AE]}$$

. Finally, Algorithm 1 perturbs the leaf mean:

$$\frac{Pr[mean(B_l) + Lap(\lambda) = S]}{Pr[mean(B'_l) + Lap(\lambda) = S]}$$

. Each operation (*Secure_cc* and *Secure_ss*) is allocated a dedicated budget for each phase of Algorithm 1 (lines 1-4).

Based on the budget distribution in Sect. 5.2 and the definitions in 4, 5, *Secure_cc* does not exceed ϵ_{cc}^1 and ϵ_{cc}^2, and *Secure_ss* does not exceed ϵ_{ss}^1 and ϵ_{ss}^2. By sequential composition:

$$\frac{Pr[B_l|T]}{Pr[B_l|T']} \leq e^{\epsilon_{cc}^1+\epsilon_{ss}^1+\epsilon_{cc}^2+\epsilon_{ss}^2+\epsilon_p} \leq e^{\epsilon}$$

This result shows that our algorithm respects the input privacy budget, regardless of the branch depth h during decomposition. By the *Parallel Composition* property of DP, this holds for all paths in the decomposition.

References

1. Abowd, J.M.: The us census bureau adopts differential privacy. In: Proceedings of the 24th ACM SIGKDD International Conference on Knowledge Discovery and Data Mining, pp. 2867–2867 (2018)
2. Acs, G., Melis, L., Castelluccia, C., De Cristofaro, E.: Differentially private mixture of generative neural networks. IEEE Trans. Knowl. Data Eng. **31**(6), 1109–1121 (2018)
3. Cormode, G., Procopiuc, C., Srivastava, D., Shen, E., Yu, T.: Differentially private spatial decompositions. In: 2012 IEEE 28th International Conference on Data Engineering, pp. 20–31. IEEE (2012)
4. Ding, B., Winslett, M., Han, J., Li, Z.: Differentially private data cubes: optimizing noise sources and consistency. In: Proceedings of the 2011 ACM SIGMOD International Conference on Management of Data, pp. 217–228 (2011)
5. Dwork, C.: Differential privacy. In: Automata, Languages and Programming: 33rd International Colloquium, ICALP 2006, Venice, Italy, July 10-14, 2006, Proceedings, Part II 33, pp. 1–12. Springer (2006)
6. Dwork, C., Roth, A., et al.: The algorithmic foundations of differential privacy. Found. Trends® Theor. Comput. Sci. **9**(3–4), 211–407 (2014)
7. Ebadi, H., Antignac, T., Sands, D.: Sampling and partitioning for differential privacy. In: 2016 14th Annual Conference on Privacy, Security and Trust (PST), pp. 664–673. IEEE (2016)
8. Fan, J., Liu, T., Li, G., Chen, J., Shen, Y., Du, X.: Relational data synthesis using generative adversarial networks: a design space exploration. arXiv preprint arXiv:2008.12763 (2020)
9. Harder, F., Adamczewski, K., Park, M.: DP-MERF: differentially private mean embeddings with random features for practical privacy-preserving data generation. In: International Conference on Artificial Intelligence And Statistics, pp. 1819–1827. PMLR (2021)
10. Inan, A., Kantarcioglu, M., Ghinita, G., Bertino, E.: Private record matching using differential privacy. In: Proceedings of the 13th International Conference on Extending Database Technology, pp. 123–134 (2010)

11. Jordon, J., Yoon, J., Van Der Schaar, M.: Pate-gan: generating synthetic data with differential privacy guarantees. In: International conference on learning representations (2019)
12. Kato, F., Takahashi, T., Takagi, S., Cao, Y., Liew, S.P., Yoshikawa, M.: Hdpview: differentially private materialized view for exploring high dimensional relational data. arXiv preprint arXiv:2203.06791 (2022)
13. Kotsogiannis, I., Tao, Y., He, X., Fanaeepour, M., Machanavajjhala, A., Hay, M., Miklau, G.: Privatesql: a differentially private SQL query engine. Proc. VLDB Endowment **12**(11), 1371–1384 (2019)
14. Kreačić, E., Nouri, N., Potluru, V.K., Balch, T., Veloso, M.: Differentially private synthetic data using kd-trees. In: Uncertainty in Artificial Intelligence, pp. 1143–1153. PMLR (2023)
15. Laouir, A.E., Imine, A.: Slim-view: sampling and private publishing of multidimensional databases. In: Proceedings of the Fourteenth ACM Conference on Data and Application Security and Privacy, pp. 391–402 (2024)
16. Li, C., Hay, M., Miklau, G., Wang, Y.: A data-and workload-aware algorithm for range queries under differential privacy. arXiv preprint arXiv:1410.0265 (2014)
17. Li, C., Miklau, G., Hay, M., McGregor, A., Rastogi, V.: The matrix mechanism: optimizing linear counting queries under differential privacy. VLDB J. **24**, 757–781 (2015)
18. McKenna, R., Miklau, G., Hay, M., Machanavajjhala, A.: Optimizing error of high-dimensional statistical queries under differential privacy. arXiv preprint arXiv:1808.03537 (2018)
19. Shaham, S., Ghinita, G., Ahuja, R., Krumm, J., Shahabi, C.: HTF: homogeneous tree framework for differentially private release of large geospatial datasets with self-tuning structure height. ACM Trans. Spatial Algor. Syst. **9**(4), 1–30 (2023)
20. Srivastava, G.C.C.P.D., Shen, E., Yu, T.: Differentially private spatial decompositions
21. Takagi, S., Takahashi, T., Cao, Y., Yoshikawa, M.: P3gm: private high-dimensional data release via privacy preserving phased generative model. In: 2021 IEEE 37th International Conference on Data Engineering (ICDE), pp. 169–180. IEEE (2021)
22. Team, A.: learning-with-privacy-at-scale. https://docs-assets.developer.apple.com/ml-research/papers/learning-with-privacy-at-scale.pdf
23. Wilson, R.J., Zhang, C.Y., Lam, W., Desfontaines, D., Simmons-Marengo, D., Gipson, B.: Differentially private SQL with bounded user contribution. Proc. Priv. Enhanc. Technol. **2020**(2), 230–250 (2020)
24. Xu, C., Ren, J., Zhang, Y., Qin, Z., Ren, K.: DPPro: differentially private high-dimensional data release via random projection. IEEE Trans. Inf. Forensics Secur. **12**(12), 3081–3093 (2017)
25. Zeidler, E., Hackbusch, W., Schwarz, H., Hunt, B.: Oxford Users' Guide to Mathematics. OUP Oxford (2004)
26. Zhang, J., Cormode, G., Procopiuc, C.M., Srivastava, D., Xiao, X.: Privbayes: private data release via Bayesian networks. ACM Trans. Database Syst. (TODS) **42**(4), 1–41 (2017)
27. Zhang, J., Xiao, X., Xie, X.: Privtree: a differentially private algorithm for hierarchical decompositions. In: Proceedings of the 2016 International Conference on Management of Data, pp. 155–170 (2016)
28. Zhang, X., Chen, R., Xu, J., Meng, X., Xie, Y.: Towards accurate histogram publication under differential privacy. In: Proceedings of the 2014 SIAM International Conference on Data Mining, pp. 587–595. SIAM (2014)
29. Zhang, Z., et al.: Privsyn: differentially private data synthesis (2021)

Correcting the Record on Leakage Abuse Attacks: Revisiting the Subgraph Attacks with Sound Evaluation

Takumi Namiki[✉], Takumi Amada, Mitsugu Iwamoto, and Yohei Watanabe

The University of Electro-Communications, Chofu, Japan
{T.Namiki,mitsugu,watanabe}@uec.ac.jp

Abstract. Searchable encryption (SE) enables efficient search over encrypted databases by allowing a predetermined amount of information leakage during operations. While this leakage is typically considered "inconsequential," its real-world impact on security remains unclear and must be carefully analyzed. *Leakage abuse attacks* aim to exploit such leakage to recover sensitive information, such as search queries or database contents. In this paper, we revisit one of the most powerful leakage abuse attacks to date, the **Subgraph** attack (NDSS 2020), and examine two critical aspects: its experimental evaluation methodology and its core algorithm.

Although empirical evaluation is essential for understanding the effectiveness of these attacks, we show that prior studies often rely on unrealistic experimental assumptions. We identify and analyze this issue and present a *sound* and realistic evaluation framework for the **Subgraph** attack. Our results show that its previously reported effectiveness was indeed overestimated. In addition, we propose two improved variants of the **Subgraph** attacks, **Subgraph+**^{ID} and **SimGraph**^{VL}, that exploit allowable leakage commonly considered acceptable in the SE literature. Under our sound experimental setting, these improved attacks achieve up to twice the query recovery performance of the original **Subgraph** attacks.

Keywords: Searchable symmetric encryption · Leakage abuse attacks · Sound evaluation

1 Introduction

In recent years, the widespread adoption of cloud computing has led to the emergence of numerous online services, including cloud-based storage platforms. These services typically operate in a client-server model, where a client outsources their data to a remote server and interacts with it through queries. In such systems, clients often require the ability to search over their stored data at

---

Y. Watanabe—A part of this work was done when the author was also at National Institute of Communications Technology, Japan.

any time. The outsourced data is generally managed on the server as a structured database.

Searchable encryption (SE) [4,18] enables keyword search over encrypted data in the client-server model while preserving confidentiality against the server. A distinguishing feature of SE is that it permits the controlled exposure of limited information, referred to as *leakage*, during search operations to enable efficient search procedures.[1] The security of SE ensures that no information about the queried keywords or the underlying database contents is revealed beyond the leakage profile, which is determined by the scheme's design. However, it remains unclear to what extent the information revealed by the leakage profile can be considered harmless, and such leakage may be exploited by adversaries to infer sensitive information about the queries or the stored data. Therefore, it is crucial not only to design secure and efficient SE schemes but also to analyze the practical impact of the allowable leakage.

1.1 Leakage Abuse Attacks

A growing line of research, known as *leakage abuse attacks* and initiated by Islam et al. [8], investigates the practical impact of leakage by constructing concrete attacks that aim to recover queried keywords or even plaintext data from the observed leakage. Leakage abuse attacks can be classified into several categories, primarily based on the attack type, target, and the availability or nature of auxiliary data.

– **Attack types.** *Passive attacks* do not require the adversary to influence or control any part of the client's data. In contrast, *active attacks*, also known as file-injection attacks [21,22], allow the adversary to inject or select specific documents to be included in the dataset. As in most prior works (e.g., [2,3,8]), this paper focuses on passive attacks.
– **Targets.** *Query recovery attacks* aim to recover the search keywords w from queries q issued by the client during the search procedure, whereas *data recovery attacks* attempt to reconstruct information about the document collection stored in the encrypted database. A large body of prior work has focused on query recovery attacks [2–7,9,12,15,16], and this paper follows the same direction. In contrast, LEAP [14] and VAL [11] are examples of attacks that aim data recovery in addition to query recovery.
– **Auxiliary data.** *Sampled-data attacks* assume access to a sample drawn from a distribution that is sufficiently close to that of the actual document collection. *Known-data attacks* and *known-query attacks*, on the other hand, require knowledge of a fraction δ of the document collection or the query set, respectively. Although sample-data attacks [5,6,8,9,12,13,15,16,20] are arguably more realistic in practice, this paper focuses on known-data

---

[1] As in previous works (e.g., [2,3,8]), this paper focuses on *non-dynamic* SE schemes. In contrast, *dynamic* SE schemes [10], which support updates to encrypted databases, have become an active area of research, but are beyond the scope of this work.

attacks [2,3,8,11,14,20], which remain the dominant setting in leakage abuse attack research.

In summary, this work aims to improve the performance of query recovery attacks conducted by passive adversaries who possess a fraction of the document collection i.e., known-data. In particular, we focus on understanding the practical impact of the *minimal reasonable leakage* in SE. Specifically, we investigate the extent to which *access patterns* and *volume patterns*, commonly considered acceptable forms of leakage in the SE literature, can be exploited to recover search queries using as small a fraction of the document collection as possible.

Although the seminal work by Islam et al. [8], known as the IKK attack, requires the adversary to know nearly the entire document collection to successfully recover queries, the Subgraph attacks [2], the state-of-the-art known-data attacks exploiting access and volume patterns, demonstrated that as little as 5% of known data can be sufficient to recover search queries.

Research Question. Did the Subgraph attacks provide a complete understanding of the practical impact of access and volume patterns in the known-data attack setting? We argue that there is still room for refinement, as existing known-data attacks, such as the IKK [8], Count [3], and Subgraph [2] attacks, have implicitly or explicitly relied on certain unrealistic assumptions in their experimental evaluations. In particular, these works assume that the adversary knows a subset of the keyword universe from which queries are drawn, although it is difficult to justify this assumption in practical scenarios (we provide a detailed discussion in Sect. 4). Relying on such additional information narrows the search space for candidate keywords, potentially leading to an artificially increased query recovery rate. Indeed, in a similar context, some prior works [5,11] raised concerns about how experimental evaluations should be conducted in the practical setting and have made efforts to address them, although their focus differs from the issues addressed in this paper.

This paper addresses two key research questions: (1) To what extent can *minimal reasonable leakage*, such as access and volume patterns, be exploited to recover search queries without relying on the aforementioned unrealistic assumption? (2) Can we design new leakage abuse attacks that exploit access or volume patterns and outperform existing known-data attacks, including the Subgraph attacks, under the same experimental conditions?

1.2 Our Contributions

In this paper, we revisit the practical effectiveness of known-data attacks against SE that exploit *minimal reasonable leakage*, specifically, *access patterns* and *volume patterns*, without relying on unrealistic assumptions often made in prior work.

Our contributions are summarized as follows:

- **More Realistic Evaluation of the Subgraph Attacks:** In Sect. 4, we identify the aforementioned limitations in the experimental methodologies of

Table 1. Comparison of query recovery rates with high selectivity among the Subgraph^{ID}, Subgraph^{VL}, and our attacks, Subgraph+^{ID}, SimGraph^{ID}, and SimGraph^{VL}. SimGraph^{ID} is a the access-pattern-based variant of SimGraph^{VL}.

	The auxiliary data rate δ										
	5%	10%	20%	30%	40%	50%	60%	70%	80%	90%	100%
Subgraph^{ID} [2] (Reevaluated in Sect. 4)	29%	35%	36%	49%	41%	49%	51%	55%	54%	51%	98%
Subgraph+^{ID} (Sect. 5.1)	59%	76%	90%	95%	96%	98%	98%	99%	99%	99%	98%
SimGraph^{ID} (App. C)	59%	76%	90%	95%	96%	98%	98%	99%	99%	99%	98%
Subgraph^{VL} [2] (Reevaluated in Sect. 4)	26%	33%	36%	49%	41%	49%	51%	55%	54%	51%	98%
SimGraph^{VL} (Sect. 5.2)	57%	74%	90%	95%	96%	98%	98%	99%	99%	99%	98%

existing attacks, including Subgraph, and demonstrate through experiments that the unrealistic assumption artificially increases the query recovery rates by the Subgraph attacks.
- **Designs of New Attacks:** In Sect. 5, we propose two leakage abuse attacks. The first one, Subgraph+^{ID}, is a new access-pattern-based attack that eliminates false negatives by avoiding the exclusion heuristic used in Subgraph^{ID}, which is a variant of the Subgraph attacks exploiting the access patterns. The second one, SimGraph^{VL}, is a volume-pattern-based attack that builds on the structure of Subgraph^{VL}, the variant of the Subgraph attack exploiting the volume patterns, but introduces a similarity-based matching strategy. This strategy ranks keywords based on their structural similarity to the query and more effectively leverages volume information, resulting in significant improvements in query recovery rates.
- **Performance Evaluation of Our Attacks:** In Sect. 6, we implemented all attacks in Rust and conducted experiments on the Enron dataset [19]. Our results demonstrate that Subgraph+^{ID} and SimGraph^{VL} significantly outperform their respective baselines without relying on the aforementioned unrealistic assumptions, achieving up to twice the query recovery rate, particularly in high-selectivity settings, where *selectivity*, introduced by Blackstone et al. [2], refers to the number of documents associated with a particular query. We summarize the performance comparison among the Subgraph and our attacks in Table 1.

2 Searchable Encryption

2.1 Notations

Although we define the basic notations used in this paper below, additional notations will be introduced at appropriate points as needed. For readability, a summary of all the main notations in the context of leakage abuse attacks is provided in Appendix A.

General Notations. Given a positive integer n, let $[n] := \{1, 2, \ldots, n\}$. We write the cardinality of a finite set $\mathcal{X}$ as $\#\mathcal{X}$. $f(\mathcal{A})$ denotes the image under a function $f\colon \mathcal{X} \to \mathcal{Y}$ of a subset $\mathcal{A}$ of $\mathcal{X}$. We denote a multiset and its multiplicity function by $\{\!\!\{\cdot\}\!\!\}$ and m, respectively. For instance, for a multiset $\mathcal{X} = \{\!\!\{a, a, b\}\!\!\}$, we have $\mathsf{m}_{\mathcal{X}}(a) = 2$ and $\mathsf{m}_{\mathcal{X}}(b) = 1$. Throughout the paper, we denote by κ a security parameter.

Keywords and Queries. Let $\mathbb{W} := \{w_1, w_2, \ldots, w_m\}$ be the keyword universe. We denote a search query for a keyword w_j by $q_{j'}$, and let $\mathbb{Q}$ be a query set corresponding to a set of searched keywords, which is a subset of $\mathbb{W}$. Note that it also does not necessarily hold $j = j'$ for a keyword w_j and its corresponding search query $q_{j'}$.

Documents. $\mathbb{D} := \{\mathrm{D}_1, \mathrm{D}_2, \ldots, \mathrm{D}_n\}$ is a set of documents over $\mathbb{W}$, and $\mathbb{ED} := \{\mathrm{ED}_1, \mathrm{ED}_2, \ldots, \mathrm{ED}_n\}$ is a set of encrypted documents of them, where those indices do not correspond one-to-one; that is, the encrypted version of D_i is not necessarily ED_i. For convenience, we often represent each document $\mathrm{D} \in \mathbb{D}$ as the set of keywords it contains, rather than as the document itself. Therefore, it holds $\mathrm{D} \subseteq \mathbb{W}$ in such a case. In practice, this can be achieved using stemming algorithms, such as Porter's stemmer [17].

Identifier. We suppose that each document $\mathrm{D} \in \mathbb{D}$ has its own identifier $\mathbf{id}(\mathrm{D})$, where $\mathbf{id}$ is a function $\mathbf{id}\colon \mathbb{D} \to [n]$. In particular, we denote D by D_i when $\mathbf{id}(\mathrm{D}) = i$ for the notational convenience. For $\mathbb{D} = \{\mathrm{D}_1, \mathrm{D}_2, \ldots, \mathrm{D}_n\}$, we define a set $\mathbf{id}(\mathbb{D}) := \{\mathbf{id}(\mathrm{D}_1), \mathbf{id}(\mathrm{D}_2), \ldots, \mathbf{id}(\mathrm{D}_n)\}$. A set of documents that contain a keyword $w \in \mathbb{W}$ is denoted by $\mathbf{D}(w)$.

Volume. Although D is sometimes represented as a set of keywords, $|\mathrm{D}|$ refers to the byte length, i.e., the *volume*, of a document D itself, not the cardinality of the keyword set. For $\mathbb{D} = \{\mathrm{D}_1, \mathrm{D}_2, \ldots, \mathrm{D}_n\}$, we define a *multiset* $|\mathbb{D}| := \{\!\!\{|\mathrm{D}_1|, |\mathrm{D}_2|, \ldots, |\mathrm{D}_n|\}\!\!\}$, since $|\mathrm{D}_i| = |\mathrm{D}_j|$ might hold for $\mathrm{D}_i, \mathrm{D}_j \in \mathbb{D}$ such that $\mathrm{D}_i \neq \mathrm{D}_j$.

2.2 Syntax

As in most previous works [2,3,8], in this work, we focus on non-dynamic searchable encryption (SE) [4], which does not support secure dynamic updates of the database. SE consists of three probabilistic polynomial-time algorithms, Setup, QueryGen, and Search. Setup takes a security parameter κ and a set of documents $\mathbb{D}$ as input, and outputs a secret key k for a client and an encrypted database EDB for a server. QueryGen takes the secret key k and a keyword w as input and outputs a search query q. Search takes a search query q for a keyword $w \in \mathbb{W}$ and the encrypted database EDB as input and outputs a search result $\mathcal{X}(q)$ and an updated encrypted database EDB'. The correctness ensures that the search result $\mathcal{X}(q)$ exactly contains identifiers of documents that include the keyword w, i.e., it holds $\mathcal{X}(q) = \mathbf{id}(\mathbf{D}(w))$.

2.3 Leakage Profiles

SE allows a predefined amount of leakage during operations in order to enable efficient search over encrypted databases. Specifically, it guarantees that no information is revealed beyond the scheme's pre-defined leakage patterns associated with the scheme. In general, the more leakage a scheme permits, the more efficiently it can support search operations. On the other hand, such leakage may introduce vulnerabilities unless it is truly "inconsequential." As such, designing SE schemes that achieve a favorable trade-off between efficiency and leakage is a central research challenge. At the same time, research on leakage abuse attacks plays a crucial role in updating our understanding of which types of leakage can be considered safe.

The set of leakage patterns permitted by an SE scheme is referred to as its leakage profile. Cash et al. [3] introduced a classification of leakage profiles into four levels, L1 through L4, where L1 corresponds to the minimal leakage and L4 to the highest level of leakage. We focus on two specific leakage patterns, *access patterns* and *volume patterns*, which are included in the L1 leakage.

Access Patterns. Roughly speaking, the *access pattern* for a keyword w refers to the set of document identifiers returned in response to a search for w, i.e., the identifiers of documents that contain the keyword w. Formally, the access pattern is the function family $\mathsf{AP} := \{\mathsf{AP}_t\}_{t \in \mathbb{N}}$ with $\mathsf{AP}_t : (2^{\mathbb{W}})^n \times \mathbb{W}^t \to (2^{[n]})^t$ such that

$$\mathsf{AP}_t(\mathbb{D}, \boldsymbol{w}_t) := \Big(\mathsf{id}(\mathbf{D}(w_1)), \ldots, \mathsf{id}(\mathbf{D}(w_t))\Big) = \Big(\mathcal{X}(q_1), \ldots, \mathcal{X}(q_t)\Big),$$

where $\boldsymbol{w}_t := (w_1, \ldots, w_t)$ and $q_1, \ldots, q_t$ are queries corresponding to $w_1, \ldots, w_t$, and we assume the correctness holds.

Volume Patterns. Roughly speaking, the *volume pattern* for a keyword w refers to the multiset of volumes (i.e., byte lengths) of the document identifiers returned in response to a search for w. Formally, the volume pattern is the function family $\mathsf{VP} := \{\mathsf{VP}_t\}_{t \in \mathbb{N}}$ with $\mathsf{VP}_t : (2^{\mathbb{W}})^n \times \mathbb{W}^t \to \mathbb{N}^t$ such that

$$\mathsf{VP}_t(\mathbb{D}, \boldsymbol{w}_t) := \Big(\{\!|D|\!\}_{D \in \mathbf{D}(w_1)}, \ldots, \{\!|D|\!\}_{D \in \mathbf{D}(w_t)}\Big) = \Big(|\mathcal{X}(q_1)|, \ldots, |\mathcal{X}(q_t)|\Big),$$

where $q_1, \ldots, q_t$ are queries corresponding to $w_1, \ldots, w_t$, and $|\mathcal{X}(q)|$ is a multiset of the volumes of documents corresponding to the search result $\mathcal{X}(q)$, i.e., $|\mathcal{X}(q)| := \{\!|D|\!\}_{\mathsf{id}(D) \in \mathcal{X}(q)} = \{\!|D|\!\}_{D \in \mathbf{D}(w)}$. Note that we assume the correctness holds.

Clearly, volume patterns can be derived from access patterns, assuming that an encrypted document ED reveals the length of the corresponding document D. Therefore, volume patterns inherently leak less information than access patterns.

3 Leakage Abuse Attacks

In this section, we define the adversarial model considered in this paper and describe the original Subgraph attacks [2], which serve as the main target of our analysis.

3.1 Adversarial Model

An adversary in SE schemes is typically modeled as an honest-but-curious server that correctly follows the SE protocol but passively observes its execution in an attempt to carry out *query recovery attacks* [2,3,8,9,15,16].[2] In this setting, the passive adversary observes all queries and obtains the corresponding leakage patterns, which it then uses to infer the keywords associated with those queries.

To enable such inference, as in prior works [2,3,8,11,14,20], we assume that the adversary possesses a *fraction of the client's ground-truth data* as auxiliary information. This auxiliary knowledge may arise, for example, from a security breach during the setup phase of the protocol, or from the adversary's prior knowledge of publicly available data, such as widely distributed emails, that are stored in the encrypted database. While this assumption enables practical attacks in experimental settings, it may be unrealistic in real-world scenarios. Therefore, the fraction δ of ground-truth data required for a successful attack should be minimized as much as possible.

In summary, we consider query recovery attacks carried out by a passive adversary who is assumed to possess the following information:

- *Leakage*: Leakage profiles obtained by observing all of t search queries $q_1, q_2, \ldots, q_t \in \mathbb{Q}$. Depending on the specific attack, this may leak access patterns AP_t or volume patterns VP_t.
- *Auxiliary data*: A fraction δ of the document collection $\mathbb{D}$, where δ is referred to as the *known-data rate*. Specifically, the auxiliary data is a subset of the document set $\widetilde{\mathbb{D}} \subseteq \mathbb{D}$ with the known-data rate δ, where $\delta := \#\widetilde{\mathbb{D}}/\#\mathbb{D}$. Note that the known-data set $\widetilde{\mathbb{D}}$ implies a known-keyword set $\widetilde{\mathbb{W}} := \bigcup_{\widetilde{D} \in \widetilde{\mathbb{D}}} \widetilde{D}$.

Then, the adversary outputs an inference result $C(q) \subseteq \widetilde{\mathbb{W}}$ for each query $q \in \mathbb{Q}$ as an inference result. That is, the adversary attempts to infer the original keyword $w \in \widetilde{\mathbb{W}}$ from which the query $q \in \mathbb{Q}$ was generated, and outputs $C(q) \subseteq \widetilde{\mathbb{W}}$ as a candidate set. We say the adversary succeeds in recovering the query q if and only if $C(q) = \{w\}$, where q is generated from w by QueryGen. Note that the inference result $C(q)$ is restricted to the *known-keyword set* $\widetilde{\mathbb{W}}$, rather than the keyword universe $\mathbb{W}$.

3.2 The Subgraph Attacks

The Subgraph attacks proposed by Blackstone et al. [2] are one of the most effective leakage abuse attacks using standard leakage profiles such as L1 leakage. The Subgraph attacks can be classified into two types depending on the available leakage patterns; the one that employs the access patterns is called Subgraph^{ID}, and the other that employs the volume patterns is called Subgraph^{VL}. In this section, we provide an overview of the Subgraph attacks, which form the basis of the attacks proposed in Sects. 5.1 and 5.2.

---

[2] Several related works [11,14] focus on *data recovery attacks*, which aim to reconstruct the contents of encrypted documents.

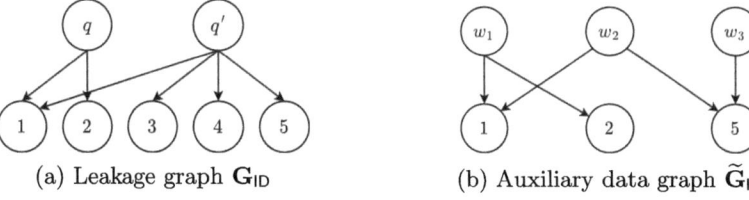

(a) Leakage graph $\mathbf{G}_{\mathsf{ID}}$ (b) Auxiliary data graph $\widetilde{\mathbf{G}}_{\mathsf{ID}}$

Fig. 1. An illustrative example of Leakage and auxilirary data graphs for $\mathsf{Subgraph}^{\mathsf{ID}}$, where d $\mathbb{D} = \{D_1, D_2, \ldots, D_5\}$ and $\widetilde{\mathbb{D}} = \{D_1, D_2, D_5\}$. The leakage graph $\mathbf{G}_{\mathsf{ID}}$ is constructed from q and q', where $\mathcal{X}(q) = \{1, 2\}$ and $\mathcal{X}(q') = \{1, 3, 4, 5\}$, and the auxiliary data graph $\widetilde{\mathbf{G}}_{\mathsf{ID}}$ is constructed from $\mathbf{id}(D_1) = \{w_1, w_2\}$, $\mathbf{id}(D_2) = \{w_1\}$, and $\mathbf{id}(D_5) = \{w_2, w_3\}$.

Crucial Tool: Bipartite Graph. The Subgraph attacks fundamentally rely on the use of *bipartite graphs*. A bipartite graph $\mathbf{G} = ((\mathcal{S}, \mathcal{D}), \mathcal{E})$ consists of two disjoint and independent vertex sets $\mathcal{S}$ and $\mathcal{D}$, and an edge set $\mathcal{E}$, where each edge in $\mathcal{E}$ connects a vertex in $\mathcal{S}$ to a vertex in $\mathcal{D}$; that is, $\mathcal{E} := \{(s_i, d_i)\}_i \subseteq \mathcal{S} \times \mathcal{D}$. We define the set of neighbors of a vertex $s \in \mathcal{S}$ by the function $N_{\mathbf{G}} : \mathcal{S} \to 2^{\mathcal{D}}$, where $N_{\mathbf{G}}(s) = \{d \in \mathcal{D} \mid (s, d) \in \mathcal{E}\}$. For a weighted bipartite graph $\mathbf{G}$, the weight of an edge $(s, d) \in \mathcal{E}$ is denoted by $W_{\mathbf{G}}(s, d)$, where the weight function is given by $W_{\mathbf{G}} : \mathcal{E} \to \mathbb{N}$.

The Subgraph attacks construct two bipartite graphs: the so-called *leakage graph* $\mathbf{G} = ((\mathbb{Q}, \mathcal{L}_{\mathsf{LP}}(\mathbb{D})), \mathcal{E}_{\mathsf{LP}})$ and the *auxiliary data graph* $\widetilde{\mathbf{G}} = ((\widetilde{\mathbb{W}}, \mathcal{L}_{\mathsf{LP}}(\widetilde{\mathbb{D}})), \widetilde{\mathcal{E}}_{\mathsf{LP}})$, where $\mathcal{L}_{\mathsf{LP}}$ denotes a function determined by the leakage patterns $\mathsf{LP} \in \{\mathsf{AP}, \mathsf{VP}\}$, and the edge sets $\mathcal{E}_{\mathsf{LP}}$ and $\widetilde{\mathcal{E}}_{\mathsf{LP}}$ are defined based on the corresponding leakage. The precise definitions of $\mathcal{L}_{\mathsf{LP}}$, $\mathcal{E}_{\mathsf{LP}}$, and $\widetilde{\mathcal{E}}_{\mathsf{LP}}$ are given below.

- The $\mathsf{Subgraph}^{\mathsf{ID}}$ attack exploits the access patterns $\mathsf{AP}_t(\mathbb{D}, w_1, \ldots, w_t) = (\mathcal{X}(q_i))_{i=1}^t$ to create the following two bipartite graphs.
  - Leakage graph $\mathbf{G}_{\mathsf{ID}} = ((\mathbb{Q}, \mathcal{L}_{\mathsf{AP}}(\mathbb{D})), \mathcal{E}_{\mathsf{AP}})$, where $\mathcal{L}_{\mathsf{AP}}(\mathbb{D}) := \mathbf{id}(\mathbb{D})$ and $\mathcal{E}_{\mathsf{AP}} := \{(q, i) \in \mathbb{Q} \times \mathbf{id}(\mathbb{D}) \mid q \in \mathbb{Q} \wedge i \in \mathcal{X}(q)\}$. That is, $\mathbf{G}_{\mathsf{ID}}$ is constructed to satisfy $N_{\mathbf{G}_{\mathsf{ID}}}(q) = \mathcal{X}(q)$ for every query $q \in \mathbb{Q}$.
  - Auxiliary data graph $\widetilde{\mathbf{G}}_{\mathsf{ID}} = ((\widetilde{\mathbb{W}}, \mathcal{L}_{\mathsf{AP}}(\widetilde{\mathbb{D}})), \widetilde{\mathcal{E}}_{\mathsf{AP}})$, where $\mathcal{L}_{\mathsf{AP}}(\widetilde{\mathbb{D}}) := \mathbf{id}(\widetilde{\mathbb{D}})$ and $\widetilde{\mathcal{E}}_{\mathsf{AP}} := \{(w, i) \in \widetilde{\mathbb{W}} \times \mathbf{id}(\widetilde{\mathbb{D}}) \mid \widetilde{D}_i \in \widetilde{\mathbb{D}} \wedge w \in \widetilde{D}_i\}$, where $\widetilde{\mathbf{D}}(w)$ is a set of *known* documents that contain a keyword $w \in \widetilde{\mathbb{W}}$, i.e., $\widetilde{\mathbf{D}}(w) := \{\mathbf{id}(D) \in \mathbf{id}(\widetilde{\mathbb{D}}) \mid D \in \widetilde{\mathbb{D}} \wedge w \in D\}$. That is, $\widetilde{\mathbf{G}}_{\mathsf{ID}}$ is constructed to satisfy $N_{\widetilde{\mathbf{G}}_{\mathsf{ID}}}(w) = \mathbf{id}(\widetilde{\mathbf{D}}(w))$ for every keyword $w \in \widetilde{\mathbb{W}}$.

  We provide an illustrative example of $(\mathbf{G}_{\mathsf{ID}}, \widetilde{\mathbf{G}}_{\mathsf{ID}})$ for $n = 5$, $t = 2$, and $\delta = 0.6$ in Fig. 1.

- The $\mathsf{Subgraph}^{\mathsf{VL}}$ attack exploits the volume patterns $\mathsf{VP}_t(\mathbb{D}, w_1, \ldots, w_t) = (|\mathcal{X}(q_i)|)_{i=1}^t$ to create, unlike the above attack, the following two *weighted* bipartite graphs.

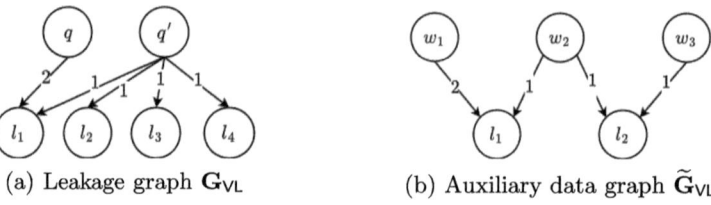

(a) Leakage graph $\mathbf{G}_{\mathsf{VL}}$ (b) Auxiliary data graph $\widetilde{\mathbf{G}}_{\mathsf{VL}}$

Fig. 2. An illustrative example of Leakage and auxilirary data graphs for Subgraph^{VL}, where $\mathbb{D} = \{D_1, D_2, \ldots, D_5\}$ and $\widetilde{\mathbb{D}} = \{D_1, D_2, D_5\}$ such that $l_1 := |D_1| = |D_2|$ and $l_i := |D_{i+1}|$ for $i = 2, 3, 4$. The leakage graph $\mathbf{G}_{\mathsf{VL}}$ is constructed from q and q', where $|\mathcal{X}(q)| = \{l_1, l_1\}$ and $|\mathcal{X}(q')| = \{l_1, l_2, l_3, l_4\}$. The auxiliary data graph $\widetilde{\mathbf{G}}_{\mathsf{VL}}$ is constructed from $\mathbf{id}(D_1) = \{w_1, w_2\}$, $\mathbf{id}(D_2) = \{w_1\}$, and $\mathbf{id}(D_5) = \{w_2, w_3\}$, where $l_1 := |D_1| = |D_2|$ and $l_2 := |D_3|$.

- Leakage graph $\mathbf{G}_{\mathsf{VL}} = ((\mathbb{Q}, \mathcal{L}_{\mathsf{VP}}(\mathbb{D})), \mathcal{E}_{\mathsf{VP}})$, where $\mathcal{L}_{\mathsf{VP}}(\mathbb{D}) := |\mathbb{D}|$ and $\mathcal{E}_{\mathsf{VP}} := \{(q, \mathsf{vol}) \in \mathbb{Q} \times |\mathbb{D}| \mid q \in \mathbb{Q} \wedge \mathsf{vol} \in |\mathcal{X}(q)|\}$. Since $|\mathcal{X}(q)|$ is a multiset representing the byte lengths of the documents matched by query q, i.e., it may contain duplicate elements, we introduce a weight function $W_{\mathbf{G}_{\mathsf{VL}}}$ to represent the multiplicity of each edge in the graph. $W_{\mathbf{G}_{\mathsf{VL}}}$ satisfies $W_{\mathbf{G}_{\mathsf{VL}}}(q, \mathsf{vol}) = \mathsf{m}_{|\mathcal{X}(q)|}(\mathsf{vol})$ for each edge $(q, \mathsf{vol}) \in \mathcal{E}_{\mathsf{VP}}$. Therefore, $\mathbf{G}_{\mathsf{VL}}$ is constructed to satisfy $N_{\mathbf{G}_{\mathsf{VL}}}(q) = \{|D|\}_{\mathbf{id}(D) \in \mathcal{X}(q)}$ (rather than $|\mathcal{X}(q)| = \{|D|\}_{\mathbf{id}(D) \in \mathcal{X}(q)}$) and $W_{\mathbf{G}_{\mathsf{VL}}}(q, \mathsf{vol}) = \mathsf{m}_{|\mathcal{X}(q)|}(\mathsf{vol})$ for every query $q \in \mathbb{Q}$.
- Auxiliary data graph $\widetilde{\mathbf{G}}_{\mathsf{VL}} = ((\widetilde{W}, \mathcal{L}_{\mathsf{VP}}(\widetilde{\mathbb{D}})), \widetilde{\mathcal{E}}_{\mathsf{VP}})$, where $\mathcal{L}_{\mathsf{VP}}(\widetilde{\mathbb{D}}) := |\widetilde{\mathbb{D}}|$ and $\widetilde{\mathcal{E}}_{\mathsf{VP}} := \{(w, |\widetilde{D}|) \in \widetilde{W} \times |\widetilde{\mathbb{D}}| \mid \widetilde{D} \in \widetilde{\mathbb{D}} \wedge w \in \widetilde{D}\}$. Let $W_{\widetilde{\mathbf{G}}_{\mathsf{VL}}}$ be a weight function for $\widetilde{\mathbf{G}}_{\mathsf{VL}}$, and it meets $W_{\widetilde{\mathbf{G}}_{\mathsf{VL}}}(w, \mathsf{vol}) = \mathsf{m}_{|\widetilde{\mathbf{D}}(w)|}(\mathsf{vol})$ for each edge $(w, \mathsf{vol}) \in \widetilde{\mathcal{E}}_{\mathsf{VP}}$, where $|\widetilde{\mathbf{D}}(w)| := \{|D|\}_{D \in \widetilde{\mathbf{D}}(w)}$. Therefore, $\widetilde{\mathbf{G}}_{\mathsf{VL}}$ is constructed to satisfy $N_{\widetilde{\mathbf{G}}_{\mathsf{VL}}}(w) = \{|D|\}_{D \in \widetilde{\mathbf{D}}(w)}$ (rather than $|\widetilde{\mathbf{D}}(w)|$) and $W_{\widetilde{\mathbf{G}}_{\mathsf{VL}}}(w, \mathsf{vol}) = \mathsf{m}_{|\widetilde{\mathbf{D}}(w)|}(\mathsf{vol})$ for every keyword $w \in \widetilde{W}$.

We provide an illustrative example of $(\mathbf{G}_{\mathsf{VL}}, \widetilde{\mathbf{G}}_{\mathsf{VL}})$ for $n = 5$, $t = 2$, and $\delta = 0.6$ in Fig. 2. Note that the settings between Figs. 1 and 2 are identical, except for the allowable leakage patterns.

The Overview of Attacks. Subgraph^{ID} and Subgraph^{VL} are essentially the same algorithms, differing only in their inputs: the former takes $(\mathbf{G}_{\mathsf{ID}}, \widetilde{\mathbf{G}}_{\mathsf{ID}})$ as input, while the latter takes $(\mathbf{G}_{\mathsf{VL}}, \widetilde{\mathbf{G}}_{\mathsf{VL}})$. Therefore, we here describe the overview of Subgraph^{ID}.

Subgraph^{ID}, which takes two bipartite graphs $(\mathbf{G}_{\mathsf{ID}}, \widetilde{\mathbf{G}}_{\mathsf{ID}})$ as input, narrows down candidate keywords $w \in \widetilde{W}$ that satisfy certain conditions and outputs candidate sets $C(q) \subseteq \widetilde{W}$ for each query $q \in \mathbb{Q}$. Setting appropriate "conditions" for narrowing down candidates is the most crucial aspect of designing the algorithm. Specifically, for each query $q \in \mathbb{Q}$, the algorithm computes a keyword set $F(q) \subseteq \widetilde{\mathbb{W}}$, where each keyword $w \in F(q)$ satisfies $N_{\widetilde{\mathbf{G}}_{\mathsf{ID}}}(w) \subseteq N_{\mathbf{G}_{\mathsf{ID}}}(q)$.[3] Since the algorithm possesses auxiliary data $\widetilde{\mathbb{D}}$, which constitutes a fraction δ of the entire document collection $\mathbb{D}$, it is natural to expect that, if a keyword $w \in F(q)$ corresponds to a query q, then the number of known documents containing w, denoted by $\#N_{\widetilde{\mathbf{G}}_{\mathsf{ID}}}(w)$, is approximately a fraction δ of the total number of documents returned by the search for q, that is, approximately $\delta \cdot \#N_{\mathbf{G}_{\mathsf{ID}}}(q)$. Following this idea, the algorithm selects keywords $w \in F(q)$ that satisfy $\#N_{\widetilde{\mathbf{G}}_{\mathsf{ID}}}(w) \geq \delta \cdot \#N_{\mathbf{G}_{\mathsf{ID}}}(q)$ and defines the selected keyword set as $C(q)$.

Subsequently, it applies refinement techniques such as *cross filtering*[4] and *eliminating duplication* to further narrow down the candidate keywords and update $C(q)$, although we omit the details of these techniques. The final set $C(q)$ obtained through this process is output as the inference result.

4 Towards Sound Evaluation of Leakage Abuse Attacks

In this section, we present experimental results for the Subgraph attacks under more practical settings.

4.1 Unrealistic Assumptions in Existing Attacks

In experiments evaluating the effectiveness of known-data attacks, it is often assumed that all queries $\mathbb{Q}$ are generated from the set of *known keywords* $\widetilde{\mathbb{W}}$, rather than from the entire keyword universe $\mathbb{W}$. This assumption is fairly reasonable, since known-data attacks only allow the adversary to recover queries associated with keywords that appear in their auxiliary data $\widetilde{\mathbb{D}}$. Thus, such experiments appropriately demonstrate the effectiveness of the attack on queries corresponding to known keywords.

In contrast, Blackstone et al. [2], in addition to assuming that the adversary possesses auxiliary data $\widetilde{\mathbb{D}}$, also assumed that the adversary knows the universe of keywords from which queries are selected. Specifically, instead of considering the entire known-keyword space $\widetilde{\mathbb{W}}$, from which queries are actually drawn, they introduced a smaller subset $\widetilde{\mathbb{W}}^\star \subseteq \widetilde{\mathbb{W}}$ and generated all experimental queries from $\widetilde{\mathbb{W}}^\star$. Moreover, they assumed that the adversary knows both the existence of $\widetilde{\mathbb{W}}^\star$ and its contents, even though *such information would not normally be available to the adversary in practice*. We emphasize that this situation is fundamentally different from the assumption described in the previous paragraph. Even if queries are generated from, say, the 5,000 most frequent keywords $\mathbb{W}^\star \subseteq \mathbb{W}$, the corresponding known-keyword set $\widetilde{\mathbb{W}}^\star := \mathbb{W}^\star \cap \widetilde{\mathbb{W}}$ should remain unknown to the adversary.

---

[3] Note that it holds $F(q) \subseteq \widetilde{\mathbb{W}}$, rather than $F(q) \subseteq \mathbb{W}$.
[4] Note that the cross filtering technique cannot be applied to Subgraph^{VL}, since it does not work well with volume patterns, i.e., with byte lengths of documents, which do not correspond to individual documents in a one-to-one manner.

Similar unrealistic assumptions have also been made in other attacks, such as the IKK attack [8] and the Count attack [3]. However, relying on such additional information narrows the search space for candidate keywords, possibly leading to an artificially high query recovery rate for known-data attacks, including the Subgraph attack. *We point out that such performance evaluations are neither accurate nor appropriate* by showing experimental results in the next section.

4.2 Experiments Without the Unrealistic Assumptions

We implemented Subgraph^{ID} and Subgraph^{VL} to evaluate their effectiveness without relying on the unrealistic assumptions that the adversary knows $\widetilde{\mathbb{W}}^*$. It should be noted, however, that we still require another unrealistic assumption, namely, that the adversary possesses some auxiliary data.

Dataset. We used 4,897 files from the `arnold-j` user directory of the Enron email dataset [19]. The Enron dataset is widely used in prior work on leakage abuse attacks, offering a standard benchmark for reproducibility. It has been publicly available for years, and the curated version used in this study includes mechanisms for user data removal upon request, helping address ethical concerns.

The text files in the dataset were preprocessed by first removing email headers, and then applying stemming using the Porter stemmer [17] and removing keywords included in the stopwords list, both implemented using the NLTK (Natural Language ToolKit) library [1]. The total number of keywords remaining in the dataset after preprocessing is 21,903.

Selectivity. The experiments relied on *selectivity*, which refers to the number of document identifiers $\#\mathcal{X}(q)$ $(= \#\mathbf{D}(w))$ associated with a particular query q (or its corresponding keyword w). We classify a query $q \in \mathbb{Q}$ (and its corresponding keyword $w \in \mathbb{W}$) into three categories based on their selectivity:

- **High-Selectivity Query/Keyword**: $15 \leq \#\mathcal{X}(q)$.
- **Middle-Selectivity Query/Keyword**: $5 \leq \#\mathcal{X}(q) \leq 14$.
- **Low-Selectivity Query/Keyword**: $\#\mathcal{X}(q) \leq 4$.

Following this classification, we obtained 3,658 keywords with high selectivity, 3,998 keywords with middle selectivity, and 14,247 keywords with low selectivity in the Enron dataset.

Experimental Settings. We present performance evaluations of the Subgraph attacks both with and without the unrealistic assumption, based on our Rust software implementation. Although we implemented both Subgraph^{ID} and Subgraph^{VL}, we provide the results for Subgraph^{ID} here due to page limitations (see Appendix B for Subgraph^{VL}). Our implementations were executed on an Ubuntu 24.04 LTS (WSL2) server equipped with an AMD Ryzen 9 7900 processor and 64 GB of RAM.

Both experiments were evaluated on 150 queries, i.e., $t = 150$. In the experiment *with* the unrealistic assumption, each query was generated from a keyword in the smaller known-keyword set $\widetilde{\mathbb{W}}^*$ ($\subseteq \widetilde{\mathbb{W}}$), where $\#\widetilde{\mathbb{W}}^* = 500$, and

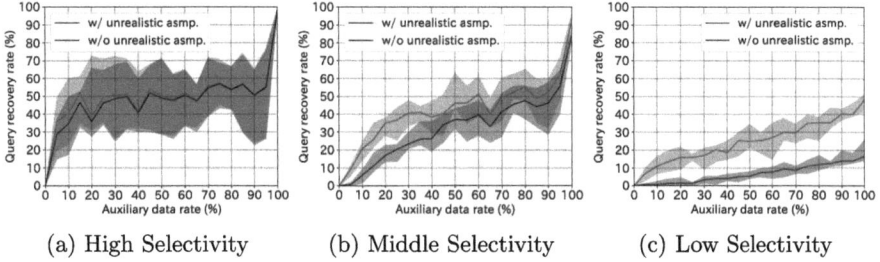

(a) High Selectivity (b) Middle Selectivity (c) Low Selectivity

Fig. 3. Performance evaluation of Subgraph^{ID} with and without the unrealistic assumption.

the Subgraph^{ID} algorithm also used $\widetilde{\mathbb{W}}^*$ as its search space. In contrast, in the experiment *without* the unrealistic assumption, although each query was still generated from a keyword in $\widetilde{\mathbb{W}}^*$, the algorithm had no knowledge of $\widetilde{\mathbb{W}}^*$ and instead used the entire known-keyword set $\widetilde{\mathbb{W}}$ as its search space. As in previous works [2,3,8], we excluded queries generated from non-known keywords, i.e., from $\mathbb{W} \setminus \widetilde{\mathbb{W}}$. Consequently, these experiments allow us to evaluate the impact of the unrealistic assumption on the performance of the Subgraph^{ID} attack, as well as the Subgraph^{VL} attack, whose results are provided in Appendix B.

In both experiments, Subgraph^{ID} attempts to recover 150 queries under varying auxiliary data rates δ, where δ is incremented by 5% from 5% to 100%. The *query recovery rate* is defined as the ratio of the number of correctly recovered queries to the total number of queries.

4.3 Experimental Results

We ran both experiments 10 times and report the minimum, median, and maximum query recovery rates in Fig. 3. Consistent with the findings of Blackstone et al. [2], our experiments demonstrated that higher selectivity leads to a higher query recovery rate. Furthermore, Subgraph^{ID} with the unrealistic assumption achieved higher query recovery rates compared to the setting without the assumption, particularly in the middle- and low-selectivity categories. Detailed discussions are provided below.

High Selectivity. At first glance, there appears to be little difference between the two experiments. However, as δ decreases, we can see the impact of the unrealistic assumption. For example, at $\delta = 0.05$ (5%), the median recovery rate of Subgraph^{ID} with the unrealistic assumption is approximately 37%, and the maximum recovery rate is around 50%, whereas for Subgraph^{ID} without the unrealistic assumption, the median recovery rate is about 30%, and the maximum recovery rate is around 37%. We now discuss the reasons behind this difference. The adversary, who possesses the known document set $\widetilde{\mathbb{D}}$, only knows a *portion* of the access pattern for each known keyword $w \in \widetilde{\mathbb{W}}$, which we refer to as the *known access pattern* for convenience; that is, the adversary observes $\mathbf{id}(\widetilde{\mathbf{D}}(w))$, not the entire access pattern $\mathbf{id}(\mathbf{D}(w))$. Therefore, a smaller auxiliary data rate δ increases the likelihood that $\mathbf{id}(\widetilde{\mathbf{D}}(w)) = \mathbf{id}(\widetilde{\mathbf{D}}(w'))$ for $w, w' \in \widetilde{\mathbb{W}}$ even when $\mathbf{id}(\mathbf{D}(w)) \neq \mathbf{id}(\mathbf{D}(w'))$. However, since the experiment under the unrealistic assumption restricts the size of the keyword set $\widetilde{\mathbb{W}}^\star$ to 500, such duplication is less likely to occur compared to the experiment without the assumption. In other words, the adversary can exclude keywords $w \in \widetilde{\mathbb{W}} \setminus \widetilde{\mathbb{W}}^\star$ from the candidate set for the searched keywords, making it easier to identify a unique match. As a result, this leads to a higher query recovery rate.

On the other hand, no significant differences are observed between the experiments for $\delta \geq 0.2$. This is presumably because, as the amount of auxiliary data increases, the likelihood of the "duplication" decreases, and the differences between the keyword spaces $\widetilde{\mathbb{W}}^\star$ and $\widetilde{\mathbb{W}}$ become less influential in the experiments.

We emphasize that the unrealistic assumption may have a more significant impact on the query recovery rate, particularly for small δ, depending on the dataset. Compared to middle- and low-selectivity keywords, high-selectivity keywords w are more likely to be unique within the keyword universe, since they satisfy $\#\mathbf{D}(w) \geq 15$. Therefore, it is expected that a more pronounced difference between the query recovery rates in the two experiments would be observed if a dataset containing a larger proportion of high-selectivity keywords were used.

Middle and Low Selectivity. Compared to the high-selectivity setting, there are significant differences in the recovery rates between the two experiments. In particular, in the low-selectivity setting, the difference in recovery rates becomes more pronounced as the auxiliary data rate δ increases. This is because the number of low-selectivity keywords, 14,247, is much larger than the number of high-selectivity keywords, 3,658. Taking into account the definition of the low-selectivity keywords (i.e., $\#\mathbf{D}(w) \leq 4$), each keyword $w \in \widetilde{\mathbb{W}}$ is unlikely to have a unique access pattern. However, in the Subgraph^{ID} attack with the unrealistic assumption, the adversary can exclude a large number of known keywords $w \in \widetilde{\mathbb{W}} \setminus \widetilde{\mathbb{W}}^\star$ by assuming that each query is generated from the *selected* known-keyword set $\widetilde{\mathbb{W}}^\star$. Consequently, recovering queries under the unrealistic assumption becomes more successful than in the setting without the assumption.

5   Proposed Leakage Abuse Attacks Based on Subgraph

In this section, we propose two new leakage abuse attacks, both built upon the Subgraph attacks. The first attack is a modified version of Subgraph^{ID} that eliminates false negatives, and we refer to it as Subgraph+^{ID}. The second attack is also based on Subgraph^{VL} in the sense that two bipartite graphs play crucial roles in its algorithm design; however, unlike Subgraph^{VL}, it focuses on the *maximum similarity* between $N_{\mathbf{G}_{\mathsf{VL}}}(q)$ and $N_{\widetilde{\mathbf{G}}_{\mathsf{VL}}}(w)$ to narrow down keyword candidates. We refer to this second attack as SimGraph^{VL}.

Algorithm 1 Subgraph+^{ID}

1: **function** ATTACK($\mathbf{G}_{\text{ID}}, \widetilde{\mathbf{G}}_{\text{ID}}$)
2: $\quad$ let $C \colon \mathbb{Q} \to 2^{\widetilde{\mathbb{W}}}$ be a mutable map
3: $\quad$ **for all** $i \in [t]$ **do**
4: $\quad\quad$ $C(q_i) \leftarrow \left\{ w \in \widetilde{\mathbb{W}} \mid N_{\widetilde{\mathbf{G}}_{\text{ID}}}(w) = N_{\mathbf{G}_{\text{ID}}}(q_i) \cap \mathbf{id}(\widetilde{\mathbb{D}}) \right\}$
5: $\quad$ **return** C

Fig. 4. Subgraph+^{ID}, the proposed attack using access patterns.

5.1 Subgraph+^{ID}: A False-Negative-Free Variant of Subgraph^{ID}

Basic Idea. As explained in Sect. 3.2, Subgraph^{ID} narrows down candidate keywords based on the known-data rate δ; that is, it selects keywords w that satisfy $\#N_{\widetilde{\mathbf{G}}_{\text{ID}}}(w) \geq \delta \cdot \#N_{\mathbf{G}_{\text{ID}}}(q)$ and defines the set of selected keywords as candidates. This procedure is reasonable and accelerates the algorithm's computation time, as it is natural to expect that the total number of *known* documents returned by a search for query q would be approximately a fraction δ of the entire search results, given that the adversary possesses a fraction δ of the document collection. However, in other words, this procedure also rules out keywords w satisfying $\#N_{\widetilde{\mathbf{G}}_{\text{ID}}}(w)/\#N_{\mathbf{G}_{\text{ID}}}(q) \leq \delta$, even if w is actually the correct keyword corresponding to the query q.

Therefore, we design our algorithm to ensure that false negatives never occur, thereby preventing the loss of correct keywords. To achieve this, we adopt the design principle of LEAP [14], a known-data attack that exploits L2 leakage. LEAP always succeeds in recovering a query q if the corresponding known keyword $w \in \widetilde{\mathbb{W}}$ has a *unique* known access pattern $N_{\widetilde{\mathbf{G}}_{\text{ID}}}(w)$, that is, if $N_{\widetilde{\mathbf{G}}_{\text{ID}}}(w)$ differs from the known access patterns of all other known keywords. As a result, no false negatives occur in LEAP.

Algorithm. We provide a pseudocode of our attack, Subgraph+^{ID}, in Fig. 4. Roughly speaking, for each query $q_i \in \mathbb{Q}$, the algorithm computes $N_{\mathbf{G}_{\text{ID}}(q)} \cap \mathbf{id}(\widetilde{\mathbb{D}})$ to remove identifiers that do *not* appear in the auxiliary data $\widetilde{\mathbb{D}}$, and then selects keywords w whose known access pattern $N_{\widetilde{\mathbf{G}}_{\text{ID}}}(w)$ exactly matches the resulting set. Consequently, no false negatives occur in the algorithm, and the ratio of known keywords with unique access patterns directly determines the performance of Subgraph+^{ID}. In particular, this ratio tends to increase dramatically in the high-selectivity setting. Indeed, as demonstrated in Sect. 6, Subgraph+^{ID} achieves significantly better performance on high-selectivity queries compared to the original Subgraph^{ID} attack, despite its conceptual simplicity.

5.2 SimGraph^{VL}: A New Attack Based on Maximum Similarity

Unfortunately, the core idea behind Subgraph+^{ID} cannot be directly applied to the volume-pattern setting. Specifically, Subgraph+^{ID} eliminates redundant information, namely, edges in the leakage graph $\mathbf{G}_{\text{ID}}$ that do not appear to correspond

Algorithm 2 SimGraph^{VL}

1: **function** ATTACK($\mathbf{G}_{\mathsf{VL}}, \widetilde{\mathbf{G}}_{\mathsf{VL}}$)
2:     let $F, C \colon \mathbb{Q} \to 2^{\widetilde{\mathbb{W}}}$ be mutable maps
3:     **for all** $i \in [t]$ **do**
4:        $F(q_i) \leftarrow \left\{ w \in \widetilde{\mathbb{W}} \;\middle|\; \begin{array}{l} N_{\widetilde{\mathbf{G}}_{\mathsf{VL}}}(w) \subseteq N_{\mathbf{G}_{\mathsf{VL}}}(q_i) \\ \wedge\, \forall v \in N_{\widetilde{\mathbf{G}}_{\mathsf{VL}}}(w), W_{\widetilde{\mathbf{G}}_{\mathsf{VL}}}(w,v) \leq W_{\mathbf{G}_{\mathsf{VL}}}(q_i, v) \end{array} \right\}$
5:        $C(q_i) \leftarrow \underset{w \in F(q_i)}{\arg\max} \sum_{v \in N_{\widetilde{\mathbf{G}}_{\mathsf{VL}}}(w)} W_{\widetilde{\mathbf{G}}_{\mathsf{VL}}}(w, v)$
6:     **return** C

Fig. 5. SimGraph^{VL}, the proposed attack using volume patterns.

to edges in the auxiliary data graph $\widetilde{\mathbf{G}}_{\mathsf{ID}}$. This elimination process is effective in the access-pattern setting because each document in $\mathbb{D}$ has a unique identifier. However, in the volume-pattern setting, multiple documents may share the same volume, and thus, the elimination strategy becomes ineffective.

Basic Idea. We begin with the access-pattern setting, and focus on an important structural property of the bipartite graphs ($\mathbf{G}_{\mathsf{ID}}, \widetilde{\mathbf{G}}_{\mathsf{ID}}$): if a query q is generated from a keyword w, then it always holds that $N_{\widetilde{\mathbf{G}}_{\mathsf{ID}}}(w) \subseteq N_{\mathbf{G}_{\mathsf{ID}}}(q)$. Given that, we have

$$N_{\widetilde{\mathbf{G}}_{\mathsf{ID}}}(w) \subseteq N_{\mathbf{G}_{\mathsf{ID}}}(q) \Rightarrow N_{\widetilde{\mathbf{G}}_{\mathsf{ID}}}(w) \cap \mathbf{id}(\widetilde{\mathbb{D}}) \subseteq N_{\mathbf{G}_{\mathsf{ID}}}(q) \cap \mathbf{id}(\widetilde{\mathbb{D}})$$
$$\Rightarrow N_{\widetilde{\mathbf{G}}_{\mathsf{ID}}}(w) \subseteq N_{\mathbf{G}_{\mathsf{ID}}}(q) \cap \mathbf{id}(\widetilde{\mathbb{D}}), \qquad (1)$$

since $N_{\widetilde{\mathbf{G}}_{\mathsf{ID}}}(w)$ is a set of identifiers of documents containing the keyword w, and therefore, it holds $N_{\widetilde{\mathbf{G}}_{\mathsf{ID}}}(w) \subseteq \mathbf{id}(\widetilde{\mathbb{D}})$ for all $w \in \widetilde{\mathbb{W}}$. Therefore, for each query $q \in \mathbb{Q}$, every keyword w in the candidate set $F(q)$ must satisfy condition (1), namely, $N_{\widetilde{\mathbf{G}}_{\mathsf{ID}}}(w) \subseteq N_{\mathbf{G}_{\mathsf{ID}}}(q) \cap \mathbf{id}(\widetilde{\mathbb{D}})$. We define the cardinality of $N_{\widetilde{\mathbf{G}}_{\mathsf{ID}}}(w)$, i.e., $\# N_{\widetilde{\mathbf{G}}_{\mathsf{ID}}}(w)$, as the *similarity* of w with respect to q. Based on the idea that *the keyword(s) with the maximum similarity with respect to a given query q are most likely to be the underlying keyword corresponding to q*, we propose an attack exploiting access patterns, which we call SimGraph^{ID}. The details of SimGraph^{ID} are provided in Appendix C due to page limitations.

Additional Condition for the Volume-pattern Setting. There is an additional hurdle to be overcome in the volume-pattern setting. In this case, the bipartite graphs ($\mathbf{G}_{\mathsf{VL}}, \widetilde{\mathbf{G}}_{\mathsf{VL}}$) are weighted, where the weight represents the number of documents that share the same volume. This makes the condition (1) insufficient for the volume-pattern setting, and thus, an additional condition regarding the weights is required. Specifically, if a query q is generated from a keyword w, it always holds that $W_{\widetilde{\mathbf{G}}_{\mathsf{VL}}}(w, v) \leq W_{\mathbf{G}_{\mathsf{VL}}}(q, v)$ for every adjacent vertex $v \in N_{\widetilde{\mathbf{G}}_{\mathsf{VL}}}(w) \cap N_{\mathbf{G}_{\mathsf{VL}}}(q)$ of both w and q. Based on this observation, we propose an attack exploiting volume patterns, called SimGraph^{VL}, which relies on the idea that *the keyword(s) with the maximum similarity and matching weight*

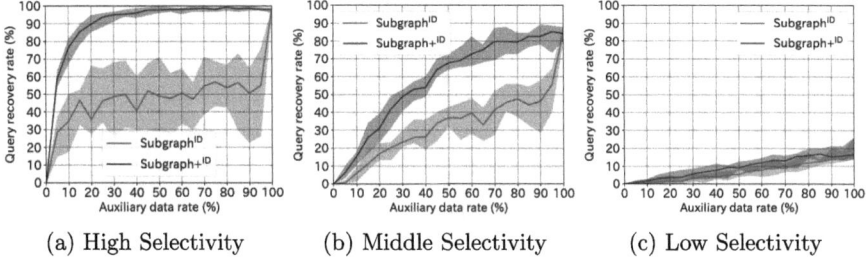

(a) High Selectivity (b) Middle Selectivity (c) Low Selectivity

Fig. 6. Performance comparison of Subgraph+^{ID} and Subgraph^{ID} (without the unrealistic assumption).

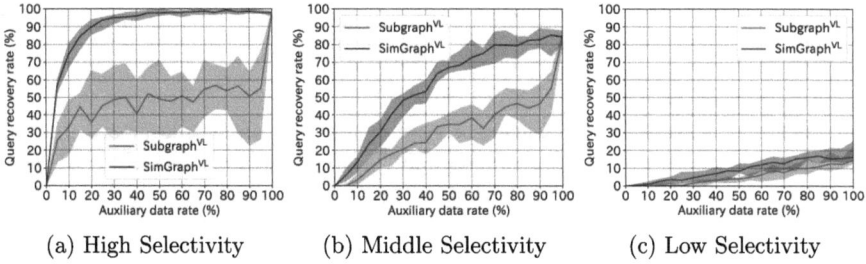

(a) High Selectivity (b) Middle Selectivity (c) Low Selectivity

Fig. 7. Performance comparison of SimGraph^{VL} and Subgraph^{VL} (without the unrealistic assumption).

with respect to a given query q are most likely to be the underlying keyword corresponding to q. The pseudocode for SimGraph^{VL} is provided in Fig. 5.

6 Experiments

We demonstrate through experiments that our attacks, Subgraph+^{ID} and SimGraph^{VL}, achieve significantly better performance compared to the original Subgraph^{ID} and Subgraph^{VL} attacks, which represent the most effective known-data attacks exploiting access and volume patterns, respectively (Fig. 10).

6.1 Experimental Settings

The experimental settings are identical to those described in Sect. 4.2. Specifically, we implemented the original Subgraph attacks and our proposed attacks, Subgraph+^{ID} and SimGraph^{VL}, in Rust, and conducted all experiments on an Ubuntu 24.04 LTS server. As before, we used the Enron dataset from Sect. 4.2 and classified the keywords into high-, middle-, and low-selectivity categories.

All experiments were conducted without relying on the unrealistic assumption and were evaluated on 150 queries. Each attack attempts to recover 150 queries under varying δ, where δ was incremented by 5% from 5% to 100%.

6.2 Experimental Results

We ran each attack 10 times and report the minimum, median, and maximum query recovery rates in Fig. 6 for Subgraph^{ID} and Subgraph+^{ID}, and in Fig. 7 for Subgraph^{VL} and SimGraph^{VL}.

Effectiveness of Our Attacks. Regardless of selectivity, our attacks recovered more queries than the original Subgraph attacks. Notably, in the high-selectivity setting, the performance gap was especially pronounced: our attacks achieved approximately twice the recovery rate of the Subgraph attacks in both settings. For example, at the lowest auxiliary data rate $\delta = 0.05$ (5%), the median recovery rates of our attacks exceeded 55.0%, whereas those of the Subgraph attacks remained around 25.0%. Our attacks also achieved roughly twice the performance of Subgraph in the middle- and low-selectivity settings, although the overall recovery rates remained low for low-selectivity queries.

The Impact of Selectivity. Based on the experiments, we observe that high selectivity tends to make the access or volume pattern of each keyword unique. The primary difference between Subgraph^{ID} and Subgraph+^{ID} lies in whether candidate keywords are excluded based on a condition determined by δ. As a result, higher selectivity leads to a larger number of unrecovered queries in the Subgraph^{ID} attack, due to its reliance on this exclusion condition. The reason our second attack, SimGraph^{VL}, outperforms Subgraph^{VL} is that, in addition to removing the exclusion condition, higher selectivity often causes the candidate-keyword set $F(q)$ to become a singleton containing the correct keyword.

7 Concluding Remarks

In this work, towards sound evaluation of existing known-data attacks, especially for the Subgraph attacks [2], we revisited experimental evaluation to rule out an unrealistic assumption that we identified in this paper, and proposed two improved attack algorithms, called Subgraph+^{ID} and SimGraph^{VL}. As a result, our attacks achieve almost twice the query recovery rate of Subgraph Attacks.

In addition to the Subgraph attacks, various other leakage abuse attacks should have also implicitly relied on the same unrealistic assumption. It would be an interesting direction for future work to experimentally evaluate these attacks under more realistic settings, where such assumptions are removed.

We plan to release our source code on GitHub to support reproducibility and facilitate future research.

Acknowledgment. We would like to thank Masayuki Yoshino for his valuable feedback. This work was supported by JSPS KAKENHI Grant Numbers JP23H00468, JP23H00479, JP23K17455, JP23K21644, JP23K21668, JP23K24846, and JST K Program Grant Number JPMJKP24U2, Japan.

A Notation Summary

Table 2 summarizes the main notations used throughout the paper in the context of leakage abuse attacks. For general notations (e.g., the cardinality of a set and multiset), please refer to Sect. 2.1.

Table 2. A summary of notations in the context of leakage abuse attacks. See Sect. 2.1 for general notations.

$\mathbb{W}$	Keyword universe, $\mathbb{W} = \{w_1, \ldots, w_m\}$	$\widetilde{\mathbb{W}}$	Known-keyword set, $\widetilde{\mathbb{W}} \subseteq \mathbb{W}$
$\mathbb{Q}$	Query set, $\mathbb{Q} = \{q_1, \ldots, q_t\}$	$\widetilde{\mathbb{W}}^*$	Subset of $\widetilde{\mathbb{W}}$, $\widetilde{\mathbb{W}}^* \subseteq \widetilde{\mathbb{W}}$
$\mathbb{D}$	Document collection, $\mathbb{D} = \{D_1, \ldots, D_n\}$	$\widetilde{\mathbb{D}}$	Known-document collection, $\widetilde{\mathbb{D}} \subseteq \mathbb{D}$
$\mathbb{ED}$	Set of encrypted documents, $\mathbb{ED} = \{ED_1, \ldots, ED_n\}$		
$\mathbf{id}(\mathbb{D})$	IDs of $\mathbb{D}$, $\mathbf{id}(\mathbb{D}) = \{\mathbf{id}(D_1), \ldots, \mathbf{id}(D_n)\}$	$\mathbf{id}(\widetilde{\mathbb{D}})$	IDs of $\widetilde{\mathbb{D}}$, $\mathbf{id}(\widetilde{\mathbb{D}}) \subseteq \mathbf{id}(\mathbb{D})$
$\mathbf{D}(w)$	Documents containing w, $\mathbf{D}(w) \subset \mathbb{D}$	$\mathcal{X}(q)$	Search results for q, $\mathcal{X}(q) = \mathbf{id}(\mathbf{D}(w))$
$|\mathbb{D}|$	Volume of $\mathbb{D}$, $|\mathbb{D}| = \{\!\!\{|D_1|, \ldots, |D_n|\}\!\!\}$	$|\widetilde{\mathbb{D}}|$	Volume of $\widetilde{\mathbb{D}}$, $|\widetilde{\mathbb{D}}| \subset |\mathbb{D}|$
$|\mathbf{D}(w)|$	Volume of $\mathbf{D}(w)$, $|\mathbf{D}(w)| = \{\!\!\{|D|\}\!\!\}_{D \in \mathbf{D}(w)}$	$|\mathcal{X}(q)|$	Volume of $\mathcal{X}(q)$, $|\mathcal{X}(q)| = \{\!\!\{|D|\}\!\!\}_{\mathbf{id}(D) \in \mathcal{X}(q)}$
δ	auxiliary data rate, $\delta = \#\widetilde{\mathbb{D}}/\#\mathbb{D}$		
$\mathbf{G}$	Leakage graph	$\widetilde{\mathbf{G}}$	Auxiliary data graph
$N_\mathbf{G}(s)$	Set of neighbors of a vertex s, $N_\mathbf{G}(s) = \{d \in \mathcal{D} \mid (s,d) \in \mathcal{E}\}$	$W_\mathbf{G}(s,d)$	Weight of an edge (s,d) in $\mathbf{G}$
$F(q)$	Set of candidate keywords	$C(q)$	Final inference result

B Experimental Result of Subgraph^{VL}

We show the results of experiments to evaluate the impact of the unrealistic assumption on the performance of the Subgraph^{VL} attack. Specifically, we provide performance evaluations of the Subgraph^{VL} attack both with and without the unrealistic assumption. The experimental setting is the same as Sect. 4.2. We ran both experiments 10 times and report the minimum, median, and maximum query recovery rates in Fig. 8.

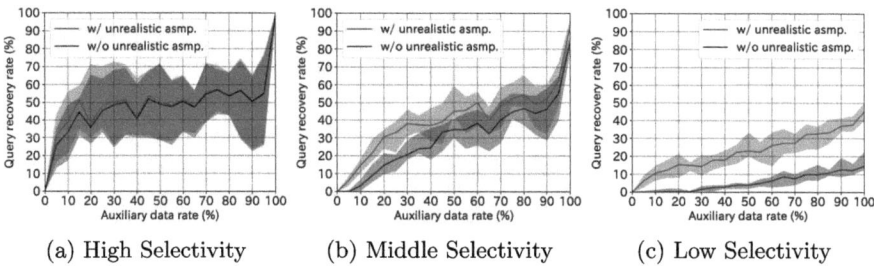

(a) High Selectivity (b) Middle Selectivity (c) Low Selectivity

Fig. 8. Performance evaluation of Subgraph^{VL} with and without the unrealistic assumption.

Algorithm 3 SimGraph[ID]

1: **function** ATTACK($\mathbf{G}_{ID}, \widetilde{\mathbf{G}}_{ID}$)
2:     let mutable maps $F, C: \mathbb{Q} \to 2^{\widetilde{\mathbf{W}}}$
3:     **for all** $i \in [t]$ **do**
4:        $F(q_i) \leftarrow \left\{ w \in \widetilde{\mathbf{W}} \mid N_{\widetilde{\mathbf{G}}_{ID}}(w) \subseteq N_{\mathbf{G}_{ID}}(q_i) \right\}$
5:        $C(q_i) \leftarrow \arg\max_{w \in F(q_i)} \# N_{\widetilde{\mathbf{G}}_{ID}}(w)$
6:     **return** C

Fig. 9. SimGraph[ID], the proposed attack using access patterns.

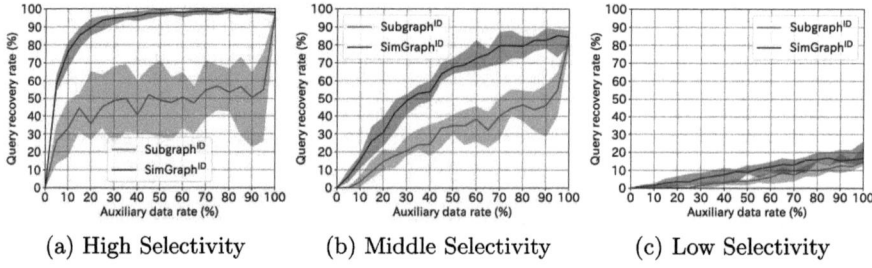

(a) High Selectivity   (b) Middle Selectivity   (c) Low Selectivity

Fig. 10. Performance comparison of SimGraph[ID] and Subgraph[ID] without the unrealistic assumption.

C The SimGraph[ID] Attack

The pseudocode for SimGraph[ID] is provided in Fig. 9, along with the experimental results for SimGraph[ID]. As in the other experiments, we ran both Subgraph[ID] and SimGraph[ID] 10 times. Interestingly, our two access-pattern-based attacks, Subgraph+[ID] and SimGraph[ID], achieved nearly identical performance (see also Table 1).

References

1. Bird, S., Klein, E., Loper, E.: Natural language processing with Python: analyzing text with the natural language toolkit. O'Reilly Media, Inc. (2009)
2. Blackstone, L., Kamara, S., Moataz, T.: Revisiting leakage abuse attacks. In: NDSS 2020. The Internet Society (2020)
3. Cash, D., Grubbs, P., Perry, J., Ristenpart, T.: Leakage-abuse attacks against searchable encryption. In: ACM CCS 2015, pp. 668–679. ACM (2015)
4. Curtmola, R., Garay, J.A., Kamara, S., Ostrovsky, R.: Searchable symmetric encryption: improved definitions and efficient constructions. In: ACM CCS 2006, pp. 79–88. ACM (2006)
5. Damie, M., Hahn, F., Peter, A.: A highly accurate Query-Recovery attack against searchable encryption using Non-Indexed documents. In: USENIX Security 2021, pp. 143–160. USENIX Association (2021)

6. Gui, Z., Paterson, K.G., Patranabis, S.: Rethinking searchable symmetric encryption. In: IEEE SP 2023, pp. 1401–1418 (2023)
7. Hoover, A., et al.: Leakage-abuse attacks against structured encryption for SQL. In: Balzarotti, D., Xu, W. (eds.) USENIX Security 2024. USENIX Association (2024)
8. Islam, M.S., Kuzu, M., Kantarcioglu, M.: Access pattern disclosure on searchable encryption: Ramification, attack and mitigation. In: NDSS 2012. The Internet Society (2012)
9. Kamara, S., Kati, A., Moataz, T., DeMaria, J., Park, A., Treiber, A.: MAPLE: markov process leakage attacks on encrypted search. Proc. Priv, Enhancing Technol (2024)
10. Kamara, S., Papamanthou, C., Roeder, T.: Dynamic searchable symmetric encryption. In: CCS '12, pp. 965–976. ACM (2012)
11. Lambregts, S., Chen, H., Ning, J., Liang, K.: VAL: volume and access pattern leakage-abuse attack with leaked documents. In: ESORICS 2022, vol. 13554, pp. 653–676. Springer (2022)
12. Liu, H., Xu, L., Liu, X., Mei, L., Xu, C.: Query correlation attack against searchable symmetric encryption with supporting for conjunctive queries. IEEE Trans. Inf. Forensics Secur., pp. 1924–1936 (2025)
13. Nie, H., Wang, W., Xu, P., Zhang, X., Yang, L.T., Liang, K.: Query recovery from easy to hard: Jigsaw attack against SSE. In: USENIX Security 2024, pp. 2599–2616. USENIX Association (2024)
14. Ning, J., Huang, X., Poh, G.S., Yuan, J., Li, Y., Weng, J., Deng, R.H.: LEAP: leakage-abuse attack on efficiently deployable, efficiently searchable encryption with partially known dataset. In: ACM CCS 2021, pp. 2307–2320. ACM (2021)
15. Oya, S., Kerschbaum, F.: Hiding the access pattern is not enough: Exploiting search pattern leakage in searchable encryption. In: USENIX Security'21, pp. 127–142. USENIX Association (2021)
16. Oya, S., Kerschbaum, F.: IHOP: Improved statistical query recovery against searchable symmetric encryption through quadratic optimization. In: USENIX Security'22, pp. 2407–2424. USENIX Association (2022)
17. Porter, M.F.: An algorithm for suffix stripping. Program **14**(3), 130–137 (1980)
18. Song, D.X., Wagner, D.A., Perrig, A.: Practical techniques for searches on encrypted data. In: IEEE S&P 2000, pp. 44–55. IEEE (2000)
19. The CALO Project: Enron email dataset (may 7, 2015 version). https://www.cs.cmu.edu/~enron/ (2015). https://www.cs.cmu.edu/~./enron/
20. Xu, L., Zheng, L., Xu, C., Yuan, X., Wang, C.: Leakage-abuse attacks against forward and backward private searchable symmetric encryption. In: ACM CCS 2023, pp. 3003–3017. ACM (2023)
21. Zhang, X., Wang, W., Xu, P., Yang, L.T., Liang, K.: High recovery with fewer injections: Practical binary volumetric injection attacks against dynamic searchable encryption. In: USENIX Security'23, pp. 5953–5970. USENIX Association (2023)
22. Zhang, Y., Katz, J., Papamanthou, C.: All your queries are belong to us: the power of file-injection attacks on searchable encryption. In: USENIX Security 2016, pp. 707–720. USENIX Association (2016)

Efficient and Secure Sleepy Model for BFT Consensus

Pengkun Ren[1], Hai Dong[1(✉)], Zahir Tari[1], and Pengcheng Zhang[2]

[1] School of Computing Technologies, Centre of Cyber Security Research and Innovation, RMIT University, Melbourne, Australia
s4038427@student.rmit.edu.au, {hai.dong,zahir.tari}@rmit.edu.au
[2] College of Computer Science and Software Engineering, Hohai University, Nanjing, China
pchzhang@hhu.edu.cn

Abstract. Byzantine Fault Tolerant (BFT) consensus protocols for dynamically available systems face a critical challenge: balancing latency and security in fluctuating node participation. Existing solutions often require multiple rounds of voting per decision, leading to high latency or limited resilience to adversarial behavior. This paper presents a BFT protocol integrating a pre-commit mechanism with publicly verifiable secret sharing (PVSS) into message transmission. By binding users' identities to their messages through PVSS, our approach reduces communication rounds. Compared to other state-of-the-art methods, our protocol typically requires only four network delays (4Δ) in common scenarios while being resilient to up to 1/2 adversarial participants. This integration enhances the efficiency and security of the protocol without compromising integrity. Theoretical analysis demonstrates the robustness of the protocol against Byzantine attacks. Experimental evaluations show that, compared to traditional BFT protocols, our protocol significantly prevents fork occurrences and improves chain stability. Furthermore, compared to longest-chain protocol, our protocol maintains stability and lower latency in scenarios with moderate participation fluctuations.

Keyword: Byzantine fault tolerance. Distributed system. Sleepy model

1 Introduction

Recent advancements in BFT have increasingly focused on addressing the challenges of dynamically available systems. BFT consensus protocols are fundamental to distributed systems, enabling reliable agreement among participants even in the presence of malicious behavior [5].

Traditional consensus protocols often assume a static set of participants who remain active throughout the entire execution of the protocol [5,16]. The Sleepy Model, introduced by Pass and Shi [23], represents a significant paradigm shift by allowing nodes to dynamically switch between active and inactive states without prior notice. This model more accurately reflects the operational realities of modern distributed systems, where node availability can fluctuate due to network instability, hardware failures, or resource optimization strategies.

Protocols based on the Sleepy Model have made notable strides in accommodating fluctuating network participation, demonstrating practical resilience and efficient latency management under dynamic conditions [10–12,14,21,22,28]. However, existing sleepy BFT models face a fundamental challenge in balancing latency and security. This latency-security trade-off manifests itself primarily in two critical aspects:

1. Multiple Round Overhead: Many existing protocols require multiple rounds of communication to reach consensus, significantly increasing overall latency. For instance, the work of [22] requires 16Δ for consensus. Although some models introduced early decision mechanisms [11,21], achieving 4Δ latency in the best-case scenario, the average latency remains considerably high.

2. Limited Resilience to Adversarial Behavior: As participation fluctuates, maintaining robust security against adaptive adversaries becomes increasingly challenging. In dynamic participation scenarios, sophisticated adversarial strategies can exploit temporary imbalances in the network [28], potentially compromising the integrity of the consensus process. These attacks underscore the difficulty of maintaining consistent security guarantees in systems where the set of active participants changes over time.

Our approach incorporates a pre-commit mechanism with PVSS into the consensus process. The protocol achieves a balanced latency-security trade-off, maintaining security guarantees against up to $1/2$ malicious nodes while achieving a latency of 4Δ in typical scenarios. Our key contributions are as follows:

PVSS-Based Message Binding Mechanism: Our approach addresses these challenges by binding messages with node identities through PVSS and integrating a pre-commit mechanism. In our protocol, nodes commit to their future participation before each consensus round, with these commitments cryptographically bound to their messages through PVSS. This design enables secure message verification in a single voting round by requiring nodes to distribute verifiable shares that can only be reconstructed with sufficient participation from the committed set, effectively preventing selective message broadcasting. When nodes plan to go offline for maintenance or upgrades, they can signal this through the pre-commit mechanism, while any unplanned deviation from commitments becomes cryptographically evident through failed PVSS reconstruction. In typical scenarios, only one secret reconstruction operation is needed, specifically for the leader's proposed block, though additional reconstructions may be required in consensus failure cases. As demonstrated in Table 1, this approach achieves competitive latency performance compared to state-of-the-art protocols.

Enhanced Security Model for Dynamic Participation Environments: We provide a rigorous mathematical model of node behavior within each Δ time interval. This model leverages PVSS properties to maintain security integrity even under sophisticated attack scenarios in dynamic settings. Additionally, the pre-commit mechanism requires that nodes must send participation commitments before joining the next consensus round, enabling dynamic threshold adjustments and enhancing the protocol's adaptability to fluctuating network conditions. We present comprehensive proofs demonstrating the protocol's resilience against a range of adversarial strategies, including adaptive corruptions and network partitioning attacks.

Table 1. Comparison of dynamically sleepy models

Protocol	Adv.Resilience	Best.Latency	Avg.Latency	Block Time	Voting Rounds
MR [22]	1/2	16Δ	24Δ	16Δ	10
MMR2 [21]	1/2	4Δ	9Δ	10Δ	9
GL [13]	1/2	6Δ	11Δ	10Δ	9
DZ [11]	1/2	6Δ	8Δ	4Δ	1
1/3MMR [20]	1/3	3Δ	4Δ	2Δ	2
1/4MMR [20]	1/4	2Δ	3Δ	2Δ	1
DNTS [10]	1/2	$O(\kappa)^*$	$O(\kappa)^*$	3Δ	1
PS [23]	1/2	$O(\kappa)$	$O(\kappa)$	Δ	0
PVSS-BFT	1/2	4Δ	4Δ	4Δ	1

Note: We compare several sleepy models in terms of their resilience and performance. The definitions of latency, block time, and voting rounds are adopted from existing literature [11]. "Adv. Resilience" refers to Adversarial Resilience. "Avg. Latency" refers to the expected time for a transaction's confirmation under random submission times. These metrics help in evaluating the efficiency and security of each protocol.
* For Goldfish [10], we show the latency in conditions of low participation.

Our experimental results demonstrate the effectiveness of our protocol in dynamic participation environments. In simulated attack scenarios, our protocol significantly reduces fork occurrences and maintains chain stability compared to traditional BFT protocols. Furthermore, latency tests show that PVSS-BFT achieves constant low latency across various participation levels, outperforming longest-chain based systems in the circumstances of low and high participation with moderate fluctuations. These findings underscore the robustness and efficiency of our approach to balancing security and performance in sleepy models.

The rest of this paper is structured as follows: Sect. 2 provides a detailed overview of related work, Sect. 3 describes our system model and definitions, Sect. 4 presents our consensus protocol, Sect. 5 provides a comprehensive security analysis, Sect. 6 presents our experimental results, and Sect. 7 concludes the paper with a discussion.

2 Related Work

Sleepy Consensus Model. Traditional BFT protocols, such as PBFT [5], were designed with the assumption of a static set of continuously participating nodes. However, node availability can fluctuate in real-world distributed systems. The *Sleepy Consensus Model*, introduced by Pass and Shi [23], addresses the challenges posed by dynamic node availability. This model allows nodes to switch between online and offline, enabling consensus protocols to function effectively even when the set of participating nodes changes over time. Daian et al. [9] extended the Sleepy Model to Proof-of-Stake (PoS) systems with their Snow White protocol. Goyal et al. [14] proposed a method for instant confirmation of transactions after their appearance in the ledger.

Building on these foundational efforts, Momose and Ren [22] further advanced the concept by introducing the notion of Dynamic Quorum. Their protocol incorporates graded agreement into the consensus process, allowing for the adjustment of quorum sizes at any given time. This innovation paved the way for subsequent research, enabling the development of Total-Order Broadcast protocols capable of accommodating inherently fluctuating node availability. Gafni and Losa [13] utilized a Commit-Adopt primitive within the sleepy model. Malkhi et al. [21] addressed the issue of potentially corrupt nodes while maintaining the integrity of the consensus. D'Amato and Zanolini [11] optimized the Sleepy Model by integrating an extended three-grade graded agreement into the consensus process. This extension streamlined the voting process, reducing the number of rounds required to reach consensus. Wang et al. [28] focused on the known participation model, where the network is aware of a minimum number of awake honest replicas. These developments have improved the ability of consensus protocols to manage dynamic participation. However, *multiple rounds of communication* can increase latency, while dynamically adjusting the quorum size increases the complexity of maintaining safety and liveness.

Security Optimizations in BFT Protocols. Though designed to withstand arbitrary faults, BFT protocols struggle to maintain security as networks scale and adversaries grow more sophisticated. Researchers have continuously sought to enhance the security of BFT systems. Algorand [7] introduced a verifiable random function (VRF) to randomly select a user committee to run the consensus in each round. ByzCoin [18] proposed the use of collective signing to reduce communication complexity and maintain safety. SBFT [15] further utilized threshold signatures based on the BLS signature scheme [4].

Secret sharing [3,25] schemes have been increasingly integrated into BFT protocols to enhance their security [2,6]. FastBFT [19] leverages trusted execution environments (TEE) to design a fast and scalable BFT protocol. It uses TEE for generating and sharing secrets, and introduces a tree-based communication topology to distribute load. Basu et al. [1] introduce an efficient VSS scheme with share recovery capabilities designed for BFT integration. COBRA [27] proposes VSSR, a VSS framework that uses hardware-assisted TEE and lightweight secret sharing to efficiently aggregate messages. These advancements demonstrate the significant potential for integrating cryptographic primitives such as VRF and secret sharing into BFT protocols to improve security. However, while secret sharing schemes have been effectively employed to improve BFT protocols, their application in environments with dynamic node participation remains limited.

3 Model and Definitions

We consider a system of n validators $\mathcal{N} = \{n_1, ..., n_n\}$ participating in a BFT protocol. The protocol proceeds in a series of consecutive views, each denoted by an integer v. In each view, one or more blocks may be proposed, but only one block can be decided [11]. Previous works [14,22,23] have demonstrated that network synchrony is a necessary condition for consensus protocols in environments where nodes can dynamically participate, as asynchronous networks cannot guarantee consensus when node participation is unpredictable. An adaptive adversary exists in the system that can corrupt nodes at any point during execution. These corrupted nodes may exhibit arbitrary Byzantine behavior, deviating from the protocol specifications and potentially colluding with other malicious nodes. Nodes that remain uncorrupted throughout execution are considered honest and follow protocol specifications faithfully.

Weakly synchronized clocks. In our model, all participating nodes maintain synchronized clocks within a maximum deviation of Δ from the global reference time, where Δ denotes the maximum tolerable network delay for message delivery and clock skew. At any global time t, each node p maintains a local time τ_p that differs from t by at most Δ, specifically $\tau_p = t - \delta_p$ where $0 \leq \delta_p \leq \Delta$. Following the definition given by [14,21,22], without loss of generality, we will consider nodes to have synchronized clocks.

Communication Channels. We assume authenticated channels for message transmission. Byzantine nodes cannot modify messages or prevent message delivery between honest nodes. Consistent with the definition provided by [22], we assume that if an honest node p is awake at global time t, then p has received all messages sent by honest nodes by global time $t - \Delta$.

The Sleepy Model. Our protocol operates in the sleepy model introduced by Pass and Shi [23]. Each validator $n_i \in \mathcal{N}$ dynamically transitions between active and inactive states over time. The awake nodes fully participate in protocol execution, while the asleep nodes suspend all protocol activities. Let $\mathcal{A}(t) \subseteq \mathcal{N}$ denote the set of active validators at global time t, with $|\mathcal{A}(t)| = n_t$ where $0 < n_t \leq n$. In line with [21,22] [11], we require that at any time t, the number of Byzantine validators in $\mathcal{A}(t)$ is bounded by f_t, where $f_t < n_t/2$, ensuring an honest majority among active participants. The protocol accommodates state transitions of honest validators under adversarial control without requiring advance notification, though our pre-commit mechanism (detailed in Sect. 4) provides a framework for planned transitions.

Atomic Broadcast. As defined in [21,22], atomic broadcast enables participants to reach consensus on an expanding sequence of values $[B_0, B_1, B_2, ...]$, which is commonly referred to as a log. Our protocol implements a variant of atomic broadcast tailored to the PVSS-BFT mechanism. In our model, clients broadcast transactions to all validators, and nodes independently propose blocks containing these transactions. In each view v, a leader is then elected based on VRF values. This order of operations influences the liveness property. We have adapted the liveness definition inspired by [28] to suit the specific mechanisms of our protocol. The protocol provides the following guarantees:

For safety: if two honest nodes decide logs $[B_0, B_1, \ldots, B_j]$ and $[B'_0, B'_1, \ldots, B'_{j'}]$, then $B_i = B'_i$ for all $i \leq \min(j, j')$.

For liveness: if a transaction tx is broadcast to all honest validators at time t, then there exists a time $t' \geq t$ such that all honest validators awake at time t' will eventually decide on a log containing tx.

Block. Blocks represent batches of transactions. Each block B contains a reference to its parent block (except the genesis block B_0), a set of valid transactions, and cryptographic proof of validity. Two blocks conflict if one of them extends the other at the same height. A chain is a growing sequence of blocks $[B_0, B_1, \ldots, B_j]$.

Fork. A fork refers to a situation in which two or more conflicting blocks (i.e., blocks at the same height that do not extend each other) are simultaneously decided or irreversibly committed by different subsets of honest validators.

3.1 Cryptographic Primitives

We assume a public-key infrastructure (PKI) with digital signatures. A message μ signed by p_i is noted as $\langle \mu \rangle_i$. $H(\cdot)$ represents a collision-resistant hash function.

Verifiable Random Functions A VRF allows a participant p_i to generate a verifiable pseudo-random value ρ_i and a proof π_i from an input μ: $(\rho_i, \pi_i) \leftarrow \text{VRF}_i(\mu)$. Anyone can verify the correctness of ρ_i using π_i and p_i's public key pk_i, i.e. $VRF.VERIFY(pk_i, \mu, \rho_i, \pi_i)$.

Secret Sharing and Verifiable Secret Sharing (VSS). Secret sharing introduced independently by Shamir [25] and Blakley [3] allow a secret s to be splitted into share distributed among multiple parties. In a (t, n)-threshold scheme, any t out of n shares can reconstruct s, while fewer than t shares reveal nothing about s. VSS schemes, introduced by Chor et al. [8], allow honest participants detect inconsistency if the dealer tries to distribute inconsistent shares.

Publicly Verifiable Secret Sharing (PVSS) PVSS [24,26] further allows anyone to verify share correctness without compromising secrecy. In our protocol, each node that proposes a block during view v plays the role of "dealer". Let G_q denote a group of prime order q, and $g, G \in G_q$ be independently selected generators. According to [24], the scheme operates as follows:

Initialization: Each participant P_i generates a private key $x_i \in_R \mathbb{Z}_q^*$ and registers a public key $y_i = G^{x_i}$.

Share Distribution: The dealer selects a random polynomial $p(x) = \sum_{j=0}^{t-1} \alpha_j x^j$ of degree at most $t - 1$, where $\alpha_j \in \mathbb{Z}_q$ and $s = \alpha_0$. The dealer publishes commitments $C_j = g^{\alpha_j}$ for $0 \leq j < t$; encrypted shares $Y_i = y_i^{p(i)}$ for $1 \leq i \leq n$ using $PVSS.SPLIT(s, n, t)$. Anyone can check that share Y_i is consistent with C_i by calling $PVSS.VERIFY(pk_i, C_i, Y_i)$.

Share Reconstruction: Any t participants can reconstruct the secret by decrypting shares: $S_i = Y_i^{1/x_i} = G^{p(i)}$ and combining the shares using Lagrange interpolation: $S = \prod_{i=1}^{t} S_i^{\lambda_i}$, where λ_i are the Lagrange coefficients. This process can be abbreviated as $PVSS.RECONSTRUCT(\{S_i\}_{i=1}^{t})$.

The scheme guarantees, for any $1 \leq t \leq n$:

Correctness. If the dealer follows the protocol, $PVSS.RECONSTRUCT$ on any t honest shares always outputs the original s.

t-Privacy. Fewer than t colluding parties obtain no information about s

Public Verifiability. Anyone, given (pk_i, C_i, Y_i), can run $PVSS.VERIFY$ without access to secret keys. Valid shares always pass, and forging an invalid share that passes is infeasible.

t-Robustness. Once C is fixed, at most one secret s can be reconstructed from any set of t verified shares. A malicious dealer cannot make two inconsistent secrets pass verification.

4 PVSS-BFT Protocol Overview

Our PVSS-BFT protocol is presented in Algorithm 1. Figure 1 shows an overview of the flow of our protocol.

4.1 Phase 1: Block Proposal and Share Distribution

In each view v, we define $\mathcal{A}(v)$ from the participant set N as the number of active participants recognized for v. $\mathcal{A}(v)$ consists of nodes that pre-committed their participation and newly awakened nodes that were confirmed in view $v-1$. Every node in $\mathcal{A}(v)$ may independently proposes a block in Phase 1 before the leader election to ensure protocol progress regardless of eventual leader availability.

Block Proposal and Pre-Commit. Each node i generates a block B_i. It also creates a pre-commit signal $PRECOM_i$ indicating its intention to participate in view $v+1$. To bind the block and pre-commit together, node i computes hash $h_i = H(B_i \| PRECOM_i)$.

PVSS Splitting. Node i now acts as a dealer for its own block. Using a PVSS scheme $PVSS.SPLIT(h_i, \mathcal{A}(v), t)$, ($t$ is the threshold required to reconstruct the secret h_i, we let $t = \lfloor \mathcal{A}(v)/2 \rfloor + 1$), node i produces: **A public commitment** C_i ensuring the validity of shares; **Encrypted shares** $Y_i = (Y_{i,1}, \ldots, Y_{i,\mathcal{A}(v)})$, where each $Y_{i,j}$ is the share sent to node j from i.

VRF Generation. Node i also generates a VRF output $(\rho_i, \pi_i) \leftarrow \text{VRF}_i(v)$, used to elect a leader in Phase 2.

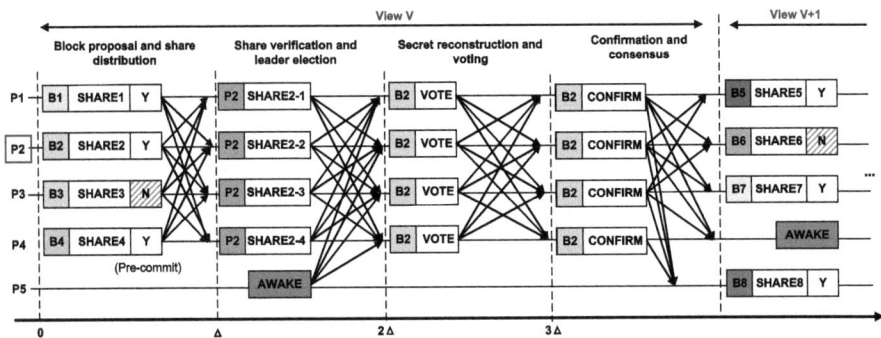

Fig. 1. The PVSS-BFT protocol flow across v and $v+1$. In the first phase, each node proposes a candidate block, splits the block's hash into multiple shares, and distributes shares along with a pre-commit signal indicating whether it intends to join the next consensus round. Nodes $P1$, $P2$, and $P4$ choose to pre-commit (Y), while $P3$ opts out (N). In the second phase, nodes determine a leader (e.g. $P2$) based on VRF values. Then every node that previously received $P2$'s share now broadcasts that share to all other nodes. During phase 3, nodes use the collected shares to reconstruct the $P2$'s block and cast votes on its validity. In the final phase, upon gathering a sufficient number of valid votes, nodes broadcast confirm messages, finalizing consensus on the leader's proposed block. As a result, by the start of View $V+1$, node P3, which did not pre-commit, is excluded, while node P5, having issued an awake message, successfully joins the protocol.

Node i broadcasts a $PROPOSE$ message $\langle v, B_i, Y_i, \rho_i, \pi_i, PRECOM_i \rangle_i$ to all other nodes. By including $PRECOM_i$ within h_i, nodes i signals possible maintenance schedules. This pre-commit mechanism ensures that a reliable set of the next-round participant for PVSS is defined. Since C_i is publicly recorded, i cannot selectively broadcast Y_i without being detected. Integrating block proposals with PVSS before the leader election ensures security by preventing equivocating or selective message broadcasting, as any inconsistency can be caught through share reconstruction and verification.

4.2 Phase 2: Share Verification and Leader Election

Upon receiving $PROPOSE$ messages, node i verifies the validity of shares and elects a leader based on VRF values.

Share Verification. For each $PROPOSE$ message from node j, node i extracts share $Y_{j,i}$ and runs PVSS.VERIFY$(pk_j, C_j, Y_{j,i})$ to ensure $Y_{j,i}$ is consistent with C_j. Node i also checks VRF.VERIFY(pk_j, π_j, v). If both verification succeed, node i deems j's message valid and include j in a set V.

Leader Election. Node i selects a leader $L \leftarrow \arg\max_{j \in V} \text{vrf}_j$. All pre-commit signals $PRECOM$ are recorded in NextRoundCommit$_i$ list to track participation intentions for round $v+1$.

Algorithm 1. PVSS-BFT Protocol

1: **Initialization:** Set $outputs \leftarrow \emptyset$. Initialize $V \leftarrow \emptyset$, NEXTROUNDCOMMIT $\leftarrow \emptyset$
2: **Phase 1: Block Proposal and Share Distribution**
3: Generate block B_i and pre-commit signal $PRECOM_i$
4: **If** receive $\langle AWAKE \rangle$ message:
5:     Add to AWAKELIST$_i$
6: Compute $h'_i \leftarrow$ HASH$(B_i \| PRECOM_i)$
7: Generate shares: $(Y_{i,1}, ..., Y_{i,n}), C_i \leftarrow$ PVSS.SPLIT$(h'_i, \mathcal{A}(v), t)$
8: Generate VRF output: $(\rho_i, \pi_i) \leftarrow$ VRF$_i(v)$
9: Broadcast $PROPOSE$ $\langle v, B_i, Y_i, C_i, \rho_i, \pi_i, PRECOM_i \rangle_i$
10: **Phase 2: Share Verification and Leader Election**
11: For each received $PROPOSE$ message:
12:     Verify VRF: $valid_{vrf} \leftarrow$ VRF.VERIFY(pk_j, π_j, v)
13:     Verify share: $Y_j \leftarrow$ PVSS.VERIFY(pk_j, C_j, Y_j)
14:     **If** $valid_{vrf}$ and Y_j: Add j to valid proposal set V
15: Select leader: $L \leftarrow \arg\max_{j \in V} \rho_j$
16: Record $PRECOM_j$ in NEXTROUNDCOMMIT
17: Update AWAKELIST$_i$
18: Prepare $M_1 \leftarrow \langle v, Y_{L,i} \rangle$
19: Prepare $M_2 \leftarrow \langle$AWAKELIST$_i$, NEXTROUNDCOMMIT$_i \rangle$
20: Concatenate and broadcast: $M_1 \| M_2$
21: **Phase 3: Secret Reconstruction and Voting**
22: Add nodes to NEXTROUNDPARTICIPANTS if they appear in $> \mathcal{A}(v)/2$ AWAKELIST and add nodes to VOTEFORNEXTROUNDCOMMITMENT if appearing in $> \mathcal{A}(v)/2$ NEXTROUNDCOMMITS
23: Reconstruct secret: $secret \leftarrow$ PVSS.RECONSTRUCT$(\{Y_{L,m}\}_{m=1}^t)$
24: **If** $secret =$ HASH$(B_l \| \text{PRECOM}_l)$: VOTE$_i \leftarrow$ true
25: Generate shares of vote: $(Y_{\text{VOTE}_i}, C_{\text{VOTE}_i}) \leftarrow$ PVSS.SPLIT(HASH(VOTE$_i$), $\mathcal{A}(v), t$)
26: Broadcast $VOTE$ $\langle v, \text{VOTE}_i, Y_{\text{VOTE}_i}, C_{\text{VOTE}_i} \rangle_i$
27: **Phase 4: Confirmation and Consensus**
28: Upon receiving $\geq \mathcal{A}(v)/2$ valid $VOTE$ messages:
29:     Broadcast $CONFIRM$ $\langle v,$ HASH$(B_l \| \text{PRECOM}_l) \rangle_i$
30: Upon collecting $\geq \mathcal{A}(v)/2$ valid CONFIRM messages:
31:     Decide on B_l

If node i receives an $AWAKE$ message from a newly active node j during phase 1 or 2, it updates AwakeList$_i$ to include j. To ensure all nodes can reconstruct L's block, node i broadcasts $Y_{L,i}$ (i.e. the share i received from the potential leader L), via $\langle v, Y_{L,i},$ AwakeList$_i$, NextRoundCommit$_i \rangle_i$.

The early distribution of blocks and shares before leader election ensures that even if the leader becomes unavailable, other nodes can reconstruct and verify the leader's block using share reconstruction. This design prevents malicious leaders from distributing inconsistent blocks or manipulating the protocol, as block verification proceeds independently of leader presence. Since the necessary data is pre-distributed, leader unavailability after the election is inconsequential.

4.3 Phase 3: Secret Reconstruction and Voting

Once the leader L is elected, nodes reconstruct and verify L's block. This process confirms both block integrity and participant adherence to pre-commit signals.

Secret Reconstruction. Node i collects at least t distinct shares $\{Y_{L,m}\}_{m=1}^{t}$. Then node i decrypts every collected share $S_{L,m} = Y_{L,m}^{1/x_m}$ and reconstructs the secret using PVSS.RECONSTRUCT($\{S_{L,m}\}_{m=1}^{t}$) and verifies it against L's block hash. If secret = Hash($B_l \| PRECOM_l$), i sets $vote_i \leftarrow$ true; otherwise $vote_i \leftarrow$ false. The successful reconstruction of the leader's block not only verifies block integrity but also confirms the adherence of participants to their pre-commits, as reconstruction requires sufficient honest nodes to contribute shares.

Voting. Each awake node i encode its vote $(Y_{i,1}^{vote}, \ldots, Y_{i,\mathcal{A}(v)}^{vote}), C_i^{vote}$ using PVSS.SPLIT($H(vote_i), \mathcal{A}(v), t$).

Node i broadcasts a $VOTE$ message $< v, vote_i, (Y_{i,1}^{vote}, \ldots, Y_{i,\mathcal{A}(v)}^{vote}), C_i^{vote} >$.

The protocol tracks node appearances in NextRoundCommitment lists - if a node i's count exceeds threshold $\mathcal{A}(v)/2$, k is added to VoteforNextRoundCommitment. Similarly, if the count for awake node k exceeds the threshold, node i preliminarily confirma k as awake for next round. The integration of PVSS with voting ensures that block verification is tied to pre-commit validation, as failed reconstruction indicates either malicious behavior or violation of pre-commits.

4.4 Phase 4: Confirmation and Consensus

Commit Rule. When node i receives $\geq \mathcal{A}(v)/2$ valid $VOTE$ messages for block B_L, it broadcasts a $CONFIRM$ message $\langle v, H(B_l)\rangle_i$. Upon collecting at least $\mathcal{A}(v)/2$ valid $CONFIRM$ messages, i decides on B_l and finalizes the participation list for round $v+1$, incorporating nodes with validated pre-commit signals $PRECOM$ and newly confirmed awake nodes.

Error Handling. When PVSS reconstruction fails or inconsistent votes are detected, the protocol initiates error correction by having all nodes broadcast their stored shares, enabling vote reconstruction to verify share-vote consistency and identify nodes whose reconstructed votes differ from their broadcast votes. This deterministic error detection approach provides cryptographic proof of both malicious behavior and commitment violations. Regarding the handling of unexpected node failures that may trigger a view change, for example, if a node receives fewer than a quorum of valid $VOTE$ or $CONFIRM$ messages, the view may be aborted. We refer readers to Sect. 6.2 and 7, where the protocol's tolerance to node failures in each phase is rigorously analyzed.

5 Security Analysis

5.1 Safety Analysis

Lemma 1. *For any honest validators $p, q \in \mathcal{A}(v)$, if p reconstructs a block B from the shares of leader L at time $t = 2\Delta$, then q either reconstructs the same block B or fails to reconstruct any block at time $t = 2\Delta$.*

Proof. We consider three possible attack scenarios.

Scenario 1 (Share forgery without modifying commits): By the *public-verifiability* property, a tuple (pk_i, C, Y) passes verification if $Y = y_i^{p(i)}$ for the unique polynomial $p(x)$ defined by C. Hence an adversary who keeps C unchanged but broadcasts $Y'_k \neq y_k^{p(k)}$ to some receiver k will inevitably fail verification.

When introducing PVSS into BFT, at the first consensus phase, every node as a dealer selects a random polynomial $p(x) = \sum_{j=0}^{t-1} \alpha_j x^j$ of degree at most $t-1$, where $\alpha_j \in \mathbb{Z}_q$ and $s = \alpha_0$. Node i has a private key $x_i \in_R \mathbb{Z}_q^*$ and a public key $y_i = G^{x_i}$, where G_q is a cyclic group of prime order q.

Node i publishes commitment $C_i = \{C_0, \ldots, C_{t-1}\}$ where $C_j = g^{\alpha_j}$. Once C_i is published, the polynomial $p(x)$ is determined. Node i's correct encrypted share is $Y_i = y_i^{p(i)}$. Every receiver n computes and verifies

$$X_n = \prod_{j=0}^{t-1} C_j^{n^j} = g^{p(n)} \tag{1}$$

$$\log_g X_n = \log_{y_n} Y_n \tag{2}$$

Suppose an adversary M broadcasts an alternative $Y'_k \neq Y_k$ for a certain node k that still passes verification to affect k's reconstruction process. Equation (1) fixes $X_k = g^{p(k)}$. For Y'_k to pass the verification, there must exist a value $p'(k)$ such that $Y'_k = y_k^{p'(k)}$ and $g^{p(k)} = g^{p'(k)}$. Because g has order q, the latter equality implies $p'(k) \equiv p(k) \pmod{q}$. Consequently $Y'_k = y_k^{p'(k)} = y_k^{p(k)} = Y_k$, contradicting the assumption $Y'_k \neq Y_k$. Hence, *no* adversary can produce a different share that still verifies against the fixed commitments.

Scenario 2 (Simultaneous forgery of commits and shares): By t-robustness, at most one secret can be reconstructed from C'. Because honest nodes accept a share only when (C, Y_i) satisfies equation (2), they will never mix shares coming from two distinct commitment vectors. Therefore, honest nodes either all stay with C or all reject the forged commitment.

Specifically, if an adversary M changes any commitment $C_j \to C'_j$, she defines a new polynomial $p'(x)$. M needs to find $p'(i)$ for each i such that: $g^{p'(i)} = X'_i$ and $y_i^{p'(i)} = Y'_i$. The challenge for M is to create consistent values X'_i and Y'_i that satisfy the proof for each i, while also ensuring that these values correspond to a valid polynomial $p'(x)$ of degree $t-1$. If M attempts to create X'_i and Y'_i that don't correspond to a valid $p'(x)$, this inconsistency will be detectable when nodes attempt to reconstruct the secret or verify the polynomial's properties.

Scenario 3 (Leader share forgery): Based on the synchronous network assumption, all honest validators select the same leader. Suppose a malicious node M attempts to broadcast an incorrect leader share $Y'_i \neq Y_i$ during the second phase. For each node i, the correct share should be: $Y_i = y_i^{p(i)} = (G^{x_i})^{p(i)} = $

$G^{x_i \cdot p(i)}$. All nodes can use the publicly published commits to compute: $Xi = \prod j = 0^{t-1} C_j^{i^j} = g^{p(i)}$

When any node receives a share claimed to be from the leader Y_i, it compute $X_i = \prod_{j=0}^{t-1} C_j^{i^j}$ and Verifies $\log_g(X_i) = \log_{y_i}(Y_i)$. If M broadcasts an incorrect share $Y_i' \neq Y_i$, then there must exist $p'(i) \neq p(i)$ such that: $Y_i' = y_i^{p'(i)} = G^{x_i \cdot p'(i)}$. This is impossible by the same argument as in scenario 2; hence leader share forgery is rejected immediately.

Now, consider honest validators $p, q \in \mathcal{A}(v)$ at time $t = 2\Delta$. If p successfully reconstruct block B. p must receive at least $t > n/2$ valid shares corresponding to B. Each share must be consistently broadcast and verified. If q receives sufficient valid shares. By Scenario 1, any share from an honest validator corresponds to the same polynomial $p(x)$. By Scenario 2, malicious validators cannot forge a consistent set of shares. By Scenario 3, all honest nodes will receive the correct share. Therefore, q must reconstruct the same block B. If q receives insufficient valid shares, q will fail to reconstruct any block.

Lemma 2. *For any honest validators $p, q \in \mathcal{A}(v)$ of view v, if p votes for block B and q votes for block B' at time $t = 3\Delta$, then $B = B'$.*

Proof. Consider the necessary conditions for honest validators to cast votes. For an honest validator p to vote for block B at time 3Δ. p must have identified the correct leader L at time 2Δ. p and q must have reconstructed B from leader L's shares. The reconstructed block hash must match L's proposed block. The reconstruction requires at least $t > n/2$ valid shares from distinct validators.

Formally, at time $t = 2\Delta$, all honest validators have received shares and VRF outputs from other validators. Since the leader L is agreed upon by all honest validators (due to the deterministic VRF selection and synchronous network), they all attempt to reconstruct the leader's block B_L using the PVSS shares. Honest validator p reconstructs block B from the shares of L at time $t = 2\Delta$. Similarly, honest validator q reconstructs block B' from the shares of L. Both p and q require at least T valid PVSS shares to reconstruct the block, where $T > n/2$. By **Lemma 1**, which states that if any honest validator reconstructs a block B from the shares of leader L, then all other honest validators reconstruct the same block B. Therefore, since both p and q are honest and have reconstructed blocks from L's shares, it must be that $B = B' = B_L$. At time $t = 3\Delta$, honest validators p and q proceed to the voting phase. They vote for the block they have reconstructed and verified, which is $B = B' = B_L$.

Lemma 3. *For any view v, if an honest validator $p \in \mathcal{A}(v)$ receives sufficient votes ($\geq n/2$) for block B at time $t = 4\Delta$, then no honest validator $q \in \mathcal{A}(v)$ can receive sufficient votes for any block $B' \neq B$ at time $t = 4\Delta$.*

Proof. By Lemma 2, all honest validators who vote at time 3Δ vote for the same block. Due to the leader election process, only the leader's block can be reconstructed and verified. Votes for any other block are invalid and will be discarded by honest validators.

Honest validators send their votes to all validators. By synchronous network assumptions, votes at time 3Δ will be received by all honest validators by time 4Δ. Even if Byzantine nodes send different votes to different honest nodes, all honest nodes will eventually receive all votes. For p to receive sufficient votes ($\geq n/2$) for block B, Some honest validators must have voted for B. By Lemma 2, all honest validators who vote must vote for B. These honest votes will reach all honest validators by time 4Δ. Therefore, no block other than B can receive sufficient votes. Any honest validator q must see the same voting result as p.

Theorem 1. (Safety) *If two honest nodes confirm blocks B and B' respectively, then B does not conflict with B'.*

Proof. Suppose two honest validators $p, q \in \mathcal{A}(v)$ decide different blocks B and B' at the same height in view v. For block B to be decided by honest validator p, p must have received sufficient votes ($\geq n/2$) for B and these votes must be based on successful block reconstruction at time 2Δ. By Lemma 1, at time 2Δ, if any honest validator reconstructs block B, all other honest validators either reconstruct B. By Lemma 2, at time 3Δ, all honest validators who vote must vote for the same block. By Lemma 3, if p receives sufficient votes for B at time 4Δ, q cannot receive sufficient votes for any $B' \neq B$. Therefore, it is impossible for p and q to decide on different blocks of the same height.

5.2 Liveness Analysis

Theorem 2. *If a transaction tx is broadcast to all honest validators at time t, then there exists a time $t' \geq t$ such that all honest validators awake at time t' will eventually decide on a log containing tx.*

Proof. Assume that tx is broadcast to all validators at time t. Due to the synchronous network assumption, all honest validators receive tx by time $t+\Delta$. Starting from the view v that begins at or after time $t+\Delta$, all honest validators include tx in their proposed blocks. The leader election is based on VRF, which is unpredictable and uniformly random among validators. Given that the set of honest validators is greater than half of the total validators, an honest validator will eventually be selected as the leader in some future view $v' \geq v$. We proceed by considering the view v' in which an honest leader L is selected.

At time t_0, all awake validators broadcast their proposed blocks and shares. Honest leader L includes tx in its proposed block B. All honest validators receive shares and VRF values from other validators by time $t_0 + \Delta$. They agree on the leader L based on the highest VRF value. At time $t_0 + 2\Delta$, honest validators reconstruct L's block B using shares. By Lemma 1, if any honest validator reconstructs B, then all honest validators reconstruct the same block B at time $t_0+2\Delta$. Since B includes tx, all honest validators now have access to a block containing tx. By Lemma 2, all honest validators vote for the same block B at time $t_0+3\Delta$. Since the number of honest validators $\geq$ half of the active validator, B receives sufficient votes at time $t_0 + 4\Delta$. By Lemma 3, no conflicting block can receive sufficient votes. All honest validators confirm and decide on block B.

Conclusion: At time $t' = t_0 + 4\Delta$, all honest validators awake at time t' have decided on a log containing tx. Therefore, for any transaction tx broadcast at time t, there exists a time $t' \geq t$ such that all honest validators awake at time t' will eventually decide on a log containing tx.

6 Experimental Evaluation

6.1 Experiment 1: Security Analysis

In this experiment, we evaluate the security performance of the PVSS-BFT system against a baseline BFT protocol that omits the PVSS mechanism. By removing PVSS from our protocol, we create a conventional BFT protocol with standard security features. The network consists of 40 nodes deployed in a cloud environment using Amazon EC2 services. We implemented both the PVSS-BFT and conventional BFT protocols on these nodes. We evaluate the resilience of our PVSS-BFT protocol against adversarial behaviors specifically designed to disrupt consensus and induce chain forks. It focuses on scenarios where malicious leaders may distribute conflicting block versions to different node groups, manipulating the consensus process to create forks. Specifically, if a malicious node is elected as the leader, it divides the entire set of nodes into two arbitrary groups without any coordination or knowledge of the honest nodes. The partitioning is solely determined by the malicious leader and is not based on any network topology or logical grouping. The malicious leader generates two different blocks with distinct transactions or data. The number of malicious nodes increased from 0 to 19 to observe the systems' behavior under adversarial conditions.

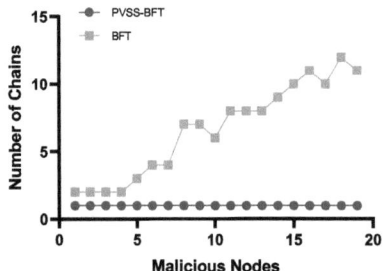

Fig. 2. Fork occurrence comparison between baseline BFT and PVSS-BFT under malicious nodes.

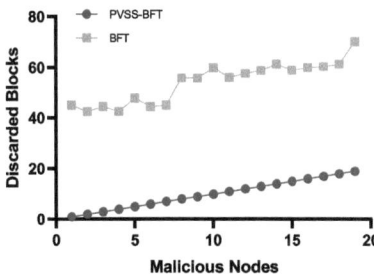

Fig. 3. Block discard rates comparison between baseline BFT and PVSS-BFT with increasing malicious nodes.

Forking Analysis. Figure 2 illustrates the relationship between the number of malicious nodes and the incidence of chain forks. We show the fork resistance capabilities of both systems under increasing adversarial presence. In the baseline BFT system, we observe a clear positive correlation between the number of malicious nodes and fork occurrences. In contrast, the PVSS-BFT system shows remarkable resilience by maintaining zero forks, demonstrating its ability to cryptographically verify and reject conflicting proposals.

Block Discard Analysis. Figure 3 presents the number of blocks discarded under varying levels of adversarial presence. The baseline BFT system demonstrates a notable increase in discarded blocks as the number of malicious nodes rises, attributed to fork resolutions and conflicting proposals. The PVSS-BFT system consistently shows fewer discarded blocks, attributed to its fork prevention and rapid invalid proposal detection capabilities.

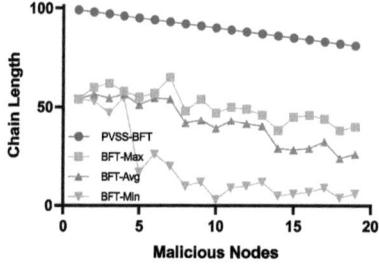

Fig. 4. Impact of malicious nodes on chain length.

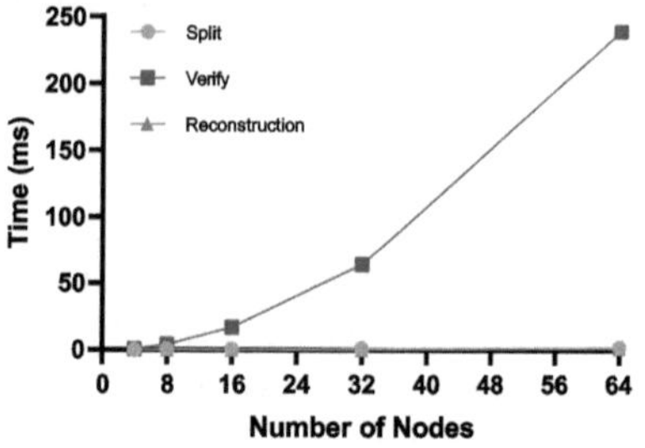

Fig. 5. Time consumption of each step of PVSS.

Chain Length Dynamics. As depicted in Fig. 4, the baseline BFT system experiences significant fluctuations in chain length as the number of malicious nodes increases. This instability can be attributed to the increasing number of forks created by malicious nodes. These forks lead to frequent chain reorganizations, causing the overall chain length to fluctuate dramatically. In contrast, the PVSS-BFT system maintains a stable and consistent chain length throughout test scenarios, proving its efficacy in countering adversarial disruptions and maintaining continuous ledger growth.

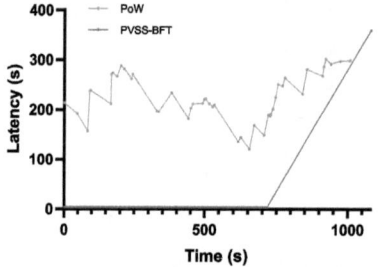
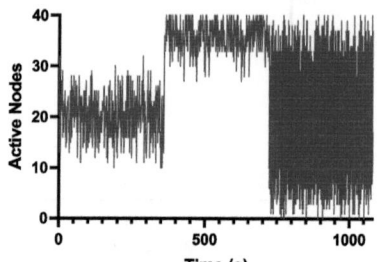

Fig. 6. The latency of both our protocol and the longest-chain protocol.

Fig. 7. The participation level over time.

6.2 Experiment 2: Latency Analysis

We first evaluated the PVSS's computational overhead by benchmarking the latency of its core operations: $SPLIT$, $VERIFY$, and $RECONSTRUCTION$. Figure 5 summarizes the results for varying numbers of nodes ($n \in \{4, 8, 16, 32, 64\}$). At $n = 64$, the average time for verification is approximately $230ms$. The splitting and reconstruction phases take negligible time. While verification is the dominant cost, its latency remains practical. It is comparable to typical cross-region network latencies observed in different AWS servers as described in the full version of [17]. Crucially, given our protocol's phase time assumption of $\Delta = 1s$ per phase (adopted based on the experimental setup in [22]), the computational overhead of all PVSS operations fits comfortably within this budget. Therefore, the PVSS computations do not impose a bottleneck.

We then evaluate how our protocol performs under varying participation levels, using the "Longest-Chain" approach from Momose and Ren [22] as a baseline. To the best of our knowledge, theeir experiment is the only publicly documented framework that models nodes switching online/offline at second-level granularity, while existing sleepy models (e.g., [11,21]) report performance only through theory. We emphasize that this comparison is strictly about latency under dynamic participation. Figure 6 and 7 illustrate how our protocol performs relative to the longest-chain protocol. For the longest-chain baseline, we configured the system to produce blocks approximately every 15 s, with a confirmation length of $k = 10$ blocks. Inspired by the experimental setup in [22], we consider three distinct participation level stages over a period of approximately 1080 time units (seconds): low participation, high participation, and unstable participation.

1. Low participation (0–360 seconds): Initially, 20 nodes are active. The total active participation then fluctuates around 50% of all nodes, following an approximate sinusoidal pattern.
2. High participation (360–720 seconds): The participation probability was consistently set at 90%, maintaining more than 30 active nodes.
3. Unstable participation (720–1080 seconds): The number of active nodes was highly volatile, fluctuating rapidly each second from 0 to 40.

In our protocol, we observe a constant latency that is significantly lower than the longest-chain protocol. This consistent low latency is maintained throughout the first two stages. However, when participation fluctuates greatly, our protocol can ensure security, but cannot make the ledger grow.

Unstable Participation Analysis: In the scenario of *unstable participation*, nodes can independently change their status every second with a probability p. In this context, an active node can become sleepy and a sleepy node can become active with equal probability. This can lead to a situation where our protocol is unable to make progress. This challenge primarily arises from the requirement of a specific threshold of nodes for secret reconstruction. We analyze the maximum tolerable probability p that allows the protocol to function correctly without compromising safety guarantees in the appendix7. Each consensus round can tolerate up to 63% of nodes being offline.

7 Conclusion and Future Work

In this paper, we have presented an advanced sleepy BFT consensus model. By integrating PVSS and VRF into a four-phase consensus mechanism, our approach offers improved efficiency and security compared to existing models.

We have provided formal proof for the safety and liveness properties of our protocol, demonstrating its robustness in the face of Byzantine adversaries and dynamic participation. Our experimental evaluations corroborate the theoretical findings. In simulated adversarial conditions, the PVSS-BFT protocol demonstrated superior fork resistance and chain stability compared to traditional BFT systems. Latency tests revealed that our protocol maintains consistently low latency across varying participation levels, only showing limitations in extreme instability scenarios.

We acknowledge that PVSS inherently adds communication overhead due to the distribution of shares and commitments. While our computational benchmarks demonstrate feasibility, optimizing communication complexity, particularly at larger network scales, remains an important consideration. Future work includes investigating techniques to reduce overall message costs.

Acknowledgment. This project is fully supported by the CloudTech-RMIT Green Bitcoin Joint Research Program.

Unstable Participation Analysis

We consider a PVSS-BFT system with n nodes. Let $X_{i,j}$ denote the number of active nodes in phase j of round i, where $j = 1, 2, 3, 4$ and $S_{i,j}$ denote the number of nodes confirmed as sleepy by phase j of round i. The expected number of active nodes in the first phase of round i is given by:

$$E[X_{i,1}] = E[X_{i-1,1}] \times (1-p)^4 + E[Y_{i-1}], \tag{3}$$

where $E[Y_{i-1}]$ is the expected number of newly activated nodes in round $i-1$ that are eligible to participate in phase 1 of round i.

For subsequent phases $j = 2, 3, 4$, since only nodes that were active in phase 1 and remain active can participate, the expected number of active nodes is:

$$E[X_{i,j}] = E[X_{i,1}] \times (1-p)^{(j)}. \tag{4}$$

For phase 2, the expected number of active nodes and sleepy nodes are:

$$\begin{aligned} E[X_{i,2}] &= E[X_{i,1}] \times (1-p)^2 \\ E[S_{i,2}] &= E[X_{i,1}] \times p \end{aligned} \tag{5}$$

For phase 3 (vote phase), the expected number of active nodes and sleepy nodes are:

$$\begin{aligned} E[X_{i,3}] &= E[X_{i,1}] \times (1-p)^3 \\ E[S_{i,3}] &= E[X_{i,1}] \times (1-(1-p)^2) \end{aligned} \tag{6}$$

The expected number of newly activated nodes eligible for the next round is:

$$\begin{aligned} E[Y_i] = &(n - E[X_{i,1}]) \times p \times (1-p)^3 \\ &+ (n - E[X_{i,1}] \times (1-p)) \times p \times (1-p)^2. \end{aligned} \tag{7}$$

To reconstruct the secret and reach a consensus, the protocol must satisfy two conditions:

$$X_{i,3} \geq 0.5 \times X_{i,1} \quad \text{(vote phase)}$$
$$X_{i,4} \geq \frac{X_{i,1} - S_{i,2}}{2} \quad \text{(confirm phase)} \tag{8}$$

Latency Analysis Using Normal Approximation. Assuming the system has reached a steady state, i.e., $E[X_{i,1}] = E[X_{i-1,1}]$, we have:

$$E[X_{i,1}] = E[X_{i,1}] \times (1-p)^4 + E[Y_{i-1}], \tag{9}$$

$$E[X_{i,1}] = \frac{E[Y_{i-1}]}{1 - (1-p)^4}. \tag{10}$$

Given the synchronous network assumption, we can deterministically detect node failures in phases 1–2. However, these detections must be confirmed through the voting process in phase 3. The success probability P_{success} depends on two critical conditions:

$$P_{\text{success\_vote}} = P(X_{i,3} \geq 0.5 \times X_{i,1}) \tag{11}$$

$$P_{\text{success\_confirm}} = P\left(X_{i,4} \geq \frac{X_{i,1} - S_{i,2}}{2} \,\Big|\, X_{i,3} \geq 0.5 \times X_{i,1}\right) \tag{12}$$

For the vote phase condition, substituting the expected values:

$$E[X_{i,3}] = E[X_{i,1}] \times (1-p)^3 \geq 0.5 \times E[X_{i,1}] \tag{13}$$

This simplifies to:

$$(1-p)^3 \geq \frac{1}{2} \tag{14}$$

Solving for the maximum tolerable probability:

$$p \leq 1 - \frac{1}{\sqrt[3]{2}} \approx 0.21 \tag{15}$$

The confirm phase threshold is dynamically adjusted based on detected sleepy nodes from phases 1 and 2, but this adjustment only takes effect after successful voting. For the confirm phase, given successful voting, we have:

$$E[X_{i,4}] \geq \frac{E[X_{i,1}] - E[S_{i,2}]}{2} \tag{16}$$

where $E[S_{i,2}]$ is the sum of sleepy nodes detected in phase 1 and 2:

$$E[S_{i,4}] = E[X_{i,1}] \times (1 - (1-p)^2) \tag{17}$$

Substituting the expressions:

$$E[X_{i,1}] \times (1-p)^4 \geq \frac{E[X_{i,1}] - E[X_{i,1}] \times (1 - (1-p)^2)}{2} \tag{18}$$

Let $p = 0.21$ (derived from vote phase constraint). Substituting this value into the confirm phase inequality shows that it is satisfied. Therefore, the vote phase constraint $p \leq 1 - \frac{1}{\sqrt[3]{2}} \approx 0.21$ is indeed the bottleneck of our protocol. Each consensus round can tolerate up to $1 - (1 - 0.21)^4 \approx 0.63$ or 63% of nodes being offline at some point during the round. This significant improvement over traditional fixed-threshold approaches is achieved through the combination of deterministic sleepy node detection in the synchronous network and dynamic threshold adjustment after successful voting.

References

1. Basu, S., Tomescu, A., Abraham, I., Malkhi, D., Reiter, M.K., Sirer, E.G.: Efficient verifiable secret sharing with share recovery in BFT protocols. In: Proceedings of the 2019 ACM SIGSAC Conference on Computer and Communications Security (CCS), pp. 2387–2402 (2019)
2. Beimel, A.: Secret-sharing schemes: a survey. In: International Conference on Coding and Cryptology, pp. 11–46. Springer (2011)
3. Blakley, G.R.: Safeguarding cryptographic keys. In: Proceedings of the International Workshop on Managing Requirements Knowledg, pp. 313–318 (1979)
4. Boneh, D., Lynn, B., Shacham, H.: Short signatures from the weil pairing. In: Annual International Conference on the Theory and Application of Cryptology and Information Security (ASIACRYPT), pp. 514–532. Springer (2001)
5. Castro, M., Liskov, B., et al.: Practical Byzantine fault tolerance. In: Proceedings of the 3rd USENIX Symposium on Operating Systems Design and Implementation (OSDI), pp. 173–186 (1999)
6. Chandramouli, A., Choudhury, A., Patra, A.: A survey on perfectly secure verifiable secret-sharing. ACM Computing Surveys (CSUR), pp. 1–36 (2022)
7. Chen, J., Micali, S.: Algorand: A secure and efficient distributed ledger. Theoretical Computer Science, pp. 155–183 (2019)
8. Chor, B., Goldwasser, S., Micali, S., Awerbuch, B.: Verifiable secret sharing and achieving simultaneity in the presence of faults. In: Annual Symposium on Foundations of Computer Science (FOCS), pp. 383–395 (1985)
9. Daian, P., Pass, R., Shi, E.: Snow white: robustly reconfigurable consensus and applications to provably secure proof of stake. In: Financial Cryptography and Data Security: 23rd International Conference (FC), pp. 23–41. Springer (2019)
10. D'Amato, F., Neu, J., Tas, E.N., Tse, D.: Goldfish: no more attacks on Proof-of-Stake Ethereum. arXiv preprint arXiv:2209.03255 (2022)
11. D'Amato, F., Zanolini, L.: Streamlining sleepy consensus: total-order broadcast with single-vote decisions in the sleepy model. arXiv preprint arXiv:2310.11331 (2023)
12. D'Amato, F., Zanolini, L.: Recent latest message driven GHOST: balancing dynamic availability with asynchrony resilience. In: IEEE Computer Security Foundations Symposium (CSF), pp. 127–142. IEEE (2024)
13. Gafni, E., Losa, G.: Brief announcement: Byzantine consensus under dynamic participation with a well-behaved majority. In: International Symposium on Distributed Computing (DISC) (2023)
14. Goyal, V., Li, H., Raizes, J.: Instant block confirmation in the sleepy model. In: Financial Cryptography and Data Security: 25th International Conference (FC)), pp. 65–83. Springer (2021)

15. Gueta, G.G., et al.: SBFT: A scalable and decentralized trust infrastructure. In: Annual IEEE/IFIP International Conference on Dependable Systems and Networks (DSN), pp. 568–580. IEEE (2019)
16. Katz, J., Koo, C.Y.: On expected constant-round protocols for Byzantine agreement. J. Comput. Syst. Sci. 91–112 (2009)
17. Kelkar, M., Deb, S., Long, S., Juels, A., Kannan, S.: Themis: fast, strong order-fairness in Byzantine consensus. In: Proceedings of the 2023 ACM SIGSAC Conference on Computer and Communications Security (CCS), pp. 475–489 (2023)
18. Kogias, E.K., Jovanovic, P., Gailly, N., Khoffi, I., Gasser, L., Ford, B.: Enhancing Bitcoin security and performance with strong consistency via collective signing. In: USENIX Security Symposium (USENIX Security), pp. 279–296 (2016)
19. Liu, J., Li, W., Karame, G.O., Asokan, N.: Scalable Byzantine consensus via hardware-assisted secret sharing. IEEE Transactions on Computers, pp. 139–151 (2018)
20. Malkhi, D., Momose, A., Ren, L.: Byzantine consensus under fully fluctuating participation. In: IACR Cryptol. ePrint Arch, p. 1448 (2022)
21. Malkhi, D., Momose, A., Ren, L.: Towards practical sleepy BFT. In: Proceedings of the 2023 ACM SIGSAC Conference on Computer and Communications Security (CCS), pp. 490–503 (2023)
22. Momose, A., Ren, L.: Constant latency in sleepy consensus. In: Proceedings of the 2022 ACM SIGSAC Conference on Computer and Communications Security (CCS), pp. 2295–2308 (2022)
23. Pass, R., Shi, E.: The sleepy model of consensus. In: Annual International Conference on the Theory and Applications of Cryptology and Information Security (ASIACRYPT), pp. 380–409. Springer (2017)
24. Schoenmakers, B.: A simple publicly verifiable secret sharing scheme and its application to electronic voting. In: Annual International Cryptology Conference (CRYPTO), pp. 148–164. Springer (1999)
25. Shamir, A.: How to share a secret. Commun. ACM, pp. 612–613 (1979)
26. Stadler, M.: Publicly verifiable secret sharing. In: Annual International Conference on the Theory and Applications of Cryptographic Techniques (EUROCRYPT), pp. 190–199. Springer (1996)
27. Vassantlal, R., Alchieri, E., Ferreira, B., Bessani, A.: COBRA: Dynamic proactive secret sharing for confidential BFT services. In: IEEE Symposium on Security and Privacy (S&P), pp. 1335–1353. IEEE (2022)
28. Wang, C., Duan, S., Xu, M., Li, F., Cheng, X.: Sleepy consensus in the known participation model. Cryptology ePrint Archive (2024)

An Algebraic Approach to Asymmetric Delegation and Polymorphic Label Inference

Silei Ren[1]([✉])[iD], Coşku Acay[2][iD], and Andrew C. Myers[1][iD]

[1] Cornell University, Ithaca, NY 14850, USA
sr2262@cornell.edu, andru@cs.cornell.edu
[2] Observe, Inc., San Mateo, CA 94402, USA

Abstract. Language-based information flow control (IFC) enables reasoning about and enforcing security policies in decentralized applications. While information flow properties are relatively extensional and compositional, designing expressive systems that enforce such properties remains challenging. In particular, it can be difficult to use IFC labels to model certain security assumptions, such as semi-honest agents. Motivated by these modeling limitations, we study the algebraic semantics of lattice-based IFC label models, and propose a semantic framework that allows formalizing asymmetric delegation, which is partial delegation of confidentiality or integrity. Our framework supports downgrading of information and ensures their safety through nonmalleable information flow (NMIF). To demonstrate the practicality of our framework, we design and implement a novel algorithm that statically checks NMIF and a label inference procedure that efficiently supports bounded label polymorphism, allowing users to write code generic with respect to labels.

1 Introduction

Information Flow Control (IFC) [23,38] is a well-established approach for enforcing information security. Using *labels*, IFC systems specify fine-grained policies on information flow that can be fully or partly enforced through compile-time analysis. These policies articulate the confidentiality and integrity goals of IFC systems, which are *security properties* [23]: hyperproperties [12] that constrain the set of system behaviors.

The most prominent security property for IFC systems is *noninterference* [18], but it is too restrictive in practice. A major challenge for adopting language-based IFC is providing developers with expressive yet intuitive ways to specify their intended security policies. To capture more nuanced security policies, the expressiveness of IFC systems is enhanced by *downgrading mechanisms* such as *declassification* of confidential information and *endorsement* of untrusted information. Misuse of these mechanisms is further mitigated by enforcing *nonmalleable information flow* [9] (NMIF), a security property controlling downgrading.

Delegation is another common mechanism for specifying security. Delegation allows one principal to grant (delegate) power to another, expressing that the first principal trusts the second. Delegation can compactly represent important aspects of the system's security policy: when there is delegation between two principals, ensuring the delegator's security also necessitates enforcing the delegatee's security. Delegation is commonly supported not only in information flow control systems [4,5,30,34], but also in a wide range of enforcement mechanisms, including access control [7,13,39] (where delegation is often referred to as a *principal* or *role hierarchy*), authorization logics [1,2,4,20,21], and capability systems [25,27].

The expressive power of delegation can be increased through what we call *asymmetric delegation*: fine-grained delegation of either *confidentiality* or *integrity*. Intuitively, when a principal Alice delegates her confidentiality to another principal Bob, she allows Bob to observe all information visible to her. When Alice delegates her integrity to Bob, she trusts that all information accepted by Bob has not been maliciously modified. With asymmetric delegation, we can model security settings like the semi-honest trust assumption in cryptographic applications and the security setting of blockchains. In the semi-honest setting, principals trust each other to follow the protocol (trust each other with integrity), but do not trust each other with their secrets (but not confidentiality). In the blockchain setting, principals do not trust each other to follow protocols, but all information is public: they effectively trust each other with respect to confidentiality.

While asymmetric delegation increases the expressive power of IFC systems, its precise role—particularly in the presence of downgrading—remains poorly understood. We address this gap by presenting a general and expressive semantic framework for IFC labels that formalizes both asymmetric delegation and its interaction with downgrading. Although prior work [5,44] develops IFC systems that support certain forms of asymmetric delegation, these systems lack sound and complete NMIF enforcement. Building on our framework, we develop algorithms for verifying the associated semantic security properties.

Experience with language-based security highlights the importance of IFC label inference to reduce the burden on programmers [3,34]. In addition, allowing programmers to write code that is generic with respect to labels enhances modularity and code reuse. We support such generic programming through an efficient label inference procedure that supports bounded label polymorphism.

To evaluate our approach, we update the label model of the Viaduct compiler [3] and extend its static information flow analysis. Our implementation features a more concise and modular syntax for specifying trust assumptions, as well as a more efficient label inference procedure.

The rest of the paper is structured as follows:

- Section 2 motivates asymmetric delegation using a semi-honest secure multi-party computation (MPC) program.
- Section 3 and Sect. 4 study the effects of asymmetric delegation on security properties using a novel semantic framework.

- Section 5 presents algorithms that statically enforce the security properties.
- Section 6 introduces an inference procedure supporting bounded label polymorphism.

```
1  host Alice : {A ∧ B←}
2  host Bob   : {B ∧ A←}
3
4  val a: {A ∧ B←} = Alice.input
5  val b: {B ∧ A←} = Bob.input
6  val w: {A ∧ B} = a > b
7
8  Alice.output(
9     declassify w to {A ∧ B←})
10 Bob.output(
11    declassify w to {B ∧ A←})
```

Fig. 1. Yao's Millionaires' problem in Viaduct [3]. The programmer must manually assign labels to hosts.

```
1  host Alice, Bob
2  assume Alice = Bob for integrity
3
4  val a: {Alice} = Alice.input
5  val b: {Bob}   = Bob.input
6  val w: {Alice ⊔ Bob} = a > b
7
8  Alice.output(
9     declassify w to {Alice})
10 Bob.output(
11    declassify w to {Bob})
```

Fig. 2. Yao's Millionaires' problem implemented with delegation. Alice ⊔ Bob is shorthand for ⟨Alice ∧ Bob, Alice ∨ Bob⟩.

2 A Case for Delegation

2.1 Semi-honest Attackers in Cryptography

Asymmetric delegation can capture a wide variety of security settings. Already mentioned is the semi-honest threat model, widely studied in the cryptography literature [45]. In this model, principals correctly follow the protocol, but attempt to improperly learn other principals' secrets. Modeling the semi-honest setting in IFC systems remains a challenge. We first give an example of modeling semi-honest security in Viaduct [3], a state-of-the-art compiler that translates information flow policies to cryptographic protocols. We then illustrate how delegation improves usability and modularity.

Consider Yao's well-known Millionaires' Problem [45], where Alice and Bob wish to compare their wealth without revealing actual numbers. Figure 1 shows a Viaduct implementation. Lines 1 and 2 declare the hosts Alice and Bob and assign them information flow labels that capture the security assumptions. The hosts are assigned different and incomparable confidentiality labels (A for Alice and B for Bob) but the same integrity label (A ∧ B) to reflect the trust relation in the semi-honest model. Lines 4 and 5 gather input from the hosts; input from a host has the same label as that host. Line 6 stores the result of the comparison in w, which has a label following standard IFC rules: the result of a computation is more secret and less trusted than all of its inputs. Specifically, w has a confidentiality of A ∧ B since it is derived using secret data from both hosts, and has an integrity of A ∧ B since that is the integrity of both inputs. Finally, lines 9 and 11 output w to Alice and Bob, respectively. Note that sending w to Alice leaks information about Bob's secret data (b), which violates noninterference. Viaduct requires an explicit **declassify** statement to indicate that information leakage is intentional.

2.2 Modeling Security with Delegation

Viaduct models security by encoding trust into labels, but this approach has problems. First, programmers must encode security assumptions by carefully crafting host labels, which becomes tricky in large systems with many assumptions. Second, this encoding pollutes the entire program. In Fig. 1, every label annotation must acknowledge the semi-honest assumption by carrying around additional integrity (i.e., $A^{\leftarrow}$ or $B^{\leftarrow}$). And third, the encoding breaks modularity. For example, to add a new host Chuck to the program, we would need to edit every label annotation to carry an extra integrity component of $C^{\leftarrow}$, requiring changes throughout the program even though Chuck is not involved in this portion of the computation. Delegation addresses all of these issues.

Figure 2 implements Yao's Millionaires' Problem using delegation. Hosts are no longer assigned cryptic information flow labels; instead, line 2 directly states the security assumption: Alice and Bob trust each other for integrity. Variables have intuitive labels that do not need to repeat the semi-honest security assumption: input from Alice has label Alice. Finally, adding a new host Chuck requires no edits to existing code; we only need to add the following lines:[1]

```
1  host Chuck
2  assume Alice = Chuck for integrity
```

2.3 Nonmalleable Information Flow

Downgrading statements (**declassify** and **endorse**) deliberately violate noninterference, so their unrestricted use poses a threat to security. Prior work [33,47] identifies cases where the attacker can exploit downgrading to gain undue influence over the execution, and proposes *robust declassification* and *transparent endorsement* to limit such cases.

Robust declassification requires that untrusted data is not declassified, and transparent endorsement requires that secret data is not endorsed. NMIF combines these two restrictions, which are key to enabling the Viaduct compiler to securely instantiate programs with cryptography [3].

Here, "secret" and "trusted" are relative to a given attacker, and NMIF must hold for all attackers. In practice, the program cannot be type-checked separately for every possible attacker, so a conservative condition is enforced: downgraded data must be at least as trusted as it is secret. For our example program, this condition means w must have integrity stronger than or equal to its confidentiality. This condition is immediate in Viaduct since w has label ⟨Alice ∧ Bob, Alice ∧ Bob⟩ in Fig. 1. On the other hand, the same variable w in Fig. 2 has label ⟨Alice ∧ Bob, Alice ∨ Bob⟩ , which seemingly has weaker integrity than confidentiality (logically, Alice ∨ Bob does *not* imply Alice ∧ Bob). However,

---

[1] In fact, we could even support separate compilation as the program need not be type-checked again: a program considered secure with fewer assumptions is secure with more assumptions.

Alice = Bob for integrity, so this label is equivalent to ⟨Alice ∧ Bob, Alice ∧ Bob⟩ using the following derivation:

$$\text{Alice} \vee \text{Bob} = \text{Alice} \vee \text{Alice} = \text{Alice} = \text{Alice} \wedge \text{Alice} = \text{Alice} \wedge \text{Bob}$$

Delegation necessitates equational reasoning under assumptions, and NMIF creates an interaction between confidentiality and integrity. The combination of these two features is what makes asymmetric delegation tricky: the cleaner syntax comes at the cost of additional technical complexity. The following sections tame this complexity by developing a semantic framework for labels, and algorithms that follow the semantics.

3 Semantic Framework

3.1 The Lattice of Principals

We build our semantic framework upon the *lattice of principals*, used in prior work in authorization logics and information flow systems [3–5,31,34,42,44].

A principal $p \in \mathbb{P}$ refers to an entity in decentralized systems that can be either concrete, such as users or server machines, or abstract, such as RBAC roles [39] or quorums [51]. In IFC systems, they are often used as labels to annotate policies on use of information [4]. For example, a: Alice in Fig. 2 requires the variable a to only be written by principals that can influence Alice's data, and to remain secret to principals who cannot observe Alice's information.

Principals are ordered by authority. When q delegates trust to p, we say p *acts for* q, written as $p \Rightarrow q$. Conjunction (the "and" logic connective) between principals $p \wedge q$ represents the least combined authority of p and q, and disjunction ("or") $p \vee q$ represents greatest common authority. The maximum authority ⊥ acts for all other authorities, and the minimum authority ⊤ trusts all other authorities. More authority is associated with elements lower in the lattice: $\bot \Rightarrow p \wedge q \Rightarrow p \Rightarrow p \vee q \Rightarrow \top$.[2]

Additionally, we use a *delegation context*, with the form $\theta = p_1 \Rightarrow q_1, \cdots, p_n \Rightarrow q_n$, to specify delegations that are not implied by the logical structure of the principal lattice. The declaration **assume** Alice = Bob **for integrity** from Fig. 2 is an example of a delegation context, specifying both Alice ⇒ Bob and Bob ⇒ Alice. Using the delegation context is compatible with much prior work in IFC. For example, the *trust configuration* from FLAM [4], *meta-policies* from the Rx model [44], *interpretation function* from DLM [29], and *authority lattice* from label algebra [28] are all delegation contexts written differently.

The lattice of principals can be interpreted as an authorization logic [1, 17] where each principal is a proposition about authorization policy. As

---

[2] It might seem odd to represent maximum authority as ⊥ and minimum authority with ⊤, since some prior work (e.g., [4]) makes the opposite choice. An intuitive justification: the "false" proposition entails everything, so no real principal can have authority ⊥. All principals are trusted with ⊤.

authorization logics are often built upon propositional intuitionistic logics, whose algebraic models are *Heyting algebra* [37], we assume $\mathbb{P}$ is distributive.[3]

3.2 Delegation and Attackers

In the MPC example, a delegation context makes some principals equivalent. In this subsection, we give delegation a precise semantics.

In systems with decentralized trust, all principals see other principals as potential attackers. In the extreme case where no principal trusts another, the attacker with respect to each principal controls all other principals. Formally, we characterize an attacker $A \subseteq \mathbb{P}$ by the set of principals it controls.

To trust a principal is to disregard the case where it is the attacker. Conversely, when a principal is attacker-controlled, so are the principals it acts for. Formally:

Definition 1 (Consistent Attackers). *A is consistent with θ ($A \models \theta$) when:*

$$\forall p, q \in \mathbb{P} \mathrel{\text{.}} ((p \Rightarrow q) \vee (p \Rightarrow q) \in \theta) \implies (p \in A \implies q \in A)$$

The set of consistent attackers is an *attacker model*: $\mathbb{A}_{|\theta} = \{A \in \mathbb{A} \mid A \models \theta\}$.

The semantic trust levels of principals can be compared based on the set of consistent attackers that control the principals. Formally:

Definition 2 (Acts-for Semantics). *p acts for q (written $\theta \models p \leq q$) when:*

$$\forall A \in \mathbb{A}_{|\theta} \mathrel{\text{.}} p \in A \implies q \in A$$

We use "$\leq$" to denote the semantics of the acts-for relation "$\Rightarrow$". When viewing principals as authorization propositions, "acts-for" stands for "implies", and a delegation context is a theory (list of propositions). Each consistent attacker is a consistent interpretation (truth assignment) of the principals and the delegation context, where 1 is assigned to the principals the attacker controls.

In fact, a delegation context determines a *congruence relation*[4] over the lattice of principals, where $p \equiv_\theta q$ is defined as $(\theta \models p \leq q) \wedge (\theta \models q \leq p)$. As a result, $\equiv_\theta$ induces a quotient lattice $\mathbb{P}/\equiv_\theta$ where mutually delegating principals are in the same equivalence class. This quotient lattice is precisely the *Lindenbaum algebra* [8] of the theory θ: the "smallest" algebraic model $\mathbb{P}$ where θ holds.

Theorem 1 (Algebraic Model). *The algebraic model of the principal lattice $\mathbb{P}$ under delegation context θ is the quotient lattice $\mathbb{P}/\equiv_\theta$.*[5]

---

[3] A Heyting algebra is a distributive lattice that supports the *relative pseudocomplement* ($\rightarrow$) operation. We do not need the $\rightarrow$ operator until label inference.
[4] A congruence is an equivalence relation that preserves the lattice structure.
[5] Full proofs of all theorems from this paper are available in the technical report [36].

The semantics of consistent attackers makes them the *prime filters* of the lattice of principals. This is a result of the Stone's Representation Theorem of Distributive Lattices [43], which says elements from distributive lattices can be fully characterized by their prime filters.

Theorem 2 (Attacker Model). $\mathbb{A}_{|\theta}$ *is the set of* prime filters *of* $\mathbb{P}/{\equiv_\theta}$.

Prime filters have intuitive interpretations, which abstracts and generalizes attacker models from prior work [9,22]. $A \subseteq \mathbb{P}$ is a prime filter when:

- $\top \in A$: All attackers control the weakest authority;
- $\bot \notin A$: No attacker controls the strongest authority;
- If $p \Rightarrow q$ and $p \in A$, then $q \in A$: Attackers are consistent;
- If $p \in A$ and $q \in A$, then $p \wedge q \in A$: An attacker controls the least combined authority of principals it controls;
- If $p \vee q \in A$, then either $p \in A$ or $q \in A$: If two principals are not controlled by an attacker, neither is their greatest common authority.

3.3 Labels

Information flow systems mainly consider two aspects of security: confidentiality (read authority) and integrity (write authority). To express differing confidentiality and integrity policies, we use *the lattice of labels*, which are pairs of principals $\mathbb{L} = \mathbb{P} \times \mathbb{P}$. For a label $\ell = \langle p, q \rangle$, p represents confidentiality and q represents integrity. Like principals, each label reflects the authority required for a principal to access information. For example, information labeled $\langle \bot, \top \rangle$ can be read by no principal except the strongest $\bot$, but it can be influenced by any principal.

A label ℓ act for ℓ' when both ℓ acts for ℓ' for both confidentiality and integrity. Similarly, conjunction/disjunction of labels is defined by the conjunction/disjunction of their confidentiality and integrity. An asymmetric delegation context is a pair of different delegation contexts $\Theta = \langle \theta_c, \theta_i \rangle$.

In general, *asymmetric attackers* $\mathcal{A} \in \mathbf{A} = \mathbb{A} \times \mathbb{A}$ may control different principals for confidentiality and integrity. We write $\mathcal{A} = \langle C \in \mathbb{A}, I \in \mathbb{A} \rangle$, where C represents the principals $\mathcal{A}$ controls for confidentiality, and I those for integrity. Consequently, the attacker model $\mathbf{A}$ is a pair of prime filters.

As visualized in Fig. 3, each attacker defines secret ($\mathcal{S}$), public ($\mathcal{P}$), trusted ($\mathcal{T}$) and untrusted ($\mathcal{U}$) sets over the lattice of labels.

$$\mathcal{P}_{\langle C,I \rangle} = \{\langle p,q \rangle \mid p \in C\}, \quad \mathcal{U}_{\langle C,I \rangle} = \{\langle p,q \rangle \mid q \in I\},$$
$$\mathcal{S}_{\langle C,I \rangle} = \{\langle p,q \rangle \mid p \notin C\}, \quad \mathcal{T}_{\langle C,I \rangle} = \{\langle p,q \rangle \mid q \notin I\}$$

4 Security Hyperproperties and Delegation

Our semantic framework formalizes a key insight relating the attacker model and delegation: more delegation means fewer attackers. In turn, fewer attackers

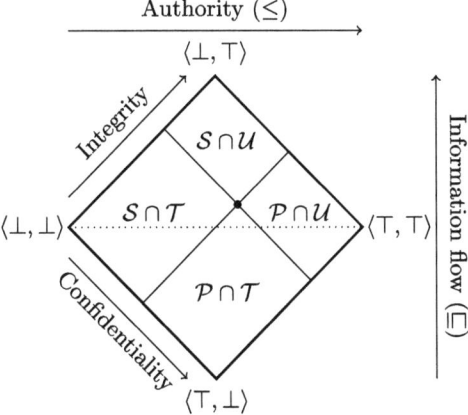

Fig. 3. The lattice of labels $(\mathbb{L}, \leq)$ and the lattice of information flow $(\mathbb{L}, \sqsubseteq)$ share the same underlying set, but use a different ordering. The dotted line depicts labels with equal confidentiality and integrity: strictly above are compromised labels, and on or below are uncompromised labels

should make it easier for programs to be considered secure. To express delegation, we extend prior definitions of IFC security *hyperproperties* [12] with our semantic framework. Rather than a standard proof of security for an IFC-typed core calculus, we abstract away from computation to concentrate on the core judgment in IFC systems: when it is safe to relabel information, under a delegation context.

The simple system has states $\sigma \in \Sigma$, intentionally left unspecified. An execution of the system emits a trace t, which is a sequence of states. Define the *behavior* $B \in \mathbb{B}$ of a program to be the *set* of possible execution traces it can emit. A hyperproperty $\mathbb{HP} \subseteq \mathbb{B}$ is a set of behaviors. A program satisfies a hyperproperty when its behavior is a member of the hyperproperty.

In decentralized IFC systems, hyperproperties $\mathbb{HP}_{\mathcal{A}}$ are parameterized by the choice of attacker: a program secure against one attacker may be insecure against another. Let the hyperproperty $\mathbb{HP}_{\mathbf{A}}$ be the hyperproperty that characterizes programs that are secure against all possible attackers from $\mathbf{A}$. A behavior B of a program falls into $\mathbb{HP}_{\mathbf{A}}$ precisely when $B \in \mathbb{HP}_{\mathcal{A}}$ for all $\mathcal{A} \in \mathbf{A}$:

$$\mathbb{HP}_{\mathbf{A}} = \bigcap_{\mathcal{A} \in \mathbf{A}} \mathbb{HP}_{\mathcal{A}} \qquad \Theta(\mathbb{HP}_{\mathbf{A}}) = \bigcap_{\mathcal{A} \in \mathbf{A}_{|\Theta}} \mathbb{HP}_{\mathcal{A}}$$

When a program assumes a static delegation context Θ, the attacker model is further restricted to the ones consistent with Θ. Therefore, a delegation context can be understood as a hyperproperty transformer. It follows that hyperproperties accept at least as many programs after a delegation context is added.

Theorem 3. $\mathbb{HP_A} \subseteq \Theta(\mathbb{HP_A})$.

This matches our intuition about static delegation: the more trust assumptions, the fewer reasonable attackers, the more programs considered secure.

4.1 Noninterference and the Lattice of Information Flow

For confidentiality, noninterference [13,38] demands that information should not flow from high to low (secret to public). Noninterference of integrity requires that information should not flow from low to high (untrusted to trusted). To illustrate how delegation affects noninterference, we adapt Clarkson and Schneider's [12] definition of *observational determinism* [18].

Definition 3 (Observational Determinism). *Let $\mathcal{L}$ be any set of low labels. Observational determinism $\mathbb{OD}$ is the hyperproperty:*

$$\mathbb{OD}_\mathcal{L} = \{B \mid \forall t_1, t_2 \in B \,.\, t_1^0 =_\mathcal{L} t_2^0 \implies t_1 \approx_\mathcal{L} t_2\}$$

State t^0 denotes the initial state of the trace t. We leave the definition of low equivalence between states unspecified, as in prior work on knowledge-based security [6,24,26,41].

Noninterference for confidentiality $\mathrm{NI}_\mathcal{A}^c = \mathbb{OD}_{\mathcal{P}_\mathcal{A}}$ and integrity $\mathrm{NI}_\mathcal{A}^i = \mathbb{OD}_{\mathcal{T}_\mathcal{A}}$ are mere instantiations of observational determinism over public and trusted labels for some attacker $\mathcal{A}$. For an attacker model $\mathbf{A}_{|\Theta}$:

$$\Theta(\mathrm{NI}_\mathbf{A}) = \bigcap_{\mathcal{A} \in \mathbf{A}_{|\Theta}} (\mathbb{OD}_{\mathcal{P}_\mathcal{A}} \cap \mathbb{OD}_{\mathcal{T}_\mathcal{A}})$$

Prior work [19,23,30] enforces low equivalence by ensuring that low-labeled information is not influenced by high-labeled information. Concretely, a dynamic *relabel* is safe when it does not relabel high-labeled information to a low label. We formalize safe relabeling as the *flows-to* relation.

Definition 4 (Flows-to). *Label ℓ securely flows to ℓ' ($\Theta \models \ell \sqsubseteq \ell'$) when:*

$$\forall \mathcal{A} \in \mathbf{A}_{|\Theta} \,.\, (\ell' \in \mathcal{P}_\mathcal{A} \implies \ell \in \mathcal{P}_\mathcal{A}) \wedge (\ell' \in \mathcal{T}_\mathcal{A} \implies \ell \in \mathcal{T}_\mathcal{A})$$

Equivalently, $\langle \theta_c, \theta_i \rangle \models \langle p, q \rangle \sqsubseteq \langle p', q' \rangle$ when $\theta_c \models p' \leq p$ and $\theta_i \models q \leq q'$.

As visualized in Fig. 3, flows-to and the acts-for define two lattices on the same underlying set of labels. The Lattice of Information operators are given by:

$$\langle p_1, q_1 \rangle \sqcup \langle p_2, q_2 \rangle = \langle p_1 \wedge p_2, q_1 \vee q_2 \rangle \qquad \langle p_1, q_1 \rangle \sqcap \langle p_2, q_2 \rangle = \langle p_1 \vee p_2, q_1 \wedge q_2 \rangle$$

4.2 Downgrading and Nonmalleable Information Flow

Some programs, such as the MPC example from Fig. 2, intentionally break noninterference. Prior work on dynamic security policies either achieve downgrading by *relabeling* or by *dynamic delegation*. Visually, relabeling moves information downward in Fig. 3 and dynamic delegation moves the attacker partition leftward.

Nonmalleable Information Flow (NMIF). To prevent misuse of downgrades by relabeling, Cecchetti et al. [9] propose NMIF, a security hyperproperty that combines robust declassification [47] with transparent endorsement.

Robust declassification requires that secret information flow to public only when the information is trusted. This restriction ensures that attackers do not influence disclosure of information to them. A declassification is only robust when it declassifies secret–trusted information $(\mathcal{S}_\mathcal{A} \cup \mathcal{T}_\mathcal{A})$.

Transparent endorsement is a dual condition that allows untrusted information to influence trusted information only when the information is public to the attacker. It only allows endorsement of public–untrusted information $(\mathcal{P}_\mathcal{A} \cap \mathcal{U}_\mathcal{A})$.

Therefore, secret–untrusted information should not be downgraded. Indeed, the key recipe to enforcing NMIF is to enforce noninterference for public or trusted information [9]:

$$\mathrm{NI}_\mathbf{A}^\blacktriangledown = \mathbb{OD}_{\mathcal{T}_\mathcal{A} \cup \mathcal{P}_\mathcal{A}}$$

A label is *compromised* when it is secret–untrusted for some attacker [9,46]. To enforce NMIF, it suffices to reject downgrading information with compromised labels, so that there is no flow out from compromised labels.

Unfortunately, NMIF against $\mathbf{A}_{|\theta}$ rejects all downgrades. Namely, all labels (except for $\langle \top, \bot \rangle$) are compromised against the attacker $\mathcal{A}_\top = \langle \{\top\}, \mathbb{P} \rangle$ (it controls every principal for integrity and controls no principal for confidentiality). Therefore, further restrictions on the attacker model are needed.

NMIF Attackers. Prior work [46,47] assumes attackers control more confidentiality than integrity. We call them *valid attackers*:

Definition 5 (Valid Attackers). $V = \{\langle C, I \rangle \in \mathbf{A} \mid I \subseteq C\}$

Restricting attackers to valid ones makes our framework mirror attacker models studied in the cryptography literature [45], where a principal is honest (not controlled by attacker), semi-honest (controlled by attacker for confidentiality), or malicious (controlled by attacker for both confidentiality and integrity). The valid attacker restriction excludes unrealistic "malicious but incurious" attackers.

In fact, much existing work satisfies the valid-attacker assumption by construction. For example, robust declassification [47] originally defines integrity and confidentiality by equivalence relations over system states. The state transitions an active attacker may perform are, by construction, observable by the attacker.

Definition 6 (Uncompromised Labels). *Label ℓ is uncompromised under Θ, written $\Theta \models \blacktriangledown \ell$, when ℓ is either public or trusted for all valid attackers:*

$$\forall \mathcal{A} \in V_{|\Theta} \,.\, \ell \in \mathcal{P}_\mathcal{A} \cup \mathcal{T}_\mathcal{A}$$

It follows that labels of principals are uncompromised: $\Theta \models \blacktriangledown \langle p, p \rangle$.

Uncompromised labels have an alternative characterization: they are the labels with at least as much integrity as confidentiality. Of course, in the presence of asymmetric delegation, we cannot directly compare a label's confidentiality and integrity components since each component has a different set of delegations. We circumvent this problem by introducing a witnessing principal r who has no more integrity than q and no less confidentiality than p.

Theorem 4. $\langle \theta_c, \theta_i \rangle \models \blacktriangledown \langle p, q \rangle \iff \exists r \in \mathbb{P} . (\theta_i \models q \leq r) \wedge (\theta_c \models r \leq p)$.

Proofs can be found in the technical report [36]. In the absence of asymmetric delegation, Theorem 4 reduces to a simple acts-for check ($\theta \models q \leq p$), which prior systems rely on [9, 47].

5 Algorithms

In IFC systems that incorporate delegation, the acts-for relation $\theta \models p_1 \leq p_2$ is frequently checked by label-inference

procedures [34] and even at run time, where it can impose significant overhead [11]. Unfortunately, its semantic definition quantifies over the potentially infinite set of all attackers, which makes direct use of the definition infeasible in practice. Similarly, the definition of uncompromised labels $\Theta \models \blacktriangledown \ell$ does not yield an algorithm.

In this section, we assume oracle access to syntactic lattice operations ($\Rightarrow$, $\bot$, $\top$, $\wedge$, $\vee$) of $\mathbb{P}$, and propose sound and complete algorithms that check for the aforementioned relations. Proofs are available in the technical report [36].

5.1 Acts-For Algorithm

Algorithm 1 gives an algorithm for deciding $\theta \models p \leq q$. We write $\theta \vdash p \leq q$ to denote this algorithmic system.

Algorithm 1 (Acts-for $\theta \vdash p \leq q$).

$$\frac{p \Rightarrow q}{\cdot \vdash p \leq q} \text{ P-Axiom} \qquad \frac{\theta \vdash p \wedge q' \leq q \quad \theta \vdash p \leq q \vee p'}{\theta, p' \Rightarrow q' \vdash p \leq q} \text{ P-Delegation}$$

The algorithm recursively applies the lattice axioms and P-Delegation until the delegation context is empty for all sub-cases. The acts-for relation holds when P-Axiom applies to all sub-cases.

Theorem 5 (Correctness of Acts-for). *Algorithm 1 terminates, and it is sound and complete with respect to Definition 2:* $\theta \vdash p \leq q \iff \theta \models p \leq q$.

5.2 NMIF Algorithm

Neither the semantic definition of uncompromised labels (Definition 6) nor their alternative characterization (Theorem 4) lends itself to an algorithmic implementation. The semantic definition quantifies over all valid attackers (a potentially infinite set), and the alternative characterization conjures up an intermediate principal. Our solution is to use the alternative characterization but with a "best principal." For that, we use $\min_\theta(p)$, the highest-authority principal in the equivalence class of p.[6]

Definition 7 (Minimal Principal). $\min_\theta(p) \in \mathbb{P}$ *is the (necessarily) unique principal such that* $\theta \models p \leq q$ *if and only if* $\min_\theta(p) \Rightarrow q$ *for any* $q \in \mathbb{P}$.

We must demand more structure on $\mathbb{P}$ to compute $\min_\theta(p)$. Specifically, we rely on an oracle that returns *join-prime* factorizations of arbitrary principals. Intuitively, a join-prime principal cannot be written as the join of other principals. In finite lattices, these are the principals of the form $p = q_1 \wedge \cdots \wedge q_n$. Factorization oracles arise trivially in existing implementations of IFC models, as these are based on lattices with a finite set of principal names [3,4,34,42].

Algorithm 2 (Min $\min_\theta(p) = q$).

MIN-BASE
$$\frac{\text{join-prime}(p) \quad \forall (p' \Rightarrow q') \in \theta \,.\, p \not\Rightarrow p'}{\min_\theta(p) = p}$$

MIN-PICK
$$\frac{\text{join-prime}(p) \quad p \Rightarrow p'}{\min_{\theta, p' \Rightarrow q'}(p) = \min_\theta(p \wedge q')}$$

MIN-FACTOR
$$\frac{\neg \text{join-prime}(p) \quad p = p_1 \vee \cdots \vee p_n \quad \forall i \in [n] \,.\, \text{join-prime}(p_i)}{\min_\theta(p) = \bigvee_{i \in [n]} \min_\theta(p_i)}$$

The rules from Algorithm 2 can be applied in any order without backtracking because of the uniqueness of $\min_\theta(p)$. Moreover, all derivations are finite since either the size of θ decreases, or we switch from a reducible element to a finite set of irreducible elements.

Theorem 6 (Correctness of Min). *Algorithm 2 terminates, and it is sound and complete with respect to Definition 7.*

Our NMIF algorithm simply combines Algorithms 1 and 2.

Algorithm 3 (Uncompromised Label Check $\Theta \vdash \blacktriangledown \ell$).

$$\frac{\theta_c \vdash \min_{\theta_i}(q) \leq p}{\langle \theta_c, \theta_i \rangle \vdash \blacktriangledown \langle p, q \rangle}$$

Theorem 7 (Correctness of Uncompromised Label Check). *Algorithm 3 terminates, and it is sound and complete with respect to Theorem 4.*

---
[6] Recall that higher authority is lower in the authority lattice, thus the use of min as opposed to max.

6 Label Inference

In practical IFC systems, label inference is an important way to avoid redundant user annotations, since it is secure to infer labels of intermediate computations from their inputs and outputs. Typically, label inference is performed by solving a system of constraints over lattice elements [34,49]. IFC systems further benefit from *bounded label polymorphism*, which allows user to write library code reusable at different security levels. In this section, we show how to do label inference directly over the algebraic model of labels using the algorithms from Sect. 5.

```
1  host Alice, Bob, Chuck
2  assume Alice = Bob for integrity
3  assume Bob = Chuck for integrity
4
5  fun average(a: int, b: int): int
6  {
7    return (a + b) / 2
8  }
```

```
8   fun main() {
9     val a = Alice.input
10    val b = Bob.input
11    val c = Chuck.input
12
13    val r1 = average(a, b)
14    val r2 = average(b, c)
15  }
```

Fig. 4. The average function is implicitly polymorphic over the labels of its arguments.

6.1 Bounded Label Polymorphism

As in traditional type systems, allowing code that is generic over labels increases expressiveness significantly. Existing IFC-based languages like Jif [34] and Flow Caml [40] support bounded label polymorphism, which allows functions to be parameterized over labels that are bounded by specified security levels. Annotation burden on users can be further reduced by assuming information flow from function arguments to return values by default.

In Fig. 4, the annotation-free polymorphic function average is applied in main to arguments with different security labels. Shown below is the same function with explicit annotations, all of which can be inferred.

```
1  fun average[X, Y, Z](a: int{X}, b: int{Y}): int{Z}
2      where (X ⊔ Y ⊑ Z)
```

Label inference assigns existential *label variables* to all unlabeled expressions and creates constraints based on IFC typing rules. The constraints are then solved by a constraint solver that uses parameter bounds as delegation contexts.

In each function, polymorphic label variables are treated as label constants, so solutions of label variables are expressed by both label constants and polymorphic label variables. Type checking at call sites ensures that the parameter bounds are satisfied. As functions have their own delegation contexts, a new constraint system is solved for each function.

6.2 Constraint Solver

We describe a novel constraint solver that computes the minimum-semantic-authority solution to constraint systems with delegation contexts. Minimum-authority solutions are desirable because they allow systems to choose cheaper security enforcement mechanisms [3,10,15,16,48,50].

L. Constants ℓ
L. Variables Y
L. Expressions $L ::= \ell \mid Y \mid L^\pi$
$\quad\mid L_1 \sqcup L_2 \mid L_1 \sqcap L_2$
$\quad\mid L_1 \vee L_2 \mid L_1 \wedge L_2$
L. Constraints $C ::= L_1 \sqsubseteq L_2 \mid \blacktriangledown L$
Projections $\pi \in \{c, i\}$

Fig. 5. Syntax of label constraints.

P. Constants p
P. Variables Y^π
P. Expressions $P^\pi ::= p \mid Y^\pi$
$\quad\mid P_1^\pi \vee P_2^\pi \mid P_1^\pi \wedge P_2^\pi$
$\quad\mid p_1 \to P_2^\pi \mid \min_{\pi'}(P^{\pi'})$
P. Constraints $D ::= P_1^\pi \Rightarrow^\pi P_2^\pi$

Fig. 6. Syntax of principal constraints.

Label and Principal Constraints. Figure 5 gives the syntax of the label constraint language. Expressions in the constraint language include label constants and label variables, authority projections, as well as standard lattice operations. A constraint either asserts that an expression flows to another, or asserts that an expression is uncompromised. We translate constraints over labels to constraints over principals to leverage algorithms from Sect. 5. Figure 6 gives the syntax of the principal constraint language. The syntax includes a principal variable Y^π for each combination of label variable Y and projection π. That is, Y^c represents the confidentiality of Y, and Y^i represents Y's integrity.

We index expressions P^π by the component π they represent. This prevents expressions like $Y_1^c \wedge Y_2^i$, whose components are mixed. Expressions include principal constants and principal variables, as well as principal-lattice operations $\vee$ and $\wedge$. The operation $\to$ is called the *relative pseudocomplement* of the meet operation: $p_1 \to p_2$ is defined as the minimum-authority principal p such that $p_1 \wedge p \Rightarrow p_2$. We use $\to$ to solve constraints of the form $Y^\pi \wedge p_1 \Rightarrow^\pi P_2^\pi$. The $\min_\pi()$ operation allows mixing integrity and confidentiality components; we use it when solving for labels that must be uncompromised. Principal constraints have the form $P_1^\pi \Rightarrow^\pi P_2^\pi$, which stands for $\theta_\pi \models P_1^\pi \leq P_2^\pi$.

Figure 7 gives rules for translating label constraints to principal constraints. The definition of $[\![L]\!]_\pi$ is a straightforward encoding of the label-lattice operations. Using $[\![L]\!]$, we translate a flows-to ($\sqsubseteq$) constraint to two acts-for ($\Rightarrow$) constraints, one for each label component. The constraint $\blacktriangledown L$ follows from Algorithm 3.

Solving Principal Constraints. Our constraint solver requires the left-hand side of each constraint to be atomic (a constant or a variable), that is, constraints of the form $p_1 \Rightarrow^\pi P_2^\pi$ and $Y_1^\pi \Rightarrow^\pi P_2^\pi$. We exhaustively apply the equational axioms of Heyting algebra (e.g., associativity, absorption, distributivity, etc.)

$$\boxed{[\![C]\!] = D_1, \ldots, D_n}$$

$$[\![L_1 \sqsubseteq L_2]\!] = [\![L_2]\!]_c \Rightarrow^c [\![L_1]\!]_c, \ [\![L_1]\!]_i \Rightarrow^i [\![L_2]\!]_i \qquad [\![\blacktriangledown L]\!] = [\![L]\!]_i \Rightarrow^i \min_c([\![L]\!]_c)$$

$$\boxed{[\![L]\!]_\pi = P^\pi}$$

$$[\![L_1 \sqcup L_2]\!]_\pi = [\![(L_1 \wedge L_2)^c \wedge (L_1 \vee L_2)^i]\!]_\pi$$
$$[\![L_1 \sqcap L_2]\!]_\pi = [\![(L_1 \vee L_2)^c \wedge (L_1 \wedge L_2)^i]\!]_\pi$$
$$[\![L_1 \vee L_2]\!]_\pi = [\![L_1]\!]_\pi \vee [\![L_2]\!]_\pi$$
$$[\![L_1 \wedge L_2]\!]_\pi = [\![L_1]\!]_\pi \wedge [\![L_2]\!]_\pi$$

$$[\![\langle p, q \rangle]\!]_\pi = \begin{cases} p & \text{if } \pi = c \\ q & \text{if } \pi = i \end{cases}$$

$$[\![Y]\!]_\pi = Y^\pi$$

$$[\![L^{\pi'}]\!]_\pi = \begin{cases} [\![L]\!]_\pi & \text{if } \pi = \pi' \\ \top & \text{if } \pi \neq \pi' \end{cases}$$

Fig. 7. Translating label constraints to principal constraints.

until no left-hand side of any constraint can be further simplified. As equational axioms are syntactic rewrites, it does not change the constraint system over the underlying algebra. Moreover, this process always terminates, and ensures that the left-hand side of each constraint either is atomic or contains a meet ($\wedge$).[7]

Constraint solving fails if the left-hand side of any constraint contains a meet, since such systems do not have unique solutions. For example, the system $Y_1 \wedge Y_2 \Rightarrow$ Alice has no minimal solution: we can assign $\{Y_1 \mapsto \text{Alice}, Y_2 \mapsto \top\}$ or $\{Y_1 \mapsto \top, Y_2 \mapsto \text{Alice}\}$, but neither solution is better than the other. Compiler implementations need to either restrict the syntax of polymorphic constraints, or report errors during constraint solving.

Once the simplification process succeeds, we extend the algorithm of Rehof and Mogensen [35] for iteratively solving semi-lattice constraints. We initialize all principal variables to $\top$, and use unsatisfied constraints to update variables repeatedly until a fixed point is reached, using the rule:

$$\text{given } Y^\pi \Rightarrow^\pi P^\pi, \quad \text{set } Y^\pi := Y^\pi \wedge \text{current-value}(\Theta, P^\pi),$$

where current-value(Θ, P^π) is the value of P^π according to the current assignment.

Note that constraints that have constants p on the left-hand side are ignored during the fixed point computation. Once a fixed-point solution is reached, we perform the following check for each constraint with a constant left-hand side:

$$\text{given } p \Rightarrow^\pi P^\pi, \quad \text{check } \theta_\pi \models p \leq \text{current-value}(\Theta, P^\pi).$$

We state and prove in the technical report [36] that this process terminates with the minimum-authority solution if all such constraints are satisfied; otherwise, there is no valid solution.

---

[7] Translation rules in Fig. 7 never generate constraints with $\rightarrow$ or $\min_\pi(\cdot)$ on the left-hand side, and the constraint simplification eliminate all joins ($\vee$) on the left.

6.3 Implementation

We modified the parser of the Viaduct compiler [3] with the delegation syntax, and extended its static analysis procedure with our label inference algorithm.[8]

Because the original Viaduct constraint solver can only make syntactic comparison ($\Rightarrow$) between labels, it instantiates polymorphic variables with constant principal names. Therefore, Viaduct has to run a *specialization procedure* to create a monomorphic copy of a function at each call site. In nested function calls, the number of monomorphic functions created grows exponentially with the depth of calls. Recursive calls need to be handled explicitly to ensure termination.

Thanks to delegation contexts, label inference no longer requires monomorphic functions and can be done in one pass. For each function call site, the specialization procedure memoizes the argument labels, and avoids creating duplicates of monomorphic functions that are instantiated with the same polymorphic argument labels, eliminating the need to treat recursive functions separately. Without duplication, our procedure creates a minimum-sized set monomorphic functions.

Empirically, type inference is fast. On all of the Viaduct benchmarks, it terminates within 300 milliseconds on a Macbook air 2023 with an M2 chip.

7 Related Work

Expressive trust delegation has been widely investigated in access control and capability systems [25,39], where delegation is called *role hierarchy* [39]. Such systems support role adoption, which is a form of dynamic delegation. However, access control systems generally do not connect to information flow security properties. Many prior IFC systems have delegation abstractions compatible with our framework, but they either lack support for asymmetric delegation [3, 9,46], or do not explore its effect over hyperproperties [4,26,32,33,47].

Our inference algorithm differs from prior implementations of syntax-directed IFC label inference [3,34,49] by operating directly over the underlying algebra. This algebraic approach enhances extensibility: adding principals or delegations does not invalidate existing analysis. Dolan [14] proposes an inference algorithm for an expressive algebraic type system with type constructors and recursive function types. However, their type system is inherently complex, and the inference doesn't produce easily interpretable representations of types. In contrast, our label system balances expressiveness with a simple and effective inference algorithm.

FLAM [4] proposes a label model and defines *robust authorization* to address security vulnerabilities arising from dynamic delegation. However, robust authorization is a proof-theoretic definition with no semantic model. Arden and Myers [5] propose the FLAC calculus, based on the FLAM label model, and prove robust declassification for a language that downgrades using dynamic delegation. Similarly, FLAC has no attacker semantics. Cecchetti et al. [9] define NMIF, but their system cannot explicitly express delegations between atomic principals.

---

[8] Code available at: https://github.com/apl-cornell/viaduct.

8 Conclusion and Future Directions

We present an algebraic semantic framework for IFC labels that models asymmetric delegation, along with sound and complete algorithms that enforce security properties and infer security annotations. Our approach provides a solid foundation for building modular, expressive and extensible IFC systems.

Acknowledgments. This work was supported by the National Science Foundation under NSF grant 1704788. Any opinions, findings, conclusions, or recommendations expressed in this material are those of the authors and do not necessarily reflect the views of the National Science Foundation. We also thank Suraaj Kanniwadi and Ethan Cecchetti for discussions and feedback.

Disclosure of Interests. The authors have no competing interests to declare that are relevant to the content of this article.

References

1. Abadi, M.: Access control in a core calculus of dependency. In: 11th ACM SIGPLAN International Conference on Functional Programming, pp. 263–273. ACM, New York (2006). https://doi.org/10.1145/1159803.1159839
2. Abadi, M.: Variations in access control logic. In: van der Meyden, R., van der Torre, L. (eds.) DEON 2008. LNCS (LNAI), vol. 5076, pp. 96–109. Springer, Heidelberg (2008). https://doi.org/10.1007/978-3-540-70525-3_9
3. Acay, C., Recto, R., Gancher, J., Myers, A., Shi, E.: Viaduct: an extensible, optimizing compiler for secure distributed programs. In: 42nd ACM SIGPLAN Conference on Programming Language Design and Implementation (PLDI), pp. 740–755. ACM (2021). https://doi.org/10.1145/3453483.3454074
4. Arden, O., Liu, J., Myers, A.C.: Flow-limited authorization. In: 28th IEEE Computer Security Foundations Symposium (CSF), pp. 569–583 (2015). https://doi.org/10.1109/CSF.2015.42
5. Arden, O., Myers, A.C.: A calculus for flow-limited authorization. In: 29th IEEE Computer Security Foundations Symposium (CSF), pp. 135–147 (2016). https://doi.org/10.1109/CSF.2016.17
6. Askarov, A., Chong, S.: Learning is change in knowledge: knowledge-based security for dynamic policies. In: 2012 IEEE 25th Computer Security Foundations Symposium, pp. 308–322 (2012). https://doi.org/10.1109/CSF.2012.31
7. Biba, K.J.: Integrity considerations for secure computer systems. Technical report, ESD-TR-76-372, USAF Electronic Systems Division, Bedford, MA (1977). https://ban.ai/multics/doc/a039324.pdf, (Also available through National Technical Information Service, Springfield Va., NTIS AD-A039324)
8. Blok, W.J., Pigozzi, D.: Algebraizable Logics (1989)
9. Cecchetti, E., Myers, A.C., Arden, O.: Nonmalleable information flow control. In: 24th ACM Conference on Computer and Communications Security (CCS), pp. 1875–1891. ACM (2017). https://doi.org/10.1145/3133956.3134054
10. Chong, S., et al.: Secure web applications via automatic partitioning. In: 21st ACM Symposium on Operating System Principles (SOSP), pp. 31–44 (2007). https://doi.org/10.1145/1323293.1294265

11. Chong, S., Vikram, K., Myers, A.C.: SIF: enforcing confidentiality and integrity in web applications. In: 16th USENIX Security Symposium (2007). http://www.cs.cornell.edu/andru/papers/sif.pdf
12. Clarkson, M.R., Schneider, F.B.: Hyperproperties. In: 21st IEEE Computer Security Foundations Symposium (CSF), pp. 51–65 (2008). https://doi.org/10.1109/CSF.2008.7
13. Denning, D.E.: A lattice model of secure information flow. Commun. ACM **19**(5), 236–243 (1976). https://doi.org/10.1145/360051.360056
14. Dolan, S.: Algebraic Subtyping: Distinguished Dissertation 2017. BCS Learning & Development Ltd, Swindon, GBR (2017)
15. Fournet, C., le Guernic, G., Rezk, T.: A security-preserving compiler for distributed programs: from information-flow policies to cryptographic mechanisms. In: 16th ACM Conference on Computer and Communications Security (CCS), pp. 432–441 (2009). https://doi.org/10.1145/1653662.1653715
16. Fournet, C., Rezk, T.: Cryptographically sound implementations for typed information-flow security. In: 35th ACM Symposium on Principles of Programming Languages (POPL), pp. 323–335 (2008). https://doi.org/10.1145/1328438.1328478
17. Garg, D., Pfenning, F.: Non-interference in constructive authorization logic. In: 19th IEEE Computer Security Foundations Workshop (CSFW) (2006). https://doi.org/10.1109/CSFW.2006.18
18. Goguen, J.A., Meseguer, J.: Security policies and security models. In: IEEE Symposium on Security and Privacy, pp. 11–20 (1982). https://doi.org/10.1109/SP.1982.10014
19. Goguen, J.A., Meseguer, J.: Unwinding and inference control. In: IEEE Symposium on Security and Privacy, pp. 75–86 (1984). https://doi.org/10.1109/SP.1984.10019
20. Hirsch, A.K., Amorim, P.H.A.d., Cecchetti, E., Tate, R., Arden, O.: First-order logic for flow-limited authorization. In: 2020 IEEE 33rd Computer Security Foundations Symposium (CSF), pp. 123–138 (2020). https://doi.org/10.1109/CSF49147.2020.00017
21. Hirsch, A.K., Clarkson, M.R.: Belief semantics of authorization logic. In: CCS 2013. Association for Computing Machinery, New York (2013). https://doi.org/10.1145/2508859.2516667
22. Hirt, M., Maurer, U.M.: Player simulation and general adversary structures in perfect multiparty computation. J. Cryptol. **13**(1), 31–60 (2000). https://doi.org/10.1007/S001459910003
23. Kozyri, E., Chong, S., Myers, A.C.: Expressing information flow properties. Found. Trends Privacy Secur. **3**(1), 1–102 (2022). https://doi.org/10.1561/3300000008
24. Landauer, J., Redmond, T.: A lattice of information. In: 6th IEEE Computer Security Foundations Workshop (CSFW), pp. 65–70. IEEE Computer Society Press (1993). https://doi.org/10.1109/CSFW.1993.246638
25. Li, N., Grosof, B.N., Feigenbaum, J.: Delegation logic: a logic-based approach to distributed authorization. ACM Trans. Inf. Syst. Secur. (TISSEC) **6**(1), 128–171 (2003). https://doi.org/10.1145/605434.605438
26. Li, P., Zhang, D.: Towards a general-purpose dynamic information flow policy (2021). https://arxiv.org/abs/2109.08096
27. Matetic, S., Schneider, M., Miller, A., Juels, A., Capkun, S.: Delegatee: brokered delegation using trusted execution environments. In: USENIX Security Symposium, pp. 1387–1403 (2018)

28. Montagu, B., Pierce, B.C., Pollack, R.: A theory of information-flow labels. In: 26th IEEE Computer Security Foundations Symposium (CSF), pp. 3–17 (2013). https://doi.org/10.1109/CSF.2013.8
29. Myers, A.C.: Mostly-static decentralized information flow control. Ph.D. thesis, Massachusetts Institute of Technology, Cambridge, MA (1999)
30. Myers, A.C., Liskov, B.: A decentralized model for information flow control. In: 16th ACM Symposium on Operating System Principles (SOSP), pp. 129–142 (1997). https://doi.org/10.1145/268998.266669
31. Myers, A.C., Liskov, B.: Protecting privacy using the decentralized label model. ACM Trans. Softw. Eng. Methodol. **9**(4), 410–442 (2000). https://doi.org/10.1145/363516.363526
32. Myers, A.C., Sabelfeld, A., Zdancewic, S.: Enforcing robust declassification. In: 17th IEEE Computer Security Foundations Workshop (CSFW), pp. 172–186 (2004). https://doi.org/10.1109/CSFW.2004.9
33. Myers, A.C., Sabelfeld, A., Zdancewic, S.: Enforcing robust declassification and qualified robustness. J. Comput. Secur. **14**(2), 157–196 (2006). https://doi.org/10.3233/JCS-2006-14203
34. Myers, A.C., Zheng, L., Zdancewic, S., Chong, S., Nystrom, N.: Jif 3.0: Java information flow (2006). http://www.cs.cornell.edu/jif, software release, http://www.cs.cornell.edu/jif
35. Rehof, J., Mogensen, T.Æ.: Tractable constraints in finite semilattices. In: Cousot, R., Schmidt, D.A. (eds.) SAS 1996. LNCS, vol. 1145, pp. 285–300. Springer, Heidelberg (1996). https://doi.org/10.1007/3-540-61739-6_48
36. Ren, S., Acay, C., Myers, A.C.: An algebraic approach to asymmetric delegation and polymorphic label inference (technical report) (2025). https://doi.org/10.48550/arXiv.2504.20432
37. Rutherford, D.E.: Introduction to Lattice Theory. Oliver and Boyd (1965)
38. Sabelfeld, A., Myers, A.C.: Language-based information-flow security. IEEE J. Sel. Areas Commun. **21**(1), 5–19 (2003). https://doi.org/10.1109/JSAC.2002.806121
39. Sandhu, R.: Role hierarchies and constraints for lattice-based access controls. In: Bertino, E., Kurth, H., Martella, G., Montolivo, E. (eds.) ESORICS 1996. LNCS, vol. 1146, pp. 65–79. Springer, Heidelberg (1996). https://doi.org/10.1007/3-540-61770-1_28
40. Simonet, V.: The Flow Caml System: documentation and user's manual. Technical Report 0282, Institut National de Recherche en Informatique et en Automatique (INRIA) (2003)
41. Soloviev, M., Balliu, M., Guanciale, R.: Security properties through the lens of modal logic (2023). https://doi.org/10.1109/csf61375.2024.00009
42. Stefan, D., Russo, A., Mazières, D., Mitchell, J.C.: Disjunction category labels. In: Laud, P. (ed.) NordSec 2011. LNCS, vol. 7161, pp. 223–239. Springer, Heidelberg (2012). https://doi.org/10.1007/978-3-642-29615-4_16
43. Stone, M.H.: Topological representations of distributive lattices and brouwerian logics. Časopis pro pěstování matematiky a fysiky **067**(1), 1–25 (1938). https://doi.org/10.21136/CPMF.1938.124080
44. Swamy, N., Hicks, M., Tse, S., Zdancewic, S.: Managing policy updates in security-typed languages. In: 19th IEEE Computer Security Foundations Workshop (CSFW), pp. 202–216 (2006). https://doi.org/10.1109/CSFW.2006.17
45. Yao, A.C.: Protocols for secure computations. In: 23rd Annual IEEE Symposium on Foundations of Computer Science, pp. 160–164 (1982). https://doi.org/10.1109/SFCS.1982.38

46. Zagieboylo, D., Suh, G.E., Myers, A.C.: Using information flow to design an ISA that controls timing channels. In: 32nd IEEE Computer Security Foundations Symposium (CSF) (2019). https://doi.org/10.1109/CSF.2019.00026
47. Zdancewic, S., Myers, A.C.: Robust declassification. In: 14th IEEE Computer Security Foundations Workshop (CSFW), pp. 15–23 (2001). https://doi.org/10.1109/CSFW.2001.930133
48. Zdancewic, S., Zheng, L., Nystrom, N., Myers, A.C.: Secure program partitioning. ACM Trans. Comput. Syst. **20**(3), 283–328 (2002). https://doi.org/10.1145/566340.566343
49. Zhang, D., Myers, A.C., Vytiniotis, D., Peyton Jones, S.: SHErrLoc: a static holistic error locator. ACM Trans. Program. Lang. Syst. **39**(4), 18 (2017). http://dl.acm.org/citation.cfm?id=3121137
50. Zheng, L., Chong, S., Myers, A.C., Zdancewic, S.: Using replication and partitioning to build secure distributed systems. In: IEEE Symposium on Security and Privacy, pp. 236–250 (2003). https://doi.org/10.1109/SECPRI.2003.1199340
51. Zheng, L., Myers, A.C.: A language-based approach to secure quorum replication. In: 9th ACM SIGPLAN Workshop on Programming Languages and Analysis for Security (PLAS) (2014). https://doi.org/10.1145/2637113.2637117

An Efficient Security-Enhanced Accountable Access Control for Named Data Networking

Jianfei Sun[1], Yuxian Li[1(✉)], Xuehuan Yang[2], Guomin Yang[1], and Robert Deng[1]

[1] Singapore Management University, Singapore 188065, Singapore
{jfsun,yuxianli,gmyang,robertdeng}@smu.edu.sg
[2] Nanyang Technological University, Singapore 639798, Singapore
s190113@e.ntu.edu.sg

Abstract. Named Data Networking (NDN) is embraced as the crucial implementation of Information-Centric Networking (ICN), enhancing content distribution and caching efficiency through edge routers. However, existing NDN architectures face significant security and privacy challenges, including: (*a*) a lack of *secure* and *efficient* access control; (*b*) inadequate support for *flexible* and *selective* content management by content publishers; (*c*) insufficient implementation of accountability and privilege revocation mechanisms. To handle these challenges, we propose ESAS, the first-ever Efficient Security-enhanced Accountable Access Control Scheme for NDN. Specifically, our ESAS incorporates anonymous authentication using group signatures at network routers to prevent unauthorized access, employs key-aggregation-based access control to facilitate selective content management, and maintains an access list at edge routers to trace and revoke privileges from content subscribers who misuse authorization tokens. Furthermore, our comprehensive security analysis and comparative studies validate enhanced security capabilities and superior features of our ESAS relative to existing access control solutions. We also conduct experiments to indicate the practicability and feasibility of our ESAS for edge routers, content publishers and subscribers, thereby confirming its effectiveness in NDN architecture.

Keywords: Named Data Networking · Access Control · Accountability

1 Introduction

Named Data Networking (NDN) is a network architecture that focuses on data itself rather than on the location of the data [5,31], which is the basis of the traditional Internet architecture that uses IP addresses. Unlike IP networking, which routes and addresses data based on the host (such as a server or computer), NDN addresses data directly by its name and every piece of data is given a unique name that is used to request and retrieve it [30,38]. NDN is part of a broader category known as Information-Centric Networking (ICN) [10,26]. Compared to other ICN architectures, NDN's hierarchical naming structure (similar to URLs) and data-centric security provide significant advantages, such as improved routing efficiency, reduced latency, and stronger protection against content tampering and unauthorized access. These features position NDN as a promising solution to meet the increasing demands of modern internet applications and services. Despite its potential benefits, NDN also faces critical security and privacy challenges [1,7,15] discussed below.

1.1 Security and Privacy Challenges in NDN

Challenge I: Current NDN Lacks a *Secure and Efficient* Access Control to Regulate Legitimate Access. Specifically, the current Internet has evolved into a business-oriented and content-oriented platform, allowing users to share content freely in NDN, regardless of its source. When network users make requests (*e.g.*, HTTP requests) to the NDN platform for certain contents, the content publisher will decide to approve or deny the requests according to an access control list. However, due to the existence of in-network caches, the requests will be fulfilled by the in-network cache rather than directly from the content publisher. This means that the content might be delivered to the user without the access approval of the content publisher if the requests match the forwarding path regulated by the routers, thus actually allowing unauthorized access to content. Hence, *no preset access control strategy in NDN may lead to the capability of unauthorized access for any requests.*

To enforce access control in NDN, potential solutions include authentication-based solutions [3,9,14,18,25,27] and encryption-based methodologies [12,13, 17,21,28,32]. With the authentication-based solutions for NDN, once the cache-enabled router encounters a cache hit (*i.e.*, content stored in its in-network cache), it initiates an authentication process to determine whether to deliver the requested content or not. Nonetheless, this solution is inappropriate since this authentication process either is performed at each cache-enabled router or involves interaction with the content publisher during content retrieval, which apparently introduces substantial computational overhead and negatively impacts forwarding performance. Besides, the authentication-based solutions suffer from a prevalent issue that authentication is required for each content request, necessitating multiple authentication processes for users to achieve the entire file retrieval. With encryption-based methodologies such as attribute-based encryption and broadcast-based encryption, and so on, the decryption capability of network users for the contents can be restricted, thus guaranteeing that the contents are accessible only to authorized users. While illegitimate users fail to access the contents, they cannot be blocked from requesting and retrieving encrypted contents from the networks, which may result in the network being overwhelmed by a flood of requests (DoS attacks [20,36]). Another recent alternative solution is to exploit an edge-based access control approach, yet this approach is vulnerable to collusion attacks between unauthorized users, thus failing to *truly* realize the authorization access to the contents. Therefore, how to efficiently and securely realize access control for regulating legitimate content access in NDN is a prime challenge.

Challenge II: Current NDN is Inadequate for *Efficiently* Supporting *Selective* Content Management by Content Publishers. In content-oriented NDN, content publishers commonly upload their files to the network for ease of sharing with content subscribers. However, the current NDN framework only supports the encryption of each file with a single encryption key. This approach is problematic because files often contain multiple contents with varying levels of confidentiality. Encrypting all contents with a single key can lead to the leakage of highly confidential information. *Therefore, it is crucial to develop an efficient mechanism to support selective content management for content publishers.* A common approach is to use distinct keys for encrypting each content and then provide corresponding authorization tokens (*i.e.*, secret keys) to content subscribers. This solution is evidently impractical, as the number of tokens would equal the number of accessed contents. Additionally, transferring these tokens necessitates a secure channel, and storing them demands highly secure and costly storage solutions. Consequently, how to efficiently and selectively manage different confidential contents of a content publisher is an unnoticed challenge.

Challenge III: Current NDN is *Seldom* Capable of *Effectively* Realizing Accountability and Privilege Revocation. In the NDN framework, effectively managing accountability and privilege revocation is crucial but challenging. An illustrative scenario is when multiple users, sharing the same decryption key, access data from the same router. Such privilege abuses can cause significant issues for the content publisher (CP), who must be able to trace each user's activity to enforce accountability and, if necessary, revoke access to mitigate damage. To combat these, intuitive methods such as logging user activities and employing more dynamic encryption techniques are typically used. Logging ensures that every access or modification to the data is recorded, allowing the CP to trace any unauthorized or malicious actions back to specific users. However, maintaining extensive logs and analyzing them in real time can be resource-intensive and may not scale well in larger networks. Another alternative solution such as traceable and revocable attribute-based encryption [11,16] not only enables the CP to embed access policies directly into the content ciphertext, thus permitting only network users who meet certain criteria to access the content, but also allows the tracking and revoking of the actual users who abuses their decryption privilege. This method indeed achieves accountability and privilege revocation but introduces computational overhead and complexity in key management, particularly when user attributes or policies frequently change. Besides, while the digital signatures and access control lists can be respectively used to ensure accountability and manage privilege revocation, existing related schemes may be easily susceptible to collusion attacks to potentially result in unauthorized data access, thereby undermining the *effectiveness* of the accountability and privilege revocation. As a result, achieving effective accountability and privilege revocation continues to be a significant challenge.

Motivation by advancements in key aggregation-based access control [6,19] and group signature technologies [4,8], we propose ESAS, the first-ever Efficient Security-enhanced Accountable Access Control Scheme for NDN to handle the above challenges. With our ESAS, content publishers can not only selectively manage their contents, but also securely deploy efficient access control on routers to restrict unauthorized access. In contrast to existing accountable access control solutions, a distinguishing merit of our ESAS approach is that it enables content publishers to manage their contents more securely, efficiently, and flexibly as well as realize robust service accountability and privilege revocation upon the misuse of authorization tokens.

1.2 Summary of Our Contributions

This work characterizes the first endeavor to devise an Efficient *Security-enhanced* Accountable Access Control Scheme (ESAS) that is *more secure and flexible, lightweight and applicable* for NDN. In detail, the ESAS decouples access control from content provisions and exploits edge routers in NDN to *anonymously* authenticate user requests, which ensures that the in-cache resources are exclusively available to authorized content subscribers. Besides, the ESAS provisions selective content management by allowing a content publisher to encrypt various contents with different encryption keys while content subscribers can efficiently access multiple contents in in-cache with a single aggregate key. To facilitate accountability and privilege revocation, signatures from an authorized subscriber serve as traceable credentials, allowing content publishers to implement the identification of users who misuse keys by referencing the user list.

To realize a more secure, flexible, efficient accountable access control scheme for NDN, the basic idea is to incorporate the principles of group signature and key-aggregate encryption, *whereas it is non-trivial to realize it securely and efficiently*. A naive approach to constructing such an ESAS would be to merge the two cryptosystems simply, *i.e.*, a group signature and a key-aggregate encryption, however, integrating the authentication keys (*i.e.*, encryption keys related to group signature) with aggregate decryption keys presents a complex challenge, as these keys are generated independently but must be unified coherently using the same master random exponent. Moreover, even if this naive approach is feasible, it is intractable to block the collusion attacks since the encryption keys and aggregate decryption keys are separately used for authentication and content access.

In order to develop a practical, accountable access control scheme for real-world NDN, we have devised a novel approach that *perfectly* integrates an authentication key with a key-aggregate decryption key. This method enhances security by incorporating the authentication key as part of the decryption key, participating in the decryption process and ensuring immunity to collusion attacks. In brief, to generate valid key pairs, a critical initial step involves producing parameters for an authentication key, which embeds one random seed of the system master secret key. Then it is integrated with the system master secret key to construct an aggregate key. During the content decryption process, the participation of two distinct types of keys is required, ensuring that the NDN architecture remains impervious to collusion attacks by closely integrating these key components.

Based on this idea, we devise an efficient security-enhanced accountable access control scheme (ESAS) for NDN. With ESAS, a content publisher can encrypt various contents with different encryption keys, but a content subscriber is selectively authorized to access partial contents with a single key-aggregate decryption key, thus realizing the flexible content sharing. Prior to the selective content access, a content subscriber is required to generate a signature with his/her authentication key and send the signature to cache-enabled routers for authentication. This authentication signature can be used as traceable credentials to actualize accountability, thereby enabling revocation by content publishers via maintaining a user list. In addition, the comprehensive proofs are also provisioned to demonstrate that our ESAS can semantically-securely realize more desirable features than the most prominent and state-of-the-art scheme including anonymous authentication, unforgeability and traceability. We have also implemented our ESAS and related solutions on a Raspberry Pi 4 Model B. The implementation is built on PBC 0.5.14 library [2], and OpenSSL 1.1.1. [29] with Python to simulate our ESAS. Our observations indicate that the computational efficiency of our ESAS is comparable to the most prominent one.

2 Related Works

Over the past few years, significant efforts have been dedicated to addressing the access control challenges in Named Data Networking. These solutions are broadly classified into two main approaches: encryption-based and authentication-based methods. The core principle of encryption-based access control methodologies is to encrypt the content such that only authorized subscribers can decode it. To date, various encryption techniques have been employed, such as Broadcast Encryption (BE) [12,17,32], Attribute-Based Encryption (ABE) [13], Identity-Based Encryption (IBE) [28], Proxy Re-encryption (PRE) [21], etc. Although these solutions enable preventing unauthorized access, they are incapable of supporting that illegitimate users cannot be blocked from retrieving contents from the networks, which may result in the network being overwhelmed by a flood of requests (i.e., DoS attacks) since routers must fairly handle every request and cannot discriminate against any request.

The fundamental concept behind authentication-based access control approaches is to verify the authenticity of subscribers' content requests either at the routers or on the content publisher side before implementing the content delivery [34,35]. Currently, numerous sophisticated initiatives in authentication-based access control [3,9,14,18,25,27] have been explored. In more detail, an access control scheme in [14] utilizes a signature mechanism to enhance network security, where routers are responsible for verifying both the integrity and authenticity of encrypted contents before caching, such that the cached ones will only be transmitted to authorized subscribers after the signature verification passes. In [9,25], each content subscriber must be authenticated by the corresponding content publisher before the transition of any content. Besides, the work [25] requires a secure channel to disseminate the network contents. In [27], it is detailed how routers confirm the authenticity of subscribers through multi-signatures generated by content publishers before proceeding with content delivery. The work [18] describes an authenticated access control framework that utilizes two distinct online entities to handle the authentication and authorization of subscribers. In [3], the subscriber identity should be authenticated by the content publisher before setting up a session key for the secure transmission of encrypted content. To summarize, current authentication-based access control schemes show some deficiencies in NDN, including escalating router overhead [14,27], curtailing NDN resource utilization [3,9,25,27], or demanding an online authority resource utilization [3,9,18,25]. Additionally, most aforementioned solutions neither address accountability for tracing key misuse by authorized subscribers nor facilitate access privilege revocation.

Initiatives have been launched to enhance accountability and privilege revocation, alongside measures to prevent unauthorized access. These primarily involve solutions based on the combination of digital signatures and either Broadcast Encryption (BE) or Role-Based Encryption (RE) approaches. Specifically, the works [12,33–35] focus on BE-related signature authentication, while the works [22–24] explore RE-related signature authentication. Compared to BE-related solutions, RE-related solutions enable flexible content share (*i.e.*, allow contents to be organized in hierarchies or support multiple content management). However, all of these schemes [12,22–24,33–35] are vulnerable to collusion attacks between the authorized subscriber and any unauthorized one. *The basic reason leading to this mainly originates from* the fact that the encryption key for signature and decryption key for authorization access are separate for respectively realizing authentication and access.

In summary, to date, no secure solution has been found that elegantly achieves secure and efficient access control, incorporating flexible and selective content management along with accountability and privilege revocation for NDN.

3 Problem Statement and Basic Knowledge

3.1 System Model

A Named Data Networking architecture primarily comprises three types of entities: Content Publishers (CP), Content Subscribers (CS), and Internet Service Provider (ISP), as shown in Fig. 1. In more detail, CPs, who are considered fully trusted, encode the contents with various public keys to generate content ciphertexts, which are then disseminated across the ISP for sharing. The ISP network mainly comprises two primary router types: edge routers and cache-enabled routers. Edge routers, which do not possess caching functionalities, are tasked with authenticating users' requests before entering the network. Conversely, cache-enabled routers facilitate the forwarding of these requests and provide direct responses if the queried contents are in their cache. The routers in ISP are deemed honest but curious, which means they honestly follow and implement the designated protocol but try to learn the contents. CS can send their interests to obtain the interested contents from CPs via the ISP network. Once two different subscribers use the identical secret key to access the same content resources, this key abuse behavior can be discerned and traced via the ISP by the CP. In this model, CSs who are assumed to be malicious may act with malicious intent, attempting to access unauthorized data through tampering, replaying, or forging operations. Besides, they are allowed to collude with other authorized ones to illegitimately acquire legitimate access privileges.

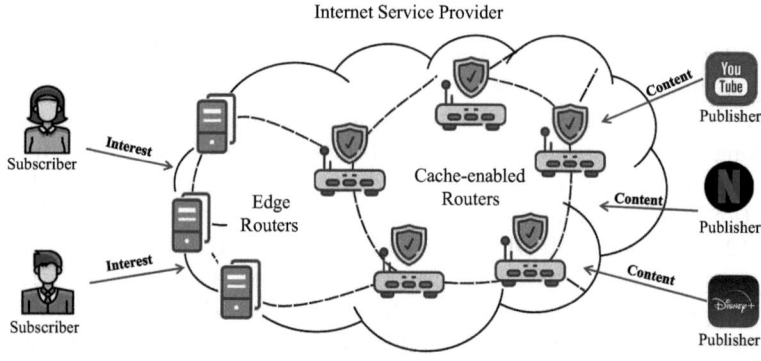

Fig. 1. System Architecture of Named Data Networking

3.2 Threat Model and Design Goal

In the threat model of our NDN, three various attacks are considered. Specifically, (a) any attackers try to launch collusion attacks to derive a legitimate secret key through the combination of partial keys, thus further enabling them to unlawfully access in-cached content they are not authorized to access; (b) malicious adversaries who intentionally launch forgery attacks aim to compromise content authenticity by intercepting-then-altering or substituting raw contents even in the absence of legitimate secret keys; (c) any adversary who deliberately compromises the secret key may intend to help unauthorized users to capture legal access. Given these threats, we have articulated the following security objectives for our NDN system:

- *Content semantic security*: Ensure that any adversary cannot derive any meaningful information from encrypted contents even if some attacks (*e.g.*, collusion attacks, replay attacks, etc.) can be launched.

- *Anonymous authentication*: Allow a user to prove that they have the right to access a service or perform an action without disclosing identifiable information.
- *Traceability*. Enable the identification and tracking of any user who misuses a secret key, facilitating effective revocation of access.
- *Content authenticity*: Guarantee that once a signature for requested content is generated, it remains invulnerable to tampering or forgery unless the adversary possesses the corresponding legitimate secret keys.

3.3 Bilinear Maps and Complexity Assumption

Definition 1 (Bilinear Maps). *A bilinear map [4] is a function* $e : \mathbb{G}_0 \times \mathbb{G}_0 \to \mathbb{G}_T$, *where* $\mathbb{G}_0$ *and* $\mathbb{G}_T$ *are groups (often cyclic groups of prime order). The function e must satisfy the following properties: (1)* **Bilinearity:** *For all* $u, v \in \mathbb{G}_0$, *and* $w, x \in \mathbb{G}_0$, $e(u \cdot v, w) = e(u, w) \cdot e(v, w)$ *and* $e(u, w \cdot x) = e(u, w) \cdot e(u, x)$ *holds; (2)***Non-degeneracy:** *there exists* $g \in \mathbb{G}_0$ *and* $h \in \mathbb{G}_0$ *such that* $e(g, h) \neq 1_{\mathbb{G}_T}$, *where* $1_{\mathbb{G}_T}$ *is the identity element of* $\mathbb{G}_T$; *(3)* **Computability:** *There exists an efficient algorithm to compute* $e(u, v)$ *for any* $u, v \in \mathbb{G}_0$.

Definition 2 (BDHE). *: Given the tuple* $(h, g^\beta, \ldots, g^{\beta^n}, g^{\beta^{n+2}}, \ldots, g^{\beta^{2n}}, T) \in \mathbb{G}_0^{2n} \times \mathbb{G}_T$, *the goal of Bilinear Diffie-Hellman Exponent (BDHE) assumption [6] is to decide* $T = e(h, g)^{\beta^{n+1}}$ *or T is a random element of* $\mathbb{G}_T$.

Definition 3 (q-SDH). *Given a* $(q + 2)$-*tuple* $(g_0, g_1, g_1^\gamma, g_1^{\gamma^2}, \ldots, g_1^{\gamma^q})$, *the goal of the q-Strong Diffie-Hellman (q-SDH) assumption [35] is to compute* $(g_0^{1/(\gamma+c)}, c)$.

4 ESAS Construction

4.1 Overview

In our scheme, CPs can encode their contents with different keys to realize the flexible selective content management for distinct contents with confidential levels. CSs are classified into different groups and are authorized an access token (*i.e.*, secret key) according to their access level, which can determine the selective contents CS can access. Specifically, we implement two advanced cryptographic solutions: group signatures and key aggregate encryption. Group signatures enable edge routers to authenticate users while preserving their anonymity, ensuring that real identities remain confidential. Concurrently, key aggregate encryption ensures that only users possessing the appropriate access privileges are able to decrypt the selective contents. Distinct from the previous solutions [12,22–24,33–35], which are easily susceptible to collusion attacks, *our methodology mandates active participation of the encryption key related to group signature for authentication in the decryption process*, thus effectively blocking the unauthorized access resulting from collusion attacks.

Intuitively, the basic idea of our scheme is illustrated in Fig. 2. Initially, a content subscriber registers with the Content Publisher (CP) and subsequently sends interest packets, which are accompanied by signatures, to retrieve desired content. The edge router authenticates these requests using the user information obtained from the CP. Upon successful authentication, the interest packets are permitted to access the cache-enabled router network, thereby facilitating the delivery of the requested content to the user. To ensure secure selective data management, the CP employs key aggregate encryption to secure the contents before they are uploaded to the network. Furthermore, the edge routers and cache-enabled routers will detect the misuse of the secret key and report this dishonest behavior to the CP, which can result in the punishment of privilege revocation for the key-misused subscribers.

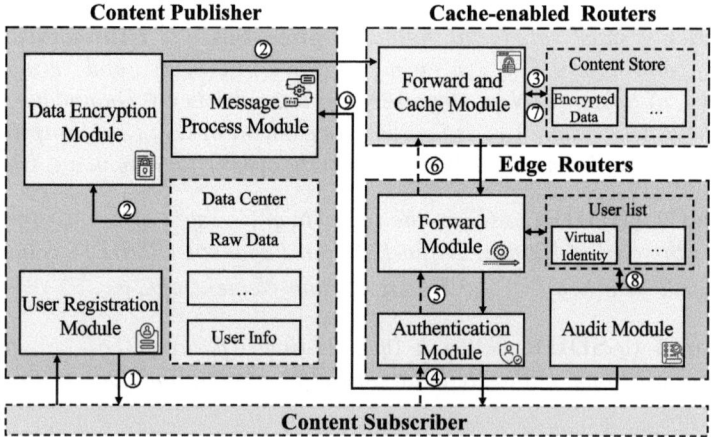

Fig. 2. System Overview

4.2 Scheme Description

System Setup: In the system setup phase, the Content Publisher (CP) as the group administration (GA) creates essential public/private parameters. Suppose the system users are classified into k groups based on access strategies. In detail, the system is initialized by CP as follows:

- Pick a bilinear group system $\mathcal{GS} = (\mathbb{G}_0, \mathbb{G}_1, \mathbb{G}_T, p, e)$ with two randomly chosen generators $g_0, g_1 \in \mathbb{G}_0$. Besides, randomly choose $\alpha \in \mathbb{Z}_p$ and compute $\mathsf{A} = e(g_0, g_1)^\alpha$, where $\mathbb{G}_0 = \mathbb{G}_1$. Besides, select $h \in \mathbb{G}_0$, $h' \in \mathbb{G}_1$, $\xi_1, \xi_2 \in \mathbb{Z}_p$ and set $u, v \in \mathbb{G}_0$, $\Theta_1, \Theta_2 \in \mathbb{G}_1$ such that $u^{\xi_1} = v^{\xi_2} = h$, $\Theta_1 = h'^{\xi_1}$ and $\Theta_2 = h'^{\xi_2}$.
- Choose k random numbers $\beta_1, \ldots, \beta_k \in \mathbb{Z}_p$ and calculate $x_i = g_1^{\beta_i}$ and $y_i = g_1^{\alpha \beta_i}$, where $i \in [1, k]$. Set $\hat{\beta} = (\beta_1, \ldots, \beta_k)$, $\mathsf{X} = (x_1, \ldots, x_k)$ and

$Y = (y_1, \ldots, y_k)$. Also, pick k random numbers $\gamma, \eta \in \mathbb{Z}_p$ and calculate $\nu = g_0^\eta$, $z_i = g_0^{\gamma^i}$, $z_i' = g_1^{\gamma^i}$, $\mathsf{B} = e(z_n, z_1')$, where $i \in [1, n] \cup [n+2, 2n]$.

– Set the public parameters $\mathsf{pp} = (g_1, u, v, h, h', z_i, z_i', \nu\ \mathsf{A}, \mathsf{B}, \mathsf{X}, \mathsf{Y}, \Theta_1, \Theta_2, \mathcal{H}_1, \mathcal{H}_2, E(.))$, where $E(.)$ is a secure symmetric encryption, $\mathcal{H}_1, \mathcal{H}_2$ is a hash function that defines $\mathcal{H}_1 : \{0,1\}^* \times \mathbb{G}_0^8 \to \mathbb{Z}_p$, $\mathcal{H}_2$ is also a hash function that is used for creating hash chains. Meanwhile, CP retains his/her master secret key $\mathsf{msk} = (g_0, \xi_1, \xi_2, \hat{\beta}, \hat{\gamma}, \alpha)$.

User Registration: For the user registration of id_i belonging to a member of group k, CP selects $t_i \in \mathbb{Z}_p$, computes $A_i = g_0^{1/(\beta_i + t_i)}$ and inserts (A_i, id_i) into the user list. For the set $\mathcal{S}$ of the level indices j the user i is authorized to access, CP computes $B_i^j = \prod_{j \in \mathcal{S}} z_{n+1-j}^\eta \cdot g_0^{\alpha t_i/(\beta_i + t_i)}$. Thus, the secret key of user i is set as (t_i, A_i, B_i), where (t_i, A_i) are used for signature generation during authentication request, (A_i, B_i) are also utilized for various content retrieval with distinct access privileges.

Content Generation: To indicate the access privilege levels of the various contents, we reserved the naming method as that in Xue et al. [35] and labeled each content with an access privilege. Different from the above method, each user does not need to pick his/her secret key but only uses his/her unique aggregate key to access various contents with different privileges.

Before the raw contents of CP are disseminated into the network, key aggregate encryption is employed to achieve data confidentiality for different contents with various access privileges. Assuming the content is labeled with the access privilege level tag j, it can be accessed by users with levels $\ell, \ldots, k$. Initially, CP randomly selects r, calculates $\mathsf{K} = \mathsf{A}^r \cdot \mathsf{B}^{-r}$, and uses K to encode each content M: $C = E_\mathsf{K}(M)$. Subsequently, CP selects z_j, y_j to encrypt K using the following calculations for $j \in [1, n]$: $C_1 = (\nu \cdot z_j)^r$, $C_2 = g_1^r$, $C_3 = y_j^r$. Consequently, the content is stored as (C, C_1, C_2, C_3) in cache-assisted routers.

Authentication Request and Verification: The group signature, which is generated in response to users' requests, undergoes authentication by the edge routers. Through a valid signature verification process, the edge routers ascertain the user's authorization to access a specific chunk of a file. Suppose a user i wishes to request access to a file chunk. In that case, she/he initiates the process by sending an interest packet containing the group identity ℓ, the file name f, the timestamp $\mathcal{TS}$, and a signature σ. Here, the file name f serves as a prefix for the chunk name. The detailed procedure for generating the signature of the user i for authentication is as follows: the user i first chooses $\tau, \epsilon, \lambda_\tau, \lambda_\epsilon, \lambda_x, \lambda_{\delta_1}, \lambda_{\delta_2} \in \mathbb{Z}_p$, computes and sets $\mathcal{M} = f \| \mathcal{TS}$, $\delta_1 = t_i \tau$, $\delta_2 = t_i \epsilon$, $\Phi_1 = u^\tau$, $\Phi_2 = v^\epsilon$, $\Phi_3 = A_i h^{\tau+\epsilon}$, $\Psi_1 = u^{\lambda_\tau}$, $\Psi_2 = v^{\lambda_\epsilon}$, $\Psi_3 = e(\Phi_3, g_1)^{\lambda_x} \cdot e(h, x_{\ell_i})^{-\lambda_\tau - \lambda_\epsilon} \cdot e(h, g_1)^{-\lambda_{\delta_1} - \lambda_{\delta_2}}$, $\Psi_4 = \Phi_1^{\lambda_x} u^{-\lambda_{\delta_1}}$, $\Psi_5 = \Phi_2^{\lambda_x} v^{-\lambda_{\delta_2}}$.

Besides, he/she also sets $c = \mathcal{H}_1(\mathcal{M}, \Phi_1, \Phi_2, \Phi_3, \Psi_1, \Psi_2, \Psi_3, \Psi_4, \Psi_5)$, $\chi_\tau = \lambda_\tau + c\tau$, $\chi_\epsilon = \lambda_\epsilon + c\epsilon$, $\chi_x = \lambda_x + c \cdot t_j$, $\chi_{\delta_1} = \lambda_{\delta_1} + c\delta_1$, $\chi_{\delta_2} = \lambda_{\delta_2} + c\delta_2$. Finally, the generated signature $\sigma = (\Phi_1, \Phi_2, \Phi_3, \Psi_3, c, \chi_\tau, \chi_\epsilon, \chi_x, \chi_{\delta_1}, \chi_{\delta_2})$ is returned.

After obtaining the interest packet from the user i, the validity of timestamp $\mathcal{TS}$ is first checked and then the signature authenticity is verified by edge routers via the following steps: the edge router sets $\mathcal{M}' = f \| \mathcal{TS}$, $\Psi_1 = u^{\chi_\tau} \Phi_1^{-c}$, $\Psi_2 = v^{\chi_\epsilon} \Phi_2^{-c}$, $\Psi_4 = \Phi_1^{\chi_x} u^{-\chi_{\sigma_1}}$, $\Psi_5 = \Phi_2^{\chi_x} v^{-\chi_{\sigma_2}}$, $t_1 = -\chi_\tau - \chi_\epsilon$, $t_2 = -\chi_{\sigma_1} - \chi_{\sigma_2}$ and checks if $\Psi_3 \neq e(\Phi_3, g_1)^{\lambda_x} \cdot e(h, x_\ell)^{t_1} \cdot e(h, g_1)^{t_2} \cdot (e(\Phi_3, x_\ell)/e(g_0, g_1))^c$ holds. If it holds, the edge router returns $\bot$; Otherwise, the edge router checks if $c = \mathcal{H}_1(\mathcal{M}, \Phi_1, \Phi_2, \Phi_3, \Psi_1, \Psi_2, \Psi_3, \Psi_4, \Psi_5)$. If this equality holds, the signature verification is validated. If the signature is successfully validated, the edge router then acknowledges that the user i is a legitimate member of group ℓ. Following successful signature validation, the edge router discerns the user i as a valid member of group ℓ. Subsequently, it elegantly derives the access privilege level ℓ' from the chunk name and judiciously contrasts it with ℓ. If $\ell \geq \ell'$, it signifies that the user has access authorization to the chunk, and the edge router injects the request into the network. Otherwise, the request is rejected and discarded by the edge router.

Content Retrieval and Access: After passing the signature verification, the requested content (C, C_1, C_2, C_3) is sent to the user i. From the content name, the user i learns access privilege level ℓ' and then picks his/her secret key A_i, B_i. After this, the encoded key K can be recovered from C_1, C_2 and C_3 by the user i by performing the following computation:

$$\mathcal{K} = e(C_1, \prod_{j \in \mathcal{S}} z'_{n+1-j})^{-1} e(C_2, B_i \prod_{j \in \mathcal{S}, j \neq i} z_{n+1-j+i}) e(C_3, A_i)$$

$$= e(z_i^r, \prod_{j \in \mathcal{S}} z'_{n+1-j})^{-1} \cdot e(g_1^r, \prod_{j \in \mathcal{S}, j \neq i} z_{n+1-j+i})$$

$$\cdot e(g_1^r, g_0^{\alpha t_i/(\beta_i + t_i)}) \cdot e(g_0^{1/(\beta_i + t_i)}, g_1^{r\alpha\beta_i})$$

$$= e(z_n, z'_1)^{-r} \cdot e(g_0, g_1)^{\alpha r} = \mathsf{K}.$$

Then, user i with the recovered K can access the content M.

Service Accountability and Privilege Revocation: When privilege abuses occur, i.e., different users with the same decryption key access the same router data, the CP is capable of tracing the identity, imposing some punishment for revoking permissions due to some damages to the CP caused.

First, the CP can make requests to an edge router to obtain the credential $(f, \mathcal{TS}, \sigma)$ of a user, then the CP holding his/her master secret key (ξ_1, ξ_2) computes $A = \Psi_3/(\Psi_1^{\xi_1} \Psi_2^{\xi_2})$ to reveal the identity of a user by looking up the user list. It is nothing that every request does not need to be checked, the batch verification method used in [34] could also be applicable for improving the scalability. Finally, to realize the punishment of privilege abuses, i.e., the users will lose any opportunity to request any content from corresponding CPs, CP should periodically update his/her revocation list $\mathcal{RL}$ for ease of user revocation. In our methodology, the signature technique is exploited to ensure the unforgeability of the revocation list sent to edge routers and the edge routers are assisted to block the authentication of revoked users prior, thus reaching the revocation motivation. In $\mathcal{RL}$, it contains some records of a revoked user $\mathcal{RD}_i = e(A_i, h')$, i.e., $\mathcal{RL} = \{\mathcal{RD}_1, \mathcal{RD}_2, \ldots, \mathcal{RD}_j\}$. Specifically, the CP produces a signature as $\mathcal{SIG} = \mathcal{F}(\mathcal{RL})^{\xi_1}$, where $\mathcal{F}$ is defined as $\mathcal{F} : \{0,1\}^* \to \mathbb{G}_1$ and sends it with the $\mathcal{RL}$ to an edge router, which then computes if $e(h, \mathcal{F}(\mathcal{RL})) = e(\mathcal{SIG}, u)$ hold to ensure the authenticity of the $\mathcal{RL}$.

Thus, prior to performing the authenticity request for validating the signature σ, the edge router first requires checking whether the user is within the user revocation list or not by implementing the *revocation verification algorithm* in the following steps: 1) set the number of revoked users in $\mathcal{RL}$ as $\mathcal{N} = num(\mathcal{RL})$ and compute $\mathcal{IM} = e(\Psi_3, h')/(e(\Psi_1, \Theta_1)e(\Psi_2, \Theta_2))$; 2) for each $i \in [1, \mathcal{N}]$, check if $\mathcal{RL}.\mathcal{RD}_i = \mathcal{IM}$ matches. If it holds, i.e., the user is listed in the user revocation list, the edge router will block the authentication. Otherwise, it implements the signature verification as stated in the authentication request phase.

5 Security Analysis

In the following theorems, we prove that our ESAS meets the four design goals described in Sect. 3. B.

Theorem 1. *Assuming the BDHE assumption holds, our ESAS achieves content semantic security.*

Proof. Suppose there is an adversary $\mathcal{A}$ that compromises our ESAS with an advantage ξ. We can construct a corresponding algorithm $\mathcal{B}$ that tackles the BDHE problem with the same advantage. $\mathcal{B}$ is given a challenge tuple $(h, g_0, z_1, z_2, \ldots, z_n, z_{n+2}, \ldots, z_{2n}, \mathcal{Z})$, where $h, g_0 \in \mathbb{G}_0$ and $z_i = g_0^{\beta^i}$ with $\beta \in \mathbb{Z}_p$. The objective for $\mathcal{B}$ is to determine if $\mathcal{Z} = e(z_{n+1}, h)$ or if $\mathcal{Z}$ is a random element in $\mathbb{G}_T$.

- **Setup:** $\mathcal{A}$ is provided with the parameters $(g_0, z_1, z_2, \ldots, z_n, z_{n+2}, \ldots, z_{2n})$. A random content index i^* from $[1, n]$ is selected and $\nu = g^r z_{i^*}^{-1}$ is defined, where $r \in \mathbb{Z}_p$. Additionally, set $y_i = g_1^{\alpha\beta_i}$ for each $i \in [1, m]$, with $\beta_i, \alpha \in \mathbb{Z}_p$.
- **Phases 1 & 2:** $\mathcal{A}$ queries for a set $\mathcal{S}$. If $i^* \in \mathcal{S}$, the process aborts; otherwise, it returns $B_i^j = \prod_{j \in \mathcal{S}} z_{n+1-j}^r z_{n+1-j+i^*}^{-1} \cdot g_0^{\alpha t_i/(\beta_i + t_i)}$ and $A_i = g_0^{1/(\beta_i + t_i)}$, where $t_i \in \mathbb{Z}_p$.
- **Challenge:** $\mathcal{A}$ outputs two equal-length messages m_0 and m_1, and an index i_c. If $i_c \neq i^*$, the process aborts. Otherwise, a bit $\tau \in \{0,1\}$ is randomly chosen and $(h^r, h, y_i^r, m_\tau \cdot \mathcal{Z})$ is returned. Let $h = g_0^t$, then $h^r = g_0^{tr} = (g_0^r z_{i^*}^{-1} z_{i^*}) = (\nu z_{i_c})^t$, indicating that this ciphertext is a valid content encryption of m_τ under the index i_c if $\mathcal{Z} = e(z_{n+1}, h)$.

- **Guess:** $\mathcal{A}$ returns a guess τ'. If $\tau = \tau'$, $\mathcal{B}$ outputs 0, indicating that $\mathcal{Z} = e(z_{n+1}, h)$. Otherwise, it outputs 1.

The probability of correctly guessing i_c is $1/n$, thereby $\mathcal{B}$ has an advantage of at least ξ/n in addressing BDHE assumption.

Theorem 2. *If our ESAS achieves content semantic security, then the group signature in our proposal is anonymous.*

Proof. If an adversary $\mathcal{A}$ can break the anonymous group signature scheme with a non-negligible advantage, an algorithm $\mathcal{B}$ can be constructed to breach the semantic security of our ESAS with a certain advantage. In more detail,

- **Setup:** $\mathcal{B}$ is given the public key (u, v, h), then the remaining parts in group public key can be produced by $\mathcal{B}$ as the steps in Sect. 4 and the generated public key (g_1, h, u, v, W) is sent to $\mathcal{A}$. Besides, the hash function $\mathcal{H}_1$ is simulated as a random oracle via a table.
- **Hash Queries:** $\mathcal{A}$ can make queries for the hash value $\mathcal{H}_1(\mathcal{M}, \Phi_1, \Phi_2, \Phi_3, \Psi_1, \Psi_2, \Psi_3, \Psi_4, \Psi_5)$, if the value has already existed in the table, then the value is directly returned to $\mathcal{A}$; otherwise, $t \in \mathbb{Z}_p$ is picked and inserted to the table. Subsequently, t is given back to $\mathcal{A}$.
- **Private Key Queries:** $\mathcal{A}$ can makes queries for the user i's secret key, $\mathcal{B}$ then returns (A_i, t_i) to $\mathcal{A}$.
- **Challenge:** $\mathcal{A}$ submits two indexes i_0 and i_1, a message M to $\mathcal{B}$. Besides, it also gives two private keys A_{i_0} and A_{i_1} to the challenger. Then, it picks a coin $\tau \in \{0, 1\}$ and returns (Φ_1, Φ_2, Φ_3) of a secret key A_{i_τ} to $\mathcal{B}$. Based on the obtained ciphertext, it produces the signature as follows: assuming that user i_τ is affiliated to group n, the random elements $c, \chi_\tau, \chi_\epsilon, \chi_x, \chi_{\delta_1}, \chi_{\delta_2} \in \mathbb{Z}_p$ are picked and then $(\Psi_1, \Psi_2, \Psi_3, \Psi_4, \Psi_5)$ can be computed in the following: $\Psi_1 = u^{\chi_\tau}\Phi_1^{-c}$, $\Psi_2 = v^{\chi_\epsilon}\Phi_2^{-c}$, $\Psi_4 = \Phi_1^{\chi_x}u^{-\chi_{\sigma_1}}$, $\Psi_5 = \Phi_2^{\chi_x}v^{-\chi_{\sigma_2}}$, $t_1 = -\chi_\tau - \chi_\epsilon$, $t_2 = -\chi_{\sigma_1} - \chi_{\sigma_2}$, $\Psi_3 \neq e(\Phi_3, g_1)^{\chi_x} \cdot e(h, x_\ell)^{t_1} \cdot e(h, g_1)^{t_2} \cdot (e(\Phi_3, x_\ell)/e(g_0, g_1))^c$, where c is set as $c = \mathcal{H}_1(\mathcal{M}, \Phi_1, \Phi_2, \Phi_3, \Psi_1, \Psi_2, \Psi_3, \Psi_4, \Psi_5)$. Subsequently, the generated signature $(\Phi_1, \Phi_2, \Phi_3, \Psi_3, c, \chi_\tau, \chi_\epsilon, \chi_x, \chi_{\delta_1}, \chi_{\delta_2})$ is given back to $\mathcal{A}$.
- **Guess:** $\mathcal{A}$ returns a guess result τ' of τ to $\mathcal{B}$, which also gives it as its guess to the challenger.

Practically, the signature of a user i_τ can be obtained from the linear encryption of A_{i_τ}, $\mathcal{B}$ can always derive a correct guess. In other words, $\mathcal{A}$ can break the anonymous group signature scheme with a non-negligible advantage, thus breaking the content semantic security of our ESAS with some advantage. Since the last theorem we have proved has indicated its semantic security of our ESAS, we can say the signature solution in ESAS can achieve the *anonymity*.

Theorem 3. *If the q-SDH assumption holds, our ESAS can realize traceability.*

Theorem 4. *If the q-SDH assumption holds, no adversaries can forge legitimate authentication information, thus ensuring content authenticity.*

Proof. Due to the space limitation, we put the security proofs of these two theorems in the Appendix.

6 Performance Evaluation

6.1 Theoretical Analysis

Table 1 presents a comparative analysis of the functionalities between our ESAS and other notable access control studies [3,9,12–14,17,18,22–25,27,32–35]. "✓" indicates supporting the feature; "✗" indicates the feature is not supported; Privacy protection ensures that authentication identities are not leaked. From Table 1, it is easily observed that our ESAS scheme offers several critical features that are absent in existing frameworks. Specifically, (i) our ESAS uniquely supports *secure* access control over *multiple* contents while effectively preventing collusion attacks, serving as the primary impetus for our research; (ii) our ESAS scheme restricts unauthorized subscribers from transmitting interest packets into the network, which helps reduce the risk of DoS attacks; (iii) our ESAS is the sole existing approach that ensures secure support for both privacy-preserving *anonymous* authentication and immediate revocation enforced by the Content Publisher (CP); (iv) our ESAS supports accountability, enabling the CP to identify subscribers responsible for key misuse.

Table 1. Functionality Comparisons

Scheme Type	Multiple Contents	Content Confidentiality	Privacy Protection	DoS Attack Resistance	Collusion Attack Resistance	Acc.& Rev.
[12,13,17,32]	✗	✓	✗	✗	✓	✗
[12,33–35]	✗	✓	✓	✓	✗	✓
[3,9,14,18,25,27]	✗	✓	✗	✓	✗	✗
[22–24]	✗	✓	✗	✓	✗	✓
ESAS	✓	✓	✓	✓	✓	✓

Acc. & Rev. : Accountability & Revocation.

Table 2. Theoretical Computation Complexity Comparison

Scheme Type	Setup	Registration	Content Generation	Auth./Verif.	Decryption	Acc. & Rev.
INFOCOM'19 [35]	$\mathcal{O}(m)$	$\mathcal{O}(n)$	$\mathcal{O}(n)$	$\mathcal{O}(1)/\mathcal{O}(1)$	$\mathcal{O}(n)$	$\mathcal{O}(\ell)$
ESORICS'20 [23]	$\mathcal{O}(\varphi)$	$\mathcal{O}(n)$	$\mathcal{O}(n)$	$\mathcal{O}(1)/\mathcal{O}(1)$	$\mathcal{O}(n)$	$\mathcal{O}(\ell)$
Our ESAS	$\mathcal{O}(m)$	$\mathcal{O}(1)$	$\mathcal{O}(n)$	$\mathcal{O}(1)/\mathcal{O}(1)$	$\mathcal{O}(n)$	$\mathcal{O}(\ell)$

Table 2 offers a theoretical computation complexity analysis of our ESAS and other notable access control solutions, including INFOCOM'19 [35] and ESORICS'20 (SRDS'21) [23]. The analysis reveals that the computational costs for system setup in INFOCOM'19 [35] and our ESAS are both $\mathcal{O}(m)$, owing to the classification of users into m groups. In contrast, the setup cost in [23] is $\mathcal{O}(\varphi)$, attributed to the association with φ roles in the content hierarchy and the necessity to generate corresponding public parameters. Furthermore, the computational demands for generating multiple content items in [23,35] and our ESAS are indicated as $\mathcal{O}(n)$, where n represents the number of contents a publisher needs to encode. Additionally, as Table 2 highlights, the computational efforts for user registration in [23,35] are $\mathcal{O}(n)$, whereas those in our ESAS are notably lower at $\mathcal{O}(1)$. Moreover, the computational cost related to the accountability and revocation processes depends on the user list length $\mathcal{O}(\ell)$.

In summary, our ESAS exhibits several advantageous properties, especially in collusion attack resistance and demonstrates superior performance than other related solutions.

6.2 Performance Analysis

The performance evaluation was conducted using Python 3.6.13, Charm 0.43, the PBC-0.5.14 library, and OpenSSL 1.1.1. The computational experiments were executed on a laptop with an Intel Core i5-11400H CPU @ 2.70 GHz (12 cores) and 16 GB of RAM, running the 64-bit version of Ubuntu 22.04.4 LTS. Additionally, a Raspberry Pi 4 Model B, equipped with a Broadcom BCM 2711 Quad-core Cortex-A72 (ARM v8) 64-bit SoC @ 1.5 GHz and 2 GB RAM running Raspbian, was employed to simulate a content subscriber/publisher scenario in a Named Data Networking (NDN) environment. In our implementation, we employ 128-bit AES keys based on a variant of the AES algorithm [37] and encode the AES keys with the encryption algorithm of our ESAS and related methodologies (*i.e.*, INFOCOM'19 [35] and ESORICS'20 (SRDS'21) [23]).

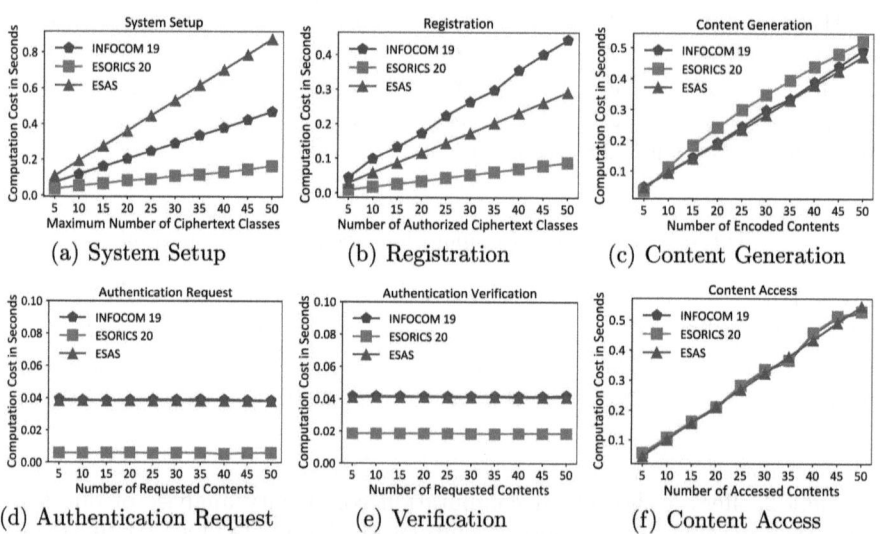

Fig. 3. Performance Evaluation and Comparison

Figure 3 shows the experimental simulations between INFOCOM'19, ESORICS'20 and our ESAS. In more detail, Fig. 3(a) gives the time of System Setup with the increasing of the maximum number of ciphertext classes (*i.e.*, contents). From this figure, one can see that the system setup time costs in INFOCOM'19, ESORICS'20 and our ESAS are linear with the maximum number of ciphertext classes, and our ESAS has lower costs than INFOCOM'19 but is slightly higher in computation cost than ESORICS'20. Figure 3 (b) shows the time of Registration with the increment of the number of authorized ciphertext classes. It is easily seen from Fig. 3(b) that the Registration time costs in all works are incremental with the number of authorized ciphertext classes, and our Registration requires slightly higher time costs than that of ESORICS'20 but needs less time costs than that of INFOCOM'19. Figure 3(c) displays the content generation time costs with the increasing number of encoded contents. From Fig. 3(c), it is straightforward to observe that the time costs for the content generation phase in all works are incremental with the number of encoded contents and our ESAS has the lowest time costs in content generation than that of INFOCOM'19 or ESORICS'20. Figures 3(d) and 3(e) respectively present the time cost of the authentication request and verification phases. From Figs. 3(d) and 3(e), our authentication request and verification take almost identical time costs as those of INFOCOM'19 since our ESAS and INFOCOM'19 adopt the same group signature technology and require much more time than those of ESORICS'20. Fig 3(f) shows the content access time cost with the number of access contents. From Fig 3(f), one can conclude that the time costs to access multiple contents in all works grow linearly with the number of decoded contents and our ESAS requires relatively less time costs than INFOCOM'19 and ESORICS'20.

In summary, the computational efficiency of our ESAS in the authentication request and verification phase is comparable to INFOCOM'19 [35] and our ESAS realizes relatively faster content generation and access than INFOCOM'19 and ESORICS'20, which makes our ESAS appropriate for NDN applications.

7 Conclusion

In this paper, we proposed the first-ever Efficient Security-enhanced Accountable Access Control Scheme (ESAS) for NDN, which efficiently handles the issues of *secure* access control, *flexible* content management, and accountability and privilege revocation. Compared to other access control solutions, our ESAS is the *first secure scheme* that realizes real collusion attack resistance. Specifically, our ESAS utilizes anonymous authentication via group signatures at network routers to deter unauthorized access. Additionally, our ESAS employs key-aggregation-based access control to enhance selective content management and our ESAS also maintains an access list at edge routers, allowing for the tracing and revocation of privileges from content subscribers who misuse authorization tokens. Our comprehensive security analysis affirmed the enhanced security capabilities of our ESAS. Additionally, we conducted experimental performance evaluations that demonstrate the practicability and feasibility of our ESAS for edge routers, content publishers, and subscribers.

Acknowledgement. This research is supported by the National Research Foundation, Singapore and Infocomm Media Development Authority under its Trust Tech Funding Initiative, and the AXA Research Fund. Any opinions, findings and conclusions or recommendations expressed in this material are those of the author(s) and do not reflect the views of National Research Foundation, Singapore and Infocomm Media Development Authority.

A Appendix

Theorem 3. *If the q-SDH assumption holds, our ESAS can realize traceability.*

Proof. If an adversary $\mathcal{A}$ can break the traceability of our scheme with a non-negligible advantage, an algorithm $\mathcal{B}$ can be constructed to solve the q-SDH assumption with the same advantage. To be specific,

- **Setup:** The generated system parameter $(\mathcal{GS}, g_0, g_1, \mathsf{X})$ generated as in Sect. 4 is given to the challenger. Additionally, a $(q+2)$-tuple $(g_0, g_1, g_1^{\beta}, g_1^{\beta^2}, \ldots, g_1^{\beta^q})$ and a collection of key pairs (A_i, t_i) for $i \in [1, q-1]$ are also given to the challenger. Some of the pairs are SDH pairs holding $e(x_n g_1^{t_i}, A_i) = e(g_0, g_1)$, where n is group identifier of a user. After that, the challenger randomly selects $h, u, v \in \mathbb{G}_0$ and $\xi_1, \xi_2 \in \mathbb{Z}_p$ such that $u^{\xi_1} = v^{\xi_2} = h$. Eventually, the public parameter $(\mathcal{GS}, g_0, h, u, v, \mathsf{X})$ and the master key (g_1, ξ_1, ξ_2) are returned to $\mathcal{A}$. Besides, $\mathcal{H}_1$ is initialized as a random oracle via a table.
- **Hash Queries:** $\mathcal{A}$ can make queries for the hash value $\mathcal{H}_1(\mathcal{M}, \Phi_1, \Phi_2, \Phi_3, \Psi_1, \Psi_2, \Psi_3, \Psi_4, \Psi_5)$, if the value has already existed in the table, then the value is directly returned to $\mathcal{A}$; otherwise, $t \in \mathbb{Z}_p$ is picked and inserted to the table. Subsequently, t is given back to $\mathcal{A}$.
- **Private Key Queries:** $\mathcal{A}$ can makes queries for the user i's secret key, $\mathcal{B}$ then returns (A_i, t_i) to $\mathcal{A}$ if the private key is SDH pair. Otherwise, it aborts.
- **Signature Queries:** $\mathcal{A}$ can make queries for a signature $\mathcal{M}$ with index i, the challenger generates a signature σ with private key (t_i, A_i) if t_i is a format of an SDH pair. Otherwise, the challenger selects $\tau, \epsilon \in \mathbb{Z}_p$, computes $\Phi_1 = u^{\tau}$, $\Phi_2 = v^{\epsilon}$, $\Phi_3 = A_i h^{\tau+\epsilon}$. In addition, $c, \lambda_\tau, \lambda_\epsilon, \lambda_x, \lambda_{\delta_1}, \lambda_{\delta_2} \in \mathbb{Z}_p$ are chosen to compute $(\Psi_1, \Psi_2, \Psi_3, \Psi_4, \Psi_5)$. Next, it sets the oracle value $c = \mathcal{H}_1(\mathcal{M}, \Phi_1, \Phi_2, \Phi_3, \Psi_1, \Psi_2, \Psi_3, \Psi_4, \Psi_5)$. If collision occurs, it aborts; otherwise, it produces a valid group signature $(\Phi_1, \Phi_2, \Phi_3, \Psi_3, c, \chi_\tau, \chi_\epsilon, \chi_x, \chi_{\delta_1}, \chi_{\delta_2})$.
- **Output:** If an adversary $\mathcal{A}$ can successfully break the traceability of our scheme with a non-negligible advantage, it can produce a forged signature $\sigma = (\Phi_1, \Phi_2, \Phi_3, \Psi_3, c, \chi_\tau, \chi_\epsilon, \chi_x, \chi_{\delta_1}, \chi_{\delta_2})$ on $\mathcal{M}$ with $c = \mathcal{H}_1(\mathcal{M}, \Phi_1, \Phi_2, \Phi_3, \Psi_1, \Psi_2, \Psi_3, \Psi_4, \Psi_5)$, which can pass the signature verification. The challenger can compute $A = \Psi_3/(\Psi_1^{\xi_1} \Psi_2^{\xi_2})$ to realize the identity tracing of a user via the master key (ξ_1, ξ_2). If $A \neq A_i$ for all users' key pairs (A_i, t_i) holds, it gives σ back; otherwise, it outputs $A = A_i$ for some user's key pair. If t_i is unknown, it also returns σ; otherwise, it aborts.

Based on the theorem, the challenger can derive another signature $(\Phi_1, \Phi_2, \Phi_3, \Psi_3, c', r'_\tau, r'_\epsilon, r'_x, r'_{\delta_1}, r'_{\delta_2})$ on $\mathcal{M}$ with some non-negligible advantage. Hence, two forged signatures hold the following equations from the signature verification:

$$\Psi_1 = u^{\chi_\tau} \Phi_1^{-c} = u^{\chi'_\tau} \Phi_1^{-c'}, \tag{1}$$

$$\Psi_2 = v^{\chi_\epsilon} \Phi_2^{-c} = v^{\chi'_\epsilon} \Phi_2^{-c'}, \tag{2}$$

$$\Psi_4 = \Phi_1^{\chi_x} u^{-\chi_{\sigma_1}} = \Phi_1^{\chi'_x} u^{-\chi'_{\sigma_1}}, \tag{3}$$

$$\Psi_5 = \Phi_2^{\chi_x} v^{-\chi_{\sigma_2}} = \Phi_2^{\chi'_x} v^{-\chi'_{\sigma_2}}, \tag{4}$$

$$\Psi_3 = e(\Phi_3, g_1)^{\chi_x} \cdot e(h, x_\ell)^{-\chi_\tau - \chi_\epsilon} \cdot e(h, g_1)^{-\chi_{\sigma_1} - \chi_{\sigma_2}} \cdot$$
$$(e(\Phi_3, x_\ell)/e(g_0, g_1))^c$$
$$= e(\Phi_3, g_1)^{\chi'_x} \cdot e(h, x_\ell)^{-\chi'_\tau - \chi'_\epsilon} \cdot e(h, g_1)^{-\chi'_{\sigma_1} - \chi'_{\sigma_2}} \cdot$$
$$(e(\Phi_3, x_\ell)/e(g_0, g_1))^{c'}. \tag{5}$$

From the Eq. (1) & (2), the challenger can get $\Psi_1 = u^{(\chi_\tau - \chi'_\tau)/(c-c')}$ and $\Psi_2 = u^{(\chi_\epsilon - \chi'_\epsilon)/(c-c')}$. From the Eq. (3), $\Psi_1^{\chi_x - \chi'_x} = u^{\chi_{\sigma_1} - \chi'_{\sigma_1}}$. Combining with Eq. (1), the challenger can further infer that $(\chi_\tau - \chi'_\tau)(\chi_x - \chi'_x)/(c - c') = \chi_{\sigma_1} - \chi'_{\sigma_1}$. With the same method, $(\chi_\epsilon - \chi'_\epsilon)(\chi_x - \chi'_x)/(c-c') = \chi_{\sigma_2} - \chi'_{\sigma_2}$ can be deduced from the Eq. (4). Finally, the challenger can get the following equation: $e(g_0, g_1) = e(\Phi_3 h^{-(\chi_\tau - \chi'_\tau)/(c-c') - (\chi_\epsilon - \chi'_\epsilon)/(c-c')}, w_n g_2^{(\chi_x - \chi'_x)/(c-c')})$, where $\hat{A} = \Phi_3 h^{-(\chi_\tau - \chi'_\tau)/(c-c') - (\chi_\epsilon - \chi'_\epsilon)/(c-c')}$, $\hat{t} = (\chi_x - \chi'_x)/(c - c')$, respectively. It can be seen that the challenger may obtain an SDH pair $(\hat{A}, \hat{t})$.

Therefore, if there is an adversary that breaks the traceability with a non-negligible probability, we can find an algorithm to solve the q-SDH problem.

Theorem 4. *If the q-SDH assumption holds, no adversaries can forge legitimate authentication information, thus ensuring content authenticity.*

Proof. If an adversary $\mathcal{A}$ can successfully forge a legitimate signature with a non-negligible advantage, then $\mathcal{A}$ can derive two valid signatures on the same message $(\mathcal{M}, \mathcal{F}, c, \sigma_1)$ and $(\mathcal{M}, \mathcal{F}, c', \sigma'_1)$ as follows, here $\mathcal{H}_1$ and $\mathcal{H}'_1$ are assumed two random oracles: $\mathcal{F} = (\Phi_1, \Phi_2, \Phi_3, \Psi_1, \Psi_2, \Psi_3, \Psi_4, \Psi_5), c = \mathcal{H}_1(\mathcal{M}, \Phi_1, \Phi_2, \Phi_3, \Psi_1, \Psi_2, \Psi_3, \Psi_4, \Psi_5), c' = \mathcal{H}'_1(\mathcal{M}, \Phi_1, \Phi_2, \Phi_3, \Psi_1, \Psi_2, \Psi_3, \Psi_4, \Psi_5), \sigma_1 = (\chi_\tau, \chi_\epsilon, \chi_x, \chi_{\delta_1}, \chi_{\delta_2}), \sigma'_1 = (\chi'_\tau, \chi'_\epsilon, \chi'_x, \chi'_{\delta_1}, \chi'_{\delta_2})$, where the above equations hold the following conditions:

$$\chi_\tau = \lambda_\tau + c\tau, \chi'_\tau = \lambda_\tau + c'\tau,$$
$$\chi_\epsilon = \lambda_\epsilon + c\epsilon, \chi'_\epsilon = \lambda_\epsilon + c'\epsilon,$$
$$\chi_x = \lambda_x + cx, \chi'_x = \lambda_x + c'x,$$
$$\chi_{\delta_1} = \lambda_{\delta_1} + c\delta_1, \chi'_{\delta_1} = \lambda_{\delta_1} + c'\delta_1,$$
$$\chi_{\delta_2} = \lambda_{\delta_2} + c\delta_2, \chi'_{\delta_2} = \lambda_{\delta_2} + c'\delta_2.$$

Due to the different hashes on the same hash content, the probability of holding $c = c'$ is negligible. Hence, $\mathcal{A}$ can calculate $\hat{t} = (\chi_x - \chi'_x)/(c - c')$ and $\hat{A} = T_3/h^{(\chi_\tau + \chi_\epsilon - \chi'_\tau - \chi'_\epsilon)/(c-c')}$ as the q-SDH tuple such that $\hat{A} = g_0^{1/(\beta_i + \hat{t})}$ holds.

References

1. Anjum, A., Agbaje, P., Mitra, A., Oseghale, E., Nwafor, E., Olufowobi, H.: Towards named data networking technology: emerging applications, use cases, and challenges for secure data communication. FGCS **151**, 12–31 (2024)

2. Ben, L., Ospanova, A.B.: Pbc library. In: https://crypto.stanford.edu/pbc/. Standfor University (2024)
3. Bilal, M., Pack, S.: Secure distribution of protected content in information-centric networking. IEEE Syst. J. **14**(2), 1921–1932 (2019)
4. Boneh, D., Boyen, X., Shacham, H.: Short group signatures. In: Franklin, M. (ed.) CRYPTO 2004. LNCS, vol. 3152, pp. 41–55. Springer, Heidelberg (2004). https://doi.org/10.1007/978-3-540-28628-8_3
5. Chaudhary, P., Hubballi, N.: Pencache: popularity based cooperative caching in named data networks. Comput. Netw. **257**, 110995 (2025)
6. Chu, C.K., Chow, S.S., Tzeng, W.G., Zhou, J., Deng, R.H.: Key-aggregate cryptosystem for scalable data sharing in cloud storage. IEEE TPDS **25**(2), 468–477 (2013)
7. Daniel, E., Tschorsch, F.: IPFS and friends: a qualitative comparison of next generation peer-to-peer data networks. IEEE Commun. Surv. Tutorials **24**(1), 31–52 (2022)
8. Delerablée, C., Pointcheval, D.: Dynamic fully anonymous short group signatures. In: Nguyen, P.Q. (ed.) VIETCRYPT 2006. LNCS, vol. 4341, pp. 193–210. Springer, Heidelberg (2006). https://doi.org/10.1007/11958239_13
9. Fotiou, N., Polyzos, G.C.: Securing content sharing over ICN. In: Proceedings of the 3rd ACM Conference on Information-Centric Networking, pp. 176–185 (2016)
10. Fu, X., Kutscher, D., Misra, S., Li, R.: Information-centric networking security. IEEE Commun. Mag. **56**(11), 60–61 (2018)
11. Han, D., Pan, N., Li, K.C.: A traceable and revocable ciphertext-policy attribute-based encryption scheme based on privacy protection. IEEE TDSC **19**(1), 316–327 (2020)
12. He, P., Wan, Y., Xia, Q., Li, S., Hong, J., Xue, K.: Lasa: lightweight, auditable and secure access control in ICN with limitation of access times. In: ICC 2018, pp. 1–6. IEEE (2018)
13. Li, B., Huang, D., Wang, Z., Zhu, Y.: Attribute-based access control for ICN naming scheme. IEEE TDSC **15**(2), 194–206 (2016)
14. Li, Q., Zhang, X., Zheng, Q., Sandhu, R., Fu, X.: Live: lightweight integrity verification and content access control for named data networking. IEEE TIFS **10**(2), 308–320 (2014)
15. Mao, B., Liu, J., Wu, Y., Kato, N.: Security and privacy on 6g network edge: a survey. IEEE Communi. Surv. Tutorials **25**(2), 1095–1127 (2023)
16. Meng, F., Cheng, L.: Str-abks: server-aided traceable and revocable attribute-based encryption with keyword search. IEEE IoTJ (2023)
17. Misra, S., Tourani, R., Natividad, F., Mick, T., Majd, N.E., Huang, H.: Accconf: an access control framework for leveraging in-network cached data in the ICN-enabled wireless edge. IEEE TDSC **16**(1), 5–17 (2017)
18. Nunes, I.O., Tsudik, G.: KRB-CCN: lightweight authentication and access control for private content-centric networks. In: Preneel, B., Vercauteren, F. (eds.) ACNS 2018. LNCS, vol. 10892, pp. 598–615. Springer, Cham (2018). https://doi.org/10.1007/978-3-319-93387-0_31
19. Patranabis, S., Shrivastava, Y., Mukhopadhyay, D.: Provably secure key-aggregate cryptosystems with broadcast aggregate keys for online data sharing on the cloud. IEEE TC **66**(5), 891–904 (2016)
20. Singh, K., Singh, P., Kumar, K.: Application layer HTTP-GET flood DDoS attacks: research landscape and challenges. Comput. Secur. **65**, 344–372 (2017)

21. Suksomboon, K., Tagami, A., Basu, A., Kurihara, J.: In-device proxy re-encryption service for information-centric networking access control. In: LCN 2018, pp. 303–306. IEEE (2018)
22. Sultan, N.H., Varadharajan, V., Kumar, C., Camtepe, S., Nepal, S.: A secure access and accountability framework for provisioning services in named data networks. In: SRDS 2021, pp. 164–175. IEEE (2021)
23. Sultan, N.H., Varadharajan, V., Camtepe, S., Nepal, S.: An accountable access control scheme for hierarchical content in named data networks with revocation. In: Chen, L., Li, N., Liang, K., Schneider, S. (eds.) ESORICS 2020. LNCS, vol. 12308, pp. 569–590. Springer, Cham (2020). https://doi.org/10.1007/978-3-030-58951-6_28
24. Sultan, N.H., Varadharajan, V., Dulal, S., Camtepe, S., Nepal, S.: NDN-RBE: an accountable privacy aware access control framework for NDN. Comput. J. **67**(4), 1572–1589 (2024)
25. Sun, R., You, L., Lu, A.A., Sun, C., Gao, X., Xia, X.G.: Precoder design for user-centric network massive mimo with matrix manifold optimization. IEEE JSAC (2025)
26. Tan, X., et al.: Hybrid-coding based content access control for information-centric networking. IEEE TWC (2023)
27. Tourani, R., Stubbs, R., Misra, S.: Tactic: tag-based access control framework for the information-centric wireless edge networks. In: ICDCS 2018, pp. 456–466. IEEE (2018)
28. Tseng, Y.F., Fan, C.I., Wu, C.Y.: FGAC-NDN: fine-grained access control for named data networks. IEEE TNSM **16**(1), 143–152 (2018)
29. Tuleuov, B.I., Ospanova, A.B.: Openssl. In: Beginning C++ Compilers: An Introductory Guide to Microsoft C/C++ and MinGW Compilers, pp. 157–163. Springer (2024)
30. Wang, X., Li, Y.: Vehicular named data networking framework. IEEE TITS **21**(11), 4705–4714 (2019)
31. Wang, X., Wu, G.: Attribute based vehicular named data networking for driving assistance. IEEE Trans. Netw. Sci. Eng. (2025)
32. Xia, Q., et al.: TSLS: time sensitive, lightweight and secure access control for information centric networking. In: GLOBECOM 19, pp. 1–6. IEEE (2019)
33. Xue, K., He, P., Yang, J., Xia, Q., Wei, D.S.: Scd2: secure content delivery and deduplication with multiple content providers in information centric networking. IEEE/ACM ToN **30**(4), 1849–1864 (2022)
34. Xue, K., et al.: A secure, efficient, and accountable edge-based access control framework for information centric networks. IEEE/ACM ToN **27**(3), 1220–1233 (2019)
35. Xue, K., Zhang, X., Xia, Q., Wei, D.S., Yue, H., Wu, F.: Seaf: a secure, efficient and accountable access control framework for information centric networking. In: IEEE INFOCOM 2018, pp. 2213–2221. IEEE (2018)
36. Yaar, A., Perrig, A., Song, D.: SIFF: a stateless internet flow filter to mitigate DDoS flooding attacks. In: IEEE SP, pp. 130–143. IEEE (2004)
37. Zeghid, M., Machhout, M., Khriji, L., Baganne, A., Tourki, R.: A modified AES based algorithm for image encryption. Int. J. Comput. Inf. Eng. **1**(3), 745–750 (2007)
38. Zhang, Z., et al.: NDNoT: a framework for named data network of things. In: Proceedings of the 5th ACM Conference on Information-Centric Networking, pp. 200–201 (2018)

Dobby: A Privacy-Preserving Time Series Data Analytics System with Enforcement of Flexible Policies

Yansen Xin[1,2], Rui Zhang[1,2(✉)], Zhenglin Fan[1,2], and Ze Jia[1,2]

[1] State Key Laboratory of Cyberspace Security Defense, Institute of Information Engineering, Chinese Academy of Sciences, Beijing 100085, China
{xinyansen,fanzhenglin,jiazer-zhang}@iie.ac.cn
[2] School of Cyber Security, University of Chinese Academy of Sciences, Beijing 100049, China

Abstract. With the proliferation of sensitive time series data being collected, stored, and queried in cloud environments, it is imperative to integrate owner-centric privacy controls with encrypted data processing to enable secure and flexible data sharing. Existing systems, however, often lack the flexibility to express nuanced privacy policies and fail to adequately protect sensitive metadata. Adversaries can exploit declared policies, query attributes, and data access patterns to infer confidential information about data owners.

In this paper, we present Dobby, a privacy-preserving time series data analytics system that enforces fine-grained and flexible access policies through function secret sharing (FSS). Dobby ensures robust privacy protection for policies, query attributes, and access patterns, while achieving malicious security in a two-party computation setting. Furthermore, we propose an optimized algorithm to streamline policy evaluation, significantly reducing communication overhead.

Our evaluation demonstrates the efficiency and practicality of Dobby. For a query involving 100 ciphertexts, the system achieves a query latency of approximately 3.3 s on 10,000 data streams, each governed by an access policy comprising eight conditions.

Keywords: Time series analytics · Access control · Metadata privacy · Function secret sharing

1 Introduction

Time series data continuously logs metrics of target systems, enabling real-time monitoring, data-driven diagnosis, forecasting, and decision-making [10]. Its applications extend to diverse domains such as health monitoring, traffic optimization, and other interconnected ecosystems [3,31]. The increasing reliance on time series data necessitates high read-write throughput and efficient analytics. However, as individuals and organizations increasingly depend on cloud services for storing and processing such data, concerns over data leakage and unauthorized sharing have escalated [1].

Sensitive time series data, such as longitudinal electrocardiographic (ECG) surveillance, provides critical physiological insights for therapeutic innovation and cardiac safety profiling but introduces significant privacy vulnerabilities. To address these challenges, recent advancements [10–12,19,21] have focused on constructing privacy-preserving frameworks that empower data owners to define and enforce privacy preferences through cryptographic techniques. Despite these efforts, two critical challenges persist: secure data sharing and the protection of sensitive metadata.

Secure Time Series Data Sharing. Data-sharing requirements vary significantly among data owners, necessitating access policies that are both flexible and fine-grained [10,36]. For instance, a healthcare provider may grant access to ECG records based on a policy such as: "(San Francisco $\wedge$ (Cardiology $\vee$ Neurology)) $\vee$ (ClinicalPrivilege $>$ 3) $\vee$ (Name = John)". Supporting such policies requires the ability to combine multidimensional conditions on attributes using logical operators (e.g., AND, OR, NOT), enabling precise access control and minimizing exposure of sensitive information. Furthermore, these solutions must integrate seamlessly with encrypted query processing to restrict queryable data, forming a comprehensive privacy-preserving framework.

Sensitive Metadata Protection. While encryption safeguards the confidentiality of time series data, the exposure of sensitive metadata–such as policies, query attributes, and access patterns–remains a critical concern.

POLICIES. Explicitly declared attributes in access policies can be exploited by attackers to infer sensitive information about data owners [35]. For example, a policy granting cardiologists exclusive access to ECG records may reveal the cardiovascular relevance of the data, even if the data is encrypted.

QUERY ATTRIBUTES. Attributes associated with data consumers' queries can inadvertently expand the attack surface. For instance, concurrent queries from distinct roles (e.g., cardiologists and pharmacists) accessing the same dataset may allow attackers to infer institutional activities (e.g., drug trials) or sensitive data semantics (e.g., medication response records), even with minimal query frequency and encrypted content.

ACCESS PATTERNS. Even with encrypted policies and query attributes, attackers can infer sensitive information by analyzing access patterns [25]. For example, frequent queries on a dataset during postprandial windows may reveal the adoption of intensive insulin therapy, exposing the owner's health conditions.

Addressing these challenges requires innovative solutions that balance efficiency and privacy, ensuring secure and privacy-preserving analytics for time series data.

1.1 Summary of Results

To address these challenges, we present Dobby, a secure and efficient system for time series data analytics. Our contributions are four-fold.

First, we introduce a two-server/multi-client model that well reflects real-world time series data analytics scenarios. In our model, data producers continuously upload encrypted time series data, data owners define corresponding access policies, and data consumers initiate analytical queries to distributed servers. We formalize the security requirements under the simulation-based paradigm [29].

Second, we present a concrete time series data analytics system, Dobby, that offers a number of desirable properties:

- *Flexible and Fine-Grained Policy Control.* Dobby enables data owners to define complex access policies through arbitrary Boolean combinations, such as conjunctions, disjunctions, and negations of conditions. Moreover, it supports various types of conditions to further enhance flexibility, extending beyond equality conditions to include range and set conditions.

- *Obliviousness with Malicious Security.* Leveraging the distributed trust setting, Dobby not only protects time series data, but also access policies (hiding the conditions rather than the Boolean formulas), query attributes, and data access patterns. Moreover, it operates in a two-server model and achieves malicious security with abort when at least one server is honest.

Third, for an efficient access policy evaluation, we propose InfixToPostfix+, as an enhancement of the state-of-the-art optimized-depth algorithm, InfixToPostfix [27], and reduces multiplication gate layers and communication rounds. The algorithm retains the ability to convert Boolean infix formulas into depth-minimized postfix formulas, while significantly reduces the circuit depth for a specific class of infix formulas with recursively nested AND and OR operators.

Finally, we implement and evaluate Dobby. For queries spanning a time window of 100 ciphertexts, Dobby processes 10,000 streams–each governed by an access policy with a single condition–in 732 ms. In comparison, Vizard achieves a lower processing time of 232 ms but does not protect the data consumer's query attributes. For access policies comprising eight conditions, Dobby attains a query latency of approximately 2.3 s, and 3.3 s under the malicious security model, with a 10 ms round-trip time between servers. Notably, Dobby maintains a lightweight client. These results demonstrate the efficiency and practicality of our system.

1.2 Technical Overview

Limitations of Existing Approaches. Oblivious RAM (ORAM) [23] and multi-party computation (MPC) [40] are prominent candidates for privacy-preserving computations. However, both face critical limitations in time series analytics. ORAM incurs significant computational overhead, while MPC suffers from excessive communication costs. In distributed-trust cloud environments, where servers operate in distinct trust domains, the high communication round complexity of these approaches results in prohibitive latency and economic inefficiencies. Our objective is to achieve the desired privacy and efficiency properties in such settings, minimizing communication overhead without imposing a heavy computational burden–an unmet goal in existing solutions.

This Work: Privacy-Preserving Access Policies via FSS. Functional Secret Sharing (FSS) [8] has emerged as a powerful tool for privacy-preserving computations. However, leveraging FSS to evaluate access policies while concealing both the policies and query attributes poses significant challenges, as FSS requires servers to evaluate keys on public inputs. Two distinct FSS-based approaches exist. The first, exemplified by Waldo [19], embeds query attributes into FSS keys, enabling servers to evaluate these keys on secret access policies. While effective for private data searches using one-hot index structures, this approach is limited to equality-based access policies and becomes inefficient for large domains due to feature size constraints. The second approach, as demonstrated by Vizard [12], embeds access policies into FSS keys, allowing servers to evaluate keys on secret query attributes. Building on prior advancements in FSS for secure computation [5,7], we adopt a variant where FSS transforms secret-shared inputs into secret-shared outputs by reconstructing masked inputs, ensuring both privacy and efficiency.

Extending the Security Model: Malicious Security. We extend Boyle et al.'s use of information-theoretic MACs for authenticating FSS evaluation outputs [5], adapting it to our setting. Instead of joint server verification, the data consumer verifies aggregated MACs from server shares. To ensure efficiency in large-scale data streams, data producers assign a fixed random MAC key per stream, while data owners independently select and update MAC keys for their access policies with each query. The primary challenge lies in privately enforcing data control under distinct MAC keys. We address this by applying a random mask to the aggregated result of each stream. Both the data producer and owner generate the MAC for this mask using their respective keys, enabling authentication of the masked result while preserving data control.

Special Recipe: Minimizing Circuit Depth of Boolean Formula. Li et al. [27] introduced a depth-optimized infix-to-postfix conversion algorithm (InfixToPostfix) to minimize communication rounds. However, the algorithm struggles with formulas containing recursively nested AND and OR operators (e.g., "$A \land (B \lor (C \land (D \lor (E \land F))))$"), where the postfix formula retains the same circuit depth. To address this, we first transform such formulas into Disjunctive Normal Form (DNF) [32], where each clause is a conjunction of literals. Each DNF clause is then converted into a postfix formula with minimal depth. Additionally, adjacent clauses are selectively merged to further reduce circuit depth, and the resulting optimized clauses are connected using OR operators. While disjunctions may increase depth, the overall optimization leads to a guaranteed reduction in circuit depth, particularly for formulas with significant initial depth.

1.3 Related Work

Privacy-Preserving Time Series Analytics. Extensive research has explored privacy-preserving time series analytics [14,16,24,26,34,37], yet many approaches fall short in analytical capabilities and fine-grained data-sharing protection. TimeCrypt [10] ensures data confidentiality and enforces privacy preferences using symmetric homomorphic encryption [13], while Zeph [11] centralizes policy enforcement via a privacy controller, generating cryptographic tokens for secure aggregation across multiple users. Vizard [12] mitigates metadata leakage in a two-server model but lacks support for complex Boolean policies and fails to prevent attribute leakage of consumers. Waldo [19] and TVA [21] enhance analytical expressiveness, with Waldo enabling secure multi-predicate queries in a three-party model and TVA introducing expressive window operators for time intervals and out-of-order records. Other works [28,30,33,41,42] focus on specific queries, leveraging specialized encryption schemes for tasks such as similarity range and interval skyline queries.

FSS for Private Queries. Splinter [39] enables efficient private queries on public databases using FSS. Dory [18] employs DPFs for private single-keyword searches on encrypted databases, hiding access patterns cryptographically. Durasift [22] distributes private databases across n servers, supporting up to $n-3$ conjunctions of arbitrary Boolean expressions through DPF-driven private information retrieval. NEMO [27] combines FSS and replicated secret sharing [2] to achieve arbitrary Boolean queries and dynamic updates without revealing search, access, or size patterns. However, these solutions are not directly applicable to our scenario, as the way clients generate FSS keys limits flexible access policy support. Additionally, existing distributed ORAM constructions [9,20,38], which focus on private read and write operations, leverage DPFs for improved performance.

2 Preliminary

Notations. Let $y \rightarrow \mathsf{Alg}(x)$ denote the execution of algorithm Alg with input x, and obtaining output y. Algorithms are probabilistic polynomial time (PPT), if not explicitly mentioned. A function $negl$ is negligible if there exists $\lambda' > 0$ and $c > 0$ such that $negl(\lambda) < \lambda^{-c}$ for all $\lambda > \lambda'$.

Access Control Policy. Recent advances in time series data access control [10, 12] indicate that attribute-based policies are ideal for flexible, fine-grained, and owner-centric access control. These policies are typically expressed as Boolean formulas combining equality conditions with AND, OR, and NOT operators. Equality conditions, such as $attr = val$, require exact value matching, where $attr$ is the attribute name and val is the specified value (e.g., "region = EU").

Data owners often need to define more complex conditions to meet secure data sharing requirements, such as ensuring attribute values fall within specific ranges or sets. To enhance the flexibility and granularity of attribute-based policy control, we introduce range and set conditions. A range condition requires an attribute value to lie within a predefined range, typically applied to numerical or time-based attributes (e.g., "$18 < \text{age} < 20$"). A set condition is satisfied if an attribute value belongs to a specified set (e.g., "region $\in \{\text{EU}, \text{US}\}$"). Sets may include multiple values, ranges, or combinations, corresponding to enumerated, range-based, and hybrid set conditions. We exclude meaningless conditions, such as redundant constraints (e.g., "$18 < \text{age} < 20, \text{age} < 30$"), assuming data owners behave honestly.

3 System Overview

In this section, we describe system model, threat model and security definitions.

System Model. As shown in Fig. 1, Dobby consists of multiple clients and two servers, S_1 and S_2. Clients can be data producers, owners, or consumers. Data producers are entities (e.g. sensors) that continuously collect time series data and update the servers' state for collective analytics. Data owners define access policies to regulate data usage, sourced from multiple producers. Data consumers initiate queries to obtain aggregated values of authorized data. Servers in different trust domains store data and execute analytical queries.

In Dobby, clients interact independently with servers and do not participate in the computation during analytics. The servers privately enforce policy control and perform secure analytics on encrypted data, supporting highly flexible and fine-grained access policies, along with a variety of foundational queries.

Threat Model. Running parallel with the non-colluding two-party computation setting [12,15], Dobby supports either semi-honest security or malicious security under a dishonest-majority model. In the semi-honest model, the servers follow the protocol but may try to infer private information. Data producers and owners are assumed to be honest, while data consumers may collude with a server to access unauthorized data. If at most one server is malicious and deviates from the protocol, Dobby ensures security with abort in the malicious dishonest-majority model. Malicious behavior is typically motivated by practical concerns, such as reducing task complexity to save resources.

Dobby provides efficient, privacy-preserving data analytics for data consumers while ensuring owner-centric policy control. Some metadata, like the data schema, is publicly available to assist query creation, as in prior works [19,21]. Only the corresponding data producers or owners can access data and policies. For each query, the data consumer's attributes remain private, but the time window and aggregation type are visible to the servers. To prevent timing-related leaks, data producers upload data at fixed intervals, achieved with synchronized epochs [12]. For certain queries, Dobby may reveal intermediate values, such as sum and count in a mean query, in addition to the result. It also protects access patterns, ensuring no party can infer which data streams a consumer is authorized to access. After the query, the consumer can verify the integrity of the results to ensure correct execution, though availability is not guaranteed if a malicious server refuses service.

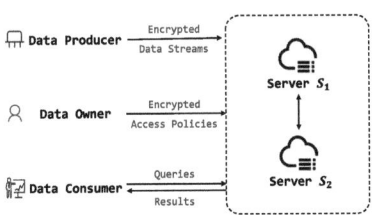

Fig. 1. System architecture.

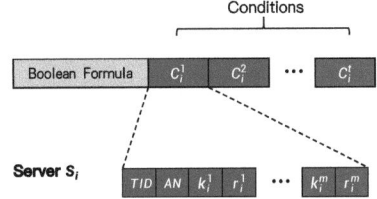

Fig. 2. The policy storage structure.

Security Definitions. Similar to previous work [19], we define the security of Dobby via the simulation paradigm [29], where a real-world protocol execution is indistinguishable from an ideal-world execution (parties only interact with an ideal functionality $\mathcal{F}$). The protocol is deemed secure if $\mathcal{A}$ cannot distinguish between the two worlds.

We allow $\mathcal{F}$ to leak $\mathcal{L}(\mathcal{F}) = (\mathcal{L}^{\mathsf{Setup}}, \mathcal{L}^{\mathsf{Append}}, \mathcal{L}^{\mathsf{Policy}}, \mathcal{L}^{\mathsf{Query}})$ in the following phases: 1) Initialization. $\mathcal{L}^{\mathsf{Setup}} = (\lambda, \tilde{s}, schema)$, where λ, $\tilde{s}$ and $schema$ denote the computational security parameter, statistical security parameter, and the schema layout, respectively. 2) Append phase. $\mathcal{L}^{\mathsf{Append}} = (t)$, where t denotes the timestamp. 3) Policy construction. $\mathcal{L}^{\mathsf{Policy}} = (\psi)$, where ψ is the Boolean formula. 4) Query phase. $\mathcal{L}^{\mathsf{Query}} = (t^1, t^2, type)$, where $[t^1, t^2]$ is the time window and $type$ refers to the aggregation type.

Definition 1. Let Π be a protocol for a time series data analytics that processes client requests $\mathcal{Q}$. $\mathcal{F}$ models the trusted execution of Π. Let $\mathcal{A}$ be an adversary who observes the view of a corrupted server during the protocol execution and obtains the final client output. Let $\mathsf{View}_{\Pi(\mathcal{Q})}^{Real}$ (as View_0) denote $\mathcal{A}$'s view in the real world. In the ideal world, a simulator $\mathcal{S}$ generates a simulated view $\mathsf{View}_{\mathcal{S},\mathcal{L}(\mathcal{F}(\mathcal{Q}))}^{Ideal}$ (as View_1) to $\mathcal{A}$ given only the leakage of $\mathcal{F}$. For all PPT adversary $\mathcal{A}$ in $\lambda, \tilde{s}$, where $\lambda, \tilde{s}$ are the computational and statistical security parameters, respectively, there exists an efficient simulator $\mathcal{S}$ such that:

$$\Pr\left[\mathcal{Q} \leftarrow \mathcal{A}(1^\lambda, 1^{\tilde{s}}); b \leftarrow \{0,1\}; \mathcal{A}(\mathsf{View}_b, \mathcal{Q}) = b\right] \leqslant 1/2 + negl(\lambda) + negl(\tilde{s})$$

4 Dobby: Flexible and Fine-Grained Policy Control

In this section, we describe how to obliviously evaluate access policies in Dobby. We start with a single condition in the semi-honest model and then extend it to support the combination of multiple conditions with malicious security.

4.1 Single Condition with Semi-honest Security

We observe that evaluating conditions in access policies mainly involves equality and comparison operations. Inspired by Boyle et al. [7], we propose a two-party FSS-based approach for secure evaluation. Recall that a two-party FSS scheme comprises two algorithms: 1) Gen, which splits a function f into two keys, k_1 and k_2, each concealing f; and 2) Eval, which reconstructs $f(x)$ for any input x by summing $\mathsf{Eval}(k_1, x)$ and $\mathsf{Eval}(k_2, x)$. DPFs are ideal for equality conditions, while distributed comparison functions (DCFs) are tailored for range conditions.

To protect attribute values in access policies, we split each condition into two shares among the servers. Each server stores its respective condition shares, along with the corresponding Boolean formula, as shown in Fig. 2. A condition share includes an identifier (TID), an attribute name (AN), and pairs of FSS keys and random shares, with TID indicating the condition type (e.g., equality, range, or set). To construct this structure, data owners need to convert conditions into corresponding FSS keys, while ensuring that logical operations in the Boolean

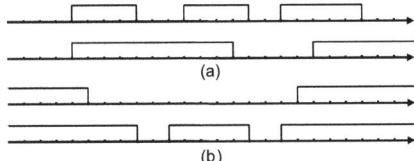
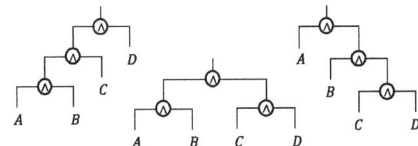

Fig. 3. Range-based set conditions.

Fig. 4. The circuit representations of a Boolean formula "A ∧ B ∧ C ∧ D".

formulas remain intact. For a condition $attr = val$, the owner generates a pair of DPF keys using $val + r$ as the secret index and 1 as the result, i.e., $(k_1, k_2 \leftarrow \mathsf{DPF.Gen}(val + r, 1))$, where r is a random mask. This mask is split into two shares, r_1 and r_2, and the condition share for S_i is $C_i = (1, attr, k_i, r_i)$. For range or set conditions, TID is set to 2 or 3, and DPF or DCF keys are generated for each masked attribute value, depending on the operation. A control value 1 is embedded at each secret's position to ensure the policy evaluates to 1 only if satisfied. Next, we describe how FSS is applied to evaluate these conditions.

FSS for Equality Condition. FSS maps secret-shared inputs to secret-shared outputs for condition evaluation. For each FSS evaluation, the servers first reconstruct the masked input in one round of interaction, then compute the output shares locally without further interaction. For evaluating an equality condition, each server performs a single DPF evaluation. Assume S_i holds the share $(1, attr, k_i, r_i)$ for the condition $attr = val$. For a query initiated by a data consumer with value x for $attr$, S_i receives the additive share x_i of x and sends $x_i + r_i$ to the other, enabling them to reconstruct $x + r = \sum_{i=1}^{2}(x_i + r_i)$. Then, they locally compute $y_i \leftarrow \mathsf{DPF.Eval}(k_i, x + r)$, which gives the share of the condition evaluation result. The sum of both shares equals 1 only if the condition is satisfied (i.e., $y_1 + y_2 = 1$ only if $val = x$).

FSS for Range Condition. There are two types of range conditions: single-sided range (e.g., $attr < val$) and interval range (e.g., $val_1 < attr < val_2$). Evaluating a single-sided range is similar to an equality condition, but with a DCF evaluation instead of a DPF. For an interval range condition $val_1 < attr < val_2$, each server S_i holds the share $(2, attr, k_i^1, r_i^1, k_i^2, r_i^2)$. Given a query with value x for $attr$, each server reconstructs $x + r^1$ and $x + r^2$, then performs two DCF evaluations to obtain shares $y_i^1 \leftarrow \mathsf{DCF.Eval}(k_i^1, x + r^1)$ and $y_i^2 \leftarrow \mathsf{DCF.Eval}(k_i^2, x + r^2)$. Each server then computes $y_i = y_i^1 + y_i^2$. One server, say S_1, subtracts 1 from y_1, i.e., $y_1 = y_1 - 1$. This gives shares y_1 and y_2 for the condition evaluation result. If $attr$ lies within the interval, the sum of the shares equals 2; otherwise, it equals 1. Subtracting 1 ensures the sum is 1 if the condition holds, and 0 otherwise.

FSS for Set Condition. To evaluate an enumerated set condition, the attribute value must match each set element obliviously. This is equivalent to performing multiple equality condition evaluations, with only one yielding 1 if satisfied.

Given a query with an attribute value, S_i reconstructs the masked values, performs DPF evaluations for each set element, and computes shares $y_i^1, y_i^2, \ldots, y_i^t$. Each server then sums these shares: $y_i = \sum_{j=1}^{t} y_i^j$, where t is the set size. If the set condition is satisfied, $y_1 + y_2 = 1$; otherwise, $y_1 + y_2 = 0$.

Next, we discuss range-based set conditions composed of single-sided and interval ranges, divided into two cases identifiable by the condition share identifier. The first case involves at most one single-sided range, as shown in Fig. 3(a). Its evaluation sums the results of all relevant conditions, as only one can be satisfied. S_i sums the DCF evaluations to compute the share y_i, and server S_1 subtracts $\lfloor \frac{t}{2} \rfloor$ to correct the result, where t is the number of DCF keys, and $\lfloor \frac{t}{2} \rfloor$ is the number of interval ranges. The second case involves two single-sided ranges, as shown in Fig. 3(b). Evaluation is similar, but server S_1 subtracts $\lfloor \frac{t}{2} - 1 \rfloor$. Subtracting 1 per interval range corrects the result, so the number of interval ranges must be subtracted for each evaluation. Any hybrid set condition can be decomposed into multiple equality and range conditions. Its evaluation is achieved by summing the results of these conditions. The servers can determine the number of interval ranges from the carefully designed identifier.

Although the FSS-based evaluation mechanism protects the confidentiality of access policies, it is still vulnerable to attribute privacy leakage in case of collusion between a data consumer and a server. This collusion allows them to derive the random secret masks and recover sensitive attribute values in subsequent queries once the FSS inputs are reconstructed. To defend against collusion attacks, data owners must update the random secret masks for each query. This can be done offline, avoiding additional computational overhead during query execution and ensuring real-time responsiveness.

4.2 Multiple Conditions with Semi-honest Security

We now address the evaluation of access policies represented as Boolean formulas comprising AND, OR, and NOT operations. AND operations are computed by multiplying the secret-shared results of individual conditions. NOT operations are performed locally by updating one share as $y_i \leftarrow -y_i$ and the other as $y_i \leftarrow 1 - y_i$. OR operations are evaluated using the equivalence "A∨B = ¬(¬A∧¬B)". Thus, evaluating Boolean formulas reduces to secure multiplications of secret-shared values. To achieve this efficiently and privately, we utilize Beaver triples, which enable two-party computation in a single interaction round. These triples, independent of input data, can be precomputed offline by data owners.

To minimize communication rounds during evaluation, we aim to reduce the circuit depths of infix formulas. The algorithm InfixToPostfix [27] converts Boolean infix formulas into postfix formulas with minimal depth (e.g., in Fig. 4, the middle circuit with depth 2 corresponds to the Boolean postfix formula "AB∧ CD ∧ ∧"). However, it does not optimize formulas with recursively nested AND and OR operators. To address this limitation, we propose an enhanced algorithm, InfixToPostfix+, building upon InfixToPostfix.

Details on InfixToPostfix+. InfixToPostfix+ enhances Boolean formula conversion by employing decomposition and reorganization techniques. It first converts the infix formula into DNF and subsequently transforms the DNF into

Algorithm 1. Merge algorithm

$postfix \leftarrow$ MergeClauses($infix$) :
1: Convert $infix$ to DNF and extract attribute sets $sets$ for each clause. ▷ For NOT operations, it is associated with the attribute in the form of $attr\|\neg$.
2: **for** len($sets$) > 1 **do**
3:    Initialize an empty two-dimensional array $nsets$ and an integer idx
4:    **for** $i = 0$ to len($sets$) $- 2$ with steps of 1 **do**
5:       **if** len($sets[i]$) and len($sets[i+1]$) are both odd and equal **then**
6:          $idx = $ len($sets[i]$) $- 1$
7:          $sets[i][idx] = sets[i][idx]\|sets[i+1][idx]\|\vee$
8:          **if** $\exists j \in [0, idx-1], sets[i][j] \neq sets[i+1][j]$ **then**
9:             Delete $sets[i+1][idx]$ from $sets[i+1]$
10:             $nsets$.Append($sets[i+1]$)
11:          **end if**
12:          $nsets$.Append($sets[i]$)
13:       **end if**
14:    **end for**
15:    **for** $i = 0$ to len($nsets$) $- 1$ with steps of 1 **do**
16:       Initialize an empty array $nset$
17:       **for** $j = 0$ to len($nsets[i]$) $- 1$ with steps of 2 **do**
18:          **if** $j = $ len($nsets[i]$) $- 1$ **then**
19:             $nset$.Append($nsets[i][j]$)
20:          **else**
21:             $nset$.Append($nsets[i][j]\|nsets[i][j+1]\|\wedge$)
22:          **end if**
23:       **end for**
24:       $nsets[i] = nset$
25:    **end for**
26:    $sets = nsets$
27: **end for**
28: **return** $sets[0][0]$

postfix form. To further minimize circuit depth, adjacent clauses meeting specific criteria are merged. The MergeClauses algorithm, outlined in Algorithm 1, processes infix formulas with nested AND and OR operators, producing a postfix formula. Lines 4–14 handle the merging of adjacent clauses, while lines 15–25 iteratively convert the merged clauses into postfix form. This process continues until all clauses are fully merged. InfixToPostfix+ operates in three stages: (1) identifying specific structures within the input infix formula, (2) processing these structures using MergeClauses to generate their postfix representation, and (3) integrating the resulting postfix formula into the output of InfixToPostfix by replacing the corresponding segments.

4.3 Multiple Conditions with Malicious Security

To defend against malicious adversaries, we employ information-theoretic MACs [17] to guarantee computational integrity during FSS-based condition evaluation.

Batch Authentication for FSS Evaluation Inputs. Let $x \in \mathcal{Z}_{2^k}$ be a secret-shared value authenticated with a MAC key $\alpha \in \mathcal{Z}_{2^{k+s}}$, where s is the statistical security parameter. The servers hold additive shares of x over $\mathcal{Z}_{2^{k+s}}$, shares of α over $\mathcal{Z}_{2^s}$, and shares of the MAC $\sigma^x = \alpha \cdot x$ over $\mathcal{Z}_{2^{k+s}}$. These MACs are additively homomorphic, satisfying $\alpha \cdot x + \alpha \cdot y = \alpha(x+y)$. All computations, including those for authenticated values and their MACs, are performed modulo 2^{k+s}. For an equality condition $attr = val$, the data owner generates the condition share $(1, attr, k_i, r_i)$ for S_i, encodes the MAC key in FSS keys $(k_1', k_2') \leftarrow \mathsf{DPF.Gen}(val + r, \alpha))$, and computes the MAC $\sigma^r = \alpha \cdot r$ for the random mask r. The data owner sends (k_i', σ_i^r) along with $(1, attr, k_i, r_i)$, where σ_i^r are additive shares of σ^r. Given a query with value x for $attr$, the servers reconstruct $x + r = \sum_{i=1}^{2}(x_i + r_i)$, evaluate the condition using k_1 and k_2 to produce u, and use k_1' and k_2' to compute σ^u, ensuring $\sigma^u = \alpha \cdot u$ for authentication. To authenticate $x + r$, each server S_i computes $z_i = \sigma_i^r - (x + r)\alpha_i$ and sends z_i and α_i to the data consumer. The consumer verifies the input by checking if $\sum_{i=1}^{2} z_i + x \cdot \sum_{i=1}^{2} \alpha_i \equiv_{k+s} 0$.

We now elaborate the batch authentication process for a large set of inputs required in FSS evaluations across all access policies. Each data owner selects a unique random MAC key, which may be reused to authenticate evaluations of multiple policies for different data streams. We begin by addressing multiple conditions for the same attribute within access policies from a single data owner. This method naturally extends to support multiple attributes and data owners.

Suppose a data owner's access policies include multiple conditions (requiring t FSS evaluations) for an attribute $attr1$. For a query with value x for $attr1$, input authentication is performed via a linear combination of the t masked inputs $(x + r^1, \ldots, x + r^t)$ and their corresponding MACs $(\sigma^1, \ldots, \sigma^t)$, using random coefficients $(\chi^1, \ldots, \chi^t)$. Each server S_i computes the commitment $z_i = \sum_{j=1}^{t} \chi^j(\sigma_i^j - (x + r^j)\alpha_i)$ and sends the coefficient $c_i^{attr1} = \sum_{j=1}^{t} \chi^j \alpha_i$ for $attr1$ to the data consumer. The data consumer verifies the authentication by checking whether $\sum_{i=1}^{2} z_i + x \cdot \sum_{i=1}^{2} c_i^{attr1} \equiv_{k+s} 0$.

We now address two cases. First, consider the case where the data owner specifies additional conditions (involving $k-t$ FSS evaluations) for another attribute $attr2$. In this case, z_i is updated as $z_i = z_i + \sum_{j=t+1}^{k}\left(\chi^j \cdot \sigma_i^j - \chi^j(y + r^j)\alpha_i\right)$, where y is the query value for $attr2$. The coefficient for $attr2$, $c_i^{attr2} = \sum_{j=t+1}^{k} \chi^j \cdot \alpha_i$, is sent to the data consumer, along with c_i^{attr1}, to enable verification via $\sum_{i=1}^{2} z_i + x \cdot \sum_{i=1}^{2} c_i^{attr1} + y \cdot \sum_{i=1}^{2} c_i^{attr2} \equiv_{k+s} 0$. For any additional attributes, z_i and the corresponding coefficients are updated analogously. Second, consider the case where another data owner, using a distinct MAC key β, imposes further conditions (involving $h - t$ FSS evaluations) for $attr1$. Here, z_i is updated as $z_i = z_i + \sum_{j=t+1}^{h}\left(\chi^j \cdot \sigma_i^j - \chi^j(x + r^j)\beta_i\right)$, where $\sigma^j = \beta \cdot r^j$. The coefficient c_i^{attr1} is also updated as $c_i^{attr1} = c_i^{attr1} + \sum_{j=t+1}^{h} \chi^j \beta_i$. This process generalizes to any number of data owners by aggregating the respective commitments and coefficients. The above approach naturally extends to support multiple attributes and multiple data owners.

Authenticating Boolean Formula Evaluation. For each FSS evaluation, the servers use the keys that evaluate to 1 to produce u and then generate its MAC σ^u using the keys that evaluate to α, as described in the previous part. To authenticate the evaluation of range or set conditions, affine operations are performed on the secret-shared outputs and MACs of the FSS evaluations, requiring only local addition and constant multiplication. To authenticate the multiplications in Boolean formula evaluations, the data owner precomputes Beaver triples and their MACs offline. Given secret-shared values u and v, S_i computes $w_i = e \cdot f + f \cdot a_i + e \cdot b_i + c_i$ with Beaver triple (a, b, c), where $e = u - a$ and $f = v - b$. This allows the multiplication to be evaluated as affine operations, once e and f are known. Consequently, the MAC σ^w for w can be computed based on these affine operations. If desired, the servers can continue computing on the shares to evaluate the Boolean formula. Note that the data owner's MAC key must be updated for each query to prevent collusion, as the data consumer may need it to verify the integrity of the query results.

5 Dobby: Secure Time Series Data Analytics

In this section, we demonstrate secure data analytics with policy control in Dobby, focusing on summation queries, while a variety of aggregation statistics are given in Appendix B. We then analyze the security of Dobby.

Policy-Controlled Private Aggregation. We have focused on evaluating access policies. Now, we present how to privately control data using these evaluations, ensuring that only matched data is used in queries. Intuitively, we can obtain the matched data for each stream through the multiplication of the access policy evaluation result and the corresponding aggregated value. However, authenticating these multiplications requires the same MAC key for both evaluation and aggregated results, which introduces significant overhead as all MACs must be updated with each new query. To address this, the servers reconstruct each aggregated value by masking it with a random value, which is jointly chosen by the producer and the data owner. It allows the values to be treated as constants and multiplied by the evaluation results. The final results are then corrected by subtracting the random values, which can be done using different MAC keys.

To protect time series data, each data producer securely shares their stream values and MACs with the servers using a 2-out-of-2 secret sharing scheme. Consider a data stream with values $(d^1, d^2, \ldots, d^n)$ and their MACs $(\varsigma^1, \varsigma^2, \ldots, \varsigma^n)$, generated using a MAC key β, which are sequentially submitted by a data producer during each epoch $(t^1, t^2, \ldots, t^n)$, as shown in Fig. 5. For a query summing values in the time window $[t^a, t^b]$, S_i computes $D_i = \sum_{j=a}^{b} d_i^j + r_i$ and $\varsigma_i^D = \sum_{j=a}^{b} \varsigma_i^j + \varsigma_i^r$, where r is a random value chosen per query. The servers

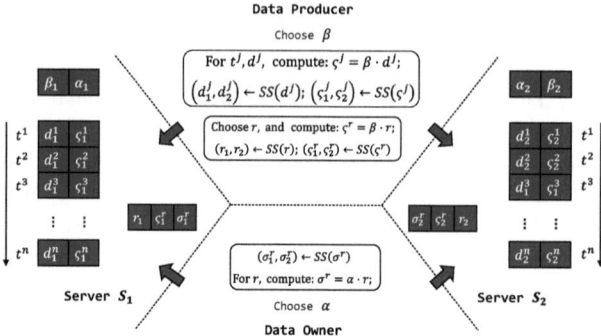

Fig. 5. Data Stream Upload.

reconstruct D and commit to $z_i = \varsigma_i^D - D \cdot \beta_i$ for authentication. S_i then multiplies the access policy evaluation share y_i by D, giving $T_i = D \cdot y_i$ and $\sigma_i^T = D \cdot \sigma_i^y$. To eliminate r, the data owner distributes shares of $\sigma^r = \alpha \cdot r$, and the servers perform secure multiplication to get $R = y \cdot r$ and its MAC σ^R. S_i locally computes the result share $T_i - R_i$ for the data stream and its MAC share $\sigma_i^T - \sigma_i^R$.

In the semi-honest adversarial model, the servers aggregate the result shares and transmit them to the data consumer, who subsequently combines them to derive the query result. Actually, in this model, the solution can be constructed by employing the two-server homomorphic stream encryption scheme [12], which utilizes the symmetric homomorphic stream encryption (SHSE) scheme [10], thereby reducing the computational overhead during the aggregation phase.

In contrast, under the malicious adversarial model, the servers transmit ω result shares along with the corresponding MAC key shares to the data consumer, where ω denotes the number of data owners in Dobby. The data consumer verifies the integrity of the MAC tags and combines the result shares only if all verification checks are successfully passed. To further obscure the involvement of the data owner, multiple data owners can utilize a shared MAC key for each query. Alternatively, this can be achieved through the use of a pseudorandom function, thereby ensuring enhanced privacy and security.

Security Analysis. We give the following theorem w.r.t. the security definition. The proof is postponed to Appendix C.

Theorem 1. *Dobby is secure under Definition 1 if it is instantiated with secure distributed point and comparison functions.*

6 Implementation and Evaluation

Implementation. We implemented Dobby in Go, comprising approximately 4,000 source lines of code (SLoC). The Distributed Point Function (DPF) and Distributed Comparison Function (DCF) constructions are adapted from [5,6],

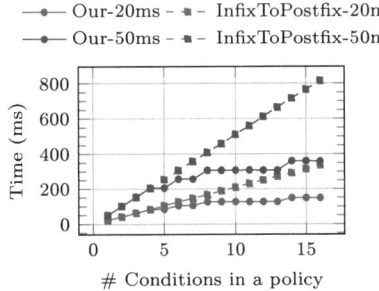
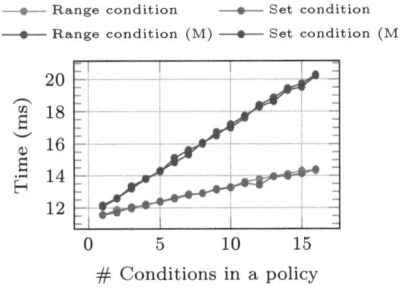

Fig. 6. Access policy evaluation benchmarking.

Fig. 7. Append latency vs. Vizard.

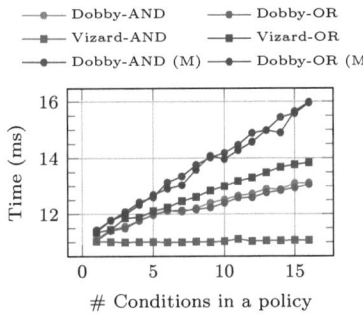

Fig. 8. Benchmarking of constructing and distributing policy storage structures.

respectively, and are instantiated following the methodology outlined in [39]. For the semi-honest and malicious security models, we utilize 64-bit and 128-bit rings, respectively. Additionally, we employ parallel query processing with load-balanced threads and implement a Kafka-free version of Vizard for comparative evaluation. The evaluation is conducted on Alibaba Cloud ECS instances. The server-side deployment uses ecs.c5.8xlarge instances (32 vCPUs, 64 GB memory, 2.5 GHz Intel Xeon Platinum 8269CY), while the client-side deployment uses ecs.r5.xlarge instances (4 vCPUs, 32 GB memory, 2.5 GHz Intel Xeon Platinum 8361). The servers are distributed across two availability zones within the same region, connected via a 5 Gbps bandwidth with a 1 ms round-trip time (RTT). To emulate inter-region deployments, we use the netem tool to introduce additional RTTs of 20 ms, 50 ms, and 100 ms between the servers. The default RTT between the client and servers is set to 10 ms.

Micro-benchmarking. Figure 6 compares the performance of the InfixToPostfix+ and InfixToPostfix algorithms in access policy evaluation, where each access policy is structured as a recursively nested combination of AND and OR operators, and the number of equality conditions is varied from 1 to 16. Our algorithm significantly improves performance. For an access policy with 16 conditions and RTT = 20 ms, it takes 149.1 ms, while InfixToPostfix takes 336.4 ms, yielding a

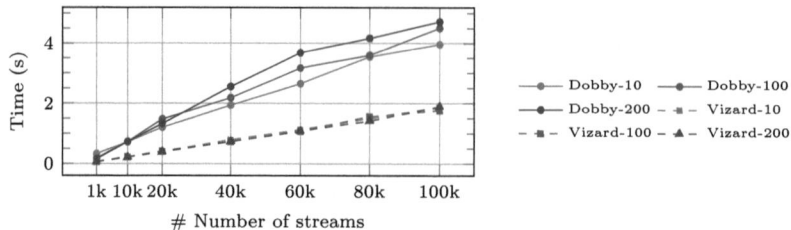

Fig. 9. Query latency comparison with Vizard (RTT = 50 ms between the servers).

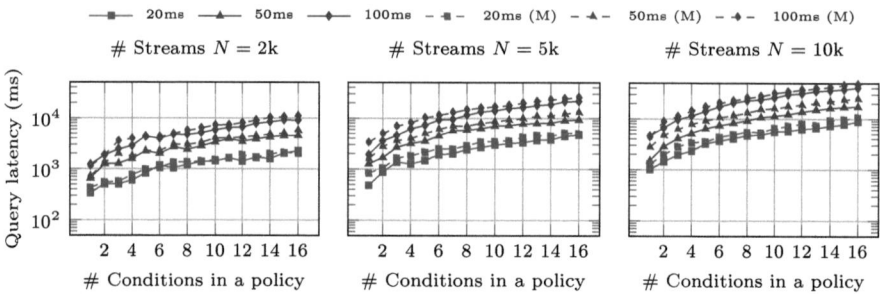

Fig. 10. The query latency with varying RTT values between the servers.

2.2× speedup. This improvement is due to our algorithm's reduced circuit depth, minimizing communication rounds (e.g., from 50 to 8, and 100 to 10). As the number of conditions increases, the performance gain grows further.

We now compare Dobby with the baseline Vizard in three aspects. Labels with an "(M)" in subsequent figures indicate Dobby under the malicious model.

Append Operations. Figure 7 shows that Dobby under the malicious model outperforms both Vizard and Dobby with semi-honest security in stream data appending. This advantage arises from its elimination of common ciphertext generation, removing the need for additional server interaction. The other two methods in the semi-honest model also perform efficiently, with network latency being the primary factor influencing append latency.

Access Policy Distribution. Given Vizard's limited support for flexible access policies, we evaluate the latency associated with the splitting and distribution of access policies. Our analysis focuses on policies that combine multiple equality conditions using AND or OR operators. Additionally, we benchmark the performance for complex policies incorporating AND, OR, and NOT operators, under the assumption that range and set conditions involve a single comparison or equality operation.

Figure 8 shows that Dobby's cost grows linearly with the number of conditions and is independent of the operators used. Dobby outperforms Vizard in computational efficiency for OR-combined access policies under the semi-honest

Table 1. The breakdown of query latency with RTT = 1 ms and the query latency with varying RTT values between the servers. §

Sts	Cds	Models	Time breakdown (ms)		Query Latency (ms)			
			Server	Client (μs)	C-S	RTT = 20	RTT = 50	RTT = 100
2k	4	Semi-honest	147.6	3.5	11.2	487.3	1115.9	2585.1
2k	4	Malicious	188.6	15.4	11.0	884.4	1634.1	3371.6
2k	8	Semi-honest	362.8	1.7	11.7	950.4	2272.6	4022.3
2k	8	Malicious	414.8	9.6	10.5	1340.5	3113.5	5891.1
5k	4	Semi-honest	338.7	1.3	11.1	1022.9	2560.7	4635.5
5k	4	Malicious	548.1	6.0	10.7	1639.1	4369.4	7804.5
5k	8	Semi-honest	717.2	1.2	12.1	2108.8	5617.1	9484.4
5k	8	Malicious	1282.4	3.3	11.0	2877.5	7460.4	13654.5
10k	4	Semi-honest	662.4	1.0	10.7	1952.5	4696.1	9461.6
10k	4	Malicious	979.6	6.1	9.9	3046.3	7486.1	14828.9
10k	8	Semi-honest	1554.9	0.4	11.6	4169.3	9965.9	19415.3
10k	8	Malicious	2695.6	3.9	10.9	5634.3	13066.4	26119.8

§ Sts and Cds denote the number of streams and the number of conditions in each access policy, respectively.

model, but is less efficient with AND-combined policies. Vizard's query optimization differentiates between logical operators, processing OR-combined policies at 1.5× the condition count and AND-combined policies at a single condition's cost. This optimization can be integrated into Dobby to enhance performance for both conjunctive and disjunctive access policies.

Query Operations. Figure 9 presents a comparison of query latency between Dobby and Vizard for access policies containing a single condition, with varying time window sizes that determine the volume of ciphertext retrieved. The results indicate that query latency increases with both the number of data streams and the time window size. Dobby provides robust privacy guarantees but necessitates an additional round of server interaction during condition evaluation, leading to increased query latency, particularly for larger data streams. In contrast, Vizard achieves higher efficiency by omitting this step. Despite this, Dobby remains practical and efficient. For example, with a time window of 100 ciphertexts, Dobby completes queries over 100k streams in 4.5 s and over 10k streams in 732.6 milliseconds.

Table 1 details the query latency breakdown for access policies with multiple conditions joined by AND operators, evaluated over a time window of 100 ciphertexts. The results demonstrate that server-side computation scales linearly with the number of data streams, while client-side processing remains negligible, measured in microseconds. Moreover, server computational overhead shows only a modest increase between the two security models, with the malicious model incurring up to 1.7× the cost of the semi-honest baseline for 10k streams. Network latency is the dominant factor in overall query latency, increasing linearly with the RTT between servers, as illustrated in Fig. 10. For example, with 2k streams, an 8-condition policy, and a 20 ms RTT, Dobby in the semi-honest model incurs a query latency of 950.4 ms, rising to 2272.6 ms when the RTT increases to 50 ms.

7 Conclusion

Dobby provides flexible, owner-centric privacy preferences and ensures the concealment of metadata, including access policies, query attributes, and access patterns. Experimental results validate its efficiency and practicality when handling large data streams. Future work will focus on further improving its efficiency and developing techniques for concealing timestamps.

Acknowledgments. This work was supported by the National Natural Science Foundation of China under Grant 62172411, and Grant U2336205, the Beijing Municipal Science and Technology Project under Grant Z231100005923047.

A Function Secret Sharing

Syntax. A ρ-party function secret sharing (FSS) scheme consists of a pair of algorithms: $\mathsf{Gen}(1^\lambda, \hat{f})$ is a probabilistic polynomial-time (PPT) key generation algorithm that takes as input a security parameter 1^λ and a description $\hat{f} \in \{0,1\}^*$ of a function $f : \{0,1\}^n \to \mathbb{G}$ (where $\mathbb{G}$ is an Abelian group), and outputs a ρ-tuple of keys $(k_1, \ldots, k_\rho)$. $\mathsf{Eval}(i, k_i, x)$ is a polynomial-time evaluation algorithm that takes as input a party index $i \in [\rho]$, a key k_i defining the function share $f_i : \{0,1\}^n \to \mathbb{G}$, and an input $x \in \{0,1\}^n$ for f_i, and outputs a group element $y_i \in \mathbb{G}$ (the value of $f_i(x)$, the i-th share of $f(x)$).

Definition 2 (Security Definition). Let $\mathcal{F} = (P_\mathcal{F}, E_\mathcal{F})$ be a function family, where $P_\mathcal{F} \subseteq \{0,1\}^*$ is an infinite collection of function descriptions $\hat{f}$, and $E_\mathcal{F} : P_\mathcal{F} \times \{0,1\}^* \to \{0,1\}^*$ is a polynomial-time algorithm defining the function described by $\hat{f}$. Let $\mathcal{L} : \{0,1\}^* \to \{0,1\}^*$ be a function specifying the allowable leakage. An ρ-party τ-secure FSS for $\mathcal{F}$ with leakage $\mathcal{L}$ is a pair (Gen, Eval) that satisfies the following requirements: 1) Correctness. For any $\hat{f} \in P_\mathcal{F}$ describing $f : \{0,1\}^n \to \mathbb{G}$, and every $x \in \{0,1\}^n$, if $(k_1, \ldots, k_\rho) \leftarrow \mathsf{Gen}(1^\lambda, \hat{f})$, then $\Pr[\sum_{i=1}^{\rho} \mathsf{Eval}(i, k_i, x) = f(x)] = 1$. 2) Secrecy. For every set of corrupted parties $S \in [\rho]$ of size τ, there exists a PPT simulator $\mathcal{S}$ such that for every sequence $\hat{f}_1, \hat{f}_2, \ldots$ of polynomial-size function description from $P_\mathcal{F}$, the following holds:

$$\{\{k_i\}_{i \in S} | (k_1, \ldots, k_\rho) \leftarrow \mathsf{Gen}(1^\lambda, \hat{f}_\lambda)\} \stackrel{c}{\approx} \{\{k_i\}_{i \in S} | (k_1, \ldots, k_\rho) \leftarrow \mathcal{S}(1^\lambda, \mathcal{L}(\hat{f}_\lambda))\}$$

B Rich Aggregation Statistics

Besides summation queries, Dobby also supports other types of aggregation statistics. For a mean query, the number of matching data streams (sum of access policy evaluation results) should be sent to the data consumer along with the summation result. Furthermore, as in prior works [10,12], we support aggregations using encoding techniques [16], mapping data values to vectors with different statistical properties. For instance, a vector containing a value and its square (d, d^2) can be used to compute variance and standard deviation. A frequency vector $(f_{d^1}, \ldots, f_{d^n})$, where each f_{d^i} tracks occurrences of d^i, supports non-additive statistics like maximum and minimum.

C Proof of Theorem 1

We construct an ideal-world simulator $\mathcal{S}$ such that the adversary $\mathcal{A}$ (controlling server S_1) cannot distinguish between the real and ideal worlds via a sequence of hybrids.

Hybrid 0. The initial hybrid $\mathcal{H}_0$ is exactly the experiment in the real world.

Hybrid 1. In hybrid $\mathcal{H}_1$, for each adaptive append request from $\mathcal{A}$, $\mathcal{S}$ samples shares of a random time series data value adhering to the *schema*, appends them to the local database, and sends S_1's shares to $\mathcal{A}$. Although $\mathcal{A}$ specifies the append request and knows the appended value, it only observes the limited shares, which are independent of the value. $\Pr \mathcal{H}_1 = 1 = \Pr \mathcal{H}_0 = 1$ holds.

Hybrid 2. In hybrid $\mathcal{H}_2$, for each adaptive request to set a policy from $\mathcal{A}$, $\mathcal{S}$ calls the FSS simulator to generate corresponding FSS keys and samples shares of randomly sampled masks. $\mathcal{S}$ then sends S_i's policy storage structure (containing these shares and keys) to $\mathcal{A}$. Since $\mathcal{S}$ knows the FSS keys and the database shares of S_2, it follows S_2's real-world query protocol. The servers compute their FSS shares locally and exchange transcripts only in access policy evaluation. In this evaluation, the $\neg$ gates consist of local computation only, and $\wedge$ and $\vee$ gates are evaluated using Beaver triples [4,17]. From the security of FSS and Beaver's protocol, the advantage of $\mathcal{A}$ in distinguishing $\mathcal{H}_2$ and $\mathcal{H}_1$ is $negl(\lambda)$.

Hybrid 3. Hybrids $\mathcal{H}_3$ and $\mathcal{H}_2$ differ solely in their reliance on MACs to detect malicious behavior. $\mathcal{A}$ observes the client's output for every query, but a distinguishing event between $\mathcal{H}_3$ and $\mathcal{H}_2$ occurs only if the client accepts an erroneous result without aborting. In our protocol, a malicious server is detected during MAC verification with probability $2^{-s+\log(s+1)}$, as shown in [5,17]. Thus, the distinguishing advantage of $\mathcal{A}$ between $\mathcal{H}_3$ and $\mathcal{H}_2$ is $negl(\tilde{s})$.

All simulation functions in $\mathcal{S}$ can be straightforwardly derived from $\mathcal{H}_3$. Thus, by combining all simulation results, there exists a PPT simulator $\mathcal{S}$ such that for any PPT adversary $\mathcal{A}$ controlling a malicious server, its advantage in distinguishing the real and ideal worlds is at most $1/2 + negl(\lambda) + negl(\tilde{s})$.

References

1. General data protection regulation: GDPR. https://gdpr-info.eu
2. Araki, T., Furukawa, J., Lindell, Y., Nof, A., Ohara, K.: High-throughput semi-honest secure three-party computation with an honest majority. In: Proceedings of CCS, pp. 805–817 (2016)
3. Babu, S., Widom, J.: Continuous queries over data streams. SIGMOD Rec. **30**(3), 109–120 (2001)
4. Beaver, D.: Efficient multiparty protocols using circuit randomization. In: Feigenbaum, J. (ed.) CRYPTO 1991. LNCS, vol. 576, pp. 420–432. Springer, Heidelberg (1992). https://doi.org/10.1007/3-540-46766-1_34
5. Boyle, E., et al.: Function secret sharing for mixed-mode and fixed-point secure computation. In: Canteaut, A., Standaert, F.-X. (eds.) EUROCRYPT 2021. LNCS, vol. 12697, pp. 871–900. Springer, Cham (2021). https://doi.org/10.1007/978-3-030-77886-6_30
6. Boyle, E., Gilboa, N., Ishai, Y.: Function secret sharing: Improvements and extensions. In: Proceedings of CCS, pp. 1292–1303 (2016)
7. Boyle, E., Gilboa, N., Ishai, Y.: Secure computation with preprocessing via function secret sharing. In: Hofheinz, D., Rosen, A. (eds.) TCC 2019. LNCS, vol. 11891, pp. 341–371. Springer, Cham (2019). https://doi.org/10.1007/978-3-030-36030-6_14
8. Boyle, E., Gilboa, N., Ishai, Y.: Function secret sharing. In: Oswald, E., Fischlin, M. (eds.) EUROCRYPT 2015. LNCS, vol. 9057, pp. 337–367. Springer, Heidelberg (2015). https://doi.org/10.1007/978-3-662-46803-6_12
9. Bunn, P., Katz, J., Kushilevitz, E., Ostrovsky, R.: Efficient 3-party distributed ORAM. In: Galdi, C., Kolesnikov, V. (eds.) SCN 2020. LNCS, vol. 12238, pp. 215–232. Springer, Cham (2020). https://doi.org/10.1007/978-3-030-57990-6_11
10. Burkhalter, L., Hithnawi, A., Viand, A., Shafagh, H., Ratnasamy, S.: TimeCrypt: encrypted data stream processing at scale with cryptographic access control. In: Proceedings of USENIX, pp. 835–850 (2020)
11. Burkhalter, L., Küchler, N., Viand, A., Shafagh, H., Hithnawi, A.: Zeph: cryptographic enforcement of end-to-end data privacy. In: Proceedings of USENIX, pp. 387–404 (2021)
12. Cai, C., Zang, Y., Wang, C., Jia, X., Wang, Q.: Vizard: a metadata-hiding data analytic system with end-to-end policy controls. In: Proceedings of CCS, pp. 441–454 (2022)
13. Castelluccia, C., Chan, A.C., Mykletun, E., Tsudik, G.: Efficient and provably secure aggregation of encrypted data in wireless sensor networks. ACM Trans. Sens. Networks **5**(3), 20:1–20:36 (2009)
14. Chan, T.-H.H., Shi, E., Song, D.: Privacy-preserving stream aggregation with fault tolerance. In: Keromytis, A.D. (ed.) FC 2012. LNCS, vol. 7397, pp. 200–214. Springer, Heidelberg (2012). https://doi.org/10.1007/978-3-642-32946-3_15
15. Chen, W., Popa, R.A.: Metal: a metadata-hiding file-sharing system. In: Proceedings of NDSS (2020)
16. Corrigan-Gibbs, H., Boneh, D.: Prio: private, robust, and scalable computation of aggregate statistics. In: Proceedings of USENIX, pp. 259–282 (2017)
17. Cramer, R., Damgård, I., Escudero, D., Scholl, P., Xing, C.: SPDZ$_{2^k}$: efficient MPC mod 2^k for dishonest majority. In: Shacham, H., Boldyreva, A. (eds.) CRYPTO 2018. LNCS, vol. 10992, pp. 769–798. Springer, Cham (2018). https://doi.org/10.1007/978-3-319-96881-0_26

18. Dauterman, E., Feng, E., Luo, E., Popa, R.A., Stoica, I.: DORY: an encrypted search system with distributed trust. In: Proceedings of USENIX, pp. 1101–1119 (2020)
19. Dauterman, E., Rathee, M., Popa, R.A., Stoica, I.: Waldo: a private time-series database from function secret sharing. In: Proceedings of IEEE S&P, pp. 2450–2468 (2022)
20. Doerner, J., Shelat, A.: Scaling ORAM for secure computation. In: Proceedings of CCS, pp. 523–535 (2017)
21. Faisal, M., Zhang, J., Liagouris, J., Kalavri, V., Varia, M.: TVA: a multi-party computation system for secure and expressive time series analytics. In: Proceedings of USENIX, pp. 5395–5412 (2023)
22. Falk, B.H., Lu, S., Ostrovsky, R.: DURASIFT: a robust, decentralized, encrypted database supporting private searches with complex policy controls. In: Proceedings of CCS, pp. 26–36 (2019)
23. Goldreich, O., Ostrovsky, R.: Software protection and simulation on oblivious rams. J. ACM **43**(3), 431–473 (1996)
24. Harvan, M., Kimoto, S., Locher, T., Pignolet, Y., Schneider, J.: Processing encrypted and compressed time series data. In: Proceedings of ICDCS, pp. 1053–1062 (2017)
25. Hu, Y., Kumar, S., Popa, R.A.: Ghostor: toward a secure data-sharing system from decentralized trust. In: Proceedings of USENIX, pp. 851–877 (2020)
26. Joye, M., Libert, B.: A scalable scheme for privacy-preserving aggregation of time-series data. In: Sadeghi, A.-R. (ed.) FC 2013. LNCS, vol. 7859, pp. 111–125. Springer, Heidelberg (2013). https://doi.org/10.1007/978-3-642-39884-1_10
27. Li, J., Wang, J., Zhang, R., Xin, Y., Xu, W.: NEMO: practical distributed Boolean queries with minimal leakage. IEEE Trans. Inf. Forensics Secur. **19**, 2594–2608 (2024)
28. Li, X., Huang, Z., Zhao, B., Yang, G., Xiang, T., Deng, R.H.: STDA: secure time series data analytics with practical efficiency in wide-area network. IEEE Trans. Inf. Forensics Secur. **19**, 1440–1454 (2024)
29. Lindell, Y.: How to simulate it - a tutorial on the simulation proof technique. In: Tutorials on the Foundations of Cryptography, pp. 277–346 (2017)
30. Liu, X., Yi, X.: Privacy-preserving collaborative medical time series analysis based on dynamic time warping. In: Sako, K., Schneider, S., Ryan, P.Y.A. (eds.) ESORICS 2019. LNCS, vol. 11736, pp. 439–460. Springer, Cham (2019). https://doi.org/10.1007/978-3-030-29962-0_21
31. Liu, X., Zheng, Y., Yi, X., Nepal, S.: Privacy-preserving collaborative analytics on medical time series data. IEEE Trans. Dependable Secur. Comput. **19**(3), 1687–1702 (2022)
32. Malluhi, Q.M., Shikfa, A., Trinh, V.C.: A ciphertext-policy attribute-based encryption scheme with optimized ciphertext size and fast decryption. In: Proceedings of AsiaCCS, pp. 230–240 (2017)
33. Ouyang, H., Zheng, Y., Wang, S., Hua, Z.: OblivTime: oblivious and efficient interval skyline query processing over encrypted time-series data. IEEE Trans. Serv. Comput. (2025). https://doi.org/10.1109/TSC.2025.3553698. Early Access
34. Rastogi, V., Nath, S.: Differentially private aggregation of distributed time-series with transformation and encryption. In: Proceedings of SIGMOD, pp. 735–746 (2010)
35. Ruan, C., Hu, C., Zhao, R., Liu, Z., Huang, H., Yu, J.: A policy-hiding attribute-based access control scheme in decentralized trust management. IEEE Internet Things J. **10**(20), 17656–17665 (2023)

36. Shafagh, H., Burkhalter, L., Ratnasamy, S., Hithnawi, A.: Droplet: decentralized authorization and access control for encrypted data streams. In: Proceedings of USENIX, pp. 2469–2486 (2020)
37. Shi, E., Chan, T.H., Rieffel, E.G., Chow, R., Song, D.: Privacy-preserving aggregation of time-series data. In: Proceedings of NDSS (2011)
38. Vadapalli, A., Henry, R., Goldberg, I.: DUORAM: a bandwidth-efficient distributed ORAM for 2- and 3-party computation. In: Proceedings of USENIX, pp. 3907–3924 (2023)
39. Wang, F., Yun, C., Goldwasser, S., Vaikuntanathan, V., Zaharia, M.: Splinter: practical private queries on public data. In: Proceedings of USENIX, pp. 299–313 (2017)
40. Yao, A.C.: Protocols for secure computations (extended abstract). In: Proceedings of FOCS, pp. 160–164 (1982)
41. Zhang, S., Ray, S., Lu, R., Zheng, Y., Guan, Y., Shao, J.: Towards efficient and privacy-preserving interval skyline queries over time series data. IEEE Trans. Dependable Secur. Comput. **20**(2), 1348–1363 (2023)
42. Zheng, Y., Lu, R., Guan, Y., Shao, J., Zhu, H.: Efficient and privacy-preserving similarity range query over encrypted time series data. IEEE Trans. Dependable Secur. Comput. **19**(4), 2501–2516 (2022)

A User-Centric, Privacy-Preserving, and Verifiable Ecosystem for Personal Data Management and Utilization

Osama Zafar[1], Mina Namazi[1], Yuqiao Xu[1], Youngjin Yoo[2], and Erman Ayday[1]

[1] Case Western Reserve University, Cleveland, OH 44106, USA
{oxz23,mxn559,yxx914,exa208}@case.edu
[2] The London School of Economics and Political Science (LSE), London, UK
y.yoo@lse.ac.uk

Abstract. In the current paradigm of digital personalized services, the centralized management of personal data raises significant privacy concerns, security vulnerabilities, and diminished individual autonomy over sensitive information. Despite their efficiency, traditional centralized architectures frequently fail to satisfy rigorous privacy requirements and expose users to data breaches and unauthorized access risks. This pressing challenge calls for a fundamental paradigm shift in methodologies for collecting, storing, and utilizing personal data across diverse sectors, including education, healthcare, and finance.

This paper introduces a novel decentralized, privacy-preserving architecture that handles heterogeneous personal information, ranging from educational credentials to health records and financial data. Unlike traditional models, our system grants users complete data ownership and control, allowing them to selectively share information without compromising privacy. The architecture's foundation comprises advanced privacy-enhancing technologies, including secure enclaves and federated learning, enabling secure computation, verification, and data sharing. The system supports diverse functionalities, including local computation, model training, and privacy-preserving data sharing, while ensuring data credibility and robust user privacy.

Keywords: Privacy-Enhancing Technologies · Decentralized Data Management · Verifiable Computation

1 Introduction

Managing personal data has become a defining challenge in modern digital systems. As organizations increasingly collect and store vast amounts of sensitive information in cloud-based centralized architectures, fundamental concerns about privacy, security, and ownership over data arise. Centralized systems, while efficient, pose vulnerabilities such as single points of failure and limited user control over data, necessitating a thorough reevaluation of data governance and management.

Traditional protocols often fall short in terms of privacy, exposing users to breaches and unauthorized access. Centralized data systems are prime targets for cyberattacks, sparking concerns among users about data security and sovereignty, particularly in sectors handling extremely sensitive personal information. Healthcare organizations manage electronic health records and data from smart devices. Educational institutions handle student records and learning analytics. Financial institutions deal with confidential transactions and personal financial information. The rise of IoT devices and increased connectivity has further accelerated the exponential growth of personal data, amplifying the need for stricter privacy regulations and innovative approaches to data management.

Existing centralized platforms face three fundamental limitations. First, they create security vulnerabilities through data concentration, making them targets for cyberattacks [7]. Second, they disenfranchise individuals from data ownership and portability, allowing service providers to manage personal data without user control [9]. Third, despite their centralized nature, these systems result in fragmented data silos that collect data within their respective domains. On the other hand, current decentralized solutions address privacy concerns [4,10]; however, significant gaps remain in developing comprehensive functionalities required for modern digital services. They struggle to perform computations on private data, facilitate controlled sharing between service providers, and maintain data utility while preserving privacy [15,21].

To address these limitations, this work proposes a privacy-preserving, decentralized, AI-enabled data ecosystem. At its core are user-controlled decentralized entities called 'data agents' that serve as secure vaults for personal data storage and computation. These data agents provide users with privacy by design, returning control while enabling complex data utilization. The proposed architecture functions similarly to a conventional model by employing a consent mechanism through access control management. This enables users to set the access permissions of service providers to their data while keeping the raw data within the user's data agent. The proposed architecture incorporates several key technical innovations. First, it implements privacy-preserving computation capabilities, allowing service providers to run analyses without accessing underlying raw data. Second, it integrates federated learning methodologies, enabling collaborative model training across distributed data sources. Additionally, it utilizes secure enclaves, enabling computations in a secure and verifiable manner protected by robust cryptographic signatures. Building on these capabilities, our architecture delivers privacy-preserving analytics by managing and leveraging personal data responsibly. It meets the dual demands of privacy and functionality, fostering trust and innovation in an increasingly data-driven world. This positions our system as a robust and future-ready platform for addressing the complex needs of modern industry applications.

From a technical implementation perspective, the system is platform-agnostic and can be easily deployed to different cloud computing platforms. We utilize

AWS services as a case study. The proposed system leverages AWS Nitro enclaves [6] for secure computation and verifiability, ensuring that even when processing user data, proprietary models and algorithms from service providers remain confidential. Our architecture includes novel data plugs that enable secure data collection from various sources while maintaining user control through comprehensive access management tools. Integrating DIDComm [3] for secure communication ensures end-to-end privacy in all data exchanges. Robust security is a cornerstone of our architecture, implemented through a multilayered approach. At its foundation, data agents implement strict access controls and secure storage using AWS security features, including multi-factor authentication. All data collection includes digital signatures for a verifiable chain of possession.

A distinctive advantage of our proposed architecture is its ability to consolidate data from various aspects of a user's life, including finance, healthcare, education, social media, entertainment activity, GPS, driving, history, and more, all while retaining ownership with the user. This holistic data integration from the user's entire life allows service providers to develop a more comprehensive profile of the user's personality and deliver enhanced personalized services without compromising the privacy of the users. For instance, content platforms like Netflix collect data on users' preferences and recommend content to watch. However, it operates within restricted visibility of user preferences due to limited user activity on the platform. This limits their recommendation capabilities to activities within their specific service. In contrast, services like YouTube and Spotify collect similar data to recommend content, benefiting from a higher activity level due to their shorter content duration. Our proposed system enables sophisticated personalization by allowing service providers to analyze patterns across platforms and contexts, all while preserving privacy and user control. In this instance, Netflix can leverage consolidated user activity data to enhance its recommendation algorithms significantly. Similarly, other service providers can deliver highly personalized content that resonates with individual tastes by analyzing user interactions across different platforms, including social media activity and cross-platform engagement.

The proposed solution protects personal and sensitive information in an open ecosystem, providing a multidirectional data flow that allows individuals and small entities to co-create meaningful value from their data. Furthermore, it presents an economic incentive for organizations to maintain and update decentralized datasets, making the overall open data ecosystem more sustainable.

Our system has been designed to address the unique challenges of key domains such as education, healthcare, and finance, making it highly practical and relevant to these critical sectors. The architecture's potential impact extends beyond immediate applications, offering a foundation for future privacy-preserving digital services across diverse industries.

We summarize our main **contributions** as follows.

- Integration of secure and privacy-preserving computation within a decentralized framework, enabling data processing without centralization;

- Support for federated learning across distributed data agents while maintaining privacy;
- Comprehensive data agent model that combines secure storage, computation, and sharing capabilities;
- Practical prototype implementation focused on specific applications such as healthcare, education, and the finance industry requirements.

The rest of the paper is organized as follows. We summarize the related work in Sect. 2. The proposed architecture is introduced in Sect. 3, and its security and privacy analyses are discussed in Sect. 4. We evaluate the feasibility of our proposed scheme in Sect. 5 and discuss its application in Sect. 6. Finally, we conclude our research in Sect. 7.

2 Related Work

Public awareness of data rights and privacy has grown significantly in recent years. Regulations such as the General Data Protection Regulation (GDPR) [22] in the European Union and the California Consumer Privacy Act (CCPA) in the United States underscore the global shift toward improved data protection standards. These legal frameworks impose stricter data management protocols and place the responsibility on organizations to ensure robust consumer data privacy.

In response to these evolving requirements, several platforms have emerged to address the need for privacy-preserving data management. Digi.me [12] offers a personal data platform that allows users to aggregate and control their data from various sources. While providing users a centralized view of their data, it lacks the advanced computational capabilities and privacy-preserving features such as decentralized model training and secure computation environments.

MIT's Solid (Social Linked Data) project [20] and OpenPDS (Personal Data Store) [17] present decentralized data storage systems that enable individuals to collect, store, and provide fine-grained access to their data. Both systems offer a solution to store and manage personal data with complete access control. However, they do not guarantee complete data ownership, as shared data with third parties becomes part of their centralized system and can not easily be recalled.

Dataswift's PDA (Personal Data Account) [11] provides an infrastructure for individual data ownership and control. It enables individuals to collect, store, process, and use their own personal data in the cloud. It allows users to permit third-party applications to read and write data. However, it lacks control over the subsequent storage, processing, and use of users' data by the authorized third parties.

PersonalData.IO [18] is a platform designed to empower individuals by providing them with tools and resources to control their personal data. It focuses on creating transparency and accountability in how companies collect, store, and use personal data. By leveraging GDPR compliance and other privacy regulations, PersonalData.IO allows users to understand what personal information companies hold about them, request data access or deletion, and maintain their privacy rights.

Meeco [14] offers a user-centric data management platform that bridges the gap between personal data ownership and ethical data usage. Focusing on secure data sharing and privacy, Meeco bridges the gap between personal data ownership and ethical data usage. Its user-centric approach ensures that individuals can actively manage who has access to their information while maintaining transparency and accountability in how their data is used.

The Databox architecture [16] offers a privacy-centric approach through a local data collection and processing system that empowers individuals to control their data while enabling secure third-party sharing. Databox focuses on the local processing of IoT data and eliminates the need to send sensitive information to third-party services. It shifts data control from centralized cloud providers to users through a hybrid system with a local physical device and cloud-hosted services that work together to manage personal data collection, storage, and processing. While being a compelling privacy-centric framework for personal data management, it has certain limitations. It primarily focus on IoT data collection and processing, which restricts its ability to aggregate and leverage multi-modal data from diverse third-party services. Although the Databox allows the execution of third-party applications in isolated environments, it lack advanced computational and model training capabilities required by complex service models like recommendation systems. It also lack robust verifiability guarantees against data tampering for the results generated by third-party applications.

Data Bank model [13] is a privacy-preserving architecture for cloud-IoT platforms designed to protect users' sensitive data by giving them control over what data their devices transmit and providing tools to manage privacy-utility trade-offs. It incorporates a category-based data access (CBDA) model for managing privacy policies, allowing data owners to define access permissions based on the data category.

P-PDS (Privacy-Aware Personal Data Storage) [19] is a user-centric system designed to automate privacy decisions for third-party access requests based on user preferences. PDS specifically offers individuals the capability to keep their data in unique logical data stores that can be connected and used by proper analytical tools or shared with third parties under the control of end users.

Current privacy-preserving data platforms generally fall into one of three categories: (i) solutions that focus primarily on decentralizing data access and ownership (e.g., Digi.me and MIT's Solid), (ii) platforms that emphasize control over data sharing mechanisms (e.g., OpenPDS and Meeco), and (iii) architectures that focus on local storage and processing capabilities (e.g., Data Bank and Databox). However, these approaches are constrained by their limited computational capabilities, which restrict their ability to perform complex analysis while maintaining privacy. Our proposed architecture distinguishes itself by enabling decentralized data control while seamlessly integrating federated learning and secure computation capabilities without centralizing or exposing personal user data. This enables scalable data analysis without centralizing or exposing personal information. Unlike existing systems that either sacrifice privacy for functionality or rely on limited local processing, our approach allows privacy-preserving data sharing and analysis. Our distinctive design safeguards user privacy and empowers individuals to retain data ownership while contributing to valuable insights and analytics. The key innovation is that users only share the computation results rather than raw data, significantly enhancing privacy and security without compromising the data utility. This approach addresses a significant limitation in existing solutions, which often sacrifice privacy for functionality and fail to deliver actionable insights without risking data exposure.

3 Proposed Framework

We present our proposed comprehensive, decentralized, privacy-preserving, AI-driven architecture for personal data management. This section details the system model and setting, threat model, and technical components that enable

Table 1. Used Notation

Notation	Description
$U = \{u_1, \ldots, u_n\}$	Set of users in the system
$SP = \{sp_1, \ldots, sp_n\}$	Set of service providers
$DS = \{d_1, \ldots, d_n\}$	Set of data sources
$RE = \{re_1, \ldots, re_q\}$	Set of computation requests
P	Data plug component
DA	Data agent component
UC	User controller component
MG	Model aggregator component
AC	Access control system
CP	Computation policies defining allowed computations
OP	Set of operations
$Auth, Cred$	Authentication system, Credential
M, M^{up}	Model, Updated model

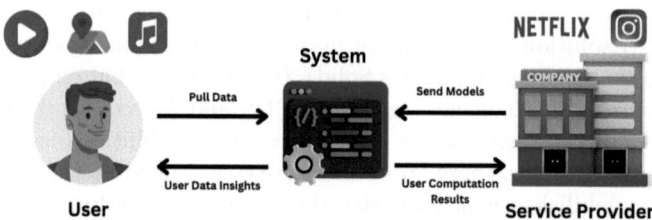

Fig. 1. Proposed decentralized, privacy-preserving, AI-driven architecture for personal data management.

secure and private data processing while maintaining utility for service providers. The used notation is introduced in Table 1.

3.1 System Model and Settings

The proposed architecture comprises two key actors: the set of users U and the set of service providers SP. Each party has a component, denoted by *data agent* DA, to securely convey, integrate, manage, and aggregate data from different platforms. The user's data agent consists of *data plugs* (P), and *user controllers* (UC). The SP's data agent consists of the service provider controller similar to the UC and a *model aggregator* (MG).

Data plugs P are the data collection components that pull user data through API integration with different raw data sources $DS = \{d_1, d_2, \ldots, d_n\}$ such as medical records, fitness activity records, financial records, and entertainment application activities. UC enforces the access control AC settings for all requests from the SP. We implemented a decentralized communication and verification mechanism called DIDComm [3] to establish the connection by exchanging decentralized identifiers called DIDs [2]. The data agent is the central part of the proposed architecture. They are self-identifiers that enable secure communication using verifiable digital identities. MG is a component that the service provider uses to manage its machine learning models and aggregate the users' computation results.

First, data plugs P establish secure connections to various service providers and data sources, pulling data into the system. When a SP intends to utilize this data (for generating personalized recommendations, training machine learning models, or performing analytics), they must submit a request to the user. Every request received is checked by the UC for permission in the AC setting to ensure the user allows the sender (service provider) access to perform a requested action. If the request is approved, UC runs the computation, producing a verifiable result, including a cryptographic attestation σ ensuring computational integrity.

Multiple data agents can participate in collaborative scenarios, such as federated learning, while preserving an individual's privacy. Each agent performs local computations (model training) on their data, and the updated trained models are aggregated through secure protocols without exposing raw data. The general framework of the proposed architecture is represented in Fig. 1.

3.2 Threat Model

We define the security of our proposed decentralized, privacy-preserving system against external adversaries and potentially curious or malicious internal parties, including service providers.

In our framework, the users are the data owners who fully trust their data agents. Service providers are considered honest-but-curious, meaning they follow protocol instructions, but might be curious to learn additional unauthorized information. Data sources are trusted to provide accurate data, but may be compromised. Secure enclaves are trusted for secure computation, and DIDComm is trusted to establish secure communications. External adversaries are considered to have complete network control and can attempt to compromise any participant except the secure enclaves. We acknowledge that securing against side-channel attacks inside secure enclaves is not our concern.

An adversary might attempt to intercept, modify, or inject communications between system components. Our framework prevents these attacks through the DIDComm protocol, which establishes authenticated and encrypted channels between parties using decentralized identifiers (DIDs). Each data source digitally signs its data, creating a verifiable chain of possession. When data agents communicate with service providers or other data agents, they use DIDComm's cryptographic protocols to verify the authenticity of each message.

Malicious actors may manipulate model training results to corrupt the system's output or gain insight into user data through modified computations. Our framework prevents this through a comprehensive verification system. Every computation executed in a secure enclave produces an attestation that cryptographically proves the calculation was performed correctly on legitimate data. For federated learning scenarios, the model aggregator verifies each contribution's attestation before incorporating it into the global model, ensuring that only legitimate, correctly computed updates are included.

Adversaries might attempt to bypass access control mechanisms to gain unauthorized access to user data or computational resources. Each request must satisfy both the permission policy and the computation policy. The system validates all credentials cryptographically and enforces fine-grained permissions through AWS attribute-based access control. Even if an attacker obtains valid credentials, they cannot exceed the explicitly granted permissions, as the user controller component validates each request against the stored access policies before allowing any data access or computation.

The system's decentralized nature, with data stored in individual data agents, eliminates vulnerabilities associated with centralized points of failure. This distributed architecture enhances the system's overall resilience and protects against large-scale data breaches that centralized systems are vulnerable to.

We define the security model of the proposed framework and formally prove it in Sect. 4.

3.3 Overview

Our framework introduces an end-to-end solution that enables service providers to derive valuable insights while allowing users to maintain control over their data. The data plug component aggregates data from external sources (such as Google Maps, Spotify, and YouTube) and stores it in the user's data agent. The user's data agent enables service providers to execute computation functions on the user's data and train machine learning models in a secure and trusted manner. The system utilizes secure enclaves on the user data agents to ensure the verifiability of computations and protect the confidentiality of functions owned by service providers.

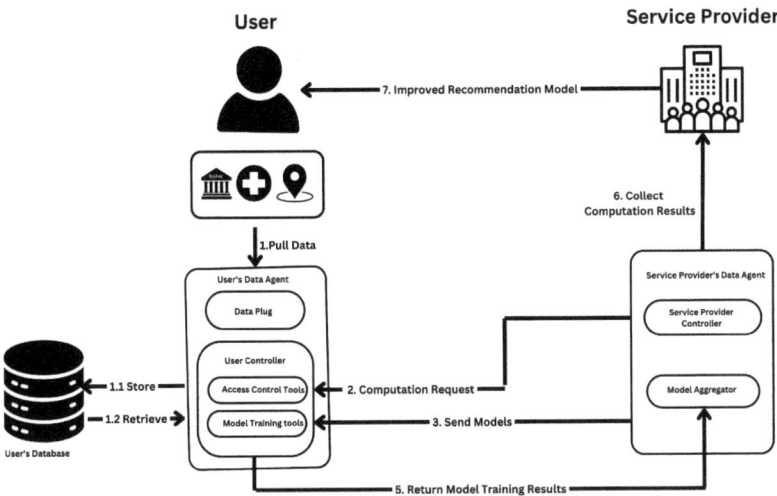

Fig. 2. General user flow diagram.

Figure 2 illustrates the general data flow within the proposed architecture, wherein the user retains control over their data through the user's data agent, while the service provider submits requests to perform computations or train machine learning models via the service provider's data agent.

3.4 Technical Details

The technical details of the proposed framework build upon the formal definitions of data agents and their interactions with service providers through secure protocols and computation mechanisms.

User's Data Agent Components

Data plug component implements a secure data collection and integration mechanism hosted with AWS Elastic Container Service (ECS) [1]. The data plug component regularly collects the data from third-party sources (such as Google Maps, Spotify, and YouTube) via their APIs and sends it to the user controller component, which pre-processes and stores it in a database for later use. The user can configure and connect the data plug (via an app) to each new data source as it requires i) proof of the user's identity, such as username and password, and ii) the access control settings for the newly added data source. This configuration process for a new data source requires a user's credentials, such as username and password *cred*, and an access control setting for the data source AC.

User controller component is the core of the entire architecture. The main functionalities of this component are secure communication and computation.

The user controller enforces access control settings for all incoming service provider requests. They check each received request to satisfy the permission in the access control setting, ensuring the user granted the sender (service provider) access to perform a requested action (building a model, computation, and sharing) using the requested piece of the user's data. The user controls the processes of connecting to the data sources and managing them through the access control settings. These settings provide the user with an interface accessible through a web browser or an app to view and manage permission levels for different types of data access. Access control can be configured for each data source, deciding which service provider can access the users' particular data and the operation types they can run. User can update these permissions according to their preferences. To protect stored data, AWS provides a robust security mechanism with two-factor authentication that requires a username, password, and a randomly generated one-time password shared via a previously registered mode of communication like email or phone text message. Furthermore, standardized protocols, such as OpenID Connect (OIDC) and OAuth, can be adopted to provide security beyond usernames and passwords.

The access control system manages data access permissions for the U through a formal specification $AC = (U, SP, DS, CP, OP, Auth)$.

The permissions are granted for each data source DS if $Perm(DS) = (SP, OP) \to 1$.

The access control function evaluates requests RE. It allows access if all the computation policies in user-defined access control settings are satisfied, namely if the $Valid$ function outputs 1 on the inputs, $Valid(RE, CP) \to 1$, and allows the process, $Allow(RE) = Valid(AC) \wedge Valid(RE, CP)$.

Service Provider's Data Agent

Model aggregator component, MG, is operated by service providers to manage machine learning models and aggregate trained model results from user data agents. When a service provider initiates a model-related request, MG first distributes the computation task to eligible users' data agents. Each user data agent performs local computations (model training) on their private data and returns results with an attestation of the correctness of the result to the MG. Then, depending on the setting, MG implements an aggregation protocol and combines individual results. The MG maintains a set of models and manages their updates based on the aggregated results. This process is advantageous for service providers to utilize distributed computations across multiple data agents, while ensuring that individual user data is protected within each data agent. As a result, the raw data of the users is not exposed to the service provider or any other participants.

Service Provider Controller is similar to the user controller, as it sends requests from the service provider side to perform tasks on the user's data. Hence, we denoted it using the same notion UC.

We deploy a DIDComm Agent [3], which is a communication middleware to establish the decentralized communication connection between parties (between user data agents or between a user data agent and service provider) via the exchange of decentralized identifiers called DIDs [2]. DIDs are self-identifiers that enable verifiable digital identities for secure communication. They are designed to be secure and privacy-preserving using cryptographic methods to demonstrate control and ensure trust in the interactions associated with them.

The DIDComm agent sends messages from the user controller to the communication agent on the service provider side, sharing them with the controller. These agents ensure secure and protected communication of information between users and service providers. Users and service providers will have interactive web interfaces connected to their respective controller components. Similarly, using the DIDComm agents, user controllers can send messages to each other to execute distributed computation. The web interface enables users and service providers to perform all operations efficiently and view responses easily.

System Functions

Compute function enables SP to analyze user data using a privacy-preserving method. It can perform custom functions on the data agent to compute and return derived values without directly exposing personal user data. When a service provider submits a computation request, the UC validates it against access control settings AC. Upon approval, the secure computation is executed (within an isolated enclave environment), preventing direct access to raw data. The enclave performs the specified analysis on the authorized subset of data. The framework utilizes compute functionality to run ML models locally and compute particular functions. The outcome of such computations, i.e., data products, can then be used to provide information to the user or the service provider (e.g., for dashboard analytics). An advantage of this approach is that a service provider can compute its functions using a wide variety of data that may be generated by other service providers and stored in users' data agents. When a SP submits a request with permitted operations OP, the compute function performs as $Cmp(SP, RE, DS) \rightarrow (r_{Cmp}, \sigma)$, if the operations are among the permitted operations.

Build is available to SP (by running their model aggregator) to perform federated learning and train new machine learning (ML) models. Figure 3 illustrates the data flow of the build functionality. The UC are distributed devices that train models using personal data without directly sharing such data with service providers. The MG and data agent communication is established via DIDComm [3]. Hence, the parties can engage in trusted communication without revealing unnecessary personal details of any participating user. Upon establishing the communication, the MG and UC must present one or more verifiable data products (e.g., attributes or credentials) to establish trust. Verifiable data products are attributes or credentials that an issuer digitally signs to enable the authenticity and validity of the records.

Once a UC receives a model from the MG, verifies the AC settings, trains the model using its data, and sends the trained model's result back to the SP. Formally, after initiating the communication between SP and MG and verification

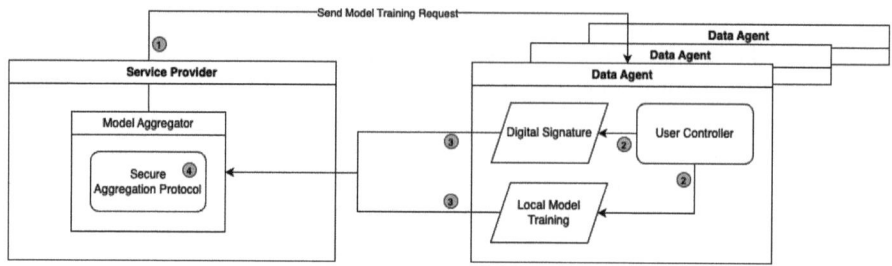

Fig. 3. Data flow of the build functionality.

of each other's credentials, consequentially, and upon receiving the request, the build function outputs M^{up} as the locally trained model update by aggregating the results running $Build((r_{cmp_1}, \sigma_1), ..., (r_{cmp_n}, \sigma_n)) \rightarrow M^{up}$.

Verify functionality validates i) the correctness (or legitimacy) of user inputs to the functions provided by service providers and ii) the correctness of computation for these functions. It runs cryptographic verifications against the data products of the input user data. Therefore, the system ensures the SP's confidence in the user's data and computation results provided by the UC through secure enclaves. Hence if the signatures on the dataset and computation results are valid, the verify function is satisfied, $Vrf(SP, UC, DS, (r_{cmp}, \sigma)) \rightarrow 1$.

We leverage the AWS Nitro enclave [8], a secure virtual environment that AWS provides for verifiable and trustworthy computations. They allow users to establish isolated computing environments, enhancing the protection and secure processing of sensitive data. It gives service providers trust and confidence in the computation output by the user controller.

4 Security and Privacy Analyses

This Section provides the security theorem of the proposed scheme π in Sect. 3 based on the threat model we provided in Sect. 3.2.

We demonstrate user data privacy by showing that service providers learn nothing beyond the computation results and proving that responses to multiple requests from service providers leak no unauthorized information. We define the real and ideal worlds of the data agent and service provider and construct a simulator that can generate views indistinguishable from real protocol executions without access to the actual user data. We show that distinguishing between real and simulated views requires breaking the security of the underlying enclave or the attestation mechanism. The privacy analyses is guarantees under standard computational assumptions and not under information-theoretic (statistical) privacy.

Theorem 1. *For any probabilistic polynomial time (PPT) adversary $\mathcal{A}$ corrupting service provider SP, in the proposed architecture π in Sect. 3, there exists a PPT simulator $\mathcal{S}_1$ such that for all user data DS and computation requests*

$re_i \in RE$, where $i = \{1, \ldots, q\}$, the views of a $\mathcal{A}$ are computationally indistinguishable with the following security properties.

- *Privacy:* For any datasets DS_0, DS_1:

$$\{\mathsf{VIEW}_\mathcal{A}^\pi(DS_0, \{re_i\}_{i=1}^q)\} \approx_c \{\mathsf{VIEW}_\mathcal{A}^\pi(DS_1, \{re_i\}_{i=1}^q)\}.$$

- *Computation Correctness:* For a valid (r_{cmp}, σ):

$$\Pr[Vrf(SP, UC, DS, (r_{cmp}, \sigma)) = 1 \wedge r_{cmp} \neq Cmp(SP, R, DS)] \leq \mathsf{negl}(k).$$

- *Access Control:* For any unauthorized request R':

$$\Pr[Allow(RE') = 1] \leq \mathsf{negl}(k)$$

- *Model Integrity:* For a valid build request:

$$\Pr[Bld(\{(r_{cmp_i}, \sigma_i)\}_{i=1}^q) \neq Agg(\{r_{cmp_i}\}_{i=1}^q)] \leq \mathsf{negl}(k).$$

We analyze the privacy proof comprehensively, and the other protocol properties follow similar arguments. We prove that for any two datasets, the views of a polynomial-time adversary corrupting a service provider are computationally indistinguishable. No polynomial-time adversary can extract additional information about the underlying user data. We guarantee that privacy holds even under multiple executions of the protocol.

Proof. We construct the proof by designing a simulator $\mathcal{S}_1(1^k, re_i, r_{cmp_i})$ for a $re_i \in RE$, where q is sequence of computation requests. The $\mathcal{S}_1$ can generate an indistinguishable view from the real protocol without access to the dataset. The $\mathcal{S}_1$ inputs the re_i, the security parameter 1^k, and a protocol's honest result $\{r_{cmp_i}\} \leftarrow Cmp(SP, RE, DS)$ at each request. Then it generates the simulated signature $\tilde{\sigma}_i$, and adds $(re_i, r_{\tilde{cmp}_i}, \tilde{\sigma}_i)$ to the simulated view which is $\mathsf{VIEW}_{\mathcal{S}_1} = \{re_i, \tilde{\sigma}_i, r_{cmp_i}\}_{i=1}^q$.

The real world's executed result follows the steps of the protocol, and the real view is $\mathsf{VIEW}_\mathcal{A}^\pi = \{re_i, \sigma_i, r_{cmp_i}\}_{i=1}^q$.

We prove in the following that the simulated view is computationally indistinguishable from the real view of the protocol.

Assume, there exists a PPT distinguisher $\mathcal{S}_2$ that can differentiate between the simulated protocol view and the real one on dataset DS with non-negligible probability ϵ:

$$\left|\Pr[\mathcal{S}_2(\mathsf{VIEW}_\mathcal{A}^\pi(DS, \{re_i\}_{i=1}^q)) = 1] - \Pr[\mathcal{S}_2(\mathcal{S}_1(1^k, \{re_i, r_{cmp_i}\}_{i=1}^q = 1]\right| \geq \epsilon$$

We can construct an adversary $\mathcal{B}$ against the enclave security using this distinguisher. $\mathcal{B}$ receives the security parameter 1^k and has access to the enclave's oracle $\mathcal{O}$. It has the honest computation results r_{cmp_i}. For each r_{cmp_i}, the $\mathcal{B}$ queries enclaves oracle $\mathcal{O}(r_{cmp_i})$. It receives θ_i that equals to a real output $\sigma_i = Sig(r_{cmp_i})$, or the simulated results $\tilde{\sigma}_i$, depending on the oracle's mode.

$\mathcal{B}$ constructs its view as $V = \{re_i, r_{cmp_i}, \theta_i\}_{i=1}^{q}$. It uses $\mathcal{S}_2$ to run the view and outputs 1 if and only if $\mathcal{S}_2$'s output is 1.

The $\mathcal{B}$ simulates the real view when the oracle provides the real enclave signature. Otherwise, when oracle provides simulated enclaves signature, $\mathcal{B}$ simulates the $\mathcal{S}_1's$ view. Therefore, $\mathcal{B}$'s advantage in distinguishing between the two worlds is non-negligible, and it can break the security of the enclaves. This contradicts the security assumption and completes the proof.

The proofs for the other defined security properties, including computational correctness, access control, and model integrity, follow similar reduction arguments.

5 Evaluation

This section presents a practical implementation and evaluation of our privacy-preserving architecture. Through a functional prototype, we assess the proposed architecture's feasibility throughout the complete lifecycle of collecting, storing, and processing individuals' sensitive information while maintaining privacy guarantees.

To demonstrate the feasibility of our architecture, we have developed and deployed[1] a prototype incorporating the core components described in Sect. 3.4. The details of implementation, deployment, and testing use cases are as follows.

The data plug component is the primary mechanism for securely retrieving information from third-party service providers. We implement specialized data plugs for multiple platforms, including: (i) a Reddit API integration that collects social media activity data (posts, likes, dislikes), (ii) a Spotify API connection that retrieves user profile and music preference data and (iii) a direct upload functionality compatible with Google Takeout exports. The modular approach allows users to connect their accounts, provide necessary authentication credentials, and designate specific service providers as authorized data sources. Data plug implementation can be readily extended to incorporate diverse source APIs for platforms such as Facebook, LinkedIn, Google Maps, or any educational information systems (as discussed in our application scenarios in Sect. 6). It makes the proposed system compatible with the most popular service providers for its use in various application areas.

We have developed a web-based interface for comprehensive access control settings using AWS Attribute-Based Access Control [5] as the underlying mechanism. This implementation gives users fine-grained permission control over their data and its usage contexts, ensuring that service providers can only access information explicitly authorized by the users.

The user controller component forms the operational core of our implementation. All incoming requests from service providers are processed through an auditing system that verifies permissions against the established access control settings. Only requests with valid permission from the user are processed and

---

[1] All implementation codes are available on GitHub and will be provided upon request.

executed, and the results are shared. The system supports both computation requests and model training operations across multiple data sources.

We evaluated our system's computation capabilities using data collected from the Reddit API (saved, liked, and disliked posts). Using data collected from the Reddit API, we apply a Natural Language Processing (NLP) technique called Name Entity Recognition (NER) to identify music artists mentioned in posts data collected from the Reddit platform. These extracted preferences were then shared with a music service provider (Spotify) to enhance recommendation relevance without exposing the user's raw data. Secondly, we implemented sentiment analysis computation on YouTube interaction data, calculating average sentiment scores across user comments on watched videos. This provided service providers with valuable engagement metrics while preserving user privacy.

Our implementation allows service providers to select from various computational approaches, including linear regression, statistical aggregations, and custom functions. They can also specify which user data portions should be included in the analysis, enhancing flexibility while maintaining privacy boundaries.

To evaluate the framework's usability, we conducted a comparative analysis of the computation runtime. Specifically, we compare the runtime of computation in a centralized setting (baseline) with that observed in our decentralized framework, considering scenarios both with and without the use of a secure enclave (for evaluation system information, see Appendix B). We also assess systems' scalability by incrementally increasing the data size. Figure 4 shows that the runtime rises linearly with the volume of processed data (number of posts), with our system demonstrating comparable performance to the centralized baseline despite its enhanced privacy protections. The runtime for computations executed within the Nitro Enclave does exceed that of the decentralized framework. This disparity can be attributed to the inherent overhead associated with loading and executing computations within the isolated environment of the secure enclave, coupled with the differential in computational resources at the time of testing. The Nitro Enclave, while providing enhanced privacy guarantees, comes with a tradeoff between efficiency and elevated security features (privacy of the SP's computation functions and verifiability of the results). As the Nitro Enclave is hosted on AWS Elastic Compute Cloud (EC2), its computational capacity (CPU and memory allocation) can be increased to potentially mitigate runtime and enhance overall efficiency. This indicates that our privacy-preserving architecture maintains efficiency without significant computational overhead.

Similarly, we successfully implemented and tested a neural network model trained on data from multiple users using federated learning. Using data collected from the Reddit API, a classification model was trained to predict user preference, specifically whether a given title would elicit positive engagement (i.e., "liked") from users. Each user's data agent receives and executes the training request independently according to the permission of its access control setting. The data agents send their respective model weight updates to the service provider agent via secure DIDComm messages.

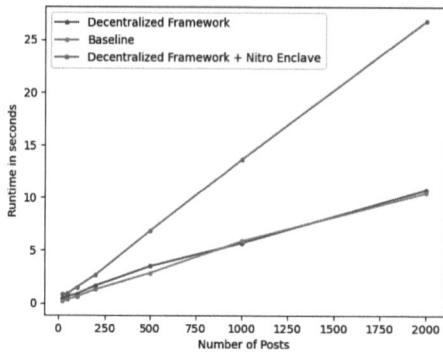

Fig. 4. Runtime of name entity recognition on Reddit data.

On the service provider side, the "service provider controller" component aggregates these weights and updates the model (detailed further in Sect. 3.4), then coordinates subsequent training rounds. This implementation offers service providers considerable flexibility in specifying data features for training, selecting from standard machine learning models or implementing custom architectures, and configuring various hyperparameters such as the number of training rounds.

Our implementation demonstrates that robust privacy protection and valuable data utilization can coexist within a properly designed architecture, addressing the fundamental limitations of existing approaches.

6 Applications

Our proposed decentralized privacy-preserving architecture finds multifaceted applications across several industries. In healthcare, technology can aid in pandemic prevention and monitoring by leveraging wearable devices and self-reported formats. Workforce development and enhancement can benefit through personalized data collection relating to an employee's work skills and well-being metrics, ensuring a healthier and more efficient workforce. Students can centralize all their academic and skill-related achievements within education and training, making it easier for prospective employers or educational institutions to evaluate their capabilities. In transportation, our architecture can help rental companies provide a seamless, secure, and customized experience for their customers by storing essential driving-related data. For more extensive details on additional applications, see Appendix A.

7 Conclusion

We introduced a groundbreaking architecture that fundamentally re-imagined personal data management, enabling users to control their sensitive information while allowing service providers to derive valuable insights through privacy-preserving computations. We proposed a decentralized, privacy-preserving architecture that addresses the inherent shortcomings of traditional centralized systems regarding privacy and security. The proposed framework mitigates data abuse or loss of privacy by allowing users to retain complete control and ownership over their sensitive data. By integrating advanced privacy-enhancing technologies, such as secure enclaves, verifiable computation, and federated learning, the framework allows service providers to execute secure and verifiable computations and model training while ensuring that sensitive information remains protected. This architecture offers significant advantages regarding user privacy, data security, and transparency, providing a scalable and trustworthy solution for the future of data-driven services across sectors such as education, healthcare, and finance.

In future work, we will extend the framework to support more complex interactions between data agents, enabling broad collaborative computations while maintaining strong privacy guarantees. The architecture will incorporate zero-knowledge proofs, secure multi-party computations, or differential privacy to support data analysis and sharing capabilities across domains, ensuring long-term sustainability and widespread adoption of privacy-preserving data management solutions.

Acknowledgment. This research was supported in part by the National Science Foundation (NSF) under awards OAC-2112606 and 2427505, and partially by the Walmart.

A Extended Applications

Healthcare data collected from the wearable devices and apps is stored in the personal data agents rather than shared directly with service providers. Collected data is then used for i) executing local AI models to provide insights to the users; ii) developing new AI models via federated learning; and iii) privacy-preserving data sharing with the medical providers.

Similarly, users can aggregate data from fitness trackers, such as Google Fitbit, which monitor heart rate, sleep patterns, and physical activity levels, along with data from health apps, nutrition tracking apps, and other related applications. Healthcare providers can access insights derived from this data while users maintain privacy and control, enabling personalized treatment recommendations without exposing raw data.

Another use case applies to collecting employee health data to promote workforce efficiency and wellness. This system: i) aggregates stress-related metrics from various sources and provides personalized recommendations to employees; ii) develops improved stress-level inference models and facilitates team-building through privacy-preserving compatibility assessments.

Furthermore, healthcare professionals can connect productivity tracking applications to generate a comprehensive profile when seeking employment opportunities. Employers can receive cryptographic proofs of the employee's qualifications and skills, ensuring authenticity while respecting privacy.

Education and training includes transcript and skill management for students. Collection of all skills a student has gained (including transcripts, training, reference letters/endorsements, books, or videos) in the student's user agent. Processing such material to extract the skills and providing a set of particular skills (in a verifiable way) to a potential future employer or school is an application of our proposed scheme. The system can also provide privacy-preserving dashboarding. It can also create AI models using the data stored in students' user agents.

Usage-Based Auto Insurance (UBI) determines auto insurance premiums based on individual driving behavior, mileage, and data collected from vehicles through a telematics device. This device records crucial metrics like speed and braking patterns. First, it sends the data to the driver's Data Agent, which processes it locally to generate a driving score without revealing raw data.

The Data Agent employs verifiable computation to protect privacy, creating a cryptographic signature for the driving score that reflects the driver's behavior. Insurance providers can assess risk and calculate premiums based on this score while maintaining data confidentiality and privacy. Drivers can selectively disclose their driving data, and as the Data Agent updates the score over time, it can adjust premiums accordingly.

This integration enhances privacy, enables accurate information sharing, and builds trust between drivers and insurers. It also allows storing driving credentials in a digital wallet linked to the driver's decentralized identity, facilitating potential sharing with other insurers and promoting fairness in premium calculation.

Personalized Treatment Planning with a Digital Twin replicas of physical entities like organs, systems, or entire patients are increasingly being used to simulate and analyze various medical conditions and treatment options. Data agents are crucial in managing and securing vast amounts of sensitive data in creating and utilizing digital twins. For example, consider a patient named Bob undergoing treatment for a complex cardiac condition. His healthcare provider creates a digital twin of his heart. A detailed virtual model that simulates how his heart functions under different conditions and treatment scenarios. Cardiologists use this digital twin to plan and optimize Bob's treatment.

Throughout this process, data agents are essential in securely managing the collection and integration of data from various sources, including Bob's medical records, imaging data, genetic information, and real-time data from wearable devices. The data agent ensures that all of Bob's sensitive health data is decentralized, giving him complete control over who can access it. During the simulation phase, the data agent facilitates the secure sharing of necessary data with simulation tools, ensuring that only authorized parties can contribute to the analysis without directly accessing Bob's raw data.

Sports Field Fan Engagement employs Decentralized Identifiers (DID) to verify credentials, thereby enhancing security, compliance, and fan engagement. The system stores digital credentials on a decentralized network, which enables tamper-proof validation at venue entry points. The system facilitates age verification at point-of-sale terminals without compromising personal information. Furthermore, this credential infrastructure supports an integrated loyalty program, allowing fans to redeem their credentials for various rewards. The system also has potential applications for regulatory compliance in sports betting platforms.

Government Services and Administration: Our system can enhance government operations by improving service delivery while protecting citizen privacy. It allows eligibility verification for social benefits without disclosing detailed income, enables secure inter-agency information sharing, and facilitates anonymous census data collection. Companies can prove contract compliance without revealing proprietary information, and a digital identity system can ensure secure e-government access. Additionally, it supports verifiable participation in public consultations and allows travelers to prove visa compliance without sharing travel history.

B Evaluation Setup

For evaluation, the system is deployed locally on a Windows machine equipped with an Intel(R) Core(TM) i7-10750H CPU and 16 GB of RAM. For a secure enclave, we deploy an AWS Nitro Enclave inside Amazon Elastic Container Service, utilizing 2 m5xlarge CPUs and 4 GB of RAM.

References

1. Amazon elastic container service. https://aws.amazon.com/ecs/
2. Decentralized identifiers (dids). https://www.w3.org/TR/did-core/
3. Didcomm messaging. https://identity.foundation/didcomm-messaging/spec/v2.1/
4. Alazab, M., et al.: Privacy and security in distributed learning: a review of challenges, solutions, and open research issues. IEEE Trans. Industr. Inf. (2024). 10.1109/TII.2024.3021234, https://ieeexplore.ieee.org/document/10278413
5. Amazon-AWS: Attribute-based access control (abac) for aws. https://aws.amazon.com/identity/attribute-based-access-control
6. Amazon.com: Aws nitro enclaves: Create additional isolation to further protect highly sensitive data within ec2 instances. https://aws.amazon.com/ec2/nitro/nitro-enclaves/
7. Aslan, Ö., Aktuğ, S.S., Ozkan-Okay, M., Yilmaz, A.A., Akin, E.: A comprehensive review of cyber security vulnerabilities, threats, attacks, and solutions. Electronics **12**(6) (2023). https://doi.org/10.3390/electronics12061333, https://www.mdpi.com/2079-9292/12/6/1333
8. AWS, A.: What is aws nitro enclaves?. https://docs.aws.amazon.com/enclaves/latest/user/nitro-enclave.html
9. Battiston, I., Boncz, P.: Improving data minimization through decentralized data architectures. arXiv **2312.12923** (2023). https://arxiv.org/abs/2312.12923
10. Bernal Bernabe, J., Canovas, J.L., Hernandez-Ramos, J.L., Torres Moreno, A., Skarmeta, A.: Privacy-preserving solutions for blockchain: review and challenges. IEEE Access **7**, 164908–164940 (2019). https://doi.org/10.1109/ACCESS.2019.2950872, https://ieeexplore.ieee.org/document/8888155

11. Dataswift: Dataswift - personal data accounts (2023). https://dataswift.io/
12. digi.me: digi.me - your data, your way (2023). https://digi.me/
13. Fernández, M., Franch Tapia, A., Jaimunk, J., Martinez Chamorro, M., Thuraisingham, B.: A data access model for privacy-preserving cloud-iot architectures. In: Proceedings of the 25th ACM Symposium on Access Control Models and Technologies, pp. 191–202. SACMAT 2020, Association for Computing Machinery, New York, NY, USA (2020). https://doi.org/10.1145/3381991.3395610
14. Meeco: Meeco: Enterprise infrastructure for the personal data economy. https://www.meeco.me/. Accessed 03 Dec 2024
15. Mireshghallah, F., Lundgren, M., Asghari, P., Ren, S., Kuzmanovic, A., Nilizadeh, S.: Privacy-preserving machine learning: Methods, challenges, and directions. arXiv preprint arXiv:2108.04417 (2021)
16. Mortier, R., et al.: Personal data management with the databox: what's inside the box? In: Proceedings of the 2016 ACM Workshop on Cloud-Assisted Networking, pp. 49–54. CAN 2016, Association for Computing Machinery, New York (2016). https://doi.org/10.1145/3010079.3010082
17. openpds: Openpds, personal data with privacy. https://openpds.media.mit.edu
18. PersonalData.IO: Home - personaldata.io. https://personaldata.io/en/home-en/. Accessed 03 Dec 2024
19. Singh, B.C., Carminati, B., Ferrari, E.: Privacy-aware personal data storage (p-pds): learning how to protect user privacy from external applications. IEEE Trans. Dependable Secure Comput. **18**(2), 889–903 (2021). https://doi.org/10.1109/TDSC.2019.2903802
20. Solid: Solid: Your data, your choice. https://solidproject.org
21. Unknown, A.: Synergizing privacy and utility in data analytics through advanced techniques. arXiv preprint arXiv:2404.16241 (2024)
22. Wikipedia contributors: General data protection regulation (2021). Accessed 30 Mar 2025

Imitater: An Efficient Shared Mempool Protocol with Application to Byzantine Fault Tolerance

Qingming Zeng[1], Mo Li[2], Ximing Fu[1,5,6(✉)], Hui Jiang[3,4], and Chuanyi Liu[1,5,6]

[1] Harbin Institute of Technology, Shenzhen, China
22S151098@stu.hit.edu.cn, {liuchuanyi,fuximing}@hit.edu.cn
[2] The Chinese University of Hongkong, Shenzhen, China
220019160@link.cuhk.edu.cn
[3] Tsinghua University, Beijing, China
[4] Baidu Inc., Beijing, China
jianghui01@baidu.com
[5] Peng Cheng Laboratory, Shenzhen, China
[6] Key Laboratory of Cyberspace and Data Security, Ministry of Emergency Management, Beijing, China

Abstract. Byzantine Fault Tolerant (BFT) consensus, a cornerstone of blockchain technology, has seen significant advancements. While existing BFT protocols ensure security guarantees, they often suffer from efficiency challenges, particularly under conditions of network instability or malicious exploitation of system mechanisms. We propose a novel Shared Mempool (SMP) protocol, named Imitater, which can be seamlessly integrated into BFT protocols. By chaining microblocks and applying coding techniques, Imitater efficiently achieves *totality* and *availability*. Furthermore, a BFT protocol augmented with Imitater ensures *order preservation* of client transactions while mitigating the risks of *over-distribution* and *unbalanced workload*. In the experiment, we integrate Imitater into the HotStuff protocol, resulting in Imitater-HS. The performance of Imitater-HS is validated in a system with up to 256 nodes. Experimental results demonstrate the efficiency of our approach: Imitater-HS achieves higher throughput and lower latency in the presence of faulty nodes compared to Stratus-HS, the state-of-the-art protocol. Notably, the throughput improvement increases with the number of faulty nodes.

1 Introduction

With the rapid advancement of blockchain technology, Byzantine Fault Tolerant (BFT) consensus has become a cornerstone of modern blockchain systems, driving extensive research and applications [1,5,9,23]. At its core, BFT consensus protocols are designed to implement State Machine Replication (SMR) in the presence of Byzantine faults, ensuring consistent transaction ordering across distributed nodes by maintaining identical state machines and logs. They provide strong guarantees of both *safety*—all honest nodes agree on a single transaction order—and *liveness*—all valid client requests are eventually processed despite Byzantine faults.

Existing methods focus on optimizing the message complexity of protocols to enhance performance [7,15,19], culminating in HotStuff [26], which achieves linear complexity. Most of these protocols are leader-based, where a designated principal node packages transactions to propose, and other replicas vote on the leader's proposal to reach consensus. Under the framework of the leader-replica structure, the leader becomes a bottleneck, thereby affecting scalability. To address this, some approaches adopt scale-out via sharding [18,24,27], dividing replicas into groups. However, these methods rely on a different fault model that limits fault tolerance within each group, rather than across the entire system.

Shared Mempool Based Protocols. The scalability bottleneck in leader-based BFT protocols primarily stems from the leader's responsibility for transaction distribution. Recent studies [8,12–14] have explored another approach to improving the scalability of BFT consensus by decoupling the block distribution and consensus phases, as described in [2,3,29], and have demonstrated significant performance improvements in recent implementations [8]. Each node independently packages its local transactions into microblocks and distributes them to other nodes. The leader then aggregates the identifiers (e.g., hash values) of these microblocks into a candidate block for consensus at the start of each consensus round. This decoupling technique improves the utilization of both computational and bandwidth resources. This decoupling approach also abstracts the microblock distribution phase as a Shared Mempool (SMP) [12,14].

Under the decoupled framework, a key challenge is ensuring the microblock availability property. When a replica receives a proposal, the microblocks it references may not be locally available, requiring it to wait until all are available before proceeding (e.g., voting). This may involve passive waiting or active requests to other nodes—both of which can significantly delay consensus.

To address this, existing Shared Mempool implementations [8,12] ensure microblock availability by having replicas to generate an availability certificate when distributing microblocks. The leader attaches these certificates to the proposal, enabling replicas to proceed with subsequent steps as soon as they receive the proposal. The certificates assure replicas that all referenced microblocks will eventually be received, eliminating the need for local availability at the time of proposal processing.

Efficient Totality. An essential property of Byzantine reliable broadcast [6] is **totality**, which ensures that if an honest node delivers a message v, then all honest nodes will eventually deliver v. This property is equally critical in BFT state machine replication (BFT-SMR). Specifically:

- **Sequential Execution.** In State Machine Replication, the execution of transactions is contingent upon the order established by consensus. However,

Byzantine faults or the asynchronous nature of the network may cause some nodes to miss certain blocks. When blocks are missing, subsequent blocks, despite achieving consensus, cannot be executed due to the sequential execution requirement.
- **Garbage Collection.** From the implementation perspective, nodes aim to release memory resources associated with a given request as soon as a decision is reached. However, because other nodes may later request this data, nodes cannot predict when it is safe to release the associated memory, forcing them to maintain these resources indefinitely.

It is worth noting that achieving totality is not inherently guaranteed by microblock availability. Most current systems do not address totality explicitly within BFT protocols. Instead, they rely on alternative mechanisms, such as state transfer (i.e., reliably broadcasting the decision value of each block) [7, 19] or a pull mechanism (i.e., requesting missing data from other nodes) [8, 14]. While resource consumption prior to reaching consensus is often a primary focus, post-consensus resource usage also deserves significant attention. Both state transfer and pull mechanisms operate after the consensus decision point, potentially contributing to further resource overhead.

However, these approaches are often communication-inefficient and may even undermine the original performance of the protocol. State transfer requires quadratic communication overhead, which remains unavoidable even in synchronous environments [10]. For the pull mechanism, considering the presence of faulty nodes, they might request every block from all nodes, regardless of whether the block is genuinely missing, thus imposing unnecessary bandwidth consumption on the system. In the worst-case scenario, if all faulty nodes request blocks from all honest nodes, this could result in quadratic bandwidth consumption, severely degrading system performance. Even one faulty node could halve the throughput, which will be confirmed in the experiments in Sect. 5

Contribution. In this paper, we pay efforts for solving the above concern. To encounter the above concerns, a series of techniques are exploited, making the following contributions.

We propose a novel Shared Mempool (SMP) protocol (Sect. 3) named Imitater that efficiently guarantees the *totality* of microblock distribution through the use of erasure codes, ensuring that all microblocks are eventually ready for execution without relying on communication-intensive request-based mechanisms.

We demonstrate how to compile Imitater into an efficient BFT protocol, Imitater-BFT (Sect. 4.1), which offers the following advantages: (i) the *totality* and *microblocks availability* can be naturally inherited from the SMP totality; (ii) by appropriately scheduling the Dispersal and Retrieval components within SMP, we achieve *bandwidth adaptability* (Sect. 4.2); (iii) the protocol ensures *order keeping* of client transactions in the final decision, effectively handles *over distribution* risks, and accommodates *unbalanced workload* scenarios without compromising protocol performance (Sect. 4.3).

We integrate Imitater into the HotStuff protocol, creating Imitater-HS, and validate it through large-scale experiments (Sect. 5). In a 100-node system with up to 1/3 faulty nodes, Imitater-HS achieves 21.5Kops/s throughput—approximately 9× higher than Stratus-HS's 2.3Kops/s—demonstrating its superior performance and practical scalability.

2 Background

2.1 System Model

In our setup, the system consists of $n = 3f + 1$ *nodes* or *replicas*, with up to f Byzantine nodes controlled by an adversary $\mathcal{A}$. Honest nodes strictly follow the protocol, while Byzantine nodes can behave arbitrarily. We assume reliable communication and a public key infrastructure (PKI). The adversary $\mathcal{A}$ has limited computational power and cannot break cryptographic primitives.

We consider a partially synchronous network as outlined in [11]. After an unknown Global Stabilization Time (GST), messages transmitted between honest nodes arrive within a known maximum bound Δ. However, the transmission of network messages can be manipulated by the adversary $\mathcal{A}$, who may delay or reorder messages. Our consensus protocol follows the *leader-replica* framework, with the leader proposing blocks and the replicas deciding to accept or deny.

External clients continuously submit transaction requests to the system, choosing replicas randomly, by proximity, or preferentially. Given that Byzantine nodes may censor transactions, clients use a timeout mechanism to resubmit transactions to other replicas until they find an honest node.

2.2 Primitives

We use a $(2f+1, n)$ threshold signature scheme [4,22], which includes algorithms $(TSign, TComb, TVerf)$. The $TSign$ algorithm allows node i to sign message m with its private key tsk_i, producing a partial signature σ_i. The $TComb$ algorithm combines $2f+1$ partial signatures for the same message m into an aggregated signature σ. The $TVerf$ algorithm then verifies σ using the public key pk, message m, and the combined signature σ.

We employ an $(f + 1, n)$-erasure code, Reed-Solomon code [21] by default, which includes a pair of encoding and decoding algorithms (Enc, Dec). The encoding algorithm Enc encodes a message into n chunks $s_1, s_2, ..., s_n$, while the decoding algorithm decodes the message using any $f + 1$ out of n coded chunks.

We utilize Merkle trees [17] to demonstrate the set relationships of coded chunks, including a set of Merkle tree generation functions and Merkle proof verification functions denoted as $(M.Gen, M.Vrf)$. We use $R(\cdot)$ to represent the root of the Merkle tree and $\boldsymbol{P}(\cdot)$ to denote the Merkle proofs. $M.Gen$ generates the Merkle root and the Merkle proofs for a set of elements $\boldsymbol{s}$, i.e., $(\boldsymbol{P}(\boldsymbol{s}), R(\boldsymbol{s})) \leftarrow M.Gen(\boldsymbol{s})$, while $M.Vrf$ verifies the validity of a proof $P_i(\boldsymbol{s})$ for an element s_i, i.e., $\{True, False\} \leftarrow M.Vrf(P_i(\boldsymbol{s}), s_i, R(\boldsymbol{s}))$.

3 Imitater Protocol

3.1 Overview

In this paper, we adopt a Shared Mempool (SMP)-based architecture [8,12–14], where each node independently packages its local transactions into microblocks and distributes them to other nodes. The leader then packages the identifiers (e.g., hash values) of these microblocks into a candidate block for consensus. The distributed microblocks is referred to as the Shared Mempool (SMP) [12,14], which conceptually represents a shared memory pool. We use the term *mempool* to denote each node's actual local storage.

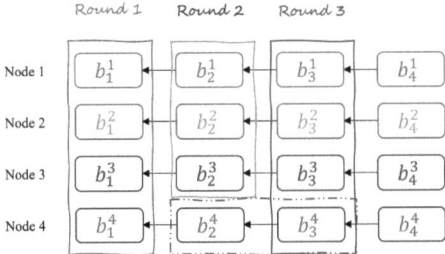

Fig. 1. Chain-based organization of a node's microblock mempool. Each node maintains n local microblock chains, where the i-th chain sequentially records microblocks disseminated by node i.

Chained Microblocks. Imitater is designed in the form of a chained structure, as shown in Fig. 1. Let $b_p^{i,j}$ denote a microblock at position p on the ith chain in the mempool of node j and $R(b_p^{i,j})$ be the identifier of $b_p^{i,j}$. In this paper, we use the Merkle root $R(\cdot)$ as the identifier of an microblock, which we will elaborate in Sect. 3.2. Since all honest nodes eventually store the same chains, as shown in Lemma 1, j is omitted, and the microblock is denoted as b_p^i for simplicity.

When node i distributes a microblock, each node receiving the distribution message replies an ack message together with a partial signature of the corresponding identifier. The partial signatures are aggregated into a threshold signature $\sigma(b_p^i)$, forming the *Availability Certificate (AC)* $C_p^i = (\sigma(b_p^i), R(b_p^i))$. Once node i has collected the AC for b_p^i, it can construct the next microblock b_{p+1}^i and distribute it, hence b_{p+1}^i implies the availability of b_p^i. Since a microblock includes the AC of its predecessor, this naturally forms a chain.

Now we formally define the structure of a microblock as $b_p^i = (R(b_p^i), C_{p-1}^i, t_p^i)$, consisting of the identifier $R(b_p^i)$, the availability certificate of the previous block C_{p-1}^i, and the content t_p^i of the current block.

A chain-based SMP efficiently maintains the order of microblocks and reduces proposal size during consensus. At the start of each round, the leader packages

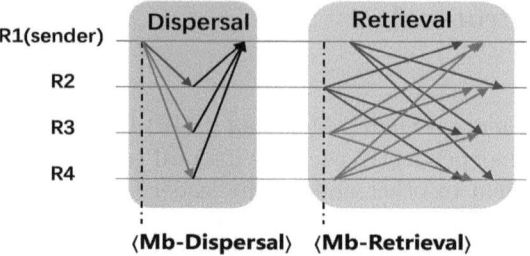

Fig. 2. The communication pattern of disseminating a microblock in SMP

the highest-position identifiers from each chain into the proposal. If some identifiers are not included, later proposals include the latest identifier, implicitly incorporating all preceding uncommitted microblocks of the chain, ensuring efficient consensus and sequential integrity.

For example, in Fig. 1, b_2^4 and b_3^4 were not included in earlier proposals. When a successor microblock such as b_4^4 is included, b_2^4 and b_3^4 are implicitly added in the correct order, preserving their sequence.

Coding and Totality. To avoid the request-based methods with high communication overhead, Imitater addresses totality by exploiting coding techniques. More concretely, our approach to microblock distribution involves distributing encoded chunks, nodes forwarding and collecting these chunks, instead of directly broadcasting the complete microblocks.

Distributing blocks via coding techniques has been extensively explored in previous works [16,20,25]. Imitater repurposes coding technique to solve the totality problem, ensuring complete microblock delivery to all nodes. In addition, this method of coding produces *bandwidth adaptability*, detailed in Sect. 4.2.

3.2 SMP Protocol

Our SMP protocol, based on the communication model in Fig. 2, consists of two phases: **Dispersal** and **Retrieval**, defined in Algorithms 1 and 2. The Dispersal phase handles chunk distribution and Availability Certificate (AC) generation, while the Retrieval phase ensures all honest nodes acquire complete microblock content.

Dispersal Phase. The Dispersal phase is initiated by an Mb-Dispersal event. When a node i distributes a microblock b_p^i, it must utilize the AC for its predecessor b_{p-1}^i. Upon triggering an Mb-Dispersal event, node i employs Enc to encode the microblock b_p^i into n chunks $s_p^{i,1}, \ldots, s_p^{i,n}$. It then uses $M.Gen$ to compute the corresponding Merkle root $R(b_p^i)$ and Merkle proof $\boldsymbol{P}(s_p^{i,j})$ for each $j \in [n]$. The Merkle root enables direct verification of the correspondence between any

Algorithm 1. Microblock Dispersal with b_p^i at node i

1: Local variables:
2: $\boldsymbol{Sigs} \leftarrow \{\}$ ▷ Signatures over $R(b_p^i)$
3: **Upon** event $\langle$Mb-Dispersal, $b_p^i, C_{p-1}^i\rangle$ **do**
4: $\quad s_p^{i,1}, ..., s_p^{i,n} \leftarrow Enc(b_p^i)$ ▷ Encode b_p^i into n chunks
5: $\quad \boldsymbol{P}(b_p^i), R(b_p^i) \leftarrow M.Gen(s_p^{i,1}, \ldots, s_p^{i,n})$
6: $\quad$ **for** $j \in [n]$ **do**
7: $\quad\quad$ Send $\langle$Mb-Dis, $R(b_p^i), C_{p-1}^i, s_p^{i,j}, P_j(b_p^i)\rangle_i$ to j.
8: **Upon** receiving $\langle$Mb-Dis, $R(b_p^i), C_{p-1}^i, s_p^{i,j}, P_j(b_p^i)\rangle_i$ for the first time **do**
9: $\quad$ **If** $TVerf(C_{p-1}^i)$ and $M.Vrf(P_j(b_p^i), s_p^{i,j}, R(b_p^i))$ **do**
10: $\quad\quad$ Store $(R(b_p^i), s_p^{i,j})$
11: $\quad\quad \sigma_j(b_p^i) \leftarrow TSign(R(b_p^i), tsk_j)$
12: $\quad\quad$ Send $\langle$Mb-Ack, $R(b_p^i), \sigma_j\rangle$ to node i
13: **Upon** receiving $\langle$Mb-Ack, $R(b_p^i), \sigma_j(b_p^i)\rangle$ **do**
14: $\quad \boldsymbol{Sigs} = \boldsymbol{Sigs} \cup \sigma_j(b_p^i)$
15: $\quad$ **if** $|\boldsymbol{Sigs}| \geq 2f + 1$ **do**
16: $\quad\quad \sigma(b_p^j) \leftarrow TComb(R(b_p^i), \boldsymbol{Sigs})$.
17: $\quad\quad C_p^i \leftarrow (R(b_p^i), \sigma(b_p^i))$. ▷ C_p^i is the AC of b_p^i
18: $\quad\quad$ Store C_p^i

given data chunk and its parent microblock, thus serving as its identifier. Node i then sends the message $\langle$Mb-Dis, $R(b_p^i), C_{p-1}^i, s_p^{i,j}, P(s_p^{i,j})\rangle_i$ to all nodes j.

Upon receiving an Mb-Dis message, node j verifies the AC C_{p-1}^i and the Merkle proof using $TVrf$ and $M.Vrf$. It also ensures that this is the first Mb-Dis message for position p from node i; otherwise, the message is ignored. After passing all verification, node j stores the data in its local SMP and signs $R(b_p^i)$ using $TSign$, sending the resulting signature $\sigma_j(b_p^i)$ in an Mb-Ack message to node i. Once node i collects $2f + 1$ Mb-Ack messages for $R(b_p^i)$ from different nodes, it aggregates the signatures into a proof $\sigma(b_p^i)$ using $TComb$. Thus, $(\sigma(b_p^i), R(b_p^i))$ forms the AC for b_p^i. Therefore, node i can utilize this certificate to initiate the Dispersal of its next microblock b_{p+1}^i.

The AC organizes microblocks from the same node into a chained structure, facilitating the resolution of the sequencing issues of microblocks from honest nodes. Secondly, once an honest node collects an AC, it can be assured that all honest nodes will eventually obtain the complete microblock. Thus, during consensus, nodes can proceed without waiting for full content, avoiding delays due to missing microblocks.

Retrieval Phase. When a node triggers the $\langle$Mb-Retrieval, $R(b_p^j)\rangle$ event, it enters the retrieval phase for $R(b_p^j)$. Upon entering the retrieval phase, node i checks whether it has previously received a chunk s_i corresponding to $R(b_p^j)$. If so, it broadcasts the message $\langle$Mb-Chk, $R(b_p^j), s_i, P_i\rangle$. It then checks whether an

Algorithm 2. Microblock Retrieval with $R(b_p^j)$ at i

1: Local variables:
2:     $\boldsymbol{Chk} \leftarrow \{\}$ ▷ Chunks corresponding to $R(b_p^i)$
3: **Upon** event⟨Mb-Retrieval, $R(b_p^j)$⟩
4:    **if** there exists a local chunk $s_p^{j,i}$ with identifier $R(b_p^j)$
5:      Broadcast message ⟨Mb-Chk, $R(b_p^j), s_p^{j,i}, P_i$⟩
6:    **if** $R(b_{p-1}^j)$ has not yet been triggered for retrieval
7:      Trigger ⟨Mb-Retrieval, $R(b_{p-1}^j)$⟩

8: **Upon** receiving ⟨Mb-Chk, $R(b_p^j), S_k, P_k$⟩ for the first time
9:    **if** the microblock corresponding to $R(b_p^j)$ has yet not been decoded
10:     $\boldsymbol{Chk} = \boldsymbol{Chk} \cup S_k$
11:    **if** $|\boldsymbol{Chk}| = f + 1$
12:     Trigger ⟨Mb-Dec, $R(b_p^j), \boldsymbol{Chk}$⟩

13: **Upon** event ⟨Mb-Dec, $R(b_p^j), \boldsymbol{Chk}$⟩
14:    $b' \leftarrow Dec(\boldsymbol{Chk})$ ▷ Decode chunks $\boldsymbol{Chk}$
15:    Mark $R(b_p^j)$ as available
16:    Compute $R(b')$
17:    **if** $R(b') \neq R(b_p^j)$
18:     Mark $R(b_p^j)$ as an empty microblock

Mb-Retrieval event for the predecessor microblock of b_p^j has ever been triggered; if not, it recursively triggers the retrieval event for the predecessor microblock.

Each node will trigger the retrieval for each microblock at most once. This means that once consensus has been reached and the microblock has been executed, it can be safely removed from memory without concerning that other nodes will need to fetch contents of the microblock.

Upon receiving an ⟨Mb-Chk⟩ message corresponding to $R(b_p^i)$, the node verifies the accompanying Merkle proof. If the verification is successful, the chunk is added to the local mempool; otherwise, the message is ignored.

When a node collects $f+1$ chunks for $R(b_p^j)$, decoding is performed to reconstruct b'. The decoded b' is then re-encoded using Enc into a set of chunks $\boldsymbol{Chk'}$ and its Merkle root is recomputed. If the recomputed Merkle root matches $R(b_p^j)$, decoding is successful. Otherwise, b_p^j is marked as empty (Nil). Future consensus on this microblock will regard it as empty.

Additionally, if a node receives $2f + 1$ Mb-Chk messages for $R(b_p^i)$ before broadcasting its own chunk, it can consider the Retrieval of corresponding microblock as completed. Since at least $f+1$ messages are from honest nodes and seen by others, all honest nodes will eventually reach the decoding threshold.

Phase Triggering. We defer the discussion on when to trigger the Dispersal phase and Retrieval phase here. By default, the ⟨Mb-Dispersal⟩ and ⟨Mb-Retrieval⟩ events are triggered automatically, but when and how to trigger them depend on the specific requirements of BFT consensus.

A straightforward approach is to periodically trigger the ⟨Mb-Dispersal⟩ event and have nodes broadcast their AC(s) once they are collected. Upon receiving an AC message, the corresponding ⟨Mb-Retrieval⟩ event is triggered. Once all nodes have triggered the Retrieval event, they can decode the complete content of the microblock, thereby achieving totality. Consequently, each node can maintain a local mempool in a chained structure, allowing microblocks to be efficiently shared among nodes.

We will discuss in Sect. 4 how we trigger the ⟨Mb-Dispersal⟩ and ⟨Mb-Retrieval⟩ events to meet our requirements when combined with BFT consensus.

3.3 Analysis of Imitater

Communication Efficiency. To achieve a Shared Mempool (SMP) with the totality property, we employ coding techniques for microblock distribution. Here, we briefly analyze the efficiency of completing the distribution of a microblock.

Assume the microblock size is m, and both signatures and hash values are of the same size λ for simplicity. During the Dispersal phase, the distributor needs to encode the microblock into n chunks, each of size $\frac{m}{f+1}$, with each Mb-Dis message containing an identifier (λ), an availability certificate (AC) (λ), a chunk ($\frac{m}{f+1}$), and a Merkle proof ($\lambda \log n$). When receiving an Mb-Dis message, other nodes send back an Mb-ack message containing a partial signature (λ). The total communication cost for this phase is $2n\lambda + n\lambda \log n + \frac{mn}{f+1}$. For large messages ($m \gg n$), the Dispersal cost approximates $3m$ with $n = 3f + 1$.

In the Retrieval phase, each node broadcasts a message with an identifier (λ), a chunk ($\frac{m}{f+1}$), and a Merkle proof ($\lambda \log n$). The total communication cost for this phase is $\frac{mn^2}{f+1} + n^2\lambda \log n$, which approximates $3mn$ for large microblocks.

In summary, the total communication overhead for completing microblock distribution is $2n\lambda + (n^2 + n)\lambda \log n + \frac{m(n^2+n)}{f+1}$, and for large microblocks, the cost is dominated by the Retrieval phase at $3mn$.

Correctness. Here we briefly show the correctness of Imitater.

Lemma 1 (Dispersal Termination). *Every honest node initiating microblock Dispersal will eventually obtain a corresponding AC after GST.*

Proof. Honest nodes distribute the Mb-Dis message to all nodes, and other honest nodes respond with Mb-Ack messages upon receipt. The sender can collect Mb-Ack messages from at least $2f + 1$ honest nodes and synthesize the final signature from the partial signatures to form the AC.

While Lemma 1 ensures that nodes engaging in honest distribution will collect a certificate, it is also essential to guarantee that all other honest nodes can obtain the corresponding microblock. Now, we show that any node could collect at most one valid AC while distributing microblock at position p.

Lemma 2 (Microblock Uniqueness). *For any position p on any mempool chain i, at most one microblock can have a valid AC.*

Proof. Suppose node i distributes two microblocks, b_p^i and $\hat{b}_p^i$, at position p, and collects valid ACs C_p^i and $\hat{C}_p^i$ for both. Since an AC is formed by aggregating partial signatures from the ack messages of at least $2f+1$ honest nodes, at least one honest node must have sent ack messages for both microblocks at the same position p. This contradicts the protocol, as an honest node should only ack one microblock per position. Therefore, at most one valid AC can be formed.

Next, we need to ensure that once an AC is formed from honest node, all other honest nodes can obtain the corresponding microblock.

Theorem 1 (SMP Totality). *If an honest node collects an AC for a microblock, then all honest nodes will eventually obtain a consistent copy of that microblock.*

Proof. We first show that any honest node will ultimately be able to decode a microblock that has the AC. As an AC comprises $2f+1$ of Mb-Ack messages, of which at least $f+1$ must originate from honest nodes, this indicates that at least $f+1$ honest nodes possess distinct chunks. These honest nodes will broadcast their chunks when triggering the retrieval, allowing all honest nodes to decode.

Since each chunk comes with a Merkle tree proof, a node will re-encode after decoding and generate a corresponding Merkle tree, then check whether the newly generated Merkle tree matches the original one. Hence, we require that either (i) every honest node's verification succeeds, or (ii) every honest node's verification fails. We can prove it by contradiction. Let's assume that for a set of segments Chk, there exist two subsets S_1 and S_2 of size $f+1$, corresponding to valid Merkle trees. Without loss of generality, we assume that decoding is successful for S_1 and fails for S_2.

Since the decoding for S_1 is successful, let the decoding result be b. Thus, re-encoding b will correctly yield $Chk' = Chk$. According to the principles of erasure codes, using any $f+1$ segments from Chk' will result in consistent decoding. In other words, any subset of Chk will obtain consistent encoding, which contradicts the fact that decoding failed for S_2.

Hence, different honest nodes decoding chunks corresponding to the same Merkle root $R(b_p)$ will obtain consistent results.

Since our SMP is maintained in a chained structure, we also need to provide a chain-based consistency constraint for microblocks.

Theorem 2 (SMP Chain-Consistency). *For any microblock chain i, where $i \in [n]$ on the SMP, if any honest node j and k have $b_p^{i,j}$ and $b_p^{i,k}$, respectively, and $b_p^{i,j} = b_p^{i,k}$, then $b_{p'}^{i,j} = b_{p'}^{i,k}$ for all $p' \leq p$.*

Proof. Given that $b_p^{i,j} = b_p^{i,k}$, it follows that the predecessor identifiers included within the microblock are also equal, that is, $R(b_{p-1}^{i,j}) = R(b_{p-1}^{i,k})$. By Lemma 1, we have $b_{p-1}^{i,j} = b_{p-1}^{i,k}$, and this logic can be recursively applied.

4 Towards Practical BFT System

In this section, we describe how to utilize Imitater to implement a partially synchronous consensus protocol, namely Imitater-BFT protocol.

4.1 Building BFT Based on Imitater

Imitater-BFT can be seen as a traditional BFT protocol where the leader's task of packaging transactions into blocks is replaced by packaging microblock identifiers. Each node then runs a Shared MemPool to share microblocks, resulting in a more efficient BFT protocol. Unlike other Shared MemPool-based protocols, Imitater-BFT follows a *dispersal-consensus-retrieval* framework (Fig. 3), where the *dispersal* and *retrieval* phases are derived from Imitater's Dispersal and Retrieval phases, respectively.

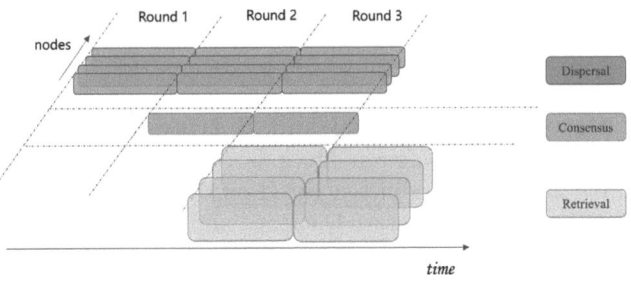

Fig. 3. The process of integrating Imitater into consensus.

The Dispersal, Retrieval, and Consensus phases run in parallel. Nodes continuously perform microblock dispersal, collect the corresponding ACs, and report the latest ACs to the leader. At the start of each round, the leader aggregates the reported ACs and microblock identifiers into a candidate block for consensus.

Once a candidate block reaches consensus, nodes initiate the Mb-Retrieval process for all microblocks referenced within it and wait for these microblocks to become available. As discussed in Sect. 3.2, retrieving a microblock recursively triggers the retrieval of its predecessor microblocks that have not yet been retrieved. This ensures that the entire chain of blocks is fully available, maintaining protocol consistency. Once all the microblocks within the block have been decoded and are available, the confirmation process for the block begins. Specifically, all requests within the microblocks are extracted and ordered based on position and timestamp to form a transaction list. Nodes then execute these transactions sequentially and return the results to the clients.

To mitigate the risk of a dishonest leader censoring certain nodes' microblocks, we adopt a consensus protocol with a built-in leader-rotation mechanism. The appendix of the full version [28] presents how Imitater can be integrated into Fast-HotStuff [15], together with a formal proof of correctness.

4.2 Bandwidth Fluctuation Adaptivity

Most BFT protocols are designed for stable network environments where communication bandwidth between nodes is assumed to be constant. However, in real-world scenarios, bandwidth often fluctuates over time. In conventional protocols that involve message distribution and vote collection, bandwidth fluctuations can lead to speed differences among nodes. As a result, faster nodes are forced to wait for slower ones, causing inefficiencies. For example, in Narwhal [8], microblock distribution progresses in rounds, each requiring $2f+1$ acknowledgment messages. The overall progress is effectively limited by the $f+1$-th slowest node, leading to underutilization of available bandwidth.

We consider an environment where the bandwidth of all nodes is governed by the same random process but varies independently across nodes.

Definition 1 (Bandwidth Adaptivity). *There exists a constant $\beta > 0$ such that, for any time t, if the bandwidth $B_i(t)$ of each node i fluctuates independently around a common mean value and satisfies $B_i(t) \geq \beta, \forall t$, then the throughput of the Imitator-BFT protocol remains constant over time.*

Benefits of Decoupling Dispersal and Retrieval. In Imitater-BFT, the Retrieval phase is triggered after a block is committed. However, the exact timing is flexible and can be adjusted based on deployment needs. Decoupling microblock distribution into separate Dispersal and Retrieval phases enables the system to better adapt to varying bandwidth conditions.

As analyzed in Sect. 3.3, Dispersal involves relatively low message volume (about $3m$ for microblock size m) compared to Retrieval ($3mn$). During the consensus phase, the messages are relatively small, consisting only of identifiers and essential information. By allocating stable bandwidth to Dispersal and Consensus messages and adjusting remaining resources for Retrieval, we eliminate the need to wait for the $f+1$-th slowest node during Dispersal as all nodes have sufficient bandwidth resources during the Dispersal phase, improving adaptability.

Assuming that for each node i, the available bandwidth $B_i(t)$ has a known and consistent mean across time, the dispersal rate can be set proportional to $1/n$ of the average bandwidth, as the size of dispersal messages in one round is approximately $1/n$ of the retrieval messages size. Hence, Definition 1 was satisfied.

Dynamic Dispersal Triggering. In more general scenarios, average bandwidth is typically unknown or fluctuates, making hardcoded rates impractical. To alleviate fluctuating bandwidth, we propose a mechanism for dynamically adapting the Dispersal phase in Imitater-BFT. We dynamically adjust the dispersal rate by monitoring the retrieval queue. Each dispersal of a microblock corresponds to a retrieval event. By observing the gap between the number of dispersals (N_d) and completed retrievals (N_r), we infer network conditions:

Algorithm 3. Triggering Mb-Dispersal for Node i

1: Local Variables:
2:   $\tau \leftarrow 0$ ▷ Time interval between dispersal events
3:   $N_d, N_r \leftarrow 0$ ▷ Completed Dispersals and Retrievals
4: **while** (true) **do**
5:   Sleep(τ)   ▷ Control Dispersal rate
6:   $b_h^i \leftarrow \langle i, h, t \rangle$ ▷ Extract a set of requests t from pending requests
7:   Wait until C_{h-1}^i formed
8:   Trigger $\langle$Mb-Dispersal, $b_h^i, C_{h-1}^i\rangle$
9:   **if** $N_d - N_r \geq t$: $\tau \leftarrow \tau + \alpha$ ▷ Increase interval
10:   **else**: $\tau \leftarrow \tau - \alpha$ ▷ Decrease interval

– If the gap is small, indicating sufficient bandwidth, the dispersal rate is increased by reducing the interval τ between events.
– If the gap is large, suggesting overload, τ is increased to reduce the dispersal rate.

Algorithm 3 outlines the dynamic triggering mechanism, which adapts dispersal frequency based on the disparity between N_d and N_r. The metrics N_d (dispersals) and N_r (completed retrievals) guide the adjustment of τ, ensuring efficient bandwidth utilization without overloading the system. Since retrieval operates asynchronously, it can be offloaded to auxiliary machines for enhanced scalability, as demonstrated in Narwhal [8].

4.3 Practical Problems

Here we discuss some practical challenges encountered in BFT systems.

Order Keeping. Maintaining the order of transactions is often overlooked in prior work, yet it is crucial when transactions depend on one another. For example, in the UTXO model, tx' may depend on funds from tx, or in the account model, tx might enable tx' by making the account balance positive. If two dependent transactions are delegated to the same node but included in different microblocks, a Byzantine leader could withhold the microblock containing tx while allowing tx' to reach consensus first, rendering tx' invalid. Thus, the final execution order must reflect the transaction submission order.

Definition 2. *Order Keeping.* *For any two transactions, tx and tx', submitted by a client to an honest node, the order in which they are submitted must be preserved in the final execution order.*

In Imitater-BFT, if tx and tx' are submitted sequentially by a client to an honest node r, and placed in the same microblock, their execution order will naturally match the submission order. If placed in different microblocks b and b', b will precede b' since honest nodes package transactions in order. In case

b is missed, b' will implicitly include b when added to a block, ensuring that b is committed before or simultaneously with b'. Thus, the transaction order submitted to honest nodes is preserved in the final execution.

Over Distribution. In decoupled architectures, some protocols [12–14] allow nodes to independently distribute blocks without round-based synchronization constraints. While this provides flexibility, it also exposes the system to the risk of flooding attacks. Malicious nodes can flood the network with an excessive number of data blocks, forcing honest nodes to store non-consensus-related blocks in memory, which increases the risk of memory overflow.

In Imitater-BFT, malicious nodes might engage solely in dispersal, disregarding retrieval. By using up available bandwidth to continually perform dispersal, they increase the retrieval burden on other nodes, while decreasing their own dispersal volume. This doesn't reduce total throughput but skews the proportion of malicious microblocks in the consensus block, compromising fairness.

We enforce a rule that the position of any microblock distributed by node i must not exceed a preset threshold k relative to the position of its latest committed microblock. If exceeded, nodes withhold ack responses until the position is within the threshold, preventing malicious flooding and network congestion.

Unbalanced Workload. In practical deployment scenarios, clients may send transaction requests to nearby or trusted nodes, causing uneven workloads across nodes. This can lead to some nodes being overloaded while others remain idle. Stratus [12] mitigates this by allowing overloaded nodes to outsource microblock distribution tasks to idle nodes. However, this introduces additional latency and may require multiple outsourcing requests to complete the task.

In contrast, the Imitater-BFT protocol handles this issue more efficiently. During microblock distribution, the retrieval phase's communication load is evenly distributed across all nodes, ensuring the distributor shares a similar load as the others. Idle nodes can participate by packaging and distributing empty microblocks, helping to balance the workload and alleviates overloaded nodes.

5 Evaluation

5.1 Implementation and Experimental Setup

We implemented a prototype of the Imitater protocol in Golang, utilizing threshold signatures[1] [4] and employing Reed-Solomon codes[2] [21] for erasure coding.

To evaluate its performance, we compared it with Stratus, a state-of-the-art protocol, using a modified version of bamboo-stratus[3], where we replaced the memory pool logic with Imitater. The comparison was made with Stratus-HS

---

[1] https://github.com/dfinity-side-projects/bn.
[2] https://github.com/templexxx/reedsolomon.
[3] https://github.com/gitferry/bamboo-stratus.

from bamboo-stratus, which, to our knowledge, demonstrates superior throughput as the number of replicas increases. The consensus part was HotStuff.

Experiments were conducted on Cloud SA5.2XLARGE16 instances within a single datacenter, each with 8 vCPUs and 3 Gbps of internal bandwidth. Each replica ran on a separate EC2 instance, and we simulated a WAN environment with 100 Mbit/s replica bandwidth using *tc*.

Four instances ran client processes, continuously sending requests to the replicas. Latency was measured as the time from when a node (the microblock proposer) receives a request to when it completes the consensus process. Throughput is the number of requests committed per second, averaged across all replicas. All measurements were taken after the system's performance had stabilized.

5.2 Performance

To evaluate the performance of Imitater, we conducted a thorough assessment of Imitater and compared with Stratus, the SOTA SMP protocol.

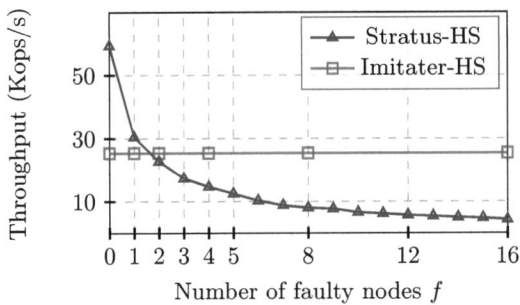

Fig. 4. Throuput with $n=49$ and bandwidth settiing to 100Mbps, varying faulty nodes number f

First, we analyzed the impact of faulty nodes on throughput. Figure 4 shows that Stratus-HS throughput declines sharply as the number of faulty nodes increases from 0 to 16, in a 49-node system with 100Mbps bandwidth. For instance, just one faulty node reduces throughput by nearly half. In contrast, Imitater-HS maintains constant throughput regardless of faulty nodes. With one faulty node, Imitater-HS achieves 0.8× the throughput of Stratus-HS, and with 16 faulty nodes, it reaches 6× the throughput.

Figure 5a demonstrates how throughput varies with the number of nodes under maximum fault tolerance, i.e., the number of faulty nodes is $n/3$. The throughput of Stratus-HS decreases much faster than Imitater-HS as the number of nodes increases. At 100 nodes, Imitater-HS achieves 21.5 Kops/s, nearly 9× that of Stratus-HS (2.3 Kops/s). The throughput decline of Stratus-HS is primarily due to all malicious nodes requesting all microblocks from each honest node, which consumes the honest nodes' bandwidth by forcing them to send these

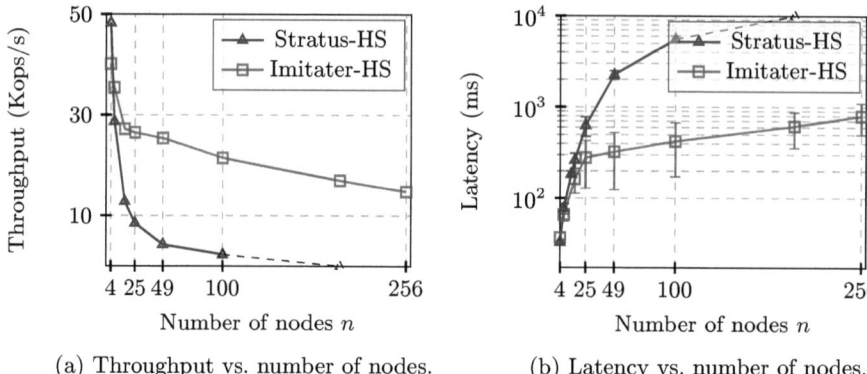

Fig. 5. Performance comparison of Imitater-HS and Stratus-HS with bandwidth setting to 100 Mbps and up to $n/3$ nodes being faulty. (a) Throughput vs. nodes. (b) Latency vs. nodes.

redundant microblocks, thereby impacting throughput. Thanks to the design of Imitater-HS, malicious nodes cannot make malicious requests, thus avoiding any performance degradation. In contrast, as the number of nodes increases under maximum fault tolerance, the number of malicious nodes also rises, leading to a noticeable performance decline in Stratus-HS.

Similarly, the latency in Stratus-HS is affected by attacks from malicious nodes. Figure 5b shows how latency changes as the number of nodes increases. It can be observed that Imitater-HS maintains a relatively low latency, while Stratus-HS experiences a sharp increase in latency as the number of nodes grows. Specifically, with 100 nodes, Stratus-HS's latency reaches 5565 ms, whereas Imitater-HS's latency remains around 550 ms.

6 Conclusion

In this paper, we propose a novel SMP protocol, namely Imitater, to improve the efficiency of microblock distribution with Byzantine faulty nodes under partially synchronous setting. Imitater ensures that all microblocks are correctly distributed, available, and ordered even in the presence of faulty nodes. Imitater is easy to integrate into a BFT protocol achieving improved performance by address specific practical problems and better bandwidth use. Our experiments, conducted in a large-scale node deployment environment, showed that the protocol is efficient, maintaining high throughput and low latency, even when some nodes are faulty.

Acknowledgment. This work was supported by National Natural Science Foundation of China (Grant 62301190), Shenzhen Colleges and Universities Stable Support Program (Grant GXWD20231129135251001), National Key Research and Development Program of China (Grant 2023YFB3106504) and Major Key Project of PCL (Grant PCL2023A09).

Disclosure of Interests. The authors have no competing interests to declare that are relevant to the content of this article.

References

1. Androulaki, E., et al.: Hyperledger fabric: a distributed operating system for permissioned blockchains. In: Proceedings of the Thirteenth EuroSys Conference, pp. 1–15 (2018)
2. Bagaria, V., Kannan, S., Tse, D., Fanti, G., Viswanath, P.: Prism: deconstructing the blockchain to approach physical limits. In: Proceedings of the 2019 ACM SIGSAC Conference on Computer and Communications Security, pp. 585–602 (2019)
3. Biely, M., Milosevic, Z., Santos, N., Schiper, A.: S-paxos: offloading the leader for high throughput state machine replication. In: 2012 IEEE 31st Symposium on Reliable Distributed Systems, pp. 111–120. IEEE (2012)
4. Boneh, D., Lynn, B., Shacham, H.: Short signatures from the weil pairing. In: Boyd, C. (ed.) ASIACRYPT 2001. LNCS, vol. 2248, pp. 514–532. Springer, Heidelberg (2001). https://doi.org/10.1007/3-540-45682-1_30
5. Buterin, V.: Ethereum: a next-generation smart contract and decentralized application platform (2014). https://ethereum.org/en/whitepaper
6. Cachin, C., Guerraoui, R., Rodrigues, L.: Introduction to Reliable and Secure Distributed Programming. Springer, Heidelberg (2011)
7. Castro, M., Liskov, B., et al.: Practical byzantine fault tolerance. In: OsDI, vol. 99, pp. 173–186 (1999)
8. Danezis, G., Kokoris-Kogias, L., Sonnino, A., Spiegelman, A.: Narwhal and tusk: a DAG-based mempool and efficient BFT consensus. In: Proceedings of the Seventeenth European Conference on Computer Systems, pp. 34–50 (2022)
9. Diem: The libra blockchain (2020). https://developers.diem.com/docs/technical-papers/the-diem-blockchain-paper
10. Dolev, D., Strong, H.R.: Authenticated algorithms for byzantine agreement. SIAM J. Comput. **12**(4), 656–666 (1983)
11. Dwork, C., Lynch, N., Stockmeyer, L.: Consensus in the presence of partial synchrony. J. ACM (JACM) **35**(2), 288–323 (1988)
12. Gai, F., Niu, J., Beschastnikh, I., Feng, C., Wang, S.: Scaling blockchain consensus via a robust shared mempool. In: 2023 IEEE 39th International Conference on Data Engineering (ICDE), pp. 530–543. IEEE (2023)
13. Hu, K., Guo, K., Tang, Q., Zhang, Z., Cheng, H., Zhao, Z.: Leopard: towards high throughput-preserving BFT for large-scale systems. In: 2022 IEEE 42nd International Conference on Distributed Computing Systems (ICDCS), pp. 157–167. IEEE (2022)
14. Hu, Z., et al.: A data flow framework with high throughput and low latency for permissioned blockchains. In: 2023 IEEE 43rd International Conference on Distributed Computing Systems (ICDCS), pp. 1–12. IEEE (2023)
15. Jalalzai, M.M., Niu, J., Feng, C., Gai, F.: Fast-Hotstuff: A fast and robust BFT protocol for blockchains. IEEE Trans. Dependable Secure Comput. (2023)
16. Kaklamanis, I., Yang, L., Alizadeh, M.: Poster: coded broadcast for scalable leader-based BFT consensus. In: Proceedings of the 2022 ACM SIGSAC Conference on Computer and Communications Security, pp. 3375–3377 (2022)

17. Kocher, P.C.: On certificate revocation and validation. In: Hirchfeld, R. (ed.) FC 1998. LNCS, vol. 1465, pp. 172–177. Springer, Heidelberg (1998). https://doi.org/10.1007/BFb0055481
18. Kokoris-Kogias, E., Jovanovic, P., Gasser, L., Gailly, N., Syta, E., Ford, B.: OmniLedger: a secure, scale-out, decentralized ledger via sharding. In: 2018 IEEE symposium on security and privacy (SP), pp. 583–598. IEEE (2018)
19. Kotla, R., Alvisi, L., Dahlin, M., Clement, A., Wong, E.: Zyzzyva: speculative byzantine fault tolerance. In: Proceedings of Twenty-First ACM SIGOPS Symposium on Operating Systems Principles, pp. 45–58 (2007)
20. Miller, A., Xia, Y., Croman, K., Shi, E., Song, D.: The honey badger of BFT protocols. In: Proceedings of the 2016 ACM SIGSAC Conference on Computer and Communications Security, pp. 31–42 (2016)
21. Reed, I.S., Solomon, G.: Polynomial codes over certain finite fields. J. Soc. Ind. Appl. Math. **8**(2), 300–304 (1960)
22. Shoup, V.: Practical threshold signatures. In: Preneel, B. (ed.) EUROCRYPT 2000. LNCS, vol. 1807, pp. 207–220. Springer, Heidelberg (2000). https://doi.org/10.1007/3-540-45539-6_15
23. Team, A.: The aptos blockchain: safe, scalable, and upgradeable web3 infrastructure (2022). https://aptosfoundation.org/whitepaper
24. Wang, J., Wang, H.: Monoxide: scale out blockchains with asynchronous consensus zones. In: 16th USENIX Symposium on Networked Systems Design and Implementation (NSDI 2019), pp. 95–112 (2019)
25. Yang, L., Park, S.J., Alizadeh, M., Kannan, S., Tse, D.: DispersedLedger: high-throughput byzantine consensus on variable bandwidth networks. In: 19th USENIX Symposium on Networked Systems Design and Implementation (NSDI 2022), pp. 493–512 (2022)
26. Yin, M., Malkhi, D., Reiter, M.K., Gueta, G.G., Abraham, I.: Hotstuff: BFT consensus with linearity and responsiveness. In: Proceedings of the 2019 ACM Symposium on Principles of Distributed Computing, pp. 347–356 (2019)
27. Zamani, M., Movahedi, M., Raykova, M.: RapidChain: scaling blockchain via full sharding. In: Proceedings of the 2018 ACM SIGSAC Conference on Computer and Communications Security, pp. 931–948 (2018)
28. Zeng, Q., Li, M., Fu, X., Jiang, H., Liu, C.: Imitater: an efficient shared mempool protocol with application to byzantine fault tolerance (2024). https://arxiv.org/abs/2409.19286
29. Zhao, H., Zhang, Q., Yang, Z., Wu, M., Dai, Y.: SDPaxos: building efficient semi-decentralized geo-replicated state machines. In: Proceedings of the ACM Symposium on Cloud Computing, pp. 68–81 (2018)

Premining in the Shadows: How Hidden Blocks Weaken the Security of Proof-of-Work Chains

Wanying Zeng[1,2,3], Lijia Xie[2(✉)], and Xiao Zhang[1,2,3,4(✉)]

[1] School of Mathematical Sciences, Beihang University, Beijing 100191, China
[2] Zhongguancun Laboratory, Beijing 100094, China
xielj@zgclab.edu.cn
[3] Key Laboratory of Mathematics, Informatics and Behavioral Semantics (LMIB), Ministry of Education, Beijing 100191, China
[4] Hangzhou International Innovation Institute, Beihang University, Hangzhou 311115, China
xiao.zh@buaa.edu.cn

Abstract. Nakamoto Consensus (NC), the foundational mechanism of Bitcoin, secures permissionless blockchains through Proof-of-Work (PoW) and the longest-chain rule. Although classical analyses suggest exponentially low success probabilities for attackers with less than 50% hash power, real-world double-spending attacks (DSAs) persist, especially when pre-mining is involved. However, existing models either neglect pre-mining or inadequately capture its trade-offs with post-transaction mining. In this paper, we first develop a pre-mining DSA model with fixed cost constraints, deriving closed-form expressions for success probability and expected revenue. Next, we propose an Adaptive Pre-mining DSA strategy that dynamically optimizes attack timing for profit maximization using Stochastic Dynamic Programming (SDP). Through comprehensive simulations, we evaluate the effectiveness of our attack strategies, demonstrating their superior performance over existing models. Based on transaction values, we propose optimal confirmation block thresholds. These insights contribute to both theoretical and practical security improvements for decentralized system protocols.

Keywords: Nakamoto Consensus · Double-Spending Attack · Pre-Mining Strategy · Stochastic Dynamic Programming · Blockchain Security

1 Introduction

Nakamoto Consensus (NC), first proposed in Bitcoin's foundational whitepaper [15], remains the most widely adopted consensus mechanism for permissionless

---

This work was supported by the National Science and Technology Major Project (2022ZD0116401), the National Natural Science Foundation of China (62141605), and the Fundamental Research Funds for the Central Universities. This work was also supported by Zhongguancun Laboratory.

blockchains [4,18]. Its core innovation lies in maintaining an immutable ledger without relying on prior knowledge of participant identities, achieved through Proof-of-Work (PoW) and the longest-chain rule. As of 2025, Bitcoin's market capitalization exceeds $1.4 trillion, securing over 40% of the total crypto market share [7].

The operational security of NC relies on *miners*—decentralized participants who validate transactions through computational puzzles (*mining*). These miners enforce the longest-chain protocol where nodes adopt the chain with maximal accumulated proof-of-work. Malicious miners exploit network latency to execute double-spending attacks (DSA) by secretly extending an alternative chain after broadcasting legitimate transactions, then overwriting the main chain when achieving length superiority. For example, between late July and early August 2020, Ethereum Classic (ETC) suffered two 51% hash rate attacks, resulting in approximately $9 million being double-spent, causing significant financial losses [6]. This vulnerability is exacerbated by mining centralization—most hash power concentrates in a few pools [12]. Such centralization introduces a high level of vulnerability to mining attacks. Concurrently, the concentration of high-value transactions on exchanges has made them attractive targets for attacks, as seen in the Mt. Gox incident that triggered severe market volatility [5]. These risks underscore the critical need to analyze double-spending attacks and their countermeasures.

The Bitcoin whitepaper and numerous analyses [15,19] suggest that, as long as an attacker controls less than 50% of the computational power, the probability of transaction reversal decreases exponentially with the number of confirmations received. However, why do double-spending attacks still occur frequently in the real world? Some studies [16,21] indicate that, in practice, attackers may attempt to create blocks before the transaction is broadcast, a phase we refer to as *pre-mining*. Given that merchants offer continuous services, attackers can choose the optimal moment to initiate a purchase, thus controlling the attack timing. However, previous basic models do not account for scenarios in which attackers have already constructed fraudulent blocks. Additionally, the cost of pre-mining is low, as the required computational effort is negligible compared to the potential gains from double-spending.

Existing models of pre-mining strategies in the literature are primarily focused on analyzing the success probability of fixed pre-mining strategies [16,21]. Pinzon [16] proposed a model that considers the success probability of a double-spending attack when an attacker adopts a pre-mining strategy with a certain time advantage. However, this model assumes that during the pre-mining period, the honest network does not generate any blocks, which is unrealistic. Sompolinsky [21] analyzed the expected number of advantageous blocks for the attacker in a long-term pre-mining process and derived the success probability under such a strategy. Nevertheless, these models neglect realistic cost considerations, such as time investment, mining power consumption, and foregone rewards from honest mining. In reality, attackers are expected to assess their potential profitability and determine the optimal timing to proceed with or abandon the attack.

In this paper, we analyze double-spending attacks with pre-mining strategies under cost constraints, incorporating more realistic system assumptions. We quantify the success probability and expected revenue of double-spending attacks, analyzing the attacker's strategy under two critical cost constraints: the pre-mining duration before launching the attack and the maximum sustained private-chain mining period during the double-spending attempt. Our findings show that, from an incentive-driven perspective, more flexible attack strategies can be analyzed. Using stochastic dynamic programming (SDP) [2,3], we identify the optimal attack strategy, which we call Adaptive Pre-mining DSA. Our results indicate that pre-mining strategies can significantly increase the success probability and profitability of double-spending attacks, thereby posing risks to blockchain consensus security.

Specifically, our contributions include:

1. We propose an enhanced double-spending attack model that considers both pre-mining time and post-transaction mining duration. Our Pre-mining DSA strategy's success probability and expected revenue are analytically derived under fixed cost constraints.
2. We develop an optimal attack strategy using an SDP framework to maximize attacker profits. This theoretical foundation facilitates the introduction of the Adaptive Pre-mining DSA, which dynamically adjusts to network conditions.
3. Through comprehensive simulations, we evaluate both attack strategies based on key network parameters, demonstrating that our attack strategies outperform existing double-spending models. Furthermore, we provide clear recommendations on the required number of confirmation blocks for merchants, depending on transaction values.

2 Preliminaries and Related Works

2.1 Naive Double-Spending Attack

The Naive Double-Spending Attack (Naive DSA) represents the foundational model for analyzing double-spending threats in PoW-based blockchains. A successful double-spending attack consists of the following steps. And the process is illustrated in Fig. 1.

- **Step 1: Transaction Broadcast and Confirmation**
  - The attacker broadcasts valid transaction TX_1 to the network, incorporated into a block.
  - The merchant waits for z-block confirmations (for example, 6 blocks in Bitcoin) before delivering goods, considering the payment irreversible.
- **Step 2: Covert Chain Construction**
  - Concurrently, the attacker initiates private mining from the pre-TX_1 block, creating transaction TX_2 that redirects funds to themselves.

- Attacker allocates computational resources to accelerate private chain growth while strategically delaying honest chain propagation through network manipulation.
- **Step 3: Chain Replacement Execution**
  - Post-delivery, attacker compares chain lengths: if private chain exceeds honest chain, broadcasts it to trigger consensus-driven reorganization, invalidating TX_1 while validating TX_2.
  - For shorter private chains, the attacker either persists in mining until achieving chain superiority or abandons the attempt after timeout thresholds.

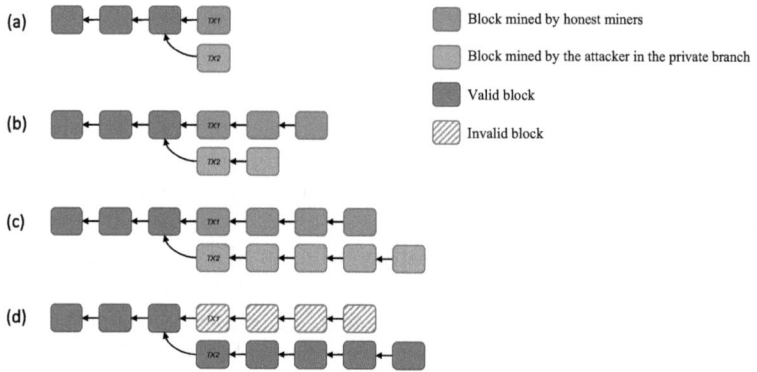

Fig. 1. Outline of the Naive DSA with $z = 3$. (a) The attacker initiates transaction TX_1 with the merchant and secretly mines a block containing a conflicting transaction TX_2. (b) The attacker continues mining on the private branch. (c) After the block containing TX_1, 3 additional blocks are added. The merchant delivers the product. (d) The attacker releases the private branch, which successfully overtakes the honest chain, causing TX_2 to be accepted and completing the double-spending attack.

2.2 Related Work

Scholarly investigations of DSAs predominantly examine two analytical dimensions: *success probability analysis* and *economic profitability assessment*. Success probability analysis quantifies attack success likelihood under fixed attack parameters while excluding cost considerations. Economic profitability assessment takes into account the attack cost, trying to minimize it while identifying the strategy that maximizes the attacker's potential profits. These approaches provide a framework for understanding and mitigating the impact of DSAs on blockchain systems. We review key works in both categories below.

Success Probability Analysis. Nakamoto [15] pioneered the analysis of DSAs in the Bitcoin whitepaper, modeling the attacker's block generation capability through a Poisson distribution. This seminal work demonstrated that when the attacker's computational power remains below 50%, the success probability of DSAs decays exponentially with increasing block confirmations. Rosenfeld [19] extended this framework by refining the expected block generation of the attacker using a binomial distribution, achieving enhanced precision in the estimation of the probability of attack. Later, Jang et al. [13] derived the probability distribution function for the success time of the DSA through rigorous probabilistic analysis.

Sompolinsky et al. [21] identified the pre-mining strategy, where attackers initiate block generation before transaction submission. Their analysis revealed that pre-mining under unbounded time constraints yields higher success probabilities than naive DSA strategies. Pinzon et al. [16] investigated time advantages in DSAs, quantifying success probabilities when attackers exploit predefined time windows for block generation. However, high success probabilities do not inherently guarantee profitability, as practical constraints, including time sensitivity, mining costs, and opportunity losses from block rewards, critically influence attack viability. Consequently, numerous studies have adopted profit-maximization frameworks to analyze optimal DSA strategies [8–11,14,21–23].

Economic Profitability Assessment. In economic profitability assessment, Gervais et al. [8] and Sompolinsky et al. [21] employed Markov Decision Processes (MDPs) to evaluate rewards in naive DSA scenarios. Another way to approach this is by using discrete-time finite-horizon stochastic processes [11], which employ optimal stopping and switching models to maximize expected rewards within a limited timeframe. Hinz et al. [10] has formalized DSA as an optimal sequential decision-making problem, introducing quantitative metrics to evaluate vulnerabilities in PoW systems. Zheng et al. [22,23] introduced adaptive DSA strategies where attackers dynamically adjust decisions per timeslot, and further developed Reinforcement Adaptive DSA (RA-DSA) by incorporating network propagation conditions. They calculate the profit-maximized attack strategy using the SDP-based theoretical framework. Additionally, Jang et al. [13] established closed-form expressions for expected DSA profits through pure probabilistic analysis, enhancing time-dependent reward predictions.

3 Pre-mining Double-Spending Attack

This section introduces the Pre-mining DSA Model under fixed and limited costs. We first outline the attack steps, then calculate the attack success probability and expected profit.

3.1 Basic Assumptions

We employ the block generation model developed by Rosenfeld [19]. Let p denote the attacker's hash power proportion and q the honest network's hash power proportion, with $p + q = 1$. Since an attacker with $p > q$ can always launch a successful double-spending attack, we assume $p \leq q$. The mining difficulty is fixed (e.g., Bitcoin's 10-minute block interval), resulting in a constant block generation rate. The block generation process is equivalent to a discrete Markov process: the attacker's chain grows by one block with probability p, and the honest chain grows by one block with probability q. Let $\Delta = j - i$ represent the honest chain's lead over the attacker's chain, where i and j are the block counts of the attacker and honest chain, respectively. At each timeslot, Δ evolves as (Fig. 2):

$$\Delta_{t+1} = \begin{cases} \Delta_t - 1 & \text{with probability } p, \\ \Delta_t + 1 & \text{with probability } q. \end{cases} \tag{1}$$

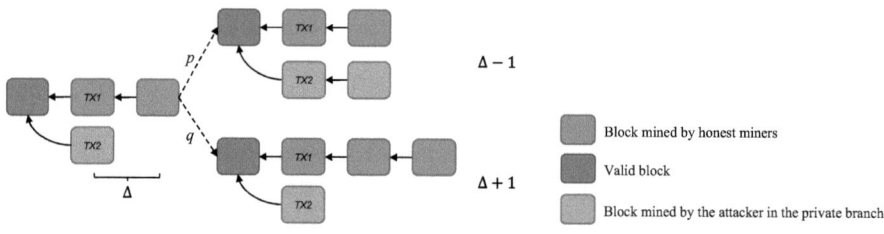

Fig. 2. The random process of block generation model.

3.2 Attack Strategy

The Pre-mining DSA draws from Sompolinsky's generalized pre-mining attack [21], an extension of the Finney attack. The key steps are as follows:

Pre-mining Phase. The attacker attempts to generate a private chain with a conflicting transaction TX_2, aiming to gain a first-move advantage and maximize success probability against the honest chain, while considering the pre-mining cost T_p and the number of pre-mining timeslots.

Observation 1. *During the pre-mining phase, if the length of the attacker's private chain becomes shorter than that of the honest chain, the attacker will promptly abandon the private chain and initiate a new fork from the honest chain to resume pre-mining.*

This strategy is dominant, as it maximizes the difference in length between the private chain and the honest chain, thereby improving the attacker's chances of success.

Confirmation Phase. After T_p rounds of pre-mining, the attacker broadcasts the transaction TX_1 to the network and waits for confirmation. At the same time, the attacker continue withholding the private chain and mining on it (Fig. 3).

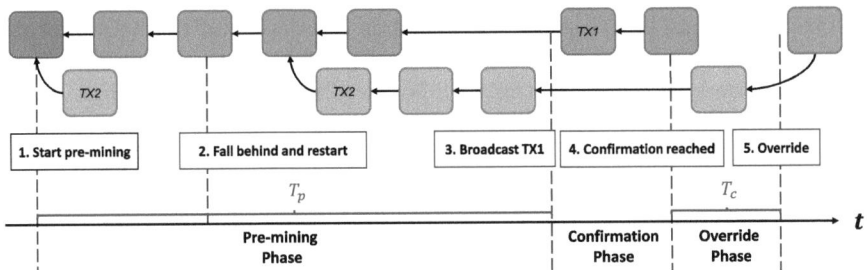

Fig. 3. Pre-mining DSA with $z = 1$. (1) The attacker starts mining a private branch containing transaction TX_2. (2) The attacker falls behind and restarts pre-mining. (3) TX_1 is broadcast. (4) TX_1 gets enough confirmations. (5) The attacker publishes the private branch and successfully double spends.

Override Phase. The merchant confirms TX_1 once z blocks are appended to its containing block, triggering goods delivery. The attacker continues mining on the private chain. If it surpasses the honest chain, the attacker releases it (attack succeeds). If unsuccessful after T_c timeslots, the attack is abandoned due to cost constraints.

3.3 Success Probability and Expected Profit

Next, we introduce the probability of success and expected profit of pre-mining DSA. The total success probability and expected profit are derived by analyzing the pre-mining, confirmation, and override phases.

Pre-mining Phase. First, we calculate the number of blocks the attacker leads in the pre-mining phase. This is a random walk problem on the non-negative integer axis. Let $P_p(n, t; p, q)$ denote the probability of the attacker leading by n blocks after t timeslots. For simplicity, we denote this as $P_p(n, t)$. At timeslot $t + 1$, if the honest network mines a block (probability q), the attacker's lead decreases to $n-1$; if the attacker mines a block (probability p), the lead increases to $n + 1$. When $n = 0$, in the next timeslot, the attacker either gains a lead of 1 with probability p or abandons the private chain and restarts mining on the honest chain (lead remains 0). Thus, the recurrence relation is:

$$\begin{cases} P_p(n,t) = qP_p(n+1, t-1) + pP_p(n-1, t-1), & n > 0 \\ P_p(0,t) = qP_p(1, t-1) + pP_p(0, t-1), & n = 0 \\ P_p(0,0) = 1 \end{cases} \quad (2)$$

We can solve this equation using dynamic programming [1], as formalized in Algorithm 2 of Appendix A.

Confirmation Phase. We calculate the expected number of blocks mined by the attacker, denoted as m, during the time period in which the merchant confirms transaction TX_1. We model m using a negative binomial distribution, which represents the count of successful events (blocks discovered by the attacker) occurring before observing z failures (blocks found by the honest network). The probability of the attacker mining m blocks during the z-block confirmation period is given by $P_w(m; p, q)$. For simplicity, we denote this as $P_w(m)$. It follows a negative binomial distribution :

$$P_w(m) = \binom{m+z-1}{m} p^m q^z. \tag{3}$$

Override Phase. The final stage involves computing the probability of the number of blocks by which the attacker lags behind the honest networks. This scenario can be modeled as a bounded random walk process. Let $P_c(k, l, t; p, q)$ denote the probability that at time t, the attacker's chain is k blocks behind the honest chain, given an initial deficit of l blocks. For notational simplicity, we write this as $P_c(k, l, t)$. For $k > 0$, the deficit evolves stochastically based on mining outcomes.

According to the definition of k and l, we have the initial conditions:

$$\begin{cases} P_c(l, l, 0) = 1, & for\ all\ l \\ P_c(k, l, 0) = 0, & for\ all\ k! = l \end{cases} \tag{4}$$

For $l \geq 0$, the evolution of $P_c(k, l, t)$ follows the recursive relations given in the governing equations. This equation can be solved by dynamic programming, as formalized in Algorithm 3 of Appendix A.

$$\begin{cases} P_c(k, l, t) = p P_c(k+1, l, t-1) + q P_c(k-1, l, t-1), & l \geq 0\ and\ k > 0 \\ P_c(k, l, t) = p P_c(k+1, l, t-1) & l \geq 0\ and\ k = 0, -1 \end{cases} \tag{5}$$

For any time t, the attack succeeds when $k = -1$, at which point the random walk terminates. The term $P_c(-1, l, t)$ thus represents the success probability of the attack at time t.

For the initial condition if $l < 0$, we assume the attacker immediately releases their private chain and the attack succeeds. We introduced notation $P_c^\delta(l, t)$ specifically for override probability at time t, given an initial deficit of l blocks.

$$P_c^\delta(l, t) = \begin{cases} P_c(-1, l, t) & l \geq -1 \\ P_c(l, l, t) & l < -1 \end{cases} \tag{6}$$

Total Success Probability. Let n be the attacker's lead from the pre-mining phase, m the blocks mined during the confirmation phase, and z the honest chain's growth during confirmation. The attacker's lag in the override phase is $z - n - m$. The total success probability of Pre-mining DSA is:

$$\mathcal{P}_{\text{total}}(T_p, T_c) = \sum_{m=0}^{\infty} \sum_{n=0}^{T_p} \sum_{t=0}^{T_c} P_p(n, T_p) P_w(m) P_c^\delta(z+1-n-m, t). \tag{7}$$

Expected Profit. Let b denote the stolen transaction value and d the fixed block reward. The attacker's cost includes computational cost (proportional to hash power p) and opportunity cost (foregone block rewards). The per-slot cost is $cost = p \cdot d$, paid regardless of mining success. The expected profit is:

$$\mathcal{R}(T_p, T_c) = \sum_{m=0}^{\infty} \sum_{n=0}^{T_p} \sum_{t=0}^{T_c} P_p(n, T_p) P_w(m) P_c^{\delta}(z+1-n-m, t) \cdot r(b, T_p, z, m, t). \quad (8)$$

where

$$r(b, T_p, z, m, t) = b - (T_p + z + 1 + m + t) \cdot cost. \quad (9)$$

4 Adaptive Pre-mining Double-Spending Attack

This section introduces the Adaptive Pre-mining Model, which identifies optimal attack strategies for double-spending. While fixed-strategy Pre-mining enhances the attacker's success probability, it exhibits limitations in dynamic scenarios. For instance:

- If the attacker rapidly accumulates sufficient lead during pre-mining, early broadcasting of TX_1 becomes advantageous.
- If the attacker's chain is significantly ahead of the honest chain during the override phase, they may choose not to release it immediately. Instead, the attacker can mine a longer private chain, leveraging a selfish mining attack.

To address these dynamics, we expand the attacker's decision space by formalizing the Pre-mining attack as a markov decision process (MDP) and solving it via SDP. Furthermore, we incorporate practical network conditions through a communication parameter w, which quantifies the proportion of honest hash power following the attacker's fork when equal-length chains exist. A higher w indicates superior network connectivity for the attacker, enabling faster propagation of newly released adversarial blocks.

4.1 MDP Formulation

The attacker observe the current length of the pre-mined private chain and the honest chain, estimating the potential profit to decide whether to broadcast the transaction and initiate an override. Therefore, typically after a block is published, the attacker reaches a decision point. We need to extract the features that influence the available actions and the attacker's potential profit and represent them as a state vector.

State. The state of the system is defined as:

$$s = (n_a, n_h, n_p) \quad (10)$$

where:

- n_a: Blocks mined by the attacker *after* broadcasting TX_1 (includes confirmation and override phases)
- n_h: Blocks mined by the honest network *after* TX_1 broadcast
- n_p: The number of blocks by which the attacker's chain is ahead of the honest chain during the pre-mining phase.

In the Adaptive Pre-mining model, the finite attack cost is reflected in two aspects:

Table 1. State transition matrix for Adaptive Pre-mining DSA.

State Condition	Decision	Next State	Probability
$n_a = n_h = n_p = 0$ (Initial state)	(0,0)	(0,0,1)	p
		(0,0,0)	q
$n_a = n_h = 0, n_p = T_p^{\max}$ (Pre-mining termination)	(1,0)	(1,0,T)	p
		(0,1,T)	q
$n_p > 0, n_a = n_h = 0$ (Pre-mining phase)	(1,0)	(1,0,n_p)	p
		(0,1,n_p)	q
	(0,0)	(0,0,n_p+1)	p
		(0,0,n_p-1)	q
$n_p > 0$, n_a or $n_h > 0$ (Active competition)	(1,0)	(n_a+1, n_h, n_p)	p
		(n_a, n_h+1, n_p)	q
	(1,1)	*	1
$n_a + n_h = T_c^{\max}$ (Attack duration limit)	(1,1)	*	1

* denotes the terminal state of state transition.

1) *Pre-mining Termination*: We set an upper bound for the number of pre-mining rounds that the attacker is willing to accept. That is, $n_p \leq T_p^{\max}$. When $n_p = T_p^{\max}$, the attacker must broadcast transaction TX_1.
2) *Attack Duration Limit*: We set an upper bound for the number of mining rounds the attacker is willing to accept during the override phase, denoted as $T_c^{\max}$. That is, $n_a + n_h \leq T_c^{\max}$.

Decision. We use d_s to denote the decision variable at state s, which is defined by two binary decisions $d_s = (d_t, d_o) \in \mathcal{D} = \{0,1\}^2$, where d_t controls transaction broadcasting during pre-mining ($d_t = 1$ broadcasts TX_1, and $d_t = 0$ continues mining), and d_o governs the release of the private chain during the confirmation/override phases ($d_o = 1$ triggers the override, and $d_o = 0$ withholds and continues mining). d_s is defined as follows:

$$d_s = \begin{cases} (0,0) & \text{if } n_a = n_h = n_p = 0 \text{ (Initial state)} \\ (1,0) & \text{if } n_a = n_h = 0 \text{ and } n_p = T_p^{\max} \text{ (Pre-mining termination)} \\ (1,0) \text{ or } (0,0) & \text{if } n_p > 0 \text{ and } n_a = n_h = 0 \text{ (Pre-mining phase)} \\ (1,0) \text{ or } (1,1) & \text{if } n_p > 0 \text{ and } (n_a > 0 \text{ or } n_h > 0) \text{ (Active competition)} \\ (1,1) & \text{if } n_a + n_h = T_c^{\max} \text{ (Attack duration limit)} \end{cases} \quad (11)$$

Decision rules are hierarchically structured based on the state of the system $s = (n_a, n_h, n_p)$. In the *initial state* (when $n_a = n_h = n_p = 0$), the attacker begins pre-mining with $d_s = (0,0)$, generating blocks without broadcasting or releasing the chain. Once the *pre-mining limit* is reached ($n_p = T_p^{\max}$), the attacker must broadcast TX$_1$ and transition to the confirmation phase with $d_s = (1,0)$.

During *active pre-mining* (when $n_p > 0$ and $n_a = n_h = 0$), the attacker faces a choice between broadcasting TX$_1$ or continuing pre-mining, represented by $d_s = (1,0)$ or $d_s = (0,0)$.

In the *override phase* (when $n_a > 0$ or $n_h > 0$), the attacker's decision space expands to $d_s = (1,0)$ or $d_s = (1,1)$, allowing the attacker to either continue mining or immediately release the private chain. Termination is mandatory once the attack duration limit $T_c^{\max}$ is reached, requiring $d_s = (1,1)$ to finalize the attack. These rules ensure the attack remains cost-bound while balancing strategic flexibility with computational constraints.

Transition Probabilities. The state transition function $T(s'|s, d_s)$ governs the probabilistic evolution between blockchain states under attack decisions. The state transition probability is determined by the current state and the decision taken, as seen in Table 1.

Reward Matrix. We denote the reward for executing a decision d_s at state s as $r(s, d_s)$. When $d_s = (1,1)$, the attacker releases the private chain, terminates the attack, and obtains the double-spending reward. The magnitude of this reward is determined by the terminal state s, which we represent through a three-dimensional matrix $R_s[n_a, n_p, n_h]$. Prior to receiving rewards, the attacker incurs mining costs. The reward function is therefore defined as:

$$r(s, d_s) = \begin{cases} R_s[n_a, n_p, n_h], & \text{if } d_s = (1,1) \\ -cost, & \text{otherwise} \end{cases} \quad (12)$$

The reward matrix $R_s[n_a, n_p, n_h]$ depends on three critical factors: the relative progress between the attacker and honest miners, the confirmation number z, and the network communication parameter w, as shown in Table 2.

(1) When the attacker's private chain length exceeds the honest chain ($n_a + n_p > n_h$) and the confirmation depth z is satisfied ($n_h > z$), full rewards

$b + (n_a + n_h)d$ are obtained; (2) If chain lengths equal $(n_a + n_p = n_h \geq z)$, the attacker cannot succeed immediately by choosing $d_s = (1,1)$. Instead, they must perform an additional mining operation. Here, we calculate the **expected reward** after one slot; (3) When the honest chain dominates $(n_a + n_p < n_h)$, rewards vanish regardless of confirmation status; (4) Under insufficient confirmation depth $(n_h \leq z)$, rewards depend solely on the attacker's chain length $((n_a + n_p)d)$ when leading, or follow a modified probabilistic model $p(n_a + n_h + 1)d + qw(n_a + n_h)d - cost$ when chains are equal.

Table 2. Stop Reward Matrix

State Conditions		$R_s[n_a, n_h, n_p]$
$n_a + n_h = T_c^{max}$	$n_h > z$, $n_a + n_p > n_h$	$b + (n_a + n_h) \cdot d$
	$n_a + n_p = n_h$	$p[b + (n_a + n_h + 1)d] + wq(n_a + n_h)d - cost$
	$n_a + n_p < n_h$	0
	$n_h \leq z$, $n_a + n_p > n_h$	$(n_a + n_p) \cdot d$
	$n_a + n_p = n_h$	$p(n_a + n_h + 1)d + qw(n_a + n_h)d - cost$
	$n_a + n_p < n_h$	0

4.2 Optimal Decision-Making Based on SDP

Let $R(s)$ denote the expected return of the optimal attack strategy at state s. In the SDP framework, the attacker's objective is to dynamically select optimal decisions that maximize the expected reward. Following the Bellman optimality principle [20], the value function is formulated as:

$$R(s) = \max_{d_s} \left\{ r(s, d_s) + \sum_{s'} T(s'|s, d_s) R(s') \right\} \quad (13)$$

In practical implementation, we represent $R(s)$ through a three-dimensional reward matrix $R[n_a, n_h, n_p]$. Based on Eqs. (11) (12) (13), the solution of $R[n_a, n_h, n_p]$ constitutes the following optimization problem:

$$R[n_a, n_h, n_p] = \begin{cases} \max\{R_s[n_a, n_p, n_h], R_c[n_a, n_p, n_h]\}, \\ \text{if } n_a > 0 \text{ or } n_h > 0; \\ \max\{R_p[n_a, n_p, n_h], R_c[n_a, n_p, n_h]\}, \\ \text{if } n_a = n_h = 0, 0 < n_p < T_p^{max}; \\ R_c[n_a, n_p, n_h], \\ \text{if } n_a = n_h = 0, n_p = T_p^{max}; \\ pR[n_a, n_h, n_p + 1] + qR[n_a, n_h, n_p] - cost, \\ \text{if } n_a = n_h = n_p = 0 \end{cases} \quad (14)$$

where:
- $R_c[n_a, n_p, n_h] = pR[n_a + 1, n_h, n_p] + qR[n_a, n_h + 1, n_p] - cost$ represents the expected rewards of continuing mining at state $s = [n_a, n_p, n_h]$.
- $R_p[n_a, n_p, n_h] = p \cdot R[n_a, n_h, n_p + 1] + qR[n_a, n_h, n_p - 1] - cost$ denotes the expected rewards of pre-ming at state $s = [n_a, n_p, n_h]$.

The optimal attack policy $D[n_a, n_h, n_p]$ and associated value function $R[n_a, n_h, n_p]$ are computed through stochastic dynamic programming (SDP) with backward induction across the state space, as formalized in Algorithm 1. The iterative backward induction in Algorithm 1 provably converges to the optimal policy due to the finite state space and contraction mapping properties of the Bellman operator [17].[1]

Algorithm 1. SDP Solver for Adaptive Pre-mining Attack

1: **Input:** $b, p, d, z, cost, T_p^{\max}, T_c^{\max}, w$
2: **Output:** Optimal decision matrix $D = \{d_s\}$, expected reward $R[0,0,0]$
3: **Initialize:**
4:    $R^{\text{cur}}, R^{\text{next}} \leftarrow$ 3D zero matrices of size $(T_c^{\max} + 1)^2 \times (T_p^{\max} + 1)$
5:    $D \leftarrow$ 3D matrix initialized with $(0,0)$ ▷ Policy storage
6:    $tol = 10^{-3}$ §
7: Generate stop reward matrix R_s using Table 2
8: **while** True **do**   ▷ Convergence loop
9:    **for** $n_p = T_p^{\max}$ **downto** 0 **do**   ▷ Reverse pre-mining progress
10:       **for** $total\_rounds = 2T_c^{\max}$ **downto** 0 **do**   ▷ Total rounds $n_a + n_h$
11:          **for** $n_a = \min(total\_rounds, T_c^{\max})$ **downto** 0 **do**
12:             $n_h \leftarrow total\_rounds - n_a$
13:             Calculate $R^{\text{next}}[n_a, n_h, n_p]$ via Eq. (14)
14:             $D[n_a, n_h, n_p] \leftarrow \arg\max$ ▷ Record optimal policy
15:          **end for**
16:       **end for**
17:    **end for**
18:    **if** $\|R^{\text{next}} - R^{\text{cur}}\|_{\max} < tol$ **then**
19:       **break**
20:    **end if**
21:    Swap R^{cur} and R^{next} ▷ Efficient update
22: **end while**
23: **return** $\{D\}, R^{\text{cur}}[0,0,0]$

---

5 Performance Evaluation

In this section, we conduct numerical experiments to evaluate the Pre-mining DSA strategy and the Adaptive Pre-mining DSA strategy.

---

[1] The value iteration terminates when the maximum difference between successive value function estimates falls below a convergence tolerance tol. We set tol = 10^{-3} throughout our experiments.

5.1 Pre-mining DSA

Pre-mining Strategy Analysis. Figure 4 illustrates the expected progression of the attacker's chain lead during the pre-mining phase $P(n)$ evaluated under varying levels of adversarial computational power p. As T_p increases, the expected pre-mined blocks grow progressively but eventually stabilize at an upper bound (annotated with circular markers), indicating that the attacker's pre-mining capacity is limited. This upper bound is derived from the following recurrence relation, $P(n) = pP(n-1) + qP(n+1)$, and the boundary condition $P(0) = pP(0) + qP(1)$. By solving this recurrence relation, we obtain the result $P(n) = \frac{1-2\alpha}{1-\alpha} \left(\frac{\alpha}{1-\alpha}\right)^n$ The result matches the finding in [21], where the attacker's lead increases with p but at a diminishing rate due to the fixed mining difficulty.

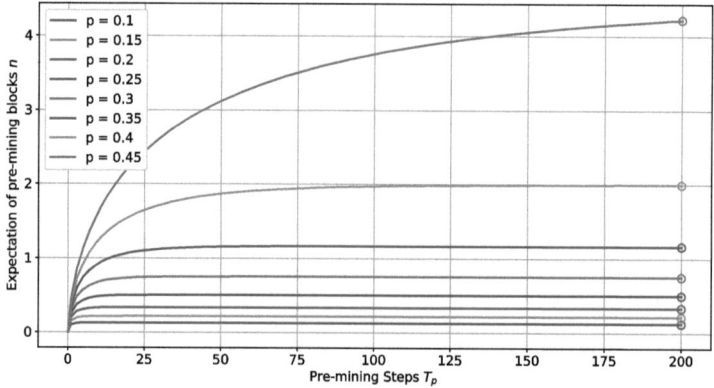

Fig. 4. Expectation of pre-mining blocks with T_p for different mining power.

Success Probability Analysis. In Fig. 5, we show the relationship between the attack success probability, the pre-mining time steps T_P and attack duration limit T_c. The results indicate that as T_c increases, the success probability increases. However, the growth rate slows down as T_P and T_c increase, eventually stabilizing at an upper bound. This suggests that the success probability of the attack is constrained even with more pre-mining steps and attack duration time.

Profit Analysis. In Fig. 6, we present the expected reward of the attacker as a function of T_P and T_c. The results show that as T_P and T_c increase, the expected reward initially rises but then decreases, reflecting the diminishing returns of the attack as it progresses.

It can be observed that although longer pre-mining durations and extended waiting rounds lead to higher attack success probabilities, they do not result in greater overall rewards. Consequently, for profit-driven attackers, determining the optimal pre-mining duration and attack timeline as strategic parameters to maximize expected returns constitutes a critical component of rational adversarial decision-making.

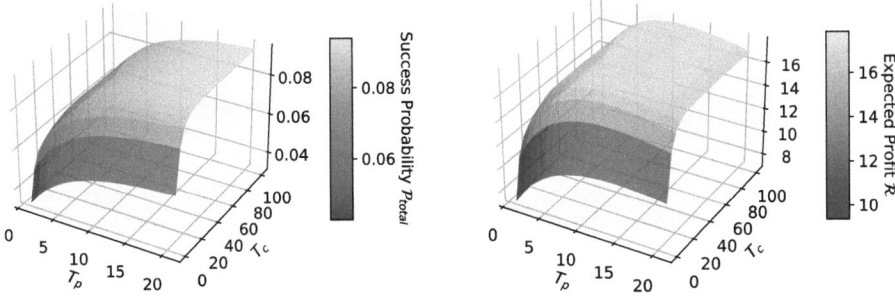

Fig. 5. Conditional Success Probability.   **Fig. 6.** Expected reward.

5.2 Adaptive Pre-mining DSA

We conduct comparative analyses of four prominent double-spending attack strategies: (1) Naive DSA [15], (2) Adaptive DSA [22], (3) Reinforcement Adaptive DSA [23], and (4) our proposed Adaptive Pre-Mining DSA. Our experimental framework establishes a default parameter configuration ($p = 0.3$, $z = 6$, $d = 6.25$, $w = 0.5$, $T_p^{\max} = 20$, $T_c^{\max} = 100$) across all comparative analyses.

Impact of the Transaction Value b. In Fig. 7, we present the relationship between the expected reward (in BTC) and parameter b. The results indicate that as b increases, the expected reward increases for all strategies. This is because when b is large enough, the DSA will make a great profit once successful. Thus, the attacker prefers to keep hiding the fork and persists in launching attacks even under adverse conditions. Adaptive Pre-Mining DSA significantly outperforms the other strategies. Especially for larger values of b, the expected reward of Adaptive Pre-Mining DSA grows faster, indicating its superior performance in larger-scale transactions.

Impact of Block Reward d. In Fig. 8, we show the relationship between the expected reward and parameter d, the reward for mining a new block. Since coinbase rewards dominate block mining rewards, we focus on d. The results indicate that when d is large, the expected reward is low, but as d decreases, the expected reward increases for all attack strategies, with Adaptive Pre-Mining DSA showing a notably higher reward as d decreases.

The expected reward is influenced by two factors. First, it consists of the coinbase reward (d) and the stolen coins (b). With b fixed, the reward depends largely on d. Second, the loss from a failed attack is proportional to d, so a smaller d leads to a higher expected reward. Furthermore, as the coinbase reward halves

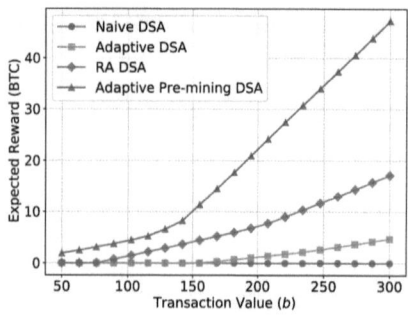
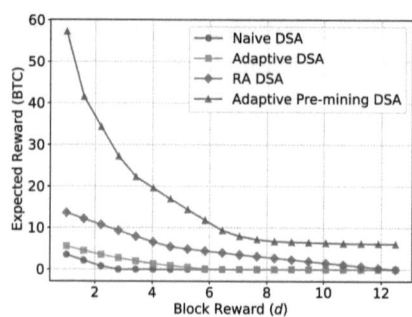

Fig. 7. Attacker's expected reward versus varying b.

Fig. 8. Attacker's expected reward versus varying d.

every four years, a decrease in d leads to a rapid increase in the expected reward, encouraging the attacker to initiate double-spending attacks.

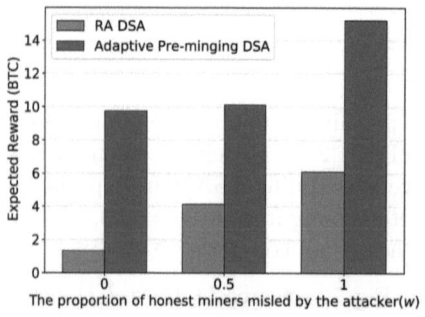
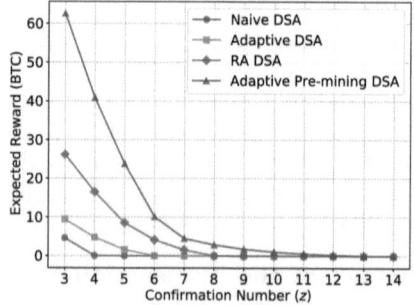

Fig. 9. Attacker's expected reward versus varying w.

Fig. 10. Attacker's expected reward versus varying z.

Impact of Network Communication Parameter w. In this experiment, we study the impact of the network communication parameter w on the attacker's expected reward. From Fig. 9, we can see that the attacker's expected reward steadily increases as w increases. This indicates that the double-spending attack becomes more favorable when the attacker controls a higher proportion of the honest hash power.

Impact of the Number of Confirmation Number z. Figure 10 illustrates the effect of the number of confirmation blocks (z) on the attacker's expected reward under various DSA strategies. As z increases, the expected reward decreases exponentially, indicating that a higher number of required confirmation blocks reduces the likelihood of a successful double-spending attack. This result underscores that merchants can significantly reduce the risk of double-spending attacks by requiring more confirmation blocks, highlighting the importance of selecting an appropriate confirmation depth to secure Bitcoin transactions.

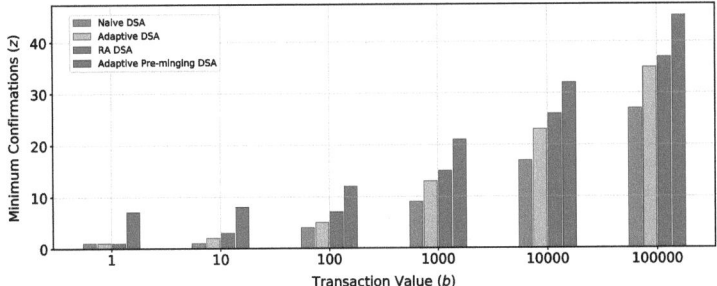

Fig. 11. Minimum of confirmation number z versus varying b.

Defense: Adaptive Confirmation Thresholds. Figure 11 illustrates the block confirmation thresholds under different attack strategies when the attacker reaches a zero-profit condition. To mitigate security risks, we recommend that merchants dynamically adjust their confirmation requirements based on transaction values, as exemplified by adopting 12 confirmations for transactions valued at 100 and 21 confirmations for those valued at 1000.

6 Conclusion

In this paper, we have developed a constrained pre-mining attack framework that identifies optimal strategies under real-world limitations. Our model integrates stochastic decision-making with practical attack scenarios, demonstrating that strategic pre-mining can fundamentally undermine blockchain security assumptions. Comparative simulation results show that our strategies achieve both high success rates and significant profitability. These findings offer new theoretical insights into the design of consensus protocols resilient to adaptive adversaries, while also highlighting previously overlooked risks in decentralized systems. Future research should incorporate dynamic network conditions, cryptocurrency price fluctuations, and competitive attacker interactions under resource constraints to improve protocol security and decentralized finance.

A Dynamic Programming Algorithms

Algorithm 2. Dynamic Programming Solution for Pre-mining Random Walk

1: **Input:** T_p, p, $q = 1 - p$
2: **Output:** Probability distribution $P_p(n, T_p)$ for all $n \in [0, T_p]$
3: Initialize $P_p[0 : T_p][0 : T_p] \leftarrow 0$ ▷ State: $P_p[\text{lead}][\text{time}]$
4: $P_p[0][0] \leftarrow 1$ ▷ Initial condition: $P_p(0, 0) = 1$
5: **for** $\tau = 1$ **to** T_p **do** ▷ Time evolution $\tau \in [1, T_p]$
6:     **for** $n = 0$ **to** τ **do** ▷ Lead $n \in [0, \tau]$
7:         **if** $n = 0$ **then**
8:             $P_p[0][\tau] \leftarrow (1-p)P_p[0][\tau - 1] + (1-p)P_p[1][\tau - 1]$ ▷ Boundary condition
9:         **else if** $n < \tau$ **then**
10:             $P_p[n][\tau] \leftarrow pP_p[n-1][\tau - 1] + (1-p)P_p[n+1][\tau - 1]$ ▷ General case
11:         **end if**
12:     **end for**
13: **end for**
14: **return** $P_p[0 : T_p][T_p]$ ▷ Final distribution at time T_p

---

Algorithm 3. Dynamic Programming for Override Random Walk

1: **Input:** l, p, $q = 1 - p$, T_c
2: **Output:** $\{P_c^\delta(l, t)\}_{t=0}^{T_c}$ ▷ Termination probability sequence
3: **if** $l < 0$ **then** ▷ Boundary case: immediate termination
4:     **return** $[1.0] + [0.0]^{T_c}$
5: **end if**
6: Initialize $P_c[\cdot, \cdot, \cdot] \leftarrow 0$ ▷ 3D array: $P_c[k, l, t]$
7: $P_c[l, l, 0] \leftarrow 1$ ▷ Initial condition
8: **for** $t = 1$ **to** T_c **do** ▷ Time evolution
9:     $k_{\max} \leftarrow l + t$ ▷ Maximum possible deficit
10:     **for** $k = 0$ **to** $k_{\max}$ **do** ▷ Current deficit states
11:         **if** $k > 0$ **then** ▷ General deficit propagation
12:             $P_c[k, l, t] \leftarrow pP_c[k+1, l, t-1] + qP_c[k-1, l, t-1]$
13:         **else if** $k = 0$ **then** ▷ Boundary absorption
14:             $P_c[0, l, t] \leftarrow pP_c[1, l, t-1]$
15:         **end if**
16:     **end for**
17: **end for**
18: **return** $P_c(-1, l, t)$ ▷ Termination probability sequence

---

References

1. Bellman, R.: On the theory of dynamic programming. Proc. Natl. Acad. Sci. **38**(8), 716–719 (1952)

2. Bellman, R.: The theory of dynamic programming. Bull. Am. Math. Soc. **60**(6), 503–515 (1954)
3. Bellman, R.: Dynamic programming. Science **153**(3731), 34–37 (1966)
4. Cash, B.: Bitcoin cash. Development **2** (2019)
5. Chen, W., Wu, J., Zheng, Z., Chen, C., Zhou, Y.: Market manipulation of bitcoin: Evidence from mining the Mt. Gox transaction network. In: IEEE INFOCOM 2019-IEEE Conference on Computer Communications, pp. 964–972. IEEE (2019)
6. Coinbase: Coinbase's perspective on the recent ethereum classic (etc) double spend (2020). https://www.coinbase.com/blog/coinbases-perspective-on-the-recent-ethereum-classic-etc-double-spend
7. coindesk.com: Coindesk (2025). https://www.coindesk.com
8. Gervais, A., Karame, G.O., Wüst, K., Glykantzis, V., Ritzdorf, H., Capkun, S.: On the security and performance of proof of work blockchains. In: Proceedings of the 2016 ACM SIGSAC Conference on Computer and Communications Security, pp. 3–16 (2016)
9. Grunspan, C., Pérez-Marco, R.: On profitability of nakamoto double spend. Probab. Eng. Inf. Sci. **36**(3), 732–746 (2022)
10. Hinz, J.: Resilience analysis for double spending via sequential decision optimization. Appl. Syst. Innov. **3**(1), 7 (2020)
11. Hinz, J., Taylor, P.: A note on optimal double spending attacks. In: de Gier, J., Praeger, C., Tao, T. (eds) 2017 MATRIX Annals. MBS, vol. 2, pp. 545–551. Springer, Cham (2019). https://doi.org/10.1007/978-3-030-04161-8_47
12. Huang, H., Kong, W., Zhou, S., Zheng, Z., Guo, S.: A survey of state-of-the-art on blockchains: theories, modelings, and tools. ACM Comput. Surv. (CSUR) **54**(2), 1–42 (2021)
13. Jang, J., Lee, H.: Profitable double-spending attacks. CoRR abs/1903.01711 (2019). http://arxiv.org/abs/1903.01711
14. Liao, K., Katz, J.: Incentivizing double-spend collusion in bitcoin. In: Financial Cryptography Bitcoin Workshop (2017)
15. Nakamoto, S.: Bitcoin: a peer-to-peer electronic cash system. Decent. Bus. Rev. 21260 (2008)
16. Pinzón, C., Rocha, C.: Double-spend attack models with time advantange for bitcoin. Electron. Notes Theor. Comput. Sci. **329**, 79–103 (2016)
17. Puterman, M.L.: Markov decision processes. Handb. Oper. Res. Manage. Sci. **2**, 331–434 (1990)
18. Reed, J.: Litecoin: an introduction to litecoin cryptocurrency and litecoin mining (2017)
19. Rosenfeld, M.: Analysis of hashrate-based double spending. CoRR abs/1402.2009 (2014). http://arxiv.org/abs/1402.2009
20. Ross, S.M.: Introduction to Stochastic Dynamic Programming. Academic Press (2014)
21. Sompolinsky, Y., Zohar, A.: Bitcoin's security model revisited. arXiv preprint arXiv:1605.09193 (2016)
22. Zheng, J., Huang, H., Li, C., Zheng, Z., Guo, S.: Revisiting double-spending attacks on the bitcoin blockchain: New findings. In: 2021 IEEE/ACM 29th International Symposium on Quality of Service (IWQOS), pp. 1–6. IEEE (2021)
23. Zheng, J., Huang, H., Zheng, Z., Guo, S.: Adaptive double-spending attacks on pow-based blockchains. IEEE Trans. Dependable Secure Comput. (2023)

Author Index

A
Acay, Coşku 334
Alhaidari, Abdulrahman 211
Amada, Takumi 294
Ayday, Erman 395

B
Bahrini, Mehrdad 1
Balioglu, Berkay Kemal 22
Bartolomeo, Giovanni 43
Bobon, Stanislav 126

C
Chekole, Eyasu Getahun 169
Chi, Jialin 63
Cortier, Véronique 86

D
Debant, Alexandre 86
Deng, Robert 354
Desharnais, Josée 233
Dong, Hai 314
Duan, Haixin 147

F
Fan, Zhenglin 374
Feng, Dengguo 63
Franza, Simone 106
Freye, Merle 1
Fu, Ximing 415

G
Gambs, Sébastien 233
Gast, Stefan 106
Gaudry, Pierrick 86
Gavenda, Jiri 126
Gruss, Daniel 106
Guo, Bingyang 147
Gursoy, M. Emre 22

H
Halim, Howard 169
Herbst, Alexander 1
Hong, Cheng 63
Hong, Geng 147
Huang, Zhicheng 190

I
Imine, Abdessamad 274
Iwamoto, Mitsugu 294

J
Jia, Ze 374
Jiang, Hui 415

K
Kalal, Bhavani 211
Khodaie, Alireza 22
Kohn, Matthias 1
Korichi, Youcef 233

L
Lafourcade, Pascal 253
Laouir, Ala Eddine 274
Li, Mo 415
Li, Ruixuan 147
Li, Wenting 190
Li, Yuxian 354
Li, ZheChen 63
Liu, Baojun 147
Liu, Chuanyi 415
Liu, Mingxuan 147
López Pérez, Elsa 253

M
Ma, Meng 190
Ma, Yihui 147
Malaka, Rainer 1
Myers, Andrew C. 334

N
Namazi, Mina 395
Namiki, Takumi 294
Neela, Sudheendra Raghav 106

O
Olivier-Anclin, Charles 253
Onete, Cristina 253

P
Palanisamy, Balaji 211
Pan, Qingfeng 147
Papon, Clément 253
Puntigam, Nora 106

R
Reijsbergen, Daniël 169
Ren, Pengkun 314
Ren, Silei 334

S
Sedlacek, Vladimir 126
Shi, Fan 147
Sohr, Karsten 1
Sun, Jianfei 354
Sun, Tianqi 63
Sural, Shamik 211
Svenda, Petr 126

T
Tari, Zahir 314
Tawbi, Nadia 233

U
Ullrich, Johanna 106

V
Vučinić, Mališa 253

W
Wang, Ping 190
Watanabe, Yohei 294
Wu, Axin 63

X
Xie, Lijia 433
Xin, Yansen 374
Xu, Chengxi 147
Xu, Fengyuan 190
Xu, Yuqiao 395

Y
Yang, Guomin 354
Yang, Jiahong 190
Yang, Min 147
Yang, Xuehuan 354
Yoo, Youngjin 395

Z
Zafar, Osama 395
Zeng, Qingming 415
Zeng, Wanying 433
Zhang, Chenbin 190
Zhang, Min 63, 147
Zhang, Pengcheng 314
Zhang, Rui 374
Zhang, Xiao 433
Zhang, Zonghua 190
Zhou, Jianying 169

MIX
Papier aus verantwortungsvollen Quellen
Paper from responsible sources
FSC® C105338

If you have any concerns about our products,
you can contact us on
ProductSafety@springernature.com

In case Publisher is established outside the EU,
the EU authorized representative is:
**Springer Nature Customer Service Center GmbH
Europaplatz 3, 69115 Heidelberg, Germany**

Printed by Libri Plureos GmbH
in Hamburg, Germany